Contents

KU-241-418

Preface   *v*

Acknowledgements   *vii*

Table of Cases   *ix*

Table of Statutes   *xi*

Tables   *xv*

Internet Web Sites   *xvii*

1   Introduction   *1*

The most important institutions and stages of the system – A statistical account of the criminal justice system – A brief account of the issue of values – Considering the nature of man, the characteristics of a particular society and the issue of crime causation – The limited amount of research that is undertaken and its problematic features – Identifying aims within the criminal justice system, with an emphasis being placed on its rather haphazard nature – The development of penal policy since 1945 – Pandering to the public – The new managerialism – Some models with which to view the criminal justice system – Factors influencing the creation of the criminal law

2   Crime Prevention   *46*

The nature of crime prevention – Some examples of crime prevention – The rational choice model – Evaluating crime prevention programmes – Current government thinking on crime prevention – Some crime prevention success stories – Displacement – Specific studies of crime prevention – Social and community strategies – Conclusions

3   The Role of the Police   *72*

Police powers – Hopes and expectations with regard to the police – Remedies and complaints – Factors influencing the practice of policing – Discretion, discrimination and stereotypes – Stop, search and arrest – The suspect in the police station – The provisions of legal services to the defendant – Community policing – What works? – Assessing the performance of the police – Conclusion

4   Pre-trial Decisions   *126*

Cautions – Official guidance on cautioning – Aims and justifications of cautions – Disadvantages of, and problems with, cautioning schemes – Diversion – The prosecution system – The reform process – The Code for Crown Prosecutors (2000) – The problems of the Crown Prosecution Service – Bail decision-making – Problems in bail decision-making

Contents

5   The Criminal Trial   *168*

Mode of trial – Pleas – Review of the criminal courts – The role of magistrates – The quality of the defence in the Crown Court – The jury – Admissibility of evidence, appeals, human rights and the Criminal Cases Review Commission

6   Sentencing   *194*

Statistics on sentencing practices – Deferral of sentence – Principles of sentencing – Factors that are taken into account in sentencing – The problem of disparity – Sentencing guidelines – Who should sentence?

7   Young Offenders   *227*

Statistics relating to young offenders – The courts – The justice and welfare models – The history of young offender systems – The youth justice framework 1982–2004 – The Youth Justice Board – Sentences and orders – Analysis of the youth justice system – Applying 'what works?' principles to young offenders – The effectiveness of interventions with young offenders – Conclusion

8   Community Sentences and Orders   *276*

The Criminal Justice Act 2003 – Statistics on community sentences and orders – Fines – Absolute and conditional discharge – Suspended sentence – Community rehabilitation orders (probation) – Community punishment orders (community service) – Community punishment and rehabilitation orders (combination orders) – Anti-social behaviour orders – Curfew orders – Electronic monitoring – Compensation orders – Forfeiture – The effectiveness of community sentences and orders – The generic community sentence

9   Prisons   *311*

The historical background and proposals for change – The statutory framework – The Criminal Justice Act 2003 – Prison statistics – The aims and functions of prisons – Overcrowding, prison conditions and prison security – Coping with long-term prisoners – Incapacitation as a benefit of imprisonment – Deterioration as a possible problem with the use of long-term imprisonment – Unwanted side-effects of prison – Praise where praise is due – The lessons of reconviction data – Should prison numbers be decreased? – Conclusion

Bibliography   *347*

Index   *367*

Preface

This book examines the major issues in relation to the criminal justice process. Clear exposition of the numerous arguments and counter-arguments within the subject has been aimed for, and the focus is very much upon the system in England and Wales at the present time. A wide range of sources has been referred to and a good variety of statistical material is provided. The book should be of value to those who study criminal justice and penology issues on law, criminology, criminal justice and other courses. Practitioners should also be able to turn to it for ideas and as a source of information.

The Criminal Justice Act 2003 has made changes to the legislative provisions for many parts of the criminal justice system. These are taken into account in the text. Whilst the Act is on the statute book much of it will not be in force immediately. You need to be vigilant in this respect. I have stated both the old and the new systems so that whatever provision is current you should have an account of it. A new feature of the book is the inclusion of a section on internet web sites that are relevant to the criminal justice system. I provide both addresses for and some information about the sites.

My thanks to my children Helen and Ian for keeping me cheerful and to the staff at Old Bailey Press for various forms of editorial assistance.

Michael Doherty
University of Glamorgan Law School
December 2003

Acknowledgements

The publishers and author would like to thank the Incorporated Council of Law Reporting for England and Wales for kind permission to reproduce extracts from the Weekly Law Reports, and Butterworths for their kind permission to reproduce extracts from the All England Law Reports.

Finally, we are indebted to the Controller of Her Majesty's Stationery Office for permission to reproduce Crown Copyright material.

Crown Copyright is reproduced with the permission of the Controller of Her Majesty's Stationery Office.

Table of Cases

Abassy v Metropolitan Police Commissioner
[1990] 1 All ER 193   *81*
Alderson *v* Booth [1969] 2 QB 216   *80*
Argent *v* R [1997] 2 Cr App R 27   *90*
Asociated Provincial Picture Houses Ltd *v*
Wednesbury Corporation [1948] 1 KB 223
78, 82
Attorney-General's Reference (No 61 of 1998)
[1999] Crim LR 428   *218, 219*
Attorney-General's Reference (Nos 62, 63, 64 and
65 of 1996), Re; sub nom R *v* Samuel; R *v*
Beresford; R *v* Jones; R *v* Murphy (1997)
(Transcripts 9608487 R2, 9608488 R2,
9608489 R2 and 9608390 R2)   *218*

Benham *v* United Kingdom (1996) 22 EHRR 293
191
Bentley *v* Brudzinski [1982] Crim LR 825   *81*

CC *v* United Kingdom (1998) Application No
32819/96, Commission Report 30 June 1998
189
Castorina *v* Chief Constable of Surrey [1988] NLJ
180   *78*
Chahal *v* United Kingdom (1996) The Times 28
November   *190*
Christie *v* Leachinsky [1947] AC 573   *80*
Collins *v* Wilcock [1984] 1 WLR 1172   *98*
Condron *v* United Kingdom [2000] Crim LR 679
90

Davis *v* Lisle [1936] 2 KB 434   *84*
Dawes *v* Director of Public Prosecutions [1994]
RTR 209   *80*
Director of Public Prosecutions *v* Hawkins [1988]
1 WLR 1166   *80*
Donnelly *v* Jackman [1970] 1 All ER 987   *81*
D'Sousa *v* Director of Public Prosecutions [1992]
4 All ER 545   *77*

Entick *v* Carrington (1765) 19 St Tr 1029   *75*

Foulkes *v* Chief Constable of Merseyside (1998)
The Times 26 June   *76*
Fuey Moy (Jim) *v* United States 254 US 189
(1920)   *44*

Gregory *v* United Kingdom (1997) The Times 27
February   *192*

Hayter *v* L (1998) The Times 3 February   *135*
Hill *v* Chief Constable of West Yorkshire [1989]
AC 53   *191*
Hood *v* United Kingdom (1999) The Times 11
March   *189*
Hussain *v* United Kingdom; Singh *v* United
Kingdom (1996) 22 EHRR 1   *190*

Kenlin *v* Gardiner [1967] 2 QB 510   *81*
King *v* Gardner (1979) 71 Cr App R 13   *78*
Krohn *v* Director of Publc Prosecutions [1997]
COD 345   *86*

Lewis *v* Chief Constable of South Wales [1991] 1
All ER 206   *80*
Linder *v* United States 268 US 5 (1924)   *44*
Liversidge *v* Anderson [1942] AC 206   *75*
Lyons *v* Chief Constable of West Yorkshire (1997)
60 JP 325   *82*

McLeod *v* Metropolitan Police Commissioner
[1994] 1 WLR 1500   *76*
Mepstead *v* Director of Public Prosecutions
(1996) 160 JP 475   *81*
Monaghan *v* Corbert (1983) 147 JP 545   *78*
Muller *v* France (1997) Reports 2:388:35   *189*
Murray *v* United Kingdom (1999) 19 EHRR 193
190

Nicols *v* Bulman [1985] RTR 236   *80*

O'Hara *v* Chief Constable of the Royal Ulster
Constabulary [1997] AC 286   *79*
O'Loughlin *v* Chief Constable of Essex (1997)
The Times 12 December   *77*
O'Reilly *v* Mackman [1983] AC 237   *98*
Osman *v* United Kingdom [1999] 5 BHRC 293
191

Percy *v* Director of Public Prosecutions [1995] 3
All ER 125   *77*
Practice Direction (Crown Court: Trial of
Children and Young Persons) (2000) The
Times 17 February   *231*

R *v* Aramah (1983) 4 Cr App R (S) 407   *222*
R *v* Brewster [1998] 1 Cr App R (S) 220   *222*
R *v* Chief Constable of Avon and Somerset, ex
parte Robinson [1989] 1 WLR 793   *89*

R v Chief Constable of Kent, ex parte Kent Police Federation and Harman [2000] Crim LR 857 *88*

R v Chief Constable of Lancashire, ex parte Parker [1993] QB 577 *85*

R v Chief Constable of Northumbria [2001] 1 WLR 1342 *89*

R v Chief Constable of Sussex, ex parte International Trader's Ferry Ltd [1997] 2 All ER 65 *99*

R v Chief Constable of Warwickshire [1997] 1 WLR 564 *98*

R v Ford [1989] QB 868 *180*

R v George (1984) 6 Cr App R (S) 211 *196*

R v Howden-Simpson [1991] Crim LR 49 *186*

R v Hurley (1999) The Times 5 August *222*

R v Inwood [1973] 2 All ER 645 *79*

R v Inwood (1974) 60 Cr App R 70 *303*

R v Kefford (2002) The Times 7 March *223*

R v Khan [1996] 3 All ER 289 *187*

R v Kulynycz [1971] 1 QB 367 *80*

R v Longman (1988) 72 Cr App R 121 *85*

R v Lowery (1992) 14 Cr App R (S) 485 *284*

R v Mason [1981] QB 881 *181*

R v Maynard [1983] Crim LR 821 *303*

R v Menard [1995] 1 Cr App R 306 *89*

R v Nottingham Justices, ex parte Davies [1981] QB 38 *159*

R v O'Keefe [1969] 2 QB 29 *283*

R v Paris [1994] Crim LR 361 *186*

R v Pendelton (Donald) [2001] UKHL 66; [2002] 1 All ER 524 *187*

R v Robinson (1992) 14 Cr App R (S) 559 *283, 284*

R v Ronchetti [1998] 2 Cr App (S) 100 *222*

R v Self [1992] 1 WLR 657 *80*

R v South Western Magistrates' Court, ex parte Cofie [1997] 1 WLR 885 *85*

R v Southwark Crown Court and HM Customs, ex parte Sorsky Defries [1996] COD 117 *87*

R v W [1999] 1 Cr App R (S) 488 *219*

R v Wijs [1998] 2 Cr App R (S) 436 *222*

Roberts v Chief Constable of Cheshire Police [1999] 2 All ER 326 *88*

Robson v Hallett [1967] 2 QB 939 *84*

Rowe and Davies v United Kingdom (1998) Application No 28901/95 (20 October 1998) *192*

Scott v Spain (1997) 24 EHRR 391 *189*

Shaw v Director of Public Prosecutions [1962] AC 220 *2*

Simpson v Chief Constable of South Yorkshire (1991) The Times 7 March *80–81*

Stafford v Director of Public Prosecutions [1974] AC 878 *187*

T v United Kingdom; V v United Kingdom (1998) Application Nos 24724/94 and 24888/94 (4 December 1998) *192*

T v United Kingdom; V v United Kingdom (1999) The Times 17 December *231*

Thompson v Metropolitan Police Commissioner [1997] 2 All ER 762 *98*

United States v Behrman 258 US 280 (1921) *44*

Webb v United States 249 US 96 (1918) *44*

Table of Statutes

Annti-social Behaviour Act 2003
    s18   *266*
    s19   *266*

Bail Act 1976   *24, 158, 161*
    s4   *158, 159*
    Sch 1   *158*
Black Act 1723   *44*

Children Act 1908   *234*
Children Act 1989   *237*
Children and Young Persons Act 1932   *235*
Children and Young Persons Act 1933   *235, 261*
    s44   *231*
    s53   *164*
    s53(2)   *219*
    s53(3)   *219*
Children and Young Persons Act 1969   *23, 24, 235, 236*
    s1   *236*
    s4   *236*
    s5   *236*
    s7   *237*
    ss11–19   *263*
Courts Act 2003   *280, 281*
Crime and Disorder Act 1998   *25, 27, 48, 127, 162, 203, 224, 237, 239, 240, 263, 266, 267, 268, 281, 296, 300, 314*
    s36   *15*
    s37   *239*
    s43   *161*
    s56   *159, 189*
    s65   *127*
    s66   *127*
    s80   *225, 226*
    s81   *225, 226*
Crime (Sentences) Act 1997   *25, 26, 27, 200, 216, 237, 239, 279, 335*
Criminal Appeal Act 1968
    s2(1)   *187*
    s23   *187*
Criminal Appeal Act 1995   *192*
Criminal Justice Act 1925   *285*
Criminal Justice Act 1948   *23, 235, 261, 285, 335*
Criminal Justice Act 1961   *23*
Criminal Justice Act 1967   *24, 281*
Criminal Justice Act 1972   *24, 195*

Criminal Justice Act 1982   *24, 234, 237, 238, 261, 263, 282, 296*
    s20   *263*
    s37   *278*
Criminal Justice Act 1987   *181*
Criminal Justice Act 1988   *24, 169, 180, 237, 238*
    s128   *263*
    s154   *159*
Criminal Justice Act 1991   *24, 25, 195, 214, 224, 237, 276, 279, 282, 283, 286, 297, 299, 301, 313, 315*
Criminal Justice Act 1993   *217, 280*
Criminal Justice Act 2003   *26, 30, 31, 32, 74, 83, 89, 96, 128, 140, 159, 162, 168, 170, 171, 174, 175, 180, 185, 188, 195, 215, 218, 219, 225, 227, 266, 276, 277, 282, 300, 306, 307, 309, 310, 311, 312, 315, 316, 335*
    s147   *306*
    s148   *307*
    s148(1)   *307*
    s148(2)   *307*
    s148(3)   *307*
    s149   *307*
    s150   *307*
    s152   *315*
    s152(2)   *315*
    s152(3)   *315*
    s153   *316*
    s177   *306*
    s199   *307*
    s201   *308*
    s202   *308*
    s203   *308*
    s204   *308*
    s205   *309*
    s206   *309*
    s207   *309*
    s209   *309*
    s212   *309*
    s213   *310*
    s214   *310*
    s215   *310*
    s225   *317*
    s227   *317*
Criminal Justice and Court Services Act 2000   *26, 237, 237–238, 238, 276, 284, 285, 296, 299, 303*
    s41   *287*
    s42   *287*

Criminal Justice and Public Order Act 1994
   25, 159, 160, 169, 237, 238
      s25   *159, 189*
      s26   *159*
      s34   *89, 90*
      s35   *89, 90*
      s36   *90*
      s37   *90*
      s48   *174*
Criminal Justice (Mode of Trial) (No 2) Bill 2000
   169, 170
Criminal Law Act 1977   *24, 169, 282*

European Convention on Human Rights and
   Fundamental Freedoms 1950   *98, 188, 296*
      art 3   *190*
      art 5   *188, 189, 190, 192*
      art 5(1)   *189*
      art 5(2)   *80*
      art 5(3)   *189, 190*
      art 5(4)   *190*
      art 5(5)   *189, 190*
      art 6   *188, 191, 192*

Harrison Act 1914 (US)   *43, 44*
Human Rights Act 1998   *98, 188, 189*

Juries Act 1974   *180, 181*
Juries (Disqualification) Act 1984   *180*

Marijuana Tax Act 1937 (US)   *42, 43*
Metropolitan Police Act 1839   *78*
Misuse of Drugs Act 1971
   s23(2)   *82*

Obscene Publications Acts 1959–1964   *99*
Offical Secrets Act 1911   *181*

Police Act 1964   *72*
Police Act 1996   *72*
Police Act 1997   *72*
Police and Criminal Evidence Act 1984   *7, 75,*
   76, 79, 82, 83, 87, 114, 115
      Part 9   *72*
      s1   *83*
      s1(1)   *82*
      s1(2)   *82*
      s1(3)   *82*
      s1(4)   *82*
      s1(5)   *82*
      s1(6)   *83*
      s1(7)   *83*
      s1(8)   *83*

Police and Criminal Evidence Act 1984 (*contd.*)
      s2   *83*
      s2(2)   *83*
      s2(3)   *83*
      s2(9)   *83*
      s3   *83*
      s8   *84*
      s8(1)   *84*
      s8(2)   *85*
      s8(3)   *84*
      s9   *85*
      s15   *85*
      s16   *85*
      s16(3)   *85*
      s16(4)   *85*
      s16(5)   *85*
      s16(6)   *85*
      s16(7)   *85*
      s16(10)   *85*
      s17   *77, 87*
      s18   *86*
      s18(1)   *86*
      s18(2)   *86*
      s18(3)   *86*
      s18(4)   *86*
      s18(5)   *86*
      s19   *86, 87*
      s19(2)   *87*
      s22   *87*
      s24   *76, 82*
      s24(1)   *75*
      s24(2)   *75*
      s24(3)   *75*
      s24(4)   *76, 82*
      s24(5)   *76*
      s24(6)   *76*
      s25   *76*
      s25(6)   *76*
      s28   *79*
      s28(3)   *79*
      s32   *86*
      s32(2)   *86*
      s34   *87*
      s36   *87*
      s37   *87*
      s37(1)   *88*
      s37(2)   *87*
      s37(3)   *88*
      s37(4)   *88*
      s37(5)   *88*
      s37(6)   *88*
      s37(7)   *88*
      s40   *88*

Police and Criminal Evidence Act 1984 (*contd.*)
 s40(1) *88*
 s41 *87*
 s42 *87*
 s55 *89*
 s56 *89*
 s58 *89, 114*
 s59 *114*
 s76 *186*
 s76(1) *186*
 s76(2) *186*
 s76(3) *186*
 s76(4) *186*
 s76(5) *186*
 s76(6) *186*
 s78 *98, 186, 187*
 s78(1) *186*
 s116 *76*
 s117 *18677, 87*
 Sch 5 *76*
Police and Magistrates' Courts Act 1994
 Part 1 *72*
Police Reform Act 2002 *73*
Powers of Criminal Courts Act 1973 *283, 296, 335*
 s7 *281*
Powers of Criminal Courts (Sentencing) Act 2000
 25, 195, 214, 218, 237, 238, 250, 264, 276, 280, 283, 301, 309, 310, 317
 s1 *196*
 ss12–15 *281*
 s16 *250*
 s16(1) *250*
 s16(2) *251*
 s16(3) *251*
 s16(4) *251*
 s16(5) *251*
 s16(6) *251*
 s16(7) *251*
 s17 *251*
 s17(1) *251*
 s17(2) *251*
 s17(3) *251*
 s17(4) *251*
 s17(5) *252*
 s18 *252*
 s18(1) *252*
 s18(2) *252*
 s18(3) *252*
 s18(4) *252*
 s18(5) *252*
 s18(6) *252*
 s18(7) *252*

Powers of Criminal Courts (Sentencing) Act 2000 (*contd.*)
 s19 *252*
 s19(1) *252*
 s19(2) *252*
 s19(3) *253*
 s19(4) *253*
 s19(5) *253*
 s19(6) *253*
 s19(7) *253*
 s20 *253*
 s20(1) *253*
 s20(2) *253*
 s20(3) *253*
 s20(4) *253*
 s20(5) *253*
 s20(6) *253*
 s20(7) *253*
 s21 *254*
 s21(1) *254*
 s21(2) *254*
 s21(3) *254*
 s21(4) *254*
 s21(5) *254*
 s21(6) *254*
 s21(7) *254*
 s22 *255*
 s22(1) *255*
 s22(2) *255*
 s22(3) *255*
 s22(4) *255*
 s22(5) *255*
 s23 *255*
 s23(1) *255*
 s23(2) *255*
 s23(3) *255*
 s23(4) *255*
 s23(5) *256*
 s23(6) *256*
 s24 *256*
 s24(1) *256*
 s24(2) *256*
 s24(3) *256*
 s24(4) *256*
 s24(5) *256*
 s24(6) *256*
 s25 *256*
 s25(1) *256*
 s25(2) *256*
 s25(3) *256*
 s26 *256*
 s26(1) *256*
 s26(2) *257*

Powers of Criminal Courts (Sentencing) Act 2000
(*contd.*)
s26(3)   *257*
s26(4)   *257*
s26(5)   *257*
s26(6)   *257*
s26(7)   *257*
s26(8)   *257*
s26(9)   *257*
s26(10)   *258*
s27   *258*
s27(1)   *258*
s27(2)   *258*
s27(3)   *258*
s27(4)   *258*
s27(5)   *258*
s27(6)   *258*
s27(7)   *258*
s28   *258*
s29   *258*
s29(1)   *258*
s29(2)   *258*
s29(3)   *258*
s35   *214*
s35(3)   *214*
ss37–40   *301*
s37   *308*
ss41–45   *284*
ss46–50   *296*
s46   *307*
ss60–62   *261*
ss63–68   *263*
ss69–72   *264*
ss73–75   *265*
s79   *214, 313*
s79(1)   *214, 313*
s79(2)   *214, 313*
ss90–92   *3, 230, 241, 261*

Powers of Criminal Courts (Sentencing) Act 2000
(*contd.*)
ss90–95   *315*
ss109–111   *313*
s109   *313*
s109(1)   *313*
s109(2)   *314*
s109(3)   *314*
s109(4)   *314*
s109(5)   *314*
s110   *314*
s111   *314*
ss118–125   *282*
ss126–129   *278*
ss130–134   *303*
s143   *304*
s152   *174*
Sch 2   *308*
Prevention of Crime Act 1908   *234*
Prevention of Terrorism (Temporary Provisions)
Act 1984
s12(1)   *79*
Probation of Offenders Act 1907   *285*
Prosecution of Offences Act 1985   *139, 142,
144, 145, 156*
s3   *144*
s4   *144*
s5   *144*
s6   *144*
Prosecution of Offenders Act 1982   *24*
Public Order Act 1936   *22*
Public Order Act 1986   *22*

Theft Act 1968
s24(2)   *83*

Youth Justice and Criminal Evidence Act 1999
25, 27, 203, 208, 237, 240, 244

Tables

1   Sentences and Orders 2000 and 2001   *2–3*

2   A Summary of Some of the Main Statistics for Notifiable Offences   *3*

3   Types of Proceedings for Motoring Offences 2001   *4*

4   Persons Aged 18 and Over Proceeded against at the Crown Court in 2001   *5*

5   Representation of Ethnic Groups at Different Stages of the Criminal Justice Process 2001–2002   *8*

6   Number of Homicides and Homicides per 100,000 of the Population in Urban Areas 1998–2000   *8*

7   Some of the Costs of the Criminal Justice System 2001–2002   *9*

8   Self-Reported Delinquency   *11*

9   Notifiable Offences Recorded by the Police 1951–2001   *20*

10   Average Prison Population 1936–2002   *21*

11   Police Service Strength in England and Wales as at 31 March 2003   *75*

12   Incidence by Race of Arrest and Self-Reported Delinquency   *104*

13   Police Source of First Information as to Crime   *110*

14   Crime Rate per 100,000 of the Population in the United States   *123*

15   Number of Reprimands and Final Warnings by Offence Type and Age in 2001 *128*

16   The Role of the Crown Prosecution Service in Magistrates' Courts   *141*

17   Crown Court Cases by Offence Type, Guilty Plea and Outcome   *141*

18   Bail Decisions by Magistrates   *157*

19   Conditions Imposed in the Five Courts   *162*

20   Persons Found Guilty or Cautioned for Indictable Offences, per 100,000 of the Population, in 2001, by Age   *228*

21   Numbers Sentenced or Cautioned in 2001 for Indictable Offences by Age Group and Gender   *228*

22   Sentences and Orders for Those under 21, by Age Group and Gender, for Indictable Offences in 2001   *229–230*

23   Community Sentences and Orders 2001   *278*

24   Persons Starting Criminal Supervision by the Probation Service   *290*

25   Percentages of Those Who Breached Orders in 1994 and 2001   *306*

26   Prison Population as at 31 December 2002   *318–319*

27   Prison Population December 2001 and December 2002 for Males and Females by Same Offence Types   *319*

28   Average Populations for Custodial Establishments   *324*

29   Percentage Reconviction Rate by Sentence   *340*

30   Percentage Reconvicted by Gender and Disposal   *340*

31   Comparative World Prison Populations   *345*

Internet Web Sites

Whilst the sites offer access to a marvellous free resource, a few words of warning are required. The addresses have been checked recently but they are subject to alteration – the Internet does not stand still for long. With the Internet you will experience some difficulties in using the material – it goes with the territory. I would also remind you that you need accurate typing as the Internet is not forgiving on this. Finally, you must remember that the material on the net is only as good as the people who put it there. As you start following links, you can end up with material of dubious quality, so it is important to provide your own quality control. Most sites are from the United Kingdom. With the United States' sites there is a considerable United States' bias, although they will offer some world coverage and often excellent material. I have concentrated on material that is available free, including the free items provided by the commercial providers. What I have listed here should operate as a good starting point. You need to get into the habit of looking for a links section in the sites that you visit as they will offer you further ideas.

Primary legal materials

Acts of Parliament
http://www.hmso.gov.uk/acts.htm
> This site provides the full text of Public Acts from the start of 1998.

Statutory instruments
http://www.hmso.gov.uk/stat.htm
> This site provides the full text of statutory instruments from the start of 1987.

House of Lords judgments
http://www.parliament.uk
> This site provides the full text of judgments starting from 14 November 1996. You may find other suggestions for a link to this site, but you will probably find this the easiest way in. You will be using the Parliament site, so you need to select Judicial Work and then Judgments.

The courts
http://www.courtservice.gov.uk
> Some recent judgments, including some from the Court of Appeal, are available here.

Incorporated Council of Law Reporting
http://www.lawreports.co.uk
> This will provide useful summaries of a wide variety of decided cases. Their view of themselves follows. 'The Daily Law Notes is a free 24-hour service from the Royal Courts of Justice and European Court of Justice, bringing you the most important updates from the House of Lords, the Privy Council, the Court of Appeal and all divisions of the High Court.

All our reporters are barristers or solicitors, so we can provide the highest quality of reporting, for which we have been the benchmark ever since our inauguration in 1865. The cases reported have been summarised and are not the full text version that will appear in due course in The Weekly Law Reports, The Law Reports or The Industrial Cases Reports. What you will find here, however, is a precise and, above all, accurate summary of those cases.

How does the service work?
Our reporters are in court for the hearing and handing down of judgments. They will summarise the case and the summary will then be published on our website within 24 hours of judgment being handed down. Access to the service is free of charge. By using the link to This Week's Cases you can see daily summaries as they appear or navigate via the monthly indexes for more in-depth lists of summaries. Alternatively, when searching for a case heard some time ago, use the A–Z listing in the Courts indexes to search for specific case names.

What is included in the service?
The aim is to provide reports of all significant decisions of the superior courts. With The Daily Law Notes you can be certain that if a case is important because it either develops or clarifies a point of law or sets legal precedent in some way it will be included. If a case merely reiterates established principles and breaks no new ground it will not merit inclusion. We do not intend to report all cases indiscriminately: we prefer to exercise strong editorial control. This means you can be assured of having direct access to those cases which are important as precedents without the distraction of irrelevant material. Accordingly, since cases will be included on the basis of their importance rather than the status of the courts deciding them, the frequency of any particular court "appearing" in the service may be irregular.'

European Court of Human Rights' decisions
http://www.echr.coe.int/Eng/Judgements.htm
   The full text of judgments is provided. When the first page comes up you need to select 'search the case law' and then use the search facility.

British and Irish Legal Information Institute (BAILII)
http://www.bailii.org
   The site provides access to the most comprehensive set of British and Irish primary legal materials that are available for free and in one place on the internet. As at 6 February 2003, BAILII includes 34 databases covering six jurisdictions. The system contains around six gigabytes of legal materials and around 475,000 searchable documents with about 15 million internal hypertext links. The databases on BAILII are derived from a number of sources. Some of the data comes from existing free-to-air sites. Most of the databases are based on published and unpublished CD–ROMs, or rely upon direct and indirect feeds by relevant courts, government departments and other organisations. All of the data has been converted into a consistent format and a generalised set of search and hypertext facilities have been added.

Major sources of data and research findings

Home Office
http://www.homeoffice.gov.uk

An excellent site for criminal justice issues, with its best feature being the provision of a wide range of full text research reports. One problem that you may experience with these is that some are in pdf format. To use these you will need Adobe Acrobat which is a piece of software. If you do not have it you could obtain it by means of a download and this will be offered to you when you try to open the file. This can be a lengthy process, over an hour, but there is a simpler alternative. Adobe Acrobat is often included as a piece of free software on the disks provided with computer magazines which you may well already have. The download from a disk will be much quicker.

Under criminal justice you can find material on prisons, probation, sentencing, the courts and the police service. Under crime reduction the sub-categories upon which information is provided include the government's crime reduction strategy and the crime reduction programme, advice and support on crime prevention, some material on the latest crime figures, urban regeneration and community crime reduction, the drug prevention and advisory service, policing and crime and other related information.

The Home Office's aims and details of its organisation are provided. There is also an A–Z Index (see below) and a search facility. The provision also includes contact details, facilities for complaints and feedback, site help, frequently asked questions, plenty of very good quality press releases, access to the full text of relevant legislation and a link to the Research Development and Statistics (RDS) web site. The RDS site, which is considered below, offers an even wider range of full text research reports. The A–Z index has hyper-text links to the relevant material and this can also operate as a means of accessing other related sites. The following are examples of the links: Action Against Drugs Unit, British Crime Survey, Correctional Policy Unit, Courts, Crime and Criminal Justice Unit, Crime and Disorder Act 1998, Crime Reduction, Criminal Cases Review Commission web site, Criminal Injuries Compensation Appeals Panel web site, Criminal Injuries Compensation Authority web site, Criminal Justice Joint Planning Unit, Criminal Law, Criminal Policy Group, Criminal Records Bureau web site, Criminal Policy Strategy Unit, Dangerous and Severe Personality Disorder Unit, Domestic Violence, Drugs and Drug Prevention, Drugs Prevention Advisory Service, Gambling, Her Majesty's Inspectorate of Constabulary, Her Majesty's Inspectorate of Prisons and Probation, Justice and Victims Unit, Juvenile Offenders, Juvenile Offenders Unit, National Criminal Intelligence Service web site, Offenders and Corrections Unit, Organised and International Crime Directorate, Parole Board web site, Police, Police Complaints Authority web site, Police Resources Unit, Police Scientific Development Branch, Policing Organised Crime Unit, Policing and Crime Reduction Group, Policing and Reducing Crime Unit, Prison Service Agency web site, Prisons, Prisons Ombudsman, Probation, Probation Unit, Sentencing, Sentencing and Offences Unit, Sentencing Advisory Panel web site, Sex Offences, Victims of Crime, Violence against Women, Youth Justice and the Youth Justice Board web site.

The Research Development and Statistics website
http://www.homeoffice.gov.uk/rds

The provision includes an explanation of the role of RDS within the Home Office, the subjects that it deals with, its research and statistical programmes and the publications that it produces. Of most interest will be the very large amount of full text reports that are available on the site. One problem that you may experience with these is that some are in pdf format: a solution is suggested above (see **Home Office**). The categories under which material is made available include the following: British Crime Survey, Crime Prevention, Crime Statistics Review, Criminal Justice System Statistics, Juvenile Offending, Notifiable Offences, The Offenders Index, Patterns of Crime, Policing, Crime Reduction, Prisons, Probation, Recorded Crime, Sexual Offending and Youth Justice.

The Law Commission
http://www.lawcom.gov.uk

The site explains the role of the Commission and provides an account of its current research projects and those of the Home Office. It is excellent for full text versions of its completed reports.

Domestic Violence Data Source
http://www.domesticviolencedata.org/default.htm

The Domestic Violence Data Source is an information co-ordinating system for projects relating to domestic violence within England, Wales, Scotland, Northern Ireland and the Republic of Ireland.

United Nations Crime and Justice Information Network
http:///www.uncjin.org

The site is of use because material is available in relation to many countries in the world, although there is much more material for the United States than for elsewhere. There is a site map and a search facility plus a good links section. Material is available relating to legislation, case law, treaties, statistics and a prison bibliography. Access is given to various units and institutions that operate in the area of criminal justice under the auspices of the United Nations.

National Criminal Justice Service
http://www.ncjrs.org

An excellent source for both American and international material, including material provided by the United Nations. There is a very good keyword search facility. A huge amount of articles can be accessed by following the links that are included. Some of the major organisational themes for the material are as follows: corrections, courts, crime prevention, statistics, law enforcement and juvenile justice.

Heiros Gamos
http://www.hg.org/crime.html

An excellent United States-based resource.

Findlaw
http://www.findlaw.com

Within this general law facility you need to go into legal subjects and then use the search facility in relation to criminal justice, criminal law or indeed your specific interest. You will normally find a range of material of good quality. Remember to make use of the general sites when looking for material on particular subjects.

The Legal Information Institute at Cornell University
http://www.law.cornell.edu

A United States-based general law facility with categories that include prisons and prisoner's rights, criminal law and criminal procedure and juvenile justice. Material can also be obtained by a keyword search for criminal justice or a more specific search term dependant on your interests. I found this to be a very good site to obtain material on juvenile gangs.

Gateways

Criminal Justice System Online
http://www.cjsonline.gov.uk/home.html

The government provides this as a useful gateway to a whole range of different criminal justice web sites. It describes itself in the following way. 'CJS Online has been developed as part of modernising government agenda, to establish a consolidated criminal justice system (CJS) presence on the Internet and reflect the continued commitment to deliver quality services which reflect both the citizens' needs and those working within the CJS. Navigation around the site has also been simplified. The site is now split into two main sections – one for those working within the CJS and another for citizens (such as witnesses and jurors) who require more general information and support. The site utilises drop down menus, and has boxes to highlight particular issues affecting the CJS. Additionally links are highlighted when the cursor is floated over them and the number of links on a page has been reduced to ease navigation.'

SOSIG
http://www.sosig.ac.uk

An excellent gateway for the social sciences.

Infolaw
http://www.infolaw.co.uk

Infolaw is a long established United Kingdom legal gateway site.

United States Department of Justice
http://www.usdoj.gov

This is excellent as a gateway to a large number of other sites and organisations in the United States in relation to criminal justice.

Sites that will provide more suggestions for legal web sites: sources of links

British and Irish Legal Information Institute (BAILII)
http://www.bailii.org
> Numerous links and general material for searches on the Internet.

Sarah Carter
http:///www.library.kent.ac.uk/library/lawlinks.default.htm
> An excellent source for links.

Clive Walker
http://www.leeds.ac.uk/law/ccjs/ukweb.htm
> A superb source for links to criminal justice arranged in four categories – United Kingdom, Continental Europe, North America and the rest of the world. There are about 180 sites for the United Kingdom arranged in A–Z order with a short description and a hypertext link to each site. This provides a comprehensive and diverse resource with numerous links to police forces, government bodies and other criminal justice organisations. For example, under A is to be found – Academy of Experts, Acts of Parliament, Aftermath (an organisation for offender's families), Amnesty International, Association of Black Probation Officers, Association of Police Surgeons, Audit Commission and Avon and Somerset Police. For Continental Europe, North America and the rest of the world the links are less detailed. There are still over 100 each for Continental Europe and North America, and more than 70 for the rest of the world. For Continental Europe, you may find a problem with links that do not work. Also, the weighting is very much towards police forces, this being the case for most of the German sites. North American sources include journals, reform bodies and links to other links. For the rest of the world, again police forces figure promptly but there is a valuable feature in the links to United Nations' material.

Home Office
http://www.homeoffice.gov.uk
> Good hypertext links.

Dr Frank Schmalleger's Cybary of criminal justice links
http://talkjustice.com
> Select cybary once you are at the site. An American offering that offers a massive 12,000 plus web sites arranged over 100 different categories.

Comparative Criminal Justice Resources
http://arapaho.nsuok.edu
> Once you are at the site select 'faculty' and then the name of the person who has supplied the site: Charles Dreveskract. In theory there are more direct routes but they may not be reliable when used. Remember to bookmark the site as a favourite once you have found it. If you run into difficulties a link may be found to this site through the various links sites, and a search of his surname by means of a search engine will get you to this site as

well. The organisation and content may strike you as idiosyncratic (Irish slang words are included) but do persist as there is a lot of good material here, particularly the links to other sites. The areas covered include criminal justice resources, material on the Native Americans, victims and victimology, comparative criminal justice and Scotland and Northern Ireland material.

Heiros Gamos
http://www.hg.org/crime.html
>   An excellent United States-based source for finding links.

Criminal Justice mega links
http://faculty.ncwc.edu/toconnor/default.htm
>   Thousands of links with a focus on the United States.

BUBL links
http://bubl.ac.uk/link/c/crime.htm
>   A general source of links for the social sciences.

Institutions

Parliament
http://www.parliament.uk
>   Much information is available in relation to the policy process.

The Courts
http://www.courtservice.gov.uk
>   See above.

Home Office
http://www.homeoffice.gov.uk
>   See above.

Department for Constitutional Affairs
http://www.open.gov.uk/lcd/lcdhome.htm
>   This took over the role of the Lord Chancellor's Department. It provides press releases, statistics, details of judges etc. Also, note that it is an excellent source of links to other useful sites.

Sectors of the criminal justice system

Her Majesty's Prison Service
http://www.hmprisonservice.gov.uk
>   Congratulations to the Prison Service for producing a welcoming and informative web site – if only it were always thus with the Prison Service. There is a site map, news, a

frequently asked questions feature and a search facility. As regards news this can be e-mailed to you on a monthly basis. Details of the Service's publications are provided and a links facility is included. Statistical material and other data is available and there are quite a number of different types of data provided in relation to each of the prison establishments.

Youth Justice Board
Address: http://www.youth-justice-board.gov.uk/youthjusticeboard

The organisation that is responsible for some of the provision in relation to young offenders. Its role is explained, contact details are available, a news and press release facility is provided, details of relevant events are included and finally of note is the detail that is given of the types of orders that can be made by the courts in relation to young offenders.

Crown Prosecution Service
Address: http://www.cps.gov.uk

This is typical of the organisations that know that they need a web presence but seem to want to say as little as possible. The content is limited and the site is not easy to use, although the Code for Crown Prosecutors is available in 15 languages, including Vietnamese. Material is provided in relation to its role, there are press releases and contact details as well as some policy documents, material for victims and witnesses of crime and the annual report which is itself a very uninspiring document.

Parole Board
Address: http://www.paroleboard.gov.uk

Annual reports and a little bit more.

Criminal Injuries Compensation Authority
Address: http://www.cica.gov.uk

As its name suggests this is the web site for criminal injuries compensation. At first sight there does not appear to be very much on offer here – a guide to the compensation scheme, the most important of the applicable rules plus details of how to apply for compensation. Once you start looking further you find that there is in fact a considerable amount of detail as regards the amount of compensation that is applicable to a wide range of injuries.

Probation Service
http://www.probation.homeoffice.gov.uk

Reports, statistics and information on probation.

Sentencing Advisory Panel
http://www.sentencing-advisory-panel.gov.uk

Very good examples of the work of this body.

Crime reduction
http://www.crimereduction.gov.uk

This provides details of research projects relating to crime reduction.

The Legal Services Commission
http://www.legalservices.gov.uk

The Legal Services Commission is an executive non-departmental public body created under the Access to Justice Act 1999 to replace the Legal Aid Board. It is responsible for the development and administration of two schemes in England and Wales, namely the Community Legal Service, which from 1 April 2000 replaced the old civil scheme of legal aid, bringing together networks of funders (eg local authorities) and suppliers into partnerships to provide the widest possible access to information and advice and the Criminal Defence Service which from 2 April 2001 replaced the old system of criminal legal aid and provides criminal services to people accused of crimes.

Avon and Somerset Police
http://www.avsom.police.uk

An example of the type of material that can be found in the various police force web sites. Included are news stories and events, contact details, frequently asked questions, recruitment material, the role of the police authority and downloadable versions of the annual report and the policing and corporate plans. Advice is given on internet matters such as viruses, electronic commerce and nanny software to prevent children accessing inappropriate material.

ACPO
http://www.acpo.police.uk

The Association of Chief Police Officers (ACPO) was set up over 50 years ago so that work on developing policing policies could be undertaken in one place, on behalf of the Service as a whole, rather than in 43 forces separately. The Association supports the philosophy of strong local policing, and believes that this must be maintained within the tripartite framework of policing which brings together the local chief constable, the local police authority and the Home Secretary. ACPO's members are police officers who hold the rank of chief constable, deputy chief constable or assistant chief constable, or their equivalents, in the 43 forces of England, Wales and Northern Ireland, national police agencies and certain other forces in the United Kingdom, the Isle of Man and the Channel Islands, and certain senior non-police staff.

Systems of accountability

Her Majesty's Inspectors of Constabulary
http://www.homeoffice.gov.uk/hmic/hmic.htm

For well over a century HM Inspectors of Constabulary (HMIs) have been charged with examining and improving the efficiency of the police service in England and Wales.

Her Majesty's Inspectorate of Prisons
http://www.homeoffice.gov.uk/justice/prisons/inspprisons/index.html

An excellent site that explains the role of the Chief Inspector and provides details of the inspection programme. The best feature is the access that is provided to the numerous full text versions of reports of prison inspections and the separate thematic reviews of issues such as suicide in prisons, women prisoners, lifers and young prisoners. A search facility, an A–Z index, contact details and some links are also available.

Prisons and Probation Ombudsman
http://www.ppo.gov.uk

The Prisons and Probation Ombudsman is appointed by the Home Secretary and investigates complaints from prisoners and those subject to probation supervision, or those upon whom reports have been written. The Ombudsman is completely independent of both the Prison Service and the National Probation Service (NPS).

Police Complaints Authority
http://www.pca.gov.uk

The old system.

Independent Police Complaints Authority
http://web.ipcc.gov.uk

The new system.

Criminal Cases Review Commission
http://www.ccrc.gov.uk

This is the web site for the body that investigates possible miscarriages of justice and it can make recommendations that the Court of Appeal should consider the matter. Details are provided as regards its role, contact details are included and information is provided for both applicants and for legal advisers. This includes an application form which can be used to raise a matter within the Commission. Press releases and annual reports are available on line. A links facility to other sites is also included.

Pressure and interest groups

NACRO
http://www.nacro.org.uk

This is one of the pressure groups in this area, and is involved in the resettlement of offenders following imprisonment. There is a limited amount of material here relating to their role, news and events, a search facility is provided and details of publications are included. Some of the publications are available on line.

The Howard League for Penal Reform
http://web.ukonline.co.uk/howard.league

Some material on its role as a pressure group, a news and press release feature, details of events and some suggestions for links.

Magistrates' Association
http://www.magistrates-association.org.uk
> Information on the role of magistrates is provided.

Neighbourhood Watch
http://web.neighbourhoodwatch.net
> Details of the work of the various schemes are provided.

Victim Support
http://web.victimsupport.org.uk
> The services provided by the organisation are detailed.

Historical material

Galleries of justice
http://www.galleriesofjustice.org.uk
> This site provides some interesting historical material.

1 Introduction

1.1   The most important institutions and stages of the system

1.2   A statistical account of the criminal justice system

1.3   A brief account of the issue of values

1.4   Considering the nature of man, the characteristics of a particular society and the issue of crime causation

1.5   The limited amount of research that is undertaken and its problematic features

1.6   Identifying aims within the criminal justice system, with an emphasis being placed on its rather haphazard nature

1.7   The development of penal policy since 1945

1.8   Pandering to the public

1.9   The new managerialism

1.10 Some models with which to view the criminal justice system

1.11 Factors influencing the creation of the criminal law

The main subject matter of this book is the system of criminal justice and penology in England and Wales in recent times, though some material from other times and places will also be utilised. Whilst the rest of the book will be an examination of the various units and stages of this system, in this chapter some background details are provided and some general issues considered.

The following matters will be examined:

1. The most important institutions and stages of the criminal justice system.
2. Some statistical data is provided.
3. A brief account of the issue of values.
4. The issues of the nature of man and society and the problem of crime causation.
5. The limited amount of research that is undertaken and its problematic features are noted.
6. An attempt is made to identify aims and concerns within the criminal justice system, with an emphasis being placed on its rather haphazard nature.
7. A recent history of the criminal justice system is offered.
8. Pandering to the public.
9. The new managerialism.

10. Some models through which the criminal justice system could be understood are examined.

11. Factors influencing the creation of the criminal law are discussed.

1.1 The most important institutions and stages of the system

The existence of criminal law is a basic prerequisite for criminal behaviour, and at the present time it is largely created by legislation. This is subject to the influence of such as the government and interest groups. Whilst there are common-law offences, such as false imprisonment, which have in the past been created by the judges, the range of criminal liability is not supposed to be added to by the judges. However, it is not difficult to find examples of such increases. An example is conspiracy to corrupt public morals (see the case of *Shaw* v *DPP* [1962] AC 220). A breach of the criminal law does not, in itself, guarantee a response by the police, who are the main investigators of criminal behaviour. They have to discover or, more likely, be informed of such behaviour. Even then, they may decide that no action is appropriate. Informants of crime may be the victim or indeed any other person who has knowledge of it. In their decisions whether or not to report offences the general public act as an important filter in relation to the criminal justice system. Possible outcomes of a police investigation include: no further action, a caution or a decision to prosecute. The latter is the task of the Crown Prosecution Service. Where a case is prosecuted it is likely that the defendant will plead guilty which will mean that there will be no need for a trial. If a trial is required it is most likely to be in the magistrates' court. Other cases, generally those that are regarded as being the most serious, are heard in the Crown Court with a judge and jury as the decision-makers. Findings of guilt are followed by the sentencing stage and there is a considerable variety of sentences. The different types of sentence and order such as community punishment orders, supervision orders and prison extend still further the already considerable amount of institutions, personnel and decisions that exist within the criminal justice system. Table 1, which is derived from the official *Criminal Statistics* (Home Office (2002a)), provides details of these sentences and orders.

Table 1

Sentences and Orders 2000 and 2001 (thousands)		
	2000	2001
Absolute discharge	15.7	15.2
Conditional discharge	106.1	101.7
Fine	1017.1	934.3
Community rehabilitation Order (1)	56.7	59.2
Supervision order	11.6	11.1
Community punishment order (2)	50.2	50.0
Curfew order	2.6	3.9
Attendance sentence order	7.1	5.8

	2000	2001
Community punishment and rehabilitation order (3)	19.3	14.7
Reparation order	4.0	8.0
Action plan order	4.4	8.7
Drug treatment and testing order	0.3	4.2
Detention and training order	5.1	7.1
Young offender institution	20.2	18.0
Immediate prison	80.6	81.1
Suspended sentence	3.1	2.8
Sections 90–92 Powers of Criminal Courts (Sentencing) Act 2000	0.6	0.5

(1) Before April 2001 this was a probation order
(2) Before April 2001 this was a community service order
(3) Before April 2001 this was a combination order

(Source: Criminal Statistics, England and Wales, 2001)

1.2 A statistical account of the criminal justice system

As regards a statistical account of the criminal justice system, the first point to be emphasised is the very large number of crimes that are recorded in a year.

The official statistics on crime (Home Office (2002a)), as presented in Table 2, reveal over five million crimes being recorded by the police. The table also allows the changes over time to be indicated. The most notable change is in the volume of crime, although the changes to the counting rules need to be taken into account.

New counting rules have been introduced for the criminal statistics – under the new system one crime per victim will be recorded. This will allow greater comparability with the British Crime Survey. Also, the number of notifiable offences has been increased. The overall effect of these changes will be to increase the number of offences recorded which makes it more difficult to show trends.

Table 2

A Summary of Some of the Main Statistics for Notifiable Offences (thousands)		
	1981	2001
Offences recorded by the police	2,794	5,500
Offences detected	1,056	1,291
Defendants proceeded against	2,373	1,840
Offenders found guilty and cautioned	2,259	1,600
Found guilty	2,105	1,370
Cautioned	144	230

(Source: Criminal Statistics, England and Wales, 2001)

Motoring offences

Table 3, which is taken from Ayres, Hayward and Perry (2003), provides data on motoring offences, which are the most common form of criminal behaviour. Given the huge amount of people involved, it is clear that being a motoring offender is a very common occurrence: 10.5 million offences in 2001, a 5 per cent increase on 2000 and the highest figure ever recorded. The number of speed limit offences was 1.4 million, a considerable change from 761,000 cases in 1996.

Table 3

Types of Proceedings for Motoring Offences 2001
(in millions)

Fixed penalty notices	3.0
Court proceedings	2.0
Penalty charge notices	5.3
Written warnings	0.1
VDRS notices	0.1
Total	10.5
Number of vehicles licensed	27.0

(Source: Motoring Offences, England and Wales, 2001)

The penalty charge notices are issued by local authority parking attendants. The fixed penalty notices are issued by the police and traffic wardens. Written warnings are issued by the police. VDRS notices are Vehicle Defect Rectification Scheme notices. More than six million of the offences, well over half of all offences, are obstruction, waiting and parking offences. Speeding accounted for over 20 per cent of offences and licence, insurance and record-keeping offences were not far behind. Roadside cameras provided evidence for 1.1 million offences (a very large increase from 319,000 in 1996), which included 72 per cent of speeding offences.

The official Criminal Statistics

The official *Criminal Statistics* for 2001 (Home Office (2002a)) provide an indication of the amount of crime during the year. They reveal that 5.5 million notifiable offences were recorded by the police in 2001. This was an increase of 2 per cent in comparison with the year before, with allowances having been made for differences in recording practices. Property crime made up 82 per cent of crime in 2001. An estimated 1.6 million people were found guilty or cautioned during 2001, a fall of 5 per cent compared to the previous year. The rate per 100,000 of the population for indictable offences was 1,007. The recorded crime statistics do not tell the whole story. Figures from the British Crime Survey suggest that the number of offences committed is more than four times the number reported to the police, and even if reported it seems that many are not recorded by the police.

The detection or clear up rate was 23 per cent in 2001, having been 24 per cent in the previous year. The rate was as high as 45 per cent in the 1960s. There were 1.3 million arrests in 2001. Of those arrested 25 per cent were under the age of 18. Where arrest was resorted to, in 56 per cent of cases this was for property offences. The number of people who were found guilty or cautioned was 1.6 million, this being a 2 per cent decrease on the year before. In total 1.37 million were found guilty whilst 230,000 were cautioned – a figure that includes reprimands and warnings. There was a slight decrease in the cautioning rate, compared to the previous year. There had been large reductions in the previous two years. Between police force areas there were big differences in cautioning rates for indictable offences, with Dyfed Powys at 51 per cent, Surrey at 50 per cent and Northamptonshire at 44 per cent having the highest rates. In contrast, Leicestershire and Merseyside had a rate of 21 per cent and South Yorkshire was even lower at 17 per cent. Ninety-eight thousand juveniles were given reprimands or final warnings – 2001 was the first year that this new system was fully operational.

In relation to court proceedings, 1.85 million people were proceeded against at magistrates' courts in 2001, a 3 per cent decrease on the previous year. Inclusive of guilty pleas, convictions in cases brought by the Crown Prosecution Service remained almost unchanged between 1992 and 2001 at 98 per cent of cases proceeding to a hearing in magistrates' courts. Convictions in the Crown Court were slightly higher at 89 per cent – in comparison with the previous year at 88 per cent. Convictions following a plea of not guilty rose gradually from 56 per cent of contested hearings in 1992 to 60 per cent in 1997, but went back down in later years being 55 per cent in 2000 and 2001. In the Crown Court 75,500 cases were tried, a large reduction from the figure of 91,000 four years earlier. Of the 75,500, 62 per cent pleaded guilty. For the remainder who pleaded not guilty as many as 66 per cent of them were acquitted. Table 4 provides data in relation to proceedings against adults in the Crown Court with information on gender and offence types also being supplied.

Table 4

Persons Aged 18 and Over Proceeded against at the Crown Court in 2001 (thousands)	Male	Female
Violence against the person	57.6	6.0
Sexual offences	6.9	0.1
Burglary	29.1	1.7
Robbery	7.5	0.6
Theft and handling stolen goods	107.2	27.4
Fraud and forgery	17.7	6.6
Criminal damage	12.3	1.2
Drug offences	43.1	5.3
Motoring offences	9.1	0.6
Other offences	64.9	9.7
Totals	355.5	59.3

(Source: Criminal Statistics, England and Wales, 2001)

Statistics on women and the criminal justice system

One of the issues for researchers is the position of women in the criminal justice system. Data was made available in relation to 2001 by a report (Home Office (2002b)) which brings together the key results from recent research and statistics that focus on the treatment of women by the criminal justice system. Criminal statistics show that in 2001 only 19 per cent of known offenders were women – the figure had been 17 per cent two years earlier. Male offenders outnumber female offenders by a ratio of around four-and-a-half to one. Women 'grow out of crime' – they are most likely to desist from offending in their late teens. The peak age of reported offending for girls was 14. Sixteen per cent of those arrested were women, but the proportion was higher for fraud and forgery (27 per cent) and theft and handling (22 per cent). Research suggests that following arrest women are more likely than men to be cautioned and are less likely to have no further action taken or be charged. This partly reflects the fact that women are more likely than men to admit their offences and to be arrested for less serious offences. According to official statistics, female offenders are also more likely to be cautioned for indictable offences.

Although women are less likely than men to be remanded in custody or committed for trial, this mainly reflects differences in offending history and type of offence. Women on remand make up a fifth of the female prison population. Women remanded in custody spend less time in custody than men. In relation to sentencing, women are more likely than men to be discharged or given a community sentence for indictable offences and are less likely to be fined or sentenced to custody. The top eight offences for women sentenced to custody in 2000 were: theft from shops (2,400 women sentenced to custody); fraud (490); wounding (460); production, supply and possession with intent to supply a class A controlled drug (450); summary motoring (430); burglary (330); robbery (320); and handling stolen goods (320). In terms of community penalties, women accounted for 13 per cent of those supervised by the Probation Service in 2001. Women starting community orders were less likely than men to have previous convictions or to have served a custodial sentence.

There were, on average, 3,740 women in prison in 2001. They made up only 5 per cent of the total prison population. Between 1993 and 2001 the average population of women in prison rose by 140 per cent as against 46 per cent for men. Theft and handling accounted for 41 per cent of sentenced receptions of women in 2000, drug offences for 14 per cent and violence against the person for 12 per cent. Among the population of sentenced female offenders the main offence groups are drug offences (39 per cent at June 2001), theft and handling (16 per cent) and violence against the person (15 per cent). Seventy women were sent to prison for fine default in 2001, but as the average stay is only five days, the average number of fine defaulters in the prison population was just two. In mid 2001 ethnic minority groups made up 26 per cent of the female prison population compared to 20 per cent of the male prison population. An estimated 20 per cent of women in prison had experienced some time in care. Over 40 per cent of sentenced women prisoners and over 50 per cent of women on remand have reported being dependent on drugs in the year before coming to prison.

Statistics on race and the criminal justice system

Data is provided on the issue of race in the criminal justice system by a recent government report: Home Office (2002c). The information relates mainly to 2000–2001, although some of the data reflects earlier time periods. Data indicates that 2 per cent of the population aged ten and over in England and Wales were of black ethnic origin, 3 per cent of Asian origin and 1 per cent other non-white ethnic groups. Six hundred and eighty-six thousand stops and searches were recorded by the police under a range of legislation, including the Police and Criminal Evidence Act 1984 (PACE), of which 10 per cent were of black people, 5 per cent Asian and 1 per cent other non-white origin. Police forces varied widely in their rates for recorded stops and searches. Compared with 1999–2000, the number of stops and searches fell by 14 per cent for white people but rose 6 per cent for black people in the Metropolitan Police Service (MPS) area. In England and Wales (excluding the MPS) the fall was less, with an average fall of about 18 per cent for white people, but a rise of 4 per cent for black people. In 1998/99, 1999/2000 and 2000/01, 2,166 homicides were recorded by the police of which 10 per cent were of black people, 5 per cent Asian and 6 per cent other non-white ethnic origin. Twenty-five homicides were recorded as being racially motivated over this three-year period. The police were statistically less likely to identify suspects for homicides involving black victims than for white or those from other ethnic groups, but differences in the type (ie the method of killing) of homicide involved may play a part here. In the same three-year period 1.3 million arrests for notifiable offences took place, of which, 7 per cent were of black people, 4 per cent Asian and 1 per cent other non-white origin. Black people were four times more likely to be arrested than white or other ethnic groups. White people showed a higher likelihood of being arrested for burglary and criminal damage, black people for robbery and both black people and Asians for fraud and forgery and drugs. The police cautioned about 209,200 persons for notifiable offences of which 6 per cent were of black people, 5 per cent Asian and 1 per cent other non-white ethnic origin. Relative to the number of persons arrested, the cautioning rate was slightly higher for white people (16 per cent) and Asians (17 per cent) than for black people (13 per cent). An offender's eligibility for a caution depends upon a number of factors, including the circumstances of an offence and whether they will admit to the offence. Information collected from six pilot areas on magistrates' court decisions indicated that, excluding those defendants committed to the Crown Court for trial, white defendants were more likely to be convicted (64 per cent) than black or Asian defendants (53 per cent and 4 per cent). In June 2000 ethnic minorities accounted for 19 per cent of the male prison population (12 per cent black, 3 per cent Asian and 4 per cent other) and 25 per cent of the female prison population (19 per cent black, 1 per cent Asian and 5 per cent other). This included foreign nationals who made up 8 per cent of the male prison population and 15 per cent of the female population. Black and Asian prisoners tended to be younger than white prisoners and white and Asian prisoners tended to be serving shorter sentences than black prisoners. Ethnic minorities are under-represented in all grades as employees in the police service, prison service and in senior posts in all the criminal justice agencies. There have been some small improvements in this representation, compared to earlier years, in most criminal justice agencies. Further information is presented in Table 5 below.

Table 5

Representation of Ethnic Groups at Different Stages of the Criminal Justice Process 2001–2002 (percentages)

	White	Black	Asian	Other	Not Known	Total
			Ethnicity			
Population (aged 10 and over)	94.5	1.8	2.7	1.1	0.0	100
Stops and searches	82.7	10.1	4.9	1.0	1.2	100
Arrests	86.3	7.7	4.4	0.9	0.6	100
Cautions	85.7	6.2	4.6	1.0	2.0	100
Prison receptions	85.6	8.9	2.4	3.1	0.0	100
Prison population	81.9	12.1	2.8	3.1	0.1	100

(Source: Statistics on Race and the Criminal Justice System)

Intenational comparisons of criminal justice statistics

Whilst it is difficult to make comparisons of crime rates across jurisdictions some guidance is provided by the following material in relation to homicide. The data is drawn from Barclay and Tavares (2002).

Table 6

Number of Homicides and Homicides per 100,000 of the Population in Urban Areas 1998–2000

City	Number of homicides	Homicides per 100,000 population
Canberra	5	0.54
Ottawa	23	0.98
Tokyo	440	1.22
Rome	98	1.24
Athens	53	0.55
Paris	181	2.85
London	538	2.38
Belfast	50	5.85
New York	1,977	8.77
Copenhagen	25	1.68
Moscow	3,863	18.20
Pretoria	1,512	41.12
Washington	733	45.79

(Source: International Comparisons of Criminal Justice Statistic)

The costs of the criminal justice system

None of the activities of the criminal justice system are cheap and some indication of the projected costs involved are given in Table 7 which is drawn from official data: Home Office (2000).

Table 7

Some of the Costs of the Criminal Justice System 2001–2002
Cost in billions

Police	7.8
Crown Prosecution Service	0.3
Criminal legal aid	0.9
Magistrates' court	0.4
Crown Court	0.2
Victim Support	0.2
Probation Service	0.5
Prison Service	2.0

(Source: The Strategic Plan for the Criminal Justice System 1999–2002)

Brand and Price (2000) provide further information as to the economic and social costs of crime. This information is also relevant to the victim perspective (on which further data is given in the next section), and the theme is picked up in later chapters as well. The data can be used to sharpen up the focus of policy-making. The research tackled the difficulties of estimating the economic and social cost of crime. Every day decisions are made by policy-makers and managers in the criminal justice system which reflect implicit judgments about the relative seriousness of different crimes, or about the benefits of pursuing one approach to reducing crime rather than another. The study represents a first step towards making such judgments more explicit and in making sure that the judgments better reflect the available evidence on the impact of different types of crime on society. Cost of crime estimates can play an important role in helping the government to achieve the greatest effect on crime for the money spent. They can be used in both appraisal and evaluation of crime reduction policies, such as those in the government's evidence-based Crime Reduction Programme, and they can help to prioritise, focusing scarce resources on policies that have the biggest impact on harm caused by crime, rather than simply the number of crimes.

'Costs of crime' cover all of the effects of crime (within the notifiable offences category), expressed where possible in monetary terms – though this does not suggest that it is either straightforward or always right to reduce the consequences of any crime into purely financial terms. Costs are incurred in anticipation of crimes occurring (such as security expenditure and insurance administration costs), as a consequence of criminal events (such as property stolen and damaged, emotional and physical impacts and health services), and responding to crime and tackling criminals (costs to the criminal justice system). Costs were measured using surveys of victims, such as the British Crime Survey and Commercial Victimisation Survey, and estimates of industry turnover and costs, such as the security and insurance industries.

Average costs of crime vary widely between offence categories. The most costly property crimes are theft of vehicles, costing around £4,700 per incident. Burglaries cost an average of £2,300, and criminal damage around £500. Personal crimes are far more costly on average than property crimes. Homicides have been estimated to cost at least £1 million, with other violence against the person crimes costing on average £19,000 per incident.

Robberies incur costs of almost £5,000 on average. Common assault is the least costly personal crime, with an average cost of around £500 per offence. The total cost of crime to England and Wales in 1999/2000 is estimated at around £60 billion, although this figure is still far from comprehensive as it does not include important costs such as fear of crime or quality of life impacts. Around £19 billion of the total cost of crime is the cost of stolen or damaged property. Nearly £18 billion of the total is the direct emotional and physical impact on victims of crime, with a little over £14 billion of this incurred as a result of violent crime. The response to crime by the criminal justice system constitutes around 20 per cent of the total cost of crime, at around £12 billion. Identifiable costs in anticipation of crime – security expenditure and insurance administration costs – come to over £5 billion, the bulk of this being security expenditure.

One example of how such data can be applied in practice is provided. The relative importance of violent crime in comparison with other crimes is marked. When we focus on the volume of offences violent crimes come to around a quarter of the total. When we focus on the cost of those offences rather than the volume, violent crimes constitute nearly three-quarters of the total cost. This finding is one example of the way in which cost of crime estimates can help illuminate potential areas where gains may be made by new policies or the switching of resources from one area to another.

Self-report and victim studies

From the data to date it is clear that many people are processed for criminality – it is equally clear that many others commit crimes without being processed. Evidence of this is provided by self-report and victim studies which deal with offences of which the police may have no knowledge. As its name suggests a self-report study of criminality involves questioning people as to their involvement in criminal behaviour. Such studies consistently indicate criminality as being more widespread in the population and more extensive than official statistics on crime would suggest. Before three United Kingdom studies are considered it has to be stated that whilst researchers have taken precautions to ensure the accuracy of their findings there are still reservations about such research. For example, those interviewed may for one reason or another exaggerate (perhaps out of bravado) or under-report (perhaps to keep their behaviour covert or through faulty recall) their criminality. Farrall (2002:58–59) provides evidence that there are high levels of honesty in what is reported in self-report studies. Belson (1975) in his study of 1,425 London boys found that:

> '... 88 per cent had at some time stolen something from school; 70 per cent had at some time stolen from a shop; 33 per cent from a stall or barrow; 30 per cent had at some time got something by threatening others; 25 per cent had stolen from a car or lorry or van; 18 per cent

had at some time stolen from a telephone box, 17 per cent a letter or parcel, 11 per cent from a meter; 5 per cent had taken a car or lorry or van.' (1975:87)

West and Farrington (1977), in their study of 389 males at age 18, provided data on both admissions of seven types of delinquency and convictions for that delinquency over the previous three years. This material is presented in Table 8: buying cheap refers to buying cheap or accepting things known or suspected of being stolen by someone else.

Table 8

	Self-Reported Delinquency Number and percentage admitting the behaviour	Number and percentage of those admitting the behaviour who were convicted of it
Damaging property	82 (21%)	9 (11%)
Taking and driving away	60 (15%)	23 (38%)
Buying cheap	268 (70%)	4 (2%)
Shop-lifting	60 (15%)	5 (8%)
Stealing from slot machines	74 (19%)	4 (5%)
Breaking and entering	42 (11%)	26 (62%)
Stealing from cars	52 (13%)	9 (17%)

(Source: The Delinquent Way of Life)

The final study is the Mori poll of 3,000 pupils, aged 10–17, and also of 172 young people who had been expelled from school: Prescott (2000). Nearly three-quarters of those who had been expelled admitted committing a crime in the last 12 months. Of those in school, 22 per cent admitted committing crime in the last 12 months. The most common offences were fare-dodging (44 per cent), shop-lifting (31 per cent), graffiti (29 per cent), criminal damage (26 per cent), assault (24 per cent) and carrying a knife or a weapon (23 per cent).

Despite the doubts that have been expressed about self-report studies, it would seem reasonable to suggest, in the light of findings such as a 70 per cent rate of shop-lifting in the Belson study and a conviction rate of only 8 per cent for shop-lifting in the West and Farrington study, that criminality is more widespread amongst the population and more extensive than an examination of official figures would indicate. Victim studies seek out previously unrecorded criminality by enquiring as to whether or not a person has been the victim of a certain type or types of criminal behaviour. Commentators are generally more positive about these studies than about self-report studies, even though they also have methodological problems. For example, it is an inappropriate method in relation to behaviour that has no obvious victim – such as drunk and disorderly and similar public order offences. It also seems that the level of crime is under-estimated by this method as people have problems of recall concerning all but the most serious of offences. A particularly valuable source of data in relation to the United Kingdom is the British Crime Survey. Data is provided from the 1998 and the 2002–2003 studies.

The 1998 British Crime Survey

This was the seventh survey of people's experiences and perceptions of crime carried out on behalf of the Home Office – the first was carried out in 1982 – Home Office (1999b). Nearly 15,000 adults were interviewed and the information from such surveys provides important insights into criminal behaviour. They certainly tell us that the official statistics do not portray anything like the whole story. They may well reveal similar trends, as with the recorded fall in crime, which is mirrored in the official statistics. The information was gathered by means of questionnaire and interview. The survey estimated that 16.5 million offences were committed against individuals and their property in 1997. Where comparisons can be made with categories used in the official statistics the survey estimated 10.2 million offences, whilst the official statistics recorded 2.5 million offences. The survey data thus records more than four times the amount of crime that the official statistics show. For 1997 the amount of crime recorded is 49 per cent greater than in 1981, but 14 per cent less than in 1995. There was a fall recorded for nearly every offence that is measured, with the figure for burglary, violence and thefts of vehicles falling by 7, 17 and 25 per cent respectively. Better security on recent makes of car is certainly making a difference and is a success for the promoters of crime prevention strategies. There were still nearly 3.5 million vehicle-related thefts. As many as 10 per cent of vehicle-owning households had a vehicle-related theft. On the issue of violence it is still the case that the source of this is likely to be an acquaintance (43 per cent of cases) or as a result of a domestic incident (another 25 per cent) rather than a stranger. Where comparisons can be made, only a quarter of the BCS crimes ended up in police records. This is because only 44 per cent were reported to the police and of these only about 54 per cent were reported and recorded. These surveys are also very valuable as a source of information on the risk of being a victim of crime. The BCS estimates that 34 per cent of adults in 1997 were victims of at least one of the crimes that the survey records – this being a fall from 39 per cent in 1995. Risks of crime are highest for youngsters, unemployed people, single parents, private renters, inner-city dwellers and those living in areas of high physical disorder associated with urban decay. Specifically on violence: 4.7 per cent had been victims with a higher rate of 21 per cent for 16 to 24-year-old males.

The 2002–2003 British Crime Survey

The authors of the 2002–2003 British Crime Survey were Simmons and Dodd (2003). The survey involves questioning a representative sample of people as to their experiences of having been a victim of crime in the previous 12 months. The present survey reports the findings from interviews carried out during 2002 and 2003. Unlike the earlier surveys these are now annual and carried out throughout the whole period of the survey. The survey estimated that 12.3 million offences were committed against individuals and their property in the survey period. Where comparisons can be made with categories used in the official statistics the survey reported nearly three times the amount of crime than is the case with the official statistics. The amount of crime reported by victims is 2 per cent less than in the previous survey and there has been a downward trend since 1995.

The British Crime Survey asked victims why they did not report incidents to the police. The most common set of reasons was that the incident was not serious enough or involved no loss or that the police would be unable to do much about it (69 per cent). These surveys are also very valuable as a source of information on the risk of being a victim of crime. The British Crime Survey estimates that 27 per cent of adults were victims of at least one of the crimes that the survey records: this being a fall from 39 per cent in 1995. Risks of crime are highest for certain groups such as youngsters, unemployed people, single parents, private renters, inner-city dwellers and those living in areas of high physical disorder.

Local victim studies

Whilst the British Crime Survey is valuable in providing further information in relation to the victim perspective at the national level important local differences are still not revealed by such data. Equally, the impact of crime on particular individuals and communities is still left not fully appreciated. Wasik (1999) offers the following insights:

> 'Important recent research has demonstrated the highly skewed nature of victimisation. For most citizens, victimisation is a quite rare event, whilst some "repeat" victims may be affected by crime routinely, almost continuously (Farrell and Pease (1993); Genn (1988)). Those living in inner city areas, for example, are much more at risk of burglary and theft than those living elsewhere. In his first speech as Prime Minister in June 1997, at a housing estate in Southwark, Mr Blair underlined this fact, observing that "nearly a half of all crimes take place in only a tenth of the neighbourhoods". Local crime surveys provide valuable data on these differential risks of crime. A person's lifestyle is known to make a significant difference to magnitude of risk. Young, fit and socially active people who go out regularly in the evenings to visit pubs and clubs and meet new people are at increased risk of violent crime. It should be remembered, however, that "lifestyle" must be broadly construed here so as to include domestic living arrangements. Much violent crime takes place in the home rather than on the streets and in public places so for those, particularly women and children, who are subjected to domestic violence, there is no safety in staying at home.' (1999:2)

Crime is pervasive

Despite the fact that there are large numbers of people dealt with each year by the criminal justice system this is only a fraction of the criminality within society. Crime is pervasive, so much so that we are all likely to engage in criminal behaviour of one sort or another. By way of example, the motor car is the setting for many offences such as speeding, parking violations and drinking and driving. Taxation systems offer the possibility of offences such as non-declaration of earnings for income tax purposes and non-payment of duty in the case of television licences. The workplace provides opportunities for crimes of dishonesty such as theft of office stationery and other materials, as well as the unauthorised use of an employer's telephone. A problem in the student context is that of students who after a drinking session have the potentially lethal desire to collect items of street furniture such as warning cones and beacons. Thus, I would hope to have persuaded most readers by now as to both their own criminality and that of other people. However, I offer fare-dodging as a final example. Andrews (1986) reported a British Rail campaign in London against fare-dodgers. The problem they were tackling was that some of their passengers who had not purchased a ticket before boarding a train subsequently transferred to the separate underground railway system, knowing that at certain stations they would not have to go through British Rail ticket inspectors. They could thus avoid payment for the British Rail part of their journey. In order to combat this an unannounced inspection system was introduced for two days at three such stations. As a result numerous fare-dodgers were detected and £4,000 in excess fares was collected. The estimated annual cost of evasion in the London commuter network is £20 million, about 3 per cent of total revenue. The comments of Mr Ken Callender, a chief ticket inspector are pertinent. 'I'm delighted that we pulled in so much revenue but this is just the tip of the iceberg. There is no way we can mount campaigns on this scale every week and the travelling public knows it. They see the railway as fair game and most of them are honest people away from the station.' Making the point that fare evasion covered the whole spectrum of society, he added, 'we have had MPs, judges, bishops, a police inspector and other people. No one is exempt' (1986:1). A retort to such material might well be that many of the offences are trivial and in some sense not really criminal. Credence can be provided for this viewpoint by referring to statistics on people proceeded against in the magistrates' courts in 2001. They reveal that 73 per cent of them were only charged with summary offences: Home Office (2002a). It should be noted, however, that the examples given above all involve dishonesty or potentially dangerous activities. Also notable is the finding that 34 per cent of men born in 1953 had been convicted for a standard list offence by the age of 40. Since the standard list offences are the more serious of the offences, this makes the trivialisation of claims of widespread criminality more difficult.

Further data on criminal careers is provided by Prime, White, Liriano and Patel (2001) who examined the criminal careers of groups of people born between 1953 and 1978. They examined data in relation to the criminal convictions of people born in the following years: 1953, 1958, 1963, 1968, 1973 and 1978. The following are their main findings. Thirty-three per cent of males and 9 per cent of females born in 1953 had been convicted of at least one 'standard list' offence before the age of 46. Two-thirds of all court appearances where a conviction occurred before the age of 46 for males born in 1953 were attributable to about one-quarter of offenders, or 8 per cent of the male population. The earlier a male offender has his first conviction the more likely he is to be convicted again; the relationship with age is not so strong for female offenders. The majority of offenders had been convicted on only one occasion: half of male offenders and three-quarters of female offenders born in 1953 had only been convicted once. Twenty-two per cent of males currently aged 10 to 45 are estimated to have a conviction for at least one standard list offence. The figure for females is much lower at 5 per cent. Fifty-five per cent of male offenders and 80 per cent of female offenders had a criminal career of less than a year in length. Nearly half of male offenders and two-thirds of female offenders born in 1953 were first convicted of theft or handling of stolen goods. The peak age of known criminal activity for males was 19, at which age 11 per cent of those born in 1953 were known to be criminally active. Over 10 per cent of males born in 1953 were criminally active between the ages of 17 and 25. Seven per cent of males and 0.5 per cent of females born in 1953 had received a custodial conviction before the age of 46. For males and females born in more recent cohort years the proportion with at least one conviction was lower than those born in earlier cohort years. This reflects the increased use of cautioning of young offenders in the pertinent time period.

One outcome of the finding of a pretty well universal criminality, for which many of us but by no means all of us will be the subject of proceedings in the criminal justice process, is that attempts to view criminals as some form of distinct group are clearly problematic. In fact such an approach has been a common strategy within criminology, the aim being to discover the alleged distinguishing characteristics of such a group. The thorny matter of crime causation is one of the issues to be considered later in this chapter. A finding of widespread criminality also raises the issue of what factors determine that some people's criminality will be the subject of official attention whilst the criminality of others manages to avoid a reaction by such as the police? This will be one of the recurring themes throughout the book. We will see that being male, black and lower class are all ways of having a better statistical chance of ending up in the arms of the law.

The response of the courts

Since capital punishment is no longer possible (final abolition, in relation to offences such as treason, was provided for by s36 of the Crime and Disorder Act 1998) immediate detention (prison or young offender institution) is the most severe sentence available to the courts. Detention cannot be used in relation to all offences and it is was only used for 8 per cent of sentences in 2001. The point can also be made that such sentences are relatively short in the sense that a system with much longer sentences would be possible. From the 2001 figures we learn that 30 per cent of adult males (the group most likely to receive a longer sentence) were given a sentence of over four years (this does not include life sentences) in relation to indictable offences. The effect of early release and parole produces a further shortening of the period of detention. In practice, the numerically most important sentence is the fine which was used in 69 per cent of cases: Home Office (2002a). Thus, the response to crime is relatively low key in comparison with the possibilities of more widespread use of detention and capital and corporal punishment. The account by Foucault (1977) of the use of torture and mutilation in France in 1757 makes this all too clear. As part of the procedure for an execution

> '... the flesh will be torn from his breasts, arms, thighs and calves with red-hot pincers, his right hand, holding the knife with which he committed the said parricide, burnt with sulphur, and on those places where the flesh will be torn away, poured molten lead, boiling oil, burning resin, wax and sulphur melted together and then his body drawn and quartered by four horses and his limbs and body consumed by fire.' (1977:3)

We have seen that whilst many people are the subject of proceedings in the criminal justice process in England and Wales this does not fully reflect the pervasiveness of criminality within the population. As seen above, the response to this criminality is not as severe as it could be. Whilst criminality is a varied phenomenon many offences involve motoring. Equally, many offences can be presented as relatively trivial. For those offences that are regarded as being the most serious, offences against property lead to both the greatest number of convictions and many sentences of imprisonment. As to offenders, two major points can be made. Firstly, they are mainly male and, secondly, in a number of respects, the younger age groups are over-represented.

1.3 A brief account of the issue of values

If the aim is to understand and assess the matters outlined above there are a number of interrelated problems to be tackled. The first of these is the question of values. The institutions in the system are clearly presenting certain values and behaviour as being undesirable. For example, there are laws designed to prevent the use of personal violence in many different circumstances. As regards this we need to ask is it possible to justify a claim that certain behaviour is undesirable? Equally, how can you justify the imposition of penalties designed to punish transgressors and attempt to deter them and others from similar actions in the future? Such questions in essence raise the issue of whether or not there is a means to satisfactorily make value judgements, or to produce an absolute code of moral precepts. In the absence of such a method, the criminal justice system (which is infested with value judgements) and its punitive effects, might be thought to be based on nothing other than the prejudices of individuals. In my view there is at present no method by which questions of value can be satisfactorily dealt with, a conclusion which is reached by means of an examination of some possible methods. Whilst clearly it is problematic to try to deal with such complex issues in a brief manner such an approach at least ensures that values have been identified as being an issue.

If an assertion is made that a particular state of affairs is or would be desirable we can ask why should such a claim be taken seriously, and if it is a mere assertion why is it preferable to counter-assertions? A popular form of vindication for moral stances, and one which has influence on criminal justice systems, is religion. Haskins (1960) offers some good illustrations of the influence of religion. There are numerous religions which offer a variety of ethical codes. Most commonly there is a belief in a supernatural power and the ethical code is accepted as a matter of faith, there being no need for positive proof. In some cases, however, there may be the claim of direct contact with the supernatural power by means of, say, a revelation. In the absence of convincing proof for just one of these religions I would suggest that the idea of basing laws upon them is problematic, if only in so far as it involves an imposition on non-believers.

Mead

A very different approach is to suggest that there are values common to all societies and that they should be regarded as absolutes. The anthropologist Mead (1961) suggested that notions of unjustified killing, incest and private property were common to all societies. Such a descriptive or anthropological approach can be challenged in certain ways. One method is to cite exceptions to alleged absolutes. Berk et al (1977:277) notes exceptions to the idea of unlawful killing, whilst Mead herself quotes other exceptions such as royal marriages contrary to the incest taboo. Mead's claim is, then, that the notions are common, though the actual behaviour in question will vary from society to society, and that there will be exceptions. As an argument for common behaviour patterns this seems to be rather weak. In any case even if behaviour common to all societies could be discovered why should this in itself be regarded as a reason to regard it as desirable activity? For example, if non-

16

consensual sexual relationships were common to all societies would it thus be a desirable activity? Mead in fact informs us that such behaviour is normally taboo.

A different approach is to argue that common agreement, or the consent of the governed, is the basis for the system of values in operation. Such ideas are seen for example in the work of the philosophers Hobbes, Locke and Rousseau. The reality, however, is that in a highly populated complex society such as that of England and Wales the whole population will not have been asked, never mind agreed, to the system of values that are in operation. Whilst of course there are political processes through which opinions can be expressed, the reality is that the role of the majority of the people will have been one of acquiescence. In the absence of complex agreement on the whole range of moral issues even the most democratic of political systems must be, at least in part, the imposition of the values of some upon others.

Rawls

Another purported method of producing moral absolutes is through the use of reason. For example, Rawls (1972) in his search for justice suggested that reasoned prudence would guarantee certain outcomes. He used the device of a person, in what he calls an original position, who has knowledge of some of the social sciences and who is asked to produce moral precepts for a society without knowledge of his own particular position within that society. He suggests that the outcome would be a set of principles which stress liberty and fairness. Whilst much has been written about this work only one point will be noted here. Probably the whole notion of an original position is unrealistic in that you would not be able to achieve the requisite state of mind. Views and knowledge other than those derived from the social sciences would be likely to impinge. More certainly it can be stressed that the contribution of the knowledge of the social sciences to such thought processes is likely to be ambivalent. In disciplines such as economics, politics and psychology much information remains ungathered, conflicting theories abound and even the question of which method or methods are likely to be productive is in issue. Where Rawls can be agreed with is that moral principles based on instinct or intuition are implausible as it leaves open the problem of choosing between conflicting instinctive and intuitive statements. Having noted Rawls as an exponent of the possibilities of reason it can be suggested that the view expressed by Hume (1969) in the eighteenth century should be adhered to. This is that reason should be used as a means to achieve ends rather than as a means of determining the desirability of such ends.

The outcome of this search for a method by which absolute principles of morality or justice could be identified is to my mind the realisation that none have as yet worked and indeed we may never discover one that does work. In order to live our lives we as individuals will have to make moral decisions and groups of people such as politicians will make decisions that affect the lives of many. The reality that we face is that if for example as individuals we decide that rape is abhorrent, or if politicians arrive at a similar decision and then go on to decide to impose a system of punishment for rape, then neither we nor the politicians can effectively claim that our decisions are right in an absolute sense.

1.4 Considering the nature of man, the characteristics of a particular society and the issue of crime causation

A further set of problems arises when questions are asked as to the nature of man and about the characteristics of a particular society. Such questions are clearly pertinent to the criminal justice system which exists within a society and which has people as its actors. Speculation has occurred, for example, as to whether human behaviour is determined or if instead we have free will? There has also been a nature-nuture debate enquiring as to which proportion of our behaviour is to be understood in terms of inherited rather than environmental factors? Our environment is the social groups that we come into contact with and the society as a whole that we are a part of. As was noted above practitioners of the social sciences, such as those of politics, sociology and psychology, have produced numerous purported accounts as to the nature of society and of human interaction. The nature of society as with the nature of man is quite simply a moot point. Whilst some of the more popular and pertinent explanations are considered in later sections of this chapter, for the moment it is best to emphasise the extent of our ignorance of such matters. Much of the rest of the book is concerned with various attempts to come to terms with criminal behaviour, and a fundamental problem for such attempts is that so much is not understood as regards the factors involved in such behaviour. The elusive ideal being sought is those empirically testable factors (or factor) which are present when crime is present and absent when there is no criminal behaviour. The position that we are in at the moment is that the practitioners of the various social sciences have failed to explain criminal behaviour. This is despite their use of the various factors mentioned above: assumptions of free-will and determined behaviour and of both inherited and environmental factors. Many texts are available which will provide an account of anomie, differential association, maternal deprivation and other purported factors in criminal behaviour. See, for example, Doherty (2002), Vold et al (2002), Downes and Rock (1997), Williams (2001) and Doherty (2004). For the most part such texts, despite any particular allegiences that they may contain, will tell you that one of the mysteries of criminology is the issue of the cause of criminal behaviour. Whilst this matter has been stated very briefly it must be stressed that it is of immense importance. If crime causation is not understood it means that attempts to deal with crime are based on dubious foundations.

In summary, the criminal justice system is composed of many people and numerous units and the nature of those people and the society of which they are a part is imperfectly understood. Competing purported explanations are defective by reason of assumption, untestability, or if testable, a lack of unequivocal empirical support. Indeed, the experience of examining research studies demonstrates both the variety of findings and the complexity of the issues involved. The data available may also be defective in other respects. For example, we have seen not only that the official statistics may underestimate the extent of criminal behaviour but also that methods such as self-report or victim studies, which were designed to alleviate such difficulties, are themselves problematic. Progress with regard to such matters is likely to be reliant on research activity but, as will be seen in a moment, there are problems here also.

1.5 The limited amount of research that is undertaken and its problematic features

Research activity is fettered in various ways. Research resources are limited and thus research will also be limited. The type of research can also be limited by the interests of, or the constraints imposed by, funding organisations. A further restriction is that access to data will often require the co-operation of agencies and individuals within the system and thus may not always be forthcoming. The levels of secrecy in relation to the most innocuous of material are notoriously high in England and Wales. I have an axe to grind on such matters – a colleague and I were denied access to the records of county court actions as it was thought that we would have too great an impact (which we estimated as likely to have been negligible) upon staff resources. The result was that the research project collapsed as alternative methods of gathering data were impractical. We then decided to undertake research on bail decisions in magistrates' courts since this did not require official sanction. This research was published as Doherty and East (1985). A further indicative example of such restrictions is provided by Ashworth (1983) in his preface. The research project on sentencing in the Crown Court, being carried out by four researchers at the Centre for Criminological Research at the University of Oxford, came to an abrupt end after only one year when the Lord Chief Justice, Lord Lane, refused his permission for the project to proceed beyond a pilot study. Lord Lane's decision, which Ashworth describes as being 'tragic', had the effect of preventing systematic knowledge being made available 'about the approach to sentencing of those who pass sentence in the courts which deal with our most serious crimes.'

1.6 Identifying aims within the criminal justice system, with an emphasis being placed on its rather haphazard nature

A major problem as regards understanding the criminal justice system is that it is not rational in the sense of having a master plan or clear aims and is also in other respects a rather haphazard system. This statement is made despite the existence of documents over the years such as *The Strategic Plan for the Criminal Justice System 1999–2000*: Home Office (1999a). In the strategic plan the following aims and objectives have been identified to:

1. reduce crime and the fear of crime and their social and economic costs;
2. reduce the level of actual crime and disorder;
3. reduce the adverse impact of crime and disorder on people's lives;
4. reduce the economic costs of crime;
5. dispense justice fairly and efficiently and to promote confidence in the rule of law;
6. ensure just processes and just and effective outcomes;
7. deal with cases throughout the criminal justice process with appropriate speed;
8. meet the needs of victims, witnesses and jurors within the system;
9. respect the rights of defendants and to treat them fairly;
10. promote confidence in the criminal justice system.

The government has also identified performance measures and targets to assess achievement against objectives. This includes targets such as reducing vehicle crime by 30 per cent within five years.

There is a need to look behind such lists, which may be no more than platitudes, and to examine the actual operation of the criminal justice system. Progress can be made initially by seeking the aims and the common concerns of the period since 1945, and by examining the way that policy developed in that period. From studying the details of the criminal justice system as a whole it is clear that there is no master plan for the criminal justice system – indeed the word system is itself misleading. A common aim of criminal justice systems is the prevention of crime through the provision of a system of stigma or punishment. A deterrent effect might be experienced by both the individual concerned and by others in society who would wish to avoid a similar experience. The individual miscreant may also be incapacitated from committing further crime by deprivation of liberty as in the case of a prison sentence. A criminal justice system may also have the aim of upholding group values by, for example, denouncing deviants, or it may seek to provide facilitative standards for a society. For example, road users may well desire the knowledge that there is a criminal law stating that traffic should keep to the left on a highway. Protection may be offered to all by some features of the system, such as restrictions on the use of personal violence. It may also offer dispassionate systems of revenge and dispute resolution, thus preventing recourse to socially divisive behaviour such as vendetta. Other concerns may be the provision of treatment, training, rehabilitation and reform, or the operation of systems of control or domination.

As regards common concerns, it is clear from Table 9 that recorded crime has risen considerably since 1951. Not surprisingly, the general increase in crime has given rise to much concern.

Table 9

Notifiable Offences Recorded by the Police 1951–2001 (thousands)	
1951	525
1961	807
1971	1,666
1981	2,794
1991	5,075
1997	4,461
2001	5,500

(Source: Criminal Statistics, England and Wales, 2001)

This rise in crime was a major factor in causing increased pressure on the criminal justice system, with pressure on the prisons being a notable example of this. Table 10 (derived from White (1999) and Hollis and Goodman (2003)) details the rise in the prison population, providing data for as far back as 1936.

Table 10

Average Prison Population 1936–2002
(thousands)

	Average prison population
1936	11
1946	15
1956	20
1966	32.1
1976	41.4
1986	46.8
1996	55.3
1998	65.3
2002	69.6

(Source: The Prison Population in 1998 and Prison Population Brief: December 2002)

Attempts to deal with these problems led to the provision of both more police and prison places. The potential for such measures was, however, affected by a conflicting common cause of concern – the cost of the criminal justice system. Other effects were that concern over cost meant that a policy would be attractive if it was cheap and unattractive if it was expensive. This clearly affected the bail system as improvements to the system, such as the development of bail hostels and information schemes, was clearly going to be expensive. Their introduction was very much delayed because of their financial implications. Similarly, measures having the effect of reducing pressure on the system were likely to be adopted, whilst those that would increase pressure would be avoided. It is for example clear that a desire to reduce the pressure on prisons has strongly influenced policy decisions in relation to bail, parole, community service, deferred sentences and, indeed, sentencing generally. As to the crime rate, it was a false hope that more police would lead to less recorded crime. As Bottomley and Coleman note, one of the established penological facts is that 'increased resources to the police are most unlikely to reduce the crime rate and may quite feasibly produce an increase in what is recorded' (1984:55). Quite simply, more police are likely to process more rather than less crime. What the steady rise in crime clearly did indicate was that policy initiatives to control it had generally ended in failure.

Analysis of policy proposals produced in recent times makes it clear that there is no long-term master plan for the criminal justice system. Measures are introduced that do not have a clear rationale, and it is not unusual to pursue a policy without any firm evidence in its favour. Equally a policy can be pursued despite the evidence against it. It seems that the facts may not matter. The increase in police numbers as an attempt to combat rising crime rates has already been noted as an unrealistic strategy given the evidence of previous such attempts. Many of the non-custodial sentences have no clear rationale. The courts were given no real guidance as regards the role of the suspended sentence and the way that non-custodial sentences interrelate is unclear. Parole offers a further example of a lack of clarity of thought. Here there was a mixture of ideas involved; the explanation for its adoption in

21

1969 was at least partly the effect it was hoped to have on prison numbers. This was also very much the reason for its extension in 1982. As for the suspended sentence Wooton (1977) pointed out that the Advisory Council on the Treatment of Offenders had stated (Home Office (1970)) that such a sentence was 'Wrong in principle and to a large extent impracticable' (1977:16). Equally, when policy is made it can be in the form of reaction management, catalysed by a particular event and without full regard to its consequences. For example, the mass killings by Michael Ryan in Hungerford in the 1980s and by Thomas Hamilton in Dunblane in the 1990s were followed by immediate policy initatives in relation to the possession of firearms. The escape of Blake (a Russian spy) and other similar events in 1966 gave rise to an outcry about the security of the prisons. Once security was highlighted as a major cause for concern, the outcome was a major change within prisons with a considerable emphasis on security. By way of further examples the Public Order Act 1936 was very much a reaction to public order disturbances at that time, and indeed the more recent Public Order Act 1986 was in part the product of similar forces. It can also be suggested that the units of the system whilst interrelated are also at times semi-autonomous. Further, that they are often not harmonised and that they can end up working against each other. The position of judges and chief constables can be noted as parts of the system of which a large measure of independence is a feature. The police and the Crown Prosecution Service have had a difficult working relationship. The sentencing stage also provides examples of competing aims as here, for example, a defendant's representative will generally seek the most lenient sentence whilst the court may have other incompatible desires such as rehabilitation, deterrence or protection of the public. Also, within units such as the police and the prison service there is evidence of different aims and concerns in the various parts of their organisations. These points are still applicable even though we are supposed to be in an era of joined up criminal justice.

1.7 The development of penal policy since 1945

In offering an account of major changes and themes in penal policy since 1945 it is hoped that at least a very basic background picture can be developed at this stage. Ashworth (1983:113–115), Hall Williams (1970:45–52) and in particular Ryan (1983) have been used as sources for the historical material prior to 1974. Newburn (2003) is very good on history generally and particularly the recent policy developments. Bottoms, Gelsthorpe and Rex (eds) (2001) are very good on the history of youth justice. By noting here numerous government reports and legislative measures this section can also act as a source for reference purposes. In the period between 1945 and the 1970s the hope and optimism that had existed before the Second World War was characteristic of the later period. This was to be evident in the 1960s with concern for the possibilities of rehabilitation. Such a spirit was also present in the measures and campaigns which were designed to liberalise the system by, for example, repealing laws which had allowed corporal punishment and also capital punishment for murder. Capital punishment was very much the dominant issue in penal policy in the period up to the 1960s, though the reform was not to come until later. Capital punishment was abolished for murder for a trial period in 1965 and complete abolition for murder came in 1969. One impact of the concentration on the issue of capital punishment was that there were few other reform measures introduced in the period before the 1960s and also in this period there was only limited legislative change. The major measure to note is the Criminal Justice Act 1948. The spirit of optimism and liberalism is seen here in that corporal punishment was to be no longer available as a sentence. The emphasis on optimism should not be overstated as the 1948 Act is clearly less optimistic than the Criminal Justice Bill of 1938 had been. Ryan describes the 1948 legislation well when he suggests that whilst it 'was indeed tough, it was by no means desperate' (1983:10).

The government White Paper, *Penal Practice in a Changing Society* (Home Office (1959)), was far from original in its suggestions. It stated that the on-going concern about overcrowding in prisons and the rising crime rate were to be tackled both by attempts to increase the efficiency of the police and also by the provision of greater resources. An idea that was developing at the time, and which had gained popularity by 1964, at which point the Labour Party formed a government, was that the aim of the system should be to rehabilitate rather than to reform. These ideas of reform were doomed to failure if only because they were never really given a chance. Limits were put on the resources that were made available and rehabilitative ideas were only half-heartedly adopted in some quarters. Also, other forces were at work – the Criminal Justice Act 1961 being a further example of the use of tougher measures in an attempt to control crime. The prison disturbances and escapes of the early 1960s led to the setting up of an enquiry into security. The report of the enquiry, commonly called the 'Mountbatten Report' after its chairman (Home Office (1966)), had as one of its conclusions that there was a need for high levels of security for certain categories of prisoner. This feature of the report was to be adopted later, as part of a security obsession, which led to a restrictive prison regime. This made nonsense of possibilities of a rehabilitative ideal. Mountbatten had in fact suggested that for those prisoners who would require it a fortress system should be used. This would have a very secure perimeter leaving open the possibility of a relaxed regime. A version of this was to be introduced many years later when Woodhill Prison was opened in 1998.

The year 1964 saw the publication of two reports, the first being the Conservative government's White Paper *The War against Crime 1959–'64*: Home Office (1964). This was an update of the 1959 report *Penal Practice in a Changing Society* (Home Office (1959)) and a notable feature of it was its recommendation of a wide-ranging and ultimately ill-fated Royal Commission on the penal system. The Royal Commission only lasted 18 months, one reason for this being that the Labour Party had formed a government in 1964. This undermined the purpose of the Royal Commission, in that the Labour Party had policy commitments already prepared in relation to issues that were part of the general remit of the Commission. Illustrations of this are to be found in the other 1964 document, *Crime – a Challenge to Us All*, a Labour Party Study Group pamphlet: Labour Party (1964). This was the work of a group led by Lord Longford and, as with the two Labour government White Papers, *The Child, the Family and the Young Offender* (Home Office (1965a)) and *Children in Trouble* (Home Office (1968a)), it was both a source of controversy and a forerunner of the Children and Young Persons Act 1969. The controversy centred on the issue of what was the correct response to juvenile delinquency? Should it be for example by means of a legalistic forum or an attempt to view delinquents as being children in need of help? In terms of the second view the traditional juvenile courts would be an inappropriate forum. *Children in Trouble* (1968) suggested the compromise of retaining the juvenile courts and adopting the caring philosophy. The 1969 Act followed this route with the juvenile courts being retained. The philosophy of care was emasculated in practice by a number of problems which included the Act never being fully implemented. Another important legislative measure in the 1960s was the Criminal Justice Act 1967. This had been influenced by the 1965 Labour government White Paper *The Adult Offender*: Home Office (1965b). The 1967 Act made provisions for a number of matters, including fines and legal aid. Also, as part of a concern about prison numbers, it introduced both parole and suspended sentences.

In the post 1960s period there was a decline in the belief in the possibilities of rehabilitation, and legislation such as the Children and Young Persons Act 1969 was viewed as being too soft and having gone too far. As an alternative, support for the idea of punishment developed with a related aim being the provision of justice through procedural safeguards. Further cross-currents and counter-currents of thought also developed and the continuing increase in overcrowding in prisons had produced a serious crisis in the prison system by the mid-1970s. One result was that a number of important reports on prisons were prepared, including: *Sentences of Imprisonment: A Review of Maximum Penalties* (Home Office (1978)); the *Report of the Committee of Inquiry into the United Kingdom Prison Services* (called the 'May Report' after its chairman) (Home Office (1979)); and *The Reduction of Pressure on the Prison Service*: Home Office (1980a). Measures to tackle overcrowding and concern over the cost of the system ensured that justice was to be a matter of expediency. For example, whilst the Bail Act 1976 introduced a presumption in favour of bail for many defendants, there were still serious deficiencies in the system. The Criminal Justice Act 1972 reflected the desire to deal with overcrowding by, for example, revising provisions in relation to the suspended sentence and parole. Parole was to be further extended in 1975 and 1982. The 1972 legislation also introduced, on a trial basis, the community service order. This had been recommended in the Wooton Report (Home Office (1970)), and by 1976 it had been made generally available. In the 1972 Act the deferred sentence was distinctive in that it was largely rehabilitative in aim rather than being an attempt to combat overcrowding. Four other Acts require attention at this stage – the Criminal Law Act 1977, Prosecution of Offenders Act 1982, the Criminal Justice Act 1982 and the Criminal Justice Act 1988. The 1977 Act was mainly concerned with administrative matters, though it created the partly suspended sentence which was not introduced until 1982 and was to be abolished again by the Criminal Justice Act 1991. The Prosecution of Offenders Act 1982 was the measure which introduced the Crown Prosecution Service, whilst the Criminal Justice Act 1982 was a more wide-ranging measure. Again, there was a desire to reduce pressure on the criminal justice system and in particular the prisons. Examples of matters dealt with were a new system of youth custody, parole, fines, attendance centres, suspended sentences, supervision orders and probation. The Criminal Justice Act 1988 provided for numerous and varied changes. These included a single type of custodial sentence for young offenders, changes to the law relating to juries, and new powers to review sentences and to confiscate the assets of offenders. The period also saw three reviews of criminal justice policy: Home Office (1977a, 1984a and 1986a). The reviews offer an account of the official view of the criminal justice system. In the 1977 document, which was produced by the Crime Policy Planning Unit, policy objectives were stated in relation to the criminal justice system as a whole, the various institutions and for particular problems such as dangerous offenders, recidivism and overcrowding. Whilst strategies were proposed for the particular problems, there was no real attempt made at general analysis though policy assumptions were stated. These were a belief in deterrence, that prison is damaging per se and that treatment can reduce recidivism. The 1984 review stated objectives which the Home Secretary, Leon Brittan, said in the Foreword were to be pursued 'in a deliberate and coherent way'. The reality was that the objectives included trite observations such as an objective of 'Convicting the guilty and acquitting the innocent' (Foreword). The assumptions and lack of an overview in the 1977 report also characterised the 1984 review. Once more the approach is piecemeal, an attempt to come to terms with particular problems in isolation. The pragmatic nature of the approach is further seen in the emphasis on good management and efficiency. Other features include stress being placed on the importance of the public having confidence in the system. This aspired to more attention being paid to the needs of victims of crime. Equally, less attention is paid to the needs of criminals and commitment to improve conditions for them within the system has declined. In the 1986 document there is an admittance that the causation of crime is a mystery and there is also a statement of the different tactics applicable to a range of particular problems. The assistance of the public is called for and details of schemes for crime prevention and community involvement are provided.

In the 1990s the government White Paper *Crime, Justice and Protecting the Public* (Home Office (1990)) had amongst its recommendations the combination order, and this was one of the new measures introduced by the Criminal Justice Act 1991 which were drawn out of that White Paper. The 1991 Act provided a new basis for sentencing. Also in 1991 was the Woolf Report (Home Office (1991)), which had been called for as a response to prison riots, and this report suggested the need for improvements in prison conditions and various forms of organisational reform. The provisions of the 1994 Criminal Justice and Public Order Act were to have impact on the right to silence, the law on bail and to introduce a system of what were to be short lived secure training orders. Numerous sub-plots operated in the period between 1960 and 1990. We saw interest in treatment and then this was ousted. Alternatives to custody became the new mantra but some of the devices used, such as the community service order and the suspended sentence, were in reality to have a net widening effect. There was then a concern that nothing worked, which was followed by a search for what worked. There was also a move to proportionality in intervention as seen in the Criminal Justice Act 1991. Interventions were to be aimed at punishment, based on proportionality, which included an era of punishment in the community. This was followed by a movement towards looking at risk factors and protecting the public. We have seen a bewildering range of ideas and of course we are still not up to date.

The years that followed the 1991 Act were to see yet more attempts to reform the criminal justice system. The government White Paper *Protecting the Public* (Home Office (1996)), from which the 1997 Crime (Sentences) Act was to be partly derived, the Crime and Disorder Act 1998 and the Youth Justice and Criminal Evidence Act 1999 were the first stages of this process. They were followed by the Powers of Criminal Courts (Sentencing) Act 2000 which provided at least a temporary consolidation of existing statutory provisions in relation to community sentences and orders – the provisions themselves were not altered to any great extent. The Criminal Justice and Court Services Act 2000 changed the names of certain dispositions. Probation orders became community rehabilitation orders, community service orders became community punishment orders and combination orders became community punishment and rehabilitation orders. The probation service itself was also reformed by this legislation. Then two consultation documents were produced: *A Review of the Criminal Courts in England and Wales* by Sir Robin Auld (Auld LJ (2001)) and *Making Punishment Work: Report of a Review of the Sentencing Framework of England and Wales*: Halliday (2001). The government White Paper, *Justice for All* (Home Office (2002d)), built on the proposals in two consultation documents. Then, in 2003, the Criminal Justice Act 2003 was produced. The details of some of these documents appear below and they are all referred to at various stages in this book. The era was also notable for two other reasons, namely, there was a further move in the direction of wanting to get tough on crime and a new managerialism could also be distinguished. These two themes are developed below.

Protecting the public

In the 1996 government White Paper *Protecting the Public: The Government's Strategy on Crime in England and Wales* (Home Office (1996)) the rhetoric is in terms of waging war on crime. Changes to sentencing are envisaged with emphasis on the problems caused by serious, dangerous and persistent offenders. The aim is to provide deterrence. Offenders would serve the sentence that they received from the court, which would mean the end of automatic early release and the abolition of parole for all but life-sentence prisoners. There would be some reduction in sentence for good behaviour. Automatic life sentences were suggested for a second serious sexual offence or second serious offence of violence. A third offence of domestic burglary would attract a three-year minimum sentence, whilst a third offence for drug trafficking would attract at least seven years. It was estimated that these changes would involve an increase in prison numbers of 10,800 by 2011–2012. Whilst these are perhaps the most important proposals, the White Paper explained more generally what the government hoped for. Their ideas include a stronger local emphasis on preventing and reducing crime, with the new police authorities and their chief constables taking a clear lead. Co-ordination of activity, as for example through the national drugs strategy, is suggested as a general tactic to be used in tackling crime. That more criminals be brought to justice is another aim. There would also be targeting of the most frequent and the most disruptive offenders. Greater fairness in procedures and practices would be sought in order to prevent miscarriages of justice. Fewer delays in processing cases would be part of this. Victims are to be paid more attention within the system. Finally, there are changes in relation to sentencing: in addition to those noted earlier there are proposals for tougher and more appropriate community sentences.

Crime (Sentences) Act 1997

The Crime (Sentences) Act 1997 which provided for some of the ideas in *Protecting the Public: The Government's Strategy on Crime in England and Wales*, was the product of a

Conservative government and the new Labour government was to leave parts of the Act dormant. Provision was made for mandatory and minimum custodial sentences in the case of repeat offending in relation to certain offences. A system of mandatory life sentences for a second serious offence was to apply for crimes such as manslaughter and rape. Seven-year minimum sentences for a third class A drug-trafficking offence and a three-year minimum for a third domestic burglary were introduced. The problem of people not paying their fines was tackled by providing for the use of a community service or curfew order for fine defaulters. A community service or curfew order for persistent petty offenders who would normally have received a fine was also introduced.

Crime and Disorder Act 1998

The Crime and Disorder Act 1998 provided for a wide range of matters. Amongst these are anti-social behaviour orders. With these certain behaviour can be prohibited and if the order is breached convictions can follow. Parenting orders are also possible where a child or young person has offended, or is subject to such as a child safety order or where poor school attendance has led to convictions. The system allows for conditions to be imposed on the parent, for up to 12 months. The aim of the order is to assist in preventing a repetition of behaviour, such as offending behaviour, by the child. Failure to adhere to the order can lead to the parent being convicted of an offence which could lead to a fine. Child safety orders apply to those under the age of ten. They are intended to control offending behaviour and allow for the supervision of and the imposition of conditions upon children. Child curfew and truancy provisions were also introduced. Cautioning for a child or young person was replaced by a system of reprimands and warnings.

Youth Justice and Criminal Evidence Act 1999

The 1999 Act provides a youth court or other magistrates' court with a new disposition, a referral to youth offender panels for many first time offenders who are under 18. It is not available where custody or an absolute discharge is appropriate. Nor is it usable in conjunction with other dispositions. Some specific powers of the courts are not affected. The Act provides for both compulsory referral conditions and discretionary referral conditions. Referral is compulsory if the offender pleads guilty and has no previous convictions or a bind over. A conditional discharge is treated as being a conviction. The discretionary conditions are different only in that they also allow referral where the offender made both guilty and not guilty pleas to the offences in issue. The order requires the offender to attend meetings of a youth offender panel, which seeks to establish a youth offender contract to provide a programme of behaviour for the offender. The aim (or principal aim) of this is the prevention of re-offending by the offender.

The following are amongst the matters that may be detailed in the contract: victim reparation, mediation, the offender to carry out unpaid work or service in or for the community, the offender to be at home at specified times, requirements for attendance at educational establishments or at a place of work, the offender to participate in specified activities (such as those designed to address offending behaviour, those offering education or training or those assisting with the rehabilitation of persons dependent on, or having a propensity to misuse, alcohol or drugs), the offender to present himself to specified persons at times and places specified in or determined under the programme and the offender to stay away from specified places or persons (or both). The above is not exhaustive, though it must be noted that the following are not possible – electronic monitoring or for the offender to have imposed on him any physical restriction on his movements. It has to be said that quite a few of the provisions have the effect of being a physical restriction on movement.

The Auld report

A major review of the criminal courts in England and Wales was carried out by Auld LJ in 2001 (Auld LJ (2001)). The main themes of the report are noted here and a number of them are covered in more detail in later chapters. The main recommendations, many of which have been enacted, include:

1. Unifying the magistrates' courts and Crown Court in a single criminal court structure with a new third intermediate District Division. Cases would be tried, according to their seriousness and the likely maximum sentence, either by magistrates, by judge and jury, or, in the new District Division, by a professional judge and two lay magistrates. The court, not the defendant, would decide which tribunal should hear a case.
2. Changes in the procedures for preparation for trial, including a shift in the respective roles of the police and the prosecuting authorities so that in the majority of cases the Crown Prosecution Service, not the police, would decide whether and what to charge, and should have more responsibility for discharging the prosecution's duties of disclosure.
3. Serious cases against young defendants should no longer be heard in the Crown Court but by a youth court composed of a judge of an appropriate level and at least two experienced youth panel magistrates.
4. Serious fraud should be tried by a judge sitting alone or with lay members drawn from a panel instead of a jury.
5. Changes to trial procedures. At the start of the trial the jurors would receive an agreed written summary of the case and a list of the issues which need to be decided.
6. Changing the technical rules of evidence so that there is no longer a reliance on magistrates and juries to decide how relevant and important the evidence is.
7. Encouraging greater public responsibility for jury service, making it harder to be excused.
8. Streamlining the appeals system and improving the procedures of the Court of Appeal to enable it to manage its caseload more efficiently.
9. The introduction of statutory exceptions to the double jeopardy rule and other extensions to the prosecutor's rights of appeal.
10. The creation of a full legislative code for criminal justice, covering offences, procedure, evidence and sentencing so that the law is clear and accessible.
11. A move to central joint direction, and local joint management, of criminal justice, supported by an integrated information technology system.

Justice for All

The Government White Paper, *Justice for All* (Home Office (2002d)) provides details of their intentions for the criminal justice system. The main themes are: a better deal for victims and witnesses, getting the process right from the start, fairer and more effective trials, putting sense back into sentencing, more effective punishment and rehabilitation, measures to engage the public and a more focused and joined up criminal justice system. Some of the detailed proposals are presented at appropriate points throughout this text, whilst the remainder are noted at this point.

Measures to engage the public
The criminal justice system relies on the participation of members of the public – as jurors, magistrates, witnesses and the thousands of individuals and community organisations who work to reduce crime and bring offenders to justice. Yet the system is seen as complex, intimidating and inaccessible to the public and less than half of those summoned for jury service actually serve. The government aims to assist this public participation by the following means:

1. By improved channels of communication between criminal justice agencies and the public.
2. By continuing to implement the findings of the Stephen Lawrence inquiry in order to reduce racism in the criminal justice system, increase diversity and build the confidence of all sections of the community.
3. By helping people to understand the criminal law by bringing it together into accessible documents available via the Internet.
4. By making jury service an important part of citizenship and ensuring that juries better reflect all sections of society and are better supported.
5. By implementing a national strategy to raise the profile of the lay magistracy and encouraging more people to apply from as wide a cross-section of the community as possible.
6. By introducing more restorative justice schemes in addition to the present use of referral orders.

Focusing the criminal justice system on fighting and reducing crime and delivering justice
While the overall crime rate has been falling and has now stabilised, street crime, anti-social behaviour and the fear of crime remains unacceptably high. Also, under-reporting and under-recording remains a concern for crimes such as domestic violence and racist crimes. The following are proposed to tackle these problems:

1. Extend the range of restraining orders.
2. Put domestic violence murder reviews on a statutory footing.
3. Make a breach of a non-molestation order a criminal offence.
4. Provide anonymity for victims of domestic violence.
5. Improve liaison between the civil and criminal courts and the family and criminal courts.

6. Extend existing drug-testing provisions to the under 18s, with parental or appropriate adult consent.
7. Arrange referral to treatment services for young people with substance misuse problems who currently either receive a reprimand or for whom the police take no further action.

Joining up the system

Each criminal justice agency still has its own methods of recording defendants, offenders, charges and cases. This makes cross-referencing, case management and tracking virtually impossible and may lead to inappropriate decisions. Getting the whole system to work together is essential to bring more offenders to justice, improve the service offered to victims and promote confidence in the work of all criminal justice agencies. To these ends the following proposals were made:

1. Deliver a strategic approach to information technology integration across the criminal justice system.
2. Strengthen the criminal justice system management framework by setting up 42 local criminal justice boards reporting to a new national Criminal Justice Board.
3. Enact legislation to integrate the management of the courts within a single courts organisation. These would replace existing magistrates' courts' committees and the Court Service.
4. Establish a new independent courts inspectorate that will have jurisdiction, for the first time, over the administration of the Crown Court.
5. Strengthen current performance measures by introducing a new information system and appoint performance officers to all criminal justice areas.

Criminal Justice Act 2003

The Criminal Justice Act 2003 makes provision for far reaching and at times controversial reform of the criminal justice system. It is important to note that most of the provisions did not come into force immediately upon Royal Assent and that they will come into effect in stages. The controversial elements include partial abolition of the double jeopardy rule, restrictions on the availability of jury trial and the introduction of a system whereby it would become possible to admit evidence of previous convictions. These made its passage through Parliament a difficult one and some of the proposals never made it to the statute book. The possibility of people opting for a trial without a jury was withdrawn from the Bill. Whilst plans to have complex fraud trials heard by a judge alone did get through, this was on the basis that they would not be implemented without further review and parliamentary approval. A further restriction forced on the government was that whilst it would become possible to admit evidence of previous convictions, juvenile convictions would only be admitted where they were very serious. In return, the clauses that provided for judge only trial where there is a real danger of jury nobbling went through. It is notable that the House of Lords continue to defeat the wishes of the government in terms of resticting access to jury trial. The Bill was based on the White Paper, *Justice for All*, which built on the proposals in two consultation documents: *Review of the Criminal Courts in England and*

Wales by Sir Robin Auld (Auld LJ (2001)) and *Making Punishment Work: Report of a Review of the Sentencing Framework of England and Wales*: Halliday (2001).

The main provisions of the Act, in outline, are indicated below.

1. Some changes to stop and search and arrest powers.
2. Police will be able to grant bail to a person on the street rather than having to bring them to a police station.
3. The detention period in a police station will change from 24 to 36 hours and other changes would be made to the detention rules.
4. Cautions with conditions, a variation on the notion of Caution Plus, will be introduced. The decision to use this will be taken by the Crown Prosecution Service and it would be run by the police. These cautions will include measures of a reparative or rehabilitative nature.
5. Greater involvement of the Crown Prosecution Service in charging decisions.
6. Magistrates to know of previous convictions before they decide as to venue.
7. Defendants to be informed of the likely sentence if they plead guilty – before they decide as to plea.
8. One of the rights of the defence, to appeal to the High Court against a refusal of court bail, will be removed. The appeal to the Crown Court would still be available. The prosecution would get enhanced rights to challenge a grant of bail. Amongst the other changes to the bail system are that there will be a presumption against bail for those tested positive for class A drugs and who refuse to go into treatment.
9. Greater duties of disclosure for both the defence and the prosecution – but much more onerous duties for the defence.
10. Changes to the hearsay rules.
11. Partial removal of the double jeopardy rule. An aquitted person could be tried again, in serious cases, where there is new evidence of a compelling nature.
12. Prosecution appeals against directed and ordered acquittals are to be introduced in relation to trials where the jury had not yet been asked to consider the evidence.
13. The rules on jury service are to be changed with the aim of involving a broader cross-section of the community.
14. Restrictions on the right to jury trial. A system of trial by judge alone where there is a large risk of interference with the jury is provided for.
15. A statement of the aims of the sentencing system – punishment, crime reduction, public protection, the reform and rehabilitation of offenders and reparation – is made. The seriousness of an offence is to be judged in terms of culpability and previous convictions, if recent and relevant, can be an aggravating factor.
16. There will be one community sentence for those who are 16 and over, which would encompass all of the presently available community order options. The Act lists the possible requirements and the court will be able to select the appropriate ones from the following list: an unpaid work requirement, an activity requirement, a programme requirement, a prohibited activity requirement, a curfew requirement, an exclusion requirement, a residence requirement, a mental health treatment requirement (with the consent of the offender), a drug rehabilitation requirement (with the consent of the offender), an alcohol treatment requirement (with the consent of the offender), a

supervision requirement and, in a case where the offender is aged under 25, an attendance centre requirement. Use of the requirements is subject to various forms of restrictions.

17. The Act extends the use of parenting orders by making them available at an earlier stage.

18. The Act provides for individual support orders for young people subject to anti-social behaviour orders and these would require them to undertake education-related activities. This seems misconceived in that the likely recipients of such orders are probably already failing to engage with the education system and will have histories of exclusion and truancy.

19. The use of sentences that would be part custodial and part community dispositions. Custodial sentences of less than 12 months will be replaced by a new sentence, which Halliday called Custody Plus. This would be a system of a short period of custody followed by release on a licence which would include community order options. This sentence would consist of a custodial period of between two and 13 weeks, followed by a period of at least six months served in the community on licence within an overall sentence envelope of less than 12 months. A variation on this is Custody Minus. With this a prison sentence of two to 13 weeks could be suspended for up to two years. There would be community requirements as set by the court, breach of which would activate the custodial element. It would then be like Custody Plus. This is a variant on suspended sentences but with more intervention. Committing a further offence during the entire length of suspension would also count as breach.

20. Sentences of imprisonment of over 12 months will be served in full, half in custody, half in the community, with supervision extended to the end of the sentence rather than the three-quarter point as now. Serious violent and sexual offenders will be given new sentences which will ensure that they are kept in prison or under supervision for longer periods than currently.

21. Suspended sentences are also to be reformed, the change coming in relation to short custodial sentences. For these the operation of the suspended sentence will include the addition of requirements of various sorts taken from the community sentence possibilities. At the moment it is a case of being told that you are free and will remain so unless you are convicted again during the life of the order.

22. New types of intermittent custodial sentence such as weekend custody are to be introduced.

23. Magistrates will be able to sentence an offender to 12 rather than six months for a single offence.

24. A Sentencing Guidance Council is to be introduced.

1.8 Pandering to the public

The 1990s was about getting tough on crime. This was a movement that was accelerated by the killing of a toddler, James Bulger, in Liverpool by two adolescents. Both the Labour and the Conservative parties decided it was worth pandering to the public. Michael Howard, whilst Home Secretary in the last Conservative government, proclaimed that prison works –

a mysterious view as the evidence seems to suggest the exact opposite. Tony Blair, as Labour Prime Minister, wants to be tough on crime and on the causes of crime. In November 1999 Jack Straw, the Home Secretary, came up with the idea of a crusade against crime. He stated in the Foreword to the *Crime Reduction Strategy* (Home Office (1999j)):

'The government is embarked on a crusade against crime. Safe and healthy communities need a strong, shared respect for the proper boundaries of the law and collective condemnation for all those who break them. Of course we need to understand the complex causes of crime and, wherever possible, offer a hand to help the offender back onto the right side. But we should all be clear that criminal behaviour is wrong. We must, in other words, be tough on crime and tough on the causes of crime. Being tough on crime means sending clear signals to criminals that a return to crime will be met with clear consequences, that the purpose of our criminal justice system is to catch and punish offenders not to make excuses for them.'

Toughening up has been seen in relation to juveniles in terms of tightening up cautions and the introduction for a short while of secure training orders. Custodial options were increased further by introducing detention and training orders (though the ideology is that these are meant to be a constructive measure). Longer maximum periods of detention for 15–17-year-olds (two years rather than one year) in young offender institutions were introduced. Provision was made for both detention and training orders for young persistent offenders aged 10–11 and that young offender institutions would be replaced by prisons. Neither of these measures was introduced immediately. Boot camps were experimented with. anti-social behaviour orders and parenting orders were introduced. The presumption that children did not have capacity, doli incapax, was removed. The provisions removing the right to silence were extended to those under the age of 14. For adults there was removal of the right to silence, moves against jury trial, tougher rules on evidence and vastly greater use of prisons.

I would endorse the view of Ashworth and Hough (1996) in terms of following public sentiment in constructing policy on criminal justice:

'The views of sentencing held by people outside the criminal justice system – "the general public" – will always be important even if they should not be determinative in court. Unfortunately, the concept of public opinion in relation to sentencing practices is often employed in a superficial or simplistic way. In this short article we have identified two major difficulties with the use of the concept. First, members of the public have insufficient knowledge of actual sentencing practices. Second, there is a significant but much neglected distinction between people's sweeping impressions of sentencing and their views in relation to particular cases of which they know the facts. When it is proclaimed that the public think the courts are too lenient, both these difficulties are usually suppressed.

To construct sentencing policy on this flawed and partial notion of public opinion is irresponsible. Certainly, the argument is hard to resist that public confidence in the law must be maintained. It is also hard to resist the proposition that public confidence in sentencing is low and probably falling. However, since the causes of this lie not in sentencing practice but in misinformation and misunderstanding, and (arguably) in factors only distantly related to criminal justice, ratcheting up the sentencing tariff is hardly a rational way of regaining public confidence.

This is not to deny that there is political capital to be made, at least in the short term, by espousing sentencing policies which have the trappings of tough, decisive action. However, the underlying source of public cynicism will not have been addressed; and once politicians embark on this route, they may be committing themselves long-term to a treadmill of toughness, "decisiveness", and high public expenditure. The political costs of withdrawing from tough policies, once embarked on, may be too high for politicians of any hue to contemplate.' (1996:786)

1.9 The new managerialism

Belloni and Hodgson (2000), who offer a very good critique of the practices of the criminal justice system, indicate the features of the new managerialism. They do this in the context of a critique of the Royal Commission on Criminal Justice (1993):

'Although denying allegiance to any model or theory, the Commission's final report is resonant with the wider discourse of "system efficiency" and "the management of risk". This begins with the terms of reference provided for the Commission. Wrongful convictions were to be considered alongside (and soon became subordinate to) wrongful acquittals and resource issues: the third of these, in the form of "system efficiency", was swiftly elevated by the Commission as the most important. Strengthening the due process rights of the accused is expensive, may result in more complex (and so more costly) proceedings and, unless public opinion is realigned, is likely to be regarded as helping the criminal, rather than the victim. More appealing are measures which streamline the processing of cases and can be measured in terms of output, rather than effectiveness – making "success" all the more achievable.

This is part of what has been dubbed the "new penology" – forged within the market ideology of new managerialism. It is attractive to policy-makers, as it is neither aspirational nor transformative: It takes crime for granted. It no longer seeks to address the causes of crime, but to manage the effects of crime. Thus, it does not appeal to external values (such as suspects' rights or crime reduction), but to its own formal rationality on the basis of which its performance can be measured easily. Performance indicators are concerned with "outputs" (what the organisation does) rather than "outcomes" (what it achieves). Due process and crime control are replaced by cost-efficiency and risk management in a form of "actuarial justice" which has pervaded most parts of the criminal justice process. Through surveillance and the effective production of knowledge, suspect populations are "managed" at minimal cost. Brownlee (1998:323) comments that "The maintenance of the criminal justice system itself and the continual striving for ever greater efficiency of operation become the inherent values which are to be pursued. Wider social or ethical values are excluded". However, the notion of "risk management" tends to de-personalise and de-politicise the handling of suspect individuals. In practice, it will be the police who, in most cases, are responsible for this task. Policing the risk society lends legitimacy to police ideologies of identifying problematic or suspect communities as part of their law-and-order function.' (2000:197–198)

Moves towards toughening up and a new managerialism have been described. These do not seem appropriate given the existing problems of the system. The first of these problems to note is cost. This has always been a major consideration, one aspect of which is a concern for efficiency and the cheaper or cheapest options. The system has long been designed to process cases and it is clearly not adversarial in nature despite being described as such. We currently have a system of conveyor-belt justice, more concerned with acquittal rates than with miscarriages of justice. There is no real commitment to rights; rather it is thought to be desirable to make it harder for defendants. The police are conviction minded and they come under pressure to get results, especially in high profile cases. The defence is not strident. Poor quality decision-making has myriad causes. The magistrates are amateurs and both the magistrates and the judges tend to side with the system. When it comes to appeals, to admit that there are problems is viewed as undermining the system. Belloni and Hodgson (2000:16–17) cite the interview that Lord Denning had with *The Spectator* in which he put the view that it would have been better if the Birmingham Six had been hanged, so as to avoid all the bad publicity that the criminal justice system was subjected to. Unbelievable!

1.10 Some models with which to view the criminal justice system

The claims of the consensus and conflict viewpoints on law and society will be examined. The aim is to raise issues and to provide a backcloth rather than being a thorough attempt to test different approaches or to vindicate a particular approach. An outline of competing perspectives is all that can be provided as a more complete account is beyond the scope of this book. Whilst some material is provided that would be of use in the making of a choice between perspectives this is not sufficient to permit definitive answers – though it will be apparent that in my view some perspectives are more persuasive than others. The first material to be examined concerns the consensus view of society. This is a common one, often being used in a matter of fact way without detailed explanation or, indeed, without even adherence to this view being made explicit. There is no definitive version of consensus theory as writers such as Durkheim, Parsons, Pound and Ehrlich have produced different accounts of it. What follows is a composite of the work of consensus theorists in order to provide a flavour of their work and to indicate key features of it. The basis of the consensus view is that society is cohesive and homogenous. There will be shared values among the people of the society which are derived from those people and their customs. The law will be a reflection of those values and the role of the political process is to enshrine those values in the law. Inevitably there will be some cases of disharmony, dispute and deviation, and in dealing with such cases the role of the courts is to recognise and to give effect to group values and thus reassert and protect those values. The courts are considered to be neutral in the sense that they do not pursue institutional goals of their own or give preference to particular individuals or groups, though clearly this is within the context of their commitment to societal values. Before the merits of this overview of consensus theory are examined a brief account will be provided of the work of some consensus theorists. This material is included as background and for reference purposes. It can be noted that their concern was not England and Wales at the present time. Also in some versions of the theory shared values are assumed or, as with other features of the theory, are regarded as being a desirable rather than necessarily being an actual state of affairs.

Durkheim

The French sociologist Durkheim wrote in the late nineteenth and early twentieth centuries. In his work *The Division of Labour in Society* (1984) a broadly evolutionary approach is adopted. The law is presented as being a reflection of the type of social solidarity in a community and that it develops with it. He identifies two types of social solidarity with corresponding types of law. The first is mechanical solidarity which is said to occur in simple, non-differentiated societies which have common aims and little division of labour. An example would be kinship groups. In these societies the legal system is repressive and punitive. The second type of social solidarity is organic solidarity. This occurs in differentiated societies which have much division of labour. Whilst the extent of shared values is reduced they are still present, having become more general as they can no longer be based on common experiences. Though individuals will have different aims they are inter-dependent and society is thus cohesive in a different way. In such a society the law is mainly restitutive, with only residual use being made of criminal law and punishment. In both these types of society the law is said to reflect the spirit of the community and it protects and gives effect to the common conscience. The use of punishment and redress accommodate the moral outrage felt by the community and gives support to the beliefs which have been threatened.

Durkheim's ideas have been challenged by a number of writers including Schwartz and Miller (1964) who undertook cross-cultural research on a sample of 51 societies. Their findings were the reverse of what Durkheim suggested. Their data showed that police are found only in association with a substantial degree of division of labour. By contrast, restitutive sanctions (damages and mediation) which Durkheim believed to be associated with an increasing division of labour, are found in many societies that lack even rudimentary specialisation. Scheleff (1975) also casts doubt on Durkheim's thesis by suggesting that the legal system is becoming more repressive rather than restitutive in character, and this in times of increased division of labour. Among a number of sound points made in this article is that it is unwise to typify civil law as being restitutive. To these studies can be added the comments of Grace and Wilkinson (1978). In their analysis of Durkheim, they point out and illustrate that 'at a number of points Durkheim provides counter evidence to his own assertions or goes directly against his own method' (1978:59–60).

Ehrlich

Ehrlich (1862–1922), the Austrian academic lawyer, examined the customs and practices of the multifarious races and groups that made up the Austro-Hungarian Empire: Ehrlich (1936). He presented law as being that which is happening in society and he suggested the study of the law in action or as he put it the living law. In his studies he noted diversity and conflicting interests, as well as the fact that the legal system was a dynamic entity which could itself influence society. However, he still argued that the law was based on custom and that there would be a group view on issues. He suggested, by way of opinion rather than fact, that the law should follow social behaviour rather than direct it and that the role of the judge should be to decide disputes in terms of the prevailing view of the group.

Pound

In examining the work of Roscoe Pound (1870–1964), the American academic lawyer, problems are inevitably encountered as a result of the great volume of his output and also the lack of clarity of his exposition: see for example Pound (1940, 1942, 1954 and 1959). That Pound views society as being based on consensus is clear from his emphasis on social cohesion. He suggests a situation of general homogeneity in which the role of the law is both to reflect the consciousness of the whole society and also to be a means of problem solving through the reconciliation of disputes. In this system the courts are a neutral machinery with the judges being engaged in the business of social engineering. The judges through knowledge of, and an application of, attitudes current within the society can ensure that law operates for social ends and gives effect to social needs. Part of his work involved the classification of various types of interest in the United States of America as well as alleged fundamental values (jural postulates) of that society. The interests (which included by way of example freedom of contract and freedom from deception) were in his view to be discovered by reference to claims made before the courts and through the political process, whilst the jural postulates were distilled out of the interests. In some, but not all, of his writings Pound claimed that the jural postulates should be used to balance or choose between competing interests. Further difficulties with his work are made evident by examining his method of identifying interests. It is never really made clear whether or not he thought that court actions and political pressure either were or should be an accurate reflection of values within the wider society. The former would seem to be an unfounded assumption of, at the least, equality of access to these spheres, whilst the latter is questionable as being a value judgement.

Parsons

In Parsons' vast, highly abstract and often difficult to follow academic output the role of law is understood in terms of the wider social structure: see Parsons (1960 and 1962). Particular importance is given to systems and society itself is presented as being an example of a system. Stress is also placed on integrative and cohesive factors with assumed shared values (consensus) being the basis of the cohesion. Society as a system is presented as having four needs for which it must strive in order to survive. These needs are: integration (a harmonising function); goal attainment (a search for progress in terms of the particular goals of the society); pattern maintenance (the provision of a dynamic within the system); and adaptation (the need to respond to changes in the prevailing circumstances). Whilst within society there are sub-systems these will be inter-dependent. In the legal system the courts engage in interpretation of the law providing stability and harmony and thus integration. In this scheme, the making of law is through legislation which is the business of a separate political sphere. In the general analysis of consensus theorists, doubts will be raised as to whether assumptions of consensus and the presentation of the role of law as being the promoter of harmony are acceptable. For the moment it can be noted that the role of judge has not been that of mere interpreter of the law as some areas of the law, such as contract, are largely the product of the judiciary.

By way of commentary on the consensus approach, it could be suggested that credence can be given to it, in that society could not exist without some degree of uniformity of viewpoint. Also the law can be considered to be functional in that it sets standards and provides a system for settling disputes. Further, that whilst it has already been made clear that breach of the law is common, in terms of the many opportunities that we have to breach the law, the general situation is in fact one of widespread compliance with the law. However, in terms of what consensus theory claimed these are not strong arguments and there are more compelling reasons as to why the consensus viewpoint must be challenged. The approach presumes a political and judicial system responsive to the values within society. Some sophisticated form of enquiry would need to be made with regard to those values. Quite simply in England and Wales the system does not work like that. General elections and the rare referendum do not amount to a sophisticated enquiry as to the viewpoint of citizens. Equally, if the law was to be a reflection of values within society we could be expected to have knowledge of that law. However, the bulk and technical nature of the law ensures that the vast majority of the population have only a layman's view (oversimplified and incomplete) of a fraction of the law. Finally, the very existence of shared values can be challenged. For example, after examining numerous empirical studies of attitudes in the United Kingdom and the United States of America, Mann was able to conclude that 'value consensus does not exist to any significant extent' (1970:9). You may well be able to arrive at the same conclusion yourself. The majority of readers will be members of society in England and Wales and as such you could be expected to know of any consensus that existed. It is my contention that after reflection upon and discussion of the issue you would conclude that consensus was difficult to discover. Differences between age groups, classes, races, creeds and the sexes would be discovered, and an examination of policy areas such as education, defence, trade unions, immigration and crime would reveal variations of, rather than uniformity of, opinion. Even when basic values are sought exceptions are numerous enough to undermine notions of consensus. Berk et al (1977) made this point well when they examined the view that Americans might take of the imperative that a person should not kill another person.

> 'Most Americans would exempt killing in time of war (though the definition of war is itself problematic) or killing in self-defense. Perhaps a smaller number would exempt killing a convicted murderer. A considerable number might exempt killing a wife's lover. Others would exempt killing by accident, killing while insane, or killing when the perpetrator was unaware of what he/she was doing. Some would exempt the killing of a fleeing suspect by a police officer using "necessary force". Others would exempt "mercy killing" and the right to die with dignity. Some would exempt killing during riot control or to maintain order. Others would exempt suicide or killing in response to trespass, insult, injustice, or during a family feud. Some would exempt killing when a larger number of lives would thereby be saved. Finally, some would exempt killing in response to terrorism, treason, espionage, kidnapping and plane hijacking.' (1977:277)

Instead of an emphasis on cohesiveness and solidarity, conflict theory offers an account of society as being typified by divisiveness, conflict, coercion and hostility. Whilst it is clear that they reject the idea of shared values this would not distinguish them from pluralist theories. What does distinguish them is that whilst the pluralists suggest competition between relatively equal groups, with the political and legal systems being neutral factors, in conflict theory both inequality and non-neutral institutions are envisaged. Thus, a part of the power struggle between opposed groups will be in order to gain control of the institutions of the law and the state. The dominant group can then utilise these institutions for its own purposes and ensure that its views are enshrined in the law. Whilst the coercive force of the criminal law and the criminal justice process are thus available to it, more subtle usage is also possible. By a portrayal of the legal institutions as being value neutral and for the benefit of all, domination can be camouflaged and indeed invested with authority. Numerous writers adopting particular perspectives, can be identified as adhering to a conflict approach: Marx (1961 and 1971), Engels (1890a and 1890b), Quinney (1970 and 1974), Chambliss and Seidman (1971), Rock (1973) and Turk (1969). As a supplement to the overview above, some details of the work of Marx, Engels and Quinney will be presented. Quinney is offered as an example of an American theorist whilst Marx and Engels are important as nineteenth-century pioneers of the approach.

Marx and Engels

In examining the work of Marx and Engels certain difficulties have to be recognised. These include the considerable extent of their writings, that their work changed as it developed and that it remained incomplete. Also of importance for present purposes is that crime and law were never central factors in their analysis of society. It is Marx's economic determination that is often turned to as being his major and most systematic theoretical statement on the relationship of law to society, on which see pp19–23 of the Preface to Marx (1971). In his economic determinism Marx presented history as a progression from primitive communism through several intermediary stages to full communism. He never attempted a complete description of full communism, though some pointers were given – there would be ownership in common, no law or state and no alienation. In the historical progression economics is the driving force and ultimate determining factor, whilst class struggle is the instrument and catalyst of it. This operates as follows. Man's need to subsist, and the available means to subsist, produce a particular relations of production. After the primitive communism stage this is best expressed as being the property relations that are prevalent in the society. This is because, in practice, a minority of the population will have gained control of the means of production. This situation is the economic base of the society. The society will require a means of social ordering, and the dominant minority will aim to establish a system by which they can legitimise, camouflage, and protect their position. It is in this situation that the seeds for class struggle are sown. To effect the above aims, the dominant minority will develop the state and other ideologies such as law, politics, and religion. The system that develops to give effect to the economic base is called the superstructure.

The above is a static account – the dynamics must now be introduced. Inevitably developments will take place as regards the means of production. The relations of production and the superstructure must also change to take account of this. But the elements in the superstructure that prospered with the old order will try to maintain it. Eventually the basis for the old order will become increasingly exhausted and the new order will have developed to a stage of maturity. At this point social revolution is inevitable and the old order will be replaced by the new order. A new relations of production and a consequent superstructure develops and the process begins again. This continues until the full communism stage is reached. In this classless society there is no further potential for class struggle, and the state and law will, through obsolescence, inevitably wither away.

In Marx's economic determinism law is presented as being only a reflection of the economic base which will inevitably wither away with the arrival of full communism. It is to legitimise, protect, and camouflage the existing relations in society and to provide a means of social ordering. It must be noted that economic determinism was only intended to be used with caution as is evident in the following quotation from Engels. 'Marx and I are ourselves partly to blame for the fact that the younger people sometimes lay more stress on the economic side than is due to it. We had to emphasise the main problem vis-à-vis our adversaries who denied it, and we had not always the time, the place or the opportunity to give their due to the other elements involved in the interaction' (1890a:683). Thus elsewhere in their work other interpretations of the role of law in society are discoverable. For instance, in Marx's (1961:231–302) analysis of the Factory Acts the movement for the shorter working day is presented as being a surprising alliance between the industrial capitalists and the workers. The former gave their support to the latter for two reasons. First, so as to get reciprocal support on the Corn Law issue and, second, so as to use legislation as a means to injure economically their less automated rivals and the traditional crafts. This work also shows how the legal system can provide an arena for conflicts and also determine the issues to some extent. Similarly, Engels (1890b) describes how law can have an autonomous, independent and important role to play in society.

Quinney

A century later Quinney (1970) offered another version of conflict theory:

'First, my perspective is based on a special conception of society. Society is characterised by diversity, conflict, coercion, and change, rather than by consensus and stability. Second, law is the result of the operation of interests, rather than an instrument that functions outside of particular interests. Though law may control interests, it is in the first place created by interests. Third, law incorporates the interests of specific persons and groups, it is seldom the product of the whole society. Law is made by men representing special interests, who have the power to translate their interests into public policy. Unlike the pluralistic conceptions of politics, law does not represent a compromise of the diverse interests in society, but supports some interests at the expense of others.' (1970:35)

He adds further as regards compromise in interest-group activity:

'Though some criminal law may involve a compromise of conflicting interests, more likely than not, criminal laws mark the victory of some groups over others. The notion of a compromise of conflicting interests is a myth perpetuated by a pluralistic model of politics. Some interests never find access to the law-making process. Other interests are overwhelmed in it, not compromised. But ultimately some interests succeed in becoming criminal law, and are able to control the conduct of others.' (1970:43)

Whilst these quotations are offered as being indicative of a conflict position, it should be noted that Quinney later developed a more radical approach in which he presents law as 'the tool of the ruling class' (1974:10).

Many examples could be provided in support of the claims made by conflict theorists. For example, in relation to the creation of law, Chambliss (1964) in his work on vagrancy laws was able to demonstrate how these particular laws arose and were developed because of the interests of certain sectors of society and to the detriment of others. Similarly, Gunningham (1974) has shown that the ineffective nature of anti-pollution legislation in Great Britain, despite the manifest need for strong legislation, is a reflection of the interests of certain interest groups. Equally, as regards policing practices, there is evidence of discrimination in favour of certain groups. However, attempts to choose between the consensus and conflict perspectives are problematic. I follow Hopkins in his suggestion that 'much of the recent effort to adjudicate between the two models of criminal law is misconceived. Neither model has been formulated unambiguously by its proponents and neither is sufficiently specific in its predictions to be falsifiable' (1975:613). Also, consensus theorists have tended to examine existing law and within that the more traditional offences, whilst conflict theorists have tended to examine law creation and more peripheral offences. I think that you should still carry forward to the later chapters a strong suspicion as regards ideas of a general system of shared values in England and Wales at the present time.

As you go through the rest of this book ask yourself the following. Do the agencies have organisational goals of their own? Are they subject to the influence or detailed control of powerful groups? Clearly then a number of images have been suggested and questions can be raised. Is the image of oppression, domination and alienation in which criminals are best seen as victims of a hostile society an accurate one? Or do we suggest that any society will require standards to work to and systems to settle disputes other than by vendetta? Further, does the criminal law serves all by the protection it offers to life, limb and property? On the other hand, do we worry that some groups may gain more than others from such a system? Are the common assumptions, that the criminal law and its enforcement are desirable, equally cause for concern? It has to be recognised that the criminal justice process is intrusive and coercive, being an attempt to prevent people behaving in a manner that they may find desirable. The police, for example, can be seen as an attempt to both deter crime and to deliver suspects to the court. The courts also have power over us, having the ability to deprive people of their property and their liberty. It can be noted that explanations of the actions of the courts also depend upon which particular one of, or mixture of, a number of penal philosophies is though to be operative. For example, sentences could be to reassert and protect norms by denouncing the wrongdoer, or they could act so as to incapacitate and deter the offender, or indeed they could operate as a general deterrent to the public at large. Alternatively, the desire might be to train, treat or rehabilitate the offender, though clearly these must also be considered to be intrusive.

1.11 Factors influencing the creation of the criminal law

Given that the political process does not provide a sophisticated form of enquiry as to the views of people generally in society, questions can be raised as to the manner in which the criminal law is produced. Since there is no behaviour that is obviously or intrinsically criminal, criminality must then be seen as the product of some person's or group's perception of certain behaviour as being criminal. In the United Kingdom the identification of types of behaviour as being criminal requires, as a first stage, the creation of law and the processes involved in this will be examined. As with the material on the consensus and conflict models the aim is restricted to identifying issues and perspectives. It is clear that government legislative proposals have a very high success rate but they may be subject to influence by such as a power elite within a society, interest and pressure groups, the media, senior civil servants and law reform bodies. A central theme adopted is an emphasis on the variety of and complexity of factors that seem to be involved in an attempt to explain the creation of the criminal law. It can be difficult to explain even a single piece of legislation.

The Marijuana Tax Act 1937

Becker (1963), Dickson (1968) and Musto (1973) analysed the Marijuana Tax Act, which became law in the United States in 1937. They offered three different accounts of the creation of this law and they also provided three possible ways of analysing the emergence of legislation in general. From its name, it would appear that the Act was intended to provide revenue functions, or that it was the result of social concern as regards drug use. In fact neither of these accounts is adequate.

Becker
Becker's analysis of the Act was intended as an illustration of his general explanation of the emergence of law. This viewed law as developing from values into specific rules and then into law. He explained this process in terms of moral entrepreneurs, who could be either individuals or groups, who crusaded for particular legislation. The methods they used were the co-ordination of interest-group activity, the creation of a favourable public opinion and the provision of the actual enterprise required. As regards the Act, Becker saw the Federal Bureau of Narcotics, formed in 1930, as being the moral entrepreneur. He suggested that the Bureau saw an area of wrongdoing, marijuana use, and moved to have it put under their jurisdiction. This would fulfil their sense of duty and satisfy their moral beliefs and to this end they produced a media campaign, co-ordinated interest-group activity and provided the necessary enterprise. Such an analysis of the Act is unsatisfactory for a number of reasons. His evidence of a media campaign is disproven by his own statistics, as articles referring to marijuana use were nearly all written after the Act and not before it as Becker suggests. Also when Musto's account of the Act is considered, it will become clear that the Bureau would actually have preferred the Act not to have been passed and to have avoided all involvement with it.

Dickson
Dickson, aware that Becker's analysis contained inconsistencies and apparent misconceptions, offered an alternative explanation. This was in terms of the relationship between organisations and their environment. He suggested that organisations tried to create a relationship between the organisation and the environment which was to the best advantage of the organisation. This could be by changes within the organisation or by attempting to engineer changes in the environment itself. He considers that the Act can be

explained in this way. When the Federal Bureau of Narcotics was set up in 1930 it had a limited role with few enforcement duties. Dickson suggests that the Bureau attempted to provide for itself a more favourable environment by pressing for federal legislation and thus creating an extended role for itself. Only some of his evidence is presented here. First, he uses the fact that there was little or no debate in Congress to disprove moral crusader explanations. Second, he explains that the Bureau would not have been satisfied with the uniform state legislation, which had been enacted by 1936, as it was only with federal legislation that they could hope for an extended role.

Musto

Musto examined the Act as part of a general analysis of anti-narcotic legislation. His view is that there are no simple explanations for such legislation, and that general cultural and institutional factors within the United States have to be considered. For instance, factors in the foreign trade sphere explain anti-opiate legislation. Also, interest groups can influence or prevent legislation. As well as the above factors, Musto pointed to what he regarded as an important general feature of the relationship between drug use and society. This was that drugs were often associated with unpopular minorities. He presented a number of examples of such associations: cocaine with negroes, heroin with communist infiltrators, opiates with the Chinese and marijuana with Mexicans. Drug use by these groups was used as an excuse to suppress them and to further arouse popular discontent with them. It is upon the above type of analysis that Musto bases his explanation of the Act. When Mexican immigrants became a threat to local workers in the west and south-west of the United States of America, they became unpopular, and their use of marijuana was a suitable excuse for their suppression and control. Local civic leaders and police chiefs pressed for federal legislation to give weight to this operation. The Bureau did not consider marijuana use to be a serious threat to the community and preferred to concentrate their attentions on the harder drugs. But pressure from the south and south-west increased, so to appease them the Bureau agreed to put the best possible case to Congress. It was in these circumstances that legislation emerged. From the available evidence it seems that the Bureau had no desire for such legislation and derived no benefit from it. It was regarded as a nuisance, it would be expensive to enforce and in fact revenue fell after the Act. From this it seems that the accounts of Becker and Dickson are disproven.

Lindesmith

The next study to be considered, which also concerns drugs, is a particularly good example of the complexity of law creation and enforcement. Lindesmith (1965) points out that the system of handling the drug problem in the United States is remarkable in certain respects. It is not the result of legislative enactments or court interpretations of such enactments. Furthermore, public and medical opinion had next to no influence in its inception. It was instead established by the decisions of administrative officials of the Treasury Department of the United States. Once these crucial decisions had been made and implemented, public and medical opinion was sought for what was already an established fact. The officials used the provisions of the Harrison Act 1914 as justification for their system of control. It should be noted that this Act was intended as a revenue measure and not as a means to control individual addicts. The Act required doctors to only have or supply drugs which were for legitimate medical purposes. The department brought a series of test cases: *Webb* v *United States* 249 US 96 (1918), *Jim Fuey Moy* v *United States* 254 US 189 (1920) and *United States* v *Behrman* 258 US 280 (1921). The test cases established that to supply drugs to addicts was not within the provisions of the Act. Whilst the Supreme Court decision in *Linder* v *United States* 268 US 5 (1924) established a contrary principle, this was to have little effect in practice, as the lower courts did not follow the decision of the Supreme Court. In conclusion, this study has revealed a remarkable situation in which law creation and enforcement has had the sanction of neither the legislature or the Supreme Court.

Platt and Haskins

Platt's (1969) study is a further example of the need to adopt a multi-factor approach in some cases. His study in Illinois shows how juvenile delinquency was invented as a means to control the children of recent immigrants and to ensure their suitability for employment. This would serve the interests of those in the economic sphere. This movement was also attractive to other groups. Legal and correctional bureaucracies would have a vested interest in such developments. It also offered the opportunity of suitable employment for some of the upper-class women at the time. It was the interaction of these factors that lead to the development of a criminal justice system for juveniles. In contrast, Haskins (1960) demonstrates that sometimes single factors can be predominant in the explanation of law creation. The factor considered by Haskins was religion and he described the Massachusetts Bay Colony in the seventeenth century in which the Bible was regarded as being indicative of the word of God and was used in the production and administration of the law. For instance, in the code of 1648, the provisions were related to chapter and verse of the Bible and in parts the literal words of the Bible were used. Whilst the colony is a good example of the influence of religion in law creation, other examples can be found throughout history – for instance, in Calvin's Geneva and the Code of Alfred the Great. The latter incorporated the Decalogue (the Ten Commandments) and much of four chapters of Exodus as part of the laws of England. At the present time it is clear that religion is still a factor in the creation of law. For instance, religious groups have considerable influence on legislatures and recent events in Iran have demonstrated the full potential of religion as a factor in law creation.

Thompson, Hay et al and Arnold

The work of Thompson (1975) and Hay et al (1975) are further examples of the study of law creation in earlier historical times. Thompson analyses the Black Act 1723 which increased the range of capital offences to the extent that it included the like of the writing of threatening letters. Much of the analysis concerns forestlands, and the conflicts between forest officials and local inhabitants and those between the established social system and the new wealthy arrivals in the social setting are detailed. An indication of the way of life of the period is the fact that population statistics were more accurate for deer than for people. This work brings out the harsh and brutal details of the period and is a view from below in the sense that it portrays the reality as experienced by the ordinary man rather than that of the people in elevated social stations. Considering the evidence that Thompson presents it is perhaps surprising that he rejects a ruling class analysis. As regards the legal system he portrays this as having some degree of autonomy. Hay et al, examining the same historical period, presents law as ideology. Whilst the legal system of the time did not always convict the least affluent, and may on occasions send the rich to the gallows, the notions of a jury of equals and equal recourse to law are revealed as ideology when account is taken of the property qualifications for the former and the expense of the latter. Arnold (1962) provides a further and more detailed example of law being considered to be ideology. He views society as a situation in which some groups are able to dominate the rest of society. These groups realise that this position must be camouflaged and a complex system of legal domination develops. This system will extol certain values – for instance the doctrines of democracy, the rule of law, separation of powers, equality before the law and freedom of contract. These values are presented as being operative, so as to try to give the impression to all groups and individuals in society that the legal system exists for their benefit. Arnold's argument is that whilst we all derive some benefit from the legal system it is equally clear that it operates as an effective ideology which disguises the power relations in society.

Gusfield

The final study to note is that of Gusfield (1963) who emphasised the symbolic dimensions of law creation and enforcement. This approach recognises that interest groups compete at the political level to have their definitions of morality recognised by the legislature and enforced by the relevant agencies. The important distinction of this perspective is that between instrumental and symbolic effects of legislation. The instrumental effect is the enforcement of the legislation, whilst the symbolic effect is the mere recognition of the legislature of a point of view. This recognition marks the ascendancy of one viewpoint over others. With the use of these dimensions it becomes clear that legislation should not be accepted at face value. Various opposed groups can derive satisfaction from a single piece of legislation. One group has its norms enshrined in the law whilst another group is allowed to continue with the now illegal behaviour. That such activity is now covert, a patterned evasion of norms in a situation of low-profile enforcement, provides symbolic support for the group whose norms have been recognised officially by the legal system. The victorious group has its norms recognised in the manner of their breach. Gusfield's account of prohibition in an example of such analysis. Prohibition in the United States was the result of middle-class Protestant groups extolling the values of temperance and managing to have these values recognised by the legislature. The resultant legislation would have been difficult to enforce in practice and such enforcement would have led to a counter-productive reaction against the legislation, thus the legislation was to serve mainly symbolic functions. In light of the above examples it is clear that explanations of law creation are both complex and varied. As a result we can say that the creation of the criminal law has to be regarded as a problem.

2   Crime Prevention

2.1   The nature of crime prevention

2.2   Some examples of crime prevention

2.3   The rational choice model

2.4   Evaluating crime prevention programmes

2.5   Current government thinking on crime prevention

2.6   Some crime prevention success stories

2.7   Displacement

2.8   Specific studies of crime prevention

2.9   Social and community strategies

2.10 Conclusions

Whilst most of this text is concerned with responses to criminal behaviour, crime prevention has the very great advantage over them in that it can hope to ensure that the crime does not even take place. Methods of crime prevention, by means of tactics such as concealing valuables and avoiding situations in which violence is likely to be encountered, have operated over the centuries. The prevention of crime has long been an aim of the criminal justice system. For example, the police have a role in the prevention of crime and sentences are designed at least in part to have a deterrent effect and thus to prevent crime. In the very broadest sense of crime prevention a successful system of rehabilitation could be said to have prevented crime. Of late the subject of crime prevention has been paid particular attention by researchers, by governments and by others. As to exactly what crime prevention is, well quite simply there have been numerous attempts at definition, none of which have gained general acceptance. I will offer a token example of such definitions. Kuhlhorn and Svensson (eds) (1982) in the editors' foreword to a collection of readings on the subject of crime prevention state that 'crime prevention measures are all technical informative and educational methods aimed at preventing criminal acts and effected in a way that allows an evaluation of the extent to which the aim is achieved' (1982:10). They have made a particular issue of the need for measures to be capable of empirical test. Whilst it is not obvious from the definition, they would exclude schemes which are aimed at the rehabilitation of the offender, which in their view have only an incidental preventative effect. Crawford (1998:Chapter 1) is valuable as a source on definitional issues.

2.1 The nature of crime prevention

This can be indicated by providing a brief initial account of some of the features of the thinking on crime prevention. Interest in crime prevention developed in the light of the general failure of other attempts to deal with the problem of crime. The search for a general cause, or causes of, crime has been largely unsuccessful. Attempts at general strategies for dealing with crime have also been largely unsuccessful. In contrast, recent strategies of crime prevention have often been highly specific in terms of particular localities, types of offence and types of offender. These activities are partly based on the idea that criminal behaviour is a rational choice on the part of offenders. If the risks of such behaviour are increased and rewards decreased then crime should be prevented. More general strategies have also been adopted and views other than the rational choice model have been followed.

2.2 Some examples of crime prevention

The provision of some examples should also help to give the flavour of what has been suggested and undertaken. The improvement in, and the use of, security devices (such as locks and alarms) for homes and cars can hope to have a crime prevention effect in that they make the commission of crime more difficult and thus riskier. Such tactics are referred to in the literature as 'target hardening'. A burglar alarm may offer a number of disincentives. It can involve a loud alarm when triggered or operate as a silent alarm at the property, providing a warning of intruders at the local police station. Risk of detection might also be increased, by the marking of property with a means of identification, such as a post code. If a person was caught in possession of such marked material, explanations would be very awkward. The stolen goods may also prove to be less marketable. This would make burglary of houses that belong to a property-marking scheme less attractive. Another possible effect of property marking is that stolen property recovered by the police could be identified and returned to their owners.

Risk may also be increased by the threat of being observed. Enhanced surveillance can be used as a means to prevent crime. This can be arranged in numerous ways by, for example, Neighbourhood Watch schemes (where neighbours keep an eye on each other's property), by patrols by the police or other groups and by manipulation of the environment. In 2003 over six million homes were in the 160,000 Neighbourhood Watch schemes. As to the latter, better lighting and generally less cover for crime, by means of reducing the availability of concealed points of entry, are possible tactics. With such strategies it is not just important to enhance the visibility of offending, it is equally important to develop a state of mind in the populace that they should both observe and report crime. Surveillance can also be carried out by employees either directly (sometimes aided by two-way or other mirrors) or through the use of remote devices such as cameras. Other tactics in relation to the environment are based on the identification and removal of a perceived factor that exacerbates the potential for crime. If violence at football matches is linked to alcohol consumption then you do not permit alcohol at football matches. If crime in city centres peaks at the closing time of public houses, then the facilitation of the swift removal of people from the setting by means of the allocation of plentiful and prompt public transport might be desirable. Equally, the lessons of research on which features of pubs and clubs are likely to increase (overcrowding is one example) or decrease (membership schemes and the provision of entertainment are some examples) the likelihood of violence and disorder can be implemented. The variety of possibilities is further demonstrated by consideration of the payment of salary by means of a cheque and the use of plastic containers for drinks in public houses. The use of a cheque amounts to target removal in that there is no longer the need for the delivery of large amounts of cash to employers with the risks that this involves. The use of plastic containers amounts to removing the means to commit an offence in a particular way. If glasses are available they provide a ready weapon in a pub brawl. Plastic containers removes the risk of terrible injuries that can result from the use of a glass as a weapon.

The campaign is another crime prevention strategy. In its most common form it warns potential victims of the risks that they run and offers suggestions as to how risks can be reduced. In other forms campaigns can be directed at offenders and potential offenders and even the parents of these two groups. In terms of parents the aim is to try to increase parental control and supervision of their children. Such thinking was clearly operative when parenting orders were introduced by the Crime and Disorder Act 1998. Schools also have a role to play in crime prevention. The Parliamentary All Party Penal Affairs Group (1983) suggested that some features of schools should be encouraged as a means to prevent crime. These include a consistent approach to discipline, an emphasis on attainment and the use of praise when targets are reached by pupils. Where measures are suggested as being desirable at the level of the school system or the home (as in the case of parental discipline), then the thrust of the policy is clearly far less specific than in some other crime-prevention measures. In essence you are at the stage of suggesting structural causes of crime within society. Other similar crime-producing factors which have been identified of late are low neighbourhood cohesion, inadequate recreation facilities, unemployment, a deterioration in family unity and inadequate housing provision for young single people. Such matters are a long way from, for example, trying to stop the stealing of wallets at bus stops in a particular city centre. It is this more specific approach to crime that is distinctive of recent thinking on crime prevention. A flavour of the various schemes being suggested and attempted under the heading of crime prevention having been provided, a little more detail on the recent thinking behind and the impetus for crime prevention is now required.

In crime prevention thinking a common attitude is that of horses for courses in which particular answers are sought to particular problems rather than hoping to develop blanket measures for a variety of crimes, offenders and settings. The aim is very much to prevent a problem arising rather than seeking a solution to a problem once it has occurred. It can be added that even if such solutions were available prevention would still be a valid strategy. Given a law of theft that is intended to protect property the response is to attempt this directly and to suggest that considerations of security are raised in relation to particular pieces of property. It is clear that the complexity of social life is accepted within this way of thinking and that its response is to try to reduce these difficulties by restricting the amount of variables to be taken into account. The approach arose, in part, as a reaction against the failure of more global attempts at dealing with crime. Both causes and cures had proved elusive and indeed labelling theory, by pointing to the stigmatising effects of the criminal justice system, suggested that this might even exacerbate rather than reduce the crime problem. Deterrence, correction and treatment were viewed as having had their day. Considerations of causation of crime are not abandoned in this new approach as knowledge of the motivation of people in particular situations is regarded as being of importance in the development of preventative strategies. Enquiries are made of offenders as to their thinking and motivation towards specific crimes in particular settings and over different time periods.

2.3 The rational choice model

This perspective was developed by Cornish and Clarke (1986) and it utilises generalisations about criminal behaviour. They see the bulk of offending as the outcome of largely reasoned decisions about the costs and benefits involved. They are taking issue with approaches which viewed criminals as being driven as a result of factors in their background or indeed in the most extreme forms as a result of biological predisposition. They do not totally reject the idea of crime as being a result of impulse or anger or passion. They see some crime as very much the result of such factors, whilst other crime is not at all explicable in these terms. In their view most crimes are in between these two positions. They make the point that it is unwise to just assume that a particular type of crime is a result of an outburst of anger or passion. They suggest for example that violence is usually a course chosen by the offender as a way of solving an inter-personal problem. Suggested examples of this are wife-battering, rape and homicide and they cite empirical studies to bolster their view. They also suggest that notions of benefit or reward should not be thought of in merely monetary terms. Apparently motiveless behaviour such as vandalism can be understood as a means to achieve status within a peer group. The law is broken because it is the law, and its very existence offers the opportunity to flaunt authority and the risk attached offers the prospect of excitement. Playing devil's advocate, Cornish and Clarke address the issue of how can crime be rational, given the risk of prosecution and conviction as evidenced by the large number of people who are subject to the proceedings of the criminal justice system? To this they suggest that the calculation of risk may in fact have been faulty, and they note that the amount of risk in some situations may in fact be very low indeed. They also make the point that they are not suggesting that calculation of risks and rewards is going to be a complete explanation of criminal and non-criminal behaviour. Rather that it offers potential as an important factor in developing crime-prevention strategies.

2.4 Evaluating crime prevention programmes

Crawford (1998:216–217) examined the problems of evaluating crime-prevention programmes. He noted that the aims and objectives of many initiatives are often poorly articulated and clouded in obscurity, as is any realistically theorised notion of the time span over which effects and outcomes may be produced and sustained. There is often little understanding of the relationship between mechanisms, contexts and outcome patterns or conception of the processes through which these are produced. These are issues programme implementers need to address in order to assist the evaluation. For those involved in evaluation he suggests that evaluation studies should address the following questions:

1. Was the initiative implemented as planned and what factors influenced implementation? (The process.)
2. Did the initiative make a difference to, or alter the size of, the problem? (The outcome.)
3. What did the initiative do which impacted on the problem and how was the problem affected by the initiative? (The relation between the mechanism and the outcome.)
4. In what ways did the context in which the mechanism was set encourage or undermine the impact of the initiative? (The relation between the mechanism, outcome and context.)
5. What else resulted from the initiative as well as the impact on the problem? (The unintended consequences or side effects.)
6. Did the benefits and/or side effects last? (The temporal durability.)
7. Were the benefits greater than the costs? (The cost benefit.)
8. How, where and for whom could the effects be replicated? (The transferability.)
9. What more do we know at the end of the evaluation about the patterns of outcome effectiveness of the initiative, and what else do we need to know? (Future evaluation.)

2.5 Current government thinking on crime prevention

This was revealed as part of the government's crime reduction strategy which was published in December 1999: Home Office (1999a). It tells us that crime prevention is a responsibility for us all as individuals and as members of communities. There is also a determination to be tough on the causes of crime by strategies aimed at the community, such as reducing welfare dependency, providing more support for families and young children, improving education in areas such as truancy and tackling environmental issues such as housing problems. Targets are being set for the agencies of the criminal justice system. For example, from April 2000 every police authority and local crime and disorder reduction partnership will have to set five-year targets (and annual milestones) for the reduction of vehicle crime. Scrutiny systems will operate to measure attainment by these bodies: the Audit Commission and Her Majesty's Inspectorate of Constabulary are to be involved in this. Particular offences and types of offender are focused upon, and burglary and vehicle crime are examples of this. For burglary they note that funding from the crime reduction programme is already helping to protect over 200,000 homes in high crime areas from burglary, with 1.8 million more to follow over the next two years. Also the Vehicle Crime Reduction Action Team has a target of a 30 per cent reduction in vehicle crime. Finally, targeted policing initiatives around the country are starting to make a reality of the commitment to tackle crimes like drug dealing, town centre disorder and racial violence. In terms of the organisation of such activities, the following developments are also noteworthy. A new national Crime Reduction Task Force has been established, chaired by a Home Office minister and drawing in senior experts from local government, the police service and other organisations to drive forward this crime reduction strategy. It provides a focus for the work of the local crime and disorder reduction partnerships and provide impetus to improving performance nationally, regionally and locally. Regional crime reduction directors are also to be appointed. The Crime Reduction Programme was a £250 million programme that ran for three years from April 1999. A further £153 million, for the Closed Circuit Television (CCTV) initiative, was announced in March 1999. The combined total of £403 million was invested in obtaining evidence on what methods are the most effective in tackling crime and its causes.

The reducing burglary initiative

This initiative involves an investment of over £50 million, over three years, in around 500 high burglary neighbourhoods, covering two million households. Already there are projects covering 223,000 households which suffered 18,000 burglaries in 1998. The second round of projects started in March 2000. By the year 2001–2002 it was anticipated that these schemes would be preventing at least 15,000 burglaries a year, rising to 25,000 a year in the longer term. Vehicle crime accounts for over a fifth of all recorded crime, with over a million thefts of and from vehicles recorded during 1998–99. It costs over £3 billion a year and causes much public concern. For tackling vehicle crime the following strategies are being adopted: £170 million investment in closed-circuit television systems to create safer car parks, town centres and residential neighbourhoods; schemes for improved security on new and used cars; and better links between information systems and new procedures at the Driver and Vehicle Licensing Agency.

2.6 Some crime prevention success stories

In the pages that follow a range of studies of crime prevention will be presented. It can be noted that both successes and failures will be encountered, though the judgment of success and failure will at times be problematic given differences of finding and interpretation. In order to whet the appetite some of the successes as noted by Cornish and Clarke (1986) are as follows. During the 1970s airline hijacks were reduced from an average of 70 a year to 15 by means of defensive measures taken by airlines and governments: Wilkinson (1977). Knutsson and Kulhorn (1981) provide an account of the decrease in cheque frauds in Sweden consequent upon the introduction of cheque guarantee cards. Mayhew et al (1976) report both the great reduction in the number of thefts from coin boxes in public telephones in Great Britain, when aluminium boxes were replaced by steel ones, and the reduction in motorcycle thefts after 1970. As to the latter it is questionable to count this as a success given that it was an unintended by-product of new legislation requiring the wearing of a crash helmet whilst riding a motor-cycle. This requirement meant that opportunist thieves, who were unlikely to be in possession of a helmet, would be deterred given the increased risk of detection. In looking at these studies some issues which will be returned to later should be kept in mind. First, it will be exasperating to find that the difficulties in crime prevention are at times not so much the finding of schemes that seem to have potential but rather the actual implementation of schemes. The organisation of the variety of people and bodies that need to be recruited, motivated and prevented from becoming demotivated, or are indeed downright deviant in relation to the scheme, has proven in some cases to be very difficult. From the work of Hope (1985) it is clear that it is not just sufficient to have a plausible idea – you also need to ensure the provision of a means to implement the idea. Bureaucracies already working in the vicinity may well wish to continue with existing practices rather than adopt a new approach. Problems such as delay, lack of co-ordination and lack of enthusiasm multiply if inter-agency contact and co-ordination are required. Hope provides examples of these problems from his own research (on preventing crime in schools and preventing disorderly and drunken behaviour at weekends in a city centre) and he also alludes to similar occurrences in the United States of America. Second, crime prevention initiatives have costs of both a monetary and a non-monetary (such as invasion of privacy and restrictions on the law-abiding) nature. Difficult issues are involved in the easily put question: what price crime prevention?

2.7 Displacement

An example of one such cost needs to be considered at this stage. This is the phenomenon of displacement. Pease (1997) is recommended as a source on this issue. Crawford (1998:81) notes that displacement can take a number of different forms. Spatial or geographic displacement occurs where the same crime is committed in a different place. Temporal displacement involves the same crime being committed against the same target at a different time. Tactical displacement involves the same crime being committed against the same target but in a different way or by a different means. Target displacement is where the same type of crime is committed but a new target is selected in place of the original (for example, a shift from robbing post offices to robbing banks). Type of crime displacement occurs when there is a change in the nature of criminal activities from the type of crime originally intended (for example, a shift from robbing post offices to street mugging).

Displacement can also be explained by means of examples. Research by Mayhew et al (1976) noted that when steering-column locks became compulsory on new vehicles in Great Britain, with the intention of preventing vehicle thefts, the overall rate of car thefts remained at the same level. Car thieves had simply concentrated their attentions on the older cars which did not have this security device. Whilst the new vehicles had been protected from crime it was only at the cost of having transferred the attention of car thieves to these older cars. Such a displacement effect was avoided in West Germany. Steering-column locks were made compulsory for all vehicles in 1963 and there was a spectacular 60 per cent reduction in the rate of car theft. A study by Chaiken et al (1974) reported that, when action was taken to prevent subway robberies, there was a displacement effect as there was an increase in street robberies. A further example is offered by Clarke and Mayhew (1980). They note that improved security in relation to safes led to a decline in safe-cracking. However, the incidence of over-the-counter robberies in banks increased, and when in turn this was made more difficult attacks on vehicles carrying money increased. Of particular concern is that each new form of crime saw an increase in the amount of violence involved. Comment can also be made about the practice of paying wages by cheque or directly to a bank account. The effect of this is that employers no longer have to have possession of large amounts of cash for wages purposes and also they do not need to have it transported to them. In both cases the potential for criminal activity in terms of wages robberies has been removed. The increased use of bank accounts that results from such measures increase the potential for crimes such as cheque and computer fraud. A further form of displacement to consider is where a crime may have been prevented at one point in time but might only have been postponed to a more opportune moment, or been replaced by a similar offence. The effect of such prevention measures on the overall level of offending is clearly difficult to calculate, but there is some evidence available as will be seen in the studies to be examined later.

Whilst further comment on the significance of displacement for crime prevention will be made in the light of such studies, it can be said at this stage that in some circumstances displacement appears to be unlikely. For example, in the case of the white-collar crime of theft by an employee, target hardening at work seems unlikely to lead to the obtaining of office supplies for private use by means of shop-lifting. It is however clearly a problem for crime prevention when a measure merely transfers the crime to a new setting (such as a house without a burglar alarm) or to a different type of offence. This is of limited use to the criminal justice system, though it may be regarded as being of great benefit by the individuals who have avoided becoming the victims of crime.

2.8 Specific studies of crime prevention

The specific studies of crime prevention that will be examined have been divided into four groups – those involving a campaign, burglary, studies of vandalism and a basket category of other studies.

Campaigns

The first group of studies to be considered are those which concern crime prevention campaigns. It has to be said at the outset that these have generally been unsuccessful. Burrows and Heal (1979) give an account of a campaign designed to increase car security in Plymouth in 1977. This included the use of newspapers, television, radio, handbills, posters and a touring car from which announcements were made. The campaign had little impact as regards getting people to lock their cars, and it appeared to be that this was because people perceived the risk involved in their approach as being negligible. It was also noted in Home Office (1986a) that in a survey of people on probation who had been convicted of stealing cars it was found that 60 per cent of the cars which they stole had been left unlocked. Unless such a campaign can be made to be successful then the tactics of suggesting the value of (or legislating for the provision of) improved locks and other security devices for cars are of little worth. Riley (1980) provided an evaluation of a campaign to reduce vandalism. A television campaign in the north-west of England in 1978 was financed by the Home Office at a cost of over £200,000. Two 45-second advertisements were prepared and transmitted. The first advert (shown 69 times) was intended to deter children from vandalism by a portrayal of the serious consequences of being found out after an act of vandalism. This included a police visit (the name given to the advert) to the child's home. The second advertisement, which was shown 57 times, was aimed at the parents. Called 'Front Room', it portrayed acts of vandalism in that setting and the hope was that it would cause parents to raise the level of parental supervision of their children. Again the campaign failed. It seemed to be that persuasion of this type would not work with children and that a more immediate risk was required. Peer group pressure in favour of vandalism had this element of immediacy and was more likely to prevail. As to the motivation of children in relation to vandalism, from evidence gathered by Brantingham (1986) and reported by Heal and Laycock (1986), self-interest can be noted as being a factor. In one community in Ontario the cost of vandalism to schools was drawn from the budget primarily intended for films in schools. In the first year of this scheme a 40 per cent reduction in vandalism was recorded.

An anti-rape campaign

The final campaign to note is that of a warning/leaflet campaign on the subject of rape which was researched by Schafer (1982). This leaflet was issued in November 1978 in Bremen in Germany as one of a number of responses to the rising number of rapes in the city. Twenty-one thousand leaflets were issued to potential victims through schools, churches, trade unions, hostels and other similar outlets. Despite the leaflet campaign the rape rate continued to rise and it was decided to reissue the leaflet. In May 1980, 243,000 leaflets were distributed by means of being inserted in a free Sunday newspaper. Yet again the number of rapes increased, and for figures gathered in 1980 only 12 (9 per cent) of the 141 victims knew of the leaflet. A higher level of awareness could have been expected given the controversy that surrounded the leaflet – particularly in the period after the re-issue. The controversial features of the leaflet will be noted shortly. As regards the above data several issues can be raised. Should the increases in the number of rapes be seen as a sign of failure? In this and similar studies it is always difficult to know what has happened – for example the rate of increase may have been greater in the absence of the leaflet. Equally, it would have been interesting to know what the level of knowledge of the leaflet was amongst women who were not attacked. The leaflet itself was largely in the form of a questionnaire. The tactic adopted was to try to communicate the information about preventing rape by means of getting people to feel good about having got the answers to the questions correct. The questions asked included:

1. Do you know the man who is escorting you and whose car you are entering?
2. When you're out at night, do you avoid dark routes where you can't see far ahead?
3. Do you and your daughter dress and behave so that a man doesn't feel he's 'being given the green light'?

Advice was also offered, such as keeping cool if you find yourself in a tight corner and if you did find yourself at a disadvantage it was suggested that you could distract him from his intention by praying out loud. The advice to pray was in part designed to provoke response which would help to ensure that the leaflet was noticed. Controversy also centred on the siege mentality involved in the advice, on the fact that popular culture exerts pressure on women to dress attractively and that warning of the dangers of associating with strangers ignores the reality that rape victims often know the assailant. Whilst many issues arise from an account of a campaign of this type, limitations of space permit only a few concluding observations. It is hard to see the campaign as having been a success and it illustrates the difficulties of both getting a message across and, indeed, the dilemmas involved in the actual selection of the message.

Burglary

Burglary has been the subject of quite a number of attempts at crime prevention and in the studies that follow accounts are offered of different types of measure, of burglary in a number of different settings and of different types of burglar.

Bennett

Bennett (1986) investigated the motivations and perceptions of convicted burglars in England. The hope was that the knowledge gained could be used to assess existing ideas about, and methods of, crime prevention and to develop others. He carried out semi-structured interviews with the burglars and also sought their views on videos and photographs of houses. Features such as alarms, signs of occupancy, the presence of cover so as to provide undetected entry and neighbours in the vicinity were amongst the features included in the video and the photographs. Security devices such as locks were rarely mentioned by the burglars as being a deterrent, and yet they are often featured in official guidance on prevention. What did deter were burglar alarms and sign of occupancy. The latter rarely features in official guidance literature. In terms of being observed burglars were most concerned about immediate neighbours, whilst they viewed police patrols and passers by as merely requiring a wait until they *had* passed by. As to environmental design factors it was an open-plan layout for housing that they avoided as it minimised the availability of cover. Bennett also found that burglars tended not to respond to opportunities to burgle but rather they got into the mood to burgle and then went looking for an opportunity. Whilst the creation of the mood is clearly complex, the main factors identified were a need for money and the influence of others – the latter being most effective whilst drinking and in public houses. The difficulties of crime prevention are illustrated by these points, in that when factors in motivation are discovered they may not in practice be manipulable. It seems unlikely that schemes to pay burglars not to burgle, or to control drinking by the general population, as a means to prevent burglary, would be implemented. Bennett asked the burglars what they did if they were put off a particular burglary. Forty per cent said that they would commit an offence that day, whilst another 40 per cent said they would not commit an offence that day. The remainder said that it would depend upon the circumstances, but over half said that they usually or sometimes gave up and went home. These findings suggest that burglary is not some sort of irresistible urge and they also offer a means to consider the issue of displacement. Bennett suggests that displacement has not occurred if an offence is not committed that day after an earlier attempt has been abandoned. Whilst there are difficulties with such a criterion (for example a once-a-week burglar remains that if a failed attempt on Monday is followed by a success on Tuesday), if we accept it, in at least 40 per cent of cases there is no displacement.

Nee and Taylor

Nee and Taylor (1988) carried out a study of 50 convicted burglars in the Republic of Ireland. The variety and complexity of factors involved in burglary start to become apparent when more than one study is available as differences can be found between them. In this particular study burglars who were merely opportunists and burglars who engaged in prior planning were noted in addition to burglars who went to search out an opportunity. The most important single factor (in 72 per cent of cases) in deciding to burgle was a need for money. Dogs and alarms at a property were seen as being a disincentive, but 92 per cent of the sample said that target hardening was ineffective as some point is likely to be left vulnerable. That a building appears to be empty was regarded as very important by only 52 per cent and, indeed, 12 per cent preferred occupancy. The latter is explicable on the basis that if the householders are present, albeit asleep, then there will be more to steal.

Wright and Logie

Wright and Logie (1988) studied a small sample of English juvenile burglars so as to learn what factors they took into account when choosing a property to burgle. The issues raised with the burglars were also addressed to a group of householders to see to what extent they were in tune with the thinking of the burglars. The burglars looked for cover, means of access, an unoccupied property, the absence of a dog and an alarm and signs of wealth. Ironically an alarm can be seen as a sign that something worth stealing is being protected and thus may turn out to be counter-productive. As to the householders, the major differences to the burglars was in relation to their misplaced confidence as to the importance of locks and they also did not appreciate the significance of the factor of wealth.

Allatt

In contrast with the above studies, Allatt (1984) found that locks could make a difference depending on the type of housing. He examined the effect of making improvements to downstairs security measures on a difficult to let council-housing estate. A comparison was made with another estate which was to act as a control (and thus did not have the improvements in security). It was found that the burglary rate held steady, whilst the rate for the control estate had increased. As to the issue of displacement, this took the form of alternative crimes on the same estate but overall the crime rate had decreased. Such studies of burglary give some indication of the factors involved in the crime and the utility of particular preventive measures.

Cornish and Clarke

Cornish and Clarke (1986:8–15) provide lots of further ideas as regards factors which may be operative as background factors, factors in the decision at any one time to commit a burglary, factors in the selection of a particular burglary and its commission and also factors involved in the continuance of, and desistance from, burglary. They also suggest models in relation to these various stages.

Thornton et al

Thornton et al (2003) examined the possibilities of crime prevention ideas in relation to distraction burglaries. An example would be where one person makes an enquiry at the front of a house so as to allow entry for an accomplice at the rear. It needs to be appreciated from the outset that the notion of a distraction burglary is a wide one and at times was extended to victims who had found a burglar in their home. One of the conclusions of the research was that attempts should be made to move towards a tighter definition of distraction burglary, perhaps by recognising a broad range of entry modes. Including a trick, action or falsehood as modes of entry offers a firm basis for a definition. This would ensure that trust crimes and the offer of over-priced goods or services are included. The specific rather than global nature of crime prevention is looked at, in that this sub category of the offence of burglary is investigated in relation to only two particular types of potential victim – older adults and ethnic minority communities.

Raising awareness. Most of the older adults in the first study (68 per cent) reported themselves to be aware of distraction burglary before the incident, largely through TV or newspapers. Fewer (35 per cent) could recall the detail of these warning messages. In contrast, Asian and African-Caribbean participants in the second study generally had little awareness of the term distraction burglary, with awareness campaigns having very little impact. Both studies have highlighted the importance of raising public awareness of distraction burglary and suggest ways in which existing awareness-raising campaigns might be improved. Recommendations for the content and dissemination of future distraction burglary awareness-raising campaigns include:

1. incorporating specific warning messages in awareness-raising campaigns rather than general cautions;
2. adding a 'keep door locked' message, which could also help reduce other forms of burglary such as walk-in burglaries;
3. adopting methods that encourage interaction rather than passivity on the part of the audience, to maximise learning effectiveness, particularly through the use of face-to-face awareness-raising strategies;
4. promoting self-confidence and feelings of personal control over victimisation, as these can minimise future vulnerability;
5. tailoring campaign strategies to meet the needs of particular communities, using mass-media strategies and more focused local campaigns using local community resources;
6. encouraging the home owner to take action and make the distraction burglary message in awareness raising campaigns more explicit and alert people to the repercussions of unsafe doorstep practices;
7. encouraging the reporting of attempted and successful distraction burglary incidents amongst all communities.

Reducing vulnerability. Older adults identified a number of environmental factors marking out a potential target. Such external property indicators of a vulnerable resident (eg neglected gardens and decor) could be minimised by:

1. Encouraging home owners to carry out external repairs, including helping them seek financial support where necessary. Registers of reputable workers may also help to reduce the extent of rogue trader crime.

2. For rented properties, simple, quick and reliable procedures for reporting repairs and upkeep to landlords, including local councils.

Poor mobility as a vulnerability factor amongst older adults. This could be minimised by ensuring that professionals visiting an older person encourage them to keep their outer doors locked and to use entry phone and remote door opening from a central control point.

Isolation as a vulnerability factor. This may be reduced by developing social networks reaching people either in their own homes or in community settings, such as day centres with an explicitly social function. Calls from utility companies or professionals should ideally be arranged in advance, with a specific date and time of appointment, in the first language of the resident. Once at the property an agreed 'doorstep code' should be employed by the visiting agency, so this practice becomes both consistent and predictable. This will reduce vulnerability to bogus callers adopting these identities.

Laycock
Laycock (1986) provides an account of the use of a property-marking scheme in 1983 in three small South Wales' communities which were situated in the same valley. The idea is that when the police recover stolen property they can check to see if it has been marked with a postcode and if so then the property can be returned to the rightful owners. Other possible benefits are that arrest rates might increase as a result of the possession of stolen goods being easier to prove, and also the property itself might be less attractive as a target for burglars if it contained marked goods which could also be more difficult to fence. Laycock's account of the evidence from similar schemes in the United States of America and Sweden suggested that the prospects for the United Kingdom would be poor. In South Wales, through a variety of publicity and recruitment methods, a high level of participation was encouraged so as to give the tactic every chance. The take up rate was 72 per cent and the outcome was a statistically significant reduction (5 per cent reduced to 3 per cent) in the levels of victimisation for the participants in the scheme. Displacement does not seem to have occurred as the non-participants did not suffer an increased incidence of burglary and there does not appear to have been displacement to alternative offences. A variety of costs were involved in the scheme (publicity costs, equipment costs and the cost of police time). These were about the same as the cost would have been for the investigation of the burglaries that had been avoided. In financial terms this scheme just about broke even but the non-financial cost of being burgled were avoided for some, and there was an additional intangible benefit of improved police-community relations.

Hope
Hope (1986) examined burglary of schools. In a survey of 59 London schools, he identified two types of school design – small, old and compact and large, modern and sprawling. The first type had low burglary rates and relevant features seemed to be an ethos of commitment to the school amongst the pupils, that there were less items available to burgle than at the other school type, that there was less access for a burglar and more potential for a burglar to be subject to surveillance. In the large, modern and sprawling schools the burglary rates

were generally higher and factors of access and surveillance were related to the incidence of burglary in particular schools. These findings do not offer much potential for design-based crime prevention measures as there is little prospect of anything other than a limited school-building programme. Some suggestions were made. For example, to target harden in relation to particular weak spots which are allowing access, to provide more surveillance by means of caretakers or other patrols and to provide more lighting and thus enhanced potential for surveillance.

Vandalism and defensible space

One of the ways in which the problems of vandalism have been tackled is by utilising the notion of an area of defensible space. Such an area is one that a person will feel personally responsible for. Newman (1972, 1976, 1980 and 1997) has analysed this notion. Newman suggests that part of the explanation for urban crime lies in a breakdown of social mechanisms which once kept crime in check, and that the inability of communities to come together in joint action hampers crime prevention. The solution he offers is one of restructuring the residential environments of our cities so they can again become livable and controlled, not by police, but by a community of people sharing a common terrain. He describes four elements of the physical design of environments which can contribute, positively or negatively, to their security. These are: territoriality, surveillance, image and milieu.

Territoriality

This is the capacity of the physical environment to create perceived zones of influence. It is claimed that the design of buildings and their sites can encourage residents to adopt proprietary attitudes and also that certain layouts inform outsiders that particular areas are for the private use of residents. Newman suggests that within the built environment there is a hierarchy of types of space – ranging from private space at one end to public space at the other. Private space is that area of space under the total control of a resident, typically the inside of a house or apartment. Semi-private space is the area under an occupant's control, which is visually and physically accessible to the public, such as the garden of a house. Semi-public space represents the area of space which is under the control of a group of residents or in their area of responsibility. Examples would be the corridors of high-rise buildings, and shared areas for recreation and parking. Public space is an area to which the public has open access. An obvious example is a public street. The explanations and examples suggested here are clearly simplistic. The points at which one type of space ends and another begins are blurred and will vary between different settings. For example, Newman suggests that in a high-rise building with low-income tenants and no doorman to control access, only the interior of an apartment will be private space, and everywhere else is a no-man's land. Newman goes on to argue that residents can extend their responsibilities beyond their front doors. He puts forward a number of suggestions which seek to increase the territorial influence of residents. One expected result is that strangers will be more easily recognised as such and will therefore be discouraged from entering. Newman's devices for defining boundaries include various types of barrier, both real (high walls, locked entry points) and symbolic (open gateways, steps, changes in texture of walking surface). Both are said to inform users of space that they are passing from a public domain to a private one where their presence must be justifiable.

Surveillance
A second element of defensible space design is the capacity to provide opportunities for surveillance. Windows should be positioned in such a way that semi-private and public areas can be kept under natural observation by residents. Newman argues that such surveillance reduces residents' fears and enables areas to be regarded as more secure, thus encouraging greater legitimate use and thereby making them still more secure. He accepts that surveillance is not a panacea for a complex problem. To be effective, it must be combined with techniques of territorial definition, since the ability to observe will not automatically cause an observer to come to the aid of a person or target being victimised. The decision whether or not to act may be affected by several conditions, including the extent to which the observer believes the activity to be happening within his sphere of influence; whether he regards the behaviour as normal within that area; whether he identifies with the victimised person or property; and the extent to which the observer feels he can have an effect on the events he is watching.

Image
A third element is image. In relation to this, Newman argues that if a building is of a distinctive height and texture it can be singled out for particular attention. Where the distinctive image is negative, stigma will arise and residents risk being victimised. Newman suggests that public housing projects are particularly affected because they are designed so as to stand out. This image combines with other design features, which reduce territoriality and surveillance opportunities, and with the socio-economic characteristics of the population to make this type of housing particularly vulnerable to crime.

Milieu
The final element is milieu, as regards which Newman suggests that if certain areas are identified as safe, other areas which adjoin them will benefit from their safety. He argues for the juxtaposition of residential areas with other areas seen as safe. However, Newman challenges the suggestion by Jacobs (1962) that residential areas should be sited alongside commercial areas in the expectation of enhancing safety because of increased activity. It is Newman's contention that the success of a particular mixture of land uses depends as much on the degree to which residents can identify with and survey activity in the related facility as it does on the nature of the users of that facility and the activities they indulge in. Newman does not rule out the mixing of commercial and residential uses of land, but he insists there must be a critical evaluation of the nature of a commercial area and of its intended users before it is located next to housing.

Criticisms of Newman's ideas
As is so often the case with ideas on criminal justice there are criticisms to be made of Newman's suggestions. Mawby describes Newman's style as 'predisposed towards political

oratory rather than serious scientific endeavour', and suggests the research findings are 'rather expertly obscured within the text' (1977:169). The use of multi-variate analysis in relation to the data obtained is accused of yielding little, and of including inaccurate calculations: Mayhew (1979). Newman is also criticised for paying insufficient attention to socio-demographic factors, such as income, and for ignoring offender rates which may have influenced variations in offence rates. It has to be said that in his later work Newman gives greater recognition to the relevance of social factors: eg Newman (1980). One serious cause for criticism of the earlier material is that Newman chose to concentrate on a comparison of just two housing projects, thus attracting suspicion that the two chosen were those which best suited his hypothesis.

Mawby used data from a study of crime in Sheffield to test whether area crime patterns varied with physical design features. He compared the crime rates of four residential areas, all council owned. Two consisted of flats, and two of conventional housing. For each type of housing, one area had a high rate of offender residence, and the other a low rate. Although some differences were found, high-rise buildings were not found to be at a disadvantage when compared with conventional housing (1977:173). In fact, for the two areas with high offender rates, the rate of residential offences was considerably higher in the area with conventional housing. Mawby points to a number of inherent contradictions in the notion of defensible space. First, the concept is so wide that the same design can incorporate both good and poor defensible space qualities. Perhaps more seriously Mawby suggests that Newman fails to consider the possibility that the four main elements of defensible space may themselves include features which threaten security, as well as others which enhance it. For example, as well as highlighting strangers, an increase in territoriality will also legitimise the presence of residents, and may increase the possibility of crime by them against neighbours. In terms of surveillability, the same building might give a good view of some areas, such as the ground below, but poor views of others, such as corridors. Mawby suggests that, using Newman's criteria, it is arguable that most private housing has poor defensible space qualities since an enclosed garden creates a private area with a visibility barrier for potential onlookers. He goes on to suggest that a flat may be less open to burglary than a conventional house because there is less choice of entry points and because although the corridor may be relatively invisible it is still a public place and therefore more open to possible interruption. This is said to make it possible to turn Newman's hypothesis on its head by suggesting that flats will be less prone to crime (1977:176). This particular suggestion seems to be criticism for criticism's sake, since Newman's recommendations include increasing visibility of as many areas as possible, and maximising the use of shared areas to increase natural surveillance. Also, literature which makes practical recommendations based on defensible space ideas tends to recognise the detrimental effect of cover around conventional housing: Poyner (1983).

Specific studies of vandalism

The first study of vandalism to consider is that by Wilson (1980) and she utilised some of Newman's ideas. She carried out a survey of 285 blocks of dwellings on inner London council-housing estates. A comparison of the rates of vandalism for the blocks was carried out in order to see if the rates could be understood in terms of the notion of an area of defensible space. Such an area is one that a person will feel personally responsible for. There will also be public areas – these are characterised as being subject to surveillance. This surveillance also provides some degree of protection from crime for activities within the area. It is the semi-public areas such as hallways in large buildings which are less likely to benefit from either type of protection and thus be more crime prone. In the London study whilst there was some support for the idea that semi-public areas seemed to be associated with vandalism, the most important factor was child density. The rate of crime per child went down as the number and density of children went up. It seems that there was only so much vandalism that could be done. Thus to reduce the density may well not do much to decrease the amount of vandalism and may have the effect of exporting the potential for vandalism elsewhere. Equally, since the housing in question was designed for families alternative usage is problematic. Some proposals to alleviate the problem were presented – more play area, reduced amounts of impersonal space and generally less use of glazing as it is a common target for vandalism. Mayhew et al (1980) investigated the effect of natural surveillance (people looking from their homes) upon vandalism to telephone kiosks. It seems that it does not appear to be a factor and that it cannot be relied upon as a defence mechanism. It seems that the most effective measure is to remove and then possibly resite those kiosks that are most at risk. A number of different types of surveillance were investigated by Sturman (1980). This study examined the problem of damage to buses by passengers. The presence of a conductor and stairs at the rear (which meant that the most frequently vandalised upstairs rear seat area would be subject to more scrutiny) both lowered rates of vandalism. Young boys seemed to be the main vandals and one tactic would be to restrict them to the downstairs area as a means to reduce vandalism. Whilst this is a reasonable idea in theory, in reality this is impractical as it would mean that the less physically able groups (such as the elderly and women with children) would then be expected to cope with the stairs.

Studies of other forms of crime prevention

Pick-pocketing

The first of these to note is that of Poyner (1986), which provides a study that shows how highly specific some measures can be. The particular crime problem was pick-pocketing of wallets at bus stops in Birmingham city centre. By observing passengers getting their fare ready before boarding a bus, a group of youths could look out for wallets being put back into the passenger's pocket. Having this information the tactic was for a group of youths to dash to the front of the queue and on to the bus platform as the queue began to board the bus. The pretext used was to ask the driver a question. This process allowed them to jostle people and pick a pocket. They would then run off and the victim would not realise his loss until later. The prevention of the crime could be achieved by removing the circumstances of it. Marshalling barriers would mean that the bus could only be boarded by people in the queue and in file. The use of a barrier could also prevent the queue being subject to scrutiny by thieves. Such tactics were found to have worked at locations examined in this study.

City centre disorder

Ramsay (1986) examined cases of violence and disorder in central Southampton in 1980. He analysed 557 such cases and found that Friday and Saturday nights were the peak periods for such incidents. Not surprisingly 21 per cent of these incidents were in or near pubs and clubs. In his work he was able to identify features of such premises that both mitigated against such disorders (provision of entertainment and refreshments and a system of membership) and also features that increased the risk of them (poor lighting and decor and overcrowding). Such knowledge provides a recipe for crime-prevention measures and details of the likely times and places of disorders can be of use to the police in manpower planning. To tell them that Friday and Saturday night are peak periods for such disorders would not of course come as news to them, but as was seen in the study the fact that there was a crime problem associated with hospitals might be of assistance.

Reducing alcohol-related violence and disorder

Maguire et al (2003) carried out research which was designed to examine strategies for reducing alcohol-related violence and disorder. They evaluated the TASC project which was designed to tackle alcohol-related street crime, particularly violence. This research provides details of initatives that were developed and used in Cardiff city centre and the Cardiff Bay area. The TASC project was launched in July 2000 and was evaluated over a period of 18 months. Its main interventions were: focused dialogue between the police and members of the licensed trade; measures aimed at improving the quality and behaviour of door staff; attempts to influence licensing policy and practice; measures aimed at publicising the problem of alcohol-related violent crime; targeted policing operations directed at crime and disorder hot spots; a cognitive behavioural programme for repeat offenders; a training programme for bar staff; a programme of education about alcohol for school age children and support for victims of alcohol-related assaults attending hospital.

An examination of patterns of violence in the city centre revealed that:

1. Alcohol-related incidents were very heavily concentrated in time, with Friday and Saturday nights between them accounting for nearly half of all incidents – not a surprising finding.
2. Sixty-one per cent of all known incidents involved physical violence, the remainder being incidents of disorder.
3. Over half of all incidents were linked to individual licensed premises, occurring either inside them or in the street directly outside.
4. Violent incidents were most common in or around specific licensed premises, while incidents of disorder were more likely to occur elsewhere on the streets.
5. Most incidents involved only one or two people.
6. Most of those involved as offenders or victims were young white males.
7. Forty-two per cent of those arrested had previous arrests for violent or public order offences.
8. Door staff were involved as victims or alleged assailants in 16 per cent of all incidents involving violence, and in 34 per cent of all such incidents taking place inside pubs or clubs.
9. Sixty-one door staff were arrested over the month period examined.
10. The most common form of assault was punching or kicking, but at least 10 per cent of cases involved bottles or glasses – the use of knives was rare.

11. Most injuries were fairly minor cuts and bruises to the face or head, but 15 per cent of victims of assault suffered broken bones and 12 per cent major cuts requiring stitches. Thirty per cent of assaults were classified as serious.

Outcomes. A comparison of the first 12 months after the launch of the project (July 2000 to June 2001) with the previous 12 months indicated that there was an overall decrease of 4 per cent in incidents involving alcohol-related assaults. By contrast, over the same period there was a 49 per cent increase in incidents of alcohol-related disorder. The fall in alcohol-related assaults (which was reflected in a variety of police record sources and in the records of A & E cases which were not known to the police) is highly encouraging for the TASC project, especially during a period when the numbers of incidents of violence against the person were rising elsewhere in South Wales and when there was a more than 10 per cent increase in licensed premises' capacity and the numbers of people drinking late at night in central Cardiff. It is impossible to say with certainty how many assaults would have occurred had TASC not been in existence, but the researchers' best estimate is that, during its first year of full implementation the project helped to reduce the expected level of violent incidents by 8 per cent – or by about 100 incidents.

By contrast, where disorder is concerned the results were disappointing. However, it must be remembered that 'alcohol-related disorder' is a much more slippery concept than 'alcohol-related assault', and that the figures given are more susceptible to changes in police activities and recording practices (there were also, unlike assaults, no figures from A & E to support or contradict them). It is possible that the increased attention to disorder created by the setting up of TASC resulted in police officers being readier to use the Public Order Act 1986 to deal with some incidents that they would earlier have defused with warnings and perhaps not recorded. Moreover, even if the figures are accepted at face value, two other important points should be noted:

1. The increase in disorder slowed considerably after the first few months of TASC commencing its operations.
2. Virtually all the rise in disorder was accounted for by one street in Cardiff – the street with the densest concentration of pubs and clubs and where a number of new premises opened over a short period.

Perhaps the most promising and clear-cut findings related to reductions in violent and disorderly incidents occurring in or just outside individual pubs and clubs which were the subject of carefully targeted policing operations. The most successful of these, lasting eight weeks, was followed by reductions of 41 per cent and 36 per cent in such incidents in and around the two clubs targeted. The reductions were sustained over time. On the other hand, operations targeted at two separate streets, rather than individual premises, appeared to be successful only in the short term, with early reductions not being sustained.

A number of examples of good practice were identified. These include:

1. A project manager at a sufficient level of seniority and a well resourced project team, including a data analyst with detailed knowledge of police data systems.
2. The full integration of the project into police objectives and priorities.

3. The creation of effective links with managers of licensed premises, especially through an active licensees' forum.
4. The maintenance of an accurate and up-to-date dedicated database, using both police and hospital data sources.
5. The use of the database not only to identify problems as they emerge, but to guide remedial visits to licensed premises by licensing officers equipped with concrete evidence with which to persuade managers to take action and, in extreme cases, as evidence to oppose licences or object to specific practices such as drinks' promotion schemes.
6. The development of an effective, proactive training programme for door staff.
7. The development of greater regulation of door staff.
8. The deployment of a member of the project team (in this case the training sergeant) on the disciplinary committee for door staff.
9. The appointment of a project nurse, based in the hospital, to support victims, encourage more reporting of assaults and assist the production of more comprehensive data.
10. Attempts to engage major players in both the public and private sectors in broader dialogue about the strategic management of the late-night economy in the city centre

Vehicle Watch

Honess and Maguire (1993) provide an account of a crime prevention measure which has been used in Gwent, South Wales. Called Vehicle Watch, it operates by means of members of the public putting a sticker on the back of their car. The sticker requests the police to stop the car if it is being used between certain night-time hours. This should reduce the car's desirability as a target for thieves during those hours, as they would run the risk of being stopped by the police. A problem that the scheme encountered was that the police could not fulfil the commitment to stop all cars carrying Vehicle Watch stickers which were active during curfew hours. The evidence from crime figures is inconclusive. Whilst crime rates for car theft in Gwent went down for a few months after the scheme was introduced, they went up again later. The decrease was also seen in other areas that did not have such a scheme. A survey in relation to the scheme was carried out with a 44 per cent response rate. From this it seems that 12 per cent of scheme members suffered from car theft, whilst the rate for non-members was twice as high. However, it seems that the Vehicle Watch members were generally less vulnerable to vehicle theft than non-members. They were older, were more likely to garage their cars overnight and during the day they were more likely to leave their car where they could keep an eye on it. A clear advantage of the scheme is that, rather like Neighbourhood Watch, it makes people feel more secure and is potentially a good avenue for facilitating police relations with the public.

Youth car crime

Research reported by Spenser (1992) provides a good example of how some depth of knowledge of offenders can lead to a variety of different strategies which are designed to tackle specific aspects of a crime problem, such as car crime involving young people. The research was carried out on Pennywell, a Sunderland housing estate. It examined the involvement of young people (those under the age of 16) in car crime. A survey of them found that over half of them knew others who were involved in car crime, and 32 per cent of those interviewed had been present when property had been stolen from a car. Involvement in car crime seemed to start at the age of ten in some cases, by, for example, acting as a lookout and other secondary participation. The motivation was complex involving a search for excitement, the gaining of status by participation and financial reward by the sale of car parts. It was very clear that the older offenders were role models for the younger boys in Pennywell which involved high-speed driving in stolen cars on the estate. Over time profit was likely to be the main motivation; there appeared to be a thriving local black market in cars and car parts and requests would be made to youths to steal specific makes of radio cassette or car parts for them. The solutions suggested by the offenders to combat the car crime were the provision of leisure facilities and the targeting of young boys aged ten years who were not yet involved in car crime but were in imminent risk of becoming so. One possibility is to use schemes in which purposeful activity is provided that involves cars. Repairing and racing old cars has been tried in some areas, and traffic-calming measures may also prevent the high-speed driving. In summary, the complex nature of car crime suggests that the most effective preventive approach is to target a number of different aspects of the problem. The findings from this research indicate the need for offender-oriented measures – diversionary activities aimed at the very young, for situational measures to frustrate displays of daring driving and for the police to remove the black market for stolen goods.

Car theft data

Information is also made available to the public as a crime-prevention strategy. An example of this is the *Car Theft Index*: Home Office (1999c). This revealed data as to which cars are most at risk of theft. The car type which was most at risk of theft was the small saloon (such as the Ford Escort or Vauxhall Astra) with 18 thefts per 1,000 registered. This was closely followed by medium saloons (such as the Ford Mondeo or Vauxhall Cavalier) with 16 thefts per 1,000 registered. The newer the car, the less likely it was to be stolen – cars registered in 1997 had a theft rate of just 4 per 1,000 registered. The type of car least likely to be stolen was the people carrier (such as the Ford Galaxy or Renault Espace) with just five thefts per thousand registered. The wider picture is that 391,271 cars were reported to have been stolen in England, Scotland and Wales during 1998 – an average of 1,072 cars per day. Overall, there were 15 cars stolen per 1,000 registered with the Driver and Vehicle Licensing Agency. Tips from the *Car Theft Index* include advice to secure the doors, windows, boot and sun-roof every time you leave the car and to take your keys with you at the petrol station when you go to pay. Never leave your credit or other plastic cards in the car. If you have to leave briefcases and other items in the vehicle, put them out of sight, preferably before you start your journey. None of this should be news to us. Less obvious is the point that even an old coat or jacket on the back seat may be a target for a thief hoping to find a wallet in the pockets.

Problem housing estates

The final study to consider is that by Morris (1996) who provides an account of research on the use of some crime-prevention strategies, that had been used with some success, on particular problem housing estates. It was suggested that the tactic of targeting key offenders was a sound one. Good information-gathering was important in this. High-profile patrols of particular problem areas could also be effective. Such activity should have clear aims and the community should be kept informed of the purpose of such operations – this can aspire to the outcome of community support for the activity. Without communication the danger is that community hostility will be produced. The research suggests that improvements in community-police relations are important in order to produce long-term solutions on problem housing estates. Getting officers integrated and exposing youngsters to positive roles for the police so as to reduce prejudice was suggested. The media should be seen by the police as a resource rather than as a threat. Where civil actions, such as evictions and injunctions, could be useful then the police should support them – local authorities are an obvious example of where support is needed for such actions.

Small shops

The Home Secretary, David Blunkett, announced in 2002 that thousands of small shops in rundown communities are to benefit from a further £5.8 million to help shops improve security. More than 5,400 shops across the country are set to receive money from the Security for Small Retailers scheme to pay for improved security measures such as burglar alarms, better locks and CCTV. It will also pay for environmental improvements to make shopping parades look better and feel safer. The funding in 2003 extended the number of shops helped to more than 12,500 over the life of the scheme. Shops can be vital to the health of local communities and provide essential services. If they become vulnerable to crime they risk closing, putting the whole community on a downward spiral.

2.9 Social and community strategies

Many of the examples to date are attempts at situational crime prevention which Crawford (1998:68) presents as being the prioritisation of the control of crime through practical, yet limited, policy-orientated measures. It also has an emphasis on alterations to the physical environment. It looks to the significance of informal social control and the offence rather than the offender as the primary focus of attention. The possibilities of social and community strategies also need to be considered. These are very likely to focus on offenders. Examples are to be found in the following report *Preventing Children Offending*: Home Office (1997a). This research examined strategies for preventing children from becoming offenders. They suggested a dual approach which offers support to children at risk of offending, backed by sanctions for parents who will not face up to their responsibilities.

Risk factors as regards potential for criminality

On the issue of what factors influence the likelihood of a child committing crime the Home Office research (Home Office (1997a)) noted the work of Graham and Bowling (1995) which had identified the following eight key factors:

1. being male;
2. being brought up by a criminal parent or parents;

3. living in a family with multiple problems;
4. experiencing poor parenting and a lack of supervision;
5. poor discipline in the family and at school;
6. playing truant;
7. associating with delinquent friends; and
8. having brothers and sisters who offend.

In the Home Office report there was an analysis of factors such as the family, the school and peer influences as regards their impact on risks of offending. In relation to the family this was presented as the single most important influence on a child's development. It is noted that those children who show signs of criminal behaviour at an early age are those who are most likely to end up as serious or persistent offenders. Such children often come from communities and families which are unstable, chaotic and suffer from a number of problems. Their parents are likely to have criminal records, to neglect their children, or to exercise low levels of supervision and harsh and erratic discipline, and themselves likely to come from similar families. Children who are exposed to abuse and neglect within a climate of hostility at home are particularly at risk of becoming violent offenders. Research has also shown that where children are brought up in a stable environment, and have a good relationship with their parents, they are less likely to display delinquent behaviour. The capacity and willingness of the parent or parents to supervise their children and exercise fair and consistent discipline is crucial.

The importance of early intervention

The government believes that it is essential to intervene with children at risk of becoming offenders as early as possible. It is also essential to develop strategies for intervention on the basis of sound knowledge about what works. One of the best-known examples of early intervention is the Perry Pre-School project (USA). It was set up with the explicit objective of reducing the risk of delinquency. The project placed a number of black children from low socio-economic families either in a pre-school child-development programme or in a control group for a period of, in most cases, two years at the age of three. The child-development programme involved pre-school supervision of children by teachers, and weekly home visits to mothers and children by teachers. Over a period of 16 years, information was collected on all the children involved in the project. The information included data on, for example, school performance, attitudes, employment record and self- and police-reported delinquency. The study found that those children who attended the pre-school programme performed better in school and adult education and were more likely to graduate and get employment. Teenage pregnancy rates were much lower (about half), and arrest rates were 40 per cent lower than for children in the control groups at the age of 19. By the age of 27, about one in three of the control group had been arrested five or more times compared with about one in 14 of those who had attended the pre-school programme. A cost-benefit analysis of the project found that it cost in the region of $5,000 per child each year. The analysis showed that, for every $1 invested, $6 was saved in future public expenditure. On that basis, early intervention to prevent children offending makes sound financial sense.

The Home Office report also presented the following as examples of our own good practice.

Home Start

This is a network of nearly 200 home-visiting schemes across the country, supported by a national consultancy. It uses trained volunteers, who are themselves experienced parents, to offer friendship, practical advice and support to families with pre-school children. It works alongside the statutory health and social services, accepting referrals from doctors, teachers and other professionals as well as from voluntary organisations such as RELATE. The families that Home Start works with may be in difficulty because of domestic violence, suspected child abuse, debt, children's behavioural problems or other reasons. Volunteers aim to share their practical experience as parents; to encourage parents to become more confident in their own abilities; and to reassure then that it is not unusual to encounter problems in bringing up children. Visits usually take place once or twice a week, but may be more frequent in times of crisis. The Home Office has recently offered Home Start a grant of £23,000 a year for three years to support two projects in Castleford and Wycombe. Ten other Home Start projects have between them received some £397,000 in the third round of grants by the National Lottery Charities Board (Health, Disability and Care Grants).

Dorset Healthy Alliance Project

This is an experimental project sponsored by the Home Office Programme Development Unit, which promoted closer parent-school links tackling a range of behavioural problems, including disruptive behaviour, truancy and bullying. An education welfare officer based at a primary school in Bournemouth was able to launch a number of initiatives, including home visits to encourage attendance at school parents' evenings; anti-bullying campaigns; and preventing exclusions and truancy by enlisting the active support of parents in setting targets for pupils to improve their behaviour.

On Track

In December 1999 a further example of such an approach was announced in the press. It was revealed that £30 million was to be used on pilot programmes to target youngsters, aged 4–12, who were at risk of becoming involved in crime. The pilot projects form part of the crime reduction programme which was launched by the government in November 1999. Up to 30 high crime areas around the country will be given extra cash for what are being called On Track pilots. The aim is to identify youngsters likely to fall into crime and then act collectively to prevent it. The aims of On Track are as follows: to reduce youth crime by developing centres of excellence in early prevention; to provide hard evidence of what works best; and to ensure better co-operation in sharing of information and co-ordination of services. The pilots will run for seven to ten years, and will involve a partnership of the main health, educational and social services providers, youth-offending teams, the police and relevant voluntary sector organisations. It is intended that improved inter-agency co-operation will mean that children at risk of offending are identified early and their families provided with consistent support as the child grows up. This will include services such as parenting skills training, home-school partnerships, home visiting by trained volunteers, family therapy and structured pre-school education. On Track will thus aim to deliver a co-ordinated, evidence-based range of preventative services.

Crawford (1998:Chapter 4) examined the possibilities of social and community strategies and concluded as follows:

'The development of social crime prevention in Britain has lagged significantly behind that of situational prevention. The long-term investment that such strategies require is often at odds with the short-term nature of much political thinking which tends to prioritise the immediacy of the question of power. Nevertheless, it appears to have recently received new impetus with the elaboration of governmental strategies aimed at encouraging early intervention with young people at risk of offending and wider community safety programmes. However, the contribution of specific social programmes to the reduction of crime remains poorly defined and ill-tested. In this context the lessons to be learnt from programmes become less evident and the problems associated with the unintended consequences of given strategies remain a significant issue. Social crime prevention is the subject of intense political debate. The nature of the relationship between crime and social policy, as well as that between community safety and social justice, remains largely unanswered. There is a clear danger that in the shift to a preventive paradigm, we may come to expect too much of social policy generally or communities specifically. Both may be ends in themselves which may become distorted if shackled around issues of crime and disorder. Of themselves they may be more important than crime prevention.' (1998:160)

2.10 Conclusions

In the provision of an overall assessment and comment on these numerous schemes of, and ideas on, crime prevention I start from the basis that much as yet remains uncertain. Some successes have been noted (for example, some firm and practical ideas on burglary), but equally there have been failures (campaigns as a general tactic seem worthy of such a description). Other findings have meant that the merit of some tactics is unclear and matters have been complicated at times by (sometimes welcome and sometimes unwelcome) unexpected outcomes. The merits of other attempts to deal with crime, as we will see later, are in fact limited. This provides the best context for an assessment of crime prevention and it comes out of a comparison with other approaches as a relative success with further potential. A summary of the problems that such tactics face is required as a valuable corrective to this praise. In terms of a basic idea behind such measures the best, the rational choice model, has its problems but is worthwhile as a working assumption. Whilst on the subject of background ideas, the material on crime prevention has been presented on the assumption that something should be done about crime. The government has been promoting the idea that individuals and groups have some form of moral responsibility in relation to crime prevention. This view has been evident for some time as illustrated by the then Home Secretary, Douglas Hurd, in his address to industry in 1988. He suggested that crime prevention is a classic example of where self-interest and community service coincide. The Hurd statement raises difficulties. Crime prevention may not in fact be identifiable with self-interest. Retail outlets prefer enticing income-maximising display areas for their goods and the vulnerability of such displays to theft is accepted and largely seen as an overhead which can be made good from income. Crime may often not be perceived as a real threat and even if it is the response may be to seek insurance in relation to the problem. Equally, crime prevention measures such as locks may threaten safety in the case, for example, of a fire. There are then, as we saw earlier, real problems of motivation in relation to crime prevention measures. Displacement has also been seen to be a problem not only in itself but also because of the difficulties involved in measuring its extent. Reliable information is vital, not just to assess crime prevention measures – its existence is also crucial in the development of such measures. Given that the cost of research projects is considerable, the potential of such measures is bound to go at least partly unexplored. Equally, there are considerable difficulties involved in balancing costs that are not readily quantifiable. What value is to be attached to the prevention and thus the avoidance of the distressing effects of having been the victim of a burglary or a rape? Do crime prevention measures increase fear of crime and is this a cost to be taken into account? Also at some stage the restrictions on the general population will be deemed unacceptable – by whom and on the basis of which criteria?

3 The Role of the Police

3.1   Police powers

3.2   Hopes and expectations with regard to the police

3.3   Remedies and complaints

3.4   Factors influencing the practice of policing

3.5   Discretion, discrimination and stereotypes

3.6   Stop, search and arrest

3.7   The suspect in the police station

3.8   The provision of legal services to the defendant

3.9   Community policing

3.10 What works?

3.11 Assessing the performance of the police

3.12 Conclusion

The police are an important part of the criminal justice system and are the main point of contact between the population at large and the system. There is a very large body of literature dealing with the many issues concerning the police and the account here is necessarily selective. It should be noted that other people and institutions have and exercise similar functions and powers the police – for example, security firms and investigative activities by such authorities as the Monopolies Commission. The Criminal Justice Act 2003 provisions that relate to the issues in this chapter are detailed below. It is important to note that since most of the provisions of the Act did not come into force immediately upon Royal Assent the earlier provisions will still be applicable for some time.

For material on the administrative structure of the police, reference should firstly be made to the Police Act 1996. This Act consolidates (principally) the Police Act 1964, the Police and Criminal Evidence Act 1984, Part 9 and Part 1, Chapter 1 of the Police and Magistrates' Courts Act 1994. The 1996 Act deals with matters such as the organisation of police forces, chief constables, police authorities, the role of the Secretary of State, police representative institutions, the Police Complaints Authority, and disciplinary and other proceedings. The reforms to the police force introduced by the Police Act 1996 have been built upon by the Police Act 1997, which establishes three new national bodies. These are: a National Criminal Intelligence Service Authority to provide criminal intelligence to other police and law-enforcement agencies; a National Crime Squad to prevent and detect serious crime which is of relevance to more than one police area; and a Police Information Technology Organisation to give advice on information technology.

Police Reform Act 2002

The Act introduced a wide variety of changes for police forces of various types within the United Kingdom. The main measures that need to be noted are the introduction of further methods of control of the local forces by central government and the alteration of methods for handling complaints by citizens and the disciplining of individual police officers. The background to this was the government White Paper, *Policing a New Century: A Blueprint for Reform* (2001). That set out the government's intentions for the future of policing in England and Wales and followed the normal consultation process. The key principles of the reform programme are: to continue the reduction in crime; to tackle persistent offenders more effectively; to improve detection and conviction rates; to tackle anti-social behaviour; to reduce the fear of crime; to provide support to victims of crime; and to rebuild public confidence in key aspects of the police service. A comment that could be made about these so-called principles is that they sound more like platitudes than principles of a criminal justice system. In the Act additional systems are introduced for the control of police forces. As part of this the Secretary of State will produce an annual National Policing Plan and present it to Parliament. There will also be various systems for giving directions to police forces, including the use of codes of practice. The National Policing Plan will set out the government's priorities for policing and how they are to be delivered, and the indicators by which performance will be measured. Provision is also made for further measures that will allow the Secretary of State to intervene in a force where Her Majesty's Inspectorate of Constabulary (HMIC) is satisfied the force is not efficient or effective. In particular, the Act introduces a new power enabling the Secretary of State to direct a police authority to produce, in conjunction with the relevant chief officer, an action plan to address the poor performance highlighted by HMIC. The Act also allows the Secretary of State to require that HMIC inspects a force or part of a force.

The Police Reform Act 2002 aims to ensure that the most effective policing methods are used by all police forces, thus tackling the variations in performance between forces. The powers enable the Home Secretary to issues codes of practice to chief officers. He can also make regulations governing the use of police equipment or requiring forces to adopt particular procedures or practices. The intention is to spread good practice throughout the police service and to help raise the standards of all forces to the level of the best.

The Act also contains provisions in relation to numerous other matters, some of which can be noted briefly. It attempts to facilitate more effective use of police support staff, and provides for community safety accreditation schemes. It also adds to the list of offences for which someone can be arrested without a warrant, and places the system of independent custody visiting, to police stations, on a statutory footing. It contains provisions regarding the taking of blood samples from those involved in road traffic incidents. It makes provision for powers for constables in relation to vehicles used in a manner causing alarm, distress or annoyance. Finally, it makes several changes to legislation regarding anti-social behaviour orders and sex-offender orders. Anti-social behaviour orders for example, will be more flexible and widely available.

It needs to be noted that there are difficulties involved in talking about 'the police'. Police officers carry out a considerable variety of functions and tasks. Special squads will deal with such as drugs, bombs and diplomatic protection. Specialisms include river police, frogmen, photographers, finger-print specialists, road-safety officers and dog handlers. Such large numbers of police officers and the diversity of tasks involved in policing, as well as the complexity of the behaviour that is involved, makes generalisations about policing difficult.

Police numbers

Cotton and Smith (2003) provide details of police numbers in the 43 forces in England and Wales in March 2003. Police numbers in England and Wales have reached record levels with 133,366 officers. This is an increase of 3,763 or 3 per cent compared to a year earlier. The Home Secretary had set targets of 130,000 police officers by March 2003 and 132,500 in 2004. Both targets were exceeded well ahead of the target date. The large growth in police numbers is further demonstrated by noting that the figure in 1960 was 72,250. There were 200,839 full time equivalent staff working in the police service in England and Wales. Police officers accounted for 67 per cent of this total, community support officers 1 per cent, traffic wardens 1 per cent and other police staff 31 per cent. Additionally, there were 11,037 special constables providing voluntary police officer resource to police forces and local communities in England and Wales. Special constables provide at least four hours a week to their force but do not have contracted hours. Table 11 provides details. A further 2,803 staff worked for the British Transport Police in England and Wales, of which 2,179 were police officers. They are the national police force for the railways throughout England, Wales and Scotland. They also police the London Underground and a number of local transport systems. In relation to the police officers, the proportion of women in more senior ranks remains low. Whereas 21 per cent of constables were female this was only true of 6 per cent of chief superintendents. There were 3,915 ethnic minority officers, 2.9 per cent of the total police strength, compared with 2.6 per cent in 2002.

3.1 Police powers

The statutory and case law provisions on police powers of arrest, entry, search and seizure and the later stage of police station detention are stated below. Issues of police accountability and remedies are raised later in the chapter. Admissibility of evidence, the human rights case law and appeal systems are covered in the chapter that deals with the criminal trial. The Criminal Justice Act 2003 provides for the following changes to procedures. The detention period in a police station will change from 24 to 36 hours and other changes would be made to the detention rules. Review of detention can take place by telephone and video link. No record need be kept of what the defendant had in his possession on entering custody. Proceedings are no longer to be commenced by a summons or the laying of an information but rather by a written charge. The Home Secretary, David Blunkett, announced in 2003 that the Fixed Penalty Notice Scheme would begin nationwide by 2004: this action being taken in the light of experimental use of the scheme. The Scheme

Table 11

Police Service Strength in England and Wales as at 31 March 2003

ACPO ranks	210
Chief superintendents	493
Superintendents	860
Chief inspectors	1,761
Inspectors	6,457
Sergeants	19,255
Constables	106,967
Total police ranks	136,003
Police staff	68,482
Traffic wardens	2,200
Community support officers	1,181
Total police service strength	207,866
Special Constabulary	11,037

(Source: Police Service Strength in England and Wales)

allows police officers to tackle minor public order and drunk and disorderly offences in the street rather than spending hours tied up in paperwork at the police station. It was presented as a sign of the government being serious about stamping out bureaucracy. However, there are still plenty of signs of bureaucracy as part of the new managerialism that is a feature of the system. A starting point in relation to police powers is the dicta of Lord Atkin in *Liversidge* v *Anderson* [1942] AC 206, ie any detention is prima facie unlawful and requires some legal justification. The Police and Criminal Evidence Act 1984 (PACE) is the main source of law and it is to that Act that references to sections relate unless otherwise indicated.

Arrest

Arrests requiring a warrant
The purpose of most such arrests is to start criminal proceedings before the courts by means of a warrant or a summons. The latter is preferable, as it is simpler. A warrant for arrest is issued by magistrates to the police. It must name the accused and the offence with which he is charged. The idea of a general warrant of arrest which does not specify the person or charge is unlawful: *Entick* v *Carrington* (1765) 19 St Tr 1029. A warrant can be executed anywhere in England or Wales. The arresting officer does not have to have the warrant in his possession but he should inform the person arrested of its existence and contents.

Arrests not requiring a warrant
Section 24(1)–(3) created the notion of an arrestable offence in relation to which later provisions provide powers of arrest. An arrestable offence is:

1. One in which the sentence is fixed by law. There are not many of these offences – an example is life imprisonment for murder.

2. Any offence that can carry a jail sentence of 5 years of more.
3. Certain other offences, such as corruption in public office, were also specified in PACE as being arrestable and later legislation added to these.

Section 116 and Schedule 5 provide for the notion of a serious arrestable offence which includes not only the obvious ones – such as murder, rape, arson, firearms and explosives offences – but others which are far less obvious. It includes, for example, an offence which involves serious harm to the security of the state or to public order. This notion is used in various parts of the legislation to increase the powers that are available in relation to such offences.

Section 24(4)–(6) states that any person may arrest without a warrant:

1. A person who is, or is reasonably suspected to be, in the act of committing an arrestable offence.
2. Where an arrestable offence has actually been committed any person can arrest anyone who they have reasonable cause to suspect of being guilty of the offence or a person who is guilty of the offence.
3. Where there is merely reasonable cause to suspect that an arrestable offence has been committed a policeman has the additional power of arresting anyone that he has reasonable cause to suspect has committed the offence. This power is not available to the private citizen. A police officer also has the power to arrest without a warrant any person he has reasonable cause to suspect is about to commit an arrestable offence, ie a preventative power.

Where s24 is inapplicable, s25 can be used so long as a general arrest condition is satisfied. A policeman may arrest for non-arrestable offences if a summons is impracticable or inappropriate and one of the general arrest criteria below is satisfied, namely:

1. The policeman does not know and cannot ascertain the identity of the person.
2. The policeman has reasonable grounds to believe the name given is false.
3. The policeman has reasonable grounds to believe the address given is unsatisfactory.
4. Where arrest is reasonably believed to be necessary to prevent physical harm to the defendant or others, or loss or damage to property, or where the person is committing an offence against public decency or obstructing the highway.
5. To protect a child or vulnerable persons.

Section 25(6) provides that the common law power of arrest for breach of the peace is saved. You should note that other statutes may provide arrest powers and that there may be purely local arrest powers in particular areas. The Court of Appeal made it clear, in the case of *Foulkes* v *Chief Constable of Merseyside* (1998) The Times 26 June, that an arrest for a threatened breach of the peace must only be used where the threat to the peace is real and imminent. Foulkes had called the police about a domestic which had led to him being locked out by his family. The arrest took place because the police officer believed that violence would occur if Foulkes went back to the house. Foulkes had failed to obtain damages for wrongful arrest and false imprisonment but this appeal succeeded.

In *McLeod* v *Metropolitan Police Commissioner* [1994] 1 WLR 1500 the right for the police to enter private property in order to prevent a breach of the peace was accepted by the

Court of Appeal. There has to be a real and imminent risk of a breach of the peace. In the case the plaintiff had been ordered to give her ex-husband some furniture. He turned up to collect it in advance of the deadline and loaded it onto a van in her absence. Upon her return a dispute arose which involved the police entering the property. Whilst such a power was to be used with care, particularly in such circumstances, on the facts of the case the police action was justified. *Percy* v *Director of Public Prosecutions* [1995] 3 All ER 125 was concerned with the power to arrest and bind over for a breach of the peace. A lady had on a number of occasions trespassed on a military base as a peaceful protest about the use of the base. The Divisional Court could not view this behaviour as amounting to a breach of the peace as there was no violence or fear of violence either from herself or likely to be provoked from the armed personnel at the base. Thus the power of arrest for breach of the peace has to be seen very much in this light.

Sections 17 and 117 state that in the use of these powers a constable can enter and search any place that he reasonably suspects a person that he wants to arrest to be. In the use of that power force can be used. A person may use such force as is reasonable in the circumstances for the prevention of crime and in the making of a lawful arrest of actual or suspected offenders or of people unlawfully at large. In the majority of cases force is not necessary. Section 17 also authorises entry in other circumstances: for example for the recapturing of a person who is unlawfully at large and who is being pursued, or for saving life or limb or preventing serious damage to property. Where ss17 and 117 permit an officer to use reasonable force to enter premises without the householder's consent, this will apply only where a demand to enter has not been complied with by the householder or where there are special circumstances applicable. These would include where the suspect is dangerous or there is a need to take him by surprise which makes it inadvisable to give warning of impending police approach.

The case of *D'Sousa* v *Director of Public Prosecutions* [1992] 4 All ER 545 illustrates the use of the power of entry for the purposes of recapturing a person who is unlawfully at large and whom a policeman is pursuing. The policeman entered premises to recapture a person who had escaped from a mental institution. He thought that the person was inside. Members of the family who were in the house told the policeman to leave but he proceeded to recapture the patient. A fight ensued and the family members were arrested and convicted of assaulting a policeman in the execution of his duty. It was held that the word 'pursuing' means that the policeman must have been chasing the person at large immediately before the forced entry. Since there was no chase the entry was unlawful as the policeman was not executing his lawful duty at the time.

In *O'Loughlin* v *Chief Constable of Essex* (1997) The Times 12 December the Court of Appeal made it clear that the police in their use of a power to enter a dwelling by means of reasonable force should, unless circumstances made it impossible, impracticable or undesirable, give any occupant present the reasons for their use of such a power. The Court presented this view in the process of dismissing an appeal by the Chief Constable against an award of damages that had been made in relation to an entry of the plaintiff's house. The plaintiff and his wife returned home after visiting a number of public houses, and it was reported that a neighbour's car that was parked outside their house was damaged during a disturbance. By the time the police arrived the couple were inside their front door, the glass of which had been broken and the door was barricaded from inside. The police asked to be allowed in but entry was denied. There was a further disturbance, during which the plaintiff was pulled outside the house by the police. This necessitated the use of force as the plaintiff struggled. The aim of the police was to speak to the wife about the damage to the car. If they had explained to the plaintiff that they wished to enter in order to arrest his wife then this would have allowed them to enter if need be by means of force. The police, however, had no power to enter merely to question the wife.

What amounts to a reasonable suspicion?

There have been a number of sources of guidance as to reasonable suspicion having to be held by policeman exercising statutory arrest powers. In *Castorina* v *Chief Constable of Surrey* [1988] NLJ 180 detectives reasonably concluded that a burglary of a company was an inside job and that documents taken would be of use to a person with a grudge. They were informed as to a person who had recently been dismissed from the employ of the company. She had no criminal record. She was arrested and then released without charge. She claimed damages for wrongful arrest and detention and received damages. The matter was then appealed to the Court of Appeal where the appeal was allowed. Woolf LJ said that there are three stages involved:

1. Did the arresting officer suspect that the person was guilty of the offence? For this there is the need to have a finding of fact as to his state of mind.
2. If he had the necessary suspicion was there reasonable cause for suspicion? This is an objective requirement arrived at by the judge in relation to facts as found by the jury.
3. Where the first two questions are answered positively the policeman has a discretion to arrest. That discretion itself is subject to control (the *Wednesbury* reasonableness principles as expounded by Lord Greene in *Associated Provincial Picture Houses Ltd* v *Wednesbury Corporation* [1948] 1 KB 223. In *Castorina* the arrest was of a middle-aged woman with no criminal record. No enquiry was made of her as to her alibi or possible motives, such as a grudge. The Court decided the arrest was reasonable on the basis of experience, motive and inside knowledge being particular characteristics of such an offence and the lady was the only person who appeared to have such characteristics. As a comment upon this it might be thought that some form of enquiry might have been a better course of action than arrest.

In *Monaghan* v *Corbert* (1983) 147 JP 545 a constable spoke to the defendant whose car was parked outside his house. The constable smelt alcohol on the defendant's breath. The next day, a Sunday, he was told by a neighbour that the defendant habitually drove for a Sunday drinking session. He waited for the defendant's return and breathalysed him. The issue arose as to whether or not the policeman had reasonable suspicion. This can be based on other sources of information but cannot be applied to wholly unrelated matters. There was nothing in itself to show any motoring offence so the conviction was quashed. In *King* v *Gardner* (1979) 71 Cr App R 13 a power under s66 of the Metropolitan Police Act 1839 to stop search and detain for reasonable suspicion of possession of stolen or unlawfully obtained property was used. Police officers received a radio message as to suspects loitering which mentioned 'two males, one female and a dog – blue jeans/long hair'. They stopped and detained Gardner with a woman and a dog. He refused to show the contents of a large canvas bag and assaulted the police during a purported arrest for which he was prosecuted. The court decided that there was nothing to constitute reasonable suspicion.

The case of *O'Hara* v *Chief Constable of the Royal Ulster Constabulary* [1997] AC 286 also provided principles on the issue of reasonableness of suspicion. In cases where a search requires reasonable grounds for suspicion the first point to be made is that this will depend on the circumstances in each case. There must be an objective basis for that suspicion based on facts or information relevant to the likelihood of finding an article of a certain kind. This can never be based on personal factors alone. Such factors include a person's race, age, appearance, or the fact that the person is known to have a previous conviction. These cannot be used alone or in combination with each other as the reason for searching that person. Reasonable suspicion cannot be based on generalisations or stereotypical images of certain groups or categories of people as being more likely to be involved in criminal activity. The comment to make about this is that research on police working practices demonstrates that suspicion can so easily be based on factors of these types. In *O'Hara* the House of Lords gave a guide to understanding provisions on reasonable suspicion. The provisions in issue were in s12(1) of the Prevention of Terrorism (Temporary Provisions) Act 1984. Section 12(1) reads as follows:

'... a constable may arrest without warrant a person whom he has reasonable grounds for suspecting to be – ...
(b) a person who is or has been concerned in the commission, preparation or instigation of acts of terrorism to which this Part of this Act applies; ...'

The guidance that was given in the case would also seem to be applicable to similar provisions in PACE which require reasonable suspicion. This requirement was satisfied, where an officer used the power, in relation to a person of whom he had been given information at a briefing prior to the arrest situation. The police constable in *O'Hara* had been told that the person had been involved in a murder. For the House of Lords having reasonable suspicion was where the constable himself had knowledge of the information, which causes the suspicion, at the time of the arrest. Acting on the request of another officer would not be sufficient, but the information that he had could come from other officers. Code A (in its revised edition (2003)), which deals with stop and search, provides further guidance on the matter of reasonableness of suspicion.

What is required for an arrest?
As to how an arrest is effected Stephenson LJ in *R* v *Inwood* [1973] 2 All ER 645 stated:

'There is no magic formula; only the obligation to make it plain to the suspect by what is said and done that he is no longer a free man.'

Section 28(3) provides that 'no arrest is lawful unless the person is informed of the ground for the arrest at the time of, or as soon as practicable after, the arrest.' Section 28 changes the position for the police; it was not intended to change the rules for citizen's arrests as it was felt to be unfair to place the higher duty that the Act now requires on a man who happens to, say, detain, until the police arrive, a burglar disturbed in his house in the middle of the night. Suffice to say that there are many other pitfalls for those who seek to uphold the law. The case of *R v Self* [1992] 1 WLR 657 is an excellent reminder of the dangers of undertaking a citizen's arrest. Whilst a police officer may arrest a person who is reasonably suspected of committing an arrestable offence, the citizen must be sure that the offence has been committed. In this case, a citizen witnessed the questioning of a suspected shoplifter, Self, by the employees of a store, outside the store. When Self ran off the citizen gave chase and, after a struggle, purported to arrest him for theft. As it turned out Self was not guilty of theft and so he could not be lawfully arrested for it. Neither had he resisted arrest as there had been no lawful arrest.

Dawes v Director of Public Prosecutions [1994] RTR 209 showed that a person could be arrested by being trapped in a car that he was trying to steal. The car was fitted with a security device that caused it to cut out after a few metres if it was being stolen. What about being told that he was under arrest I hear you say? Well this happened as soon as was reasonably practicable. In the future a similar security device could be developed that contained an audible message informing a person as to their situation. The case of *Director of Public Prosecutions v Hawkins* [1988] 1 WLR 1166 confirms that the reason does not have to be given at once if it is impracticable to do so. Article 5(2) of the European Convention on Human Rights 1950 states that 'everyone who is arrested shall be informed promptly, in a language which he understands, of the reasons for his arrest and of any charge against him.' In *Alderson v Booth* [1969] 2 QB 216 the policeman said 'I shall have to ask you to come to the police station for further tests' to a suspect who had just given a positive breath test. This was viewed as not being an arrest as it sounded like a request rather than a command, and the person would not have known that he was no longer free. In *Nicols v Bulman* [1985] RTR 236 the words 'I arrest you' were found to be insufficient to constitute an arrest; they must be accompanied by a physical arrest indicating compulsion.

We learn from *Christie v Leachinsky* [1947] AC 573 that where an arrest is made without warrant the arresting officer must do two things. First, in ordinary circumstances he must inform the person arrested of the true ground of arrest. He is not entitled to keep the reason to himself or to give a reason which is not the true reason. A citizen is entitled to know on what charge, or on suspicion of what crime, he is seized. Second, if the citizen is not so informed but is nevertheless seized, the policeman is liable for false imprisonment. In the case a Liverpool policeman purported to exercise a local power of arrest. He knew the conditions needed to exercise the power did not exist. The police officers were sued for wrongful arrest and false imprisonment. In court it was argued on behalf of the police that the arrest was lawful because at the time of the arrest the police had information about Leachinsky that would have justified his arrest at common law for another offence. The House of Lords decided that the arrest was unlawful and that it was a condition of the law of arrest that the person should be told the reason for the arrest. In *R v Kulynycz* [1971] 1 QB 367 a constable purported to arrest the accused without giving him a reason. A little later at the police station he was told that he had been arrested on suspicion of handling stolen goods in Kings Lynn. Eventually he was charged with the unauthorised possession of controlled drugs in Cambridge. The court decided that whilst the original arrest was unlawful, in the police station he was given sufficient information to make his detention lawful. Similarly, in *Lewis v Chief Constable of South Wales* [1991] 1 All ER 206, where two ladies were detained and not given a reason for this until later at a police station: their detention became lawful from that point on. From *Simpson v Chief Constable of South*

Yorkshire (1991) The Times 7 March we learn that the use of unreasonable force does not necessarily make the arrest unlawful. However, if the police exceed their legal powers they may be open to a variety of remedial systems as utilised by defendants, including a civil action in tort for trespass to the person (for assault, battery or false imprisonment). In *Abbassy v Metropolitan Police Commissioner* [1990] 1 All ER 193 a policeman told the defendant that he was under arrest for unlawful possession without specifying what was being unlawfully possessed The court decided that in the circumstances, which were that the defendant knew she was being questioned about the ownership of the car she was driving, the arrest was lawful. The precise technical reason for the arrest did not have to be provided.

Police questioning

The principle here is that there is no power to detain for questioning short of arrest. In *Kenlin v Gardiner* [1967] 2 QB 510 two schoolboys were going from house to house to remind members of their rugby team about a game. Two police officers became suspicious and, producing a warrant card, asked what they were doing. The boys did not believe they were police officers. One boy made as if to run away. The police officer took hold of his arm. The boy struggled violently, punching and kicking the officer. The other boy got involved and struck the other officer. Both were charged with assaulting a police constable in the execution of his duty. The court decided that what the police had done was not as an integral step in the process of arresting them. There is no power to detain for questioning yet that is what they had attempted to do. In *Donnelly v Jackman* [1970] 1 All ER 987 a uniformed police officer approached Jackman, who was lawfully walking along a pavement, at 11.15 am, about offences which the police officer thought Jackman had committed. The police officer asked if he could 'have a word' with him. The request was ignored with Jackman continuing to walk away from the police officer. The police officer followed him, repeated the request, and eventually tapped him on the shoulder. Shortly afterwards, Jackman turned around and in turn tapped the officer on the chest saying: 'Now we are even, copper'. The police officer touched Jackman on the shoulder a second time but Jackman's response was to strike the police officer with some force. This was an assault on a police officer in the execution of his duty. Not every trivial interference with a citizen's liberty takes a police officer outside the course of his duties. *Mepstead v Director of Public Prosecutions* (1996) 160 JP 475 is a further case dealing with the ability of the police to physically restrain a person whom they have not arrested without the behaviour amounting to an assault by the police officers concerned. In this case it was regarded as permissible that a policeman took hold of a person's arm in order to be able to explain to him the consequences of his actions. The policeman needed to be able to control the person to that extent in order to do this. In *Bentley v Brudzinski* [1982] Crim LR 825, during the early hours of the morning, two brothers were stopped in the street by a police officer. They answered his questions truthfully and identified themselves. After waiting ten minutes for the officer to unsuccessfully verify their identities by radio they decided to walk off. At that moment another officer came along and tried to stop one brother, who then punched the policeman in the face. This was viewed as being not guilty of assaulting the officer in the course of his duty. There was more than a trivial interference with the defendant's liberty: it amounted to an unlawful attempt to stop and detain him.

Wednesbury unreasonableness

Many police powers are discretionary: for example, s24(4) states 'Any person may arrest ...'. In the exercise of these statutory powers police officers are subject to the principles expounded by Lord Greene in *Associated Provincial Picture Houses Ltd v Wednesbury Corporation* [1948] 1 KB 223, which is that officers must not exercise statutory discretions for improper purposes; they must not take legally irrelevant matters into account or fail to have regard to legally relevant matters and an exercise of discretion must not be so unreasonable that no reasonable authority or officer could so decide. In the case of *Lyons v Chief Constable of West Yorkshire* (1997) 60 JP 325 the Chief Constable was appealing against an award of damages to Lyons for wrongful arrest and false imprisonment. Two officers, whilst investigating a burglary, went to a house looking for Lyons. He was not there but a friend of his was and he told the officers that Lyons could not have committed the robbery as he had been with him at the time. Lyons was later arrested. The arrest and detention were challenged and damages awarded on the basis that the decision to arrest under s24 was unreasonable (*Wednesbury* unreasonableness) in light of the friend's evidence. The Chief Constable's appeal was allowed on the basis that the two officers had reasonable cause for their suspicion and that the judge had no basis for finding that their discretion was undermined by a failure to consider the friend's statement.

Stop and search of people and vehicles

The power to stop and search persons arises under statute. There are specific statutes that give such powers: for example, in relation to drugs, the Misuse of Drugs Act 1971, s23(2). There are also more general powers provided by PACE. The police have a general power to search a person or a vehicle (or anything which is in or on a vehicle) and to detain the person or vehicle for the purpose of such a search. This is provided by s1(2). It is necessary, however, for the constable to have 'reasonable grounds for suspecting that he will find stolen or prohibited articles' as a result of the search: s1(3).

Additionally, s1(1) provides that the search may only be carried out if the person or vehicle is:

'(a) in any place to which at the time when [the constables] proposes to exercise the power the public or any section of the public has access, on payment or otherwise, as of right or by virtue of express or implied permission; or
(b) in any other place to which people have ready access at the time when he proposes to exercise the power but which is not a dwelling.'

In relation to searches of persons or vehicles on land adjacent to a dwelling house, the Act provides by s1(4) and (5):

'(4) If a person is in a garden or yard occupied with and used for the purposes of a dwelling or on other land so occupied and used, a constable may not search him in the exercise of the power conferred by this section unless the constable has reasonable grounds for believing –
(a) that he does not reside in the dwelling; and
(b) that he is not in the place in question with the express or implied permission of a person who resides in the dwelling.
(5) If a vehicle is in a garden or yard occupied with and used for the purposes of a dwelling or

on other land so occupied and used, a constable may not search the vehicle or anything in or on it in the exercise of the power conferred by this section unless he has reasonable grounds for believing –
(a) that the person in charge of the vehicle does not reside in the dwelling; and
(b) that the vehicle is not in the place in question with the express or implied permission of a person who resides in the dwelling.'

Section 1(6) states that 'if in the course of a search a constable discovers an article which he has reasonable grounds for suspecting to be a stolen or prohibited article ... he may seize it.' The purpose of the search is to locate stolen goods or prohibited article. However, stolen goods is not a term defined in PACE. Thus, it is submitted, it is likely to be interpreted as being analogous to s24(2) of the Theft Act 1968 so that goods are stolen goods if they are goods originally stolen, or which directly or indirectly represent or have at any time represented stolen goods, or are the proceeds of any disposal or realisation of stolen goods, or are goods obtained by blackmail or by deception. The meaning of prohibited articles is provided by s1(7) and (8). Section 1(7) states:

'(7) An article is prohibited for the purposes ... of this Act if it is –
(a) an offensive weapon; or
(b) an article –
(i) made or adapted for use in the course of or in connection with an offence to which this sub-paragraph applies; or
(ii) intended by the person having it with him for such use by him or by some other person.'

The Criminal Justice Act 2003 adds items that are made, adapted or used for criminal damage to the notion of prohibited articles.

As soon as a constable is satisfied that the provisions of s1 have been met, then a constable who takes the decision to exercise his powers of search must follow the procedure laid down by s2 and usually make a record of it in accordance with s3. The procedure in s2(2) provides that 'If a constable contemplates a search ... in the exercise – (a) of the power conferred by s1 ... (i) to search a person without first arresting him; or (ii) to search a vehicle without making an arrest [then he has] to bring to the attention of the appropriate person ... documentary evidence that he is a constable' if he is not in uniform; and, whether or not he is in uniform, the following matters specified in s2(3), namely:

'(a) the constable's name and the name of the police station to which he is attached;
(b) the object of the proposed search;
(c) the constable's grounds for proposing to make it; ...'

R v Fenneley (1989) Crim LR 142 makes it clear that a search is unlawful unless the grounds required under s2(3)(c) are given.

Section 2(9) imposes limits on the extent of the search. It states:

'Neither the power conferred by section 1 ... nor any other power to detain and search a person without first arresting him or to detain and search a vehicle without making an arrest is to be construed –
(a) as authorising a constable to require a person to remove any of his clothing in public other than an outer coat, jacket or gloves; or
(b) as authorising a constable not in uniform to stop a vehicle.'

Entry, search and seizure

When a police officer has been allowed to enter a private house to make enquiries, but is then asked to leave, he must be given a reasonable time to do so. In *Robson* v *Hallett* [1967] 2 QB 939 a police sergeant was told to leave a private house where he was making enquiries. He at once turned and walked towards the front door but was then jumped upon. The sergeant had not become a trespasser the instant he was told to depart. When a licence is revoked as a result of which something has to be done by the licensee, a reasonable time must be implied in which he can do so, in this case to get off the premises. The amount of time that would be allowed would be a short time. But he has to be allowed time to leave the premises, and he was making every effort to do so in this case. Two constables assisted the sergeant. The constables had been in the front garden, and lawfully so, as they like any other members of the public had an implied licence to walk up to the front door. That implied licence had never been revoked. They were acting in the execution of their duty in assisting the sergeant and avoiding any further breach of the peace. *Davis* v *Lisle* [1936] 2 KB 434 makes it clear that if an officer persists in making enquiries and does not attempt to leave private premises when requested he becomes a trespasser.

Search warrants

Section 8 permits a constable to enter and search premises on the authority of a warrant if he suspects the commission of a serious arrestable offence and the presence on those premises of evidence relevant to that suspected offence. Section 8 provides:

'(1) If on an application made by a constable a justice of the peace is satisfied that there are reasonable grounds for believing –
(a) that a serious arrestable offence has been committed; and
(b) that there is material on premises specified in the application which is likely to be of substantial value (whether by itself or together with other material) to the investigation of the offence; and
(c) that the material is likely to be relevant evidence; and
(d) that it does not consist of or include items subject to legal privilege, excluded material or special procedure material; and
(e) that any of the conditions specified in subsection (3) below applies, he may issue a warrant authorising a constable to enter and search the premises.'

These conditions are (s8(3)):

'(a) that it is not practicable to communicate with any person entitled to grant entry to the premises;
(b) that it is practicable to communicate with a person entitled to grant entry to the premises but it is not practicable to communicate with any person entitled to grant access to the evidence;
(c) that entry to the premises will not be granted unless a warrant is produced;
(d) that the purpose of a search may be frustrated or seriously prejudiced unless a constable arriving at the premises can secure immediate entry to them.'

The specific references to items subject to legal privilege, excluded material and special procedure material in s8(1)(d) above mean that a magistrate cannot issue a warrant which authorises entry and search for any of the following classes of evidence:

1. Documents subject to legal professional privilege. This preserves a person's right not to incriminate himself by the disclosure of any information which is given in confidence by or to his legal advisers.
2. Excluded material includes personal records of any person's physical or mental health or personal welfare acquired or created in confidence and any journalistic material held in confidence.
3. Special procedure material includes journalistic material other than that comprised in the definition of excluded material, together with certain business records held in confidence or subject to an obligation by statute not to disclose them. This material and excluded material can be the lawful object of police search and seizure on the authority of a circuit judge under s9.

Safeguards in the use of warrants

A search warrant remains in force for only one month after it has been issued. If it is not executed within that time it lapses and it must be returned to the court office from which it was issued: s16(3) and (10). The warrant should be executed 'at a reasonable hour unless it appears to the constable executing it that the purpose of a search may be frustrated on an entry at a reasonable hour': s16(4). When a constable is on the premises to be searched he must produce the warrant to the occupier (if present), leave a copy of it with him and also produce documentary evidence that he is a constable: s16(5). In the absence of the occupier the constable can effectively exercise the same procedure with some other person who appears to be in charge of the premises: s16(6). The constable has a duty to leave a copy of the warrant in a prominent place on the premises if no one is present who appears to be in charge of those premises: s16(7).

The case of *R v Chief Constable of Lancashire, ex parte Parker* [1993] QB 577 states that the police must identify themselves, produce the warrant and give a copy to the occupier. *R v Longman* (1988) 72 Cr App R 121 provides that in some circumstances merely to say 'police' and that you have a warrant is sufficient if speed is of the essence. The other matters can be dealt with when it becomes possible to do so. In *Longman* police officers with a search warrant gained entry to a house by deception, as a result of difficulties they had encountered in the past. A woman police officer in plain clothes pretended to deliver flowers. When the door was opened to her, other officers in plain clothes immediately entered the house, with one shouting 'Police, got a warrant' which he held in his hand. The Court of Appeal held that this procedure complied with ss15 and 16 of PACE. The Court rejected the contention that before entering the premises a police officer must not only identify himself but also produce his warrant card and the search warrant and serve a copy of the search warrant on the householder. It is enough that these things are done after entry to the premises. To hold otherwise would mean that the whole object of a search could be defeated. In *R v South Western Magistrates' Court, ex parte Cofie* [1997] 1 WLR 885 it was provided that where a building is divided up, as in the case of flats, then any search warrant must specify the part of the building to which it applies. Authority for the constable to seize evidence, connected with the suspected offence for which the warrant is issued, is given by s8(2).

Power to search upon arrest

Section 18 provides that if a suspect is arrested for an arrestable offence a power is conferred on a constable to:

'... enter and search any premises occupied or controlled by that person if he has reasonable grounds for suspecting that there is on the premises evidence, other than items subject to legal privilege, that relates –
(a) to that offence; or
(b) to some other arrestable offence which is connected with or similar to that offence.
(2) A constable may seize and retain anything for which he may search under subsection (1) above.
(3) The power to search conferred by subsection (1) above is only a power to search to the extent that is reasonably required for the purpose of discovering such evidence.
(4) Subject to subsection (5) below, the powers conferred by this section may not be exercised unless an officer of the rank of inspector or above has authorised them in writing.
(5) A constable may conduct a search under subsection (1) above –
(a) before taking the person to a police station; and
(b) without obtaining an authorisation under subsection (4) above,
if the presence of that person at a place other than a police station is necessary for the effective investigation of the offence ...'

In the case of *Krohn v Director of Public Prosecutions* [1997] COD 345 a search authorised by an acting police inspector under s18(1) was in issue. Police officers had arrested Krohn's son on suspicion of handling stolen property and they wished to search the father's property. He refused entry and they returned with a s18(1) warrant. Krohn still refused entry and his actions led to his conviction for assaulting a police officer in the execution of his duty. The acting inspector failed to make any further record in writing regarding the grounds of the search and the nature of the evidence sought. The issue was whether this rendered the search unlawful. The court decided that it did not as this did not affect Krohn's position and that he had had an opportunity to inspect the written authority that the inspector had signed but had not done so. The provisions as to record keeping were regarded as being directory rather than mandatory. The appeal against the conviction for assaulting a police officer in the execution of his duty was not allowed. No evidence was found as a result of the search.

Section 32 provides for a further power of search upon arrest. Search is permitted away from a police station if there is a reasonable belief that a person presents a danger to himself or others. The search may also be to look for anything which he might use to escape from lawful custody or which might be evidence relating to an offence. The officer may seize and retain articles discovered during the search if the material is not privileged. Under s32(2) the search may also extend to premises in which the suspect was arrested, or in which he was present immediately before his arrest, in order to discover evidence relating to the offence for which the arrest was made, if the arresting constable has reasonable grounds for believing that such evidence exists.

Powers of seizure

Section 19 confers a general power of seizure on constables who are lawfully on any premises. Before anything is seized under s19 the 'reasonable grounds for believing' proviso should be satisfied, although no material subject to legal privilege should be seized. Remember the entry powers provided in relation to arrest under ss17 and 117. By providing a lawful entry these can in conjunction with s19 provide a means of seizing material. When a constable invokes the sl9 power and seizes articles, s22 provides that the articles may be retained so long as is necessary in all the circumstances.

Section 19 provides that:

> '(2) The constable may seize anything which is on the premises if he has reasonable grounds for believing –
> (a) that it is has been obtained in consequence of the commission of an offence; and
> (b) that it is necessary to seize it in order to prevent it being concealed, lost, damaged, altered or destroyed.'

The case of *R v Southwark Crown Court and HM Customs, ex parte Sorsky Defries* [1996] COD 117 states that where there is an entry by means of a warrant under PACE then the s19 power of seizure will cover not just the items mentioned in the warrant but also evidence of other offences.

Detention

Limits on detention without charge

Section 41 provides that a person can only be held at a police station, without charge, for a maximum of 24 hours. Where arrest took place away from a police station the time would run from the time of arrest. There is a system of designated police stations, regarded as suitable for custody – the period of permitted detention is only 6 hours if it is not a designated police station. Extensions to the period are possible, up to 96 hours in relation to designated police stations, though the person would have had to have been brought before magistrates after 36 hours. The first extension up to 36 hours is possible, in certain circumstances, under s42 where an officer at the rank of superintendent or above authorises it. The extensions up to 96 hours require the authorisation of magistrates from the 36-hour point. Section 36 provides for a system of custody officers who are responsible for managing the detention.

Sections 34 and 37 provide that the custody officer should order release if grounds for detention no longer apply. The grounds would be those under s37. The duties of a custody officer before charge, under s37, include that where a person is arrested for an offence without a warrant or under a warrant not endorsed for bail he must firstly see if the person should be charged. For this there would have to be sufficient evidence to charge that person with the offence for which he was arrested. Detention is permitted in order to allow that decision to be made. Section 37(2) states:

> 'If the custody officer determines that he does not have such evidence before him, the person arrested shall be released either on bail or without bail, unless the custody officer has reasonable grounds for believing that his detention without being charged is necessary to secure or preserve evidence relating to an offence for which he is under arrest or to obtain such evidence by questioning him.'

If the custody officer has reasonable grounds for so believing, he may authorise the person arrested to be kept in police detention: s37(3). The custody officer has to, as soon as is practicable, make a written record of the grounds for the detention: s37(4). This should be in the presence of the person arrested who shall at that time be informed by the custody officer of the grounds for his detention: s37(5). This would not apply if the person being detained 'is incapable of understanding what is said to him; or is violent or likely to become violent; or is in urgent need of medical attention': s37(6). If the custody officer 'determines that he has before him sufficient evidence to charge the person arrested with the offence for which he was arrested, the person arrested shall be charged; or released without charge, either on bail or without bail': s37(7).

Review of detention

Section 40 provides for review of detention at regular intervals. This will be by the custody officer after charge but by a review officer (an officer of the rank of inspector or above) before charge. In the case of *Roberts v Chief Constable of Cheshire Police* [1999] 2 All ER 326 Roberts was arrested on 30 July 1992 at 10.50 pm on suspicion of conspiracy to burgle. He was taken to Northwich police station where his detention was authorised at 11.25 pm. At about 1 am on 31 July 1992 he was transferred to Macclesfield police station where his continued detention was authorised by the custody officer there at 1.45 am. He was checked on every hour between 4 am and 8 am. At 7.45 am an inspector conducted a case review and authorised further detention to obtain evidence by questioning. During the afternoon the respondent was interviewed in the presence of his solicitor. Following a case review at 5.20 pm Roberts was interviewed in the presence of his solicitor, and was further detained with the intention of preserving evidence and to question other suspects. At 6.55 pm on the grounds of insufficient evidence the respondent was released. He was not subsequently charged with the offence. Roberts had been detained at 11.25 pm on 30 July 1992, therefore under s40 a review of his detention should have taken place by an officer of the rank of inspector or above at 5.25 am on 31 July 1992. Under s34 a person should not be kept in police detention except in accordance with the relevant provisions of the Act. Therefore, the respondent's detention had been unlawful after 5.25 am unless some event occurred to have made it lawful. The absence of a review before 5.25 am meant that Roberts was subject to false imprisonment. The Court of Appeal thought that detention became lawful again after the review that took place at 7.45 am. The trial judge had awarded £500 damages for false imprisonment between 5.25 am and 7.45 am and this stood when the appeal was dismissed.

In the case of *R v Chief Constable of Kent, ex parte Kent Police Federation and Harman* [2000] Crim LR 857 it was decided that reviews of police detention under s40(1) could not be conducted by video link. This was because Parliament had contemplated face-to-face confrontation between review officers and suspects. For the purpose of the continuing detention of a person whose detention was under review by a review officer, a written record of the grounds for his detention must be made by the review officer 'in the presence of the person whose detention is under review'. It was not possible to hold that a record was made by a review officer in the presence of a person whose detention was under review if they were not in the same place and in each other's company at the time. Further, as a matter of statutory construction, s37(1) of the 1984 Act pointed to the physical presence of the review officer being at the police station where the person whose detention was under review was detained. Parliament could not have contemplated the proposed procedure in this case, the use of a video link, since they had legislated for face-to-face confrontations between the review officer and the suspect. If important rights enacted to protect a suspect were to be modified it would be for Parliament to make the change. The Criminal Justice Act 2003 contains provisions that would, if in force, allow for such as review by telephone and video link.

Access to legal advice and additional provisions

There are rights to consult a solicitor under s58 and to have a person informed of their detention under s56. A superintendent or above can delay access to the solicitor for up to 36 hours in limited circumstances. In *R v Chief Constable of Northumbria* [2001] 1 WLR 1342 the Court of Appeal decided that s58 gave a person arrested and held in custody in a police station the right to consult a solicitor privately at any time subject to certain specified limitations. Code C provided that 'If a solicitor wishes to send a ... probationer representative to provide advice on his behalf, then that person shall be admitted to the police station ... unless an officer of the rank of inspector or above considers that such a visit will hinder the investigation of crime'. In *R v Chief Constable of Avon and Somerset, ex parte Robinson* [1989] 1 WLR 793 the Divisional Court decided that there was no reason why senior police officers should not advise their subordinates as to what action they should consider taking as to the presence of solicitors' clerks at interviews as long as the instructions were advisory and did not pre-empt the actual decision of the appropriate officer based on a particular investigation of a crime. The Deputy Chief Constable was not entitled to make a blanket direction such as was made here. Advice could be given and when giving advice the character of the representative could be taken into account. If, because of his character, a representative was likely to hinder an investigation, then advice could be given that indicated that state of affairs. The appropriate officer could then reach a decision as to whether the attendance of a representative was likely to interfere with a particular investigation. The advice could provide guidance as to what the decision should be, but the decision had still to be in relation to the individual case.

Search of the suspect is permitted under s56 and seizure of items found during the search is also permitted where, for example, it is evidence relating to the offence. Intimate searches are permitted in more restricted circumstances under s55. Section 56 provides for the taking of fingerprints. In relation to protections available for interview situations, with questioning being the characteristic ingredient of an interview, these protections will not be applicable if the police merely record what a suspect says. Such was the gist of the Court of Appeal decision in *R v Menard* [1995] 1 Cr App R 306.

Right to silence

The Criminal Justice and Public Order Act 1994, ss34–35, allows a court or jury to draw inferences from the failure of an accused to mention during questioning, or when charged, a matter that he then seeks to rely upon in his defence. This is where the failure to mention the matter is unreasonable and the drawing of an inference is reasonable. Section 34 deals with the questioning stage and s35 with the silence of the accused at trial. Sections 36–37 make similar provision in relation to the failure of the accused to explain such as objects, substances or marks on his person or elsewhere or his failure to account for his presence at a particular place.

In *Argent* v *R* [1997] 2 Cr App R 27 factors that were required for the use of s34, at the questioning stage, were identified:

1. there must be proceedings against a person for an offence;
2. the alleged failure to mention a fact must occur before a defendant is charged;
3. the alleged failure must occur during questioning under caution by a constable;
4. the constable's questioning must be directed towards trying to discover whether or by whom the alleged offence had been committed;
5. the alleged failure must be to mention any fact relied on in his defence in those proceedings; and
6. the fact which the accused failed to mention must be one which in the circumstances existing at the time he or she could reasonably have been expected to mention when so questioned.

The European Court of Human Rights in *Condron* v *United Kingdom* [2000] Crim LR 679 made the point that the inference should not be drawn where a person had acted upon the advice of their solicitor and the advice had been correctly given. The notion of the right to silence is that you should not have to self-incriminate. How can its removal be justified? Well it protects the guilty and what have the innocent to fear? Indeed, they should be willing to help the police and they have access to a lawyer if they want one. That is one view. However, a person may want to be silent if they do not understand what is going on, or they may be bewildered and may wish to consider their options. The situation is one of pressure and coercion where the suspect may feel trapped in a hostile environment and the interview situation is designed to put the suspect at a disadvantage. Thus, the change to the law on the right to silence and adverse inferences at trial might perhaps be justifiable if the present system was a more acceptable one in other respects. It might be better to operate on the premise that the system is quite simply not to be trusted.

3.2 Hopes and expectations with regard to the police

A starting point for an examination of the police is to note some hopes and expectations that might be held as regards the police. First, that they would keep order. Second, that their existence would deter and prevent criminal activity. Third, that where the law was broken that they would enforce it. Fourth, that they would provide a variety of services such as directing traffic, providing information and assisting with problems such as missing persons or property. Finally, that in the exercise of such functions the considerable powers that the police have, are not abused. Some points need to be made as regards these hopes and expectations. Whether or not a person would agree with them clearly depends upon their own standpoint.

Order maintenance

Whilst the keeping of order for some is a mutually beneficial (we all get some benefit), continuation of a largely harmonious society for others it is a part of a system of domination. Bowden (1978) describes the police as the operating arm of the ruling class. On this issue Bunyan (1976) is a particularly good source of evidence of the political role of the police. The literature on the 1984 miner' strike also provides some evidence for those who share Bowden's view: see for example Fine and Miller (eds) (1985), Welsh Campaign for Civil and Political Liberties and the NUM South Wales (1985) and the whole issue of the *Journal of Law and Society*, volume 12, number 3, Winter, 1985. That such activities should attract such attention surprises me somewhat. I would expect that a police force would be used to uphold the existing order. Complaints about such police action are somewhat misdirected – it is the system that they protect that is the appropriate target if criticism is to be raised.

Law enforcement

As to the expectation that the law should be enforced the reality is that only a small part of the law-breaking activity that occurs becomes the subject of court proceedings. Apart from the fact that full enforcement would be impossible, major reasons for the courts dealing with only a part of the legal infractions include the following. The police are heavily reliant on members of the public for information about criminal behaviour. Most particularly, they need to have crime reported to them. In the absence of such information being provided, the police may not ever become aware of some criminal behaviour. Where the police become aware of incidents the use of police and prosecution discretion as regards decisions to arrest, summons, charge and prosecute suspects also helps to determine who will be the defendants in court proceedings. These factors operate as an important selection and filtering system for the later stages of the criminal justice system.

The role of the public

On the issue of reporting practices, the importance of the public is made clear by McConville et al (1991), where in a study of three police forces areas 70 per cent of arrests were the result of information being provided by the public. Similarly, Mawby's (1979) data from Sheffield revealed that 82 per cent of crime was reported by the victim, whilst the police made the report in only 6 per cent of cases. Mitchell (1984) notes that in Sellin and Wolfgang's Philadelphia study in 1964 for serious crimes the victim was the reporter in 48 per cent of cases whilst friends and relatives reported an additional 14 per cent. Mitchell also notes Bottomley and Coleman's (1981) study in Northern England, which found that, for offences of personal violence, 90 per cent of the reporting was the work of the victim. Since the public has such a vital role to play in reporting crime, the factors that affects such reporting are important. There is by no means anything like full reportage of crime, Southgate and Ekblom's (1984) study in England and Wales noted that only 30 per cent of offences were reported. They found that the most common reason for such inaction were that the offence was considered to be trivial (43 per cent of cases) and that the victim was of the view that the police would not be able to do anything effective about the matter (23 per cent of cases). Other factors to note are that in some cases victims of crime may wish to avoid the involvement of the criminal justice system. For example, because the potential defendant is a friend or relative, or in the case of a crime such as rape there might be a desire to avoid further hurt and humiliation. These latter examples point to at least some evidence of a limited expectation that the law will be enforced.

Service functions

As well as reporting crime the public also make demands of the police for the provision of services of the type noted above. Indeed, most of the requests made by the public do not concern crime. Southgate and Ekblom (1984) recorded that roughly two-thirds of calls made on the police in their study were not concerned with crime. They also quoted the figures recorded in other studies: Ekblom and Heal (1982) (three out of ten were crime-related); Punch and Naylor (1973) (41 per cent of requests for police help were crime-related); Comrie and Kings (1975) (34 per cent of calls concerned crime); Hough (1980) (36 per cent of incidents involve crime); and Jones, S (1983) (who noted that 43 per cent of contacts made by the public were crime-related). The United States literature on the police contains similar findings and also provides some points to consider in relation to England and Wales. Cumming et al (1965) analysed calls to a police department and noted: that over half the calls were for some sort of help; that a car would be sent to about 75 per cent of these; and that the police would then try to solve the problem themselves or get someone who could. Hence, the title of the article 'The Policeman as Guide, Philosopher and Friend'. Reiss (1971) in his observational study of the police in three United States cities found that 87 per cent of police mobilisations were in response to requests by the public. He makes the point that many of these calls were from the elements of the community that are portrayed by others as downtrodden and overpoliced. Bittner's (1967) study of the policing of skid row also provides an account of the performance of welfare functions by the police. Interestingly it is also made clear in the article that such work is carried out as part of a strategy to keep control in the area by preventing further deterioration of the circumstances there which would otherwise have been likely to have led to trouble. In England and Wales the work of the police is also very much consumer led, commonly being described as being reactive rather than proactive. Mawby (1979) in his Sheffield study stated that the police were rather more concerned with acting as receptive vessels to public complaints and organising their area in terms of people who could give information, than they were actively engaged in proactive policing.

It is clear from such as Smith et al (1983) who carried out research in London, that the public want to be policed in order to combat such as street violence and burglary. The research was published in four volumes. Volume 1: A Survey of Londoners, Volume 2: A Group of Young Black People, Volume 3: A Survey of Police Officers and Volume 4: The Police in Action. The observation can be made at this stage that this desire for policing, linked with the portrayal of the police as responding to public demands and providing services, does not readily marry up with the idea of the police as the instruments of a dominant group within society. This is the type of point made by Reiss (1971) but which requires caveats such as those made by Bittner (1967). As well as being a means to keep order, the provision of services may amount to little more than showing the flag by merely answering a request for help. To measure the effectiveness of such police action would be very difficult. Remember that the making of a request is as least, in part, a function of the perceived expectation of a satisfactory outcome. Analysis of requests would be an analysis of a loaded sample. For some types of crime, victims may have already given up on the police as a source of assistance. Another implication of the police involvement in the provision of services is that it dilutes their potential for work in relation to the criminal law. This does not correspond with the wishes of the police who often see such activity as being not real police work – despite the fact that they do so much of it! Real police work is regarded as being matters concerned with the criminal law such as making arrests. This is seen in the study by Southgate and Ekblom (1984) in that when the police initiated contact with the public it was in crime-related areas – mainly in relation to motor cars.

The views of the police and the public

In research carried out by the Joint Consultative Committee of Police Staff Associations (1990) they found that police officers' views are at variance with those of the public on a number of important points. Respondents in both groups were asked to identify five offences, from a given list of 15, on which they thought the police should expend most time and energy. Rankings were close for residential burglary and identical for parking and general traffic offences, but otherwise there were marked variations. The Review gave more examples of differences of opinion. The public wanted to see more officers patrolling on foot, whereas the police thought the existing balance was right. In relation to the investigation of crimes, 68 per cent of officers felt the police should concentrate on those crimes which they had a better chance of solving. Thirty per cent of officers believed all crimes should be investigated equally, whatever the likely outcome. The responses from the members of the public were almost a mirror image. Seventy-three per cent said that all crime should be investigated equally, whereas 23 per cent thought the police should concentrate on offences which, they were more likely to solve. Policing is sometimes presented as being based upon, or that it should be based upon, the notion of policing by consent. This notion implies the existence of a consensual relationship between the police and the community it polices. It presupposes that there is, or can be, a mutuality of aims and obligations between the parties. There is widespread support for the concept of community policing, as formulated by Alderson (1979), which places an emphasis on proactive policing and consultation with the community. The above Joint Consultative Committee findings suggest that if the police are to receive the support of the community and to police by consent, they must obtain a representative range of views and act upon them. Or, alternatively, and more logically, the public need to be educated so that they will be able to accept that foot patrols, for example, are a very inefficient form of policing. Giving the public what they want and what they need are at present incompatible aims.

Abuse of power

As to the issue of abuse of power, this has been a major theme in the literature and is a popular subject for media attention. There is no doubt that there is abuse: the literature abounds with examples some of which are noted later. A result of such literature is that it can lead to a distorted view of the police emerging and some measure of corrective is required. First, quite simply, much police behaviour does not involve abuse. Second, society expects the police to deal with many of its unpleasant situations. Examples include dealing with violent and sometimes armed people, dealing with such as traffic accidents, suicide attempts, informing people of bereavements and more mundanely clearing drunks from public places. Such behaviour generally goes unnoticed in media reports. A further point to consider on the issue of abuse concerns what are called norms of due process. They consist of restrictions on police use of their powers. An example in relation to arrest being that a constable must have reasonable grounds for suspecting that a person has committed an offence before an arrest can be made. From the police point of view such restrictions mean that they are being asked to do a difficult job with their hands tied. Their response is an attitude that they have to break the rules to some extent if they are to get the job done. Abuse is thus built into the police view of their role. Our expectation as citizens is that the abuse would not take place. In relation to such abuse, systems of accountability have been provided and these are detailed later. The problem with these systems of accountability is that it is very difficult for them to have an impact. It is no good making rules and developing systems of accountability if they cannot actually penetrate into and affect the practice of policing. Much policing is low visibility, attitudes towards rule-breaking within the police are facilitative and supervision by senior officers is very limited. Changes in police attitudes are the key to changes in police behaviour.

Three sets of illustrative information on police abuse will be presented. Material from Rose (1996) on the Guildford Four and other matters, the lessons of the Carl Bridgewater case and an account of factors that cause miscarriages of justice.

The Guildford Four

Gerard Conlon, Paul Hill, Patrick Armstrong and Carole Richardson, the Guildford Four, were convicted for planting a bomb in a Guildford pub in 1974. The bomb killed five people. They were released in 1989 when it was concluded that the convictions were unsafe. One of the revelations of the investigations into the case revealed that there were draft typewritten notes of an interview with Armstrong and that these notes were covered with corrections. At the trial the police relied on their original handwritten notes taken during the interviews. No problem with this you may think. There was a problem, however, and it was that the handwritten notes were the same as the typewritten notes. The typewritten notes had a series of corrections and alterations on them. This meant that the typewritten notes must have been produced first, that the hand-written notes were copies of them and that the police had lied. The book contains other similar examples and it allows Rose to make very strongly the point that there is a real problem of innocent people being convicted. In similar vein he presents material that suggests that there are categories of criminal that are able to escape conviction because of problems with the system. Examples are noted in the areas of organised crime and serial rapists.

The Carl Bridgewater case

In February 1997 three of the defendants (Michael Hickey, Vincent Hickey and James Robinson) in the Carl Bridgewater case were released. They had been in prison since 1979.

The fourth defendant (Patrick Molloy) died in prison during his sentence. They were convicted for the killing of Carl Bridgewater who was a 13-year-old newspaper-delivery boy. It is thought that Carl was killed when he disturbed a burglary at Yew Tree Farm near Stourbridge, Staffordshire. The convictions for murder of Vincent Hickey and James Robinson produced a sentence of life with a recommendation that they serve a minimum of 25 years. Michael Hickey was detained at Her Majesty's Pleasure as he was under 18 years of age. Patrick Malloy received 12 years for manslaughter. The three were released because of what appears to have been a miscarriage of justice. This is far from being a novel event as can be seen from other cases such as the Birmingham Six, Tottenham Three and the Maguire Seven.

The Carl Bridgewater case was investigated by the discredited West Midlands Crime Squad, which was wound up in 1989 having been involved in 23 cases of fabricated evidence in the 1980s. A major factor in the police case was the confession of Patrick Molloy, in which he said that he had been upstairs at the cottage at the time of the offence: he named the other three as having been downstairs when, and where, the shooting took place. He later asserted that the confession was not freely given, in that he was abused in various ways. A further problem suggested by Patrick Molloy was that the confession had been given after he had been shown a confession that had been made by Vincent Hickey. The court has ordered the release of the prisoners because it seems that Patrick Molloy was shown a fabrication of a confession by Vincent Hickey, which tricked him into confessing and implicating the others. When the issues were raised later the police denied that a confession had been fabricated. Whilst numerous investigations were carried out, in the years after the convictions, it is only now that the evidence is such that a court would order the release of the prisoners. Esda tests (electrostatic document analysis) were carried out on the confession document in 1990. The sort of things that were being looked for were items that had been added after the original document was written. The fact that there were impressions of other confessions was not thought to be significant – indeed that is what you would expect to find on a pad used for statements made by defendants. It was during the preparation for what was to be a new appeal that Jim Nicholl, the solicitor who was acting on behalf of the prisoners, spotted that the tests had in fact uncovered what at first sight was a Vincent Hickey confession. This was not a very plausible document given that Vincent Hickey and Patrick Malloy were interviewed in different police stations and would not have used the same pad for confessions. Once alerted to this, further tests suggested that one policeman had written a Vincent Hickey confession whilst a second had signed it. All four defendants at the trial had criminal records and Michael Hickey and James Robinson received 12-year concurrent sentences for armed robbery. However, they should not have been imprisoned for a killing unless they had been convicted by an acceptable investigation and trial process. It is this that the Bridgewater Four do not appear to have received.

A large part of the problem is the culture of the police. Having a stake in the result of cases, with a conviction being the benchmark of success, leads to an ends justifying the means type of approach. What is needed, especially in the most serious cases, is an ethos that the most important thing is that the court is provided with the best opportunity to discover the truth in relation to an offence and offenders. That falsifying evidence and obtaining evidence by inappropriate means is not acceptable. All levels of the police must be made to understand this. Changes in police recruitment, training and supervision seem to be called for. The threat of severe penalties, and a likelihood of their imposition, should become the norm as a deterrent for potential offenders. This should hit all levels of the command structure, with senior officers taking responsibility when things go wrong. The quality of supervision would probably improve in such circumstances. Perhaps a more inquisitorial system would also be desirable. At present there is a risk that matters are not discovered by the defence and the court. The Criminal Cases Review Commission, which started work in 1996, investigates potential miscarriages of justice. It may have some value but really it misses the point as the important thing is to stop problems happening in the first place. As far as discovering police malpractice and delivering penalties to offenders the prospects are gloomy without major reform and new attitudes. In the Carl Bridgewater case there had been a six-week appeal in 1989 and six separate police enquiries. There is a major problem of the lack of an effective system of police accountability. It is clear that the police investigate themselves to too great an extent. Finally, the question should be asked why is so much importance attached to confessions? This is especially so given the amount of pressure that can be used to obtain them. Is there no merit in the idea that if they wish to confess they can do so in court or indeed plead guilty if that is their desire? In court they can hope to have access to a higher regard for notions of due process.

Factors in miscarriages of justice

Walker (2002) identified the main factors in miscarriages of justice. The most obvious danger is thought to be the falsification of evidence by either a co-accused or the police. Identification evidence is also unreliable especially where the sighting was momentary and in a situation of stress. Over-reliance on the value of expert testimony and unreliable confessions are also problematic. The latter may be caused in various ways, such as police pressure or physiological or mental instability. The disclosure rules may mean that the defence is unable to access information. The Criminal Justice Act 2003 makes the situation worse. Whilst there are greater duties of disclosure for both the defence and the prosecution, the duties are much more onerous for the defence. The inequality of arms of the parties means that there may not be effective investigation of the issues on behalf of the defence. At the trial the judge may be unfair to the defendant in terms of summing up and in the rulings and directions that are made. Defence lawyers may also fail their clients. The position of the defendant can be prejudiced by media comments and by the setting for the case in terms of its presentation as a terrorist case or with high levels of security. Prejudice can also arise through media commentaries. Finally, appeal processes have proven to be difficult to access and funding is precarious.

3.3 Remedies and complaints

The possibilities for remedies and complaints' procedures are noted below and some matters are considered in detail. The Criminal Cases Review Commission, the human rights dimension and admissibility of evidence are covered in Chapter 5.

1. Self-help, in the sense of breaking out of false imprisonment as in the case of *Kenlin* v

Gardiner [1967] 2QB 510. Here two schoolboys resisted unlawful detention. One boy made as if to run away. The police officer took hold of his arm. The boy struggled violently, punching and kicking the officer. The other boy got involved and struck the other officer. Neither had been lawfully detained and so they could use force in order to free themselves.

2. Habeas corpus which is a system whereby the legality of detention can be challenged.

3. Complaints to the police. Povey and Cotton (2003) provide an account of the police complaints and discipline system in the 12 months to March 2002. There were 12 per cent fewer complaints than in the previous year which had also seen a 10 per cent year-on-year decrease. Of the 16,654 complainants, 898 were substantiated – five fewer than in the previous year. About a quarter of these were for oppressive behaviour and more than half involved a failure in duty. Disciplinary/misconduct charges against 1,353 officers were proven and this led to 97 officers being dismissed or required to resign. Of complaints investigated 12 per cent were substantiated. More than a third (35 per cent) of the complaints were informally resolved and a further 36 per cent were withdrawn or dispensed with. The informal resolution system is designed to provide a quick and simple system and the complainant has to agree to this. It is appropriate where an explanation of the behaviour or an apology will suffice. The figure for police officers convicted of criminal offences in this period was 188 and of these 52 were for non-traffic offences.

A new system of complaints to the police is to operate from April 2004. The Independent Police Complaints Commission will take over responsibility from the Police Complaints Authority. With the old system cases could be dealt with informally by an explanation being provided or an apology being offered. If this was inappropriate an investigating police officer would be appointed. The Authority had a role in the approval of the appointment. It could also undertake supervision of the complaint but this only happened in the most serious cases and only amounted to examining the paperwork in relation to the case. The Independent Police Complaints Commission will have the powers to investigate complaints separately from the police service. This would happen with managed investigations where they will be able to choose to direct a police team that is investigating alleged police misconduct. This is a major change to procedures for dealing with complaints but is likely to be only used for serious cases. With supervised investigations they will be able to oversee a police investigation, checking certain decisions that the police take throughout the course of the investigation. This is also an improvement on the existing system. The two existing systems whereby the matter is resolved locally or the paperwork is examined will also be utilised. Complainants will have rights of appeal to the Commission where the police have not recorded a complaint about misconduct or there is concern about the handling or outcome of a complaint that has been investigated locally. The Commission will be able to present a case against a police officer in a disciplinary hearing. The Commission is not part of any government department and is independent of the police service. Its decisions cannot be overruled apart from by a court of law. The 18 Commissioners must not have worked for the police. The Commission will have its own investigation teams that will enable it to choose to investigate incidents of alleged police misconduct even when no complaint has been made. The investigators will be mostly civilians. The Commission will be looking for investigative experience and expertise for these appointments. The Police Reform Act 2002 provides for the new system. The background to the new provisions was a consultation paper in May 2000: *Complaints against the Police: A Consultation Document*, London: Home Office. As regards the removal, suspension and disciplining of police officers, the Act broadens the circumstances in which senior officers can be removed in the interests of the efficiency or effectiveness of the force. It also provides for the issue of regulations regarding the procedure for removing senior officers and makes provision for the suspension of senior officers.

4. Admissibility of evidence. Section 78 PACE provides that in any proceedings the court may refuse to allow evidence on which the prosecution proposes to rely 'if it appears to the court that, having regard to all the circumstances, including the circumstances in which the evidence was obtained, the admission of the evidence would have such an adverse effect on the fairness of the proceedings that the court ought not to admit it.' This provision is clearly applicable to search and seizure situations as well as to other police practices, such as the interrogation of suspects.

5. The Criminal Cases Review Commission.

6. A tortious action for damages. If the police exceed their legal powers they may be open to a civil action in tort for trespass to the person for assault, battery or false imprisonment. In *Collins* v *Wilcock* [1984] 1 WLR 1172 it was stated that an assault is an act which causes another person to apprehend the infliction of immediate, unlawful, force on his person; a battery is the infliction of unlawful force on another person; and false imprisonment is the unlawful imposition of constraint on another's freedom of movement from a particular place. In contrast with the very important general principles expounded by the House of Lords in *O'Reilly* v *Mackman* [1983] AC 237, the case of *R* v *Chief Constable of Warwickshire* [1997] 1 WLR 564 needs to be noted. It was stated in the latter case that complaints about the use of a warrant, where for example it was used to enter property, should take the avenue of an action for trespass rather than an action for judicial review. In *Thompson* v *Metropolitan Police Commissioner* [1997] 2 All ER 762 Court of Appeal guidelines were provided as to the level of exemplary damages that were awardable by juries in relation to civil actions against the police. Fifty thousand pounds was the maximum for the worst cases involving officers of at least the rank of inspector. The guidance was given as juries had been prepared to award much more – over £300,000 in one case of police brutality.

7. The use of the European Convention on Human Rights in the light of the Human Rights Act 1998.

3.4 Factors influencing the practice of policing

The reality of policing is a result of the complex interaction of hopes and expectations about policing held by various groups and institutions and the response to these and the attitudes held at various levels of the police organisation. Emphasis will be placed on the impact of the attitudes within the close-knit working group to which policemen often belong. These attitudes seem to influence the usage of the autonomy, discretion and power of individual police officers. Attention will also be directed to the different types of work that the police engage in such as community policing, arrests, stops and interrogations. These matters will be rounded off with a brief account of the issue of assessing police behaviour.

The chief constable

Whilst police forces are subject to the control, influence and direction which results from the actions of institutions – such as the government, the legislature, the courts and police authorities – in constitutional theory it is the chief constable who is responsible for the direction of the force. In *R* v *Chief Constable of Sussex, ex parte International Trader's Ferry Ltd* [1997] 2 All ER 65 the Court of Appeal restated the principle that decisions as to the disposition of the resources of a police force rest with the chief constable. The case involved animal rights protesters who were interfering with the activities of livestock exporters. Decisions were taken by the Chief Constable of Sussex, which were based on the inability of the police to provide resources to ensure that the trade could continue. Thus, it is clearly very difficult to challenge this form of police discretion. An example of the impact of the power and autonomy of individual chief constables is provided by James Anderton who was the Chief Constable of Manchester. Kettle (1979) noted that as a result of his policy initiatives the 1977 figures for traffic offences being reported were 35 per cent less than the 1976 figures and the arrest figures for offences under the Obscene Publications Acts showed a five-fold increase in the same period. Despite such directions and initiatives much of a policeman's time has not in any real sense been structured as a result of direction from the upper ranks. This is in part, as Smith et al revealed, a result of the fact that the senior officers themselves find it difficult to state their policy, objectives and priorities except in the most general terms. It was also noted in the survey that 'there is little direct supervision of the junior ranks by senior officers or constables by sergeants and inspectors' (1983, Volume 4:343). This did not leave a haphazard vacuum but rather a situation in which the practice of policing was the outcome of 'preoccupations, perceptions and prejudices that develop amongst groups of constables and sergeants in response to the people and problems they have to deal with' (1983, Volume 4: 49).

Pressures on the police organisation

Before such attitudes are explored some material on the pressures upon police organisations will be presented. This is drawn mainly from the work of Chambliss and Seidman (1971), who are writers in the United States. The police as an organisation are presented as attempting to maximise their resources and minimising strains on their organisation. They depend upon the politically and economically powerful sectors of the community for their resources. As a result, they act so as to fulfill the expectations of such groups. This has several results. First, the police have found that policing the unlawful behaviour of such respectable citizens produces negative evaluations of such police work by the citizens concerned. The police will tend to minimise such activity. Second, where the police have to take action against such citizens they will handle them very carefully. This is because such people are in a position to complain effectively about police malpractices, which could cause organisational strain. Third, given an expectation that the police will achieve a high level of law enforcement, but not in respect of the powerful, and taking account of their limited resources, the police have to adopt strategies to maximise their efficiency. They concentrate their activities in high crime areas (to some extent a self-fulfilling prophecy) and upon the most visible offences. This means the areas in which the poor are to be found. In the policing of this group of citizens efficiency can be increased by ignoring the norms of due process. This is possible because such people are not influential within the community and if they are unable to complain effectively, then the police can cut corners without fear of comeback.

O'Reilly and Stevens (2002) examined other forms of pressure on the police, arising from the large volume of crime that they are called upon to contend with and the bureaucratic demands within which they must operate:

'Jason Hansford-Adams, 30, a businessman from Warlingham, Surrey, tried to alert police that a number of youths were using rocks to smash up a parked car outside his house. He was told that Surrey police had a new policy of no longer responding to such incidents. "I couldn't believe it," he said. "Just how serious does it have to be for officers to turn out?" Police chiefs argue that with limited resources, having officers patrolling the streets on foot is not a practical way of reducing crime. But there is a growing feeling that officers are not close at hand even in police stations. In the past two years 12 police stations in England and Wales have closed every month. Since Labour came to power in 1997, one in five stations has closed. Only 272 stations are open 24 hours a day – just 15 per cent of the total number. Victims of night-time crime must contact remote call centres. Even some 999 calls do not always find a helpful voice. Research by Her Majesty's Inspectorate of Constabulary (HMIC) found that in some areas 40 per cent of all calls were being put through to recorded messages. Those officers who do fight crime get sidetracked into vast amounts of paperwork. A government study found that on average officers spend just 17 per cent of their time on patrol. More than two-fifths of their time was spent inside police stations and 40 per cent of this time was taken up with paperwork. "As a sergeant it dawned on me that I was operating like a clerk, like someone sitting behind the counter in a post office, filling in forms and documents that were more to do with compiling statistics for the Home Office than enforcing the law," said Glen Smythe, chairman of the Metropolitan Police Federation.' (2002:12)

Cop culture

The lower ranks in the police receive only limited direct supervision of their actions and the system of supervision involves a lot of turning a blind eye to their activities. As Holdaway (1983) observes, at best it can control the worst excesses. Holdaway's study was of urban policing in a deprived inner city area in the mid-1970s. He was a police sergeant at the time and engaged in covert participant observation. Holdaway's account looked at policing as it was over 20 years ago, the work of Rose (1996) suggests that there has been some change for the better. A police officer's work also lacks direction in that it is largely unstructured from above. Without such direction and supervision their exercise of discretionary powers in low-visibility situations leaves much to trust. The actual practice of policing is considerably shaped by the occupational cultural of the lower ranks, variations of which develop in different working situations. Goals are developed in this setting and they reflect commonly found male peer group norms. These are characterised by macho attitudes of glorying in violence and acting hard, and sexually orientated banter involving the degradation of women, and derogatory attitudes towards homosexual behaviour and blacks and other ethnic groups. The fostering of these attitudes is assisted by the fact that the lower ranks are close knit and relatively socially isolated groups who will not only work together but will also tend to socialise together – presenting sensationalised and exaggerated versions of their working day at the end of their shift. The solidarity and group loyalty is seen in the swift and mob-handed response to a call for assistance from an officer in trouble. Equally, the solidarity is seen in the collusion involved in covering up for each other in cases of malpractice. Tolerance of such malpractice is however limited and individuals may decide not to work with such policemen again. That the system will often accommodate such decisions just further highlights the limited amount of control that is exercised by the upper ranks. Even if an officer is put with someone that they do not trust, they can do their level best to ensure that they avoid situations in which action has to be taken. In terms of group norms, much value is placed upon the ability to keep control of situations, to maintain order, to engender respect and not to lose face. Bowling and Foster (2002:1012–1013) give a good account of various aspects of police culture and the problems which they can lead to. The features that are identified are a sense of mission, action orientated, cynicism and pessimism, suspicion, isolation and solidarity, conservatism, machismo, racial prejudice and pragmatism. Studies from the United States have also stressed the importance of such factors: see for example Bittner (1967), Black (1971), Skolnick (1966), Westley (1970), Reiss (1971) and Wilson (1968). As will be seen later these outcomes can be attempted in a variety of ways. Commonly an impassive slow-to-respond stance will be adopted, the citizen will be looked in the eye and any slight will not be avoided, though equally there will not be an over-reaction. Threats and aggressive behaviour, including violence as a means of control, is one possible response but officers with better people skills will find other ways.

Real police work
A further feature of the group culture are notions of real police work, which they identify as being matters concerning the criminal law. For the uniformed branch this would be, for example, an arrest in which some skill had been shown, particularly if it involved a successful villain, whereas dealing with domestic disputes would be regarded as rubbish. The clearing of drunks from city centre streets is demoralising in terms of their idealised image of the job, though at least it offers some action. The police crave excitement, being action hungry, a consequence of the reality of police work actually often involving mundane and boring situations. Action on the streets is not a policeman's daily lot. Instead, much time can be spent in the police station dealing with paperwork, or appearing as a witness in court. Most of their time does not involve action or 'real' work and in their eyes this is wasted time. For some patrols nothing at all will happen, there may not even be any contact with other people. As Smith et al noted 'much patrolling by police officers on foot and in vehicles is apparently aimless. The officers are waiting for something to happen, which mostly means hoping that they will have a call to respond to.' (1983, Volume 4:345). Clearly this is not the whole story – for example, the best officers will manage to spot things of

significance. However, it is also clear that in this action-hungry state there can be an over-response when something does occur. This is best illustrated in terms of the police obsession with cars. Cars offer warmth and a means to get to action but they are also clearly regarded as intrinsically interesting. Smith et al (1983) relate an incident in which 13 police vehicles ended up at the end of a chase of a Ford Fiesta. Examples of unnecessary high-speed driving are also provided, and also recorded was the practice of one police driver who chased any other police car that was being driven quickly or which had its flashing light and siren on. Similar behaviour was reported by Holdaway (1983). He recalls patrolling with a colleague at about 3.00 am when they saw the area car, driven by a member of the same shift. The sergeant positioned his car behind and then in front of the other vehicle, encouraging a chase. The following 20 minutes were spent racing round the street, the car at the head of the chase signalling left to turn right, driving on the wrong side of the road and so on. The area car is a large powerful vehicle intended for rapid response situations. Another response to the tedium is to engage in what is called easing behaviour, which has been reported by numerous observers: see for example Cain (1973). It involves seeking out and frequenting suitable places for a rest and refreshment. This is of course covert behaviour and its practice further strengthens solidarity within groups. Hospitals and public houses are common venues and they provide this facility on a reciprocal basis, expecting swift assistance when it is called for.

Complexity and variety

Reiner (1997:1016–1018) presented material that is of use in stressing the complexity and variety of policing. In relation to police culture, he emphasised the differences that can exist within any one force and it is also clearly possible to see differences between forces. Differences within a particular force are likely in terms of differences in rank, function, age, ethnic origin, educational and social background, street or management cop, uniformed or detective. In fact, even within a group of constables who are all engaged in patrol functions it is possible to find sub-divisions of police culture. Reiner notes four types of variant: peace-keepers, law-enforcers, alienated cynics and managerially inclined professionals. Peace-keepers are as keen on the service role of the police as on their control functions, but they neglect neither of them. As you might expect with law-enforcers their motivation is the control of crime and criminals. Tasks like dealing with domestic disputes are not seen as real police work. Alienated cynics are timeservers who have become frustrated with failure in the job and are looking forward to their pension. They attempt to avoid work and are referred to as uniform-carriers or coat-hangers, wearing the uniform but not pursuing its purposes. Managerial professionals are those who want to get on, rank-and-file officers ambitious for promotion. As Reiner tells us: 'In a form of anticipatory socialisation they already exhibit attitudes associated with management rather than street cops. They see the virtue of all arrangements and policies ordained from on high and refrain from the general canteen chatter at the expense of the "bosses". If frustrated in his ambitions this type of constable is prime material for the uniform-carrying coterie' (1997:1020).

Kilburn: London in the 1990s

Rose (1996) is a journalist who, whilst researching his book, was allowed six months unrestricted access to a London police division – Kilburn. This provided very good material, suggesting a need to reconsider some of the previous analysis of British policing.

His Chapter 6 is devoted to the culture of the police. In previous accounts this has been portrayed as being macho, sexist and racist. It also contained an 'us against them' attitude in which colleagues would collude in, or at least turn a blind eye to, malpractice. This culture was seen as being problematic as it affected the type of policing that the public received and it was also perceived as being a barrier to changing police practices. Rose found evidence from his observations in Kilburn that this culture was changing and breaking down. For example, he found that there were openly gay and lesbian officers. Rose makes the very good point that even where police officers hold intolerant views it does not necessarily mean that they act upon them. Finally, mention needs to be made of what Rose has to tell us about police accountability. It is not a happy tale and problems are discovered at numerous stages of the investigation processes. The individual cases that are discussed also leave much cause for concern. The West Midlands Serious Crime Squad which had been involved in numerous discredited investigations of cases, including murder, did not have a single officer prosecuted. Indeed, Rose notes that 'Not one police officer accused of malpractice arising from the many miscarriages of justice put right by the Court of Appeal since 1989 has been convicted of a criminal offence' (1996:296).

London in the new millennium

Fitzgerald and Hough (2002) undertook a major study of policing in London. They gathered data primarily by means of interviews so as to obtain a representative sample of the London population over the age of 15. Additional interviews were carried out amongst ethnic minorities, and further interviews were used in relation to the police. Secondary data and focus groups were also utilised. The study was undertaken in 2000 2001. It is the first major independent study of policing in London since that mounted by the Policy Studies Institute 20 years ago. It found that Londoners did not simply want more patrol officers on the beat, but called for a style of policing that was more responsive to local problems and local needs. Though Londoners were no more fearful of crime than 20 years ago, there were rising concerns about disorderly teenagers, litter, graffiti and drug dealing.

Over a third of the public had sought police help in the previous 12 months, and a quarter were approached by the police as suspects. Though two-thirds of those who sought police help were satisfied with the response, levels of satisfaction were lower than in 1981. The majority of those who were stopped as suspects were satisfied with the way they were treated; but dissatisfaction was greatest amongst the young, amongst black suspects and those who lived in poor areas. Confidence in police effectiveness in London fell between 1982 and 2000 – and markedly between the mid-1990s and 2000 – but not as steeply as in other police forces. The falls in public satisfaction and confidence can be attributed, at least in part, to reductions in the capacity of uniformed officers to respond to everyday demands on the police and falls in staff morale. Rising public expectations may also be a factor. The failure of the service to be more responsive to local needs and the fall in staff morale can both be traced in part to performance-management regimes that emphasise quantified performance targets, and as a result ignore the complexities of police work. The researchers concluded that the Metropolitan Police needs to achieve a better balance between 'crime fighting' objectives and the equally important ones of 'peace-keeping' and 'order maintenance' if it is to retain the consent of Londoners. The force also needs to be able to develop ways of managing performance that place greater emphasis on achieving professional standards and less emphasis on hitting numerical targets. The current emphasis on quantitative measures is distorting performance and reducing the quality of service. The legacy of discrimination and over-policing continues to overshadow relations between the police and black people and there is a danger of similar tensions arising with other groups; but improving police relations with minority groups cannot be achieved in isolation.

3.5 Discretion, discrimination and stereotypes

The influences upon the police use of discretion has been a major theme in the literature and it is clear that there is some discrimination and some questionable use of stereotypes. Smith et al (1983) found a lot of evidence of racial prejudice amongst police officers, only rare overt prejudice in their work and only some bad behaviour because of it. The police use of stereotypes involves holding ideas of the type of person who is to make up their clientele. This will be most particularly the inadequate, the accident prone, the disorganised, the uncontrolled and those with such associates. Given the vast reservoir of crime within society, basing the policing of almost any group on a stereotype view of who is criminal is very much a self-fulfilling prophecy. A study in the United States by Chambliss and Nagasawa (1969) reveals the problems involved in the use of such tactics. They compared the incidence of arrests in certain racial groups and compared them with the incidence of self-reported delinquency for the group. Table 12 presents their findings.

Table 12

| Race | Incidence by Race of Arrest and Self-Reported Delinquency | |
	Percentage of each group arrested during 1963	Percentage of each group classified as having high delinquent involvement on the basis of self-reported delinquency
White	11%	53%
Black	36%	52%
Japanese	2%	36%

(Source: Policing and People in London)

What the police were doing was operationalising their view of the Japanese as law-abiding, and thus not requiring police attention, and the blacks as law-breakers and requiring police attention. Use of stereotypes led to disproportionate amounts of blacks being arrested and the Japanese not being arrested.

Factors in arrest decisions

Black (1971) provides an account of the impact of a number of factors upon police arrest decisions. The data was gathered in three American cities in 1966 and the conclusions presented below are based on an analysis of 5,713 incidents. Much of what Black reported still holds true and it is still a very valuable source. He presents a profile of police behaviour in routine situations where arrest is a possibility. First, the point is made that most arrest situations arise through citizen rather than police initiative. The public operate a filtering system before the state assumes its enforcement role. A major portion of the responsibility for criminal-law enforcement is kept out of police hands. Arrest practices sharply reflect complainant preferences, particularly when the desire is for leniency. The idea of the police responding to broad social forces could be questioned by the finding that the greater part of the police workload is case-by-case, isolated contacts between individual policemen and individual complainants. These individual encounters can become patterns of police behaviour. Black also stresses that the police are lenient in their routine arrest practices – they have opportunities to arrest many more people than they do. As a factor in arrest decisions evidence is not surprisingly important. The stronger the evidence the more likely is an arrest. Even where the evidence is very strong it is often the case that there will be no arrest. Arrest has to be rationed and saved for the most important cases, the seriousness of the offence affects the use of arrest. The degree of intimacy between the complainant and a suspect, that is the extent to which they normally interact, will also affect arrest decisions. Where it is a domestic dispute arrest is less likely than in other forms of assault. Disrespect to the police is also clearly a factor in arrest probability. This phenomena extends to disrespectful complainants who may have their preferences as a factor in the arrest decision downgraded as a result of the disrespect. Black suggests that the higher arrest rates for blacks can be explained to a large extent by the higher levels of disrespect shown to the police by black suspects.

Attitude and demeanour

Piliavin and Briar (1964), another early American study, is instructive in a number of ways. For example, it reinforces the point about demeanour that Black made. It also demonstrates the power that the police have in the criminal justice process and how certain groups can become over policed. Finally, it provides an account supportive of the labelling perspective. The study was of police encounters with juveniles. The police officers had very considerable discretion and they very largely decided which juveniles came to the attention of the courts and were labelled as delinquents. The police officers were strongly guided by the demeanour of the juveniles. Over one-third of negroes showed an unco-operative demeanour towards the police, whilst this was the case for only one-sixth of the white juveniles that were encountered by the police. This led to negroes being treated more severely than other juveniles for comparable offences. The observations made in this study serve to underscore the fact that the official delinquent, as distinguished from the juvenile who simply commits a delinquent act, is the product of a social judgement, in this case a judgment made by the police. He is a delinquent because someone in authority has defined him as one, often on the basis of the public face he has presented to officials rather than of the kind of offence he has committed.

Studies of discretion in England and Wales

The first material to consider is a field manual produced by Powis (1977) who was a Deputy Assistant Commissioner in the Metropolitan Police. The text was an attempt to provide guidance as to how to identify criminals. The material is far from reassuring, the more so since the text is not only still on sale but has attracted favourable reviews on the internet. The following indices of suspiciousness are suggested:

1. Young people generally, but especially if in cars (and even more so if in groups in cars).
2. People in badly maintained cars, especially if they have a tatty, dog-eared licence; people of untidy, dirty appearance – especially with dirty shoes (even manual workers, if honest, he says, are clean and tidy).
3. People who are unduly nervous, confident or servile in police presence (unless they are doctors, who are naturally confident).
4. People whose appearance is anomalous in some way – eg their clothes are not as smart as their car.
5. People in unusual family circumstances.
6. Political radicals and intellectuals, especially if they 'spout extremist babble', and are in possession of a 'your rights' card (as supplied by the NCCL). These people are also particularly likely to make unjust accusations against the police.
7. Normal, unsuspicious people are those outside the above categories, especially if they are of smart conventional appearance (which commands natural authority and respect) and even more so if they smoke a pipe.

On the other hand, as Southgate and Ekblom (1984) report, when the number of vehicle offences which respondents admitted to British Crime Survey interviewers was compared with the number of times they had been stopped, the indication was that the police did seem to be stopping those individuals who offend most on the road.

The police as gatekeepers to the criminal justice system

Phillips and Brown (1998) carried out research on factors influencing entry into the criminal justice system. The study developed out of a desire to provide information as to the 1.75 million people who are arrested by the police every year in terms of their characteristics, the eventual outcome of the arrest up to conviction and the influences upon the outcomes. It proceeded by examining a sample of over 4,000 cases. A third are arrested for relatively minor offences usually concerned with public disorder. Most are arrested for intermediate offences, with burglary, motor crimes and shop-lifting being important examples. Most arrests are not the result of proactive policing but rather calls upon the police by the public. In the majority of cases the evidence relied upon by the police is eyewitness evidence. As many as 6 per cent of arrests are for domestic violence. The arrest population is not typical of the population as a whole. It is largely male, 13 per cent black and 6 per cent Asian, with 75 per cent aged under 30 and over 60 per cent have previous convictions. It should be noted that blacks make up 1 per cent of the population and Asians 3 per cent. Arrests are not always in relation to an offence that has just taken place, they can for example be a means to protect vulnerable people. As to the main outcomes, conviction was the outcome for 40 per cent of the sample of those arrested and in all 51 per cent were charged. Many of those convicted had pleaded guilty and only 2 per cent of cases involved a trial. A further 17 per cent were cautioned by the police, 20 per cent involved no further action, 12 per cent were other police disposals, whilst 7 per cent of cases were terminated by the Crown Prosecution Service. The Crown Prosecution Service played an important role in terms of charge reduction, particularly in relation to certain offence types. For example, over a third of cases of violence and nearly a quarter of the fraud cases were so affected. The reasons offered for this were most commonly to reflect the available evidence, to get a guilty plea and to end up dealing with an offence that was simpler in terms of criminal intent.

More recent similar data was provided by Ayres, Hayward and Perry (2002). They note that 1,272,000 persons were arrested for notifiable offences in 2001–2002, a 1 per cent increase over 2000–2001. Recorded crime was estimated to have increased by 2 per cent over the same period (after changes in police recording practices are taken into account). A 2 per cent increase in arrests for violent crime compares with an estimated decrease of 1 per cent in the number of recorded violent crimes. The police stopped and searched 740,700 persons and/or vehicles, 4 per cent more than in 2000–2001. Only 13 per cent of searches led to an arrest, the same as in 2000–2001 and continuing at the (not very impressive) highest rate since 1993. Only 95 road checks were carried out which was a considerable reduction from the figure of 181 in 2000–2001. As many as 697 persons were detained for more than 24 hours and subsequently released without charge, 172 more than in 2000–2001. One hundred and two intimate searches, mostly for drugs, were carried out, 29 fewer than in 2000–2001.

Overall there was a 2 per cent increase in arrests for violent crimes (violence against the person, sexual offences and robbery), up 5,700. This compares with an estimated decrease in the number of recorded violence offences of 1 per cent. Arrests for property offences (burglary, theft, fraud and forgery and criminal damage) accounted for 56 per cent of all arrests for notifiable offences, a decrease of one percentage point from 2000–2001. In total the number of arrests for these offences fell slightly, by just under 1 per cent, to 718,000. In contrast, recorded property offences increased during this period by 6 per cent, but this rate of increase is smaller than the statistics suggest as most of the rise is accounted for by an increase in recording resulting from changes in recording practice.

In 2001–2002, 84 per cent of those arrested for notifiable offences were males, the same proportion as in 2000–2001. The number of male arrests remained the same at 1,066,300, whilst the number of female arrests increased by 7,600 (4 per cent). There were increases in the number of females arrested within all offence categories except for sexual offences (down 18 per cent to 900) and fraud and forgery (down 4 per cent to 10,500). Females are more often arrested for theft than for other offences: in 2001–2002 47 per cent of females were arrested for theft (50 per cent of 10–17-year-olds arrested). The second most common category for which females were arrested was violence against the person (18 per cent). Theft (32 per cent) and violence against the person (21 per cent) were also the most common offence groups for males in 2001–2002. Of all persons arrested, one quarter were aged 17 or under and 41 per cent were under 21. Arrests of males aged under 21 fell by 11,800, whereas arrests of males aged 21 or over increased by 14,300. Arrests of females increased for most age groups: by 600 for 10–17-year-olds, 400 for 18–20-year-olds and 7,200 for 21 or over. Theft is the most common offence for arrestees across all age groups, particularly for 10–17-year-olds (38 per cent). A larger proportion of those aged over 21 were arrested for violence against the person offences (23 per cent) than 18–20-year-olds (19 per cent) and 10–17-year-olds (16 per cent).

Social groups as police property and the police use of suspicion

Reiner (1997) provides an account of the unfairness of patterns of policing that results from the phenomena of police discretion:

'Some groups are much more likely than others to be at the receiving end of the exercise of police powers. A general pattern of benign under-enforcement of the law disguises the often oppressive use of police powers against unpopular, uninfluential, and hence powerless, minorities. Such groups have been described graphically as "police property" (Cray, 1972; Lee, 1981:53–54). The social powerlessness which makes them prey to police harassment also allows the police to neglect their victimisation by crime. They tend to be over-policed and under-protected.

The main grist to the mill of routine policing is the social residuum at the base of the social hierarchy (Brogden, Jefferson, and Walklate, 1988:chapter 6). Those who are stopped and searched or questioned in the street, arrested, detained in the police station, charged, and prosecuted are disproportionately young men who are unemployed or casually employed, and from discriminated against ethnic minorities. The police themselves recognise that their main business involves such groups and their mental social maps delineate them by a variety of derogatory epithets: "assholes" Van Maanen (1978), "pukes" Erickson (1982), "scum", "slag" Smith et al (1983:vol IV, 164–165), "prigs" Young (1991). In turn public attitude surveys show that such groups have the most negative views of the police (Smith et al (1983:vol I, 314–315, vol IV, 162–168); Jones and Levi (1983); Hough and Mayhew (1983) and (1985); Kinsey (1984); Jones et al (1986); Crawford et al (1990); Skogan (1990) and (1996)). The basic organisation and mandate of the police in an industrial society tend to generate this practical concentration on policing what has currently come to be known as the underclass.' (1997:1010–1011)

Dixon et al (1989) provide examples of how the police construct suspicion. An example:

'... comes from observation of a car-patrolling officer in the City Centre sub-division of our Research Force. At 9.35 on a Friday night, a researcher and the officer are discussing stop and search. On an industrial street, they pass a man walking with a canvas bag. The PC states that, if it were later at night, he would routinely stop and search a man walking with a bag in such an area. But at this time, a man carrying a bag is still not incongruous, and therefore not suspicious: he is probably someone going home from work. The PC comments that, if he stopped and attempted to search the man, strong objection would be likely. This makes a point suggested by the historical material noted above: that the construction of suspicion must be understood as taking place in the context of relations and negotiations of power. The man would not have regarded himself as "fair game" to be stopped and searched: the officer would have been acting out of order if he had done so. The categories of suspicion are not created unilaterally by the police: they are a product of negotiation and interaction with their public.

A few minutes later, the officer's suspicion is aroused by three people. They are not carrying anything, or doing anything other than standing on a street corner. If the time had been 5.45 rather than 9.45, they would have been unremarkable. However, they are incongruous here at this time of night because of their age: they are all early teenagers. They are asked to account for themselves by the PC, who asks where they are from and what they are doing. They tell him that they are from a large council estate which is some distance away. They are now regarded as being out of place as well as out of time, and have to explain their presence. They are visiting a friend. This account satisfies the PC's suspicion: nothing that they have done or said, or that he has seen, has served to increase it. Similar examples are evident in the grounds provided on some PACE stop and search forms for the exercise of stop and search powers by officers in our Research Force: eg, "Time of day and location (being far from home address)" and "Suspicion of reason to be in area because of age (15 years) and also because not direct route home for him."' (1989:188)

3.6 Stop, search and arrest

Sanders (2002) provides further insight into the police use of discretion:

'Discretion is at the root of criminal justice practice. McConville et al (1991) identify several "working rules" which structure police decision-making. The first is previous (ie being known to the police). Sometimes this "bureaucratic" mode of suspicion, Matza (1969), is sufficient on its own. As an arresting officer told McConville et al: "When you get to know an area, and see a villain about at 2.00 a.m. in the morning, you will always stop him to see what he is about", (1991:24). The second concerns disorder and police authority. Dealing with disorder is a prime police task. Although Shapland and Vagg (1988) found that the police do not usually arrest when they intervene in disorderly incidents, arrests are usual if the disorder does not cease even when it is trivial and only the police are involved, Brown et al (1994). This is in part because of the challenge thereby presented to police authority, even if no specific charge fits the facts. Hoyle (1997) found the same in relation to domestic violence incidents. Other working rules include consideration of types of victims and their wishes, information received and workload. But perhaps the most important working rule is "suspiciousness". This entails the suspect "being in the right place at the right time", or being "out of the ordinary" or "unco-operative", or keeping the wrong company, or its being "just a matter of instinct" on the officer's part, "something undefinable" (all these phrases are from officers quoted in McConville et al (1991:26–28).' (2002:1038 and 1042)

3.7 The suspect in the police station

From an interrogation of a suspect the police can hope for a number of things. They might obtain a confession or other evidence, details of accomplices might be provided, stolen property might be recovered and TICS might be arranged. The latter is a process in which defendants who are intending to plead guilty reveal other crimes and these are taken into consideration at the time of the sentence. The advantages for the defendant are that these matters will no longer be hanging over him. Equally, whilst the sentence he receives will as a result be increased, this will not be to the same extent as would have been the result of separate convictions. For the police it provides a means to clear up offences that might otherwise have remained unsolved. Doubt will be cast upon the effectiveness of, and the acceptability of, interrogations for these purposes. Mitchell (1984) carried out a survey of 400 cases heard at Worcester Crown Court in 1978. He notes the reactive role of the police as illustrated by the data in Table 13.

Table 13

Police Source of First Information as to a Crime

Victim	54%
Police present (sometimes acting on information received)	17%
Professional people (doctor, teacher, fireman etc)	9%
Victim's relative	6%
Passer-by or witness	12%
Defendant or that person's friend or relative	3%
Not known	1%

(Source: 'The Role of the Public in Criminal Detection', Criminal Law Review)

As well as having crimes reported to them the police are also provided with other assistance. In 43 per cent of cases the police will be told the full identity of a suspect. In only 14 per cent of cases, and only 10 per cent in a study by Zander (1979a), will the police have no information as to identity at the start of an investigation. Mitchell makes the point that by the time the suspect is apprehended the evidence that will be used by the prosecution will often have already become available and that the interrogation can only hope to provide a confession. A confession will of course in practice make the job of the prosecution easier. More generally on interrogation, McConville and Baldwin (1982a) were of the view that whatever claims might be made about the importance of interrogation, the pay-off is as a rule slight. This view is based, for example, on the fact that sufficient evidence for a prosecution will already be available before the interrogation. They also note that there is little support for the idea that other offenders will be revealed by interrogations or that stolen property will be recovered. Steer (1980) has a more positive view of interrogations, seeing them as a means to get an admission of guilt and finding merit in a device by which a significant minority of offences are first brought to light. He found that nearly a quarter of the less serious offences are cleared up as a result of TICS Willis (1984) notes that generally 20–25 per cent of offences are cleared up by TICS. Figures from other studies are Mawby (1979) (as many as 40 per cent) and Bottomley and Coleman (1981) (about a quarter). As to TICS this system still leaves the problem of the real doubt as to whether a conviction could have been obtained in relation to the offence, and this system is perhaps best seen as a vice in relation to interrogation rather than a virtue of it.

Inequality of arms

The police arrest those that they think have committed a crime and then their aim is a conviction. The police will be searching for material to reinforce their suspicion and will not be probing for that which undermines it and which might be of interest to the defence. The danger in all of this is that there is inequality of arms. This is particularly so in relation to gathering and challenging forensic material. Finding people to do the work and securing payment of an adequate amount in a timely fashion are all in practice problematic. Also, there may be very little time between disclosure of such evidence and the trial date, with the court having little willingness to grant adjournments. The limitations of lawyers in terms of understanding such evidence is another factor. That they will know very little is a real possibility. In terms of disclosure, the giving up of material to the defence may in many cases depend upon decisions being made by personnel without the necessary legal training. Also, they are not likely to be as well motivated and focused in the performance of the task as the defence might have been. Also, for a legal representative, the idea of planning a defence and preparing a defendant seems like a good idea. The reality is that they may be given only ten to 15 minutes to see the defendant prior to police interview. It may then take the Crown months to get their case in order.

The interview environment

The police station is a hostile environment for the suspect and he naturally wants out. Conversely, the police station is home territory for the police and they will have a high degree of familiarity with what is going on. They will desire a confession. Unless the suspect is very experienced he is unlikely to be familiar with the laws of evidence and the intricacies of the criminal law. Access to a lawyer for the suspect's time in a police station would offer the chance of some assistance in these respects. However, the quality of the provision can be problematic. Also, for the client, the presence of the lawyer offers an immediate disadvantage in the sense that when issues of police malpractice are considered there is a higher threshold if the person is represented rather than unrepresented. He might also be concerned if he knew that defence work is an industry and that the simplest and most economically rewarding way to get through the caseload is by offering guilty pleas. The interview situation and the investigation as a whole is not designed to establish the truth but rather to obtain evidence to secure a conviction. The defendant will have had the opportunity to plead guilty and indeed there will be pressure to do so. The system appears geared to prevent trial and defence lawyers seem to do little to help. We need to consider the police/suspect interaction as a process which starts long before the actual interrogation. The suspect may have been groomed for the interview, ie, softened up, sweetened up, threatened etc. One solution would be for the police to be tape-recorded throughout their shifts. Belloni and Hodgson (2000:59) looked at this, as did the Royal Commission in 1993. This may be a great idea and, of course, it would also protect officers from false complaints.

Some material will be presented on the types and extent of pressure exerted upon defendants in the interrogation situation. Softley et al (1980) took the view that, whilst there may be some evidence of malpractice, the situation overall is one of fairness in what he views as being a pressure situation. As part of this he notes that suspects will face persistent and determined police officers. He also notes that juveniles can be interviewed without a protecting adult being present, that the police are slow to get a solicitor for defendants, that cautions may not be given and that statements may be encouraged. Bottoms and McClean (1976) and Smith et al (1983) take a dimmer view of such matters. Bottoms and McClean record that 4 per cent of those who plead guilty claim that in some sense they were forced to confess, for example by means of a physical assault or by threats that a remand in custody would be arranged. Smith et al (1983) noted that at the time of arrest suspects are frequently neither cautioned nor told they are being arrested. Juveniles are often questioned without a responsible adult being present. Whilst a degree of pressure is implicit in the fact of being arrested, it is not uncommon for officers to use bullying tactics in interrogation and to use threats, especially the threat of being kept in custody for a long time. These kind of pressures go well beyond what is necessary or inevitable within the current framework or procedure. They also suggested that it is common for officers to make bargains with subjects in which an offer not to press charges or to help the suspect to get bail is traded for information. Such behaviour by the police might be regarded as problematic – certainly to my mind what is problematic are the implications of such behaviour. Evidence or a confession obtained in such circumstances might induce a guilty plea or lead to an eventual conviction. The police desire a confession and they may secure one from someone who may only be confessing in order to protect someone else or from a desire for notoriety, or from a fantasist, or from someone who cracked under the pressure and just wanted to get out of the situation. Why do the police need to ask a question more than once? Then if there are four 'no' responses and one 'yes' why is the 'yes' preferable? There are then reasons why confessions can be unreliable – yet a confession is likely to be regarded as enough to convict. The idea of a contested confession (one which the defendant wished to refute at trial) being accepted without a requirement of corroboration and being sufficient to convict is the present reality, but is it an acceptable reality? The realities of the situaton are explained to the defendant by his lawyer and thus he decides to plead guilty. Thus, the merits or demerits of what has happened are never examined as the issue is never tried. Confessions may not be admissible before a court if they are a result of oppressive behaviour, but as Mirfield (1985) notes the Court of Appeal has set at a very high level the point at which custodial interrogation becomes oppressive. Whilst the onus is upon the prosecution to prove that there was no oppression, the procedure becomes one in which the defence have to challenge the prosecution's account of the matter. The reality is thus that in essence the trial/the determination of guilt takes place in the police station without safeguards such as the presence of a solicitor being guaranteed. This makes a mockery of the elaborate safeguards that surround the trial situation. Textbook accounts of interrogations, based as they are on statements by judges, often adopt a take-it-for-granted attitude towards the interrogation situation and the pressures it involves. Unless I missed the point somewhere along the line, I can see merit in a view such as the following. That pre-trial statements made by the accused should not be admissible unless the defendant agrees to this at the trial. None of this is likely to happen as at the moment of course, given the fate of the right to silence. The introduction of tape-recording for interrogations can be welcomed as it offers some additional protection for defendants. The use of tape-recorders is of course not a fool-proof method, as pressure can be applied before recording starts or during a break in recording.

3.8 The provision of legal services to the defendant

The present system provides assistance to some extent, with the means of the defendant and the seriousness of the case being operative factors in relation to some of the forms of provision. Whilst this may provide assistance for representation and advice in police stations, the same sort of investigative facilities that assist the prosecution in the preparation of their case are not available to the defence. Also, it is clearly difficult to cope with the legal system without the assistance of a lawyer. Yet, that is what the criminal justice system expects many defendants to do at present. The existing provisions are far from generous given the way that the thresholds for eligibility and the payment of contributions have been set. Where provision is made, as we will see later, there are reservations about the quality of the service that is provided. The final introductory point to make is that you need to be aware of the Access to Justice Act 1999. This statute contains sections that could eventually be used to introduce a Criminal Defence Service. This Service would be responsible for providing defendants with such advice, assistance and representation as the interests of justice require. The situation at present is that the idea is being used on an experimental basis. Trials started in Liverpool, Middlesbrough, Birmingham and Swansea in 2001, and earlier in Scotland, using a system of public defenders. In England and Wales solicitors on the staff of the new public defender service will act as duty lawyers advising suspects in police stations, representing them in magistrates' courts and organising their defence in the Crown Court. So defendants will be able to choose to be defended by US-style public defenders in those areas. Cases will be prosecuted and defended by state lawyers. The public defenders will have to compete for clients with the private practice law firms. The fear is a repeat of the Crown Prosecution experience, where the funding was never sufficient to deliver a good service and to attract the best lawyers.

Types of assistance that are available

1. There is a duty solicitor scheme for advice in police stations and this is free.
2. The green form scheme provides an initial two hours of advice. It can be used for advice in the police station. There is a means test. The form is now white rather than green, and is known as a Claim 10 form. The scheme is still being referred to as the green form scheme.
3. ABWOR is advice by way of representation and it is an extension of the green form scheme. There is a means test.
4. Legal aid gives help with the preparation of the case and also with going to court. There is a means and merits test and contributions can be required. The criteria developed by Lord Widgery provide the merits test. The following factors are amongst the considerations that would allow a decision to be made as to whether or not the interests of justice require legal aid to be made available.

   a) Where the offence is a serious one, which if proved would mean that defendants are likely to lose their liberty or livelihood, or to suffer serious damage to their reputations.
   b) Where the case raises a substantial question of law.

c) Where defendants are unable to follow the proceedings or state their own case because of language difficulties, mental illness or some other mental or physical illness.

d) Where the nature of the defence demands the tracing and interviewing of witnesses, or expert cross-examination of a prosecution witness.

e) Where legal representation is desirable in the interests of someone other than the accused (for example, the victim in a child-abuse case, who would clearly suffer from being cross-examined by the defendant in person).

5. There is also a duty solicitor schemes for the courts which gives only a partial safety net as not all proceedings are covered.

Not everyone is covered by the above provisions, which is of course a cause for concern. Also worrying are the reservations that have been expressed about the actual quality of the service that is provided by defence lawyers.

Baldwin

Baldwin (1992), as a result of his research on defence solicitors in police stations, suggested that they should be more assertive on behalf of their clients. He stated:

'There is a good deal of scope for them to do so, and there were only a few lawyers on the video tapes who demonstrated that they could wield much authority in the interview room if the need arose. Some lawyers were more tolerant than were others of police officers who adopted harrying tactics, who persisted doggedly with certain lines of questioning or who made crude assumptions of guilt. Searching questions need to be asked, therefore, about how far legal representatives – who are in most instances unqualified legal personnel – can be said to be providing adequate protection to their clients in the police station. The lawyers' view of their role at the police interviews reflects the way that their attitudes have been moulded by the history of their relations with the police. The interview takes place on police territory and it is police officers who are in charge of it. Officers often describe it as their interview, and the lawyers contacted in this study did not commonly see it in other terms. Although police attitudes towards the presence of solicitors have shifted in the course of the past decade – reflecting to a considerable extent the changes brought in by the PACE legislation – lawyers continue to be treated with circumspection and suspicion. While they are no longer regarded as gatecrashers at interviews, they are nonetheless only tolerated at police stations if they behave appropriately. Advising clients not to answer questions or intervening at interviews are not seen by police as reasonable forms of behaviour. It is only if they toe the line that lawyers are regarded as acceptable participants at police interviews.' (1992:52)

Sanders

Similar concerns were raised by Sanders (2002) about police-station advice:

'The most striking due-process provision of PACE is the provision, in ss58–59, of free legal advice to all suspects who request it.

The research, the most recent being conducted by Brown et al (1992) and McConville et al (1994), is summarised by Sanders and Young (1994) and by Brown (1997). First, some suspects do not request advice because they are not informed (wholly or partly) of their rights.

Secondly, some suspects' requests are denied, ignored, or simply not acted upon. Sanders and Bridges (1990) estimated that in some 10.5 per cent of cases (which the police knew the researchers were observing) the police actually broke the law, this being the Code of Practice made under the authority of PACE. Custody records recorded some of these malpractices but failed to record the majority, records made by the police are inevitably a feeble safeguard for suspects against the police. Thirdly, the police often use ploys to attempt to dissuade suspects from seeking advice and to persuade them to cancel their requests. These ploys ranged from the incomprehensible reading of rights to scare stories, such as "You'll have to wait in the cells until the solicitor gets here." The problem does not lie wholly with the police. Many suspects have negative attitudes towards solicitors, which is not surprising, given their level of service. Advice is frequently provided by telephone, rather than in person, in many cases solicitors do not attend interrogations, and when they do they are usually passive. Legal aid lawyers have a generally non-adversarial stance and take their lead from the police. They routinely allow the police to use intimidatory tactics, such that in one notorious case the suspect's lawyer had not objected to intimidation which the Court of Appeal condemned without hesitation (this was the Cardiff Three case). Sometimes defence lawyers are actually sought by the police to put their case to recalcitrant suspects! McConville et al (1994:8) found one firm, which specialised in criminal work, advising-over the telephone – "Tell the truth, son you won't go far wrong on that advice."' (2002:1045–1046)

Whilst advice may be available that does not mean that you will get it. There are very many mundane cases and for many of these there is no one providing legal advice. Belloni and Hodgson (2000:42) note the study by Bucke and Brown (1997) where only 34 per cent of detainees asked for and 34 per cent eventually got advice – 82 per cent face to face and 18 per cent by telephone. Cape (2002) makes similar points:

'A significant minority of suspects who ask for legal advice subsequently withdraw their requests. In part this may be attributed to delay by the police in contacting the chosen lawyer, but it can also be partly explained by the fact that in some cases solicitors either do not respond, or are slow to respond, to the request for advice. There is evidence that in recent years the performance of solicitors in this respect has improved, but it is of particular importance, given that most suspects hate delay and want to get out of the police station as quickly as possible. If the solicitor contacted fails to respond to the request or is slow to respond, such suspects will be susceptible to suggestions by the police that they proceed with the police interview without having obtained legal advice. There are various explanations for solicitors' failure to provide advice or failure to provide it quickly, including the fact that they may be engaged on other cases (although this is, in part at least, a consequence of inadequate organisation of their work by solicitors' firms) and a reluctance on the part of many solicitors to attend the police station until the police are ready to interview the client.' (2002:107)

McConville et al

Doubts about the role of defence lawyers are also raised by McConville et al (1994). Their view was that for the most part solicitors do not see magistrates' courts as trial venues but as places where defendants can be processed through guilty pleas without, in general, any risk of severe sanction. The idea that the prosecution should be put to the proof – required to establish a case against the defendant – is not accepted as valid or realistic by defence solicitors. Whilst it would be misleading and unfair to argue that solicitors do not care about their client, so strong is their presumption of guilt and their faith in the prosecution's case that they fail to see their own role in the production of pleas and their implication in ambiguous or inconsistent pleas of guilt. But it is not right to argue that solicitors are socialised, through court and prosecutorial inspired disciplinary mechanisms, into non-adversarial practices: they join hands with prosecutors not out of fear of sanction but because they share similar social and crime control values.

We should note that in recent years payment is only available for the work of advisers in police stations who are qualified and who have either passed or commenced an accreditation scheme. The accreditation scheme must be passed within six months of its commencement. These changes are very likely to have improved the quality of police-station advice but as yet we do not know how much of an improvement there has been. In relation to the accreditation scheme Cape (2002) has the following comments:

'The discovery that a large proportion of suspects were being advised, not by solicitors, but by unqualified representatives led to the creation of an accreditation scheme which is designed to ensure, through a system of testing, that all non-solicitors who give legal advice at police stations can demonstrate a minimum level of competence. Research on the impact of this accreditation scheme has shown that it has had a significant impact on the quality of police station advice and, interestingly, that the improvement extends to solicitors as well. It is likely that one reason for this improvement is that, in devising the scheme, the Law Society had to develop and articulate standards of competence by which candidates for accreditation could be judged. The standards confirmed the adversarial role of defence lawyers, set out in detail both the knowledge and skills required to perform the role effectively and articulated the steps to be taken by defence lawyers in advising clients at the police station. The accreditation scheme has now been adopted in a modified form for determining whether solicitors are sufficiently competent to become duty solicitors. Furthermore, since the accreditation scheme is, in effect, run jointly by the Law Society and the Legal Service Commission (the government body responsible for administering legal aid), it has helped to legitimise the adversarial role of defence lawyers, making it less vulnerable to challenge by the police and other law enforcement agencies, and by the government itself.' (2002:111)

Belloni and Hodgson (2000) draw together a number of the issues that have been considered in relation to interrogations, confessions and the provision of legal services for the defendant in the following quotation:

'The right to have a lawyer present both before and during interrogation has been given greater effect by the universal provision of Legal Aid for custodial legal advice. Unfortunately the profession has not responded adequately to the possibility of pre-charge involvement in the investigation. Until recently, the majority of legal advisers were neither qualified nor trained. Most were clerks of some form or other, with little or no knowledge of criminal law and procedure. Even solicitors themselves were generally passive and cursory in their dealings with suspects. Clearly, custodial legal advice has been considered routine and mundane work for which non-qualified individuals might inexpensively be employed. Recent initiatives to improve the quality of service provided are the result of financial sanctions for those failing to comply, rather than conscious standard-raising by lawyers themselves. Recent reforms such as curtailment of the right to silence mean that non-adversarial defence lawyering, both at the police station and during case preparation, has a greater impact upon the construction and running of the defence case. ... The police station is the key site in the construction of the

116

case against the accused and is therefore central in understanding and tackling some of the major causes in miscarriages of justice.' (2000:64)

3.9 Community policing

The 1986 Working Paper (Home Office (1986a)) suggested that the police must gain the trust and confidence of the communities which they serve. Community policing was presented as being a means to achieve this. This is seen as being a system in which police officers get to know their 'patch' and to understand the people whom they serve and protect. Community policing is in their view a form of knowledgeable policing which is not an alternative to law enforcement but a condition for its success.

Bowling and Foster (2002:990–992) note some of the issues that have been raised in the development of community policing ideas. The prior history to these developments was how the barriers between the police and community were created by the use of technology. The police went mobile in police cars rather than walking a beat. They relied on radio contact for communication and these developments were aimed at a wider coverage of areas and faster response times. The lack of communication with the public which resulted was added to by the poor quality of interaction with the public that was taking place. This was especially so with urban black young males and a further dimension was an outbreak of urban riots.

Community policing was one response to these problems. It can be linked to information-gathering and even used as part of a zero-tolerance strategy. The latter can be problematic given the high degree of intervention that such an approach can entail. Community policing involves notions such as policing by consent, policing with the community and public policing. It would seek to address the concerns of the community and Trojanowicz and Bucqueroux (1998) suggest that it involves the following ten principles: change, leadership, vision, partnership, problem-solving, equity, trust, empowerment, service and accountability. Some evidence suggests that it can reduce fear of crime, change the attitudes of police officers and help to develop the community in positive ways. In the view of others it is ill-defined, poorly implemented and not properly evaluated.

Weitekamp, Kerner and Meier (2003:306–307) suggest the following as principles of community policing: that every citizen has the responsibility that the police perform on a full time and salaried basis and that they will work together; that it is an on-going and problem-solving approach rather than being event driven; and that the system is based on communication and that it involves decentralisation thus becoming grassroots. The aim is to improve quality of life and the police are to be responsive to community needs which will not just be crime and disorder orientated. Rather, as with the broken windows thesis, the police will respond to signs of disorder or incivility such as vandalism, graffiti, abandoned housing or cars, rubbish in the street and similar issues. The bobby on his beat is the way to deliver this. Other organisations will have similar responsibilities. The police should operate as an organising and integrating force in the community. Community policing aims to be inclusive of all the members of the community with social cohesion and peace-keeping being key goals. Crime control is seen as an important, but subsidiary, role.

That such ideas are no panacea for the disease of crime, in that problems clearly exist with such schemes. Brown and Iles (1985) examined initiatives in five forces and noted a number of problems, amongst which was the very limited amount of contact that such schemes actually involved. For police officers involved in such work other calls on their time meant that under 14 per cent of their time could be regarded as community involvement. The police themselves tended to dislike this work. It certainly isn't seen as 'real' police work and it threatened their desire for control of situations. Breaking down the barrier between them and the public meant that they would have to let their guard down which they would not desire. Also career prospects in the force can be furthered by specialisation, so police officers would be keen to be transferred into a specialism such as the Drug Squad. A result of this would be that any contact between an individual police officer, who had been doing community work, and a community would be lost. This latter problem would seem to be solvable by linking career prospects with community policing if community policing was to be regarded as a desirable form of policing. Weatheritt (1986:Chapter 3) provides an account of a number of community policing schemes and notes reasons why appraisals of them have to tend towards the equivocal and the gloomy. The Parliamentary All Party Penal Affairs Group (1983:Chapter 4) provides a more optimistic account. More recently Fielding (1994) carried out research into community policing as practised in two inner-city divisions of the Metropolitan Police in London. He found that numerous occupational and organisational problems arose from the attempt to use this style of policing and that the work was not recognised and supported to any great extent. The following extract from Fielding, that records the view of a community officer, is a very clear indication that the various elements of the force are pulling in different directions.

'Even when one warned the reliefs during temporary assignments that one would be keeping a beat appointment they expect you to be there fifteen minutes. It was not just that seriousness and time had different meaning for relief and homebeat. The mode of relief policing and overtime constraints were also askew. While you're there you can't have your radio blurting out (a la relief). If you are not heard of for an hour so when you finally put your battery in you get "where the hell have you been?" The constable had a tenants' association meeting that evening and had promised the NW coordinator he would attend, but the meeting was to begin just half an hour before his shift ended. Wouldn't it be nice if they gave me an hour's pay to sit at this tenants' association meeting? Oh no, cutbacks and all that. Can't have an hour's time for the public. It was hard to excuse an organisation which distorted its own explicit priorities. The priority, the main priority, is for homebeat men to be out there. Everybody wants it, from the Commissioner down, but when it comes to the nitty-gritty its all out the window.' (1994: 312)

Also the community officers would also be redeployed to fill a vacuum in other operations as they occurred. For the community constables there was the problem of accountability in that the things that they were doing were not recognised by the established systems of record-keeping. This was despite the particular form of community policing that had been adopted having crime control and order maintenance as prime concerns. There was a desire to use the system for intelligence-gathering. Social service and community outreach were not prioritised. The community officers also reported a lack of clarity as regards exactly what they should be doing and it was clear that any direction that was available varied over time.

3.10 What works?

One starting point might be the tasks that the police are to perform, though it is clear that, even when identified, they are going to be difficult to operationalise in their entirety. A national plan for policing priorities was issued in 2003. The primary objective for the police service nationally is to deliver improved police performance and greater public reassurance. This is with regard to the following: tackling anti-social behaviour and disorder; reducing street, drug-related, violent and gun crime in line with local and national targets; increasing the number of offences brought to justice; and combatting serious and organised crime operating across force boundaries. That is a gloss on what is required. The reality of what the detail is, is frightening, especially as there is meant to be a war on bureaucracy as it pertains to criminal justice. The following is the tip of the iceberg of the requirements. The national policing plan requires all 43 police forces in England and Wales to produce three-year plans which incorporate ten public service agreements with 17 key performance indicators; four strategic priorities with ten core actions, 17 local actions and 19 more key performance indicators; six performance domains, with 21 best value performance indicators; and three reform-priority areas with 51 local planning points. The 17 key performance indicators, which are linked to the ten public service agreements, include violent crime, youth crime, organised crime, anti-social behaviour, seizure of assets, efficiency, drugs, and feelings of public satisfaction and safety. They also require police to cut burglaries, robberies and car crimes, measured per thousand of population. The 19 performance indicators which are attached to the four strategic priorities also require police to cut the number of burglaries, robberies and car crimes, but measured this time by the absolute number which are recorded by police without reference to population. These 19 targets also cover efficiency (to go up by 2 per cent a year), road traffic deaths (to go down 40 per cent in ten years), community participation (up 5 per cent by 2006), sick days (down to 11.5 for each officer by 2006), value for money (up), overtime (down), police visibility (up), ill-health retirements (down), recruitment of women (up), child road deaths (down) and so on. In producing these local plans, the 43 forces are required to consult local police authorities, the other criminal justice agencies, the crime and disorder reduction partnerships, youth offender teams, drug action teams and the new criminal justice boards, all of whom have their own multiple sets of priorities, performance indicators and targets etc.

The issue of how to evaluate the police was considered by Horton and Smith (1988); the ideas that follow are based on what they had to say. Whilst it is possible to identify broad desires as regards policing, identifying aims that are isolatable and measurable is difficult. Clearly policing is concerned with a range of tasks so the use of one measure alone is inappropriate. Each task seems to invite a separate measure which is fine if you want to know something like the cost per mile of police patrols by car. Other matters are more difficult. Can the success of police crime prevention work be measured by counting the number of talks delivered to the public or the number of people advised? Probably not satisfactorily – but to actually measure the number of crimes prevented by police action is very difficult. Similar problems of assessment arise in relation to tasks such as police reassurance of burglary victims, the contribution of the police to maintaining public harmony and the impact of schools liaison work. As well as looking at the impact of police practices the issue of value for money can also be raised. But sometimes things are done not because of their utility in a monetary sense but rather because it is thought that they must be done. For example, the huge expenditure on murder hunts is for the meeting of public expectations. If we are concerned about the value of life a draconian enforcement of the law on speeding would save numerous lives and generate revenue as well. When deciding how to allocate resources and measure the effectiveness of such decisions it becomes necessary to be able to distinguish between the merits of such diverse tasks as reassuring the elderly, investigating drugs suppliers, apprehending burglars and catching speeding motorists. Broad goals such as crime prevention and peace-keeping, as we have seen, are very difficult to measure. They also interact with each other. Indeed, a crime prevention campaign may increase fear of crime and reduce public harmony. Narrow goals such as arrest rates also have their problems. Arrest rates as a measure is fine in the sense that you would know that arrests had, for example, increased; but then is such an increase good or bad? Is it down to increased diligence and efficiency or the failure of crime prevention strategies? Using a measure such as crime rates is clearly problematic as the police are only one of the variables. If they ran a successful campaign to increase reporting behaviour of a crime such as rape then the crime rate would suggest that the have failed because crime has increased. In reality the actual number of rapes may have decreased but the level of reporting may have gone up. If you go to the micro level you face the reality that the police may be performing a number of tasks at the same time. For example, the officer on point duty may be improving the traffic flow, giving directions to motorists, improving public relations and helping to prevent crime. To measure issues of effectiveness for such practices is clearly difficult. In relation to particular crimes it is going to be difficult to work out the different contributions to success or failure of an investigation. In reality the public are the great detectives who will discover the crime, by being the victim, and are also likely to provide the evidence, for example, by saying who they thought the offender was. A further difficulty is the low visibility of policing and the high levels of autonomy that they possess in their daily work. It is difficult to measure what is unlikely to be seen, although there may be some potential in self-assessment.

Horton and Smith (1988) provide a quotation from Ann James (1987:13) on the issue of performance indicators, that is 'they tend to become an end in themselves. They tend to measure a level of activity rather than a level of achievement.' In relation to this Horton and Smith comment as follows:

> 'Because the existence of performance indicators can cause a distortion in the pattern of policing, it is important that the chosen indicators measure activities which should be encouraged. In the words of the Deputy Director of the National Consumer Council, "... bad performance indicators will lead to badly directed resources": Healey (1985:14).' (1988:23)

The actual business of recording data in order to measure performance can of course consume resources that could have been used to produce better performance. Finally, the fashion for such as better response times, as was the case in the 1970s, may be the pursuit of an aim and a measure that is of little or no value. One thing that we have discovered is that speed of response was critical in only a tiny proportion of cases.

Bowling and Foster (2002:998–999) reviewed research on different aspects of police effectiveness, particularly their ability to reduce crime. Some of the main conclusions are noted below and they make rather depressing reading. Their work provides much more detail than the points below.

Strategies

1. Increasing police numbers in order to reduce crime – the findings are inconclusive.
2. The use of random patrol in order to offer deterrence – it is ineffective.
3. Mandatory arrests as a means to reduce crime – mixed findings depending on the context.
4. Community contact in general – inconclusive findings, although it may make people feel better and aids police legitimacy.
5. Contact with young people as a way to reduce crime is ineffective as a strategy.
6. Rapid response – the findings are inconclusive.
7. Intelligence-led policing by targeting prolific offenders or major crime problems – may be effective in some contexts.
8. Directed patrolling with a focus on hot spots and hot times may be effective in some contexts and ineffective in others.
9. The targeting of repeat victims may be effective in some contexts and ineffective in others.
10. Multi-agency working for a joined-up criminal justice system – the findings are inconclusive.
11. Problem-orientated policing involves analysing crime patterns and attempts to deal with underlying problems which then produces less crime by solving the problems – inconclusive findings.
12. Zero tolerance, including aggressive order maintenance. The theory is that by being strict in relation to all forms of crime, including the minor offences, this will reduce even the more serious crime. The findings are inconclusive as the aggression can be counter-productive, although there is some support for the broken windows thesis. This involves the need to protect and repair all aspects of a community's infrastructure and in this a broken window would be a sign of decay.
13. Proactive stop and search – the findings are inconclusive. Whilst it may be effective in some contexts it will alienate the parts of the community that are being regularly searched.

Weitekamp, Kerner and Meier (2003) note the following suggestions for a problem-orientated policing approach (point 11 above):

'(1) Focus on problems of concern to the public.
(2) Zero in on effectiveness as the primary concern.
(3) Be proactive.
(4) Be committed to systematic inquiry as a first step in solving substantive problems.
(5) Encourage the use of rigorous methods in making inquiries.
(6) Make full use of the data in police files and the experience of police personnel.
(7) Group like incidents together so that they can be addressed as a common problem.

(8) Avoid using overly broad labels in grouping incidents so separate problems can be identified.
(9) Encourage a broad and uninhibited search for solutions.
(10) Acknowledge the limits of the criminal justice system as a response to problems.
(11) Identify multiple interests in any one problem and weigh them when analysing the value of different responses.
(12) Be committed to taking some risks in responding to problems.' (2003:309–310)

The following sources provide clear guidance as regards best practice for policing. Effective policing strategies were sought by Jordan (1998) as part of research by the Home Office to find strategies for reducing crime. An examination was made of research that has been carried out to date on different policing strategies and the work of the American researchers (Sherman et al (1997)) was utilised in relation to the methodology to be followed. Much of the evidence relied upon was also from the United States. First, as regards what doesn't work in reducing crime, random patrols clearly belong in this category. Such patrols may have other impacts, such as reducing fear of crime. Higher charging rates are also ineffective in reducing crime, particularly where highly legalistic systems were used in relation to juveniles. This reinforces the practice of cautioning juveniles for the early stages of their offending. Some forms of community policing do not work – for example, neighbourhood watch and community policing that does not have a clear focus. Disrupting drug dealing in the hope that related crime will also be driven out is also a strategy that seems to be ineffective. Proactive work with children and the very different strategy of increasing the proportion of fast response times are two other tactics to regard as ineffective. In contrast, the following have been shown to be effective strategies: the targeting of repeat offenders, targeting repeat victims, targeting drink driving and police patrols directed at hot spots. Some other strategies are in 'the worth a closer look and more research' category. These are community participation in setting priorities, improving police legitimacy with the community, domestic violence strategies, order maintenance which avoids damage to legitimacy and problem-orientated policing.

Beating Crime

In a report by HM Inspectorate of Constabulary which was called *Beating Crime* (HM Inspectorate of Constabulary (1998)), a large study was undertaken in order to try to discover both the present state of play and suggestions for good practice in relation to crime reduction and prevention activity. They noted at the outset that some police areas have seen large falls in recorded crime – 40 per cent over a five-year period. This had been achieved without any real increase in police numbers. It was a result of focusing their own activities more effectively and through collaboration with a variety of partners, particularly local authorities. They compare this 40 per cent improvement with the much publicised 37 per cent reduction over three years in New York City which was preceded by a 20 per cent plus increase in police establishment.

In New York the police reclaimed the streets and went for zero tolerance. Crime has been reduced generally in recent years in the United States: as noted in Table 14. A recent feature of policing in the United States has been the expansion of community policing tied in with the idea of problem-solving and targeted policing

Table 14

	Crime Rate per 100,000 of the Population in the United States				
	All crime	Violent crime	Murder	Rape	Burglary
1990	5,820.3	731.8	9.4	41.2	1,235.9
2000	4,124.0	506.1	5.5	32.0	728.4

(Source: Bureau of Justice Statistics 2001)

The following strategies were suggested in the 1998 report for reducing crime and the fear of crime:

1. Make crime reduction a core policing function and manage its performance by the provision of a clear strategy followed through with leadership, robust accountability and management support.
2. Use a problem-solving approach which is based on good quality information. This should mix innovation with tried and tested methods to produce effective solutions tailored to meet local needs. They noted that at the present time problem-solving was not the usual approach. Instead there was much unfocused and misdirected effort which had an unknown impact on crime. They suggested that if police forces did no more than better direct that unproductive effort, the results would be significant.
3. Develop partnerships which can agree joint priorities and broaden the range of potential solutions, ensuring that action is taken by the most appropriate partner.
4. Make best use of resources in relation to its strategy and priorities. Decisions should be informed by cost-benefit analysis.

3.11 Assessing the performance of the police

One starting point is the official criminal statistics which reveal that the clear-up rate for 2001 was only 23 per cent, a figure that has fallen since the 1960s when it was 45 per cent: Home Office (2002a). The situation is worse than it might at first appear because the total number of offences has also been increasing. In 1950 the figure was half a million offences, whilst it is now eleven times that amount (5,527,000 offences), and of course many other offences are never reported to the police. There are very notable variations in the performance of the different police forces. Humberside only manages to clear up 20 per cent of offences and the Metropolitan Police were even worse at 14 per cent. This last figure can be compared with Dyfed-Powys where 68 per cent are cleared up. The performance for some important offences is also poor – for example, the average clear-up rate for burglary in Greater Manchester was only 7 per cent in 2001.

A variety of other tactics can be adopted in order to provide an assessment of the police. Assessment in terms of what the public think of them produces outcomes such as 'generally satisfied' (Southgate and Ekblom (1984)) and as having a reasonably favourable view of the police: Smith et al (1983). In both these studies, however, evidence was provided of some groups who felt they were persecuted by the police. For example, Smith et al (1983, Volume 1:particularly Chapter 6) reported that this was the case as regards West Indian youths. Individual police officers will at times (whilst probationers or seeking promotion or otherwise under scrutiny) have to be seen to be performing well in terms of such as number of arrests and stops of vehicles. As Holdaway (1983) notes this means in practice that easy targets will be sought out. Public toilets can be investigated so as to arrest people for gross indecency. Clearing the streets of drunks is also an easy means of making arrests. Standing at the end of a bus lane will ensure a ready supply of offenders, as will a search for vehicles without tax discs on display. This is a very crude form of assessment and a method in which the merits of an arrest was a central issue would seem preferable to a simple counting of the numbers arrested. In recent decades there has been increased spending on policing but no improvement in crime rates or public confidence – indeed quite the contrary. Also the trend has been towards centralisation and control whilst talking about going local in emphasis. Clarke and Hough (1984) provide a general account of the effectiveness of police methods, and both Hough (1987) and Chatterton (1987) provide additional views on the issue of effectiveness. Clarke and Hough's work is an indictment of traditional methods of policing such as foot patrols, car patrols and detective work. Clarke and Hough are of the view that an increase in provision of such policing offers no real prospects of crime reduction. They do see some hope for certain innovations such as community policing (which may help with crime prevention and lead to the provision of information) and the use of specialised patrols. The latter would include the use of saturation policing and decoy patrols which of course involve quandaries of their own. Conventional forms of patrol could hope to be present when a crime is committed, to offer a police presence, or to offer a quick response. Car patrols were meant to be of use for the last two and particularly the latter. Foot patrols carried the hope of contact with the community and information thus being made known to the police. This point is a matter of supposition and is certainly not a proven valuable feature of foot patrols. All of these forms of patrol might well give some feeling of security and confidence to members of the community. As to actually being present at the scene of a crime, they note data on foot patrols in London. A constable will be within one hundred yards of a burglary about once every eight years – this does not mean that they knew about it and certainly not that they caught anyone. Similar doubts are raised about car patrols, which offer little chance of coming across such as a robbery. The importance of response time should also not be over-estimated as it is often not of real importance. Finally, some similar data from a variety of studies as recorded by Mitchell (1984:459) can be noted. Figures for the percentage of crimes unearthed by the police were as follows: Black (1981) 13 per cent, Bottomley and Coleman (1981) 13 per cent and Sellin and Wolfgang (1964) 29 per cent.

3.12 Conclusion

Some final comments by way of conclusion on the police seem to be called for. Some things seem clear. When necessary the police will act in an overtly political manner in order to protect the establishment. For most of the time their importance is in terms of playing a part in determining which breaches of the law will be subject to enforcement activity. In examining their part in this filtering process the importance of the activities of members of the public becomes clear. For the public the police are their main point of contact with the criminal justice system. Research indicates that they are generally happy with the policing that they receive, that they would like more of it and in particular they look to the police for services rather than with regard to overtly crime-related matters. Police behaviour is clearly a complex and varied phenomenon. When research is carried out, to some extent, all that you capture is a snapshot of that particular time and place. I recommend Graef (1990) for further examples of this complexity and variety. In his book he provides an account of what the police themselves have to say about their experiences of policing: thus he presents many more snapshots for us. There is also plenty of evidence that policing is to a considerable extent consumer led. It is equally clear that police behaviour is in many respects unsavoury. This is a result of the operationalisation of views fostered and developed by largely autonomous groups of policemen at the local level. The reality of policing is often what they decide it should be. If change is desirable its implementation will depend upon the ability to penetrate into and neuter the self image of the police. In terms of assessing police behaviour it is clear that by several measures they are ineffective. In arriving at your own views on the police you really have to decide what you expect of them. For example, the public want services to be provided which the police are both reluctant to, and to some extent unable to, deliver. Who, if anybody, should deliver such services?

4 Pre-trial Decisions

4.1 Cautions

4.2 Official guidance on cautioning

4.3 Aims and justifications of cautions

4.4 Disadvantages of, and problems with, cautioning schemes

4.5 Diversion

4.6 The prosecution system

4.7 The reform process

4.8 The Code for Crown Prosecutors (2000)

4.9 The problems of the Crown Prosecution Service

4.10 Bail decision-making

4.11 Problems in bail decision-making

In this chapter three forms of pre-trial decision making are examined – these are the various forms of cautioning and diversion, the prosecution process and bail decision-making. They can all have implications in terms of the later stages of the criminal justice system. This is most notable when the decision taken means that a person will not proceed to the next stage of the system. The government White Paper, *Justice for All* (Home Office (2002d)), provides details of their intentions for the initial stages of the criminal justice system. They see this as getting the process right from the start and the major aim is to take some of the delay out of the process. This would, for example, help to deal with the problem of defendants who commit offences whilst on bail awaiting trial. The White Paper makes the following proposals:

1. Give the Crown Prosecution Service responsibility for charging in all but routine cases.
2. Improve case preparation by, for example, further improving the interaction of the police and the Crown Prosecution Service.
3. Give the police power to impose conditions on bail before charge, coupled with measures to prevent offending while on bail.
4 Provide incentives and sanctions to promote effective and focused case preparation.
5. Radically improve the disclosure of information, with both the prosecution and defence obliged to disclose all information necessary to ensure the trial addresses the real issues.
6. Make better use of technology and forensic and technological expertise to enable the police to obtain the evidence to make an effective case.

Many of these ideas were incorporated in the Criminal Justice Act 2003 and the provisions that relate to the issues in this chapter are detailed below. It is important to note that, since most of the provisions of the Act did not come into force immediately upon Royal Assent, the earlier provisions will still be applicable for some time.

4.1 Cautions

The system of official cautions is a specific example of diversion and this will be examined prior to a more general account of the notion of diversion. An official caution has to be distinguished from the type of situation in which an informal warning is given to an apologetic motorist stopped for speeding. Such behaviour is an example of the use of police discretion and its extent is unknown. The system of official cautions is one in which a person receives counselling as to their future conduct, as an alternative to a charge. Whilst procedures vary, an oral caution by a policeman of the rank of inspector or above at a police station is the most common form. Steer (1970) notes that the idea was being used as early as 1833 by the Metropolitan Police, so it is far from being a new idea. Most forces developed the idea as being suitable for the treatment of the elderly and for motoring offences. A major expansion took place in usage between 1968 and 1972 but this was almost entirely a consequence of changes in relation to the treatment of juveniles. The police developed cautioning systems for juveniles to the extent that, as Stanley and Baginsky (1984) indicate, the ratio of court appearances to cautions changed from 1/1 in 1965 to 1/3 in 1979. Over that period the number of cautions of juveniles virtually quadrupled. There is at present a move away from such extensive cautioning of youngsters and the cautioning system has been replaced by one of reprimands and warnings. Further details as to the characteristics of those cautioned are provided by Ditchfield (1976) and Steer (1970). Ditchfield (1976) stated that, excluding motoring offences, there are many juveniles and that most offenders are cautioned for minor property offences. Steer (1970) noted the large amount of motoring offenders and youngsters. He also drew attention to the greater proportion (almost double) of female to male offenders that are cautioned. The explanation for this is not completely clear, but some part of this difference can be explained in terms of the previous criminal record of the offender and the characteristics of the present offence. A cautioning scheme for drunks in Hammersmith led to an extension of the scheme throughout London and to the setting up of a cautioning scheme for adults generally, on which see Light (1984). Anthony (1984) reported the use of a scheme in Devon, and Dickens (1970) described the use of cautions by local authorities. Dickens noted that authorities in seeking an effective strategy in areas such as consumer protection and public health have found that warnings may often be the best tactic to use.

Crime and Disorder Act 1998

One major point to note at the outset is the impact of the Crime and Disorder Act 1998. Sections 65 and 66 provided that cautioning for a child or young person is replaced by a system of reprimands and warnings and the system was fully operational in June 2000. As an alternative to prosecution, for those not previously convicted or warned, a reprimand may be given by the police. If a reprimand has been given then a warning may be appropriate in relation to a later offence. A warning may be appropriate without a reprimand having been given. After that prosecution would have to be used: except that if two years have passed since a warning another warning is possible. This system of a further warning can be used only once. Warnings would be reported to the youth-offending team and they would normally prescribe a rehabilitation programme. Reprimands and warnings will be treated by a court as previous convictions for two years and conditional discharges will not be a possibility for the court.

A major review of the Criminal Courts in England and Wales was carried out by Auld LJ in 2001: Auld LJ (2001). Auld suggested that consideration should be given to the wider use of conditional cautioning or Caution Plus alongside existing and future restorative justice schemes, for which a national strategy should be devised. The Criminal Justice Act 2003 provides for cautions with conditions. The decision to use this will be taken by the Crown Prosecution Service and it would be run by the police. These cautions will include measures of a reparative or rehabilitative nature.

Statistics on cautioning

In 2001, 229,000 offenders were cautioned for offences other than motoring offences. This was 4 per cent fewer than in 2000. Twenty two per cent of males were cautioned and 26 per cent of females. This data includes reprimands and warnings. Table 15 provides further details of reprimands and warnings: Home Office (2002a).

Table 15

Number of Reprimands and Final Warnings by Offence and Type and Age in 2001

	Age 10–11	Age 12–14	Age 15–17	Age 10–17
Indictable	4,020	25,740	33,745	63,505
Summary (excluding motoring)	2,381	13,211	18,945	34,537
Total	6,401	38,951	52,690	98,042

(Source: Criminal Statistics, England and Wales, 2001)

4.2 Official guidance on cautioning

One of the problems of cautioning systems as carried out by the various police forces is that there is evidence of disparity between them and thus some injustice for individuals. This disparity arose in part because of the limited guidance that was made available to the police. Semi-official guidelines published in 1983 (Attorney General (1983)) were one of a number of attempts to limit disparities by the provision of guidance as to the use of cautions.

Further versions appeared later and the latest version is the 1994 guidelines (Circular 18/1994). In most respects the guidance in the 1994 Circular, and in the revised national standards for cautioning which accompany it, are similar to those contained in Circular 59/1990 which it supersedes. The police are described in the Home Office *Annual Report for 1995* (Cm 2808), presented to Parliament in March 1995, as having discretion whether to charge an offender or formally to caution him or her. It goes on to say that cautioning, properly used, is an effective deterrent to those who have committed minor offences or who have offended for the first time. However, it states that multiple cautioning can lead to an offender becoming an habitual criminal before even coming to court, suggesting that those who abuse the chance offered by a caution should generally be prosecuted. Data from the official statistics (Home Office (1998a)) indicates that the use of both repeat cautions and cautions for those with convictions has declined in recent years, which was the effect that was intended when the circular was issued. But the decrease has only been in the order of 5 per cent, which is certainly not a large impact. Evans and Ellis (1997) in their 1995 research noted a similar small decrease in repeat cautions. In March 1995, new guidance was issued to the police aimed at curbing the inappropriate use of cautioning. The use of cautioning was ruled out for the most serious offences and repeat cautioning was strongly discouraged. Evans and Ellis (1997) report that 25 out of 42 forces did not implement the new requirement on gravity (ie serious) offences. They doubted the ability of such circulars to affect police behaviour.

Home Office Circular 18/1994

The aim of the Circular is to provide guidance on the cautioning of offenders and in particular:

1. To discourage the use of cautions in inappropriate cases, eg offences which are triable on indictment only.
2. To seek greater consistency between police force areas.
3. To promote the better recording or cautions.

The purpose of a formal caution
A formal caution is intended to:

1. deal quickly and simply with less serious offenders;
2. divert such offenders from the criminal courts;
3. reduce the chances of their re-offending.

The Circular emphasises that a formal caution is not the only alternative to prosecution. For example, in certain cases it will be appropriate for the police to give an offender an informal warning, or for them to take no further action.

The criteria to be met before cautioning
Several conditions must be met before a caution can be given:

1. The evidence must be sufficient to give a realistic prospect of conviction. If the evidence is insufficient, cautioning is ruled out.

2. The offender must admit the offence. The admission must be clear and reliable. If the offender's mental health or intellectual capacity were in doubt, a caution would not be appropriate but prosecution would not be inevitable in such a case – the police might take no further action or consider referral to another agency which could help the offender.

3. The offender (or in the case of a juvenile his parent or guardian) must consent to a caution being issued. Consent should not be sought until a decision has been made that a caution is the appropriate course of action – in other words it is not possible to offer a caution as an inducement to admit the offence. When consent is sought, the offender (or parent/guardian) must have the significance of the procedure explained to him.

4. A record of the caution will be kept and, if the person offends again, the caution may influence the decision whether to prosecute for the new offence. If the person is convicted of another offence in the future, the caution may be cited in court.

The public interest

If the first two of the above conditions are met, consideration should be given to whether a caution is in the public interest. The factors which should be taken into account are:

The nature of the offence. Cautions must never be given for the most serious indictable-only offences. Their use for other indictable-only offences will only be appropriate in exceptional circumstances. A caution will not be appropriate when the victim has suffered significant harm or loss. The term 'significant' is to be construed with reference to the circumstances of the victim. In cases of doubt, the assistance of the Crown Prosecution Service should be sought.

The likely penalty if the offender were to be convicted by a court. The circular refers to the Code for Crown Prosecutors which suggests that prosecution may not be appropriate where the offence is not particularly serious and the probable sentence would be an absolute or conditional discharge. The likelihood of a more substantive penalty being imposed does not mean that a caution could not be given.

The offender's age and state of health. The circular retains a presumption in favour of not prosecuting the elderly or infirm and people suffering from a mental illness or a severe physical illness. It goes on to state that the presumption against prosecution should be extended to other groups of adults where the criteria for cautioning are met.

The offender's previous criminal history. An offender's previous record is important but is not decisive on its own. The existence of a previous caution or conviction does not rule out a further caution if other factors exist which suggest that a caution would be appropriate. For example, there might have been an appreciable lapse of time since the last offence, the previous and most recent offences might be different in character and seriousness, or a previous caution might have had a noticeable effect on the pattern of offending. However, the circular suggests that a caution should not be given when there can be no reasonable expectation that it will curb the recipient's offending.

The offender's attitude to the offence. Two factors are to be considered. The first is the wilfulness with which the offence was committed. The second is the offender's subsequent attitude. A demonstration of regret, such as apologising to the victim or an offer to put matters 'right, are features which might support the use of a caution.

The views of the victim

The Circular suggests that before a caution can be given the victim should normally be contacted to assess such factors as:

1. His view of the offence.
2. The extent of any damage or loss. The significance of the loss or damage should be considered in relation to the victim. The effect of the caution should be explained to the victim.
3. Whether there is any continuing threat from the offender. Although cautioning might otherwise be appropriate, in some cases a prosecution may be necessary in order to protect the victim from the future attentions of the offender.
4. Whether the offender has paid any compensation or made any form of reparation. The police must not become involved in negotiating over the making of reparation or the provision of compensation. The consent of the victim to a caution is desirable but not essential.

Disparity in decision-making

There has been more research on this than on other issues. Most studies find disparity of one sort or another and this is not surprising since the decision-makers, as we will see, have so little regard for the criteria they are supposed to apply. Ditchfield (1976), for example, found evidence of disparity between different areas. He reported that 68 per cent of juveniles were being cautioned in Devon and Cornwall whilst only 24 per cent were cautioned in Kingston upon Hull. For adults a 0 per cent rate for Manchester can be contrasted with 20 per cent for Suffolk (1976:19). Evans and Ellis (1997) found that there were 35 percentage points difference between forces for the use of cautions in relation to males aged 14–17. Most forces could not explain why their rate was different to the average and 25 forces did not know how their figure compared with the national one. The official statistics for 2001 (Home Office (2002a)) reveal that things have not improved. Whilst Dyfed-Powys had a cautioning rate of 51 per cent and Surrey 50 per cent, in contrast the rates elsewhere were 17 per cent in South Yorkshire and 21 per cent in Merseyside. There is no doubt that there is geographical disparity in cautioning.

Understanding cautioning rates

In studies by both Steer (1970) and McClintock and Avison (1968) the policy of the force and especially of the chief constable were found to be important in understanding cautioning rates. In the Steer study of five police forces, four main reasons for giving cautions were discovered. These were that the complainant did not want a prosecution, that the crime was what is called a victimless crime, factors in the offender's circumstances and finally and

131

most disconcertingly – insufficient evidence! The latter was a factor in one in four cases in three of the five forces. Landau (1981) in a study of the Metropolitan Police found that the most important factors in deciding whether or not to caution were the offence and any criminal record of the person concerned. Age and race also seemed to be factors. For certain offences blacks seemed to be considered less suitable for a caution. A later study by Landau and Nathan (1983) also uncovered the use of illegitimate criteria such as race. Data is collected (Home Office (1999d)) to discover how different racial groups are treated in the criminal justice system and this indicated that in the 1998–1999 period the cautioning rate was slighly higher (14 per cent) for white people and Asians than for black people (12 per cent). This data is not proof of discrimination as it may well be that other factors are operative. In studies by Bennett (1979) and Farrington and Bennett (1981), the seriousness of the offence and age were the major factors. Some evidence of the middle class being favoured was also revealed. The attitude of the parents in terms of their willingness to exercise control of their children was also a variable. The latter was also revealed in a study by Fisher and Mawby (1982). As to variations between forces uncovered by Sebba (1967), these could not be explained by reference to such as population characteristics. Somerville (1969) found that the policies in use in different forces were important, whilst Rainton (1974) even found evidence of disparity existing within one force. A study by Mawby (1979) can be contrasted with much of the above evidence. After making allowances for factors such as age, sex and previous convictions of offenders he found that most of the differences in cautioning levels disappeared.

Controlling discretion

Evans and Wilkinson suggested the following as ways in which discretion could be better regulated:

> '... by defining tight criteria for judging the seriousness of offences in terms of monetary values or degrees of violence scale, by subjecting individual decisions to consistent gatekeeping or by centralising decision making. Perhaps for guidance to be effective in producing uniform approaches to cautioning in practice greater attention needs to be given to this level of detail and to the question of enforcement. Finally, our research suggests that another potential source of a lack of a uniform approach to juvenile cautioning concerns consultation arrangements. These vary both between and within forces. For a major plank in cautioning policy surprisingly little is know about the effect of different systems on outcomes or about how discretion is exercised by the various professional interests involved although our findings, like other recent research, suggests that difference professionals may have very different agendas.' (1990:174–175)

4.3 Aims and justifications of cautions

The remaining material to be considered on cautions is presented in terms of aims of and justifications for cautioning systems followed by an account of disadvantages and problems that occur with their use. Aims of cautioning schemes vary, schemes themselves vary and this is part reason for the fact that some of the arguments actually contradict each other. My intention is to allow you to become familiar with the arguments. Cautions provide a response to crime and there is still some condemnation. They are also a cheaper and quicker alternative to the overburdened courts and thus seem particularly suited to the less serious offence. The cost factor is important – as Alderson (1979) notes cautions are 'considerably cheaper than mounting prosecutions.' A point made generally, but particularly well, by Steer (1970) is that cautioning can be a humane means of disposal for the mentally ill, the young and the old. It also provides an option for offenders for whom a conviction would be disastrous no matter how trivial the offence. Finally, it seems suitable for victimless crimes and where the complainant does not wish to press the matter. In relation to juveniles, studies by Patchett and McClean (1965) and Tweedie (1982) provide grounds for optimism. For adults cautioning might have value as a warning particularly for first offenders. For persistent offenders, unless there is some system of referral, cautions may be able to do little more than save the courts the problem of having to deal with them. The use of a referral to some other agency (for example to a detoxification centre in the case of a drunk) has the potential for some form of beneficial outcome but this cannot be assumed. Systems of what is being called 'caution plus' have been introduced in recent years and this has involved such as reparation, counselling and therapy. Ditchfield (1976) thought that considerable numbers of minor adult offenders could be diverted by increased cautioning, particularly in the cities. He had in mind the value that this would have for reducing pressure on courts and penal institutions. Leon Brittan (1984) also found merit in adult cautioning and in his capacity as Home Secretary he pressed for its development. He pointed to the success of the Hammersmith scheme for dealing with drunks. Here three-quarters of the cases were cautioned and most of these offenders did not reoffend often enough to have to go to court. Often enough is three times in the previous month, which on the face of it appears to me to be quite frequent. However, it is clear that the aim of this scheme was to clear the drunks off the street and to avoid pressure on the courts and prisons. In such circumstances, the use of a caution is little more than a façade disguising a money-saving exercise. Others claims of the potential of cautioning are made by Alderson (1979) who suggests that it may lead to less recidivism and Stanley and Baginsky (1984) who claim that it works in terms of recidivism. Stanley and Baginsky base their claim on data which shows that relatively few offenders reoffend after a caution: only 20 per cent of first offenders for example.

4.4 Disadvantages of, and problems with, cautioning schemes

The existence of disparity in decision-making with consequent injustice for individuals was noted above. A further problem is that as Pratt (1986) notes there are few safeguards, the police having the power to confer the label of delinquency without recourse to the formalities and intricacies of the legal process. He further notes that a delinquency-processing apparatus has been developed which is not hidebound by the need for legal formalities and ritual, nor designed to assess the individual need and welfare of each child in the mode of the juvenile court. In fact, this machine does just the opposite: it can note, record and monitor the delinquencies of whole groups of the youth population.

McConville et al (1991) note some of the general problems of the system of cautioning and provide a concrete example from their research:

'For the police the caution is essentially a let off having few if any adverse consequences for the subject. From the police point of view the utility of the caution is in identifying individuals who will be suitable for prosecution should they re-offend, and as a means of warning a juvenile about undesirable conduct and associations. Thus, for the police there is no pressing need to apply rigorous standards of proof in caution cases, and the caution is seen as having utility not only for offenders but also for their associates or those on the periphery of crime. The consequence of this is that where cases are processed with a view to caution, exculpatory remarks short of a flat claim to innocence are routinely ignored as being irrelevant to the caution decision.

J33 had been named by another boy as having been involved with a group of children who had stolen a bicycle. In interview J33 described how the bicycle had been stolen by another boy who had then shown it to him. J33 did not admit having ridden it or even having touched it. J33 was cautioned for the offence of taking a vehicle without consent.' (1991:78)

The emphasis on legal rights as the cornerstone of juvenile justice (but within more relaxed and 'caring' surroundings than the adult court) has been replaced by emphases on efficiency, expediency, crime prevention (in the sense of general surveillance rather than individual treatment) and public policy. But, at the same time, a juridical flavour is maintained: the cautioning framework exists as an appendage to the juvenile court. A reminder of Steer's (1970) finding that insufficient evidence was a reason for police usage of cautions is valuable here. The possibilities of caution-copping (ie taking a caution in order to end the process even though the person does not believe that they have committed an offence) are also real. Ashworth makes it clear that people may feel pressure to admit an offence:

'If the suspect denies knowledge of a certain fact, he or she might wish to decline a caution and have the point adjudicated in court; and yet the disincentives to taking that course are so great (delay, risk of not being believed, risk of conviction) that acceptance of the caution is likely. The National Standards state that "a caution will not be appropriate where a person does not make a clear and reliable admission of the offence"; but there is the additional problem that the police may not fully understand the relevant law, such as the mental element required for the crime or the possible defences. In effect, whenever a person knows or believes that there will be a choice between accepting a caution and risking a prosecution, there is bound to be pressure to accept the caution. The disadvantages of this must be minimised by ensuring, as far as possible, that cautions are only offered if the conditions are strictly met. This would require far greater supervision within the police, or the provision of legal advice, or the transfer of the function to the Crown Prosecution Service.' (1998:158)

A related problem is that a person's record of cautions are revealed to the court prior to sentence. For those with a history of cautions the sentence is likely to be more severe. To suggest the introduction of further safeguards would to a great extent be futile. It can be noted that the Crown Prosecution Service do not provide a quality control function here, though it has been suggested that they should. Indeed, it has been suggested that they should take over the whole function from the police. As noted earlier, the Crown Prosecution Service wouild be the decision-makers in the new system of cautions with conditions. A large part of the attraction of cautioning is that it is relatively straightforward and cheap. Safeguards would offend against both these ideas. A police officer at the level of inspector or above makes cautioning decisions at the moment. Further expansion of cautioning schemes may lead to lower grade and cheaper personnel and thus potentially more dangers for citizens. Another problem is that it seems that cautioning systems produce what is called net-widening in that more people end up being processed by the criminal justice system. This is particularly a matter for regret given that one of the basic ideas of cautioning is to reduce official response to criminality. The case of *Hayter* v *L* (1998) The Times 3 February also deserves a mention. L had accepted a caution in relation to an assault on Hayter's son. A caution is meant to be an alternative to a charge and prosecution. Hayter was allowed to bring a private prosecution against L. This to me is unfair. The final cause for concern to mention in relation to cautioning is that, as Farrington and Bennett (1981) note, some scepticism has to be raised as to its effectiveness. Their finding was that police cautions were no more effective than court appearances in preventing re-arrest. They note generally that use of cautioning is really a matter of faith rather than being based on unequivocal evidence in its favour. The official statistics do however indicate that the reconviction rates are lower for those who are cautioned than for those who are charged. The objection to this is that the group who are charged are a higher risk group and indeed that is why they were charged. Ashworth (1998:157) cites a study by Mott (1983) in which the two groups (charged and cautioned) were matched and the cautioned group was still less likely to offend. As Ashworth tells us, it is sufficient for the purposes of supporting cautioning to be able to say that cautioning produces no worse results than going to court.

An interesting piece of research was carried out by Tweedie (1982). He made a comparison of two styles of cautioning. The first was an admonitory style in which a harsh warning was delivered by a uniformed policeman at a police station. The policeman was seated whilst the juvenile stood. The juvenile was told that this was his last chance and emphasis was placed upon the offence. In the second style, a plain-clothes policeman visited the juvenile's home. The aim was to provide advice and guidance in a relatively relaxed manner and to get involved both the juvenile and his parents. All participants would be seated and the emphasis would be upon positive suggestions as to the future behaviour of the offender. The re-offending rate over a two-year period was 9 per cent for the more formal system and 22 per cent for the other. For the juvenile it seemed that simple messages which carried a threat worked best, though the advice and guidance did seem to be beneficial as far as the parents were concerned. What is to be made of the following example, provided by Smith et al (1983), of a caution, given by a chief inspector to three 11–13-year-old boys who had admitted exposing themselves to a housewife?

'You have been very lucky. If I'd been that woman's husband I might have dealt with you myself whether or not I'd called the police. You were lucky – he simply called us. Every man has nothing but contempt for what you've done and if you go on doing it someone will give you a damn good hiding one day. People who molest ladies and children have to be kept separately in prisons. Do you know why? Because all the other prisoners might do them a very serious injury if they were allowed to mix. Next time you fancy doing this why don't you do it to your sisters ... your 22-year-old sister (looking through the papers), your 18-year-old sister, your 17-year-old sister. Then you see what your fathers and brothers think of you. Or do it to your mum, eh? Why not do it to your mother's? It's not funny.' (1983:207)

Do we view this as a particularly fine example of the admonitory style or worry about the merits of mid-ranking police officers?

4.5 Diversion

In terms of the criminal justice system the notion of diversion is difficult to deal with because of the numerous and varied schemes worldwide to which the term has been applied. An avoidance of, or the provision of an alternative to, some stage or feature of the criminal justice system is some guidance. McKittrick and Eysenck (1984) suggested the halting or suspending of proceedings against an accused person in favour of processing through a non-criminal disposition as a convenient definition.

Diversion is fashionable, particularly in the United States. Brantingham and Blomberg (1979) note for example the growth of such schemes in the United States after the 1967 President's Commission critique of the official court system and the recommendation of informal community-based alternatives. In the United Kingdom, Ashworth's address to the Howard League for Penal Reform in 1984 (see Ashworth (1984)) and the Report of the Stewart Commission for Scotland (1983) all indicated interest in the possibilities. The developments since then have not matched the initial enthusiasm. The Stewart Commission recommended the use of both traditional methods, such as cautions, and more radical methods. Ashworth (1984) similarly saw advantages in diversion. He suggested that minor property offences might be best dealt with on a pro-rata financial basis (£10 value of property would lead to a £10 financial penalty) plus any compensation deemed necessary for the victim. Marshall (1985), who wishes to see the courts only dealing with matters that are absolutely essential, indicates the scope for diversion as he sees it:

> 'As far as absolute numbers are concerned, the greatest impact on the work load of the courts would be obtained by reducing the vast number of summary motoring offences presently prosecuted ... representing as they do exactly half of all the business of magistrates' courts. Fixed penalties and administrative processing offer cheaper and more efficient methods for dealing with this huge caseload. Extension of such methods to some of the indictable motoring offences should also be investigated, as these constitute the next largest category, 17 per cent of the overall workload of magistrates' courts. Removing all offences that are identified and often processed by agencies (public or private) other than the police would affect a further 13 per cent of the courts' business. Even the remaining 20 per cent could be reduced in less dramatic ways by removal of many vagrancy offences, drunkenness and minor property offences. Where appropriate reparation can be secured without prosecution.' (1985: 180)

Similarly, Dodge (1979) as part of a general argument for reduced use of, and thus diversion from, custody indicates the possibilities of non-custodial sentences. In the following quotation he clearly has in mind reparation and mediation. 'While the offender works to repay his victim, he receives on-the-job training, counselling, or education in life skills that so many offenders do not at present receive. At the same time, the victim may keep in touch with the rehabilitation of his offender, and in some cases ... actually involve themselves in the offender's rehabilitation' (1979:164).

The various stages at which diversion is possible will be examined next. One possibility would be to suggest that certain types of behaviour could be decriminalised by the legislature. Another approach is to have some matters dealt with by a body other than the police. For example, in Saskatchewan they have peace officers to deal with domestic disturbances. Alternatives to the court process, of which cautioning is an example, is another possibility. This could be by the use of another body to hold a hearing. An example is the Colombus Night Prosecutor's Office. This is an informal hearing used as an alternative to arrest in cases such as wife-battering. It is intended to, and was found to, diffuse and calm situations and to prevent formal steps being taken. It was also found to be useful as a referral system. The Stewart Committee recommended, in relation to Scotland, that the Procurator Fiscal could fix a penalty instead of a court hearing. Ashworth (1984) developed similar ideas in relation to England and Wales. Other possibilities include the use of referral and screening systems. A scheme in Scotland which made use of reporters (officials who decide if a hearing is necessary) produced a 60 per cent reduction in hearings between 1969 and 1975. With such schemes, numerous variations are possible involving such as mediation, counselling, restitution and various programmes of self-development. Schemes have been designed to take place within the family, the school, the community and also with the victim. In the United States, as well as providing an alternative to the courts, the Youth Service Bureau provide a co-ordinating function for these activities. For example, a scheme in British Columbia involved short-term counselling by such as probation officers or special programmes. Examples of the latter are outward-bound courses, vocational and educational schemes, restitution and victim service. The New York City Employment Project developed with the support of the Vera Institute was an attempt to remedy vocational disadvantage. Whilst it failed in this respect its clients were less likely to reoffend than court-processed offenders.

Dingwall and Harding (1998) in a wide-ranging analysis of diversion examined the practices of regulatory agencies such as the National Rivers Authority and also bodies such as Customs and Excise, the Inland Revenue and the Benefits Agency. They found that their motivation could well be to do with matters such as future compliance or the recovery of money. Some of the differences are seen in the following extract:

'It may even be asked in what way the phenomenon discussed in this chapter is in any sense a kind of diversion and how relevant criminal law and criminal proceedings may be considered to be in such a context. There is a striking preference for "settlement", in the interests of longer-term compliance and both recovering loss and preventing future damage. This is manifest in the enforcement strategies of the main revenue departments and in the traditional conciliatory style of enforcement in the context of health and safety and environmental regulation. In the area of welfare fraud the "non-prosecution interview" technique has been adopted with enthusiasm in recent years; and despite the confrontational approach espoused by the NRA, prosecution is still used only in a minority of cases to deal with water pollution. A range of cultural and pragmatic considerations render it unlikely that criminal proceedings will emerge as much more of a significant option for these types of enforcement agency.' (1998:84)

It is difficult to provide an effective overview on the subject of diversion as aims, attitudes, assumptions and schemes vary so much. Diversion schemes might offer quicker and cheaper methods of disposal in some cases, they may have beneficial effects on crime rates, they might rehabilitate, they might reduce or avoid stigma and more certainly it is difficult for them to be the worst option if the alternative is a custodial sentence. Where such claims are made however they need to be vindicated if they are to be taken seriously. Morris (1978) makes the point that many current practices are unproven acts of faith. Stanley and Baginsky (1984) suggested that diversionary programmes have not been an unqualified success. Evaluation research has not always demonstrated the effectiveness of such programmes. Furthermore, any success they have is perhaps because they are dealing with low-risk people, or of more concern, no-risk people. That is people who had not offended and would not offend and who have thus engaged in what is called diversion-copping. In the view of Brantingham and Blomberg (1979), the tide of diversion programmes continues to expand despite both the absence of empirical justification and the critical speculation that they have attracted. That is, that no desirable effect on crime rates has been demonstrated and that the schemes may even accelerate the development of offenders' personal problems. Sarri (1979) found that Australian juvenile aid panels did not succeed in screening minor juveniles offenders out of the courts and the scheme did not produce a desirable effect on crime rates. Pasternoster (1979) investigated the issue of whether or not diversion schemes would produce less feeling of having been stigmatised than custodial measures. From the self-perception of juveniles on diversion schemes it was clear that they felt no less stigmatised than those juveniles that had been incarcerated. Other problems, other than the effectiveness of such schemes, have also been identified. The idea of treatment, rehabilitation and reform, which is central to some diversion schemes, which even if they were successful in such respects would still have to face the challenge of being unpalatable social engineering. Such intervention is doubly worrying given the clear net-widening effects of diversion schemes. Also, again as with cautioning schemes, diversion schemes have attracted criticism because of the lack of safeguards for the individual in what at times are secret systems of control. In some cases people have to admit guilt, without a hearing, as a precursor to starting a diversion scheme. Apart from any intrinsic problems with this there is certainly a real difficulty when individuals do not fit in with the diversion scheme. What happens next is a dilemma several schemes have had to face.

Diversion schemes and cautioning in particular are now a major feature of the criminal justice system. They have considerable impact as a filtering mechanism, with regard to later stages of the system. Their development has been greatly assisted by pragmatism because of the savings in time and money that they offer. Limiting intervention, both as a goal in itself and particularly where outcomes are largely negative, whilst at the same time recognising the possibility of worthwhile intervention, are factors that need to be applied in the consideration of these innovations. The ideas explored in this section offer possibilities as regards both of them. Whilst clearly there are problems with such schemes, they offer hope and it would seem worthwhile to invest resources in exploring and developing their potential. A net increase in resources need not be involved as funding could be made available by some reductions in the use of the expensive and ineffective police forces and the prison system. It can be noted that interest in, and use of, the ideas of restorative justice, on which see below, has fostered further interest in diversion.

4.6 The prosecution system

Most prosecutions are the responsibility of the Crown Prosecution Service, which was introduced in 1996 by means of the Prosecution of Offences Act 1985. Other bodies still engage in prosecutions within particular spheres, and private prosecutions are still possible. The system since 1995 has been subject to change and review on a number of occasions, most notably by, and as a result of, the Glidewell Report into the Crown Prosecution Service in 1998. It is this report and some statistics in relation to prosecution decisions that will be examined before other material and issues are explored.

The Glidewell Report into the Crown Prosecution Service (1998)

This report into the Crown Prosecution Service (Home Office (1998b)) had been commissioned because of perceived problems with the discontinuance rate, the failure rate at trials the use of charge reduction and an overly bureaucratic and centralised system. The report itself found the Crown Prosecution Service to be too centralised and too bureaucratic. Major reorganisation of the prosecution system was suggested. Before the new structure is considered some of the other concerns need to be explored. There was a desire to clarify the aims of the Crown Prosecution Service and its proper relationship with other agencies of the criminal justice system, these being the courts and the police. What was required was for these bodies to work together more effectively. Thus, the setting up of criminal justice units for co-ordinating the activities of agencies with similar prosecution-related concerns in particular localities was suggested. It was thought that this could be a police unit with some Crown Prosecution Service staff permanently based within it or, their much preferred option, a Crown Prosecution Service unit with some police officers permanently working within it. They supported the idea of fast-tracking cases and thought that this work could be a task for the legally non-qualified but experienced Crown Prosecution Service personnel who have limited rights of audience from April 2000. As to recommendations on structure, decentralisation was the aim with power going to a system of local prosecutors in 42 local areas, each with its own chief Crown prosecutor. Crown Prosecution Service lawyers would be allowed to concentrate more on court work in the future rather than paper work. Also suggested were integrated teams, which would include the police, to be used to deal with cases in a more streamlined system. Whilst previous reform of the Crown Prosecution Service had been intended to produce efficiency this has not happened in practice. The changes introduced in 1993 are now seen as having been a mistake. These had produced a system of 98 local branches, 13 area offices and the London Headquarters. Previously there had been 38 area offices. The process of restructuring commenced and the new system for the area organisation is in force. Details of the reforms in relation to joint working with the police are provided below.

A major review of the criminal courts in England and Wales was carried out by Auld LJ in 2001: Auld LJ (2001). Auld suggested changes in the procedures for preparation for trial, including a shift in the respective roles of the police and the prosecuting authorities so that in the majority of cases the Crown Prosecution Service, not the police, would decide whether and what to charge, and should have more responsibility for discharging the prosecution's duties of disclosure. The Criminal Justice Act 2003 provides for much greater involvement of the Crown Prosecution Service in determining whether proceedings should be instituted and if so on which charge. Most of the present police role will be taken over. In certain circumstances the police will have to charge as it is envisaged that the defendant would be released on bail whilst they await the decision of the Crown Prosecution Service. Thus, in a case where detention seems to be required the police will charge as part of the process through which the defendant is brought before the court. The police role in relation to charges also remains in other circumstances, including such as minor and routine offences.

The Crown Prosecution Service and the police have been involved in pilots to work together more closely and to improve efficiency. Gloucestershire has been involved in these experiments which followed the recommendations contained within the Glidewell Report. In Gloucestershire this originally led to the setting up of a Glidewell unit in June 2002. The unit involved certain staff from the Crown Prosecution Service working alongside police staff to make pre and post court file preparation easier and more cost effective. The process was improved further in September 2003, with between six and eight members of Crown Prosecution Service staff – some caseworkers and some lawyers – being moved into the Constabulary's Criminal Justice Department. It will mean the end of the current dual file system, where every case has two files which are exact replicas, but with one held by the police and one held by the Crown Prosecution Service in separate offices. The new system will mean duplication and photocopying costs are reduced, file transport between the police, Crown Prosecution Service and courts is reduced and communication flows are improved. Whilst this seems like an obvious improvement to make, it is really about the streamlining of processes. The central aim still needs to be to achieve a system in which Crown Prosecution staff and the police are truly working together. This is being worked towards and in Sheffield and elsewhere there are examples of the police and prosecutors being based in the same building.

Statistics on prosecution

The *Criminal Statistics 2002* (Home Office (2002a)) reveal that 1.84 million cases were prosecuted in the year, which is a very large workload. About 42 per cent of these cases are summary motoring offences and another 31 per cent are also summary cases. Details of the work of the Crown Prosecution Service in magistrates' courts and the Crown Court are provided in Tables 16 and 17: Home Office (2002a). The variations by offence in Table 17 are marked.

Table 16

The Role of the Crown Prosecution Service in Magistrates' Courts

	1996	2001
percentage discontinued	12	13
percentage written off	8	6
percentage committed for trial	8	7
percentage bound over	2	2
percentage heard in court	71	72
Outcome where a hearing		
percentage where a guilty plea	81	82
percentage proof in absence	11	12
percentage convicted after a trial	6	4
percentage dismissed	2	2

(Source: Criminal Statistics, England and Wales, 2001)

Discontinued proceedings include cases where witnesses fail to appear, refuse to give evidence or change their story, or evidence is excluded because of material irregularity in its collection, and where defendants wait until the day of the hearing to produce driving documents showing that no offence has been committed. They also include cases discontinued on public interest grounds. The Crown Prosecution Service can proceed only where sufficient evidence exists to provide a realistic prospect of conviction. The Crown Prosecution Service also writes off from its record of current cases a number of proceedings where it is not possible to proceed directly. The most common reason is that the defendant cannot be found.

Table 17

Crown Court Cases by Offence Type, Guilty Plea and Outcome

	Total tried (thousands)	percentage pleading guilty	percentage pleading not guilty who were convicted
Indictable offences			
Violence	18.7	49	30
Sexual offences	4.9	32	34
Burglary	8.1	75	34
Motoring	1.3	71	55
All indictable offences	72.8	60	34
Summary offences	2.6	93	70
Total	75.5	62	34

(Source: Criminal Statistics, England and Wales, 2001)

Further statistical data is provided from the *Crown Prosecution Service Annual Report 2002–03*: Crown Prosecution Service (2003). This report as with much of the material produced by the Crown Prosecution Service is an attempt to defend the Service by maximising the positive and minimising the negative. As such it needs to be considered in the context of other material which is available in relation to the Crown Prosecution Service. This is commonly produced by the news media and as only bad news is newsworthy that is equally one-sided. The report tells us that in 2002 they received 77,000 more cases from the police than in the previous year – a total of 1.44 million. They also prosecuted an extra 65,000 cases – 1.08 million in the magistrates' courts and 80,000 cases in the Crown Court. In the magistrates' courts the conviction rate was 95 per cent but this would have been very largely a by-product of guilty pleas. Where the matter was contested they had a success rate of 70 per cent. This is a higher rate than in the Crown Court where only 62 per cent of those who pleaded not guilty were convicted. The budget was £453 million and 7,046 people were employed.

The Crown Prosecution Service present the following view (Crown Prosecution Service (2003)) as to their role.

'We are completely independent of the police although we work closely with them at all times.
1. We prosecute people in England and Wales who have been charged by the police with a criminal offence.
2. We advise the police on possible prosecutions.
3. We review prosecutions started by the police to ensure the right defendants are prosecuted on the right charges before the appropriate court.
4. We prepare cases for court.
5. We prosecute cases at magistrates' courts and instruct counsel to prosecute cases in the Crown Court and higher courts. In some cases our own lawyers appear in the Crown Court and other higher courts.
6. We work with others to improve the effectiveness and efficiency of the criminal justice system, for example through the Trials Issues Group.
7. The Crown Prosecution Service also provides legal and administrative support services to deliver: guidance to prosecutors and police on application of the Code for Crown Prosecutors, updated information about changes to statute and case law, and prosecuting procedure, full administrative support, including all aspects of personnel, finance and performance management and specialist legal, administrative and management training for staff.'

4.7 The reform process

The Prosecution of Offences Act 1985 provided for a new system of prosecution which was introduced in 1986. A brief account of the deficiencies of the previous system and the hopes for the new system is provided as background material. In the old system many prosecutions were handled by individual police forces, either by the use of police officers or by appointing lawyers to act on their behalf. Justice (1970), in the first of a number of investigations into the prosecution process, found a variety of defects in this system. In particular they thought that the role of the police should be limited to investigating crime, whilst prosecution considerations should be transferred to an independent body. The police it was thought were likely to be result-orientated and may be over-zealous in proceeding with a prosecution. The problem with this would be that weak cases might be proceeded with, producing both economic and human costs. As to the latter, quite simply being put on trial is a painful business and safeguards are desirable. An independent body could hope to be fair to all parties and could also produce consistency on what would have to be, at times, policy decisions. The chances of securing a conviction could never be the only consideration. Factors such as the effect on the defendant (where they are old or seriously ill), where the sentence is likely to be nominal, where the offence happened a long time ago and prohibitively high costs of a prosecution are amongst those that might be considered.

The Royal Commission on Criminal Procedure (1981)

The Royal Commission suggested an end to police advocacy and the introduction of local prosecution services. Such a system, it was hoped, would meet their criteria for a prosecution system. This contained notions of fairness (this included an absence of arbitrary decisions being made and that weak cases would not be prosecuted), accountability and efficiency. The Commission indicated the problems that existed in relation to efficiency when it pointed to delays in preparing cases for trial with consequent court adjournments, inadequately prepared cases leading to their early collapse, and the employment of professionals upon tasks for which they are not trained. These were just a few examples of how resources can be and, as we know from our evidence, are wasted in the prosecution system. And this inefficient use of resources can also provide equally undesirable consequences: injustice to the accused, inconvenience to witnesses and frustration to those employed in the system.

The 1982 White Paper

The government response was firstly to seek views and to this end a Consultative Memorandum was issued. In 1982 a working party was established and 1983 saw the publication of a White Paper entitled *An Independent Prosecution Service for England and Wales*: Home Office (1983). The White Paper included the report of the 1982 working party as an annex. The working party suggested, an independent national prosecution service for which they prescribed the following objectives. Such a prosecution service has to be, and be seen to be, independent of the police. Decisions on prosecution must not be susceptible to improper influence, either in individual cases or in categories of cases. The structure of the service should be such as to promote the greater consistency of policy across the country that the Royal Commission saw as important if there is to be public confidence in the fairness of prosecution arrangements. At the same time, however, the structure should provide some measure of flexibility to take appropriate account of relevant variations in local circumstances. It should also make for a higher quality of decision-making and case preparation; to the fullest extent possible standards in these two respects should be uniform across the country. The effects should be that cases which are unlikely to succeed should be weeded out at an early stage. Proceedings which are pursued should be conducted as vigorously and effectively as fairness and the merits of the case allow. In its handling of cases the service must be efficient and cost-effective. Arrangements must also be devised to secure the necessary accountability for the efficiency, effectiveness and financial probity of the service.

The White Paper accepted the arguments in favour of an independent national prosecution service and the Prosecution of Offences Act 1985 followed this model. The conclusion to the White Paper stated that the government was satisfied that such a system would promote consistency, efficiency and accountability. Further, that the proposals are designed to produce a workable, effective and fair system which consumes the minimum of public resources while meeting the criticisms to which the present arrangements give rise. The essence of the above documents is that police involvement and local systems of prosecution did not lead to consistency of policy and action being avoided in weak cases. The hope was that a national system independent of the police could achieve these and other goals.

The Prosecution of Offences Act 1985

This Act established a Crown Prosecution Service for England and Wales with the Director of Public Prosecutions as its head. The Director of Public Prosecutions was to be both appointed by and supervised by the Attorney-General. The functions of the Director of Public Prosecutions are stated in s3, of which the following is an overview. Criminal proceedings instituted on behalf of a police force are to be taken over (subject to exceptions) and other proceedings may also be taken over for reason for example of their importance or difficulty. This section notes that other statutes call for his appearance for the prosecution. A final function is to provide advice as thought appropriate to police forces on all matters relating to criminal offences. Section 4 provides for the introduction of Crown prosecutors who have the powers of the Director of Public Prosecutions in relation to the institution and conduct of proceedings but subject to his instructions. Section 5 allows for the use of other lawyers to assist with this work. The final section that needs to be noted is s6, which provided for the continuation of prosecutions being brought by private individuals and institutions.

Prosecutions by private individuals and institutions

In terms of the impact of the 1985 Act it is prosecutions by private individuals and institutions that will be commented upon first. Lidstone, Hogg and Sutcliffe in their research for the Royal Commission noted that 'the ten leading types of non-police prosecutor were (in descending order of their use of the courts): the Post Office (including television licence cases), the British Transport Police, the Department of the Environment (vehicle excise licences), the local authorities, retail stores, the DHSS, London Transport, Customs and Excise, private individuals, and the Regional Transport Commissioners' (1980: 179). As to private prosecutions by individuals these are most likely to be cases in which wives prosecute husbands for common assault and where shops prosecute for shop-lifting. The latter is clearly most likely to occur in those areas where as a matter of policy prosecutions are left to the shops. The role of private prosecutions had been considered prior to the 1985 Act, and the Royal Commission (1981) noted problems with such a system and called for further safeguards to be introduced if prosecutions by individuals were not to be abolished. One such problem is vexatious litigants who may for example commence proceedings whilst having the intention of later discontinuing it. As regards prosecutions by agencies, such a system produces inconsistency in prosecution policy both within and between agencies. Some agencies for example will only use prosecution as a last resort. Dickens said of local authorities that they:

> '... appear to regard their statutory duties as imposing upon them an obligation to act to achieve prescribed results, and not simply an obligation to enforce the strict provisions of the law per se.' (1970:631)

Samuels notes a similar attitude on the part of the Health and Safety Executive and the Inland Revenue, as well as recording that some agencies, such as the DHSS, are quick to prosecute. He also makes the major point that 'The diversity of practice does raise important questions of public interest and social justice. For example, tax frauds are not prosecuted, thefts from shops are' (1986:36–37). In work by Sanders (1985) such material is analysed along the lines that there is a class bias in prosecutions. Samuels (1986) suggests the limitation of such prosecutions and consequently the limitation of injustice caused by inconsistencies. This could be achieved, for example, by the Crown Prosecution Service taking on such work. Equally, by removing the excise licence for motor vehicles and the licence for televisions, 40 per cent of non-police prosecutions could be removed at a stroke. Samuels suggests a further tax on fuel to cope with the former and I would suggest limited advertising on the BBC to cope with the latter. Such strategies are designed to limit problems and to provide for consistency. In some fields Crown prosecutors may well end up agreeing that prosecution should be used sparingly. The latter points assume of course that the new Crown Prosecution Service is working and can fulfil the hopes that existed in relation to it. As we will see, such assumptions are highly problematic at the end of the day. Comparisons will be made with the old system which Timmons (1986), a chief prosecuting solicitor, described as producing tolerably acceptable results.

4.8 The Code for Crown Prosecutors (2000)

A full account of the tests to be used in making decisions as to prosecution is presented. These are from the new Code as produced in 2000.

'5. The Evidential Test
5.1 Crown Prosecutors must be satisfied that there is enough evidence to provide a realistic prospect of conviction; against each defendant on each charge. They must consider what the defence case may be, and how that is likely to affect the prosecution case.
5.2 A realistic prospect of conviction is an objective test. It means that a jury or bench of magistrates, properly directed in accordance with the law, is more likely than not to convict the defendant of the charge alleged. This is a separate test from the one that the criminal courts themselves must apply. A jury or magistrates' court should only convict if satisfied so that it is sure of a defendant's guilt.
5.3 When deciding whether there is enough evidence to prosecute, Crown Prosecutors must

consider whether the evidence can be used and is reliable. There will be many cases in which the evidence does not give any cause for concern. But there will also be cases in which the evidence may not be as strong as it first appears. Crown Prosecutors must ask themselves the following questions:

Can the evidence be used in court?

1. Is it likely that the evidence will be excluded by the court? There are certain legal rules which might mean that evidence which seems relevant cannot be given at a trial. For example, is it likely that the evidence will be excluded because of the way in which it was gathered or because of the rule against using hearsay as evidence? If so, is there enough other evidence for a realistic prospect of conviction?

Is the evidence reliable?

2. Is there evidence which might support or detract from the reliability of a confession? Is the reliability affected by factors such as the defendant's age, intelligence or level of understanding?

3. What explanation has the defendant given? Is a court likely to find it credible in the light of the evidence as a whole? Does it support an innocent explanation?

4. If the identity of the defendant is likely to be questioned, is the evidence about this strong enough?

5. Is the witness's background likely to weaken the prosecution case? For example, does the witness have any motive that may affect his or her attitude to the case, or a relevant previous conviction?

6. Are there concerns over the accuracy or credibility of a witness? Are these concerns based on evidence or simply information with nothing to support it? Is there further evidence which the police should be asked to seek out which may support or detract from the account of the witness?

5.4 Crown Prosecutors should not ignore evidence because they are not sure that it can be used or is reliable. But they should look closely at it when deciding if there is a realistic prospect of conviction.

6. The Public Interest Test

6.1 In 1951, Lord Shawcross, who was the then Attorney General, made the classic statement on public interest, which has been supported by Attorneys General ever since: "It has never been the rule in this country and I hope it never will be that suspected criminal offences must automatically be the subject of prosecution." (House of Commons Debates, volume 483, column 681, 29 January 1951.)

6.2 The public interest must be considered in each case where there is enough evidence to provide a realistic prospect of conviction. A prosecution will usually take place unless there are public interest factors tending against prosecution which clearly outweigh those tending in favour. Although there may be public interest factors against prosecution in a particular case, often the prosecution should go ahead and those factors should be put to the court for consideration when sentence is being passed.

6.3 Crown Prosecutors must balance factors for and against prosecution carefully and fairly. Public interest factors that can affect the decision to prosecute usually depend on the seriousness of the offence or the circumstances of the suspect. Some factors may increase the need to prosecute but others may suggest that another course of action would be better.

The following lists of some common public interest factors, both for and against prosecution, are not exhaustive. The factors that apply will depend on the facts in each case.

Some common public interest factors in favour of prosecution

6.4 The more serious the offence, the more likely it is that a prosecution will be needed in the public interest. A prosecution is likely to be needed if:

1. a conviction is likely to result in a significant sentence;

2. a weapon was used or violence was threatened during the commission of the offence;

3. the offence was committed against a person serving the public (for example, a police or prison officer, or a nurse);

4. if the identity of the defendant is likely to be questioned, is the evidence about this strong enough?

5. the defendant was in a position of authority or trust;

6. there is evidence that the offence was premeditated;

7. there is evidence that the offence was carried out by a group;

8. the victim of the offence was vulnerable, has been put in considerable fear, or suffered personal attack, damage or disturbance;

9. the offence was motivated by any form of discrimination against the victim's ethnic or national origin, sex, religious beliefs, political views or sexual orientation, or the suspect demonstrated hostility towards the victim based on any of those characteristics;

10. there is a marked difference between the actual or mental ages of the defendant and the victim, or if there is any element of corruption;

11. the defendant's previous convictions or cautions are relevant to the present offence;

12. the defendant is alleged to have committed the offence whilst under an order of the court;

13. there are grounds for believing that the offence is likely to be continued or repeated, for example, by a history of recurring conduct;

14. the offence, although not serious in itself, is widespread in the area where it was committed.

Some common public interest factors against prosecution

6.5 A prosecution is less likely to be needed if:

1. the court is likely to impose a nominal penalty;

2. the defendant has already been made the subject of a sentence and any further conviction would be unlikely to result in the imposition of an additional sentence or order, unless the nature of the particular offence requires a prosecution;

3. the offence was committed as a result of a genuine mistake or misunderstanding (these factors must be balanced against the seriousness of the offence);

4. the loss or harm can be described as minor and was the result of a single incident, particularly if it was caused by a misjudgment;

5. there has been a long delay between the offence taking place and the date of the trial, unless: the offence is serious; the delay has been caused in part by the defendant; the offence has only recently come to light; or the complexity of the offence has meant that there has been a long investigation;

6. a prosecution is likely to have a bad effect on the victim's physical or mental health, always bearing in mind the seriousness of the offence;

7. the defendant is elderly or is, or was at the time of the offence, suffering from significant mental or physical ill health, unless the offence is serious or there is a real possibility that it may be repeated. The Crown Prosecution Service, where necessary, applies Home Office guidelines about how to deal with mentally disordered offenders. Crown Prosecutors must balance the desirability of diverting a defendant who is suffering from significant mental or physical ill health with the need to safeguard the general public;

8. the defendant has put right the loss or harm that was caused (but defendants must not avoid prosecution solely because they pay compensation); or

9. details may be made public that could harm sources of information, international relations or national security.

6.6 Deciding on the public interest is not simply a matter of adding up the number of factors on each side. Crown Prosecutors must decide how important each factor is in the circumstances of each case and go on to make an overall assessment.

The relationship between the victim and the public interest

6.7 The Crown Prosecution Service prosecutes cases on behalf of the public at large and not just in the interests of any particular individual. However, when considering the public interest test Crown Prosecutors should always take into account the consequences for the victim of the decision whether or not to prosecute, and any views expressed by the victim or the victim's family.

6.8 It is important that a victim is told about a decision which makes a significant difference to the case in which he or she is involved. Crown Prosecutors should ensure that they follow any agreed procedures.

Youths

6.9 Crown Prosecutors must consider the interests of a youth when deciding whether it is in the public interest to prosecute. However Crown Prosecutors should not avoid prosecuting simply because of the defendant's age. The seriousness of the offence or the youth's past behaviour is very important.

6.10 Cases involving youths are usually only referred to the Crown Prosecution Service for prosecution if the youth has already received a reprimand and final warning, unless the offence is so serious that neither of these were appropriate. Reprimands and final warnings are intended to prevent re-offending and the fact that a further offence has occurred indicates that attempts to divert the youth from the court system have not been effective. So the public interest will usually require a prosecution in such cases, unless there are clear public interest factors against prosecution.

Police Cautions

6.11 These are only for adults. The police make the decision to caution an offender in accordance with Home Office guidelines.

6.12 When deciding whether a case should be prosecuted in the courts, Crown Prosecutors should consider the alternatives to prosecution. This will include a police caution. Again the Home Office guidelines should be applied. Where it is felt that a caution is appropriate, Crown Prosecutors must inform the police so that they can caution the suspect. If the caution is not administered because the suspect refuses to accept it or the police do not wish to offer it, then the Crown Prosecutor may review the case again.'

4.9 The problems of the Crown Prosecution Service

In looking at the problems of the Crown Prosecution Service the tendency will be to overstate them. This is because it is the problems that have been publicised. Allan Green, a former Director of Public Prosecutions, made the point, in an interview with Morton (1989), that bad news meant good copy and the net result was a chorus of criticism. What is very clear is that there have been staff shortages in the Crown Prosecution Service. The press have in recent years found new targets for bad publicity and the knocking press has diminished; the problems are still there. Staff shortages were a result of poor pay and a poor image. Ironically, the shortages were tackled by the use of agency lawyers as a partial solution. The cost was high in monetary terms and the use of temporary staff mitigates against the development of a coherent organisation. Overwork also results, a factor made worse by their inexperience within the ranks of Crown prosecutors. Suggestions have also been made that recruits joined the service in order to gain experience and then to use this as a stepping stone to other employment. Similarly, that local firms would poach the most promising and they would end up doing defence work. These problems led to lost files, cases being thrown out of court because they have not been prepared properly and delays. The following incidents were reported by Kavanagh:

'In Highbury Corner Magistrates' Court a case had been listed for trial on 30 June. On that date it was adjourned at the prosecution's request. At the next appearance, on 18 August, the bench granted a defence application for an adjournment but said that the trial must go ahead on 15 October. The Crown Prosecution Service agent appeared in court on the trial date five minutes before the court was due to begin saying that she had been given the file only five minutes earlier and she felt "too inexperienced" to handle the case. The bench adjourned for one hour for the prosecution to read the file but eventually threw the case out and ordered costs out of central funds. Defence costs alone were estimated at £1,200. At Clerkenwell Magistrates' Court a case in which there had been four previous appearances was thrown out when the Crown Prosecution Service, on the day set for committal, lost all the papers.' (1986:8)

Other newspaper reports centred on the cases in which the Crown Prosecutors have declined to prosecute. The *Sunday Times* provided some typical examples of the complaints:

'In Streatham, south London, a constable was hit over the head with a crowbar. He was furious when the Crown Prosecution Service offered no evidence at his attacker's trial. In a memorandum, an inspector wrote: "This type of incident does nothing for the morale of officers who are at the butt end. Officers feel there is no meaning to the commissioner's promise that their role should be enhanced and supported by all."

Carol and Robert Awcock were outraged when the Crown Prosecution Service brought only charges of driving with excess alcohol against a motorist who knocked down and killed their son. The couple from Crowborough, Sussex, then spent two years and £7,000 on a private prosecution, which culminated in September when the driver was jailed for two years for causing death by reckless driving. As a result of this case the Attorney General has ordered the Crown Prosecution Service to review policy on the prosecution of drunken drivers.' (1988: A12)

O'Reilly and Stevens (2002) examined the problems that prosecution lawyers have in court, with inadequately prepared files which they have not had sufficient time or even opportunity to get to grips with before they appear. Also, that some of the staff who prepare the files can lack the ability to speak English competently and bring little in the way of legal skills to the task. Some view such problems as being caused by a lack of money, whilst others suggest that staff at all levels lack commitment. They also investigated:

'The late delivery of files to frontline lawyers means mistakes are made. Last week Thames branch caseworkers complained about files being handed to them by their lawyers only the day before they were due to go to court. One caseworker sighed after reassembling a file that he described as a "dog's dinner". Another admitted that Crown Prosecution Service staff were "flying by the seat of their pants" in turning round cases for court. One said: "If I have got time

I try to do the job properly even though I cut corners. I seem to scrape through just enough to get everything at least looked at". Errors or omissions in the paperwork can mean alleged criminals go free without having to face trial. Recent failed CPS cases nationally have included:

A man accused of car-jacking a £75,000 Mercedes whose trial collapsed after lawyers admitted they had failed to obtain adequate evidence showing his mobile phone had been left in the car.

Three youths accused of mugging two young children were released after the Crown Prosecution Service repeatedly failed to produce available closed-circuit television evidence of the alleged attack.

In the south London borough, of Camberwell this month, a judge was forced to adjourn a trial for assault amid complaints about missing Crown Prosecution Service memos and evidence not passed on to the defence. The judge claimed it was "an unhappy state of affairs, and sadly all too common".

Four months ago, the Thames branch – which handles more than 8,000 cases a year – was criticised for blunders that meant cases had to be cancelled at the committal stage. A report by the Crown Prosecution Service inspectorate concluded: "We were told this was as a result of a, combination of the quality and timeliness of committal files received from the police together with the lack of time available to prosecutors and caseworkers to prepare the necessary papers."' (2002:12)

The police view of the Crown Prosecution Service

A repeated police complaint is that the Crown Prosecution Service fails to prosecute unless it has a cast-iron case. Tendler (1989) noted the case of burglary where a suspect's fingerprints were found at the scene of a burglary and the case was dropped because the Prosecution Service wanted more evidence. This sounds outrageous until you realise that at a jury trial fingerprint evidence may be distrusted. Tendler was reporting the proceedings of the Police Federation during which one speaker labeled the Crown Prosecution Service a 'Criminals Protection Society'. Complaints raised were that a worryingly high number of cases were being dropped in the interests of economics and to keep the Crown Prosecution Service success rate up. There was also a feeling that the service were taking upon themselves the tasks of judge and jury and that all this was having a poor effect on police morale.

The Crown Prosecution Service are also criticised for downgrading charges, but such criticism assumes that the earlier police decision as to the charge was appropriate. However, it can be noted that the police themselves may well have taken the lower charge option because they are aware that it will be more likely to stick. So there are pressures and desires to downgrade at various stages and yet still we have discontinuance and acquittals at high levels.

Acquittals

Whilst there were complaints about a failure to prosecute, at the same time a major problem of the present system of prosecution has been acquittals. Rates of acquittal have risen to record levels. In England and Wales in 2000, 68 per cent of those who pleaded not guilty at Crown Court were acquitted by either the judge or the jury. In Liverpool, 79 per cent of those pleading not guilty were acquitted. One point to note though is that in using a 51 per cent rule as to whether to prosecute then anything in the region of half the cases failing should not be a surprise. Some insight into acquittals is provided by Block, Corbett and Peay (1993) who examined a sample of acquittals with the following results:

'Of the sample of 100 non-jury acquittals, there were 71 ordered acquittals, 28 directed acquittals and one mixed acquittal, where there were two indictments and one was acquitted by order and one by direction. Although fewer than half of ordered acquittals were considered definitely or possibly foreseeable, three-quarters of directed acquittals were so classified. This supports our view, derived from the study, that directed acquittals result largely from weak cases that should have been discontinued, whereas ordered acquittals often result from unforeseeable circumstances. This may be considered to challenge Zander's (1991) assertion that ordered acquittals represent an even weaker category of case than where the judge directs an acquittal. Our study shows that in fact there are at least two categories of ordered acquittals: those weak cases that are spotted by the Crown Prosecution Service immediately after committal, and others – seemingly good cases – which weaken unpredictably before committal or trial. Of all ordered acquittals in our sample (71), 14 were listed for mention (the former category) and 37 weakened nearer or on the day of trial (the latter category). Use of the term weak cases implies criticism of the Crown Prosecution Service, but this is misleading. The real basis for criticism is the distinction between predictably weak cases which the Crown Prosecution Service fail to spot and unpredictably weak cases. Of fundamentally weak cases, the Crown Prosecution Service may be held responsible for those resulting in ordered acquittals that should have been spotted even before committal, and for those ending in directed acquittals due to weaknesses not spotted at all. Any analysis of the national statistics which is used as a basis for assessing the performance of the Crown Prosecution Service needs to take account of these distinctions.' (1993:100)

In 1995 a similar study was carried out by Baldwin (1997). He noted that it is very difficult to judge how good the witnesses are going to be prior to the trial. The failure of a witness to arrive at the court, or the witness retracting a statement, was a major factor in 48 per cent of the acquittals he examined. But in as many as 76 per cent of the cases that were acquitted, there had been some form of reservation expressed by the prosecution as to the merits of the case. Baldwin suggests that many prosecutors lack confidence and so may let cases just carry on for fear of letting the police down or 'copping out' in serious cases by leaving the decision to the jury. He suggests that case review is a 'hurried even perfunctory exercise' and that the attitude is 'play safe and allow the case to proceed to the next stage'. (1997:554). Belloni and Hodgson (2000) make a similar point: 'The picture which emerges is not one of the careful evidential scrutiny of cases, but of Crown Prosecution Service lawyers wading through large numbers of poorly organised files, making hurried and inconsistent decisions which fail to test out the initial police view' (2000:110). So the custody officer goes with the initial police view, the Crown Prosecution Service go with the charge, magistrates believe them and even the defendant is likely to join in. Indeed, guilty pleas are the major problem in the whole process as the acquittal system will never be able to operate as a safeguard in such cases. Throughout all of this the defence (if we can call it that) has been largely passive.

151

As between the agencies there have also been problems in terms of blaming each other for mistakes – for example, the Prosecution Service complain of poor quality files being delivered late in the day by the police. Despite this chorus of woe the real issue of how bad things are has not been established. The media have emphasised the bad news and one-off mistakes, if that is what they are, would provide a poor basis for generalisations. Allan Green, a former Director of Public Prosecutions, in an interview with Morton (1989) gave the following view:

> 'There are bound to be setbacks when you consider we handle over one million cases annually in the magistrates' courts and 250,000 at the Crown Court. It would be totally unreal to expect there to be no cases where things went wrong. The picture I have seen is one of substantial improvement in the service we provide and this is increasingly being recognised by judges, magistrates, their clerks and the police.' (1989:6)

In January 1989 a speech by the Attorney-General, Sir Patrick Mayhew, was reported by *The Magistrate* (1989). He made the point that it was the bad that was being concentrated upon with the exclusion of the good work that was being done. Both Allan Green and Patrick Mayhew may have been right but they did not provide a detailed justification for what are best seen as being assertions. Indeed, the Crown Prosecution Service has never been quick to volunteer information, its Annual Report for example is a bland and unhelpful document.

Some matters are clear. Acquittal rates are still problematic, indicating quite a high failure rate. How much this is the fault of the Crown Prosecution Service is another matter; some of the fault will lie with the police and the lack of resources to which it has been subjected. The failure rate is over 50 per cent in the Crown Court. There are also still delays. It seems that the comments of the Royal Commission (1981) on the old system seem equally applicable to the new – that we have continued to have delays in preparing cases for trial with consequent court adjournments, inadequately prepared cases leading to their early collapse, and the employment of professionals upon tasks for which they are not trained.

It is plausible to suggest that weak cases are still being proceeded with. It is also worth considering the extent to which the police are still involved in the prosecution process, which would mean that the idea of prosecution independence can also be doubted. For the prosecution to offer advice to the police about a particular case they would of course have to be aware of it. If the police are keen to see a case prosecuted despite its weakness then they are very unlikely to ask for advice or to make the case known at an early stage. The problems of the Crown Prosecution Service, as noted earlier, mean that by the relatively late stage that they receive a complete file they may have only limited time to look to the merits of a prosecution. Even where they discover weak cases there will still be a reluctance to go against the police decision. As Sanders notes:

> 'Police and prosecutors naturally avoid causing each other problems. They necessarily share similar goals, they spend a considerable amount of time in each other's company, and each can make the other's job more or less difficult at will. American research shows that police-prosecutor relationships are generally characterised by co-operation, consensus and compromise. ... Both the Director of Public Prosecutions and Scottish procurators fiscal generally fail to drop cases which the police want prosecuted. Prosecuting solicitors are also entitled to refuse to prosecute cases – if doing so would breach their duty as officers of the court (for instance, where there is no prima facie case). Prosecuting solicitors claim they do

this occasionally. But it never happened in the 1,109 prosecutions encountered in this research, despite several opportunities:

D1 and D2 were arrested and charged with burglary. The prosecuting solicitor's "advice" to the police regarding D1 was: 'I'm pleased to see that DC mentions in his report that this accused has intimated a guilty plea. As the file stands there is not a scrap of evidence against him apart from the admissions made by the co-accused' (who could not be compelled to give evidence against D1). Both pleaded guilty and were sentenced to three months' detention.

This illustrates one particularly powerful reason why prosecutors will always be unwilling to drop cases, however weak: there is always a chance that the defendant might plead guilty! And even trials which prosecutors fully expect to lose sometimes produce convictions.' (1986:24–25)

This material of course also offers some reasons as to why the notion of Crown prosecutors being independent of the police is clearly problematic. Such ideas and material need to be considered in the light of the comments of the police, noted earlier, in which the failure of prosecutors to adopt an approach that they would have found desirable was the subject of critical comment. From this we know that the police are sometimes unhappy with prosecution decisions. As yet we do not really know the exact extent of continuing police involvement in prosecution decisions. An examination of two different sets of views on these matters is instructive.

A retreat from prosecution

The main message that Rose (1996) tries to get across is that there has been a retreat from prosecution. Rose examined the Crown Prosecution Service code which provides discretion as to prosecution decisions. The code requires the use of two principles, the first of which is evidential sufficiency. This requires a realistic prospect of conviction and it is a much higher standard than the pre-Crown Prosecution Service test used by the police which was: Is there a prima facie case? This requires a subjective judgment to be made as to how witnesses will come across, and the prosecutor also has to predict the future reaction of a jury or magistrate. Rose has doubts as to the ability of the prosecutors to be able to give a meaningful answer to these questions:

'The real answer to these questions is that it is simply impossible to know how a witness will react before he gets into the box and gives evidence. Juries are not homogenous: their reactions to witnesses will differ widely. The performance any witness may give is also likely to vary according to many factors beyond the prosecutor's control. It may be simply a question of health or general well-being. Some witnesses may behave very differently according to whether a defendant is in custody, or has been given bail ... in almost every case, the prosecutor will never have met the witnesses he is supposed to assess, but will merely have read their statements, taken by the police. It is difficult to see how anyone could meaningfully evaluate "the impression a witness is likely to make" on this basis.' (1996:134)

Rose also doubts the ability of a prosecutor to be able to apply the public interest criterion:

'It is difficult to believe that the 2,000 salaried solicitors and barristers who make up the ranks of the Crown Prosecution Service spend much time dwelling on lofty notions of "public morale and order". The pre-eminent public interest here is not justice, but cost.' (1996:135)

153

One of Rose's main themes is that the Crown Prosecution Service are quick to discontinue cases and reluctant to prosecute full stop. The reason for early discontinuance is that they are judged in financial terms and they can save the most money by stopping the case at the earliest possible point. They are also criticised for failures, so it does not encourage them to take chances – to the contrary, they will look for certainties. One problem with this is that decisions may have been made before vital evidence is available – some scientific evidence just cannot be made available quickly.

The bureaucratic and other pressures faced by prosecutors

Rose does take account of the difficulties that the Crown Prosecution Service has faced in relation to funding. He quotes David Faulkner, who was Deputy Secretary at the Home Office from 1982 to 1992 and who played a greater part in setting up the Service than anybody else:

> 'It started disastrously because the costing was all wrong and it has struggled to catch up ever since. Crown Prosecution Service funding was initially determined by the management consultants, Arthur Andersen, who conducted a study of police prosecution work to calculate how much money the new service would need ... they got it wrong by a factor of almost fifty per cent.' (1996:145)

The bureaucratic burden that the Crown Prosecution Service has to face is also commented upon by Rose. He notes that for a criminal damage case against a man who had got drunk and broken one of his ex-wife's windows the following documents were required:

> 'The forms in the file were as follows: form MG1, the "front sheet", containing the basic details of the defendant; form 67a, the charge record; form MG17, a list of previous formal cautions, of which the defendant had none; form MG16, his previous criminal record, also blank; form MG3, with information about the defendant's employment situation and income; form MG5, a summary of evidence; form MG6, the "confidential information form", the place to put comments about the strength of the case, possible problems with witnesses or whether there might have been an accomplice; form MG7, the initial remand application form, used as a summary in the case of a court appearance before the main hearing (in this case it merely repeated what was in form MG5); form MG9, the witness list; form MG10, a calendar on which dates when witnesses would not be available should be blocked out; and finally, form MG 12, the list of (in this case non-existent) exhibits.' (1996:147)

The defendant was pleading guilty and had no previous convictions and the outcome was a conditional discharge, and orders for costs and compensation. The police and the Crown Prosecution Service had still had the burden of completing all of that paperwork.

The power of the police and the passivity of the prosecution

Sanders (1997) examine the problems of the prosecution system and suggested that there is evidence that the prosecution process does not always adhere to the formal rules that are designed to control it. This can lead to the continuation of cases that should have been discontinued. The material can be contrasted with the view noted earlier from Rose (1996) who argued that there has been a retreat from prosecution. What is certainly true in what

Sanders has to tell about cautioning is that the Crown Prosecution Service has no meaningful role in relation to it (though this may change in the future) there is no system by which they check to see if cases are being cautioned that should not be:

'The police continue to charge, summons, caution, and NFA as before. Once charged or summonsed, though, the accused becomes the responsibility of the Crown Prosecution Service, which decides whether to continue the prosecution. ... McConville et al (1991) found, from research in three police-force areas, that the Crown Prosecution Service rarely dropped cases which were evidentially weak, and that when they did so this was usually on the initiative of the police and/or only after several court appearances. There were three main reasons for this: policy (the furtherance of police working rules, shared by both prosecutors and police officers); the chance of a freak conviction (because verdicts are so hard to predict); and guilty pleas (just because a case is evidentially weak it does not follow that the defendant will contest the case; weak cases are continued in the often correct expectation of a guilty plea). If the Crown Prosecution Service is passive in relation to weak cases where case failure is a measure of institutional efficiency, it is not surprising to discover that it is even more passive in relation to cautionable cases. McConville et al (1991) found no cautionable cases at all being dropped on grounds of cautionability alone, despite many similar cases being cautioned by the police. Again, where police working rules point to prosecution, the Crown Prosecution Service is reluctant to stop the case, Gelsthorpe and Giller (1990). In more recent years there has been a significant rise in discontinuances, both on evidential and "public interest" grounds, although the former outnumber the latter by two to one, Crisp and Moxon (1994). However, many "public interest" discontinuances are of trivial cases, and are made on cost grounds. That there is scope for far more diversion by the Crown Prosecution Service has been confirmed by Crisp and Moxon (1994), who found that cases which went through experimental "Public Interest Case Assessment" (PICA) schemes were far more likely to be discontinued than normal. Despite this, many cases which were assessed as cautionable were not discontinued and yet received nominal penalties. McConville et al's argument that the police and Crown Prosecution Service insist on prosecuting when they have extraneous reasons for so doing would appear to hold firm.

The Crown Prosecution Service is in a structurally weak position to carry out its ostensible aims primarily because of police case construction. The Crown Prosecution Service reviews the quality of police cases on the basis of evidence provided solely by the police. This is like the problem of written records, where those who are being evaluated write their own reports. Cases being prosecuted are usually presented as prosecutable; the facts to support this are selected, and those which do not are ignored, hidden, or undermined. Thus weaknesses or cautionable factors, whether known by the police or not, often emerge only in or after trial, Leng (1992). This situation is exacerbated when the Crown Prosecution Service relies on police summaries, which are very selective indeed, Baldwin and Bedward (1991). Moodie and Tombs (1982) and Duff (1997) in Scotland (Duff in relation to psychiatric cases), and Gelsthorpe and Giller (1990) in England cite prosecutors who agree that the police present them only with what seems relevant to them as prosecutors (as distinct from neutral intermediaries). Similarly, when the police seek advice from the Crown Prosecution Service, they can obtain the advice they want by carefully selecting the information they present (Sanders et al 1997). This is why PICA schemes, which present prosecutors with information from non-police sources, lead to increased numbers of discontinuances.' (1997:1074–1075)

National Audit Office Report on the Crown Prosecution Service (1998)

Further information on the working of the Crown Prosecution Service was provided by an Audit Commission report published in November 1998. It noted the increased collaboration between the Crown Prosecution Service and the police. Initiatives include: joint monitoring of the timeliness and quality of police files, prosecutors visiting police stations to give officers face to face advice and joint training programmes. They also noted that the Crown Prosecution Service discontinuance rate of 12 per cent of the cases submitted by the police includes local variations which need to be investigated. Consultation with the police is possible in 95 per cent of such cases. The report also notes that the severe staff shortages which the Crown Prosecution Service experienced when it was first established have been overcome. Staff numbers have in fact been reduced in recent years. Counsel returning briefs is a problem that needs to be tackled. Early results from monitoring the timeliness of case processing show wide variations in local performance. Early results from monitoring the quality of prosecution decisions show that decisions meet the Crown Prosecution Service's quality standards in 97 per cent of cases.

From the available evidence it seems that the Prosecution of Offences Act 1985 cannot be said to have succeeded in terms of removing the pre-Act problems. The structural factors such as the role of the police which were seen to be at the root of such problems may also have survived. With the new administrative structure in the post-Glidewell era we have moved a further step back to where we were before the 1985 Act.

4.10 Bail decision-making

The police have to decide if detention is needed, prior to a person going before the courts, and this is called police bail. For cases in which a court is at that point in time unable to complete the matter before it, a remand will be necessary. The court will then have to decide if this is on bail or in custody and this system is not surprisingly called court bail. Both types of bail may be subject to conditions. The official statistics provide information on bail decision-making. The data from the criminal statistics (Home Office (2002a)) are only estimates because of problems in data collection. For proceedings before magistrates in 2001, 54 per cent were summoned, the other 46 per cent being arrested and charged. Where arrested, 14 per cent were held by the police until the first court appearance. Of those summoned, 7 per cent failed to appear at court. Where bail was granted by the courts 45,000 defendants were proceeded against for failing to appear; in all 13 per cent failed to appear. The magistrates granted bail in cases that for 5 per cent of them there was eventually a custodial sentence. This indicates lenient use of bail perhaps. On the other hand, where remand in custody was used only 45 per cent got a custodial sentence and 23 per cent were acquitted. The figures in Table 18 provide a breakdown of some of the data. It can be noted that the bail rate in 1967 was much lower at 67 per cent, so there has been a considerable improvement over the years.

Table 18

	1987		2001	
Bail Decisions by Magistrates (thousands)	Bailed	Remanded in custody	Bailed	Remanded in custody
Indictable offences	300 (88%)	40	319 (84%)	60
Summary offences (other than motoring)	67 (94%)	4	125 (95%)	7
Summary motoring offences	62 (95%)	3	79 (88%)	11
All offences	429 (89%)	51	523 (90%)	78

(Source: Criminal Statistics, England and Wales, 1987 and 2002)

The need for a further hearing in a court case can arise in a number of ways. For example, either one or both of the prosecution and the defence may need further time in which to prepare their case or the court may require a report on a defendant prior to sentence. In such circumstances the courts have to decide whether the remand should be on bail (the defendant being released until the next hearing) or in custody. It is clear that most of the remands in custody are the result of proceedings for indictable or triable either way offences in the magistrates' courts. Such proceedings will be concentrated upon for both that reason and also because most of the research that has been done has been in relation to these proceedings. Where custody is used it will normally mean a period in prison. Where they are available, bail hostels and remand centres can be used as alternatives to prison. Also at times police cells have been used if there is nowhere else to send people. For those who are bailed this may be subject to conditions (such as place of residence) or sureties (where someone agrees on a defendant's behalf that they will have to pay a sum of money if the defendant absconds). In the making of their decisions the court will hear objections to bail by the Crown prosecutor and also listen to any representations from the defendant or his representative. Before the introduction of Crown prosecutors, the police had a larger role in relation to court bail.

4.11 Problems in bail decision-making

Researchers and commentators have noted numerous problems with regard to bail or custody decision-making. The problems have their root in the attitude of expediency adopted by those who have responsibility for the system. The main causes of official concern have been considerations of cost and the exacerbation of the overcrowding problem in prisons that custodial remands involve. The actual quality of such decisions has been largely neglected. As a result, the way in which decisions are arrived at is suspect by reason, for example, of the decisions being based on insufficient information. This may mean that defendants, often unconvicted, may be unnecessarily remanded in custody. Some of these defendants are subsequently declared innocent having in the meantime suffered custody, and the situation is made worse by the fact that remand prisoners experience some of the worst of generally poor prison conditions. Also problematic is that for cases in which a defendant is found guilty, after a remand in custody, a custodial sentence may be deemed to be unsuitable in the particular case. As will be seen later, such occurrences have to be balanced against the fact that a court in refusing bail may quite rightly be concentrating on issues such as ensuring that the defendant is present at the next hearing. Other problems include the possibility that being in custody may impair the preparation of a defendant's defence. It is also possible that the very situation of custody may lead to a guilty plea and thus prevent a trial from taking place. Defendants remanded in custody are also likely to suffer adverse consequences in terms of their abode, their personal relationships and their employment. A further problem is the real possibility of defendants who would be best remanded in custody being released on bail. Such defendants are by their nature likely to offer a threat to the operation of the criminal justice system and to the community generally. Where those who could have been bailed are through bad decision-making sent to prison this causes further pressure on those establishments. During the 1960s and early 1970s a number of commentators – for example Davies (1971), Bottomley (1970) and King (1971) – had criticised the bail system in such terms and the official response was first to set up a Home Office Working Party. The report of that body (Home Office (1974)) was followed by the Bail Act 1976 which is the main source of law in relation to the bail system at the present time. It is clear that the pre-Bail Act problems have to a great extent continued until the present time. Before such material can be explored, an account of the most important of the legal provisions on bail needs to be provided.

The Bail Act 1976

The Act came into force in May 1978 and s4 created a rebuttable presumption in favour of bail. Part I of Schedule 1 of the Act details the circumstances in which bail need not be granted. The main points to note from this are that where an offence is imprisonable, bail need not be granted if there are substantial grounds for believing that, if released on bail, a defendant would fail to surrender to custody, commit an offence, interfere with witnesses or otherwise obstruct the course of justice. Bail may also be refused for the protection of a defendant, to ensure the welfare of a defendant who is a child or young person, where a defendant is in custody in pursuance of the sentence of a court or of any authority acting under any of the Service Acts and where the defendant has in relation to the proceedings absconded or breached bail conditions. Bail may also be refused where the court is satisfied that it has not been practicable to obtain sufficient information, for the purpose of making such decisions, for want of time, since the institution of proceedings against the defendant. Finally, if reports would not otherwise be practical without a remand in custody this may be ordered. Paragraph 9 of this part of the Schedule states the sort of factors that would be relevant to such decisions. These include the nature and seriousness of the offence and the strength of the evidence in the case and the character, antecedents, associations, community ties and record on bail of the defendant.

The retreat from the presumption

The presumption in favour of bail provided by s4 has been undermined in a number of ways. One of these was a time-saving device adopted by the courts and recognised by the decision in *R v Nottingham Justices, ex parte Davies* [1981] QB 38. Courts would not consider bail unless there had been a change in circumstances since the previous hearing. An exception was allowed in the case of the second hearing where there had been insufficient opportunity to prepare for the issue of bail at the first hearing. Section 154 of the Criminal Justice Act 1988 gives statutory force to a restricted version of the above system. This applies to defendants who have a general right to bail under s4 of the 1976 Act where a court has decided not to grant bail. The court must, at each subsequent hearing at which a person appeared from custody and at which he still has the general right to bail, consider whether the person ought to be granted bail. At the first such hearing any argument as to fact or law (whether previously used or not) may be advanced to support the bail application. At subsequent hearings the court need not hear arguments that it has heard previously. Sections 25 and 26 of the Criminal Justice and Public Order Act 1994 further restricted the power of the courts to grant bail. Any person charged with murder, manslaughter, rape or attempted rape who already had a conviction for such an offence could not be granted bail. This absolute ban was changed to bail only being possible in exceptional circumstances by s56 of the Crime and Disorder Act 1998. A person who is charged with any indictable offence will not have the presumption in favour of bail where it seems that the offence was committed whilst the person was on bail. It can be noted that it was the 1994 Act that made it possible for the police to grant bail subject to conditions.

The Criminal Justice Act 2003 provided for the following changes to the bail system:

1. There will be a presumption against bail for those tested positive for class A drugs and who refuse to go into treatment.
2. When deciding whether to grant bail in respect of an offence which appears to have been committed whilst an adult defendant was on bail for another offence, the courts are required to refuse bail unless they are satisfied that there is no significant risk that he will offend again if released on bail.
3. Where there has been a previous failure of an adult to surrender to court bail then a court should refuse bail unless they are satisfied that there is no significant risk that he will abscond again.
4. That the police will be able to grant bail to a person on the street rather than having to bring them to a police station. This change has been made in order to maximise the police use of resources as taking people to police stations takes a lot of time out of shifts.
5. One of the rights of the defence, to appeal to the High Court against a refusal of court bail, will be removed. The appeal to the Crown Court would still be available. The prosecution would get enhanced rights to challenge a grant of bail. The rhetoric is that these changes are designed to produce a better bail system. The concern is that all of these changes favour the state rather than the defendant.
6. Finally, it provides that bail conditions are to be made possible for the protection and welfare of defendants.

The impact of custodial remands on the individual

For those remanded in custody a number of points cause some concern. Where a conviction follows a remand in custody, a non-custodial sentence may be used. Some defendants are not convicted. In relation to such matters, in 1987 a dossier of cases of particularly long remands in custody, which was collated by the National Association of Probation Officers, was sent to Members of Parliament. These included the cases of: John R, aged 34, held for 390 days on drug offences before being acquitted on all charges; Robert T, aged 19, held in a youth-custody centre for 218 days (as regards the charges he faced, he was either acquitted or no evidence was offered against him at the trial); and Brian C, acquitted after being held for 119 days on a charge of burglary involving goods valued at £10. That such events are not followed by compensation for defendants is a disgrace.

Offending on bail

Offences being committed by those on bail has also been a cause of concern. One of the points made by Vogler (1983) is that Lord Goddard, in a series of decisions in 1955 in the Court of Criminal Appeal, invented the idea that a fear of offences being committed if bail was granted was an acceptable reason for refusing bail. Clearly, as Vogler points out, preventative detention of the unconvicted can be regarded as unpalatable. In his view bail decisions should be about the offences with which the defendant is charged and not previous or possible future offences. Equally, the point can be made that the aim of the decision making should be concerned with attendance at trial and matters directly connected thereto. Whatever the merits of Vogler's view the reality is that such considerations are frequently used by the courts.

People who offend whilst on bail are called bail bandits by the popular press. In 1991 Avon and Somerset Police reported that between 24 per cent and 39 per cent of crime in their area was committed by offenders on bail. Morgan and Henderson (1998) thought that the figure for those convicted for another offence which had been committed whilst they were on bail was about 11 per cent. The Criminal Justice and Public Order Act 1994 removed the right to bail for those who appeared to have committed an indictable or either-way offence whilst on bail.

Brown (1997) reported the findings of research into offending on bail which was gathered by examining a sample of 1,283 suspects remanded in Northumbria and Greater Manchester. Of those bailed, 24 per cent committed one or more offences but the offending rate was much higher for juveniles (38 per cent) than for adults (18 per cent). The highest rates by offence were for vehicle crime (44 per cent) and shop-lifting (40 per cent). The offending rate was also much higher for juveniles (30 per cent) than for adults (7 per cent) where police bail had been used. There was a failure to appear at court in 7 per cent of cases where the police had granted bail and 9 per cent where a court had granted bail.

Morgan and Henderson (1998) identified groups who had higher offending rates on bail. Information such as this would clearly be of use to bail decision-makers as it would indicate both the high-risk and the low-risk categories. They found that 42 per cent of those who had no fixed abode offended whilst on bail. Certain offence groups were worse risks than others: burglary had a rate of offending of 29 per cent and car theft was even higher at 32 per cent, whilst fraud was 8 per cent and assault 7 per cent. The period of remand was also important as a less than one-month wait for trial had a 4 per cent rate whilst more than six months had a 32 per cent rate. Section 43 of the Crime and Disorder Act 1998 provides for a system of new time limits, which have as one of their intentions the reduction of remand delays. Morgan and Henderson suggested a need for better quality information, in terms of having ready access to records relating to previous offending, as an area for improvement in decision-making. Merit was also seen in bail-information schemes, bail support schemes, a fostering scheme for juveniles on remand and diversion schemes for mentally disordered offenders. Also suggested were the training of magistrates in risk assessment and greater clarity in explaining conditions to defendants. Attempts were made to test some of these ideas in five areas with beneficial effects being found in two of them.

Pressure on prisons

One of the hopes for and aims of the Bail Act 1976 was to increase the use of bail and thus to reduce pressure on prisons. Despite the fact, that in general, a greater percentage of people are now being bailed than was the case in the past, the remand population still causes considerable pressure on the prison system. This was a point made strongly in the Woolf Report (Home Office (1991)), and this was commented upon by Morgan and Jones (1992). Woolf was investigating the causes of prison riots and he saw that remand prisoners have the capacity to cause serious problems. This was particularly where they were the object of excessive security and the control measures to which they were subject were inappropriate. Moreover, they suffered a grave deficiency of justice. Woolf also doubted that so many remand prisoners need be held in custody for so long. He pointed out that, in procedural terms, the question of bail is dealt with by the courts more casually than sentencing. Decisions are sometimes made hurriedly, without adequate information, by lay magistrates. He stressed that the amenities and services available to untried prisoners should be different from those for convicted and sentenced prisoners. For example, the untried, subject to the presumption of innocence, should not be compelled to work. On the other hand, there is no case for denying them access to programmes on the ground that they have not been convicted of an offence.

Bail hostels

One of the Woolf Report recommendations was for an increase in bail hostel facilities. As well as taking the pressure off prisons they will save people from unnecessary custodial detention. In 2003 there were about 2,000 places available, but clearly there is a need for more. The provision of facilities other than prison would often be appropriate for those remanded in custody. Research on bail hostels does however reveal some cause for concern. Pratt and Bray (1985) found some evidence of hostels being used in cases where people would have been granted bail in any case. White and Brody (1980) found that 38 per cent of their sample of people in bail hostels broke bail in some way – for example, by failing to report to the hostel, by absconding or by committing offences. It should also be noted that the motivation for the development of bail hostels was not the desire to spare defendants unnecessary custody but rather to save money by replacing the use of prisons with the use of hostels. Similarly motivated was the use, on a trial basis, of electronic tagging for people on bail. The idea is that, by providing a means of electronically monitoring the whereabouts of those on bail, such devices could allow a greater use of bail. The trials had mixed results in relation to bail, but this did not stop the idea being reborn in relation to early release and as a sentencing option.

Conditional bail

Both the police and the courts can make bail subject to conditions. The Crime and Disorder Act 1998 introduced a system of securities which involves the defendant in putting money up before release. This supplements the use of a surety system in which another person puts up money on behalf of the defendant. The Act also introduced a possible requirement of having to attend an interview with a solicitor. Tagging can also be used in relation to bail, although it has been little used and has proved problematic (on which see Hucklesby (2002:131)). The Criminal Justice Act 2003 provides that bail conditions are to be made possible for the protection and welfare of defendants.

Raine and Willson (1996) carried out an investigation of the use of conditions in bail decision-making in five courts. Conditions were imposed in about half of the cases. The type of conditions used and the degree of use of conditions is indicated in Table 19. On conditional bail: see also two earlier studies by Cutts (1982) and East and Doherty (1984).

Table 19

Conditions Imposed in the Five Courts		
Particular condition imposed	Percentage of cases involving conditions in which it was used	Maximum and minimum per cent use in the five courts
Residence	79	65/85
No contact with witnesses or co-accused	46	36/73
Keep away from a specific address	24	19/29
Curfew	21	15/30
Report to police	17	8/28
Exclusion from an area	4	0/8
Abide by hostel or bail scheme rules	4	0/11
Sureties/securities	4	0/10
Surrender passport or restrict travel	3	1/6
Not to drive or enter a motor vehicle	3	2/4
No alcohol or entry to licensed premises	2	0/7
Other	4	1/8

(Source: 'The Imposition of Conditions in Bail Decisions', Howard Journal of Penal Reform)

The research by Raine and Willson revealed that there was inadequate enforcement of conditions, which raises the question why have them if they are not enforced. One answer would be to have them as a form of illegitimate punishment, whereas their aim should be better behaviour on remand. Perhaps surprisingly the defendants who were interviewed, indicated that conditions had a positive effect on their behaviour. In terms of the decision-making process, the first step is that the need for custody should be considered if this issue is thought to be appropriate. If bail is to be granted, the issue of conditions could then be raised. In practice, bail with conditions actually seems to exist as a third option. It was common for conditional bail to be imposed without the requirement of reasons being given for them being met. On the issue of the enforcement of bail conditions Raine and Willson suggest that much greater priority be given to this and that:

> '... the courts should be satisfied that compliance with the requirements imposed is routinely monitored and enforced. If the police are unable to satisfy the courts in this respect, perhaps another enforcement agency has to be considered; certainly it is important that the courts' authority is not undermined by defendants knowing that the decisions are not enforced. At the same time, however, magistrates have to recognise their part in the enforcement process and to give careful consideration to the possible interaction, both by defendants and by the police, of decisions to re-bail those brought back to court for non-compliance. A combination, then, of wise decision-making and diligent monitoring and enforcement actions can help to ensure that decisions to grant defendants bail with conditions are less "hit and miss" and more often achieve the desired objective of better behaviour while on remand.' (1996:269)

Hucklesby (2002) provides the following analysis of the use of conditional bail:

> 'Critical comment on the use of conditions of bail is rare. This is because it provides an alternative to remands in custody. However, it is an important issue for a number of reasons. Conditional bail restricts the liberty of defendants who are legally innocent. Defendants can be subject to the conditions imposed for considerable lengths of time. Conditions, whether singly or as a package, can be unjustly restrictive and would not be imposed as part of a sentence on conviction. Packages of conditions may be overly restrictive, making defendants' lives impossible. The more conditions imposed, the more restricted defendants are, and arguably the more likely they are to breach their bail.
>
> Several concerns with the use of conditions have been highlighted. First, that the conditions imposed have very little relevance to the exceptions to bail in individual cases, for example, a night-time curfew attached to the bail of a defendant who is known to commit all her offences of shoplifting in daylight hours. This problem is worsened by defence solicitors who propose packages of conditions in an attempt to persuade magistrates to release defendants on bail. If bail is then granted, magistrates impose all the proposed conditions without checking their relevance to the exceptions. In these circumstances, the specific conditions are unlikely to be challenged because of the relief that defendants have avoided being remanded in custody and from fear of being so remanded. Secondly, conditions do not necessarily prevent absconding, offending, or witness intimidation. For example, a curfew may simply result in defendants changing their hours of operation. Other conditions, such as reporting to the police station, simply seem to miss the point entirely, as defendants can abscond immediately after reporting and have several days to abscond before their next reporting session. Finally, many of the conditions cannot be enforced effectively. This partly reflects the lack of resources of the police and the low priority which checking compliance with conditions necessarily has. However, just as important is that some conditions, such as a requirement to keep out of the city centre, are practically impossible to enforce. Enforcement

is an important part of the deterrence value of conditions. If defendants perceive that the likelihood of getting caught is negligible then they are less likely to abide by the conditions imposed.

Unsurprisingly, the longer defendants are on bail the more likely they are to breach conditions. There is no evidence available to indicate exactly why this occurs. Defendants may simply forget what conditions they are required to observe, or they may realize that conditions are not enforced as no checks have been conducted. Breaches may be made all the more likely by the practice of not restating every single condition attached to bail on each court appearance, but simply stating that defendants are subject to the same conditions as previously imposed. This is a further practice, highlighted by the Law Commission's review of bail law, which may be in a breach of human rights legislation.

Delays in the criminal justice process have arguably made breaches more likely, although there are no statistics on the length of time that defendants spend on bail awaiting trial. However, requiring legally innocent people to abide by restrictive conditions over a period of months raises civil liberties issues. One way of limiting these problems would be to introduce time limits for defendants on bail. The result of this would be that if cases were not completed within a specific time the case would be discontinued.' (2002:129–130)

Disparity in decision-making

There is evidence of several forms of disparity in bail decision-making. This must be regarded as worrying if only in so far as it means injustice between accused. Jones (1985) noted that the court custody rate varied by area. Whilst the figures for all areas was 16 per cent there were lows of 7 per cent (Bedfordshire) and 8 per cent (Gwent) and highs of 37 per cent (North Yorkshire) and 31 per cent (Dorset): Jones (1985:113). The Prison Reform Trust (1986) also reported geographical disparity in relation to indictable offences in 1984. An average use of custody of 14 per cent saw a high of 36 per cent in Dorset and a low of 4 per cent in Bedfordshire. Even within areas there were variations – for example, custody was used for three in ten cases in Uxbridge, whilst it was thought appropriate in only one in 20 cases in nearby Harrow. The same point was made by Gibson (1987) who reported Home Office data from the period 1980–86 in which Bournemouth was noted as using custody in 313 of 1,000 indictable proceedings. Nearby Blandford and Weymouth recorded figures of only 43 and 76 respectively. Portsmouth had a figure of 31, whilst the nearby and similar city of Southampton recorded 179.

Empirical studies of bail

An examination of such studies provides material in relation to the factors that are of most importance in bail decision-making and other insights. In the large study by Jones (1985) reliance was placed on court records of hearings, thus information is not available on matters such as the role of the police or defendant's representatives. He found that the most important factors in the court's decisions were the police decision whether or not to grant police bail, the offence group and court policy. Other factors such as age and sex of defendants had only a marginal impact. This fits generally with the findings of other research.

The police

In the past the issue of the role of the police has received much attention. Studies reported different rates of police opposition to bail: Bottomley (1970) (55 per cent), King (1971) (25 per cent), Bottoms and McClean (1976) (50 per cent), Cutts (1982) (54 per cent for 1976 and 43 per cent for 1981), Zander (1979b) (25 per cent) and Doherty and East (1985) (18 per cent). It was noted in Doherty and East (1985:255) that the earlier studies found the police role to be dominant in court proceedings – for example, Bottoms and McClean remarked that magistrates everywhere generally accept the police view. In Doherty and East, however there was less evidence of the police view being dominant. For example, 27 (31 per cent) of the 88 cases in which the police objected to bail saw the defendant being released. The role of the police will not be considered in the depth it would have been in the past because of the arrival of the Crown Prosecution Service. Having taken over the role of objectors to bail, they have moved the police from centre stage in bail decision-making.

The Crown Prosecution Service

As to the role of the Crown Prosecution Service, Hucklesby (1997) is a good source of information. She carried out research in relation to 1,524 remand hearings in three South Wales courts in the early 1990s. In 85 per cent of cases there was no request for a remand in custody by the Crown Prosecution Service. In the 229 cases where there was a request the defence only responded in 132 cases. So, in reality, there was only an issue in 9 per cent of cases. The system of police bail was influential as where this is granted the court are virtually certain to grant bail. Information was available in relation to 145 cases where the police had granted bail, and in only one of these was there a remand in custody by the court. The impact of the Crown Prosecution Service can also be seen, in that the court agreed in 95 per cent of the cases in which they made a request for a remand in custody. As to the character of the process, this is portrayed in the following terms:

> '... the decision-making process is largely an administrative process conducted in private by participants other than the magistracy according to discretionary and hidden rules. This process is generally characterised by uncontested court remand hearings where the effective decisions are made out of court, by professional practitioners, prior to the court hearing. The magistrates' role is limited simply to "rubber stamping" their recommendations in the majority of cases.' (1997:269)

The quality of decision-making

Material from Doherty and East (1985) portrays the system of bail decision-making as being of a poor quality. The criteria for refusal of bail are numerous and various and at some point the risk in relation to these becomes unacceptable. In reaching a decision the court can be asked to consider a variety of matters. Doherty and East carried out a study in Cardiff and found that in 77 cases the police suggested reasons as to why bail should be refused. They averaged two reasons per case and used 21 reasons in all. Emphasis was upon the defendant's past and potential criminality and the needs of the criminal justice system. Defendants' representatives used 24 reasons as to why bail should be granted, these being

165

broadly similar to those used by the police but with emphasis being placed on the circumstances of the defendant. The court was a very busy court and most bail decisions are made in similarly busy courts. Decision-making was rapid even where bail was refused. In such cases 38 per cent of cases were disposed of in less than two minutes and 87 per cent in less than ten minutes. The lay magistrates, who heard 25 per cent of these cases, very rarely enquired into the assertions made by the parties. The proceedings in most cases could not be described as being adversatorial. Given that lay magistrates are amateurs who receive only limited training not much should be expected of them. This produces a situation in which 'decision-makers, often amateurs with limited training who are working under a time-pressure, have to make subjective decisions on the basis of limited unsubstantiated information' (1985:263).

The realities of bail applications is also revealed by Plowden (2003). His intention was to provide a guide for trainee practitioners. He tells them to: 'Deal with each prosecution ground in turn. Be thorough, but be concise. Normally your application should not exceed three or four minutes' (2003:78). They could be locked up for months.

The problem of low-quality information

The Woolf Report (Home Office (1991)) also expressed concern about the lack of information in the bail system:

> 'Magistrates would not regularly, if ever, sentence a defendant to imprisonment on the limited information which is usually available on a bail application. Yet frequently the question of whether or not to refuse bail has an important influence on the sentence which is eventually passed. The refusal of bail can result in a defendant, for example, losing his employment or his accommodation, both of which may be important considerations in determining his ultimate disposal. We propose, therefore, that there should be a clear expectation that magistrates should not make a final decision to remand a defendant in custody until they have received at least the information which will be available to the Crown Prosecution Service in those areas where a Bail Information Scheme is in operation. We would expect magistrates to insist on more information than that which is made available at the present time to the Crown Prosecution Service where there is no Bail Scheme in operation. They should develop the practice of requiring a report on the community ties which the prisoner has. In addition, we propose that magistrates should attach considerable significance to whether or not the offence which the defendant is alleged to have committed is one which, if proved, would justify a sentence of imprisonment. While it is in order to grant bail irrespective of the likely sentence, to remand a defendant in custody for an offence for which he would never be sentenced to imprisonment can be questionable, unless there is some reasonable justification such as possible interference with justice or a persistent failure to surrender to his bail or to comply with its terms.' (1991:10.82–10.84)

More assistance could be provided to decision-makers in the form of more and better information and training which should form part of a national standardised system. Decisions could then hope to be more uniform and accurate and thus limit the problem of disparity. Where problems exist in the system, as for example with absconders, then this should be investigated and tackled. Further information as to any identifying characteristics of absconders would be of use in the development of more sophisticated methods of making

166

bail decisions. Equally, information as to how much and what types of difficulty arise from absconding would be desirable so that the costs of this could be balanced against the costs of prison and of depriving a person of his liberty. In terms of providing better quality information to the court a number of attempts have been made and schemes are in use. An early impetus for such ideas was the success (in terms of preventing absconding and increasing the use of bail) in the United States of variants of the Manhatten Bail Scheme. In such a scheme defendants are investigated as to their community ties and a prediction can then be made as to their suitability for bail. Such schemes clearly have potential but little future if sufficient finance is not made available.

Bail information schemes have in fact been much expanded of late and they are mainly operated by the probation service. The system includes the citing of negative information. Provision has depended upon what has been inconsistent funding. Hucklesby (2002:132–133) provides further information on such schemes.

5 The Criminal Trial

5.1   Mode of trial

5.2   Pleas

5.3   Review of the criminal courts

5.4   The role of magistrates

5.5   The quality of the defence in the Crown Court

5.6   The jury

5.7   Admissibility of evidence, appeals, human rights and the Criminal Cases
        Revision Commission

In this chapter it will be possible to examine just some of the features of the criminal trial –
these are the decisions as to mode of trial, pleas and the role of magistrates and the jury.
The magistrates' courts deal with the bulk of the work of the criminal justice system, whilst
the Crown Court deals with the more serious cases.

The Criminal Justice Act 2003 provisions that relate to the issues in this chapter are
detailed below. It is important to note that, since most of the provisions of the Act did not
come into force immediately upon Royal Assent, the earlier provisions will still be applicable
for some time. The government White Paper, *Justice for All* (Home Office (2002d)), provides
details of their intentions for this stage of the criminal justice system. Many of these
proposals appear in the Criminal Justice Act 2003. They seek fairer, more effective trials.
Their actual concerns are not immediately apparent from the title. It is thought that there
are too many cases in which tactical manoeuvres disrupt the process so a verdict is not
reached and justice not done. That courts are deliberately over-booked on the basis that
some cases will not go ahead as scheduled. This means that over 40 per cent of victims and
witnesses who attend to give evidence are not called to do so on the day. The proposed
answers, so as to ensure swifter, fairer and more efficient trials that balance the rights of
victims and the accused, include the following.

1. A unified administration, as part of the Lord Chancellor's Department, for the Crown
    Court and the magistrate's court.
2. An increase in magistrates' sentencing powers from six to 12 months.
3. Reform of the youth courts to enable them to deal with young offenders accused of
    serious crimes.
4. More use of preparatory hearings so issues can be clarified in advance.
5. Allowing trial by judge alone in serious fraud and jury intimidation cases.
6. Encouraging early guilty pleas by introducing a clearer tariff of sentence discount for

pleading guilty, and arrangements where defendants could seek advance indication of what the discounted sentence would be if they pleaded guilty.

7. Ensuring appropriate safeguards so that innocent defendants are not put under pressure to plead guilty.

8. An overhaul of the rules of evidence, including making available to judges and juries information on previous convictions and conduct where it is relevant and extending the reported evidence available to magistrates, judges and juries. Evidence of previous convictions is very controversial – a person with a dozen previous convictions for burglary may find it difficult to find a jury that will give him a fair trial if the charge is burglary.

9. Another controversial proposal is that the rule against double jeopardy would not operate in grave cases where compelling new evidence has come to light. This would mean that a person who has already been tried and acquitted would be tried for a second time for the same offence. To make it worse this will operate with retrospective effect.

5.1 Mode of trial

Jury trials cause delay and are more expensive than summary proceedings and an issue to consider is to what extent should jury trial be available? Magistrates can decide whether they think that an either-way case is suitable for the magistrates' court. In relation to such decisions, guidelines have been issued by the Lord Chief Justice, ie the National Mode of Trial Guidelines 1995. At present defendants can still insist on jury trial in relation to either way offences. Legislation determines access to jury trial and it can, for example, restrict the categories of either-way offences. This happened with the Criminal Law Act 1977. The 1977 Act removed offences such as some drink driving offences and assault on a police constable from the either-way category. The Guidelines in both 1995 and 1991 were also designed to stop cases being sent for jury trial. The Criminal Justice Act 1988 saw more offences being removed from the either-way category, for example criminal damage cases under £2,000. The £2,000 limit for criminal damage was further increased to £5,000, by the Criminal Justice and Public Order Act 1994. A number of other legislative strategies to limit jury trial have also been attempted.

The Criminal Justice (Mode of Trial) (No 2) Bill 2000 sought to restrict access to jury trial in a more fundamental manner. Magistrates would make the decision as to where the trial would take place in the case of either-way offences. The Royal Commission on Criminal Justice (1993) had recommended such a reform, as indeed had the Narey Report on reducing delay in the criminal justice system: Home Office (1997e). The Narey Report made the point that 20 per cent of cases that go to the Crown Court are cases that the magistrates would have been happy to deal with. In those cases two-thirds end up as guilty pleas and three quarters of the remaining third end up in convictions. The proposals in the 2000 Bill were controversial and an earlier Bill had been withdrawn from the House of Lords after a defeat at committee stage. The new amended Bill, the Criminal Justice (Mode of Trial) (No 2) Bill 2000, was introduced into the House of Commons and was again defeated. A House of Commons briefing paper, Baber (2000), is a useful guide to the issues involved both then and now. Whilst there has been controversy it needs to be emphasised that of those who are sent for trial at the Crown Court, many end up pleading guilty – in 2001 the figure was 60 per cent. So defendants very often deny themselves trial by jury. The factors that influence such decisions are of course another matter and they are considered later.

The Criminal Justice (Mode of Trial) (No 2) Bill 2000 stated that the following matters should be considered by the magistrates when they make a decision as to venue:

1. the nature of the case;
2. any of the circumstances of the offence (but not of the accused) which appears to the court to be relevant;
3. whether the magistrates' powers were sufficient in relation to the case.

Representations would have to be heard from the defence and the prosecutor before a decision is made. It is interesting to note that in other jurisdictions the prosecution makes the decision as to venue. We at present have to resort to trusting lay magistrates rather than give the task to the Crown Prosecution Service. Where the defence makes representations at the hearing as to venue, there would be a right of appeal to the Crown Court in relation to the decision of the magistrates, where that decision was summary trial. The aim of the proposals is to reserve jury trial for the most serious and important cases and to ensure that petty cases do not end up there. This will reduce delay and save money. Baber (2000) notes that it would mean 14,000 fewer jury trials and a saving of about £128 million per annum. The proposal may well be controversial but it is not an unusual arrangement and it is our present system that is unusual.

As I noted earlier the Criminal Justice (Mode of Trial) (No 2) Bill 2000 was defeated. The government did not give up on the issue. A major review of the criminal courts in England and Wales was then carried out by Auld LJ in 2001: Auld LJ (2001). Auld suggested that the court, not the defendant, would decide which tribunal should hear a case. The defendant should no longer have an elective right to trial by judge and jury in either-way cases. The allocation should be the responsibility of the magistrates' court alone and exercisable where there is an issue as to venue by a district judge. The Criminal Justice Act 2003 amends the procedure to be followed by magistrates' courts in determining whether cases triable either way should be tried summarily or on indictment, and provides for the sending to the Crown Court of those cases which need to go there. The new procedures are designed to enable cases to be dealt with in the level of court which is appropriate to their seriousness, and to ensure that they reach that court as quickly as possible. These provisions give effect to a number of recommendations from Auld, including: making magistrates aware, when they determine allocation, of any previous convictions of the defendant; removing the option of committal for sentence in cases which the magistrates decide to hear; allowing defendants in cases where summary trial is considered appropriate to seek a broad indication of the sentence they would face if they were to plead guilty at that point; and replacing committal proceedings and transfers in serious fraud and child-witness cases with a common system for sending cases to the Crown Court, based on the present arrangements for indictable-only cases. The upshot will be less cases going to jury trial, an outcome that many defendants would not have chosen if they had not had the choice in the matter taken away from them. This is not supporting the particular virtues of jury trial but rather noting the further erosion of the position of defendants.

Strategies have been adopted to prevent too many cases getting through to jury trial. The arguments in favour of this can be summarised as being that jury trial introduces delay, involves extra cost, adds to prison overcrowding and has higher acquittal rates than with the use of magistrates. Also, if they could have given the same sentence as the Crown Court it is not expedient to use the Crown Court. With this view the Crown Court is to have symbolic importance and is to be used to show that a case is serious. The Royal Commission in 1993 thought that the removal of the right to jury trial would save the need for 35,000 cases a year and a further impact would be more convictions. In effect this is saying that they would be using a system that would convict people a jury could have freed. We should not be surprised at this argument as the system generally is all about expediency, cost, economies, speed of processing and, of late, various moves to undermine defendants. For the defendant, he would have favoured the acquittal rates of jury trial, he may think that he would get a fairer hearing and he might have a notion of the importance of a right to trial by jury. Defendants may also think that they will receive a lower quality trial in the magistrates' court. An editorial in *The Times* newspaper (2000) pointed out that in the Crown Court there is a professional judge who will ensure that the trial is properly conducted according to law and will give the appropriate rulings. In the Crown Court there is also full disclosure. To balance the developments that have taken place elsewhere in the jury system, we now have not simply the disclosure of witness statements, which has always been part and parcel of the higher courts, but also primary disclosure of documents. There has also been the introduction of defence statements and there is now secondary disclosure where documents are brought out by the prosecution and handed to the defence. Another advantage of jury trial is that legal argument takes place in the absence of the jury; for example, on whether character should be an issue or whether admissions are admissible. Previous convictions or admissions which are not admissible are not heard by, and do not in any way prejudice the minds of, the jury. Some undermining of this principle may arise from the Criminal Justice Act 2003. Furthermore, the legal principles that a judge in a Crown Court trial applies, both on matters in the absence of the jury and in a summing up, are stated and discussed openly in court and any error that there may be will be rectified on appeal. Finally, in the Crown Court there is a full record of the proceedings. All of this can be contrasted with the magistrates' courts. Baroness Kennedy, in a House of Lords debate, looked at the issue of people wanting to play the system and she examined the other side of the coin. She made the following observation:

> 'Sometimes dishonest witnesses decide to retract their statements, or want to avoid being cross-examined and found wanting. Sometimes, alibis are found, and that makes all the difference. Sometimes, when the Crown Prosecution Service has had time to review the case, evidential issues come to light to show that the case could never succeed. So there are very good reasons why cases are dropped or original charges reduced due to over-charging.' (HL Deb, 2 December 1999, c9704)

The acquittal rate is a further cause for concern. It is lower in the magistrates' courts (at 25 per cent) than in the Crown Court (where it is 40 per cent). The civil liberties pressure group (Liberty (2000)) thought: that restricting access to jury trial would lead to a decline in the standard of criminal justice, an increase in the number of wrongful convictions and a wide perception of unfairness and discrimination; that jury trial is fundamentally more democratic and likely to achieve a fairer result than trial in a magistrates' court; that it is more important to deliver the very best and highest standards of criminal justice, rather than the cheapest; and that limiting access will have a disproportionate effect on black defendants because they are more likely to choose jury trial, less likely to have confidence in the system and more likely to plead not guilty.

Finally, it needs to be noted that if the aim is to reduce the use of jury trial, the numbers for which have been increasing, then the defendant is only one variable. As Hedderman and Moxon (1992) indicate, the magistrates are also an important variable. Hedderman and Moxon carried out research into decision making for either way offences in 1990. The following are some of the more important of the points that they made.

1. Almost 60 per cent of cases dealt with in the Crown Court were sent there because magistrates declined jurisdiction. The impact of magistrates in terms of the percentage of cases in which they determine venue has been variously reported and 60 per cent is in the middle. For example, Riley and Vennard (1988) stated that the rate was 40 per cent. In 2001 of the either-way cases that were sent for jury trial 81 per cent were there because the magistrates declined jurisdiction. Hedderman and Moxon also made the point that in their sample magistrates' sentencing powers would have been sufficient to deal with a majority of the cases that were sent to the Crown Court.

2. Nearly three-quarters of defendants who were denied a choice of venue by magistrates would have wanted summary trial to expedite the matter and in expectation of a lighter sentence.

3. Most of those who chose to be dealt with at the Crown Court were influenced by the prospect of acquittal; yet the majority (82 per cent) ended up pleading guilty to all charges on which they were convicted. This is a very common finding and there is clearly something peculiar in the decision-making process. The sentence discount is reduced when you leave it till late in the process to plead guilty. It is of course possible that charge reduction may have taken place by the time that they plead guilty. Research by Choongh (1997) pointed out that there is a real problem with charge reduction not happening until the last possible moment and indeed decisions to change the plea to guilty happening on the day of the trial. For the defendants there are factors that encourage them to wait till the last moment. They can wait to see if the witnesses turn up and they can also wait to see if they get a judge that they perceive as being a lenient one.

4. More than half of those who elected Crown Court trial said that the possibility of a lighter sentence at the Crown Court influenced their decision. The reality in fact is that the Crown Court made far more use of custody than magistrates' courts. This remained true when cases were matched on a number of factors.

5. A substantial number of defendants, including some who intended to plead guilty from the outset, chose to be dealt with at the Crown Court because they did not trust magistrates to give due weight to their case, often feeling that the magistrates would be biased in favour of the police.

Conclusion on mode of trial

My own view is largely influenced by a very great concern about the use of juries in the first place, so the issue of restricting access to jury trial could be perceived as a plus point in itself. Any decision as to the merits of such restrictions on your part, would be the better if it came after material on the day-to-day workings of the jury system had been examined.

5.2 Pleas

Guilty pleas

Within the criminal justice system many defendants will be guilty as a result of their own plea of guilty. The figures are particularly high for the magistrates' courts where in 1997 the following figures were recorded: 82 per cent were guilty pleas, in a further 12 per cent of cases the case was proven in the absence of the defendant, 2 per cent of cases were discontinued and in only 4 per cent of cases was the defendant convicted after a trial. The figure for the Crown Court was 60 per cent guilty pleas in 2001: Home Office (2002a). The criminal justice system relies on these guilty pleas and that is why there is a discount on sentence for a timely guilty plea. In many cases of course people plead guilty because they know that they are guilty and they see no percentage in acting in any other way than pleading guilty. The issue of concern is that as Sanders and Young (1994) indicate there are forces at work that may lead to some innocent people pleading guilty. Some of the reasons that people plead guilty, apart from thinking that they are guilty, are: a desire to get it over with; that the odds are poor; the outcome is unpredictable even with a good case; worries about access to a lawyer; there are no transcripts to aid an appeal; and the inducements of charge bargains, plea bargains and the sentencing discount. In reality, the inducements offer most reward to the guilty. Also, the people who are at most risk are the innocent who rely on the trial and may lose out and then end up worse off than if they had pleaded guilty! The outcome is that the trial as a safeguard is largely mythical as trials happen so rarely. Sanders and Young point out that there would be more tolerance of features of the criminal justice system – such as charge bargaining, sentence discounts and sentence bargains – if the net result was more convictions of the guilty and no corresponding increase in convictions of the innocent. The ends would be sufficiently desirable to render the means acceptable. The problem is that there is a real risk that the innocent are being induced to plead guilty. The danger that the factually innocent will be induced to plead guilty is partly a product of the law that states that the weaker the evidence against a defendant, the greater the discount given for a plea of guilty should be. A sentencing discount for a guilty plea has been a feature of our system for some time and the earlier the plea the greater the discount. It is interesting to note that there is no discount in Scotland where it would be regarded as an improper inducement. Here we regard it, for good or ill, as a sign of remorse, a reward for saving the expense of the trial and for avoiding further pressure upon the witnesses. The Auld review of the criminal courts (Auld LJ (2001)) supported the idea and suggested that a graduated scheme of sentencing discounts should be used so that the earlier the plea of guilty the higher the discount for it. This should be coupled with a system of advance indication of sentence for a defendant considering pleading guilty. The White Paper, *Justice for All* (Home Office (2002d)), promoted a similar message and suggested introducing a clearer tariff of sentence discount for pleading guilty and arrangements where defendants could seek advance indication of what the discounted sentence would be if they pleaded guilty. The Criminal Justice Act 2003 provides for a graduated discount to encourage early guilty pleas. The provision re-enacts s152 of the Powers of Criminal Courts (Sentencing) Act 2000 which in turn followed s48 of the Criminal Justice and Public Order Act 1994. The effect of this aspect of the discount principle is to make a trial less attractive to the innocent. The innocent have more discount to lose than the guilty in contesting their cases. It seems that innocent people do plead guilty. Baldwin and McConville (1977) noted that nearly half of the late plea changers in their study made substantial and credible claims of innocence. In a substantial number of these guilty plea cases independent assessors judged the evidence against the defendant to be weak.

Royal Commission on Criminal Justice (1993)

In contrast with the view of Sanders and Young the Royal Commission on Criminal Justice (1993) saw less dangers in the use of sentencing discounts for guilty pleas:

> 'For many decades defendants who plead guilty in the Crown Court have been regarded by the Court of Appeal as usually entitled to a discount or reduction in their sentence. The usual range of discount is 25 per cent to 30 per cent. The primary reason for the sentence discount is to encourage defendants who know themselves to be guilty to plead accordingly and so enable the resources which would be expended in a contested case to be saved. A subsidiary reason, applicable in some types of cases, is to recognise that the defendant by pleading guilty has spared witnesses the trauma of having to give evidence at court. Provided that the defendant is in fact guilty and has received competent legal advice about his or her position, there can be no serious objection to a system of inducements designed to encourage him or her so to plead. Such a system is, however, sometimes held to encourage defendants who are not guilty of the offence charged to plead guilty to it nevertheless. One reason for this is that some defendants may believe that they are likely to be convicted and that, if they are, they will receive a custodial sentence if found guilty after a contested trial but will avoid such a sentence if they plead guilty. The risk cannot be wholly avoided and although there can be no certainty as to the precise numbers it would be naive to suppose that innocent persons never plead guilty because of the prospect of the sentence discount.' (1993:110)

5.3 Review of the criminal courts

In the review of the criminal courts by Auld LJ in 2001 (Auld LJ (2001)) he suggested unifying the magistrates' courts and Crown Court in a single criminal court structure with a new third, intermediate, District Division. Cases would be tried, according to their seriousness and the likely maximum sentence, either by magistrates, by judge and jury, or in the new District Division by a professional judge and two lay magistrates. Magistrates and district judges should continue to exercise their established summary jurisdiction and the work should continue to be allocated between them much as at present. If the recommendation for the establishment of a new unified criminal court with a District Division is adopted, they should also sit together in that Division exercising its higher jurisdiction. Steps should be taken to provide benches of magistrates that more broadly reflect the communities they serve. Auld also suggested that in trials by judge and magistrates in the District Division, the judge should be the sole judge of law, but he and the magistrates should together be the judges of fact, each having an equal vote. The judge should not sum up the case to the magistrates but should retire with them to consider the court's decision. The judge should be solely responsible for sentence. The Courts Act 2003 contained some of these ideas and the Criminal Justice Act 2003 incorporated others. In both cases they were not implemented on Royal Assent and so will have to await implementation in the future. We can note at this stage the important change that the Criminal Justice Act 2003 provides for. This is that magistrates will be able to sentence an offender to 12 rather than six months for a single offence. This is one of a number of features of the legislation that will mean that jury trial will not be used – for good or ill. A further extension to their powers is that where sentences are to be served consecutively the maximum period is increased from 12 months to 65 weeks.

5.4 The role of magistrates

There are over 24,000 lay magistrates. Certain groups are excluded – such as members of the armed forces, the police and their relatives, those with certain types of criminal conviction and undischarged bankrupts. There are also professional magistrates who were called stipendary magistrates but they have been renamed as district judges. They are designed to help with the workloads and they are essential in some areas such as the major cities. The recruitment problem in relation to lay magistrates is seen in the recent increase in the maximum age at which you can be appointed – it is now 65. You can apply to be a lay magistrate but most people are nominated by organisations such as trade unions and political parties. In 1998 new criteria for the appointment of lay magistrates were announced by the Lord Chancellor. The characteristics to be sought were good character, understanding and communication, social awareness, maturity and sound temperament, sound judgement and reliability. There are problems with their background as they are disproportionately middle class, middle aged and conservative-minded. They are part-timers who are only required to sit 24 times a year. They are also amateurs in the law who receive only limited training. As we will see in a moment, there are many criticisms of the lay magistrates but their advantages are said to be the very fact that they are a lay element, their local knowledge and that they help to make possible a cheap and quick system. As Derbyshire (2002:286) notes, magistrates hear many more cases than juries and do much more sentencing than the judges. The idea of the cases that they deal with being trivial or low level is also in a good number of cases inaccurate. Public confidence is said to be in their favour, yet when we looked at the issue of mode of trial they were not trusted.

Criticisms of lay magistrates

1. Their background. However, Morgan and Russell (2000) found that lay magistrates are ethnically representative of the population at a national level. They are also balanced in terms of gender.
2. Their lack of expertise, though they do have a court clerk to offer legal advice. Vennard (1981) in research on magistrates found that their decisions were based upon the credibility of witnesses and the evidence that had been presented to them in the case. Whilst the 1993 Royal Commission on Criminal Justice felt that there was no problem of any significance with the decision-making of magistrates, as evidenced by the fact that there are so few appeals, Belloni and Hodgson (2000) felt that this is misleading. You cannot appeal if you plead guilty, which is what the vast majority of defendants will have done. Also, the vast majority of cases are motoring cases which people may just let go as small fry. Of the rest they are still likely to be doubtful of winning if they appeal, reflecting a lack of faith in the system. They are also likely to get discouragement rather than encouragement from the system in terms of funding an appeal. Despite all this, their data from 1997 revealed that a quarter of those who pleaded not guilty and who were convicted appealed and of those 42 per cent got their appeal allowed or a sentence variation – so there is a problem.
3. It is a conveyor-belt system of justice with limited safeguards for defendants. This is particularly so in comparison with Crown Court procedures. There is not same level of disclosure and legal representation.
4. Magistrates are said to suffer from case-hardening and also that they are too inclined to believe the police and the prosecution. They hear implausible tales offered to them on a regular basis from people who lack skills and come over badly. They start to assume that the defendants are guilty whilst realising that there has to be some evidence to support the assumption. But they believe the police and disbelieve the defendants so that is not too hard. They are not blind to the possibility of problems with police evidence but in the round the police are quite simply more credible. A belief that most defendants are lying whilst only some of the police are lying might reflect their attitude. Lets be clear that at a trial at least one side is lying. Belloni and Hodgson (2000) make very similar suggestions:

> '... magistrates are very strongly disposed to believe and rely upon the integrity of the police and the veracity of their evidence. This was explained to us by a solicitor-advocate as follows:
>
>> "I think the police are more believable to the magistrates than the defendants. They think: 'The police don't have to come here and tell lies. On the other hand, the defendant comes here because he's in trouble and he might tell lies to get out of trouble.' I think they work on that basis too often: so it is an uphill struggle for us solicitors to persuade them otherwise." (Interview, February 1995)
>
> Hedderman and Moxon (1992) found that the majority of both defendants and their solicitors believe that "magistrates are on the side of the police"; and Gifford (1986:36) asserts that the impression most often given by magistrates to defence solicitors "is of total partiality towards the prosecution. The burden of proof seems to be reversed: if the

police say you are guilty, you will be found guilty unless you can prove your innocence." McConville et al (1994) also gained the impression that in magistrates' courts "there is a reverse onus of proof under which it is for the defendant to establish innocence rather than for the prosecution to prove guilt" (211–38). Thirdly, defence solicitors are often poorly pre-pared and disinclined to function in an adversarial capacity. According to McConville et at (1994), they operate in a way which assumes the client's guilt. The extent to which defence lawyers share the values of magistrates in this respect is supported by a number of our own interviews with solicitor-advocates, as in the following example.

> "My view is that probably 90-plus percent of defendants are guilty; and as you pointed out, about 95 per cent of defendants get convicted, so it probably works out just about right – but whether for the right reasons I don't know. I suspect that the vast majority of people who are charged are guilty of an offence, and I think that's probably the view taken by most magistrates. ... Unlike jurors, I think magistrates tend to become ... perhaps the word isn't cynical, but hardened to a certain view. I think they probably expect and believe that most defendants are guilty. Their decisions, not always based upon the evidence, reflect that ... I think it's a rough-and-ready result that comes out [in magistrates' courts] at the end. But in most cases, happily, I think it is probably justified. However, the magistrates' way of dealing with it doesn't necessarily equate with it being correct and unbiased." (Interview, February 1995). (2000:4–5)

5. There is disparity between benches in relation to decisions on a range of matters such as legal aid, sentencing and bail applications.
6. There is more disclosure in the Crown Court.
7. The amount and type of training that they receive: its about making the process work rather than the rights of defendants.

The alternatives to the present system include the use of more professionals to replace or reduce the need for lay magistrates. A greater use of district judges is one possibility or court clerks who are legally qualified or sufficiently trained could perform the additional role of arbiter of fact. Both the district judge and the clerks could sit with one or two lay magistrates.

Auld LJ favoured retention of the lay magistracy and also saw a role for a mixed bench. Cost is the big deterrent for a wholly professional set-up. Morgan and Russell (2000) carried out research on magistrates and whilst during 2000 the name for stipendiary magistrates was changed to district judges, during the research for the report the old name was still being used and it has been used in the report. At the time of the research in the year 2000 the magistracy comprised approximately 30,400 lay magistrates, 96 full-time stipendiaries and 146 part-time stipendiaries. The lay magistracy was found to be gender balanced, ethnically representative of the population at a national level, overwhelmingly drawn from professional and managerial ranks and comprises a high proportion (two-fifths) who have retired from full-time employment. In comparison, stipendiaries are mostly male and white and tend to be younger. Lay magistrates sit in court an average 41.4 occasions annually (although many sit a good deal more frequently), and additionally spend the equivalent, on average, of a full working week on training and other duties. The stipendiaries sit in court about four days per week. Lay magistrates usually sit in panels of three whilst stipendiaries nearly always sit alone. Stipendiaries tend to be allocated more complex, prolonged and sensitive cases and concentrate on triable either-way cases. Even with more difficult cases they are about 22 per cent faster than the lay magistrates. The greater speed of stipendiaries is not achieved at the expense of inquisition and challenge; on the contrary, hearings before stipendiaries typically involve more questions being asked and more challenges being made. They are more efficient and will be less likely to use adjournments. Lay magistrates are less likely to refuse defendants bail in cases where the prosecution seeks custody and the defence applies for bail (19 per cent compared to 37 per cent) and make use of immediate custody as a sentence (12 per cent of triable either-way cases compared to 25 per cent). This is probably a reflection of the stipendiaries seeing the more serious cases.

If only directly attributable costs (salaries, expenses and training) are considered, lay magistrates are much cheaper because they are not paid directly and many do not claim loss of earnings. A sizeable minority does not even claim their allowable travelling expenses. A lay magistrate costs on average £495 per annum compared to the £90,000 per annum total employment costs of a stipendiary. These translate into a cost per appearance before lay and stipendiary magistrates of £3.59 and £20.96 respectively.

As to the views of the public they do not have strong feelings about the precise role of magistrates; they think that summary offences, particularly if not contested, can be dealt with by a single magistrate but that panels should make the more serious judicial decisions. Cost considerations suggest that this could only be achieved (in the short term at least) by continuing to make extensive use of lay magistrates. They also found that at no stage during the study was it suggested that in most respects the magistrates' courts do not work well or fail to command general confidence. Thus, eliminating or greatly diminishing the role of lay magistrates would not be widely understood or supported.

5.5 The quality of the defence in the Crown Court

There is a problem with barristers in the Crown Court. Not only may their quality be low, they may well not get the brief until the morning of the trial. This compounds the fact that the brief may well be, and probably has been, prepared by unqualified staff. For the defendant the difficulty is that it is very hard to persuade an appeal court that the incompetence of your lawyers is a reason for your conviction to be overturned. Even the 1993 Royal Commission on Criminal Justice (1993:174) thought that injustice was being done to defendants. With the split profession there is little or no contact with the barrister by the solicitor and little or no familiarity with the case by the barrister. The solicitor is not going to court and he does not know how the barrister will play it, so it is hard to know what to do in terms of preparation. This is a disincentive for the solicitor to do much in preparing a case and he may end up doing just the basics. Also file preparation is likely to be delegated to those who are cheaper than qualified staff: the profit motive. Many lawyers still do a good job, but the concern has to be for the defendants who end up with the less competent. Last-minute changes of barrister are also common. Zander and Henderson (1993) report that it happens in 48 per cent of cases and that 25 per cent received the files the afternoon before the trial and some even on the day of the trial. This may encourage deals, as the lack of preparation means that the barrister will be more likely to be put on the spot. So you go for a negotiated sentence but have lost out on a timely plea of guilty and indeed the chance to be acquitted.

5.6 The jury

The jury is a popular topic for writers and it has plenty to offer interest, but its importance to the criminal justice system should not be overestimated. Most trials take place in the magistrates' court rather than the Crown Court, and for both courts the impact of guilty pleas is important. Statistics for 2001 (Home Office (2002a)) reveal that 79,200 defendants were sent for jury trial, 75,500 appeared before the court (6 per cent of cases were written off) and of the 75,500 62 per cent pleaded guilty and only 34 per cent of the rest were convicted. Thus, two-thirds of defendants decide against a trial but of the third that do go to trial two-thirds of them also win. The major role of the judge at trials in the Crown Court also needs to be appreciated, as about half of the not-guilty cases are directed and ordered acquittals. Ordered acquittals occur before the trial where the prosecution says it will not be offering evidence. Directed acquittals will be during a trial where the judge forms the view that the prosecution case could not hope to succeed.

The functions of the jury at the criminal trial will be explained and criticised and thought will be given to the need for reform of or a reduction in the use of or indeed abolition of the jury system. Whatever the merits of the latter suggestion it is not in reality going to be on the political agenda. Lord Denning and others tell us that the jury has been the bulwark of our liberties for too long for any of us to seek to alter it and the jury seems to be regarded as a good thing. The jury in its present form is in fact a very modern institution. Until 1974 you had to be a property owner to be eligible to be on a jury – so many people, particularly women, would not have qualified. Also you should note that those who suggest that the jury protects our liberties provide little in the way of evidence for the proposition.

Functions of the jury

The jury are the arbiters of facts and a finding of guilt or innocence should arise from those facts on the basis of material presented to them during the trial and as guided by directions of the judge. The problem is that they may well have no particular expertise in these matters and ignorance does not seem to be an attractive virtue in those who are to decide guilt or innocence. There are I suppose worse systems – trial by ordeal and trial by battle to mention two. Maybe we should aspire to the best possible system. Juries do provide certainty – the finding will normally be either guilty or not guilty. Nothing is left to dispute, especially as we are not allowed to know how the jury made its decision. Justice is said to be delivered in that there is a verdict according to conscience. Jury duty is an important public duty providing judgment by one's peers. For that reason the aim should be to provide a panel that is independent, impartial and representative.

Qualifications and disqualifications

These are provided for in several pieces of legislation, but principally the Juries Act 1974, the Criminal Justice Act 1988 and the Juries (Disqualification) Act 1984. You have to be 18–70 years old, on the electoral roll and ordinarily resident in the United Kingdom for at least a five-year period from the age of 13. You need sufficient level of understanding of the language to be able to serve effectively as a juror. The categories who are ineligible are: those who have served a sentence of life or five years' or more detention, the judiciary, those involved in the administration of justice, the clergy and the mentally ill. There are further groups who are disqualified, such as those who in the last ten years have served a custodial sentence, including a suspended sentence, and those who have been subject to orders such as probation orders in the last five years, and those on bail. The sense in the above is clear, but it results in the loss of some good potential jurors and it is not fully representative of society. Whilst juries are now more representative than in the past. some groups such as ethnic minorities are under-represented. On this however the Royal Commission on Criminal Justice (1993) noted that for 1991 the non-white component of juries in the study by Zander and Henderson (1993) was 5 per cent, whilst the rate for the population as a whole was 5.9 per cent. The same research found that it is common to have all-white juries.

People are called for jury service and they make up panels for the courts, with the jury being selected from the panel by a ballot. A person can defer jury service once as of right. If you did defer you would be called again shortly afterwards. You can be excused from jury service because of previous service or if you are entitled – this covers groups such as the over 65s and doctors. There is also a discretion to excuse people on the grounds of inconvenience. It may also be necessary to excuse a juror with knowledge of, or a vested interest in, the case.

A major review of the criminal courts was carried out by Auld LJ in 2001: Auld LJ (2001). In the review he suggested that there was a need to encourage greater public responsibility for jury service and to make it harder to be excused. Jurors should be more widely representative than they are of the national and local communities from which they are drawn. Qualification for jury service should remain the same, save that entitlement to, rather than actual, entry on an electoral roll should be a criterion. Potential jurors should be identified from a combination of a number of public registers and lists. While those with criminal convictions and mental disorder should continue to be disqualified from service, no one in future should be ineligible for jury service or excusable as of right. Any claimed inability to serve should be a matter for discretionary deferral or excusal. Provision should be made to enable ethnic minority representation on juries where race is likely to be relevant to an important issue in the case. The Criminal Justice Act 2003 provides for the rules on jury service to be changed, with the aim of involving a broader cross-section of the community. The Act includes provisions to abolish the categories of ineligibility (with the exception of mentally disordered persons and certain groups of convicted persons) for, and excusal as of right from, jury service. This means that certain groups of people who currently must not, or need not, do jury service would be required to do it unless they can show good reason not to.

It was made clear in the case of *R* v *Ford* [1989] QB 868 that the trial judge cannot interfere with the selection process to try to produce a racially balanced jury. The judge can discharge people – for example, the stone deaf. Also, the judge can discharge once the trial has begun – for example, if they are drunk or they fall asleep or engage in frivolous behaviour, or if they learn of the defendant's antecedents. You need nine members of the jury to keep the trial going. Jury-vetting, a system whereby the background of the jury is investigated, would undermine the randomness of the selection process. This occurred in relation to the ABC trial in 1978 which was concerned with the Official Secrets Act 1911. It was discovered that the jury panel had been investigated and a second trial was started as a result. Attorney-General's guidelines were produced on the practice of jury-vetting and these were subsequently amended in 1989. The guidelines reaffirm the basic principles – jury selection should be a system of random selection. Vetting is to be restricted to cases involving issues of national security and the Attorney-General's authorisation would be required. Exclusion is to operate by being called upon to stand by for the Crown or by challenge for cause. The system of stand by for the Crown is technically a challenge for cause but there is no requirement to provide proof until the panel is exhausted. A search of criminal records can be used for the above purposes. In security cases the above methods are supplemented by the investigation of particular beliefs, and evidence in camera can be used. Investigations can include the use of Special Branch. The legality of vetting was upheld in the case of *R* v *Mason* [1981] QB 881. In all of this there is a clear inequality of resources and in many ways the defence are disadvantaged. They do not get access to relevant information and it is common that checks that would be desirable are not carried out for the defence. The system of peremptory challenge, the right to remove jurors without reasons being established, was finally removed completely by the Criminal Justice Act 1987.

The verdict

A unanimous verdict is desirable, but the Juries Act 1974 states that if there are not less than 11 jurors then ten must agree and if there are not less than ten then nine must agree. If there are only nine jurors they must be unanimous. A majority verdict can be resorted to after a reasonable time and this can be after two hours and ten minutes. The deliberations of the jury are supposed to be secret. A number of justifications for secrecy can be suggested, one of which is that freedom of discussion is ensured. There may also be a reluctance to participate without secrecy as harassment and other reactions might be feared – secrecy protects finality and certainty. It is also said that you would lose faith in the jury if their discussions became known – this is not a strong argument. It prevents false reporting by jurors as to what they had done in a case and there is no pressure to justify the verdict. Against secrecy is the view that there is the exercise of power without responsibility and accountability. Injustices would be easier to cure if mistakes were more apparent. An understanding of the jury system and any move towards reform would be aided if we knew better what was going on.

Are juries up to the job?

1. It is said that juries acquit too often – the evidence on this is at least equivocal. In the Clive Ponting case, a civil servant passed documents to a Labour Party Member of

Parliament. The documents concerned the sinking of an Argentine warship, the Belgrano, during the Falklands War. Under the Official Secrets legislation the passing of such information to unauthorised persons was clearly an offence. It was not in dispute that the documents had been passed to an unauthorised person. The issue was raised at the trial that there was a public right to be informed on the matter and the government should not be able to conceal the information. The jury were directed by the judge that Ponting had clearly had no right to act in the way that he did. The jury acquitted Ponting despite this direction.

2. Should conscience as the basis for a decision be allowed? The view has been put that even if a jury is arbitrary and prejudiced that this proves that the jury is independent.
3. Can they understand the evidence?
4. There is irritation in being a juror and this may affect their behaviour.
5. Case hardening may occur where a jury had only just managed to arrive at a decision to convict a defendant in a case and then they hear a long list of previous convictions. At the next trial they may well be more prosecution orientated.

Research on the competence of the jury

McCabe and Purves (1972) arranged for experts to examine 173 cases in which the defendant was acquitted and in only 15 cases was the decision to acquit regarded as being against the evidence. They also used a shadow jury, a replica of a real jury, that listened to 30 cases and their deliberations were observed. The research found that the shadow jury looked carefully at the evidence and used it as the basis for their verdict. Baldwin and McConville (1979) in their research found the decision-making by the jury to be an arbitrary and unpredictable business. There were a small number of cases where there were doubtful verdicts, both convictions and acquittals. Zander and Henderson (1993) in a survey of over 8,000 jurors reported that 56 per cent of jurors said that all the jurors understood the evidence and 41 per cent said that most did. Ninety per cent of barristers reported that jurors would be able to understand the evidence in relation to particular cases. And ninety-four per cent of judges reported that they thought that the jury would be able to understand scientific evidence. The study also reported that the vast majority of trials are not long the average being under seven hours.

Barber and Gordon provided and edited a set of personal reactions to having been a juror. The manner in which contributors were sought, meant that they were professional writers in the main. A common observation was that jury members switched their point of view so as to fit in with the majority. The danger is that they are doing this in order to expedite the matter. It should be made clear that being a hung jury is an acceptable, if not perfect, outcome of a trial. Brooks noted that 'five of these jurors could not read the oath without verbal prompting from the usher' (1976:27). Harry Cohen noted that when the issue of whether there was prejudice at work, in a jury that was considering a case in which there had been white defendants and black victims, prejudice was denied in the following manner: 'I've got no racial prejudice whatsoever, but you can't believe a word they say, can you?' (1976:44). Harry Cohen also had the following tale to tell. It was as regards a fellow juror who had also taken notes:

'... he started asking questions based on the evidence we had heard with regard to identification etc. After speaking to quite a few of the jurors he suddenly stopped and looked across the table at me with an expression of blank amazement on his face. It had become painfully obvious that most of the jury had not even remotely followed the case. Some did not even remember the names of the individuals ... the juror said it was useless to try to discuss the case in detail if hardly anyone seemed to be aware of the details. In these circumstances I asked the juror sitting next to me how he arrived at his verdict, to which he replied "well, I just got the general impression that they were not guilty and that's good enough for me."' (1976:45)

The worst has been saved till last. Elwyn Morris noted that 'Three of the women in the jury upon entering the jury room ... immediately secured chairs in a far corner of the room where they sat, their knees almost touching, puffing deeply on their cigarettes.' When asked to take their seats at the jury table, 'Oh you men settle it amongst yourselves,' said one of the women, and they took no part in and showed no interest in what followed and only five people really took part in the deliberations. At the end 'One of the men sitting at the top of the table who had not uttered a word said loudly "Thank God the bloody thing's over"'(1976:87,88).

Devons (1965) was an economics professor who had been called for jury service on two occasions in Manchester. He was thus able to provide a first-hand account for us of the operation of the jury as part of the decision-making process within the criminal justice system. The jury of course decide upon the very important issue of guilt or innocence and evidence such as this causes me to doubt the wisdom of such a system of decision-making. His first general observations were that nobody really told the jury what it was supposed to do and that much went over the head of the jury. Devons recounted his experience of one case he sat in as follows:

'The "Case of the Officious Bureaucrat" concerned a man who was being prosecuted for re-selling used national insurance stamps. The accusation was that the man had got hold of some national insurance cards, steamed off the stamps, rubbed off the cancelling dates, and had used them again, thus avoiding paying the national insurance contribution and defrauding the Insurance Fund. The main evidence came from a Ministry of National Insurance expert, who told us of tests he had done on the gum which had been used to stick on the stamps, and the small bits of fibre that were still attached to the stamps. ... The official, who seemed to me to be quite a junior one, gave his evidence clearly, but somewhat disdainfully, cryptically and officiously – or so it seemed to me – in answer to questions by prosecuting counsel. He was almost the prototype of the petty bureaucrat. ...

In his summing up the judge concentrated on the evidence of the technical expert, pointing out that it had not been seriously challenged, and that the defence had no explanation for it. He hardly mentioned the officious clerk's evidence since this was on quite a minor point. And he pointed out to us that the onus was on the prosecution to prove guilt.

The point of all this is its influence on the jury. When we retired to the jury room the jurymen turned to each other saying: "Did you hear that little pip-squeak of a civil servant"; "These petty bureaucrats, they need to be taught a lesson"; "I would not like to have to work for him." When the self-appointed foreman asked for our views on the case, I said that the technical evidence seemed to me to show conclusively that the stamps had been re-used, that this was not rebutted by the defence, and that the accused had given no explanation whatsoever except just flatly to deny having used old stamps. This seemed to me conclusively to point towards his guilt. The others disregarded this altogether and just said one after

183

another: "But look at that tinpot dictator"; "these officials"; "it might happen to us any day"; "I'm not going to find him guilty"; "let's teach these civil servants a lesson." So they all argued for "Not guilty". I argued with them for about twenty minutes that they were not directing themselves to the evidence; I called attention to the judge's summing-up and argued that the officiousness of the civil servant was really quite irrelevant. But it was no use; this was what impressed them and they were determined to do the official world one in the eye. I gave way and we returned a verdict of "Not Guilty".' (1965:565–566)

Conclusion

The jury has already been largely eliminated from the civil trial (an experience that we have all survived) and is under some attack in the criminal trial. If we wanted alternatives to the present system of jury trial these include: allowing the judge to make the decision, or a bench of judges, or a composite tribunal in which the judge would retire with the jury in order to assist them or to become a member of the jury, or having a trained jury that may sit for an extended period of time – perhaps a year. Some final and further arguments that have been suggested for and against the jury can be noted.

Advantages of the jury
1. It saves us from the state and its ability to make and prosecute laws.
2. Magistrates may know the past form of those who may well be old customers of the courts – jury members are unlikely to be in this position.
3. There will be a better quality trial available to the defendant in the Crown Court, though this has to be paid for.

Disadvantages of the jury
1. Juries are said to be swayable by advocates – that however is surely the point of having the advocates.
2. Are people too inexperienced at 18 to be on a jury? They could have been a parent by this age of course.
3. There is no test of abilities or suitability. Should there be selection tests, qualifications and training?
4. There may be local or other prejudices operative.
5. For some cases there may be the problem of jury nobbling. The Criminal Justice and Public Order Act 1994 offered further protection to juries, by allowing a retrial after a tainted trial, in relation to which a person has been convicted for interfering with jurors or witnesses. The Criminal Justice Act 2003 makes provision for this, as well as allowing for complex fraud trials to be heard by a judge alone. The latter provision was on the basis that it would not be implemented without further review and parliamentary approval. In return the clauses that provided for a judge-only trial where there is a large risk of interference with the jury went through. In 2003 the Prime Minister, Tony Blair, told an international conference that it was wrong that the Metropolitan Police should have to spend the equivalent of 26,000 officer days a year protecting juries from intimidation by the defendant when such trials should continue with the judge sitting alone. The defendant will be able to appeal against a decision to try a case by judge alone.

Where a trial is conducted or continued without a jury, and the defendant is convicted, the judge will be required to give a reasoned verdict.

6. Long trials are both expensive and daunting, however the average length is seven hours.

7. The idea of the jury has been undermined by reforms such as majority verdicts, disqualification systems and jury-vetting. Juries are, as a result, less representative of society.

8. The jury does not give trial by peers. Most defendants are young working-class males which is not the typical jury.

9. Juries acquit the guilty and convict the innocent. As part of this argument it is noted that all of the miscarriage of justice cases were jury trials. I think it is wrong to blame the jury for these cases as problems clearly existed elsewhere in the criminal justice system in relation to those cases.

10. Juries add to the length of the trial and thus the cost.

11. Note the provision in the Criminal Justice Act 2003 which will allow juries to be able to hear about a defendant's previous convictions and other misconduct where this is relevant to the case and where the value of the evidence is not outweighed by its prejudicial effect. However, you do wonder how it will be possible for a person standing trial for rape to have a fair trial if it were revealed that he had say two previous convictions for rape.

5.7 Admissibility of evidence, appeals, human rights and the Criminal Cases Revision Commission

In Chapter 3 a number of sources of remedy that were most relevant to the role of the police were considered, including the complaints system against the police. Admissibility of evidence, appeals, human rights and the Criminal Cases Revision Commission offer other possibilities and they impact most directly in relation to the criminal trial. The route of appeal for a defendant who was tried in the magistrates' court are firstly to the Queen's Bench Division, on a case stated basis, arguing that there has been an error of law. A further appeal to the House of Lords would be possible if leave to appeal was granted. There is also an appeal to the Crown Court with regard to both sentence and conviction. Finally, judicial review can be used. Where the case was tried in the Crown Court there is an appeal, normally subject to leave to appeal, to the Court of Appeal and thereafter to the House of Lords. The appeal can relate to sentence and conviction. The prosecution can use the case stated method of appeal and can also ask the Court of Appeal to consider whether the sentence was unduly lenient.

Admissibility of evidence

Our system is one in which there are not hard and fast rules which has the purported justification that cases differ and so judges must have wide discretion. A problem with the system is that much of the work in preparing a defence file/brief will be in the hands of the unqualified and so the requisite material may not be there to help put the trial barrister on alert. How to prove malpractice in low visibility situations is the problem. The statutory basis of the system is ss76 and 78 of the Police and Criminal Evidence Act 1984 (PACE). Section 76 states:

'76(1) In any proceedings a confession made by an accused person may be given in evidence against him in so far as it is relevant to any matter in issue in proceedings and is not excluded by the court in pursuance of this section.

(2) If, in any proceedings where the prosecution proposes to give in evidence a confession made by an accused person, it is represented to the court that the confession was or may have been obtained –

(a) by oppression of the person who made it; or

(b) in consequence of anything said or done which was likely, in the circumstances existing at the time, to render unreliable any confession which might be made by him in consequence thereof;

the court shall not allow the confession to be given in evidence against him except in so far as the prosecution proves to the court beyond reasonable doubt that the confession (notwithstanding that it may be true) was not obtained as aforesaid.

(3) In any proceedings where the prosecution proposes to give in evidence a confession made by an accused person, the court may of its own motion require the prosecution, as a condition of allowing it to do so, to prove that the confession was not obtained as mentioned in subsection (2) above.

(4) The fact that a confession is wholly or partly excluded in pursuance of section shall not affect the admissibility in evidence –

(a) of any facts discovered as a result of the confession; or

(b) where the confession is relevant as showing that the accused speaks, writes or expresses himself in a particular way, of so much of the confession as is necessary to show that he does so.

(5) Evidence that a fact to which this subsection applies was discovered as a result of a statement made by an accused person shall not be admissible unless evidence of how it was discovered is given by him or on his behalf.

(6) Subsection (5) above applies –

(a) to any fact discovered as a result of a confession which is wholly excluded in pursuance of this section; and

(b) to any fact discovered as a result of a confession which is partly so excluded, if the fact is discovered as a result of the excluded part of the confession.'

Section 76 requires exclusion if there has been oppression or the effect is such as to render the evidence unreliable. It is very difficult to satisfy this test and the defence is more likely to try to succeed under s78.

Section 78(1) provides that the court may refuse to allow evidence that having regard to all the circumstances of the case, including the circumstances in which the evidence was obtained, '[may have] such an adverse effect on the fairness of the proceedings that the court ought not to admit it.'

R v Howden-Simpson [1991] Crim LR 49 is a reminder that confessions cannot be extracted by means of an inducement. In this case a defendant was told that other offences would not be pursued if there was a confession to two offences. This led to an exclusion of the confession under s76. In *R v Paris* [1994] Crim LR 361 a confession was excluded after 13 hours of hostile questioning, which included the police shouting at the defendant the responses to questions that they desired. In *R* v *Khan* [1996] 3 All ER 289 the police obtained some evidence by planting a surveillance device. The view of the House of Lords was that that alone would not mean that the evidence should be excluded under s78.

Appeals

Appeals following a trial on indictment

In *R* v *Donald Pendelton* [2001] UKHL 66; [2002] 1 All ER 524 the proper approach for the Court of Appeal, in cases where there is new evidence that had not been available when the matter was tried by jury, was considered by the House of Lords. Section 23 Criminal Appeal Act 1968 provides for an appeal against conviction in cases where there is fresh evidence. The legal question raised was whether the House of Lords had correctly defined the test to be applied in such cases in *Stafford* v *Director of Public Prosecutions* [1974] AC 878. The House of Lords suggested that the question for the Court of Appeal on an appeal against conviction was whether the conviction was safe and not whether the accused was guilty. When assessing fresh evidence in a case of any difficulty it would usually be wise for the Court of Appeal to test its own provisional view by asking whether the evidence, if given at trial, might reasonably have affected the decision of the trial jury to convict. If so, the conviction would be unsafe. Trial by jury did not mean trial by jury in the first instance and trial by judges of the Court of Appeal in the second. The Court of Appeal was entrusted with a power of review to guard against the possibility of injustice, but that power had to be exercised with caution, mindful that the Court of Appeal was not privy to the jury's deliberations and should not intrude into territory that properly belonged to the jury. The House of Lords thought that since the Court of Appeal had directed itself in accordance with the *Stafford* case, its approach had been correct in law. However, given the uncertainties in the case and the fresh psychological evidence, these made it impossible to be sure that the conviction was safe. In holding otherwise the Court of Appeal had strayed beyond its true function of review and had made findings that had not been open to it in all the circumstances, coming perilously close to considering whether the appellant was, in its judgment, guilty. For these reasons the appeal from the decision of the Court of Appeal should be allowed – the Court of Appeal had refused the appeal from the decision in the Crown Court. The following extract from Lord Bingham states the principles lucidly:

'It is undesirable that exercise of the important judgment entrusted to the Court of Appeal by s2(1) of the 1968 Act should be constrained by words not to be found in the statute and that adherence to a particular thought process should be required by judicial decision. Thus the House in *Stafford* were right to reject the submission of counsel that the Court of Appeal had asked the wrong question by taking as the test the effect of the fresh evidence on their minds and not the effect that that evidence would have had on the mind of the jury ([1974] AC 878 at 880). It would, as the House pointed out, be anomalous for the court to say that the evidence raised no doubt whatever in their minds but might have raised a reasonable doubt in the minds of the jury. I am not persuaded that the House laid down any incorrect principle in *Stafford*, so long as the Court of Appeal bears very clearly in mind that the question for its consideration is whether the conviction is safe and not whether the accused is guilty. But the test advocated by counsel in *Stafford* and by Mr Mansfield in this appeal does have a dual virtue to which the speeches I have quoted perhaps gave somewhat inadequate recognition.

First, it reminds the Court of Appeal that it is not and should never become the primary decision-maker. Secondly, it reminds the Court of Appeal that it has an imperfect and incomplete understanding of the full processes which led the jury to convict. The Court of Appeal can make its assessment of the fresh evidence it has heard, but save in a clear case it is at a disadvantage in seeking to relate that evidence to the rest of the evidence which the jury heard. For these reasons it will usually be wise for the Court of Appeal, in a case of any difficulty, to test their own provisional view by asking whether the evidence, if given at the trial, might reasonably have affected the decision of the trial jury to convict. If it might, the conviction must be thought to be unsafe.' (para 19)

The Auld report

The review of the criminal courts by Auld LJ in 2001 (Auld LJ (2001)) suggested a streamlining of the appeals system. Also suggested was that the procedures of the Court of Appeal should be streamlined in order to enable it to manage its caseload more efficiently. The introduction of statutory exceptions to the double jeopardy rule and other extensions to the prosecutor's rights of appeal were also on the agenda. This was in support of the general thrust of the Law Commission's recommendations for the introduction of statutory exceptions to the double jeopardy rule, save that a prosecutor's right of appeal against acquittal should not be limited to cases of murder and allied offences, but should extend to other grave offences punishable with life or long terms of imprisonment. There should also be provision for appeal by the defence or the prosecution against a special verdict of a jury which on its terms is perverse.

Criminal Justice Act 2003

The Act provides the prosecution with two new possibilities in terms of reopening issues. First, prosecution appeals against directed and ordered acquittals are to be introduced in relation to trials where the jury had not yet been asked to consider the evidence. Second, there is a partial removal of the double jeopardy rule. An acquitted person could be tried again, in serious cases, where there is new evidence of a compelling nature. This has to be such that it strongly indicates that an acquitted person is in fact guilty of that offence and it is right in all the circumstances of the case for that person to be retried. A number of safeguards would be included in the legislation and this system of retrial could only be used once. The DPP's consent would be needed before a suspect can be re-investigated and before an application can be made to the Court of Appeal to quash the acquittal. This change would not have been welcomed amongst those of the criminal fraternity who have written their memoirs and revealed their involvement in serious offences for which they have stood trial and been acquitted.

Human rights

Illustrations of the application of the European Convention on Human Rights and Fundamental Freedoms 1950 to the criminal justice system are provided. Not all of them concern the United Kingdom as a party to the proceedings but they do provide us with guidance as to the applicable standards. The examples are based on arts 5 and 6 of the European Convention. The Convention rights were, prior to the Human Rights Act 1998, an influence upon the domestic courts. As a result of the 1998 Act they are to be applied by the domestic courts. Whilst they are mainly concerned with the trial stage and some of the consequences of it, there are also some examples of earlier matters such as arrest, bail and pre-trial detention.

Article 5
This provides for a right to liberty and security of the person with exceptions which permit lawful detention by means of such as a sentence of imprisonment following due process of the law. As part of this process there is a right to be informed of the reason for detention, a right to be taken before a court expeditiously, mechanisms to question the lawfulness of detention should be available and a system of compensation provided for breach of such rights.

Applying art 5(3) to bail decisions. The decision of the European Commission on Human Rights in *CC v United Kingdom* (1998) Application No 32819/96, Commission Report 30 June 1998, was concerned with pre-trial detention. Section 25 of the Criminal Justice and Public Order Act 1994 stated that those brought before the criminal courts, in relation to any of the offences of murder, attempted murder, manslaughter and rape, would not be granted bail if they had previously been convicted for one or more of these offences. The applicant had been arrested for attempted rape and had a previous conviction for manslaughter: he was automatically remanded in custody. It was argued for the applicant that there is a right to liberty under art 5(1). If this is to be refused it must be through the use of art 5(3), which required that he be brought promptly before a judge or other officer authorised by law to have the matter heard. The failure to do this was presented as being a breach of art 5(3) and the lack of a system of compensation was also suggested to be a breach of art 5(5). The Commission found for the applicant on these matters. They viewed s25 as being a system, whereby the court was deprived of the ability to make its own decision. Section 56 of the Crime and Disorder Act 1998 has amended the legislation by providing that bail would only be granted for such repeat offenders where there were exceptional circumstances to justify it. It is quite possible that this is also a breach of art 5(3).

The need to bring a case to trial with special diligence. Scott v Spain (1997) 24 EHRR 391 concerned Scott, a British citizen, who was arrested for rape in Tenerife in March 1990. He was detained until March 1994 when he was acquitted. Articles 5(1) and 5(3) were considered by the European Court of Human Rights. The justification for his detention was that he was being held pending trial and this satisfied the requirements of art 5(1), but the length of his detention was a breach of art 5(3). Scott had not caused the delay and the authorities were required to show special diligence in bringing the case to trial. The case itself was not a complex one and the evidence to be considered was limited. Four years was regarded as too long a period of delay. Similarly, in *Muller v France* (1997) Reports 2:388:35, four years on remand was considered an unreasonable period to have to wait for trial.

The need for impartial decisions. Hood v United Kingdom (1999) The Times 11 March concerned detention prior to a court martial, the decision to detain being made by the applicant's commanding officer. There was found to be a breach of art 5(3), in that since the commanding officer would be involved in the prosecution he could not be viewed as an impartial decision-maker for the purposes of pre-hearing detention. Given that there was no domestic right to compensation for a breach of art 5(3), there was also a breach of art 5(5).

Challenging detention after sentence. Hussain v United Kingdom; Singh v United Kingdom (1996) 22 EHRR 1 was concerned with art 5(4) which requires systems for the challenging of the legality of detention. The applicants were being detained during Her Majesty's pleasure, having been found guilty of murder and being under the age of 18. Hussain had been considered for release by the Parole Board on four occasions. However, he had not had access to a court, other than through the process of judicial review, in order to have his post-conviction detention considered. Their sentences were presented as being akin to that of discretionary life sentence prisoners, thus their detention must be reviewed periodically to take account of any new circumstances. The European Court of Human Rights viewed an indeterminate sentence of detention for a young person as being justified by the need to protect the public. There was a need to have a review system once the tariff element of such a sentence had been completed. The role of the Parole Board would not suffice as it does not give an oral hearing or allow legal representation and the calling of witnesses and, most importantly, it cannot order the release of a prisoner. The Court held that there had been a violation of art 5(4) in each case.

Arrest and extradition. In the case of *Murray v United Kingdom* (1999) 19 EHRR 193, there was no breach of art 5 where there was a delay of two hours between an arrest and the provision of the reason for that arrest. The context was important here as Murray had been arrested by soldiers in Northern Ireland and she was suspected of involvement with terrorist organisations. *Chahal v United Kingdom* (1996) The Times 28 November was an extradition case. Chahal was an Indian citizen who had entered the United Kingdom illegally, but in 1974 he had been given indefinite leave to remain. In 1984, during a visit to the Punjab, he was involved in a political movement, which led to him being detained and tortured by the police. He returned to the United Kingdom and then later, in 1990, the Secretary of State decided to deport him, pending which he was to be detained. These actions were to combat terrorism and in the interests of national security. He sought political asylum and this was refused. Since there was an issue of national security he could not have access to an independent tribunal; instead there was an advisory panel to look at his case. At this hearing he was not allowed representation or to know the evidence against him. Judicial review of the deportation order that was made was equally unsuccessful – this was largely because the court was unable to examine the material used in the making of the decision. The European Court of Human Rights felt that the key to the case was the risk that Chahal would be tortured if he was sent to India. They decided that the decision to deport was a breach of art 3, which gives a right not to be tortured. They also declared a breach of art 5(4), as this requires an acceptable system for challenging the legality of detention to be in place. Their view was that it should be possible to find a method of protecting confidential information without denying access to the court system.

Article 6

This provides for a right to a fair and public hearing in relation to civil rights and obligations or criminal charges. The hearing should be within a reasonable time, it should be by a body established under the law and that body should be independent and impartial. The judgment must be issued in public but the press and public may be excluded from all or part of the hearing in certain circumstances. These are in the interest of morals, public order or national security, in the interest of juveniles, the protection of the private life of the parties or to prevent publicity that would prejudice the interests of justice. Article 6 also provides for a presumption of innocence. In relation to criminal offences, a person must be given a detailed account of the nature and cause of the accusation against him. Adequate time and facilities for the preparation of a defence must be allowed. A person also has the right to defend himself in person or through legal assistance of his own choosing. Where he does not have the means to pay for this and the interests of justice so require, he must be provided with it. He must also be able to call and examine, or have examined, witnesses and to examine, or have examined, witnesses against him. Provision must be made for those who do not speak the language of the jurisdiction.

The requirement of access to a court. Osman v *United Kingdom* [1999] 5 BHRC 293 was a case in which access to a court was felt to be required. A child and his father were shot, with the father dying as a result, by a former teacher of the child. The child had been the subject of an infatuation by the former teacher. This had manifested itself in a variety of ways and there had been complaints to the police. Legal action was attempted by the child and his mother against the police. This was for negligence in terms of their failure to prevent the shootings. The action was not allowed. Public policy provided absolute immunity in such circumstances, this being based on the House of Lords decision in *Hill* v *Chief Constable of West Yorkshire* [1989] AC 53 (the case involved a claim by a mother of one of the victims of the Yorkshire Ripper). The manner in which crime was investigated could not be subject to such a court action. A variety of issues were raised before the European Court of Human Rights, but it was only in relation to art 6 that the applicants succeeded. The failure to consider any competing public interest to that protected by the immunity principle amounted to too great a restriction on the ability of the applicants to receive a judgment on the merits of their claim against the police. Clearly, this raises the possibility of other similar actions against public officials, although there are criteria to be satisfied before such an action would be allowed.

The duty to provide legal representation. The case of *Benham* v *United Kingdom* (1996) 22 EHRR 293 saw the European Court of Human Rights decide that since there was no provision for legal aid this was a failure to provide legal representation and thus a breach of art 6. Benham was sent to prison by magistrates for a failure to pay the community charge. Where the liberty of the individual was at stake there was a need for legal aid provisions. The need for legal representation also arose because of the complexity of the issues and proceedings.

Alleged racial bias in a jury. In *Gregory* v *United Kingdom* (1997) The Times 27 February a black defendant was convicted of robbery on a majority jury verdict. During the trial, the jury had sent the judge a note asking for one of them to be excused because of racial bias. The judge reiterated his direction that they must act impartially. The complaint to the European Court of Human Rights was that the failure to discharge the juror had denied Gregory a fair trial, a point of view that seems very plausible on the face of it. The Court did not agree with this. The difficulty is that since it cannot be known what happens in the jury room, all that can be looked to are the directions to the jury. The redirection was as far as it was possible to go in order to ensure a fair trial.

The nature of the court proceedings. *T* v *United Kingdom; V* v *United Kingdom* (1998) Application Nos 24724/94 and 24888/94 (4 December 1998) was an application that concerned the two boys who had murdered a two-year-old when they were ten. They were being held at Her Majesty's pleasure following a public Crown Court trial. Given their age they could not be expected to participate meaningfully in such a trial. The European Commission on Human Rights heard an application in relation to a variety of issues and found a breach of art 6, ie that the circumstances of the trial had denied them a fair hearing. There was also a breach of art 5 in that there had been a failure to provide the opportunity to have their detention reviewed.

Public interest immunity. The European Commission on Human Rights found violations of art 6 in the case of *Rowe and Davies* v *United Kingdom* (1998) Application No 28901/95 (20 October 1998). The applicants had been convicted of murder and robbery and then appealed to the Court of Appeal. During these proceedings the issue arose as to the status of a document. To reveal it might have put people at risk, for example by identifying those who had obtained a reward (though in fact the nature of the document was not identified). Equally, non-disclosure might have prevented a fair trial. Counsel for the defence would not undertake not to reveal the contents of the document to their clients. At trial it was decided, in the absence of the defence, that there should be public interest immunity. The Commission decided that there was a breach of art 6. At the trial, the judge had not been able to consider the matter and the defence had had no knowledge of the document and no opportunity to make representations.

The Criminal Cases Review Commission

The Commission investigates suspected miscarriages of justice in England, Wales and Northern Ireland. It is an independent body set up under the Criminal Appeal Act 1995. Since 31 March 1997 the Commission has received over 6,008 applications and 5,345 cases have been completed. Convictions are referred to the appellate courts if the Commission believes that there is a real possibility that they will be found to be unsafe. A high proportion of applications involve only simple points of fact or law and can be reviewed within a month or two. Where there are complex issues to investigate, the review may take a year or more. There have been 201 referrals, of which the Court of Appeal have made decisions in 148 cases – in 97 of these cases the sentence was quashed. Some examples of its impact are, first, in the case of James Hester, who was convicted of burglary in 1995 and sentenced to four-and-a-half years. The case was received in 1997 and in 1998 the case was referred to the Court of Appeal. This was because of concern over alibi evidence that had not been called at trial and other matters. By December 1998 the conviction had been quashed. For Raymond Cook a conviction in 1996 for aggravated burglary also produced a sentence of to four-and-a-half years. The case was received in July 1997 and in 1998 the case was referred to the Court of Appeal. This was because of an error concerning previous convictions. By February 1998 the Court of Appeal had reconsidered the issue and the sentence was reduced to three-and-a-half years.

6 Sentencing

6.1   Statistics on sentencing practices

6.2   Deferral of sentence

6.3   Principles of sentencing

6.4   Factors that are taken into account in sentencing

6.5   The problem of disparity

6.6   Sentencing guidelines

6.7   Who should sentence?

This chapter is concerned with the manner in which the sentencing decision is arrived at, rather than the way that the various sentences and orders actually operate in practice. The following three chapters are concerned with the operation of custodial and community sentences and orders as well as the systems applicable to young offenders. A statistical account of sentencing is provided as background material. The following issues are then considered in turn: deferred sentences, principles of sentencing, factors that are supposed to influence sentencing, the impact of race and gender, disparity in sentencing and methods of providing guidance for sentencers.

The government White Paper, *Justice for All* (Home Office (2002d)), provides details of their intentions for this stage of the criminal justice system. The White Paper notes that one of the key purposes of custody is to reduce crime once offenders are released, yet half of all convicted criminals are reconvicted within two years. Prison can break up families, impede resettlement and have a devastating effect on children. At the same time there is no consistency in approach to sentencing, with extreme cases of variation in sentencing for similar crimes across the country. The government wants to put the sense back into sentencing and ensure sentences work to both protect the public and punish and rehabilitate offenders. To these ends the following proposals are made.

1. Sentences to be based on what has been shown to work in reducing re-offending.
2. Create a sentencing framework and establish a Sentencing Guidelines Council, chaired by the Lord Chief Justice, to achieve greater consistency.
3. Introduce a new graded framework to tailor sentences to the offender and the offence.
4. Introduce within this framework a series of new and innovative sentences, ranging from:

   a) a new suspended sentence called Custody Minus, reform of short custodial sentences and the introduction of Custody Plus;
   b) a new intermittent custody sentence that denies liberty, for example at the weekend, but allows the offender to continue working and maintain family ties;

c) introduce an extended version of the Intensive Supervision and Surveillance Programme so there is a greater opportunity for rehabilitation coupled with a reduced chance of reoffending;

d) ensure that, like adults, young offenders sentenced for serious offences will be released at the halfway point of the sentence and supervised all the way until the end of sentence.

The Criminal Justice Act 2003 provisions that relate to the issues in this chapter are detailed below. It is important to note that, since most of the provisions of the Act did not come into force immediately upon Royal Assent, the earlier provisions will still be applicable for some time. The Criminal Justice Act 1991, which is now consolidated in the Powers of Criminal Courts (Sentencing) Act (2000), provided the basis for the sentencing system. Proportionality as part of a punishment or a just desserts approach was provided for. The Criminal Justice Act 2003, when implemented, would introduce a new approach. Whilst being based on just desserts, the system under the 1991 Act also found room for other factors to be operative: rehabilitation, restoration, incapacitation and deterrence for example. As noted in Chapter 1, in the years that followed the 1991 Act steps were taken to toughen up the system – most notably through a much greater use of prisons. Also numerous new innovations were introduced.

6.1 Statistics on sentencing practices

Information from the criminal statistics provides a background for the issues that follow in this chapter: Home Office (2002a). A total of 1.35 million offenders were sentenced in 2001 for indictable and summary offences. At magistrates' courts, 30 per cent of those sentenced for indictable offences were fined, 33 per cent were given a community sentence, 19 per cent were sentenced to a conditional or absolute discharge, 14 per cent were sentenced to immediate custody and 4 per cent were otherwise dealt with. At the Crown Court, 63 per cent of those sentenced for indictable offences were sentenced to immediate custody, 27 per cent were given a community sentence, 3 per cent were fined, 3 per cent received an absolute or conditional discharge and 4 per cent were otherwise dealt with. Persons sentenced to immediate custody numbered 106,300, an increase of 84 per cent since 1992. The average custodial sentence length for male offenders convicted of indictable offences was 15 months in 2001. The numbers sentenced to immediate custody for summary offences was 5,800 in 2001.

6.2 Deferral of sentence

A court can decide to defer a sentence in relation to a convicted offender for a period of up to six months. This provides the opportunity for the person's conduct during the period to be considered at a later hearing. The power to do this was introduced by the Criminal Justice Act 1972, though a similar but more limited power had existed before that. Section 1 of the Powers of Criminal Courts (Sentencing) Act 2000 deals with the matter at the present time. The intention of this device is reformative. The court at the later hearing will look for evidence of some positive change in circumstances, such as the making of amends to the victim. If the person has done what was hoped for then normally a severe sentence would not be imposed. The offender has to consent to the deferment. The main guideline case from the Court of Appeal is *R* v *George* (1984) 6 Cr App R (S) 211. The case tells us that deferment should not be a means to avoid making a difficult decision and that the court must have specific reasons for taking this course of action. A record of what is hoped for should be kept and the situation must be made clear to the offender. It should not be used where a specific matter that is desired could have been part of an order that the court has the power to make. It may well be useful in circumstances where something like reparation was hoped for but could not be prescribed. The present rate of deferment for the Crown Court is 2 per cent, which, given the limited amount of cases that it could be expected to be used for, means that it being used quite frequently. Jones, R (1983) after a review of research in the area provides the following conclusions:

> 'The typical offender for whom sentence is deferred is likely to be male, aged 17–25, with previous convictions and already known to the probation and after-care service. His latest offence will probably involve some kind of dishonest appropriation of property, although not of a very large amount. The period of deferment is likely to be six months and he stands an even chance of re-offending in that period. He will probably appear before a different bench from the one that deferred sentence. If he has not re-offended he will almost certainly receive a non-custodial sentence.' (1983:392)

The question can be asked, is a system of deferment unnecessary? If supervision is required probation is the answer, and if it is not then use could be made of a conditional discharge. On the other hand, some probation officers have been keen on it as it provides for specific requirements within a particular period of time. The Criminal Justice Act 2003 will require more of the offender on a deferred sentence. He may have to complete undertakings in the community as set by the court. An example would be a requirement of reparation.

6.3 Principles of sentencing

Sentences are generally unpleasant experiences for those who are subject to them so the question arises: How can they be justified? In short, what are the aims of sentencing? If harder questions are desired we could ask which aims are appropriate for which offences and which aims are appropriate for which offenders? There are many ideas to be found in relation to these issues, but in reality most sentences have no particular intellectual justification for them. The criminal justice system should perhaps be able to do better than that. Duff and Garland warn us that we should not expect too much:

> '... how far should we even hope, or aim, for a penal system which is structured by just one coherent normative theory of punishment? Should we not rather recognise that punishment is inevitably a locus both of conflicting principles, and of conflicts between principles and more pragmatic considerations? Von Hirsch (1993) argues, for instance, that the principle of proportionality should be the primary guide to sentencing: legislators, policy-makers, and

sentencers should strive to ensure that each offender receives a sentence whose severity is proportionate to the seriousness of the crime, in order that the punishment can express the appropriate degree of censure. Critics have objected, first, that we cannot in practice hope to achieve a proper proportionality between crime and punishment; second, that there are other principles such as that of parsimony in punishment which may conflict with the demands of proportionality; and third that an undue emphasis on strict proportionality stands in the way of making effective use of the wide range of intermediate sanctions (such as intensive probation or supervision, substantial fines, and community service, which fall between imprisonment and traditional probation) which are finding favour amongst penal policy-makers.' (1994a:19)

Some of the possible aims of sentences

1. To provide punishment. A system of retribution often described as being based on the principle of 'just desserts'. A tariff-based system in which there should be a punishment to fit the crime.
2. Individual and general deterrence.
3. The reduction of crime in society
4. To show the disapproval of society, a system of denunciation, condemnation and censure. Given that we all offend to at least some extent, who is there left to do the denouncing if there is not to be hypocrisy? This approach also carries with it the danger of labelling.
5. To prevent vendetta.
6. The rehabilitation of the offender.
7. To incapacitate offenders and to sanitise society.
8. Paternalism.
9. Restorative justice.

A number of these aims will be discussed below.

Retribution

This suggests the need for sentencing being designed to provide punishment and, more particularly, that the punishment should fit the crime. Our system certainly provides punishment in a whole variety of ways but most particularly by the use of fines and custody. Retribution involves the notion of just desserts. It favours set tariffs to reflect the differing levels of seriousness of offences. The problem is that even particular crimes vary in their severity so you would need a very complex tariff. A tariff system concentrates on the offence not the offender, and notions of discretion and the individualisation of sentences do not fit well within it. When treatment declined as an ideal in sentencing, retribution filled the void it left behind. The Criminal Justice Act 1991 was built on these ideas. In *Crime, Justice and Protecting the Public* (Home Office (1990)) the intentions of the government were made clear. The first objective for all sentences is the denunciation of, and retribution for, the crime. Depending on the offence and the offender, the sentence may also aim to achieve public protection, reparation and reform of the offender, preferably in the community. This approach points to sentencing policies which are more firmly based on the seriousness of the offence, and just desserts for the offender.

Retribution provides revenge as a response to the offence. Why should we punish for this reason, since it appears to be a hypocritical response by the society? If you kidnap someone and are caught you would be deprived of your liberty, if you steal you may well have money taken from you by means of a fine. It has been suggested that the punishment is the means to repay a fictional debt or that the slate is wiped clean. Punishment is also viewed as being acceptable, in that by your criminal behaviour you have gained an advantage or avoided a disadvantage. The retribution approach is not the same as the reductionist approach, though they have similar features and both would hope to see deterrence. Reductionism as a philosophy sounds attractive, the aim is to reduce the amount of crime in a society. However, it soon runs into difficulties. In particular, there is the difficulty that sentences struggle to reduce crime. You can view deterrence, incapacitation and reform as types of reductionism. In conclusion, retribution does not come across as a good basis for sentencing though it has considerable appeal for the general public.

Deterrence

There are two types of deterrence – individual and general. The aim is to reduce or prevent crime. With individual deterrence the penalty that is inflicted is an experience that the individual would not want to repeat. It is a use of the notion of utilitarianism, that people would avoid pain, and is based on the idea of people making rational choices, and thus the extent to which crime is a matter of rational choice has to be considered. Some crimes may result from such as impulse or be spur of the moment decisions. Such factors may well be operative with crimes of violence. In seeking the individual deterrence of the offender, repeat offending would justify increases in punishment. This system sacrifices the individual for the sake of the society. It carries with it the danger of labelling. Also doubts have to be raised about its efficacy. With some offenders repeated sentences have little or no impact, or certainly not in the short to medium term. For them, the strategy of individual deterrence fails. We know that for petty persistent offenders it is very difficult to deter them from crime; custodial sentences are really only to show disapproval and to give society a short rest from such offenders. If the motivation is supposed to be the avoidance of pain then an unwanted outcome could be displacement, a phenomenon in which the offender seeks a less risky crime to commit.

General deterrence relies on the system of penalties offering a disincentive to the population as a whole. The police force was disbanded in Denmark whilst the country was occupied during the Second World War and the crime rate went up. This is seen as a situation in which the deterrent was taken away. A similar phenomenon has been seen with recorded instances of the police going on strike. Capital punishment as a penalty for murder has been examined as a test of general deterrence. In the United States, the retentionist states fared no better than the abolitionist states in terms of the murder rate. Also, in the United Kingdom, abolition of the death penalty for murder did not increase the murder rate. The reality is that a long period of detention worked as well as capital punishment. Murder was in fact a bad offence to use as a test of general deterrence given that it is so often a spur of the moment form of behaviour. You need offences that are much more calculated.

Deterrence research

A problem for deterrence research is the amount of variables that can be operative. There will be variations amongst people and groups as to perceptions of risk. These may be accurate or false. The willingness to take risks may also vary with time, place, company and state of mind. The latter could be influenced by drink and drugs. Experience may tell you that you can get away with the behaviour and the risk may be part of the attraction of the behaviour as in the case of joy-riding. The mechanics involved in deterrence are demanding. For general deterrence to operate you would need to know about the general system of sanctions and to have that knowledge in mind when opportunities for criminal behaviour were present or were being considered. A person would have to know about the particular sanction if the claim is that that particular sanction is to operate as a deterrent. It seems that most offenders do not have sanctions in mind when they are considering offending. They are very unlikely to have particular sanctions in mind and are more likely to have a general fear of being caught. This fear has to compete with more immediate influences such as peer group pressure. You must also be fairly convinced that there is a real prospect that punishment would follow the crime. The reality is that for many offences no one will be found liable. For those who are caught they can balance the times that they are caught with the times that they get away with the offence. The material by Murray (1997) in relation to the use of prisons as a form of the deterrence, which is examined in Chapter 9, should be referred to. His thesis is that if the sanction is severe enough the crime rate will go down. He argues that you have to be prepared to send sufficient people to prison to convince the rest of society that the punishment is a reality for those who offend. This does not get round the problem of low detection rates for offences. Also, as we will see in Chapter 7, there was still offending when there was a general use made of capital punishment for quite a range of offences. So harsh was the regime that it was even applicable to children.

Von Hirsch et al (1999) looked at the role of the degree of certainty of a punishment being delivered and also the effect of changes in sentence severity. They note that there may be reasons other than deterrence that produce law-abiding behaviour. A person's moral views may mirror the legal norms or the view may be held that the law should be upheld as a good in itself. They also realise that the issues are complex. A new prohibition on what at the moment is popular behaviour may produce compliance based on fear which may eventually be replaced by changed attitudes towards behaviour. This was probably the case with the introduction of increased control of drink driving. Von Hirsch et al see deterrence as the avoidance of prescribed activities for fear of the penalty. They were particularly interested in marginal deterrence, that is the ability to prevent behaviour by increasing sentence severity. Increased certainty of punishment is likely to work better than increased severity, but it is much harder to deliver. It is also made clear that what is important is not the real risk but the perceived risk. Equally, it is the subjective view of the penalty that is important. The short, sharp shock regime in detention centres had features that were positively liked by offenders. The drill sessions and the physical education were regarded as being much better than the earlier regime. This is not what was intended and neither I suppose were the fitter recidivists that also materialised.

Von Hirsch et al suggest that there are five hurdles that marginal general deterrence has to cope with:

1. The audience of potential offenders must know that there is a new and more severe penalty that is to be operative.
2. This information must be taken into account when a person is deciding whether or not to offend.
3. There must be a belief on the part of the offender that there is a risk of being caught.
4. The particular potential offender must believe that the new penalty would be applicable for his particular offending. Again it is not the reality that is relevant but the subjective state of mind of the potential offender who may be an optimist.
5. There must be a willingness to act on all of this information. If the criminal behaviour is too attractive to particular offenders, if it is irresistible or if there is little choice as to the behaviour then there are problems. The situation of drug addicts is a case in point.

Consideration was also given to the type of changes in sentencing that might be introduced. Increasing small penalties of a financial nature by, for example, making a £20 fine a £50 fine may have very little impact, though it is a huge 250 per cent increase. If the penalty is already severe, as in the case of a 20-year jail sentence, it is difficult to see what impact the threat of a 30-year sentence would have.

In conclusion it is clear that there are other problems for deterrence arguments. We all offend to at least some extent and we are aware that most crime does not go before the courts. We also know that there are many more offences than convictions so the chances of being caught for some offences must be low.

Incapacitation and sanitising society

Sentencing can be intended to protect society. As we will see in Chapter 9, a justification that is suggested for imprisonment is that it could provide the means to incarcerate those who are considered too dangerous to be free within society. This may apply to serial killers, terrorists and paedophiles and other serious sex offenders. The idea may offend considerations of just desserts in that you may be operating on what a person might do rather than what he has done. The sentence would be in terms of the need to protect society and would not be wholly tariff-based. In reality it is likely that for such offenders a long custodial sentence would have been appropriate on dessert principles. Its influence has been seen in the general lengthening of sentences for the more serious offenders, and it was used in the Crime (Sentences) Act 1997 in relation to repeat offending in the spheres of sex and violence offences. Other forms of incapacitation are used in that electronic monitoring and disqualifications from driving could be viewed in this way.

Rehabilitation

This is based on positivist notions, that there is a defect of the individual. The aim is to change attitudes and to provide skills or education. The emphasis is on the offender rather than the offence and it produces the individualisation of sentencing. It can lead to the use of sentences that are not for specified periods of time. This is called indeterminate sentencing. Such sentences would be required as it would not be clear at the start of the treatment how long it would take. The issue is whether this is fair to the offender. Rehabilitative ideas were a feature of the borstal system and they have also been evident in probation practice. The welfare model which is considered in Chapter 7 suggests that they should be used for youngsters. In the same chapter the opposing arguments of the justice model are presented and they need to be considered here. Ideas of rehabilitation have been very largely abandoned in relation to prisons given the prevailing conditions in prisons. Also there are problems in finding effective treatment programmes. Where rehabilitation was used, the problem was that often the programmes did not deliver, that is there was still recidivism. There is also the problem of experts. What expertise do they have and what safeguards are there for offenders if these supposed experts are really only building on sand? In short rehabilitation is not a dominant idea at the present time, yet despite its negative press some programmes may well have something to offer. Rex (1998) developed this theme and looked at the possibilities of a new form of rehabilitation. This would utilise what is known about offending and provide a strategy to tackle it. For example, impulsiveness is a feature of the offending behaviour of youngsters who are petty persistent offenders. The eventual onset of maturity alleviates this so the aim is to find ways to bring the process forward. One method is to improve their reasoning skills. Rex notes that:

> 'The aim of these techniques is to teach offenders to stop and think before acting, to consider the consequences of their actions for themselves and others, and to consider alternative ways of behaving. Evaluation of the STOP programme in Mid-Glamorgan suggests that reasoning-based approaches can be effective in reducing recidivism, though the effects may wear off over a period of time if this kind of work is not complemented by attempts to assist offenders with the problems that they encounter in their everyday lives in the real world.' (1998:36)

Paternalism

The approach suggests that punishment is of value in helping people to understand the difference between right and wrong and that it can assist in our moral development. So rather as with a parent and a child the guidance is given for the offender's own good. An extract from Morris (1993) gives an idea of the thinking involved in this idea:

> 'I have claimed that to have as one's aim in punishing the good of the wrongdoer counts strongly in favour of the moral legitimacy of punishing. I do not claim, of course, that this is the sole justification for punishment, though I do believe that what it seeks to promote is among the most important, if not the most important, of human goods. The practice of punishment is complex and any justification proposed as an exclusive one must, in my judgment, be met with scepticism, if not scorn. There is, too, as I earlier briefly noted, a significant logical overlapping of this theory with retributivism, though at a certain point, when one considers types of punishment, they diverge. A paternalistic theory, given the good as defined, would support principles that are familiar dictates of retributivism-that only the guilty may be punished, that the guilty must be, and that the punishment inflicted reflect the degree of guilt. Failure to comply with the demands of retributivism would preclude realisation of the paternalist's goal. I have also, however, suggested that retributivism needs supplementing if it is to meet our intuitions of what is morally permissible punishment. But, of course, this overlapping of justifications for punishment includes as well some form of utilitarianism, for it our goal is as I have defined it, and punishments are threatened and imposed, deterrent values are also furthered. I do not question the rich over-determination of

goods promoted by the practice of punishment. I do urge that weight be given, and on the issue of restrictions on punishment, determinative weight, to paternalistic ends.' (1993:110)

Restorative justice

The material examined here is concerned with the principles of restorative justice. The specific examples of its operation in the criminal justice system, such as referral orders, reparation orders and compensation orders, appear in later chapters. Ideas of restorative justice have become popular in recent years for both the prospects that they offer to the criminal justice system and as an alternative to the prevailing ideas which have emphasised punishment and which have been widely criticised by commentators. Instead of punishing the offender the aim is for the person to make good, to engage in reparation, either to the community as a whole or to the victim of the crime. Where there is a requirement of, for example, work for the community this is to operate as a means of making good rather than as punishment. The concern with the victim is part of a wider movement that has taken place in terms of recognising the needs of victims. As we will see the ideas and schemes vary quite considerably in the various jurisdictions in which they have been utilised.

Victim offender mediation in Canada in the mid 1970s was one of the earliest features of the rise in ideas for restorative justice. It then spread particularly to the United States and Australasia. Daly (2001), unlike a number of other writers, suggests that restorative justice was not based on indigenous practices; rather that it is aware of a need to include elements that reflect and are sympathetic to cultural diversity so it is an influence upon rather than the basis of restorative ideas. In reality there would not have been one pure model to have copied if only because of the impact of colonialism. We should also note the view that the state historically took over from practices that were previously predominantly restorative in nature. So by using restorative ideas we are only reintroducing what had been the norm. Braithwaite (2001), for example, presented restorative justice as being the dominant model of criminal justice throughout most of human history. Strang (2002) states that

'... restorative justice has historically been the dominant paradigm of criminal justice, by which I mean that the response to crime until the rise of the modern state involved offenders making amends to their victims, so as to restore order and peace as quickly as possible and to avoid vengeful blood feuds. The diminished role for victims in criminal justice which now obtains began in Europe in the late Middle Ages as the Crown increasingly assumed the right of both adjudication and compensatory benefit for wrong-doing. This decline continued through the centuries in the West, until victims retained almost no rights in the justice process, which became exclusively a struggle between the offender and the state.' (2002:192)

As Morris and Maxwell (eds) (2001) tell us, restorative justice appears in numerous guises in different systems and that it is in flux: not being possessed of crystal clear foundations. The needs of the offender are also recognised and as an example of the variation they may be dominant in some of these schemes. The aims for the offender will not be to punish or alienate, which can happen with punishment-based systems, rather to reintegrate. With reintegrative shaming, which is one form of such thinking, the aim is to reject the offence but embrace the offender. In restorative systems there is also an expectation that responsibility will be taken by the offender for the offence. A further dimension is that steps can be taken to help the offender in terms of asking what caused the offence and then attempting to remedy the problem.

Developments in England and Wales have included more sensitive treatment for victims including, particularly, child victims and victims of sexual offences, and more information and involvement for victims, including the use of victim impact statements and the introduction of a system of state compensation. The Crime and Disorder Act 1998 and the Youth Justice and Criminal Evidence Act 1999 were the first big attempts to set up a statutory scheme with a delivery system in terms of the Youth Justice Board at the national level and a youth offending team at the local level. Before that there had been ad hoc experiments and various elements of the ideas in use. As well as referral orders restorative justice can now be part of final warnings, reparation orders and action plan orders, and can also be used in supervision. Compensation orders are also available as a disposal and in a sense there were elements of restorative justice in community service orders.

The government made the following statement as to their policy on victims in the White Paper, *Justice for All*: Home Office (2002d). That victims and witnesses, who are often the same person, can be left feeling ill informed and badly treated by the criminal justice system. Proposals in the White Paper address this so as to aim for a fair balance between defence and prosecution and also that the needs of victims and witnesses are considered at every stage. The following are some of the ideas being considered:

1. A national strategy for victims and witnesses.
2. A victims' code of practice setting out what victims can expect from the criminal justice agencies.
3. Every service that comes into contact with victims should have a responsibility under the new code to provide protection, support and information.
4. A right of complaint to the Parliamentary Ombudsman for Victims and Witnesses.
5. A new Independent Commissioner for Victims and Witnesses supported by a National Victims Advisory Panel to champion their interests.
6. The introduction of more measures for vulnerable and intimidated witnesses, including pre-recorded video evidence and screens around the witness box.
7. Adopting some of the ideas being developed as part of the Street Crime Initiative, for example victim volunteers being available to accompany victims when giving statements.
8. The extension of specialised support to victims of road traffic incidents and their families.
9. The appointment of victim liaison officers to join youth offending teams as resources become available.

A more distant example of such activity is family group conferences in Australia and New Zealand. The victim and his family would interact with the offender and his family. The interaction between victim and offender is to aid mutual understanding. This may not be attractive to victims, particularly where children are involved or the offences are sex offences. In the case of the latter, it may in fact be one of the better areas for such initiatives, as a great problem with sex offenders is their inability to recognise that there are victims of their behaviour.

In the traditional system the state is the victim and its response will be to take revenge against the offender or to apply the treatment or rehabilitative model. The victim is at most a witness and the offender is the object of the process (often largely passive) as events unfold around him. With restorative justice rather than the crime belonging to the state it belongs to the community and they respond because of the injury to it. Restorative justice gives a role to the victim and seeks to involve the offender, whereby the offender may be confronted with the offence. Restorative justice takes in those affected by the offence: it aims to bring people together and to remove the distance and the damage caused by the offence. Marshall (1996) emphasises the bringing together dimension:

> 'Restorative Justice is a process whereby all the parties with a stake in a particular offence come together to resolve collectively how to deal with the aftermath of the offence and the implications for the future.' (1996:37)

In bringing groups and individuals together, or back together, it clearly has reintegration as a function of the process. It also clearly has a community dimension and it is presented as being good for the wider community and also for both the offender and the victim. An observation that can be made is that community-based conferencing or circles, for a variety of purposes including sentencing, may well be appropriate where there are real communities, but that this is not perhaps the case in the United Kingdom. Whilst the systems do vary commonly there would be some form of meeting or meetings at which the offender would interact with the victim or community representatives and this probably would be aided by a facilitator. Again in terms of a somewhat idealised set of generalisations the system would be voluntary for the parties, it would be forward looking and the parties would be seeking a constructive agreement. They should offer each other respect and understanding and it should be a bonding and healing process. The offender should be taking responsibility for the offence and should gain self awareness. The system would also aim to have the effect of reducing offending behaviour.

Having identified some of the common features it is necessary to further emphasise the variations that occur and to identify the problems and dilemmas that can be involved in these ideas. Morris and Maxwell (2001:267–268) is a valuable source in relation to such issues. The following are some of them which they raise. What is the theory at the root of restorative justice if any and is it verified and verifiable? We will see that it is based on different things and that different systems seek different things. Is it designed to fit in with the culture or cultures that it encounters and is it able to do so? Should it replace the old system completely or to a degree or should it be integrated with it? The focal concern can be a variable: is it and should it be the offender or the victim? What is in it for the victim, the offender and the community – the good and the bad? What about the people operating the system? What background and training do they require? Do community participants need preparation and training? What legal and administrative set-up is desirable? What of rights and accountability? What type of offence and which career stage or age of offender are suitable candidates for restorative justice or is it capable of universal application. Does it cause labelling by such as confronting and shaming: hopefully not if the aim is to move on to a new scenario in which the status of offender is to be left behind. Does it net widen (ie cause more people to be brought into the criminal justice system) or divert (ie cause people to avoid or limit the amount of contact they have with the criminal justice system)? Does it work and, more fundamentally, what was it supposed to do? We will see that outcomes vary and that these can be intended and unintended. Many questions have been asked: there are not clear answers to all of them. Smith (2001) further emphasises the variation in answers to the question what sort of justice is restorative? He notes that:

'... its advocates (including quite a few prominent corrections officials) use the phrase to include everything from family group conferencing to Native American sentencing circles, from victim-offender mediation to re-integrative shaming, from monetary restitution and community service orders to a smorgasbord of victims' rights within the ordinary criminal process. The roots of the restorative justice movement are also many, but the durable ones run deep – in religion, culture, political ideology, and spirituality, as well as in common sense. To its proponents, it is a new paradigm, a rejection of the criminal law's focus on culpability and retribution and an embrace of the idea that punitive responses aggravate the harm that flows from crime. In the new paradigm, justice's purposes are: restoration of the victim and the victim's intimates, who suffer the harm; restoration of the community whose fabric is torn by the crime; and restoration of the offender who, after all, will remain part of that community and, if unrestored, a continuing threat to it. The key mechanisms appear to be respectful hearing of the story of the harm caused (as told directly by the victim and by those who support the victim in this process), voluntary acceptance of responsibility and making amends by the offender (also heard respectfully, lest stigmatisation and self-loathing block his return to full membership in the community), and collaboration, consensus and caring all around in the fashioning of solutions.' (2001:207)

Examples of restorative justice

Weitekamp (2001) suggests a division of restorative justice into three major types of programme – victim offender mediation, conferencing and circles. Victim offender mediation can be a face-to-face talk through of the offence in order to aid understanding and to come up with a package to repay in some way. A system to check and ensure compliance would also be included. Other forms of victim input are also possible – they may just make comments or ask for information and this could happen several times. A trained mediator may be used during or before the process in terms of such as preparatory work with some or all of the parties. Weitekamp states that conferencing came from Maori practices and invites in more people in than victim offender mediation. This would be all those affected, so the families and friends of both would be included. Circles go even further so as to include those in the neighbourhood in so far as they have some sort of stake in the matter. This might be the parent of a teenager in an area where an offender has been subjecting others to peer pressure. Such systems can be used as a form of diversion and in relation to a range of forms of dispute which have included the sphere of complaints against the police

Daly (2001) is a good source in relation to practices in Australia and New Zealand. She points to the various forms of conferencing that have been undertaken. She notes that these are often based on statute and are mainly intended to divert juveniles from the criminal justice system, and that they are part of a welfare and preventative ideology. She tackles what she describes as three misconceptions of the Australasian experience. First, that there are not many programmes. She answers this by saying that there are about 5,300–5,800 conferences a year in Australia. My retort is that this is still not that many and it will be interesting to see

205

Learning Resources Centre

how many hearings our recently introduced referral order system produces. Second, that police-led conferencing is the norm. She notes that there are other systems as well. Third, as noted earlier, that care has to be taken in seeing conferences as being based on indigenous practices. She stresses variety in what takes place across the jurisdictions, for example, it can range from six weeks to a year to deliver on what was promised. There is also variation in terms of the type and the percentage of offences that are included. She gives a good account of the research to date, of which the following is an example:

> 'Conferencing was first researched in New Zealand (Maxwell and Morris (1993, 1996)). Interviews with 157 young offenders and 176 of their parents attending family group conferences between August 1990 and May 1991 show that 84 and 85 per cent, respectively, were satisfied with the outcome of the family group conference (satisfaction decreased to 70 per cent for young offenders receiving the most severe penalties) (1993:115). By comparison, just half of victims reported being satisfied with the outcome (the level of satisfaction was even lower for sentencing advice to courts) (Maxwell and Morris 1993: 120). When examining the sources of dissatisfaction in the open-ended portions of the interview (1993:121), one sees that victims were critical of too lenient outcomes. Moreover, some were "simply never informed about the outcome" (1996:100). A quarter of victims said "they felt worse as a result of attending" the conference. While many reasons were given for this, Maxwell and Morris suggest that the most frequent was the victim's sense that the young person and his/her family did not feel "truly sorry" (1996:100).
>
> Studies of conferences in Queensland, New South Wales and Western Australia, focused mainly on participants' perceptions of fairness of the process and on their satisfaction with the process and outcome. Collectively these studies show that conferences receive high marks on the fairness and satisfac-tion variables. In Queensland, Palk et al (1998) analysed survey data collected by the Department of Justice over a thirteen-month period. Of the 351 offenders, parents (or carers), and victims interviewed, 98 to 100 per cent said the process was fair, and 97 to 99 per cent said they were satisfied with the agree-ment made in the conference (1998: 145). To statements such as "I was treated with respect", "I got to have my say", and "The conference was just what I needed to sort things out", 96 to 99 per cent of participants agreed (1998:146).
>
> In New South Wales, Trimboli (2000) gathered data from 969 victims, offenders, and offenders' supporters across all state regions during 1999. Overall, 92 to 98 per cent of the groups said that the conference was "somewhat" or "very fair" to victims and to offenders, with more detailed procedural justice variables (such as "You were treated with respect" and the "Conference respected your rights") showing similar results (2000:36-40). Across the three groups, 80 to 97 per cent agreed that they were "satisfied with the conference outcome plan" (2000:45).' (2001:70–71)

McCold (2001) also provides accounts of examples of restorative justice practices.

Youth Justice Family Group Conferences in New Zealand

These were based on legislation made in 1989, are an alternative to the courts and are used for serious and persistent young offenders. As the name suggests the family of the offender is involved. The victim also attends with a Child, Youth and Family Services Co-ordinator. The system allows for the views and experiences of the parties to be expressed and they also discuss how to put matters right. The family would then meet privately in order to come up with a proposal in terms of such as apologies and restitution. Their proposal may or may not be acceptable and the proposal may have to be fine-tuned after feedback. The research of Maxwell and Morris (see above extract) revealed both positive and negative features of the process. For example, whilst it was a voice for the victims they only attended about half of the conferences and were marginal participants in the proceedings and at worst would be further victimised. The professionals also appeared to have too great a role. Changes were eventually introduced which were designed to focus more on the victim's perspective.

Police-led conferencing

This has been developed in Australia and was an extension of police cautioning. It was based upon Braithwaite's ideas of reintegrative shaming: Braithwaite (1989). It allows for a role for the victim and reflection by the offender. It is inclusive in terms of encouraging those affected to participate and aims to provide an agreement to make amends. One feature of this system is that it became scripted, that is that the people running the conference would have a script to work from. It is but one form of the conferencing system in Australia, though it has tended to get most of the publicity. Thames Valley Police have used this as a part of cautioning practices. Young (2001) deals with police-led conferencing involving victims, particularly low tariff cases which were referred to the police as an alternative to a caution in the Thames Valley area. He observed 23 cases and did interviews with the parties. The meetings were in the form of Braithwaite-type shaming set-ups and can be criticised as giving too much power to the police. It may not be appropriate for the police to be handing out the shame – the community would seem more appropriate for the purpose. However, the context is that this is an alternative to a caution so they already had power over the offender, including the power to cause shame. You do wonder if the police would have the skills to ask the right sort of questions or would they be offence-orientated?

Victims

Victims have always had a role to play – indeed they are the great detectives in that they discover virtually all of the crime by virtue of being the victim of it. They also provide evidence and act as witnesses. The crime was however against the state and the needs of victims was a marginal issue. The victim movement called for rights for victims; that their voice should be heard and their position protected. When their interests started to be realised it was in terms of such as restitution and compensation, when in fact their focal concerns were to have a voice or to be emotionally restored. The interest that has been taken in victims and the agitation for rights on their behalf has made some other changes to the traditional situation. Through movements for rights for victims in the United States various groups were politicised, such as feminists with regard to the plight of women in terms of domestic violence and rape. It is still the case, however, that they are bit players and whilst the system has improved in a number of respects it is a matter of degree only. Strang (2002) notes the movements from the 1970s onwards with regard to victim rights and suggests that they have got as much as they can hope for through that route. Restorative justice can give them a better voice and deliver restoration, especially emotional restoration. One of the main themes that will be developed is the role of restorative justice schemes that aim to meet the needs of the offender as in the case of victim offender mediation. Victims are at least clearly on the agenda now as the following statement indicates. In November 1999 Jack Straw, the Home Secretary, stated in the Foreword to the *Crime Reduction Strategy* (Home Office (1999j):

'*A fair deal for victims*

'Putting the public's protection first also means putting the needs of victims first. Offenders cannot be brought to justice unless victims and witnesses report crimes to the police and are willing, if necessary, to give evidence in court. Yet the criminal justice system has been far too slow in recognising its responsibilities towards victims and witnesses. The needs of victims and witnesses should be at the heart of the criminal justice system. Funding for Victim Support has now been substantially increased. Services are being improved for victims and witnesses in the magistrates' courts. And we have introduced legislation to protect and support vulnerable victims and witnesses, including those in rape or serious sexual offence cases.'

In England and Wales a Victims Charter was introduced in 1996 but this consists of aspirations rather than rights and duties. The Victim's Charter tells you what you can expect at the various stages of the system. A leaflet is also available as a source of information. The charity, Victim Support, will provide information and assistance to victims. We have also had experiments with the One Stop Shop, an attempt to co-ordinate provision for victims. The Victims Virtual Walkthrough (http://www.cjs.gov.uk/virtual/victims.html) is an interactive virtual tour on the internet of the criminal justice system process as it relates to a victim of a crime. It provides information to guide any victim of crime through the processes that they will encounter, from the time a crime is reported, through the police investigation, prosecution decision-making, court processes and sentencing. It also provides information on the personal support that is available at all stages, including, when relevant, after the court case. The Youth Justice and Criminal Evidence Act 1999 introduced various forms of protection for vulnerable or intimidated witnesses. We now have victim statements prior to sentence, which operate as an influence in that victims can say what the effect has been on them, but they do not determine the sentence – it is a lottery for the offender as the effect can be subjective and they cause variations in sentence. Problems include when should the information be gathered and what if there is more than one victim? The research that was carried out before they were used on a national basis from 2001 had been lukewarm but they were still introduced. The crime surveys are also an example of interest in victims and there have also been studies of the victimisation process and the phenomena of repeat victimisation – these have all contributed to crime prevention ideas.

Victim offender mediation

Umbreit, Coates and Vos (2001) undertook an analysis of 27 North American and United Kingdom studies of victim offender mediation. There was little or no pressure on victims to participate in the schemes and very roughly across studies about 50 per cent took part in restorative systems where the victim could have a role. The vast majority of these volunteers were satisfied with the process. The researchers note that the systems were used for just about all ages and offence types and at various stages of the process. Different formats were used that had different aspirations: some were more interested in victim rights, others in payback and others in terms of turning round the offender.

They identified the following factors in a victim wanting to meet, or making it more likely that they wanted to meet, the offender: to get restitution, to help the offender, to participate, to understand the whys of it all, to have a voice and to ask questions, to teach the offender a lesson, if the offender is white, if it is a minor offence, that it is a property rather than a personal type offence, if the victim is an institution. In contrast the factors that made a meeting less likely or desirable were: a longer time lapse, hassle and fear. Other research has identified additional factors. Victims may want the offender to have a hard time, they may desire revenge through punishment. By going into a process which asks for empathy with the offender may deny the victim in that respect. Victims may also just want closure, to get on with their lives and to have nothing to do with the offender. The process could however have provided closure, removed desires for revenge, led to forgiveness and restored the peace.

Umbreit, Coates and Vos (2001) also reported that victims like to know what will happen, they want to be safe and to have direct dialogue. Since they want to talk to the offender, the mediator playing a limited role in the interaction is preferable. Systems which are not heavily scripted would be best. They also want to feel that their time has achieved something and would like follow up. Strang (2002:193) adds to this and tells us that victims want: a less formal process where their views count; more information about both the processing and outcome of their cases; participation in their cases; fair and respectful treatment; and material and emotional restoration, including an apology.

Morris and Maxwell (2001) suggest that the advantage that exists for victims with restorative justice is that they are more likely to receive the things that they desire from a criminal justice system and that restorative justice is more inclusive than conventional systems and they will receive more information. They can gain better understanding of the offending behaviour and can learn that the offender is not a monster, and that the crime was not personal and may have been a result of the offender's circumstances. They can vent anger and lose fear. They are more likely to get compensation or a similar outcome, including apologies or another form of payback. Higher satisfaction levels are also reported as are less negative feelings as an outcome. It also offers a way to achieve closure.

There is also a downside. As Morris and Maxwell (2001) state:

> 'Obviously, restorative justice processes do not always "work" for victims – some angry or distressed victims will remain so, and some victims will find it difficult to cope with what will happen in the restorative justice meeting and the range of emotions – anger, hurt, sadness, fear and so on – which they are likely to experience there. They may, therefore, leave the meeting feeling revictimised and unsupported. But these failings are likely to be the result of poor practice or of differences in the circumstances or attitudes of particular victims, rather than the result of some inherent defect in restorative justice processes.' (2001:268)

Other problems include revictimisation, apologies being offered that appear to be insincere and the offender not being able to offer anything by way of recompense for reasons such as having no talent or money.

Restorative justice can also be offender orientated and thus be a different version of ignoring the victim – can such a strategy be justified? Victim groups in particular are worried about putting more pressures on victims and they suggest that they should not be a means to an end. There is no doubt restorative justice can produce more demands and fear. However research by Strang (2002) found that restorative justice was better than conventional systems in terms of the following criteria: levels of fear of the offender re-offending against them, more likely to help with closure and self esteem and much more likely to get an apology which was a very common desire. We must remember that the reasons to be disillusioned are plentiful if you are a victim faced with a traditional system of criminal justice, namely: charge bargains, acquittal rates and what they may perceive as derisory sentences.

The parameters of restorative justice

The issue arises as to whether restorative justice should be part of the existing system or an alternative to it? We can also ask at what stage, or stages, it should operate and in relation to what offences and offenders? The short answer is that it has been very widely used even in relation to very serious offences. Van Ness, Morris and Maxwell (2001) note its use in prisons and also to deal with such as complaints against the police as in Fresno, California, and for Thames Valley Police. Morris and Maxwell (2001) put the common suggestion that victims must opt in and also the less commonly expressed view that mandatory referral for offenders should not be seen as problematic. There are clearly arguments against forcing either offenders or victims to meet against their will. Yet at a trial the interests of the victim are sacrificed in their use as witnesses, so in an offender-orientated system the compulsory attendance of the victim would not be such a different system. Whether this would still be restorative justice is problematic. There is always the danger that the offender may opt in as a way to avoid another form of intervention.

Philosophical considerations

Ashworth (1986:97) suggests that any pay back should be proportionate to the offence and not to the harm to the victim. We again have to ask who are we trying to be fair to – the victim or the offender? Ashworth has chosen the offender. You take your victim as you find them in tort and in contract and you have to give damages in terms of the consequences of the breach. What ever you do there are problems. A very bad action can produce the lowest possible level of injury and vice versa. For serious crime, Ashworth tells us that we should focus on intent and look to mens rea. On the general issue of restorative justice, Von Hirsch and Ashworth (1998) offer the following thoughts:

> 'This readiness of modern restorative theorists to recognise the wider community's interests in crime should not, however, deflect attention from the question of the nature of the victim's interest. Is it not arguable that one key element in modern states is that the state takes over the responsibility for government and law; that it does so in order to ensure efficiency and consistency, and especially to displace vigilantism and to prevent people from "taking the law into their own hands"; that therefore the state ought to control adjudication and sentencing; but that its doing so ought not to deprive victims of their right to compensation (as happened for some centuries, and happens in some cases now)? It may be true that one of the driving forces behind modern restorativism is dissatisfaction with the "conventional" punishment paradigm, as developed in many criminal justice systems. But the question is whether what is wrong is the paradigm or the way in which it has been developed. How convincing are Christie's (1977) arguments that "conflicts" should be taken back from the state and returned to the victim and her or his community? To what extent does Pettit and Braithwaite's (1993) conception of dominion, in the context of their wider republican theory, imply that the

particular victim has an interest going beyond compensation and "recognition", and do they accept that it is the state's function to decide on the measure and form of "recognition, recompense and reassurance"?' (1998:303)

Walgrave (2001) takes an equally philosophical view of the issues and he compares ideas of restorative justice with the notion of punishment. Punishment is the imposition of pain as a response to an infraction of the criminal law. The punisher intends to cause pain. He notes that whilst restorative justice can involve pain that was not the intention of the intervention and it seems that that is probably the difference between restorative and punishment-based systems. In relation to restorative justice the state may well act as a back up for non-compliance and restorative justice is retributive in that respect. To adopt the point of view of the offender, as an alternative approach to the intention of the delivery of restorative justice, is unhelpful: there could be many subjective responses to societal interaction. These can be unintended and some people will like being sent to prison or indeed having pain inflicted upon them. Other writers such as McCold (2001) would not allow for any coercion in restorative justice. This would thus exclude such as community service. In reality it would leave nothing, as given a real choice offenders would be likely to choose hanging out with their mates rather than meeting the victim of the offence.

Guidance as to good practice

Morris and Maxwell (2001:278–280) provide guidance as to good practice in restorative justice. Whilst these ideas are of use, they are very idealistic and would be difficult to achieve in practice. The system of restorative justice should be based on clear ideas. The participants should all be committed to these ideas even though this may require major changes of mind set for some. Training is probably needed. The aim should be to repair and restore. The meeting should look to the behaviour of the offender. Preparation is required in terms of the provision of information, allowing people to know what their expectations should be and what is likely to happen. They should also be told what is and what is not acceptable behaviour: the ground rules. Confidentiality should be a principle but probably not an absolute one. The meeting should be when it is appropriate for the participants so it should avoid times when people are in school or employment. The professionals involved should aim to empower the participants rather than marginalising them. There should be a means to provide a voice for those not present. Time to do the task should be provided, although there has to be a limit: for example children will lose concentration and get tired. Monitoring and review should be a feature of the system and rights should be safeguarded within it. There should be follow up for all parties so that they know the outcomes. For the offender, involvement should not just cease abruptly as this would be cutting off the lifeline. A few further thoughts are desirable in relation to facilitators.

It is clear that the people who facilitate have to be suitable so they should be trained and motivated for the work and not be hindered by a prior mind set. We can ask how suited are the various professional groups in terms of the cultures that they come from? The police may be overbearing and perhaps destroy rather than build rapport – they may also be viewed in a hostile fashion by the offender. The police, even if they only sit as observers, will impact on offenders. The police at least may be victim conscious whilst social workers may side with the offender.

Accountability

Roche (2003) is valuable in terms of providing a clear account of both the dangers of restorative justice and in making suggestions for avoiding such problems. He looked at 25 programmes in six countries: United States, Canada, England, Australia, New Zealand and South Africa. He notes that restorative justice can be cruel and that it needs safeguards for all concerned. It also carries the dangers of promoting and justifying unacceptable practices and in making a virtue of informal justice which may be nothing other than a system without safeguards. He gives the following examples of the problems that can arise:

'In the summer of 2002 hundreds of fierce bushfires raged for weeks across New South Wales, Australia, forcing the evacuation of thousands of people, destroying over 100 homes, and burning out huge expanses of bush land. When a number of children caught lighting fires were referred to restorative justice conferences, the New South Wales Premier Bob Carr proclaimed on national television: "I think sending them to a juvenile prison is in some respects too good for them. What is better is to rub their noses in the ashes they've caused, by making them clean up the mess, work with the victims and go into a burns ward and talk to people who've suffered from fire" (ABC (2002)). A few years earlier in Canberra, Australia, a restorative justice conference was convened for a 12-year-old boy caught shoplifting, who agreed to the proposal by his mother and the store manager that he should wear outside the shop a T-shirt emblazoned with the words "I am a thief" (Braithwaite (2001:160)). Elsewhere, in Milwaukee, USA, a restorative justice programme was inundated with community volunteers when flyers were distributed with the heading "It's payback time!" (Walsh (2000).' (2003:1)

Later (2003:14–15) he also has material that allows us to guard against romanticised notions of the community resolution of disputes in terms of the behaviour of lynch mobs and the sometime historical practice of burning witches.

Roche suggests the need for systems of accountability at the various stages of restorative justice systems and in relation to all the participants. The issue is: does restorative justice fail to control the power that is given to the participants? The risk for the victim is perhaps obvious; that of the offender less so. The danger is that the power will be abused against offenders who in some senses are victims themselves. Is shame and humiliation a good idea? Anything that is on the 'putting in the stocks' side of things can seem dubious in terms of labelling perspectives. Perhaps showing the offender the problem and the offender understanding it with a view to adopting different attitudes and behaviour is acceptable. Roche says that the face-to-face meeting prevents offenders from denying the harm that they have done, but in reality what they can do is admit the harm but deny their part in it in various ways. He notes that there should be a consensual meeting but maybe the offender has no real choice in that he fears a worse alternative if he does not opt in to restorative justice. Someone to referee or facilitate the interaction and to review agreements are suggested as being valuable.

The effectiveness of restorative justice

Morris and Maxwell (2001) suggest that it make offenders aware of the consequences of their behaviour, they can feel remorse and they are not being made to feel a bad person (or a bad parent) at the end of the process. For the victim there can be meaningful repair of harm and

212

they seem to be satisfied with the agreements reached. The suggestion is that it works best in relation to serious and repeat offenders.

Rex (2003) examined and quoted the research of Daly (2002) in relation to the issue of the empirical support for restorative justice:

'Daly (2002) overviews the evidence to examine some "myths" about restorative justice, including the one that the experience can produce transformations in people. She cites the "most robust finding" as being the high levels of procedural justice perceived by victims and offenders alike (who generally view the process and outcomes as fair). However, her own research on the South Australian Juvenile Justice project found relatively less evidence of "restorativeness": of offenders giving sincere apologies, and victims being able to understand that apologies are sincere.

As Daly (2002) remarks, the conferencing effect everyone asks about is whether it reduces offending. Here, the RISE (Reintegrative Shaming Experiments) project in Canberra found that for one of four major offence categories (violence, but not drink-driving, property offences or shoplifting), those offenders who were assigned to a conference had a significantly reduced rate of re-offending compared with those assigned to court . In the South Australian Juvenile Justice project, and in New Zealand, links were found between what happened in conferences (for example, expressions of remorse by offenders, agreement over the outcomes) and reduced reconviction during follow-up periods.' (2003:50)

Roche (2003) illustrating the realities of what might be commonly achieved, which is something but not everything, describes one conference as follows:

'One conference I convened illustrates this point well. The case concerned a car theft by a young offender. The offender spoke about his actions, the victims described the impact of the theft of their only car, and all participants expressed their disappointment at the offender's action but also their faith in him for the future. The offender showed remorse, and then in crescendo, the victim expressed his forgiveness. By way of conclusion the victim asked the offender "So, do you think you'll ever steal a car again?" "Well", he said, "I'm definitely not going to steal your car again."' (2003:12)

A further issue that can be raised is that restorative justice is a soft option. Walgrave (2001) suggests not:

'Restorative justice is not a soft option. In the traditional criminal justice procedures, confrontation is indirect, impersonal and filtered through judicial rituals. Restorative processes, on the contrary, are personal, direct and, often, very emotional. For the offenders, being confronted directly with the suf-fering and harm they have caused and with the disapproval of their family is a deeply touching burden. Apologising in front of others may be experienced as very difficult and humiliating. Experiencing pressure to make up for the harm done may be hard to cope with. Through their personal relations with the participants and empathy with other persons, including the victim, offenders are brought to feel intensely a mixture of all kinds of unpleasant emotions like shame, guilt, remorse, embarrassment and humiliation.' (2001:17)

6.4 Factors that are taken into account in sentencing

The principles of sentencing

These may have a general influence on sentencers.

Legal limits

Sometimes the sentence is fixed by law or there may be other parameters within which the sentencer has to work, such as the maximum penalty for the offence.

Powers of Criminal Courts (Sentencing) Act 2000

The 2000 Act, which consolidated the Criminal Justice Act 1991, provides thresholds for the use of custodial and community penalties and the 2000 Act is the statutory basis for sentencing. The sentencing system is arranged in terms of the seriousness of the offence. The statute envisages non-custodial sentences or orders being utilised wherever possible. The length of a custodial sentence is to relate to the seriousness of the offence, though for violent or sexual offences a longer term to protect the public from serious harm is possible.

Custodial sentences
Section 79 relates to restrictions on imposing custodial sentences:

'(1) This section applies where a person is convicted of an offence punishable with a custodial sentence other than one –
(a) fixed by law ...
(2) Subject to subsection (3) below, the court shall not pass a custodial sentence on the offender unless it is of the opinion –
(a) that the offence, or the combination of the offence and one or more offences associated with it, was so serious that only such a sentence can be justified for the offence; or
(b) where the offence is a violent or sexual offence, that only such a sentence would be adequate to protect the public from serious harm from him.'

Community sentences
In relation to community sentences the 2000 Act provides in s35:

'(1) A court shall not pass a community sentence on an offender [that is to say, a sentence which consists of or includes one or more community orders] unless it is of the opinion that the offence, or the combination of the offence and one or more offences associated with it, was serious enough to warrant such a sentence.'

Where a court passes a community sentence, s35(3) states:

'(a) the particular order or orders comprising or forming part of the sentence shall be such as in the opinion of the court is, or taken together are, the most suitable for the offender; and
(b) the restrictions on liberty imposed by the order or orders shall be such as in the opinion of the court are commensurate with the seriousness of the offence, or the combination of the offence and other offences associated with it.'

It must be noted that an alternative system is provided for by the Criminal Justice Act 2003. This provides a statement of the aims of the sentencing system as it relates to adults. These aims are: punishment, crime reduction, public protection, the reform and rehabilitation of offenders and reparation. There are exceptions to these aims as certain offences have provisions relating to them that require particular disposals. The seriousness of an offence is to be judged in terms of culpability and the harm caused. Previous convictions, if recent and relevant, can be an aggravating factor, as can the offence having been committed whilst on bail.

Information for sentencers

Information will be made available to sentencers from a variety of sources – such as the defence, the police, the prosecution and probation and social workers. This will include a pre-sentence report, a statement of the facts of the case and a police antecedents statement. The antecedents statement will not just contain previous convictions but also data on age, employment, education and domestic circumstances.

Pre-sentence reports

The probation service or social workers prepare a pre-sentence report when it is required or requested. It will be required when custody is in issue or to determine the correct length of custody or prior to some of the community sentences such as community service or a combination order. The report should produce a balanced picture providing an account of both strengths and weaknesses. The risk of reoffending and the risk of harm to the public should be addressed. The report may make a suggestion as to a suitable disposition. National Standards as to the preparation of pre-sentence reports have been introduced, and the latest are the 2000 Standards.

The 2000 National Standards for pre-sentence reports

This tells us that the purpose of a pre-sentence report is to provide information to the sentencing court about the offender and the offence(s) committed and to assist the court to decide on suitable sentence.

The requirements for a pre-sentence report

These are as follows:

1. to be objective, impartial, free from discriminatory language and stereotype, balanced, verified and factually accurate;
2. to be based on the use of the Offender Assessment System, and when implemented to provide a systematic assessment of the nature and the causes of the defendant's offending behaviour, the risk the defendant poses to the public and the action which can be taken to reduce the likelihood of re-offending;
3. to be based on at least one face-to-face interview with the offender;
4. to specify information available from the CPS, any hostel placement or from any other relevant source;

5. to be written, and a copy provided to the court, the defence, the offender and (where required by the Crime (Sentences) Act 1997) the prosecution; and
6. to be prepared within, at most, 15 working days of request; or such shorter timescale as has been agreed in protocols with the court.

Offence analysis
Every pre-sentence report has to contain an offence analysis which has the following tasks:

1. an analysis of the offence(s) before the court, highlighting the key features in respect of the nature and circumstances of offences;
2. to assess the offender's culpability and level of premeditation;
3. to assess the consequences of the offence, including what is known of the impact on any victim, either from the CPS papers or from a victim statement where available;
4. to assess the offender's attitude to the offence and awareness of its consequences, including to any victim;
5. to indicate whether or not any positive action has been taken by the offender to make reparation or address offending behaviour since the offence was committed.

Offender assessment
Every pre-sentence report must also contain an offender assessment which has to:

1. state the offender's status in relation to literacy and numeracy, accommodation and employment;
2. assess the implications of any special circumstances, eg family crisis, substance abuse or mental illness, which were directly relevant to the offending;
3. evaluate any patterns of offending including reasons for offending and assess the outcome of any earlier court interventions, including the offender's response to previous supervision;
4. where substance misuse is relevant, provide details of the nature of the misuse and the offender's response to previous or current treatment;
5. give consideration to the impact of racism on the offender's behaviour where directly relevant to the offence;
6. include any relevant personal background which may have contributed to the offender's motive for committing the offence.

Risk factors
Pre-sentence reports also have to contain an assessment of the offender's likelihood of re-offending (based on the current offence, attitude to it, and other relevant information), contain an assessment of the offender's risk of causing serious harm to the public and identify any risks of self-harm.

Conclusion
This is also required in a pre-sentence report and it must have a content that:

1. evaluates the offender's motivation and ability to change and identifies, where relevant action required to improve motivation;

2. explicitly states whether or not an offender is suitable for a community sentence;
3. makes a clear and realistic proposal for sentence designed to protect the public and reduce re-offending, including for custody where this is necessary;
4. where the proposal is for a probation order or combination order, include an outline supervision plan containing a description of the purposes and desired outcomes of the proposed sentence, the methods envisaged and interventions likely to be undertaken, including attendance at accredited programmes where appropriate, the level of supervision envisaged (which for offenders at high risk of causing serious harm to the public is likely to be higher than the minimum required by the Standards);
5. where a specific condition is proposed, sets out the requirement precisely as it is proposed to appear in any order, and gives a likely start date;
6. where the proposal is for a curfew order, include details of the suitability of the proposed curfew address and its likely effects on others living at the offender's address;
7. for all serious sexual or violent offences, provide advice on the appropriateness of extended supervision;
8. where custody is a likely option, identify any anticipated effects on the offender's family circumstances, current employment or education.

Response to previous sentences and orders

The use of and failure of non-custodial dispositions in the past would help to move the offender towards the use of a custodial disposition. Some offenders receive custody for their persistence. The Criminal Justice Act 1993 made it clear that the previous criminal record of the offender should be a factor in sentencing and the 2003 Act also provides for this.

Age

This can be a factor, particular as regards youngsters. For them particular options may or not be available. Also old age could be a mitigating factor, especially where it is accompanied by serious or terminal illness. For youngsters some of the particular rules as to the availability of dispositions are as follows: attendance centre orders are only for those under 21; supervision orders are for those aged 10–17; and, finally, action plan orders, reparation orders and referral to a youth-offender panel are for those under 18.

Mitigating factors

Age, remorse (a timely guilty plea) and factors in the person's personal circumstances, such as caring for a sick relative, could be an influence on the sentence that is chosen by the court. Wasik (1993) suggests the following as some other mitigating factors. Provocation, duress, intoxication and other factors that may impact upon culpability. Previous good character and the assistance given to the police could be factors. The impact of the sentence on a particular offender may be taken into account. An offence involving a breach of trust may cause a person to lose his career and pension entitlement, a sexual offence may break up a marriage and a family. The long length of time since the offence, in the sense of it being a stale offence, might be a consideration.

Aggravating factors

The Criminal Justice Act 2003 provides that racial and religious dimensions are aggravating factors. This continues the system under the Powers of Criminal Courts (Sentencing) Act 2000.

As an example, aggravating factors of a burglary of a dwelling would include where the victim is in the house at the time and indeed more so when the burglar confronts the victim. Wasik (1993) suggests the following as some other aggravating factors. A particularly vulnerable victim by reason of age, handicap or infirmity. A breach of trust by a carer, teacher, nurse or parent, by an employee against an employer or by an office-holder in the performance of his responsibility. Premeditation and professionalism. Gratuitous violence and injury. Group offending as in the case of sexual and public order offences.

Examples of the operation of aggravating and mitigating factors

The first example is provided by the following jointly heard cases. In *Re Attorney-General's Reference (Nos 62, 63, 64 and 65 of 1996)*; sub nom *R v Samuel; R v Beresford; R v Jones; R v Murphy* (1997) (Transcripts 9608487 R2, 9608488 R2, 9608489 R2 and 9608390 R2) the first defendant was driving a car with the fourth defendant as a passenger. Speeds of 38–47 mph were reached in a 30-mph limit. There was a collision with a pedestrian who suffered a range of serious injuries including head injuries. Instead of stopping, the car was driven off, abandoned and set fire to. They then went to the house of the other two defendants where they all agreed to say that the car had been stolen earlier and thus avoid liability for the offences. Samuel pleaded guilty to offences, including dangerous driving, and it is this that will be concentrated on. In favour of the driver was the plea, his remorse, the time interval between the incident and the sentence and that the driving was on the borderline of careless and dangerous driving. Aggravating features were the serious injuries, the attempt at deceit, the excessive speeding and the failure to stop. The suspended sentence of six months was referred, as unduly lenient, by the Attorney-General. The Court of Appeal stated that exceptional circumstances would be needed to justify a suspended sentence and since none were present a sentence of six months immediate custody was substituted, with a one-year period of disqualification from driving.

The next two cases show the use of further factors of aggravation and mitigation in relation to the offence of indecent assault. Also seen to be operative are public policy considerations. The cases also demonstrate the complexity of the issues that can be involved in sentencing. The *Attorney-General's Reference (No 61 of 1998)* [1999] Crim LR 428 concerned a 40-year-old man who pleaded guilty to eight counts of indecent assault of the child of a woman that he was living with at the time. The mother had left the offender after the issue of indecent assault had been raised. Some years later the mother was told by the daughter that the assaults had been serious ones which included putting a finger in her vagina and requiring her to perform oral sex on him. He pleaded guilty and received a probation order for three years with a requirement of treatment. The court accepted that judges had to have discretion and respond to the particular facts of a case – here they were clearly influenced by a need for treatment. However, their discretion only goes so far and public policy required a custodial sentence here. Sentences should reflect the clear intention of Parliament that offences of this kind were to be met with greater severity than might have been the case in the past. Three years would have been appropriate but two years was substituted, allowing for the work on the probation order and the element of double jeopardy. Double jeopardy recognises that a person has run the risk of being sentenced twice and that he may for example end up with a custodial rather than a non-custodial sentence. In contrast to the approach seen in *Attorney-General's Reference (No 61 of 1998)* (above) is the case of *R* v *W* [1999] 1 Cr App R (S) 488. This case involved an indecent assault by a 13-year-old boy on a 12-year-old girl whilst they were walking home. This included putting his hands inside her clothing and simulated intercourse. The original sentence was eight months' detention under s53(2) and (3) of the Children and Young Persons Act 1933. Whilst the attack had to be viewed as a serious one, the needs of such a young offender indicated a community penalty and a supervision order was substituted.

Reasons to be given for sentences

The Criminal Justice Act 2003 provides that courts are under a duty to give reasons for and to explain the effect of the sentence.

Gender as a factor in sentencing

Gender is of course not meant to be a factor that influences sentencing. Research shows that for indictable offences women are more likely than men to be discharged or given a community sentence or order and are less likely to be fined or sentenced to custody than males of the same age. Custody rates for indictable offences are higher for men than for women at magistrates' courts and at the Crown Court. Women also receive shorter sentences on average. These differences partly reflect the different types of offences committed by women. However, even within offence groups, the above tends to hold (although offence group is a crude control as the seriousness of offence can vary greatly within a group). Some of these offences that women tend to commit have low custody rates, but the large volume of offences means that even a low custody rate delivers a large number to prison.

Some information on the sentencing of women was provided by Hedderman and Gelsthorpe (1997) who noted that in the research that had been carried out for the Home Office there were differences in the patterns of sentences for males and females. These differences may of course have been a result of factors other than gender in the background of the offender. Offence variables may also be involved. They suggested that sentencers, in order to avoid discriminatory practices, should use the same approach and ask the same questions in relation to offenders, regardless of sex. This may still not produce the same outcomes. They argue that if there was discrimination then it would be found consistently. They point out that women stand the same chance as men of going to prison for a first offence of violence but that women repeat offenders were less likely to be imprisoned than their male counterparts. The main factor in sentence decisions was clearly the offence. The factor that was more likely to be operationalised in relation to women was that they were more likely to be perceived as troubled rather than troublesome. In relation to shop-lifting, which was the most common offence for women before the courts, their behaviour was seen as being in order to provide for themselves and their children in a situation in which they had a low or a precarious source of income. This perception of the women having a troubled status could work to their disadvantage. There was a reluctance to use fines in such circumstances, which carried with it the risk that the next stage of the sentencing ladder would be arrived at prematurely, by the use of probation for example. Hedderman and Gelsthorpe also noted the impact of the following factors:

'Turning to the offender in the courtroom, while some magistrates recognised that body language is open to misinterpretation, most stressed the importance of seeing the offender in court, and a number were confident that they would not themselves misinterpret nonverbal cues. The research also indicated that, based on perceptions of body language and appearance, men – ethnic minority men in particular – may come across as having less respect for the court, while women are generally perceived to be inexperienced, deferential and (therefore) honest.

The internal politics of the courtroom also seem to shape magistrates' decision-making. The same information could be viewed quite differently according to which courtroom player provided it – most weight was accorded to information from prosecutors or the Clerk, who were regarded by magistrates as being impartial. Not only defence solicitors but probation officers were seen as siding with the offender.

Interaction between magistrates was also important, with experience weighing more heavily than training. Moreover, virtually all the magistrates mentioned "common sense" or "gut feelings" at some stage of their assessment as to who was respectful or rebellious, remorseful or rancorous; and "common sense" was what magistrates used to explain any decision that seemed to have no other explanation or, at least, no easily expressed explanation. Yet notions of what is "common sense" and what reliable indicators of honesty and remorse differed among magistrates.

Taken as a whole, these findings suggest that there remains a risk that some magistrates will resort to their "common sense" (and a gendered "common sense" at that) as the best arbiter of what is right, despite the fact that new magistrates receive training designed to inform them of the inherent dangers of making decisions on the basis of stereotypes and on the dangers of relying on non-verbal cues.' (1997:57–58)

Race as a factor in sentencing

Research by Hood (1992) provides an account of the impact of race as a factor in sentencing decisions in the Crown Court. It is well known that the rate of custody is higher for some groups than others, the important issue, and the one that Hood tackles, is whether or not this can be explained in terms of characteristics of the offence and of the offender. Taking such factors into account does remove some of the difference in custody rates but some still remains. So it seems that a person's race can on the face of it be an operative variable. The impetus for Hood's work was the over-representation of Afro-Caribbeans in prisons and young offender institutions. He investigated the possibility of a racial factor in sentencing, mainly by examining Crown Court records for 1989 in a variety of courts in the West Midlands. A total of 1,441 ethnic minority males went through the courts in the period and a sample of 1,443 white males was drawn for comparative purposes. Differences in the proportions of each ethnic category – white, black or Asian – given a custodial sentence were marked. Taking the sample as a whole, the proportion of blacks sentenced to custody was just over 8 percentage points higher than for whites (56.6 per cent versus 48.4 per cent). Asians, on the other hand, were sentenced to custody less often than either whites or blacks (39.6 per cent). To what extent could these disparities be accounted for by variability in the nature of the cases dealt with by these judges at the various courts covered by the study? A comparison was first made of the nature and circumstances of the offences and the legally relevant characteristics of the defendants in each ethnic group. Factors that increased a person's risk of getting custody were identified and applied to the defendants. A higher proportion of blacks than whites fell into the category with the highest risk of custody, and fewer in the category with the lowest probability of receiving such a sentence. Asian offenders, on the other hand, were much less likely to be in the highest risk of custody group and were much more frequently in the lowest. The black to white difference in the proportion sent to custody was at its greatest in the band of cases which could he described as of medium seriousness (with a probability of custody ranging from 45 to 80 per cent). Here the 68 per cent custody rate for blacks was significantly higher than the 60 per cent rate for whites: a difference which amounts to a 13 per cent greater probability of a black offender receiving a custodial sentence than a white in the range of cases.

6.5 The problem of disparity

Wasik (1992) noted the belated official recognition of the unacceptable degree of sentencing disparity which exists in England and Wales. He stated that:

> 'The existence of sentencing disparity, in the sense of unprincipled differences in sentencing outcome from court to court and from sentencer to sentencer, has been confirmed in numerous empirical studies. Most have been carried out in magistrates' courts (Tarling 1979; Moxon et al 1985; Turner 1992). Much of this disparity is probably explained by differing bench norms, arrived at in isolation, without reference to neighbouring benches, and sustained by the views of court clerks and senior magistrates, who train and constrain newer magistrates in their sentencing practices (Henham 1990; Parker et al 1989). There are fewer studies of Crown Court sentencing, but nobody doubts that disparity exists there, too. One reason for the lack of information about Crown Court sentencing has been the reluctance of the higher judiciary to submit its sentencing practices to outside scrutiny. (See Moxon (1988), though this study was not aimed at identifying disparity.) Studies of Crown Court disparity in specific areas of sentencing have been carried out by Walmsley and White (1979) and McConville and Baldwin (1982b). A large-scale exploratory study of sentencing in the Crown Court was begun by Ashworth et al. (1984) but was halted at a preliminary stage by Lord Lane's opposition.' (1992:128)

Once the issue of disparity is revealed the question to ask is how could the situation be improved? One answer is to have a system of sentencing guidelines. Some examples of the practice of the Court of Appeal in this respect are provided below.

6.6 Sentencing guidelines

Sentencing guidelines for drugs

The case of *R v Ronchetti* [1998] 2 Cr App R (S) 100 saw the Court of Appeal issue sentencing guidelines in relation to the importation of cannabis. This was to supplement the guideline case of *R v Aramah* (1983) 4 Cr App R (S) 407 and it reflected the increased problem with the offence in recent years. Where the amount was 100kg at a trial and the role of the defendant was a major one, then the starting point should be seven to eight years. This should increase to ten years for 500kg and rise, with increases in the amount of the drug, to the maximum permitted sentence of 14 years. The Court of Appeal also issued sentencing guidelines in relation to the importation of amphetamine in the case of *R v Wijs* [1998] 2 Cr App R (S) 436. The guidelines needed to be quite different to those for cannabis, given both the greater street value of the drug, for a particular weight, and that it is very likely to be sold in an adulterated condition. After a trial the expectation would be a custodial sentence, unless the amounts were very small so as to indicate personal use. Where the drug was at 100 per cent purity then at up to 500g amounts two years should be the norm, two to five years for 500g to 2.5kg, four to seven years for 2.5kg to 10kg and seven to ten years for 10kg to 15kg. Sentences of ten years to the statutory maximum of 14 years would be for amounts of more than 15kg. Sentencing guidelines, for the offence of possession of LSD with intent to supply, were provided in the case of *R v Hurley* (1999) The Times 5 August. In relation to 25,000 50 microgram units, the sentence should be ten years or more. Where the amount was 250,000 50 microgram units, it should be 14 years or more. Variation would occur depending on the facts of each case. For example, in this case the 280,000 31 microgram units should have produced a 12- to 13-year sentence, which was further reduced by a guilty plea to ten years.

Sentencing guidelines for burglary

Whilst burglary as an offence covers various forms of property and entry of them for a variety of purposes, sometimes involving violence, the aim here is to provide insight as regards sentencing guidelines in cases where entry is to a dwelling for the purposes of theft. Such cases are commonly called domestic burglary. *R v Brewster* [1998] 1 Cr App R (S) 220 saw the Court of Appeal provide sentencing guidelines for domestic burglary.

The *Brewster* case

In the *Brewster* case Lord Bingham CJ stressed the seriousness of the offence of burglary, given the impact upon the victim. This can involve property that has been lost which may be irreplaceable and of sentimental value. Also, some victims may not be insured. There is also the impact of the invasion of privacy and the undermining of a feeling of security. The offence causes fear, particularly where the victim is in the house at the time and indeed more so when the burglar confronts the victim. Entry to an unoccupied house, whilst it is less frightening for a victim, might however indicate evidence of careful planning and preparation. Whilst the offence is a serious one, in some cases it may only require a non-custodial sentence. Lord Bingham also noted the variety of actions that can be involved –

ranging from an impulsive act, such as reaching through a window to take a bottle of milk, to a professionally planned operation, directed at objects of high value. Other dimensions can include preying on the elderly or the disabled, repeated burglaries of the same premises or the presence of soiling and vandalism. Another factor is the background of the particular offender, though this will be of less importance than the aggravating and mitigating factors. Professional burglars with many convictions, who have behaved as predators, require substantial terms of imprisonment. Burglars of a different character, whose careers may lack any element of persistence or deliberation, are entitled to treatment that is more lenient. For drug addicts, who burgle in order to raise money to satisfy their habit, this cannot be relied on as mitigation.

Aggravating and mitigating factors in burglary

Lord Bingham stated that the following increase the seriousness of the offence, if the burglaries

> '... are of occupied houses at night; if they are the result of professional planning, organisation or execution; if they are targeted at the elderly, the disabled and the sick; if there are repeated visits to the same premises; if they are committed by persistent offenders; if they are accompanied by vandalism or any wanton injury to the victim; if they are shown to have a seriously traumatic effect on the victim; if the offender operates as one of a group; if goods of high value (whether actual or sentimental) are targeted or taken; if force is used or threatened; if there is a pattern of repeat offending. It mitigates the seriousness of an offence if the offender pleads guilty, particularly if the plea is indicated at an early stage and there is hard evidence of genuine regret and remorse.' (p243)

These factors provide us with general indicators, Lord Bingham's view was, that given the variety of factors that can be operative, it is not possible to establish sentencing brackets.

Sentencing guidelines for thefts and false accounting

These were provided by the Court of Appeal in *R* v *Kefford* (2002) The Times 7 March. The case concerned a series of thefts and offences of false accounting by a building society employee. The offences, which were more than 30 in number, totalled over £11,000. They led to the imposition of sentences of 12 months per offence to operate concurrently. The Court was of the view that the appropriate period would have been four months. The main point of interest in the case is the impact of the overcrowding of prisons upon sentencing decisions. Great emphasis was placed upon the importance of only using prison where it was appropriate and for a period no longer than was necessary. It is only in this way that the prison population will remain at anything like manageable levels. This call by the higher judiciary for restraint on the part of sentencers in the lower courts echoes similar sentiments that have been expressed in the past. Whether the message is being delivered by the appellate judiciary or by legislators it is difficult to influence the punitive obsession that is at work in the United Kingdom.

The Court was keen to establish as a context for sentencing decisions, the problem of increases in the prison population. The prison system should not have to operate so close to its overcrowded capacity. The stage had now been reached where it would be highly undesirable if the prison population were to continue to rise. The overcrowding situation was not only a matter of grave concern for the prison system, but also for the criminal justice system as a whole. The ability to tackle a prisoner's offending behaviour and so reduce reoffending was adversely affected if a prison was overcrowded. Those responsible for imposing sentences had to take into account the impact on the prison system of the number of prisoners the service was being required to accommodate at the present time. The aim was not to deter courts from sending those who committed offences involving violence or intimidation or other grave crimes to prison for the appropriate period. However, there were other categories of offences where community punishment or fines were more appropriate. Prison was not necessarily the only appropriate form of punishment for economic crimes, particularly where the offender was of previous good character.

6.7 Who should sentence?

The issue of disparity in sentencing and the system of sentencing guidelines raise the wider issue of: who should impose sentences and who should be allowed to provide them with direction? At the moment our sentencers are the magistrates and the judges, and sentencing is thus a judicial function. Concern for rights suggests that there is some merit in it remaining a judicial function. A problem of course is that our present sentencers know little about sentencing. The judges receive only limited training in sentencing and indeed in terms of judicial independence even that is not entirely welcome.

Guidance to sentencers comes from the Court of Appeal and legislation also attempts to set parameters. Whilst the Court of Appeal provides guidelines, these mainly deal with the high tariff offences and most sentencing is at the other end of the sentencing scale. Change in relation to much of the above has been suggested – there could instead be specialist sentencers or a specialist sentencing body. A very mechanical perhaps even a computerised system could be introduced. In Minnesota a system is used which calculates an offence score and an offender score (predicting what he may do) which indicates a point on a table or graph which indicates whether or not custody is required. The Criminal Justice Act 1991 used a very loose version of such ideas. Another approach is to use indeterminate sentencing so that an offender would get a sentence of say one to five years and then the matter is left in the hands of a review body.

A number of the above matters will be considered in more detail. Ashworth (1982) and (1987) explored how a system of sentencing guidance could be devised for England and he also proposed that a Sentencing Council should be introduced. The Crime and Disorder Act 1998 made provision in relation to both of these ideas. Ashworth's conclusion on the issue of sentencing guidance was as follows:

'This Chapter amounts to little more than a brief sketch of the proposed guidance. It recommends as its main feature the offence tabulation, sub-dividing offences into categories and indicating recommended sentences. For serious offences there would be a grid showing a range of recommended measures according to the number of previous convictions, from none to five. For less serious offences it might be preferable to leave courts to use a number of alternative measures, but it would remain necessary to indicate both a recommended normal penalty (eg for an offender with one previous conviction) and a ceiling above which the sentence should not go. For both approaches, the court should have regard to the principles relating to previous record. Having located the offence in the offence tabulation, the sentencer would then have to consider further matters. There would be the list of aggravating and extenuating factors, which would help the sentencer to decide whether to go higher or lower than the recommended penalty. There would be the list of mitigating factors, to be considered in conjunction with any representations made on behalf of the offender. There would be the guidance on non-custodial measures, to be considered in conjunction with any report on the offender by a probation officer (or, where appropriate, psychiatrist). And, lastly, there would be principles of totality of sentence which would give guidance on whether the sentence should be concurrent or consecutive, and on how the court should assess the totality of consecutive sentences, for cases in which an offender is sentenced for more than one offence. It is envisaged that guidance of these kinds should be addressed to the Crown Court and to magistrates' courts.' (1987:101)

Ashworth put the following arguments for a Sentencing Council:

'What is needed is a body which can consider sentencing practice from all these points of view, can instigate research which will provide systematic knowledge about the reasoning of judges and magistrates, and can then reformulate sentencing policy so that it is no longer reliant on custodial measures. The question of policy just outlined must be tackled by whatever body is assembled for the purpose. The Court of Appeal, I submit, is not the appropriate body. It lacks a wider appreciation of penal policy, and it is imperfectly informed about sentencing practices in the lower courts ... My proposal is for a Sentencing Council, chaired by the Lord Chief Justice himself and producing recommendations which would be issued as practice directions ... Its membership should draw on persons with considerable experience of the penal system, from magistrates, to a circuit judge sitting in second- and third-tier centres, to a probation officer, a prison governor, a Home Office official and an academic ... it would be essential that there should be a number of sentencers who fairly represent the range of English courts, so as to bring a wider experience than a few senior judges can muster.' (1982:122)

Crime and Disorder Act 1998

Section 80 of the 1998 Act makes provision for the existing system of sentencing guidelines by the Court of Appeal to be put on a statutory footing, in an amended form. Section 81 was innovative in that it provided for a Sentencing Advisory Panel. In providing for a Panel, a watered-down version of what Ashworth had suggested in terms of a Sentencing Council can be introduced. Both sections were implemented in spring 1999. Auld LJ in his review of the criminal courts (Auld LJ (2001)) suggested that the law should be amended: to widen the remit of the Sentencing Advisory Panel to include general principles of sentencing, regardless of the category of offence; and to enable the Court of Appeal to issue guidelines without having to tie them to a specific appeal before it. The Criminal Justice Act 2003 makes provision for a Sentencing Guidelines Council to be introduced. The aim is to standardise sentencing. It will consist of seven judicial members and five non-judicial members. The courts will be required to have regard to sentencing guidelines and they will have to explain why they depart from a guideline if they do so. Courts generally will be required to explain and give reasons for sentences The Sentencing Advisory Panel will continue to operate and it will be able to offer advice to the Sentencing Guidelines Council.

Section 80: sentencing guidelines

The Court of Appeal, if it is hearing a sentencing appeal or they receive a proposal from the Sentencing Advisory Panel as to the need for sentencing guidelines in respect of a particular category of offence, must act as follows. The Court has to consider whether to frame guidelines as to the sentencing of offenders for offences of that category. If there were already guidelines in existence they must consider whether it would be appropriate to review them. The Court of Appeal in producing or amending guidelines is to have regard to:

1. the need to promote consistency in sentencing;
2. the sentences imposed by courts in England and Wales for offences of that type;
3. the cost of different sentences and their relative effectiveness in preventing reoffending;
4. the need to promote public confidence in the criminal justice system; and
5. the views expressed by the Sentencing Advisory Panel.

The guidelines that are produced are to include criteria for determining the seriousness of offences, including (where appropriate) criteria for determining the weight to be given to any previous convictions of offenders or any failures of theirs to respond to previous sentences.

Section 81: the Sentencing Advisory Panel

The Sentence Advisory Panel can suggest to the Court of Appeal that there is a need for guidelines in a particular area of sentencing. Where appeals on sentencing go to the Court of Appeal and the Court is minded to produce or alter guidelines, the Panel will be informed of this. This will allow the Panel to inform the court of its views on the matter. The Panel will also inform the court of its views where it makes a proposal as to the need for guidelines. The Panel started work in 1999 with the aim of promoting consistency in sentencing. Its work has involved offering advice to the Court of Appeal on offences such as child pornography and causing death by dangerous driving. Also, in 2001 the Sentencing Advisory Panel decided to propose to the Court of Appeal that it should frame a sentencing guideline for the offence of handling stolen goods. A further example is the proposal for a guideline on robbery in 2003.

7 Young Offenders

7.1   Statistics relating to young offenders

7.2   The courts

7.3   The justice and welfare models

7.4   The history of young offender systems

7.5   The youth justice framework 1982–2004

7.6   The Youth Justice Board

7.7   Sentences and orders

7.8   Analysis of the youth justice system

7.9   Applying 'what works?' principles to young offenders

7.10 The effectiveness of interventions with young offenders

7.11 Conclusion

The age of criminal responsibility is ten and the criminal justice system in England and Wales makes special provision for those between the ages of ten and 21 in a variety of ways. As the Audit Commission (1997) recognises, crime committed by young people is a major problem. In some neighbourhoods about a quarter of known offenders are aged under 18 and youth crime costs public services £1 billion. Whilst young offenders constitute a major part of the crime problem, the good news is that they will generally grow out of crime – maturational reform is the name for this. The bad news of course is that the next generation of youngsters will also become a problem that society will have to contend with. The main theme to consider in this chapter will be how should society respond to this criminal behaviour and what allowances should be made for the youthfulness of offenders? The numerical importance for the criminal justice system of young offenders is illustrated further by material from the criminal statistics in the next section. The Criminal Justice Act 2003 provisions that relate to the issues in this chapter are detailed below. It is important to note that, since most of the provisions of the Act did not come into force immediately upon Royal Assent, the earlier provisions will still be applicable for some time. Pickford (2000) is valuable as an introduction to youth justice issues and the collection of readings in Pickford (ed) (2000) is also of use.

7.1 Statistics relating to young offenders

Table 20 gives further information on the age patterns of offending.

Table 20

Persons Found Guilty or Cautioned for Indictable Offences, per 100,000 of the Population, in 2001, by Age		
Age	Male	Female
All persons	1,666	371
10–11	519	136
12–14	2,388	1,086
15–17	5,891	1,541
18–20	6,623	1,251
21 and over	1,184	247

(Source: Criminal Statistics, England and Wales, 2001)

Table 21 provides figures from which you can work out that 41 per cent of indictable offenders are under the age of 21. This proportion of offenders is very much more than their percentage of the general population would suggest. As self-report studies demonstrate the participation rate of youngsters in criminal activity is even higher than the official statistics indicate and indeed some form of delinquent activity can be regarded as quite normal for youngsters.

Table 21

Numbers Sentenced or Cautioned in 2001 for Indictable Offences by Age Group and Gender (thousands)			
Age	Male	Female	Total
10–11	3.7	0.9	4.6
12–14	25.0	10.8	35.8
15–17	58.9	14.5	73.4
18–20	66.6	11.9	78.5
Over 21	225.1	49.4	274.4

(Source: Criminal Statistics, England and Wales, 2001)

Table 22

Sentences and Orders for Those under 21, by Age Group and Gender, for Indictable Offences in 2001
(thousands)

	Male	Female
Discharge		
10–11	0.1	0.01
12–14	1.4	0.4
15–17	5.2	1.2
18–20	15.0	22.0
Fine		
10–11	0.02	0.002
12–14	0.5	0.1
15–17	4.7	0.5
18–20	12.7	1.4
Supervision order		
10–11	0.12	0.003
12–14	1.9	0.3
15–17	4.4	0.9
Attendance sentence order		
10–11	0.04	0.002
12–14	0.7	0.1
15–17	2.2	0.2
18–20	0.3	0.0
Curfew order		
10–11	0.01	not applicable
12–14	0.2	0.0
15–17	0.6	0.1
18–20	0.4	0.0
Reparation order		
10–11	0.01	0.001
12–14	1.2	0.2
15–17	2.3	0.5
Action plan order		
10–11	0.01	0.001
12–14	1.5	0.3
15–17	3.0	0.6
Detention and training order		
12–14	0.6	0.0
15–17	4.8	0.3

	Male	Female
Sections 90–92 Powers of Criminal Courts (Sentencing) Act 2000		
12–14	0.1	0.0
15–17	0.4	0.0
Community rehabilitation order (1)		
15–17	1.4	0.3
18–20	5.6	1.6
Community punishment order (2)		
15–17	2.6	0.2
18–20	8.0	4.0
Community punishment and rehabilitation order (3)		
15–17	1.2	0.1
18–20	1.8	0.2
Drug treatment and testing order		
15–17	0.1	0.0
18–20	0.4	0.1
Young offender institution		
18–20	12.5	0.9

(1) Before April 2001 this was a probation order
(2) Before April 2001 this was a community service order
(3) Before April 2001 this was a combination order

(Source: Criminal Statistics, England and Wales, 2001)

Further data is presented in Table 22 in relation to specific sentences and orders. Some of the main points to note are as follows. For males aged 18–20, 57,100 were sentenced for indictable offences. Of these 23 per cent received immediate custody, whereas in the early 1990s the rate would have been 15 per cent.

7.2 The courts

Those over the age of 18 are tried in the same way as adults but the dispositions that are available are different. Juveniles are normally tried in a special magistrates' court called the youth court. This is meant to provide a more relaxed forum and other differences from the adult court include a different oath, plea and finding. The juvenile is not convicted but rather found guilty and the juvenile is not sentenced, receiving instead an order upon a finding of guilt. The youth court is meant to be separate from the adult court, though this may only amount to a hearing at the same place at a different time. The youth court is not open to the public and there are limitations upon the reporting of hearings. Other features include the presence of both a male and a female magistrate, though this requirement can be waived.

Practice Direction (2000) The Times 17 February

Practice Direction (Crown Court: Trial of Children and Young Persons) (2000) The Times 17 February was issued as a response to the judgment of the European Court of Human Rights in *T* v *United Kingdom*; *V* v *United Kingdom* (1999) The Times 17 December in which the arrangements for the trial of young defendants in the Crown Court were criticised. The case concerned the juvenile killers of James Bulger in 1993. The Practice Direction stated that the steps taken in any given case should have regard to the age, maturity and development (intellectual and emotional) of the young defendant on trial and all other circumstances of the case. Some young defendants, accused of committing serious crimes, might be very young and very immature when standing trial in the Crown Court. The purpose of a trial is to determine guilt (if that was in issue) and to decide the appropriate sentence if the young defendant pleaded guilty or was convicted. The trial process should not itself expose the young defendant to avoidable intimidation, humiliation or distress. All possible steps were to be taken to assist a young defendant to understand and participate in the proceedings. The ordinary trial process should so far as is necessary be adapted to meet those ends. Regard should be had to the welfare of the young defendant as required by s44 of the Children and Young Persons Act 1933.

Before trial

If a young defendant was indicted jointly with an adult defendant, the court should consider at the plea and directions hearing whether the young defendant should be tried on his own. It should normally order this unless a joint trial would be in the interests of justice and would not be unduly prejudicial to the welfare of the young defendant. If a young defendant was tried jointly with an adult the ordinary procedures would apply, subject to such modifications (if any) as the court might see fit to order. At the plea and directions hearing before the trial of a young defendant, the court should consider and so far as practicable give directions on the matters noted below. It might be appropriate to arrange a private visit to the court in advance of the trial. Arrangements should be made to try to ensure protection from hostile members of the public and a direction should be made as to the control of pre-trial publicity.

The trial

The trial should, if practicable, be held in a courtroom in which all the participants were on the same or almost the same level. A young defendant should normally, if he wished, be free to sit with members of his family or others in a like relationship and in a place which permitted easy, informal communication with his legal representatives and others with whom he wanted or needed to communicate. The court should explain the proceedings to a young defendant in terms he could understand and remind those representing a young defendant to act in the same manner. The trial should be conducted according to a timetable that took full account of a young defendant's inability to concentrate for long periods. Robes and wigs should not normally be worn. Police officers would similarly normally be in plain clothes. The court should be prepared to restrict attendance, perhaps limited to some of those with an immediate and direct interest in the outcome of the trial. Facilities for reporting the trial should be available but may need to be restricted. A separate audio, and perhaps video, link for reporters would be a suitable alternative for those not admitted.

Auld suggested (Auld LJ (2001)) that serious cases against young defendants should no longer be heard in the Crown Court but by a youth court composed of a judge of an appropriate level and at least two experienced youth panel magistrates.

7.3 The justice and welfare models

An account of the justice and welfare models in the context of youngsters is presented below. The themes developed in these models should assist when considering past, present and indeed future strategies in relation to the offending behaviour of youngsters. The question of what to do about the misbehaviour of youngsters has produced a variety of different answers over the years. A particular focus has been the competing claims of the welfare model and the justice model. The material is based on analysis by Stewart and Tutt (1987) who in turn relied upon the work of the Black Committee (1979). The Black Committee produced a report on the system of criminal justice for young offenders in Northern Ireland.

The assumptions of the welfare model

1. Delinquent, dependent and neglected children are all products of an adverse environment, which at its worse is characterised by multiple deprivation. Social, economic and physical disadvantage, including poor parental care, are all relevant considerations.
2. Delinquency is a pathological condition; a presenting symptom of some deeper maladjustment out of the control of the individual concerned.
3. Since a person has no control over the multiplicity of casual factors dictating his delinquency, he cannot be considered responsible for his actions or held accountable for them. Considerations of guilt or innocence are, therefore, irrelevant and punishment, is not only inappropriate, but is contrary to the rules of natural justice.
4. All children in trouble (both offenders and non-offenders) are basically the same and can be effectively dealt with through a single unified system designed to identify and meet the needs of children.
5. The needs or underlying disorders, of which delinquency is symptomatic, are capable of identification and hence treatment and control are possible.
6. Informality is necessary if the child's needs are to be accurately determined and his best interests served. Strict rules of procedure or standards of proof not only hinder the identification of need but are unnecessary in proceedings conducted in the child's best interests.

7. Inasmuch as need is highly individualised, flexibility of response is vital. Wide discretion is necessary in the determination and variation of treatment measures.
8. Voluntary treatment is possible and is not punishment. Treatment has no harmful side effects.
9. Whilst the child and his welfare are of paramount importance considerations of public protection cannot be ignored. A system designed to meet the needs of the child will in turn protect the community and serve the best interests of society.
10. Prevention of neglect and alleviation of disadvantage will lead to prevention of delinquency.

The assumptions of the justice model

1. Delinquency is a matter of opportunity and choice. Other factors may combine to bring a child to the point of delinquency, but unless there is evidence to the contrary, the act as such is a manifestation of the rational decision to that effect.
2. Insofar as a person is responsible for his actions, he should also be accountable. This is qualified in respect of children by the doctrine of criminal responsibility as originally evolved under common law and now endorsed by statue.
3. Proof of commission of an offence should be the sole justification for intervention and the sole basis of punishment.
4. Society has the right to re-assert the norms and standards of behaviour both as an expression of society's disapproval and as an individual and general deterrent to future similar behaviour.
5. Sanctions and controls are valid responses to deviant behaviour both as an expression of society's disapproval and as an individual and general deterrent to similar behaviour.
6. Behaviour attracting legal intervention and associated sanctions available under the law should be specifically defined to avoid uncertainty.
7. The power to interfere with a person's freedom, and in particular that of a child, should be subject to the most rigorous standard of proof which traditionally are found in a court of law. Individual rights are most effectively safeguarded through the judicial process.
8. There should be equality before the law and like cases should be treated alike.
9. There should be proportionality between the seriousness of the delinquent or criminal behaviour warranting intervention and the community's response to it and between the offence and the sentence given.

Pickford (2000) examined the various responses, in criminal justice for juveniles, of the competing justice and welfare principles. These responses have taken the form of a variety of compromise strategies whereby elements of justice and welfare have been distributed over the system in a bid to resolve this inevitable tension. In summary, these are:

'1. bifurcation strategy – distinguishing between different types of children and young people who come before the justice system. This involves differentiating those who need help from those who deserve punishment; serious offenders from non-serious offenders; and persistent offenders from those whose behaviour can be "nipped in the bud";
2. sequencing strategy – creating different types of procedures/processes which utilise

divergent approaches; for example, a justice approach in relation to trial and conviction; a welfare approach in relation to mitigation and sentencing; pre-trial court diversionary schemes, and so on;

3. institutional strategy – developing practices whereby different institutions or organisations will deal with different types of young offenders; for example, informal tribunal-style hearings such as the new Youth Offender Panels as opposed to the courts; social services as opposed to the formal youth justice system, etc;

4. double-edged strategy – the introduction of measures which have both a welfare and justice function; for example, the criminal care order introduced by the Children and Young Persons Act 1969 (now abolished);

5. career criminal strategy – a young offender may experience a more welfare oriented approach at the start of their offending careers for example, by the use of cautions/reprimands and final warnings or other diversionary measures; if he or she continues to offend, more justice orientated procedures and sanctions will be implemented.' (2000:xxxiv)

7.4 The history of young offender systems

Morris and Giller (1987) make the point that until recently there was no developed notion of a separate category of juvenile. They quote Pinchbeck and Hewitt (1973) who noted that one day in 1814 five children between the ages of eight and 12 were hanged for petty larceny. The nineteenth century saw the first real attempts to make separate custodial provision for youngsters, for example in 1838 a separate prison was built. The nineteenth century also saw notions of reform developed as an alternative to ideas of deterrence. This does not fit well with a society that was much concerned with order. A part explanation is that at the time ideas of free will, which deterrence theory relies upon, were being replaced by ideas of determinism. Notions of reform developed as a response to the idea that individuals had personal faults that required a cure. Reformatories and industrial schools were introduced to provide this correction. As regards such developments Morris and Giller (1987) suggest that explanations in terms of both humanitarian intentions and a conspiracy of the upper class attempting to control the lower class are both probably overplayed. For example, that whilst there was some concern for the lower classes the humanitarian endeavours were authoritarian and conservative in effect. The reformatories and the industrial schools, for example, provided harsh regimes. They were reorganised as a result of the Children Act 1908. The 1908 Act also introduced a separate system of juvenile courts. The courts were in many ways similar to those of the present day, though criminal jurisdiction extended as low as the age of seven.

The era of borstals and approved schools

The Prevention of Crime Act 1908 gave official recognition to borstals which had been the subject of a number of experiments in earlier years. Borstals were introduced for youngsters over the age of 16 to provide a system of custodial education and training. They were eventually replaced by youth custody centres by the Criminal Justice Act 1982. Borstals were in the past viewed as being a success. For example, on a two-year follow-up the reconviction rate was only 30 per cent in 1936. However, by 1960 the reconviction rate was high as 64 per cent. The demise of borstals is a story that is not easy to tell in a few words. The loss of most of their staff and accommodation at the start of the Second World War, probable differences in pre- and post-war youth as seen in an increasing problem of escapes by trainees and the criticisms by some of what were viewed as harsh and paternalistic regimes were certainly factors. After the legislation in 1908 the next significant development was the report of the Molony Committee (1927) on the treatment of offenders. The report was in favour of a criminal jurisdiction for youngsters. This would provide a hearing of the issues and, if the matter was a serious one, such a forum would ensure that he was made aware of this. The Molony Committee also wished to retain the notion of offence because they felt crime was a result of wickedness. However, once guilt had been proven then they thought a welfare function was required so as to provide treatment in line with the needs of the child. For this reason they thought that magistrates who would deal with such cases should have particular qualifications. The Children and Young Persons Act 1932, which was consolidated by the Children and Young Persons Act 1933, introduced some of these ideas. They included a system of qualifications for the magistrates who were to be concerned with the welfare of the child in what was a criminal court. The 1933 Act also replaced reformatory and industrial schools with approved schools. These institutions were aimed at a younger age group than in the case of borstals, and they were to provide education and training. Many of the approved schools were managed by religious and voluntary groups. They became part of the community homes, which were incorporated into the care system, after the Children and Young Persons Act 1969. To go back slightly in history, the Criminal Justice Act 1948 was the next major piece of legislation. This both increased (introducing detention centres as a form of short-term punishment and attendance centres) and decreased (abolishing corporal punishment and limiting the use of imprisonment) the dispositions available for youngsters.

The 1960s

The Ingleby Committee Report (1960), on children and young persons, pointed to the problem of the juvenile court having to exercise both a criminal and a welfare function. Their answer was to remove criminal considerations in relation to those under 13, with the age limit to be eventually raised to cover those under 15. The older age groups would be subject to a criminal procedure with welfare considerations being minimised. The report of a group chaired by Lord Longford, *Crime – A Challenge to Us All* (Labour Party (1964)) had even more radical ideas. They wanted the juvenile courts to be abolished as unsuited to the needs of children who might need care. Such need for care was to be dispensed by a family service and, if necessary, a family court, as part of a decriminalisation of children. The Labour Party White Paper, *The Child, the Family and the Young Offender* (Home Office (1995a)), adopted many of the Longford proposals. Both documents produced controversy. It was suggested, for example, that by removing the criminal jurisdiction, the rights and safeguards that this entails would be lost. Also that by not having to face such a forum respect for the law amongst children would be diminished. The Labour government, which was in a weak parliamentary position, tried to produce a compromise that would retain the juvenile courts whilst adopting the care provisions. Their ideas were stated in *Children in Trouble*, a 1968 White Paper (Home Office (1968a)), and this document was used as the basis of the Children and Young Persons Act 1969.

The Children and Young Persons Act 1969 and the reaction to it

The intention of the 1969 Act was that care considerations were to be the primary response to juvenile delinquency. Section 1 provided for a general system of care for both offenders and non-offenders. A feature of this was that an offence alone would not be sufficient reason for intervention; there would also have to be a need for care and control. Section 4 provided for a system of a gradual increase of the age at which criminal proceedings could be used to 14. Section 5 provided a series of restrictions, including consultation with the local authorities, which had to be satisfied before criminal action could be taken in relation to 14–17 year olds. Section 7 provided for a system whereby the use of borstals, detention centres and attendance centres could be reduced. When the Conservatives came to power in 1970, they prevented the legislation from having much impact by their non-implementation of key sections of the Act. For example, ss4, 5 and 7 were never implemented. The result was that criminal proceedings for those of ten and over were still possible. Criminal proceedings were used instead of the care system under s1. The care system was to have been the basis of the new system. Some of the reforms of the 1969 Act were introduced. These included community homes (which were to be involved in the care system to provide residential care) and supervision orders. These measures were not that different to earlier measures. For example, the new care orders were very similar to the earlier fit person orders. Any differences that there were had to contend with the non-implementation of the major sections of the 1969 Act. One new feature was the introduction of intermediate treatment as part of the supervision system. This was a community-based system of activities, involving the development of skills and interests as part of a participation in constructive activities. Given the philosophy of the 1969 Act, an increase in the use of treatment disposals and a decrease in the use of custody would have been expected. This did not occur, both the proportionate use of custody and absolute numbers for those sent to custody increased. Where changes did occur that were in line with the philosophy of the 1969 Act, as in the increased use of cautioning, these changes were a continuation of an earlier trend. What the 1969 Act had intended never took place. It was not so much that the policy failed rather that it never really occurred. Despite this, the Act was to be criticised in the 1970s. The criticisms were that the Act had weakened the position of magistrates and also that it had produced a situation in which youngsters could commit crime with impunity. This was because a child who was given a care order could be sent home. Such complaints ignored the reality. Some children were sent home but the 'powerless' magistrates were in fact avoiding care orders and making greater use of custody. The 1969 Act was considered to be problematic and changes were envisaged. The welfare model was under attack and the importance of safeguards within courts which were to be given teeth (increased powers) were the ideas that were in the ascendancy. For example, the Labour Party White Paper of 1976 (Home Office (1976)) looked at the 1969 Act and, whilst it reaffirmed its commitment to the Act, proposed further emasculation of it. Ideas were moving towards notions of there being real criminals who needed to be dealt with as such. At the same time, the increased use of custodial dispositions was regarded as being unacceptable. Change was to come with the Criminal Justice Act 1982.

Criminal Justice Act 1982

The Conservative Party White Paper *Young Offenders* (Home Office (1980b)) stated that there was a need for more diversion from custody. This could be by means of a greater use of existing methods such as cautions and the provision of further non-custodial dispositions. Also suggested in the White Paper was the replacement of borstals by youth custody and the removal of imprisonment as a sentence for those under 21. The courts were also to be given more teeth. The 1982 Act duly replaced borstal with youth custody and imprisonment was removed as a sentencing option for those under 21. Shorter periods of detention-centre custody were made possible – as short as 21 days rather than three months. This was in the hope that shorter sentences would be passed. Beefed-up care orders, by for example providing for change and control conditions (so as to remove parental influence for a time), were introduced. Provisions were also made for restrictions on activities to be part of supervision orders and parents were to be generally responsible for their offspring's fines. Also widened was the availability of community service. The aim of the legislation was less intervention for the majority and tougher measures in relation to a minority. Safeguards were introduced, which reflected the influence of justice model considerations and its relative eclipse of the welfare model. For example, where care orders were to be used the offence had to be both a serious one and the juvenile had to be in need of care and control which would otherwise not be available. Equally, before custody could be used the offender had to be unable or unwilling to respond to non-custodial penalties or custody was to be needed for the protection of the public or because of the seriousness of the offence. Where such criteria or reasons for custody were to be used they had to be recorded as such. Normally a social inquiry report would be required and the opportunity of obtaining legal representation was to be provided before a custodial sentence could be passed.

7.5 The youth justice framework 1982–2004

The Crime and Disorder Act 1998 finally replaced the system established by the Criminal Justice Act 1982. The system established by the 1982 Act had, however, been amended on several occasions in the interim. The legislative changes include those of the Criminal Justice Acts 1988–1991 (the main impact of the 1991 Act was to simplify and in some senses restrict the rules on custodial detention for youngsters – also the juvenile court was renamed the youth court), the Children Act 1989 (which removed the system of criminal care proceedings but left the family court jurisdiction in place), the Criminal Justice and Public Order Act 1994 and the Crime (Sentences) Act 1997.

The Crime and Disorder Act 1998 was itself supplemented by the Youth Justice and Criminal Evidence Act 1999, the Powers of Criminal Courts (Sentencing) Act 2000 and the Criminal Justice and Court Services Act 2000. Whilst the Criminal Justice and Court

Services Act 2000 is examined in more detail in the next chapter, some of its main features are noted here. The Act aimed to reform the probation service, to provide further community dispositions (an exclusion order and a drug abstinence order), to toughen up the enforcement of community dispositions, to make further use of electronic tagging, to further control truancy and to increase the powers to carry out drug tests within the criminal justice system. The latter should allow the provision of treatment for those who have a drug problem. Finally, some of the orders were renamed. Probation orders became community rehabilitation orders, community service orders became community punishment orders and combination orders became community punishment and rehabilitation orders. The Powers of Criminal Courts (Sentencing) Act 2000 was a consolidation measure in relation to the numerous pieces of sentencing legislation that were operative.

The Criminal Justice Act 1988

The 1988 Act introduced changes that were a result of the experiences of the 1982 Act. It became clear that considerably fewer ten to under 21 year olds were being sentenced than was the case in 1982. The figure for indictable offences in 1982 was 216,500 and for 1987 154,100. All other things being equal this was a considerable diversionary effect on the part of the 1982 Act. The proportion, though not the total amount, of sentences which result in immediate custody increased from 14 per cent (29,800) in 1982 to 16 per cent (25,300) in 1987. This would appear to be a failing of the 1982 Act. This figure hides a considerable change in the proportion of such sentences which were to detention centres rather than to borstal or youth custody. This was 61 per cent in 1982 and only 29 per cent in 1987. It seems that magistrates had a more positive viewpoint of youth custody centres than they did of detention centres and this was reflected in their sentencing patterns. The result was that detention centres were half empty whilst youth custody centres were bursting at the seams. The Criminal Justice Act 1988 provided for the amalgamation of detention centres and youth custody centres, to produce a new system of young offender institutions. The intention was that the particular features of detention centres and youth custody centres would be retained. Such differences as there were should not be over-emphasised, as from 1982 it had been difficult to distinguish the regime at a detention centre from that of a youth custody centre.

Criminal Justice and Public Order Act 1994

The 1990s saw a growth in the desire to protect the public from the activities of delinquents. One manifestation of this was the introduction of secure training orders by the Criminal Justice and Public Order Act 1994. This was designed as a means to control 12–14-year-old males who had a history of at least three imprisonable offences and a history of failure on non-custodial dispositions. It provided a half-and-half mix of detention and supervision and the order could be from six months to two years in length. The secure training order was replaced by the detention and training order in June 2000. The 1994 Act also doubled the maximum sentence for 15–17-year-olds in a young offender institution, to two years, and parents could be bound over for the failings of their children on community orders.

Crime (Sentences) Act 1997

Further change came with the Crime (Sentences) Act 1997 which allowed electronic tags to be available for use in relation to the 10–15 age category. More generally, the 1997 Act increased the community sentencing options that were available in relation to youngsters and also had impact upon the use of custody for youngsters.

The Crime and Disorder Act 1998

Major changes to the administration of youth justice and further new powers for the courts were provided for in this legislation. On the administrative side the development of crime and disorder strategies, the local provision of youth justice services, youth offending teams, youth justice plans and a Youth Justice Board are all provided for. Section 37 states that the principal aim of the youth justice system is to prevent children offending.

New systems of control in the 1998 Act

A further system of control was introduced by the provision of anti-social behaviour orders which apply to those aged ten and over. This can lead to certain behaviour being prohibited and if the order is breached convictions can follow. A detention and training order becomes possible for a child or young person where prison would have been possible for an adult. It can even be used for those under 12 in certain circumstances. The length of the order can be the equivalent of what would have been possible for an adult. Half of it will be in secure accommodation with the rest being a system of supervision. Action plan orders for a child or young person are also introduced. They provide a new (additional to possibilities such as probation and community service orders) form of order. It allows for the imposition of prescribed requirements and supervision. Child safety orders apply to those under ten and they are intended to control offending behaviour and allow for the supervision and imposition of conditions upon children. Child curfew and truancy provisions and reparation orders for a child or young person are also part of the new scheme of things.

Reprimands and warnings

The Crime and Disorder Act 1998 also provided for changes in relation to the cautioning system. In June 2000 cautioning for a child or young person was replaced by a system of reprimands and warnings. As an alternative to prosecution for those who had not previously been convicted or warned the police may give a reprimand. If a reprimand had been given then a warning may be appropriate in relation to a later offence. A warning may be appropriate without a prior reprimand. After that prosecution would be used: except that if two years had passed since a warning then another warning is possible on one occasion. The youth offending team is informed of warnings; it would normally prescribe a rehabilitation programme. Courts treat reprimands and warnings as previous convictions for two years. Conditional discharges will not be a possibility for the court.

Parenting orders

The Crime and Disorder Act 1998 made provision for parenting orders. They are possible where a child or young person has offended, or is subject to such as a child safety order or where poor school attendance has led to convictions. Parenting orders allow for conditions to be imposed on the parent for up to 12 months. The aim of the order is to assist in preventing a repetition of behaviour, such as offending behaviour, by the child. Failure to adhere to the order can lead to the parent being convicted of an offence and this can lead to a fine.

Other changes in the 1998 Act include the removal of the presumption that children, the ten to under 14 age group, cannot commit an offence (doli incapax) and the right to silence has been removed for those under 14 as well.

Youth Justice and Criminal Evidence Act 1999

This Act provides a youth court or other magistrates' court with a new disposition, a referral to youth offender panels for many first time offenders who are under 18. It is not available where custody, or an absolute discharge, is appropriate. The Act provides for both compulsory referral conditions and discretionary referral conditions. Referral will be compulsory if the offender pleaded guilty and has no previous convictions or a bind over. A conditional discharge is treated as being a conviction. The discretionary conditions are different only in that they also allow referral where the offender made both guilty and not-guilty pleas to the offences in issue. The order will require the offender to attend meetings of a youth offender panel, which will seek to establish a youth offender contract, which will provide a programme of behaviour for the offender. The aim (or principal aim) of this will be the prevention of re-offending by the offender.

7.6 The Youth Justice Board

The Board, a product of the Crime and Disorder Act 1998, was established in October 1998. Its main work will focus on early intervention with young offenders, speeding up youth justice and better programmes for stopping offending. One of its first tasks was to help create the new infrastructure for youth justice by April 2000. This included setting up local youth offending teams, final warning schemes and the new reparation and action plan orders and the programmes to underpin them. The early work of the Board was concerned with the following:

1. stimulating more and better intervention programmes in areas like parenting, reparation and mentoring;
2. developing a national training and development programme for youth offending team managers;
3. encouraging more bail supervision and support schemes to underpin the new statutory duty on local authorities;
4. speeding up youth justice, especially reducing the time from arrest to sentence for persistent young offenders;
5. identifying information needs and promoting better information systems at local level; and
6. advising the government on the regimes, standards and placement arrangements needed

in secure juvenile facilities to implement the new detention and training order, together with a new contracting system for places for remanded and sentenced offenders.

The Board's objectives for the youth justice system

In 1998 the Youth Justice Board produced a document called *Preventing Offending by Young Persons* (Report of the Youth Justice Board (1998)), in which the following objectives for the youth justice system were suggested:

1. the swift administration of justice so that every young person accused of breaking the law has the matter resolved without delay;
2. confronting young offenders with the consequences of their offending, for themselves and their family, victims and the community;
3. punishment, proportionate to the seriousness and persistency of the offending behaviour;
4. encouraging reparation by young offenders for victims;
5. reinforcing parental responsibility; and
6. helping young offenders to tackle problems associated with their offending and to develop a sense of personal responsibility.

7.7 Sentences and orders

A checklist

The material here is intended for quick reference. A more detailed account of some of the provisions that relate solely to those under 21 appears in the next part of this chapter. The non-custodial measures which also apply to those over 21 are considered in Chapter 8.

Sentences and orders that only apply to age ranges under 21
1. Young offender institution
   For those aged 18–20. A minimum of 21 days with the adult maximum being applicable.

2. Detention and training order
   For those aged 12–17. It was introduced in June 2000.

3. Sections 90–92 of the Powers of Criminal Courts (Sentencing) Act 2000
   For those under 18 in relation to grave offences.

4. Attendance centre orders
   For those under 21.

5. Supervision orders.
   For those aged 10–17.

6. Action plan orders
   For those under 18.

7. Referral to a youth offender panel
   For those under 18.

8. Reparation orders
   For those under 18.

9. Parenting orders
   For those under 18.

10. Parental binding over and parental liability for financial orders.

11. Referral orders.

Sentences and orders that also apply to those over 21

1. Absolute or conditional discharge
   They can be used for any age group.

2. Fines
   They can be used for any age group. In the magistrates' court for those aged 10–13 fines can be up to £250. For those aged 14–17 fines can be up to £1,000. In the Crown Court there is no upper limit. Normally for those under 16 the parent will be ordered to make the payment. This is also possible for those aged 16–17.

3. Compensation orders
   They can be used for any age group. Normally for those under 16 the parent will be ordered to make the payment. This is also possible for those aged 16–17.

4. Restitution and forfeiture orders
   They can be used for any age group.

5. Confiscation orders
   They can be used for any age group.

6. Curfew orders
   These apply once a person is 16.

7. Community rehabilitation orders
   These apply once a person is 16.

8. Community punishment orders
   These apply once a person is 16.

9. Community punishment and rehabilitation orders
   These apply once a person is 16.

10. Drug treatment and testing order
    These apply once a person is 16.

This checklist is now followed by some detail on specific institutions and orders.

Reprimands and warnings

These provide the notion of a caution for those under 18. The person must admit the offence and not have been found guilty of an offence in the past. They are in stages, with the reprimand coming first and then the final warning – unless the behaviour merits an immediate final warning. Final warnings are a variant on Caution Plus: the person is referred to a youth offending team, he will get help in reducing offending behaviour and reparation can be arranged. This can include conferences at which parents, victims and other adults could be present – thus an example of the use of restorative justice ideas. Newburn (2002:562) suggests that the evidence to date indicates that these innovations may have caused net widening, that they are not being reported as more participative by offenders, that questions have been raised about some of the content of the programmes and that many young offenders and youth offending team workers saw the warning system as arbitrary, unfair and disproportionate.

Guidance to the use of final warnings

A report by the Home Office/Youth Justice Board (2002) provided guidance for the police and youth offending teams as to the use of final warnings:

'How the system is to operate

Has the young person previously been reprimanded or finally warned?

If the young person has previously been convicted of an offence, he or she cannot be reprimanded or finally warned and should be charged.

The Crown Prosecution Service will then consider, in the light of the facts of the case and in line with the Code for Crown Prosecutors, whether to proceed with the prosecution.

If the young person has been finally warned for one offence more than two years previously or reprimanded, he or she cannot be reprimanded but may be warned or charged.

If the young person has previously been finally warned for two offences or warned at all in the past two years, he or she cannot be reprimanded or warned and should be charged.

The Crown Prosecution Service will then consider whether to proceed with the prosecution.

How serious is the offence?

The ACPO Gravity Factor System

The decision whether to reprimand, finally warn or charge will depend on the seriousness of the offence. To help the police assess the seriousness – or gravity – of offences, the Association of Chief Police Officers (ACPO) has devised a Gravity Factor System, under which all offences can be given a gravity score of between "1" for the most minor offences and "4" for the most serious.

Other factors – either aggravating (eg the offence was motivated by the victim's racial or ethnic origin) or mitigating (eg the offender was influenced by others more criminally sophisticated) – may raise or lower the score for a particular offence.

The Gravity Factors will help in assessing whether a young person should be charged for an offence. They reflect the public interest principles in the Code for Crown Prosecutors.

The different gravity scores, and the police action that should normally be taken in response to them are:

With a gravity score of 1 the appropriate police action is: always the minimum response applicable to the individual offender, ie reprimand, warning or charge.

With a gravity score of 2 the appropriate police action is: normally reprimand for a first offence. If offender does not qualify for a reprimand but qualifies for a warning then give warning. If offender does not qualify for a warning then charge.

With a gravity score of 3 the appropriate police action is: normally warn for a first offence. If offender does not qualify for a warning then charge. Only in exceptional circumstances should a reprimand be given. Decision maker needs to justify reprimand.

With a gravity score of 4 the appropriate police action is: always charge

Further detail, of the scoring system, is provided in Annex D of the Report.

Public interest considerations

Is it in the public interest for the young person not to be prosecuted?

A reprimand or final warning may be given only if the police are satisfied that it would not be in the public interest to prosecute.

Where the option to prosecute has not been ruled out and where there are risk factors present, the police should consider bailing the young person for a Youth Offending Team assessment to inform the police's decision.

The use of bail enables full consideration of the public interest test. The Youth Offending Team can explore whether all the aggravating and mitigating factors have been identified and correctly applied to the gravity score. It also enables information from victims to be taken into account and the final warnings and interventions to be tailored to the offender and the offence.'

Referral orders

The Youth Justice and Criminal Evidence Act 1999 introduced a new order (a referral order) which will be used for virtually all 10–17-year-olds who are pleading guilty and who are convicted for the first time by the courts. It is thus a major new feature of the youth justice system. Whilst it is may be the first conviction for these people they may previously have received a caution, reprimand or a final warning. The latter may well have involved previous intervention. The disposal involves referring the young offender to a youth offender panel. It is an example of the use of the principles of restorative justice and Hancock (2000) is useful in relation to the thinking behind referral orders. The orders have been available nationally since April 2002, having been used on an experimental basis in some areas from the summer of 2000. The order is not going to be available where custody or an absolute discharge are appropriate. Nor will it be usable in conjunction with most other dispositions. One thing a court can do is make provision for compensation and indeed the court must turn its mind to issue of compensation when dealing with offenders. However, this part of the system has not been fully thought out. It seems that this obviously restorative action cannot be taken into account by the panels. The alternative is for the panels to deal with monetary compensation, but the youth offending team probably could not manage the demands of such a system. Compliance with financial orders is notoriously problematic and indeed the whole idea of getting youngsters to deliver financial payback is undermined by their very likely lack of income and resources.

Referral orders, as made by the courts, should include the name and address of the offender, the details of the offence, the length of the order and the name of the youth offending team responsible for the referral order (this will be the youth offending team for the area in which the young offender is living, or is expected to live in the future), details of those parent(s)/guardian(s)/local authority representative(s) required to attend panel meetings and details of any ancillary orders. A copy of the order must be given to the offender, and sent on the same day to anyone required by the court to attend panel meetings, but not in court when the order was made. A copy of the referral order must also be sent on the same day to the youth offending team named in the order. It is important that the panel has the full facts of the offence. The Crown Prosecution Service is responsible for supplying youth offending teams with a pre-sentence report package whenever a referral order is made.

Referral orders are being used mainly for cases that previously would have received fines or conditional discharges. The Act provides for both compulsory referral conditions and discretionary referral conditions. Referral will be compulsory if the offender pleaded guilty and has no previous convictions or a bind over. A conditional discharge is treated as being a conviction. The discretionary conditions are different only in that they also allow referral where the offender made both guilty and not guilty pleas to the offences in issue. The order will require the offender to attend meetings of a youth offender panel, which will seek to establish a youth offender contract, which will provide for both reparation and activities that are designed to tackle issues in the lives of the offenders that have been linked to their offending behaviour. One advantage of successful completion of the order is that for most purposes the youngster would not have a criminal record. The effect of the order is to be explained to the offender, in ordinary language. This will also apply as to the consequences if no youth offender contract takes effect between the offender and the panel or if there is a breach of the contract. The order will last between three and 12 months. During the order there will be monitoring which can lead to referral back to the court for re-sentencing. In practice, 12-month orders are unlikely to be used as there will be a desire to leave open the option of adding additional months to the order in cases of breach.

The following are amongst the matters that may be detailed in the contract: victim reparation, mediation, the offender to carry out unpaid work or service in or for the community, the offender to be at home at specified times, requirements for attendance at educational establishments or at a place of work, the offender to participate in specified activities (such as those designed to address offending behaviour, those offering education or training or those assisting with the rehabilitation of persons dependent on, or having a propensity to misuse, alcohol or drugs), the offender to present himself to specified persons at times and places specified in or determined under the programme and the offender to stay away from specified places or persons (or both). The above is not exhaustive, although it must be noted that the following are not possible: electronic monitoring or for the offender to have imposed on him any physical restriction on his movements. It has to be said that quite a few of the provisions would have the effect of being physical restriction on movement.

Youth offending teams both provide the infrastructure for the orders and operate as facilitators and deliverers of the orders. This is an example of multi-agency working and is part of the government's aspiration to joined-up criminal justice. In reality, whilst a number of agencies such as the police and health and education workers are involved, most of those involved are from the probation and social services. Youth offending teams are responsible for: recruiting, training and supporting community panel members; assessing offenders prior to initial panel meetings; engaging with victims; convening youth offender panels; facilitating panel meetings; supervising compliance with contracts; and arranging the referral back of offenders to court where necessary. Essentially, therefore, youth offending teams have four main tasks in the youth offender panel process: assessing offenders and producing reports for youth offender panels; engaging with victims, offering them the opportunity to participate, depending on informed consent and risk assessment; attending and advising youth offender panels; and adopting the case supervisor role in terms of monitoring the compliance of offenders with contracts.

With restorative justice, instead of punishing the offender, the aim is for the person to make good, to engage in reparation, either to the community as a whole or to the victim of the crime. Where there is a requirement of, for example, work for the community this is to operate as a means of making good rather than as punishment. Rather than the crime belonging to the state it belongs to the community and they respond because of the injury to it. Restorative justice gives a role to the victim and seeks to involve the offender. The offender may be confronted with the offence, perhaps by the victim. Restorative justice takes in those affected by the offence and aims to bring people together and to remove the distance and the damage caused by the offence. There are numerous possibilities as to systems of restorative justice and referral orders are geared more to the needs of offenders rather than victims. This is particularly the case where, as reports have noted, the participation of victims is at a low level. The orders aim to be inclusive, involving the community, victims, the offender and his family. They give a role to the offender and expect him to take responsibility for his behaviour.

The offender will be required to attend a community meeting where they will make a contract whereby they will agree to do certain things. A suitable person can attend with the offender – for example, a parent. This may be a requirement in relation to the younger offenders. A member of the youth offending team (a professional person such as a social workers or a policeman) will operate as a facilitator in order to provide professional expertise and guidance. The community are also involved as community panel members. Two or three of them will be present and they will run the panel, with one of them as chairman. The community panel members are meant to be a cross section of the community. There are certain people who are unable to be panel members, including certain categories of past offenders. The community panel members receive training of approximately 40 hours. They tend to be older rather than younger, female rather than male and the middle class are also over-represented. Ethnic minorities are few and far between.

The victims are also given the opportunity to be present so that the victim and the offender can meet. In my experience of being a community panel member the victim rarely attends personally and may not even have an indirect input as to their feelings and desires. The offender can still volunteer to write a letter of apology, although care has to be taken in order to ensure that these letters are suitable in terms of not causing further hurt to the victim.

Several meetings are held. The first meeting is an initial meeting which lasts 50–60 minutes. An agreement is drawn up between the panel and the offender. In the agreement it must be stated that something is given back to the victim directly (possibilities include money, work to be carried out or a letter of apology). Since victims often do not want to be part of the process, usually the offender will end up doing something that is needed in the community such as repair and maintenance work. Health and safety issues have to be looked into with regard to such work. What is decided upon has to be workable and there are controls – for example, where there is an offence of violence a requirement to work with children is very unlikely. The delivery of the orders can be expensive as placement arrangements have to be made and supervision provided. Travel arrangements also have to be made and paid for. Given the low skill levels of the offenders they do not in any real sense give to the community as it will cost more to provide the placement than the work that is done is actually worth. Indeed, the more these people do for the community the more it costs. The justification seems to be in terms of it being good for them to have given to the community. The offender will also hopefully benefit by becoming aware that there is a victim in these processes, and by taking responsibility for their actions. Review meetings are also held to see how things are going. At the end there will be a final meeting to acknowledge completion of the contract. At a number of stages problems may have arisen and, eventually, after attempting to solve the problems, breach proceedings would be implemented and the person would go back to court.

Newburn et al (2002) provides an account of the operation of referral orders when they were used on a pilot basis prior to national implementation in 2002 which offers a valuable insight into their operation. Referral orders were piloted in 11 areas: Blackburn, Cardiff, Nottingham (city), Nottinghamshire (county), Oxfordshire, Swindon, Suffolk, Wiltshire, Hammersmith and Fulham, Kensington and Chelsea and Westminster. The principal findings are noted below.

Community panel members
The need to attract a representative group of community panel members took second place in most areas to the need to recruit enough panel members to begin operations within the deadlines that were to operate. Two-thirds of community panel members from the first recruitment round were women and there were relatively few community panel members from manual backgrounds or the unemployed. Subsequent recruitment rounds have targeted particular sections of the local community deemed to be under-represented previously.

Referral orders and the courts
Magistrates, justices' clerks and youth offending team staff endorsed the restorative justice approach that was assumed to characterise referral orders. During the course of the pilots, magistrates became more concerned about the loss of discretion brought about by referral orders. Magistrates displayed relatively high levels of dissatisfaction with the information they were provided with regarding the implementation of referral orders and the workings of the panels, particularly in relation to what happened to the young person once they had left court.

Youth offender panels
Less than one-third of panels took place within the national standard of 15 working days

following the making of the referral order, though slightly over half occurred within 20 working days. Most panel meetings involved one offender and three panel members. In 68 per cent of cases the young person attended with only one other person (usually their mother) and in 15 per cent the young person attended alone. Observation suggests that many young people played an active role in panel meetings. Young people were more likely to offer an apology in panel meetings where a victim was present.

The experience of community panel members

Sixty-two per cent of community panel members said that they had a 'very good' and a further 32 per cent a 'reasonably good' working relationship with the youth offending team panel members. Community panel members appear to be becoming more confident and more assertive of their central role and position in steering panels, particularly in relation to the role of the youth offending team panel member. Seventy per cent of community panel members who had experienced at least one panel at which a victim had been present said that a victim's presence at a panel was either 'very beneficial' or 'beneficial'. Eighty-five per cent of all community panel members agreed (40 per cent) or strongly agreed (45 per cent) with the statement that 'more should be done to encourage victims to attend' panel meetings.

Young offenders and their parents

The young people were generally happy with their experience of attending an initial panel meeting. The majority felt the purpose of the meeting was fully explained to them (72 per cent) and that they understood what was going on at that meeting (91 per cent). Eighty-four per cent felt they were treated with respect and 86 per cent that the panel members treated them fairly. Three-quarters responded that they did not feel pushed into anything they disagreed with. Over two-thirds of young people said they had a clearer idea of how people had been affected by their offence after attending the panel meeting. Of those young people who attended panels at which a victim was present, three-quarters said it was right that they should have been there. However, of those who attended panels with no victim, a majority said they would not have wanted the victim there. Three-quarters of young people agreed that their contract was useful (including 12 per cent who 'strongly agreed') and an even larger number (78 per cent) agreed that it had helped keep them out of trouble (including 28 per cent who 'strongly agreed'). Compared with their experience of the youth court, parents understood the referral order process better, felt it easier to participate in the process and perceived it to be fairer. Of the parents interviewed 97 per cent agreed that the initial panel had treated them with respect and the same number felt that the panel members were fair. Fifty-five per cent of parents said that they thought victims should always be invited to panel meetings. Three-quarters of parents felt that the panel took account of what they said in deciding what should be done. Seventy-two per cent agreed that the contract elements were 'useful'. However, somewhat ambiguously, 45 per cent believed that the contract had not made any difference to the young person's behaviour.

The involvement of victims

The involvement of victims and in particular their attendance at panel meetings across the pilot areas has been both lower than was originally anticipated and significantly lower than comparative experiences from restorative justice initiatives around the world. A victim attended a panel in only 13 per cent of cases where at least an initial panel was held. In 120 cases victims made some other form of input into the panels, such as a statement or consent to personal reparation. In only 28 per cent of appropriate cases was there any form of victim involvement. The higher number of victims attending panels in some pilot areas was in large part due to the higher priority accorded to victim contact. Seventy-eight per cent of victims who decided to attend a panels said that the opportunity to express their feelings and speak directly to the offender had been very important in their decision. One area of dissatisfaction about the panel process expressed by a significant number of victims concerned the limits to their involvement and participation in the whole panel meeting. Of particular concern is that 70 per cent of victims who did not stay for the entire panel meeting did not receive any information about the content of the eventual contract. I would add to this that the system that was introduced nationally in 2002 was designed so that victims would leave after the 'pay back' issue was resolved which is the half-way stage. Half of the victims interviewed who had not attended a panel meeting had not been offered the opportunity to do so. Almost half of these indicated that they would have attended if they had known about it or had been offered the chance.

Contracts

The most common compulsory element in all contracts was some form of reparative activity (40 per cent). This was followed by offending behaviour work (9 per cent), attending supervision/assessment sessions with a youth offending team officer (6 per cent), exploring employment and career options (6 per cent), and education (5 per cent) and victims awareness work (5 per cent). Education and reparation also formed the most common voluntary elements in contracts. The most common form of reparation was community reparation (42 per cent), followed by written apology (38 per cent), indirect reparation (10 per cent), direct reparation to victim or the payment of compensation (7 per cent) and then various forms of unspecified activity. The most common youth offending team activities were meetings with a youth offending team officer (20 per cent), attending offending behaviour sessions (17 per cent), anger management sessions (13 per cent), drugs/alcohol awareness sessions (9 per cent), victim awareness sessions (8 per cent) and attending courses on the consequences of violent behaviour (3 per cent). Young people completed the contract successfully in three-quarters (74 per cent) of cases where a panel had met. Higher completion rates were associated with shorter orders, fewer elements in the contract and the type of offence committed. In just under a quarter (23 per cent) of those closed cases where there had been an initial panel meeting, the young person was convicted of a further offence. In three-quarters of such cases, the order was revoked and the offender was resentenced.

The costs of referral orders

Average panel costs varied between £130 and £350 for initial panels and £50 to £130 for review or final panels. The average cost of contracts varied from under £100 to over £400 across the pilot areas, with an overall average of £110. The mean cost per referral order was

£630 outside London. Including London the average cost was £690 per order. Higher costs were associated with longer referral orders, victim involvement in the process and type of offence (burglary for example).

Some problems with referral orders

One problem that may arise is that these orders are going to be used for people who have already had a very similar experience as part of a final warning – an experience that failed to the extent that they have reoffended. Youngsters may think that referral orders are a soft option and engage in referral order copping – that is pleading guilty in order to dispose of the matter. The danger of such an approach is that they have advanced to a higher stage of the system of interventions in relation to delinquency. Throughout the system there needs to be a desire for due process and accountability and systems may not be that developed at the moment. Another problem is that as a response it may be too serious or too light at the extremes. And some offences appear to be too serious for this type of intervention and others too trivial. There are also insufficient resources to deliver the orders adequately. A further feature of the system has been delay; this is fatal because a response to the offending behaviour of youngsters needs to be very quick or otherwise it is unlikely to have much of an effect. Other problems include meetings that should take place do not always do so. This is mainly because offenders fail to turn up and this is at times when taxis have been provided for them. Reports that are written can be incomplete, or out of date or not in a standard format. There are also indications that experiences are not the same across the country which point to a lack of consistency in approach both in and between areas. This arises in a number of different ways. For example, whilst the panels are trained they have not all received the same training. The style of the meetings used may also be different and people's attitudes will also influence the meeting.

Scottish youth hearings

These have a longer history than referral orders and they provide an indication as to how referral orders may develop. The Scottish system seems to involve higher levels of training than is the case with referral orders. They also seem to have recruited good quality panel members and eventually they got over the initial problem of these not being representative. They have to give reasons in writing for what is decided upon and offenders are able to have a representative, including a legal one.

Legislative provisions

The legislative provisions on referral orders are now provided by the Powers of Criminal Courts (Sentencing) Act 2000.

> **'16 Duty and power to refer certain young offenders to youth offender panels**
>
> (1) This section applies where a youth court or other magistrates' court is dealing with a person aged under 18 for an offence and –
>
> (a) neither the offence nor any connected offence is one for which the sentence is fixed by law;
>
> (b) the court is not, in respect of the offence or any connected offence, proposing to impose a custodial sentence on the offender or make a hospital order (within the meaning of the Mental Health Act 1983) in his case; and

(c) the court is not proposing to discharge him absolutely in respect of the offence.

(2) If –

(a) the compulsory referral conditions are satisfied in accordance with section 17 below, and

(b) referral is available to the court,

the court shall sentence the offender for the offence by ordering him to be referred to a youth offender panel.

(3) If –

(a) the discretionary referral conditions are satisfied in accordance with section 17 below, and

(b) referral is available to the court,

the court may sentence the offender for the offence by ordering him to be referred to a youth offender panel.

(4) For the purposes of this Part an offence is connected with another if the offender falls to be dealt with for it at the same time as he is dealt with for the other offence (whether or not he is convicted of the offences at the same time or by or before the same court).

(5) For the purposes of this section referral is available to a court if –

(a) the court has been notified by the Secretary of State that arrangements for the implementation of referral orders are available in the area in which it appears to the court that the offender resides or will reside; and

(b) the notice has not been withdrawn.

(6) An order under subsection (2) or (3) above is in this Act referred to as a "referral order".

(7) No referral order may be made in respect of any offence committed before the commencement of section 1 of the Youth Justice and Criminal Evidence Act 1999.

17 The referral conditions

(1) For the purposes of section 16(2) above the compulsory referral conditions are satisfied in relation to an offence if the offender –

(a) pleaded guilty to the offence and to any connected offence;

(b) has never been convicted by or before a court in the United Kingdom of any offence other than the offence and any connected offence; and

(c) has never been bound over in criminal proceedings in England and Wales or Northern Ireland to keep the peace or to be of good behaviour.

(2) For the purposes of section 16(3) above the discretionary referral conditions are satisfied in relation to an offence if –

(a) the offender is being dealt with by the court for the offence and one or more connected offences;

(b) although he pleaded guilty to at least one of the offences mentioned in paragraph (a) above, he also pleaded not guilty to at least one of them;

(c) he has never been convicted by or before a court in the United Kingdom of any offence other than the offences mentioned in paragraph (a) above; and

(d) he has never been bound over in criminal proceedings in England and Wales or Northern Ireland to keep the peace or to be of good behaviour.

(3) The Secretary of State may by regulations make such amendments of this section as he considers appropriate for altering in any way the descriptions of offenders in the case of which the compulsory referral conditions or the discretionary referral conditions fall to be satisfied for the purposes of section 16(2) or (3) above (as the case may be).

(4) Any description of offender having effect for those purposes by virtue of such regulations may be framed by reference to such matters as the Secretary of State considers appropriate, including (in particular) one or more of the following –

(a) the offender's age;

(b) how the offender has pleaded;

(c) the offence (or offences) of which the offender has been convicted;

(d) the offender's previous convictions (if any);

(e) how (if at all) the offender has been previously punished or otherwise dealt with by any court; and

(f) any characteristics or behaviour of, or circumstances relating any person who has at any time been charged in the same proceedings as the offender (whether or not in respect of the same offence).

(5) For the purposes of this section an offender who has been convicted of an offence in respect of which he was conditionally discharged (whether by a court in England and Wales or in Northern Ireland) shall be treated, despite –

(a) section 14(1) above;

(b) article 6(1) of the Criminal Justice (Northern Ireland) Order (corresponding provision for Northern Ireland),

as having been convicted of that offence.

18 Making of referral orders: general

(1) A referral order shall –

(a) specify the youth offending team responsible for implementing the order;

(b) require the offender to attend each of the meetings of a youth offender panel to be established by the team for the offender; and

(c) specify the period for which any youth offender contract taking effect between the offender and the panel under section 23 below is to have effect (which must not be less than three nor more than twelve months).

(2) The youth offending team specified under subsection (1)(a) above shall be the team having the function of implementing referral orders in the area in which it appears to the court that the offender resides or will reside.

(3) On making a referral order the court shall explain to the offender in ordinary language –

(a) the effect of the order; and

(b) the consequences which may follow –

(i) if no youth offender contract takes effect between the offender and the panel under section 23 below; or

(ii) if the offender breaches any of the terms of any such contract.

(4) Subsections (5) to (7) below apply where, in dealing with an offender for two or more connected offences, a court makes a referral order in respect of each, or each of two or more, of the offences.

(5) The orders shall have the effect of referring the offender to a single youth offender panel; and the provision made by them under subsection (1) above shall accordingly be the same in each case, except that the periods specified under subsection (1)(c) may be different.

(6) The court may direct that the period so specified in either or any of the orders is to run concurrently with or be additional to that specified in the other or any of the others; but in exercising its power under this subsection the court must ensure that the total period for which such a contract as is mentioned in subsection (1)(c) above is to have effect does not exceed twelve months.

(7) Each of the orders mentioned in subsection (4) above shall, for the purposes of this Part, be treated as associated with the other or each of the others.

19 Making referral orders: effect on court's other sentencing powers

(1) Subsections (2) to (5) below apply where a court makes a referral order in respect of an offence.

(2) The court may not deal with the offender for the offence in any of the prohibited ways.

(3) The court –

(a) shall, in respect of any connected offence, either sentence the offender by making a referral order or make an order discharging him absolutely, and

(b) may not deal with the offender for any such offence in any of the prohibited ways.

(4) For the purposes of subsections (2) and (3) above the prohibited ways are –

(a) imposing a community sentence on the offender;

(b) ordering him to pay a fine;

(c) making a reparation order in respect of him; and

(d) making an order discharging him conditionally.

(5) The court may not make, in connection with the conviction of the offender for the offence or any connected offence –

(a) an order binding him over to keep the peace or to be of good behaviour;

(b) an order under section 150 below (binding over of parent or guardian); or

(c) a parenting order under section 8 of the Crime and Disorder Act 1998.

(6) Subsections (2), (3) and (5) above do not affect the exercise of any power to deal with the offender conferred by paragraph 5 (offender referred back to court by panel) or paragraph 14 (powers of a court where offender convicted while subject to referral) of Schedule 1 to this Act.

(7) Where section 16(2) above requires a court to make a referral order, the court may not under section 1 above defer passing sentence on him, but section 16(2) and subsection (3)(a) above do not affect any power or duty of a magistrates' court under –

(a) section 8 above (remission to youth court, or another such court, for sentence);

(b) section 10(3) of the Magistrates' Courts Act 1980 (adjournment for inquiries); or

(c) section 35, 38, 43 or 44 of the Mental Health Act 1983 (remand for reports, interim hospital orders and committal to Crown Court for restriction order).

20 Making of referral orders: attendance of parents etc

(1) A court making a referral order may make an order requiring –

(a) the appropriate person, or

(b) in a case where there are two or more appropriate persons, any one or more of them,

to attend the meetings of the youth offender panel.

(2) Where an offender is aged under 16 when a court makes a referral order in his case –

(a) the court shall exercise its power under subsection (1) above so as to require at least one appropriate person to attend meetings of the youth offender panel; and

(b) if the offender falls within subsection (6) below, the person or persons so required to attend those meetings shall be or include a representative of the local authority mentioned in that subsection.

(3) The court shall not under this section make an order requiring a person to attend meetings of the youth offender panel –

(a) if the court is satisfied that it would be unreasonable to do so; or

(b) to an extent which the court is satisfied would be unreasonable.

(4) Except where the offender falls within subsection (6) below, each person who is a parent or guardian of the offender is an "appropriate person" for the purposes of this section.

(5) Where the offender falls within subsection (6) below, each of the following is an "appropriate person" for the purposes of this section –

(a) a representative of the local authority mentioned in that subsection; and

(b) each person who is a parent or guardian of the offender with whom the offender is allowed to live.

(6) An offender falls within this subsection if he is (within the meaning of the Children Act 1989) a child who is looked after by a local authority.

(7) If, at the time when a court makes an order under this section –

(a) a person who is required by the order to attend meetings of a youth offender panel is not present in court, or

(b) a local authority whose representative is so required to attend such meetings is not represented in court,

the court must send him or (as the case may be) the authority a copy of the order forthwith.

Youth offender panels

21 Establishment of panels

(1) Where a referral order has been made in respect of an offender (or two or more associated referral orders have been so made), it is the duty of the youth offending team specified in the order (or orders) –

(a) to establish a youth offender panel for the offender;

(b) to arrange for the first meeting of the panel to be held for the purposes of section 23 below; and

(c) subsequently to arrange for the holding of any further meetings of the panel required by virtue of section 25 below (in addition to those required by virtue of any other provision of this Part).

(2) A youth offender panel shall –

(a) be constituted,

(b) conduct its proceedings, and

(c) discharge its functions under this Part (and in particular those arising under section 23 below),

in accordance with guidance given from time to time by the Secretary of State.

(3) At each of its meetings a panel shall, however, consist of at least –

(a) one member appointed by the youth offending team from among its members; and

(b) two members so appointed who are not members of the team.

(4) The Secretary of State may by regulations make provision requiring persons appointed as members of a youth offender panel to have such qualifications, or satisfy such other criteria, as are specified in the regulations.

(5) Where it appears to the court which made a referral order that, by reason of either a change or a prospective change in the offender's place or intended place of residence, the youth offending team for the time being specified in the order ("the current team") either does not or will not have the function of implementing referral orders in the area in which the offender resides or will reside, the court may amend the order so that it instead specifies the team which has the function of implementing such orders in that area ("the new team").

(6) Where a court so amends a referral order –

(a) subsection (1)(a) above shall apply to the new team in any event;

(b) subsection (1)(b) above shall apply to the new team if no youth offender contract has (or has under paragraph (c) below been treated as having) taken effect under section 23 below between the offender and a youth offender panel established by the current team;

(c) if such a contract has (or has previously under this paragraph been treated as having) so taken effect, it shall (after the amendment) be treated as if it were a contract which had taken effect under section 23 below between the offender and the panel being established for the offender by the new team.

(7) References in this Part to the meetings of a youth offender panel (or any such meeting) are to the following meetings of the panel (or any of them) –

(a) the first meeting held in pursuance of subsection (1)(b) above;

(b) any further meetings held in pursuance of section 25 below;

(c) any progress meeting held under section 26 below; and

(d) the final meeting held under section 27 below.

22 Attendance at panel meetings

(1) The specified team shall, in the case of each meeting of the panel established for the offender, notify –

(a) the offender, and

(b) any person to whom an order under section 20 above applies,

of the time and place at which he is required to attend that meeting.

(2) If the offender fails to attend any part of such a meeting the panel may –

(a) adjourn the meeting to such time and place as it may specify; or

(b) end the meeting and refer the offender back to the appropriate court;

and subsection (1) above shall apply in relation to any such adjourned meeting.

(3) One person aged 18 or over chosen by the offender, with the agreement of the panel, shall be entitled to accompany the offender to any meeting of the panel (and it need not be the same person who accompanies him to every meeting).

(4) The panel may allow to attend any such meeting –

(a) any person who appears to the panel to be a victim of, or otherwise affected by, the offence, or any of the offences, in respect of which the offender was referred to the panel;

(b) any person who appears to the panel to be someone capable of having a good influence on the offender.

(5) Where the panel allows any such person as is mentioned in subsection (4)(a) above ("the victim") to attend a meeting of the panel, the panel may allow the victim to be accompanied to the meeting by one person chosen by the victim with the agreement of the panel.

Youth offender contracts

23 First meeting: agreement of contract with offender

(1) At the first meeting of the youth offender panel established for an offender the panel shall seek to reach agreement with the offender on a programme of behaviour the aim (or principal aim) of which is the prevention of re-offending by the offender.

(2) The terms of the programme may, in particular, include provision for any of the following –

(a) the offender to make financial or other reparation to any person who appears to the panel to be a victim of, or otherwise affected by, the offence, or any of the offences, for which the offender was referred to the panel;

(b) the offender to attend mediation sessions with any such victim or other person;

(c) the offender to carry out unpaid work or service in or for the community;

(d) the offender to be at home at times specified in or determined under the programme;

(e) attendance by the offender at a school or other educational establishment or at a place of work;

(f) the offender to participate in specified activities (such as those designed to address offending behaviour, those offering education or training or those assisting with the rehabilitation of persons dependent on, or having a propensity to misuse, alcohol or drugs);

(g) the offender to present himself to specified persons at times and places specified in or determined under the programme;

(h) the offender to stay away from specified places or persons (or both);

(i) enabling the offender's compliance with the programme to be supervised and recorded.

(3) The programme may not, however, provide –

(a) for the electronic monitoring of the offender's whereabouts; or

(b) for the offender to have imposed on him any physical restriction on his movements.

(4) No term which provides for anything to be done to or with any such victim or other affected person as is mentioned in subsection (2)(a) above may be included in the programme without the consent of that person.

(5) Where a programme is agreed between the offender and the panel, the panel shall cause a written record of the programme to be produced forthwith –

(a) in language capable of being readily understood by, or explained to, the offender; and

(b) for signature by him.

(6) Once the record has been signed –

(a) by the offender, and

(b) by a member of the panel on behalf of the panel,

the terms of the programme, as set out in the record, take effect as the terms of a "youth offender contract" between the offender and the panel; and the panel shall cause a copy of the record to be given or sent to the offender.

24 First meeting: duration of contract

(1) This section applies where a youth offender contract has taken effect under section 23 above between an offender and a youth offender panel.

(2) The day on which the contract so takes effect shall be the first day of the period for which it has effect.

(3) Where the panel was established in pursuance of a single referral order, the length of the period for which the contract has effect shall be that of the period specified under section 18(1)(c) above in the referral order.

(4) Where the panel was established in pursuance of two or more associated referral orders, the length of the period for which the contract has effect shall be that resulting from the court's directions under section 18(6) above.

(5) Subsections (3) and (4) above have effect subject to –

(a) any order under paragraph 11 or 12 of Schedule 1 to this Act extending the length of the period for which the contract has effect; and

(b) subsection (6) below.

(6) If the referral order, or each of the associated referral orders, is revoked (whether under paragraph 5(2) of Schedule 1 to this Act or by virtue of paragraph 14(2) of that Schedule), the period for which the contract has effect expires at the time when the order or orders is or are revoked unless it has already expired.

25 First meeting: failure to agree contract

(1) Where it appears to a youth offender panel to be appropriate to do so, the panel may –

(a) end the first meeting (or any further meeting held in pursuance of paragraph (b) below) without having reached agreement with the offender on a programme of behaviour of the kind mentioned in section 23(1) above; and

(b) resume consideration of the offender's case at a further meeting of the panel.

(2) If, however, it appears to the panel at the first meeting or any such further meeting that there is no prospect of agreement being reached with the offender within a reasonable period after the making of the referral order (or orders) –

(a) subsection (1)(b) above shall not apply; and

(b) instead the panel shall refer the offender back to the appropriate court.

(3) If at a meeting of the panel –

(a) agreement is reached with the offender but he does not sign the record produced in pursuance of section 23(5) above, and

(b) his failure to do so appears to the panel to be unreasonable,

the panel shall end the meeting and refer the offender back to the appropriate court.

26 Progress meetings

(1) At any time –

(a) after a youth offender contract has taken effect under section 23 above, but

(b) before the end of the period for which the contract has effect,

the specified team shall, if so requested by the panel, arrange for the holding of a meeting of the panel under this section ("a progress meeting").

(2) The panel may make a request under subsection (1) above if it appears to the panel to be expedient to review –

(a) the offender's progress in implementing the programme of behaviour contained in the contract; or

(b) any other matter arising in connection with the contract.

(3) The panel shall make such a request if –

(a) the offender has notified the panel that –

(i) he wishes to seek the panel's agreement to a variation in the terms of the contract; or

(ii) he wishes the panel to refer him back to the appropriate court with a view to the referral order (or orders) being revoked on account of a significant change in his circumstances (such as his being taken to live abroad) making compliance with any youth offender contract impractical; or

(b) it appears to the panel that the offender is in breach of any of the terms of the contract.

(4) At a progress meeting the panel shall do such one or more of the following things as it considers appropriate in the circumstances, namely –

(a) review the offender's progress or any such other matter as is mentioned in subsection (2) above;

(b) discuss with the offender any breach of the terms of the contract which it appears to the panel that he has committed;

(c) consider any variation in the terms of the contract sought by the offender or which it appears to the panel to be expedient to make in the light of any such review or discussion;

(d) consider whether to accede to any request by the offender that he be referred back to the appropriate court.

(5) Where the panel has discussed with the offender such a breach as is mentioned in subsection (4)(b) above –

(a) the panel and the offender may agree that the offender is to continue to be required to comply with the contract (either in its original form or with any agreed variation in its terms) without being referred back to the appropriate court; or

(b) the panel may decide to end the meeting and refer the offender back to that court.

(6) Where a variation in the terms of the contract is agreed between the offender and the panel, the panel shall cause a written record of the variation to be produced forthwith –

(a) in language capable of being readily understood by, or explained to, the offender; and

(b) for signature by him.

(7) Any such variation shall take effect once the record has been signed –

(a) by the offender; and

(b) by a member of the panel on behalf of the panel;

and the panel shall cause a copy of the record to be given or sent to the offender.

(8) If at a progress meeting –

(a) any such variation is agreed but the offender does not sign the record produced in pursuance of subsection (6) above, and

(b) his failure to do so appears to the panel to be unreasonable,

the panel may end the meeting and refer the offender back to the appropriate court.

(9) Section 23(2) to (4) above shall apply in connection with what may be provided for by the terms of the contract as varied under this section as they apply in connection with what may be provided for by the terms of a programme of behaviour of the kind mentioned in section 23(1).

(10) Where the panel has discussed with the offender such a request as is mentioned in subsection (4)(d) above, the panel may, if it is satisfied that there is (or is soon to be) such a change in circumstances as is mentioned in subsection (3)(a)(ii) above, decide to end the meeting and refer the offender back to the appropriate court.

27 Final meeting

(1) Where the compliance period in the case of a youth offender contract is due to expire, the specified team shall arrange for the holding, before the end of that period, of a meeting of the panel under this section ("the final meeting").

(2) At the final meeting the panel shall –

(a) review the extent of the offender's compliance to date with the terms of the contract; and

(b) decide, in the light of that review, whether his compliance with those terms has been such as to justify the conclusion that, by the time the compliance period expires, he will have satisfactorily completed the contract;

and the panel shall give the offender written confirmation of its decision.

(3) Where the panel decides that the offender's compliance with the terms of the contract has been such as to justify that conclusion, the panel's decision shall have the effect of discharging the referral order (or orders) as from the end of the compliance period.

(4) Otherwise the panel shall refer the offender back to the appropriate court.

(5) Nothing in section 22(2) above prevents the panel from making the decision mentioned in subsection (3) above in the offender's absence if it appears to the panel to be appropriate to do that instead of exercising either of its powers under section 22(2).

(6) Section 22(2)(a) above does not permit the final meeting to be adjourned (or re-adjourned) to a time falling after the end of the compliance period.

(7) In this section "the compliance period", in relation to a youth offender contract, means the period for which the contract has effect in accordance with section 24 above.

Further court proceedings

28 Offender referred back to court or convicted while subject to referral order

Schedule 1 to this Act, which –

(a) in Part I makes provision for what is to happen when a youth offender panel refers an offender back to the appropriate court, and

(b) in Part II makes provision for what is to happen when an offender is convicted of further offences while for the time being subject to a referral order,

shall have effect.

Supplementary

29 Functions of youth offending teams

(1) The functions of a youth offending team responsible for implementing a referral order include, in particular, arranging for the provision of such administrative staff, accommodation or other facilities as are required by the youth offender panel established in pursuance of the order.

(2) During the period for which a youth offender contract between a youth offender panel and an offender has effect –

(a) the specified team shall make arrangements for supervising the offender's compliance with the terms of the contract; and

(b) the person who is the member of the panel referred to in section 21(3)(a) above shall ensure that records are kept of the offender's compliance (or non-compliance) with those terms.

(3) In implementing referral orders a youth offending team shall have regard to any guidance given from time to time by the Secretary of State.'

Young offender institutions

These institutions are the main means to provide custodial detention for those under 21 and they apply to those who are aged between 18 and 20. The sentence is possible in cases where prison would have been possible if an adult had committed the offence. There is a 21-day minimum period of detention with the adult maximum being applicable. In August 1999, the government announced that it was considering the abolition of the Young Offender Institution as a custodial disposal and the use of imprisonment instead. Section 61 of the Criminal Justice and Court Services Act 2000 made provision for this but it has not been implemented to date.

The system in practice

Feltham Young Offender Institution and Remand Centre. Reports by the Chief Inspector of Prisons provide insight into the day-to-day workings of young offender institutions. A report on Feltham Young Offender Institution and Remand Centre (Home Office (1997c)) provided the following information. Dedicated staff and volunteers had worked hard at providing a caring environment. This was despite the many pressures of providing a regime, for an over-large population of sentenced and convicted young offenders, at a time of inexorably increasing numbers and shortage of resources. This had turned the prison into a gigantic transit camp, in which day-to-day activities are dominated by the process of finding beds for ever-increasing numbers. The prison contained a rapidly growing number of juveniles and a disturbingly increasing number of 15 and 16 year olds. There were insufficient day-time activities for the hundreds of remand prisoners who spent long hours in their cells awaiting trial; and although the regime for convicted prisoners was better, there were still too many locked in their cells.

There was a lack of background information about convicted prisoners and despite the efforts of the staff, the personal officer scheme was almost doomed to failure because of the rapid turnover of prisoners. Prisoners rarely knew who their future probation officer would be, which was not conducive to the throughcare process. Lack of resources for education meant that the obligation to provide all prisoners under school leaving age with 15 hours of education a week was not met. The regime in the health-care centre was impoverished and much of the physical environment was shabby and dirty. The inspectors identified serious problems in transferring prisoners to NHS facilities. They also called for the cessation of the inappropriate and damaging practice of secluding those at risk of self-harm.

However, Feltham had tackled most of its problems with vigour and imagination and there was a sense of vigour and purpose. Positive aspects of the regime included the facilities for PE and recreation and the inspectors praised the leisure industry PE course for unconvicted prisoners. The prison also had its own prison radio run by prisoners and overall the prison benefited a great deal from the efforts of volunteers. The attempt to engage and involve parents in their children's progress was commended, as were the visiting arrangements for juveniles, convicted sex offenders and vulnerable youngsters.

Additional resources were needed and the Chief Inspector called for a second young offender remand centre to relieve the intolerable pressures on Feltham. Once again, the Chief Inspector called for a separate director for young prisoners to ensure that their distinct needs are met. A thematic study of young prisoners is now under way.

Werrington Young Offender Institution. A report was also carried out in relation to Werrington Young Offender Institution in 1998 (Home Office (1998d)) which revealed the following situation. Over 190 15–17-year-olds were kept in 96 single cells in what amounted to warehouse conditions. The cells were described as little more than lavatories and they had to eat in their cells. They were only allowed association on two evenings a week on the landings where they had no chairs to sit on. The conditions were described by the Chief Inspector Sir David Ramsbotham as being quite incredible and he stated 'I have not come across such totally deliberate and unnecessary impoverishment of children anywhere.'

Sir David criticised the Prison Service for replacing dormitories at the institution with a large cellular house block in which the accommodation was made of metal and all the noise was amplified, making it like an echo chamber. He added that to find that adult prison conditions have been deliberately introduced, overturning previous and appropriate treatment and conditions for children, is nothing short of disgraceful. Also criticised were:

1. the sports hall having no lavatories or showers;
2. the lack of 24-hour healthcare cover, the availability of a doctor for only 11 hours a week and the absence of a health centre; and
3. reception arrangements for new inmates were 'appalling' – youths arriving at night were subjected to a torrent of abuse from other inmates.

Farrington et al (2002) report the results of research on intensive custodial regimes for young offenders. Two regimes were established at Thorn Cross Young Offender Institution in July 1996 and at Colchester Military Corrective Training Centre in February 1997 and there was also a control group. The Thorn Cross regime contained offending behaviour, education, employment, mentoring and throughcare components, as well as drilling and physical training components. In the latter respects it had features of a boot camp. The Colchester regime emphasised physical activities without the other features. The aim was to test the impact of demanding, highly structured regimes on attitudes, behaviour and recidivism. The Thorn Cross group was the most successful in that whilst the recidivism rates were not that different between the groups, the Thorn Cross group took longer to reoffend and committed significantly fewer crimes. The Colchester group was the second most successful in terms of recidivism in that they committed slightly fewer crimes than the control group. Also the Colchester group had significantly more positive attitudes towards staff and other inmates at the end of sentence and were significantly more hopeful about the future than the control group. The success of the Thorn Cross regime in reducing reconviction offences is probably due to its offending behaviour, education, employment, mentoring and throughcare components rather than to its drilling and physical training components. The Colchester regime, which emphasised physical activities, was not successful in reducing reconvictions.

Stewart and Tutt (1987) paint a bleak picture as regards the help that is given to children in custody. In a survey of those carrying out such work it was found that nearly four-fifths of the children in penal institutions were not receiving any significant help from the workers who responded to the survey. Reasons given for this were that help had been rejected or was likely to be unwelcome, that the institutions were viewed as being to deter rather than to help and, most commonly, that the short period of detention makes attempts at such work pointless. Providing insight for the offender, helping with adjustment to custody and assisting with additional problems and education were mentioned by respondents as being features of their remit.

It seems that there is little good work with these youngsters whilst they are in custody and they get insufficient support upon release. Other problems include suicide, recidivism and loss of contact with their community, family, job, abode etc. A short rest from them for society during their worst years seems to be the desire. The Crime and Disorder Act 1998 and its aspiration to preventing offending seems to have been confused in this regard.

Detention and training order

A detention and training order was introduced in June 2000. It can be used for a child or young person where prison would have been possible for an adult. The orders are intended for those aged 12–17 but it can even be used for those under 12 in certain circumstances. For the under-12 age group the aim would be to protect the public. For those aged 13–15 the order is intended to provide a means of dealing with persistent offenders. The length of the order can be the equivalent of what would have been possible for an adult. Half of it will be in secure accommodation, with the rest being a system of supervision. This order replaced the secure training order and also the use of young offender institutions for those aged 15–17.

Long-term detention

A number of systems need to be noted. Custody for life is imposed for those aged 18–20 who commit murder. This system may also be used for that age range in relation to other offences where the maximum sentence for an adult is life.

Powers of Criminal Courts (Sentencing) Act 2000, ss90–92

This replaces the earlier provisions of the Children and Young Persons Act 1933. The 2000 Act provides a system of detention during Her Majesty's pleasure as a sentence for those who are under 18 when they commit murder. The Act gives a power to impose a sentence up to the maximum applicable in the case of a person aged 21 or above. This is applicable to 10–13-year-olds who are convicted of manslaughter and for 14–17 year olds who commit certain grave offences. These grave offences are those that are punishable with a sentence of 14 years or more. Additionally, for those who are 16 or 17, it applies to indecent assault on a woman, and for a person who is 14 or more it also applies to death by dangerous driving and death by careless driving. The latter where the person was under the influence of drink or drugs.

Attendance centres

Attendance centres became available as a sentencing option, in relation to those under the age of 21, as a result of the Criminal Justice Act 1948 and the Criminal Justice Act 1982. Sections 60–62 of the Powers of Criminal Courts (Sentencing) Act 2000 provides the current legislation. In the past the main provision of centres had been for boys under the age of 17. Lord Templeman during the debate on the 1948 Criminal Justice Bill saw their role as follows. That the objective was to deprive young offenders of a half holiday, to prevent them going to a football match or a cinema and, perhaps not less important, to make them look ridiculous to their friends and relatives. Whilst at that time it was viewed as a punishment, welfare notions crept in. Confusion as to its role has been added to by confusion as to its place in the tariff. Policy-makers and sentencers have varied in their views as to whether or not it is suitable as an alternative to a custodial sentence. The Home Office (1986a) in a review of criminal justice policy stated that the purpose of the centres was to impose a significant loss of leisure and to encourage more constructive use of leisure time. The review also notes that they are normally run by the police for two to three hours on Saturdays. Examples of activities engaged in are disciplined physical education instruction and constructive activities such as first aid or craft work. Normally 12 hours' attendance will be prescribed, though a smaller amount is possible for the under-14s and larger amounts are also possible – up to 24 hours for the under-17s and up to 36 hours for those aged 17 and over. The trend is for an increased use of orders of over 12 hours. Dunlop (1980) carried out research on 14 junior centres in 1976 by means of questionnaires completed by officers in charge of the centres. The features noted earlier were found to be standard, though some differences such as three- rather than two-hour periods, some not run by the police and some not on Saturday afternoons were also noted. The conclusion of the research was that the centres were relatively effective and efficient given their 60 per cent record of achieving satisfactory attendance by those subject to the orders and a level of offending during the order of 29 per cent. It was found that the orders were used for a wide variety of offenders and it was suggested that further widening was possible and that it could be used as an alternative to custody. Gelsthorpe and Morris (1983) examined the workings of a junior centre from 1979–1981. This was an atypical set-up with a clear welfare orientation amongst the staff who hoped to offer something positive. They wanted the centres to be used early in the tariff so as to maximise the chances of providing help, whilst the authors saw its role as being more useful as a last resort before the use of custody. The boys who were subject to the order generally felt lucky that they had not received custody. In other respects they were ambivalent as to its effect. The following are a sample of the observations recorded.

'It's better than a fine ... 'cos you still have your money.

It takes your Saturday afternoon, that's the worst thing, when you could be with your mates or out in town.

This is harder because it takes so long, you have to keep clean for a long time and you know they're watching your every move.

With the supervision order you don't do anything, the social worker just talks, this involves you more, demands effort from me so it's worse.

You know after this place its detention centre so it just makes you give it all up ... you don't hang around with the same mates.

Whatever this place does to people, it's up to them in the end. This place scares you but it won't stop you.'

The material gathered by Burney (1985) reveals a considerable amount of variation on a number of matters. For example, some magistrates saw attendance centres for punishment whilst others would welcome a more purposive regime; some see them as alternatives to custody (this is most likely for the junior centres), whilst others do not. Usage is also limited by availability, a nearby facility being required; though one chairman of a juvenile bench saw an extra distance to be travelled as useful in terms of being a further punishment! Variation was also revealed by a study of six local juvenile justice systems in 1984 by Gelsthorpe and Tutt (1986). Rate of use varied from 6.6 per cent of dispositions to 21.1 per cent. The courts used the centres for the full age range of offenders and for the full range of offences. It was not normally used as an alternative to custody but rather instead of a fine or a supervision order. Two of the centres in the centre were run by the social services and one by the education department.

Supervision orders

The Children and Young Persons Act 1969, ss11–19, introduced supervision orders (now community rehabilitation orders) as a probation-type disposition for the under-17s. They are rather like probation orders but for a younger age group. The Crime and Disorder Act 1998 made a number of changes to these orders, including the introduction of reparation as an element of them. Sections 63–68 of the Powers of Criminal Courts (Sentencing) Act 2000 contains the current provisions. Supervision is commonly carried out by social workers, though some orders involve probation officers. The order typically involves weekly meetings with less regular meetings after the first few months, and the maximum period for an order is three years. Restrictions may be included in the order. Supervision orders also include the notion of intermediate treatment, which may be residential or non-residential. This can include specified activities in the spheres of education, work and skill development and socially valuable activities. The period away from home, if this is used, may be in the form of trips and expeditions – for example, taking part in an outward-bound programme. Whilst the supervision order itself can last for up to three years, the intermediate treatment element can only be for up to 90 days. Pessimism was a common response to intermediate treatment in its early years. Rutter and Giller (1981) examined the research on the early years and concluded that whilst it would be premature to conclude that these intensive community-based approaches are without value, the results so far are contradictory and inconclusive. Section 20 of the Criminal Justice Act 1982 attempted to tackle one particular problem with this disposition – a lack of confidence on the part of the courts with regard to it. This was because the supervisor largely determined what, if anything, would be done and the court was worried that little would be done. Gelsthorpe and Morris (1983) reported the observation of one boy on such an order: 'With the supervision order you don't do anything, the social worker just talks ...'. To try to remove such disquiet the 1982 Act allowed the court to limit the discretion of the supervisor by determining the content of an intermediate treatment package if the court chose to do so. The Act also provided for additional restrictions that could be imposed, such as a curfew system. Section 128 of the Criminal Justice Act 1988 extended the range of requirements to include school attendance and also tightened up the breach procedure so that where specified activities have been provided as an alternative to custody the court dealing with the breach proceedings have all the power of the court that imposed the original sentence. The trend is for tougher, more intensive, programmes to be offered to, and prescribed by, the courts so as to increase the use of this disposal and in particular to get it used as an alternative to custody.

Action plan orders

They were introduced by ss69–72 of the Powers of Criminal Courts (Sentencing) Act 2000 for those under the age of 18. They are to rehabilitate or to prevent further offending. The order is for three months and it contains requirements such as:

1. being under the supervision of the responsible officer who is named in the order – that person would be a probation officer, a social worker or a member of the youth offending team;
2. to participate in specified activities;
3. to present himself to a person or persons specified in the requirements or directions at a place or places and at a time or times so specified;
4. to attend at an attendance centre;
5. to stay away from a place or places as specified in the order;
6. to comply with any arrangements for education;
7. to make reparation.

The order should avoid any conflict with the offender's religious beliefs and any interference with the times, if any, at which he normally works or attends school or any other educational establishment. They should provide tailored intensive intervention.

Reparation orders

These were introduced in 2000 for those under 18. They require the offender to make reparation, as specified in the order, to a person or persons who are victims of the offence or who are otherwise affected by it, or the order can be to make reparation to the community at large. It will not be applicable for use in conjunction with a custodial sentence, a sentence under the grave crimes provision of the 2000 Act and some community orders. A reparation order shall not require the offender to work for more than 24 hours in aggregate or to make reparation to any person without the consent of that person. Requirements specified in a reparation order should be commensurate with the seriousness of the offence. The order should avoid any conflict with the offender's religious beliefs and any interference with the times, if any, at which he normally works or attends school or any other educational establishment.

Reparation can be viewed as a form of restorative justice and a number of methods already exist to achieve reparations. This part of the book has considered different functions of sentencing, including retribution, deterrence and rehabilitation. Almost exclusively, the sentences discussed are intended to serve the aims of society or to affect the offender. The role of victims is frequently ignored. Indeed, it is a feature of a developed criminal justice process that once proceedings are commenced, the needs of the system are paramount and the victim is relegated to a minor role. Justice would perhaps be better served if we concentrated on meeting the needs of victims, society and the offender instead of the meting out of punishment. The role that reparation could play is that a reparative schema would demand the abandonment of culpability of the offender as the central focus of sentencing and, in its place, pay much closer attention to the issue of harm delivered to victims, society and perhaps also offenders. Restoring individual damage and repairing social bonds rather than inflicting pain on the offender is the aim. In this we would invite (or perhaps demand) the involvement of the community in the process of restoration. Wright (1982) proposes that the aim should be making amends by means of victim compensation or service to the state, but a wider approach is possible. For example, a system in which the offender manages to empathise with the victim could be regarded as being an acceptable outcome.

With such schemes, although the victim can never be put back into the position he was in before an offence, it must surely be to his benefit both to receive compensation and to feel his needs are recognised. Offenders are not allowed to escape scot free and some may recognise that making reparation is not intended as a punitive exercise. A few may even reflect on the experience and benefit from atoning for their wrongdoing. Within this broader definition, reparation may take one of four forms: individual reparation, reparation to the community, restitution and compensation. With individual reparation as a concept, instead of, or as well as, paying monetary compensation, the offender performs some service for his victim – perhaps by repairing damage he has caused. Sections 73–75 of the Powers of Criminal Courts (Sentencing) Act 2000 makes provision for the system that is available in our jurisdiction; it is a continuation of earlier systems of reparation. The reparation order requires payment to specified victims or to the community at large. The person who is to benefit has to be willing to receive the work, ie to consent, and the reparation order should be commensurate with the seriousness of the offence.

Wasik (1999) contrasts the enthusiasm of the government for reparation with some of the difficulties that can be envisaged in putting the ideas into practice. He noted that in the White Paper, *No More Excuses*, the government suggested that reparation 'can be a valuable way of making young offenders face the consequences of their actions and see the harm they have caused. It can be a catalyst for reform and rehabilitation and can also benefit victims … The reparation might involve writing a letter of apology, apologising to the victim in person, cleaning graffiti or repairing criminal damage': Home Office (1997d). Wasik asks who will count as a victim for these purposes and notes the problems of determining priority amongst victims and persons who are otherwise affected by crime, and the tailoring of sentence in accordance with the preference of victims. He argues that these matters, and others, require urgent clarification if reparation orders are to be integrated successfully within the existing sentencing framework. The new order is to operate as a punishment and the penalty should fit the seriousness of the offence. Reparation and desert are not easy to reconcile. Wasik tells us that this is because the main emphasis in desert is on proportionality between offender and offender, and not between offender and victim. Proportionality involves the infliction of comparable penalties for comparable crimes, and this creates two immediate problems for reparation orders. These are that reparation turns both upon the differing practical abilities of offenders, and the differing predilections of victims. One young offender may be able to make a good practical job of repairing the window which he has smashed, but another would make a bad situation worse. Also, allowing victims to influence the form that reparation should take can lead to inconsistency and injustice. The operation of reparation orders within a desert framework is bound to create significant problems of principle. There is little discussion of these issues in the existing writings on reparation. Much of that literature is strong on general rhetoric, but weak on addressing issues of principle, and vague on the practicalities. If reparation is now to claim a more central place in sentencing practice, the questions which emerge from the analysis presented by Wasik need to be confronted and resolved.

Parenting orders

They were introduced in 2000 as a result of the Crime and Disorder Act 1998. They reflect the desire of the government to get parents to face up to their responsibilities for the offences committed by their children. The view of the government is that parents have the primary responsibility for ensuring that children know the difference between right and wrong and that they are brought up to respect the law. It believes that most parents would want to take up the offer of a referral to a suitable scheme if that reduced the risk of their children offending.

Parenting orders amount to criminalising parents for the behaviour of their children. It may well be that the parents just do not have the ability to control their children and, indeed, how can they actually do it? Once children are out of the parent's sight there is the influence of peer pressure. How can you keep them at home, how can you ensure that teenagers go to school and stay in school? Breach of a parenting order is a criminal offence and there is a compulsory part in terms of parenting skills and also ensuring such as school attendance. This is in reality will commonly mean that these regimes are being imposed upon single parent families where there are other younger children to be cared. Parents in this situation are unlikely to benefit much from a few hours of classes and would probably be stigmatised by the process. Despite this the principle has been extended in a number of ways. For example, the Criminal Justice Act 2003 extends the use of parenting orders by making them available at an earlier stage in relation to the parents of offenders who receive referral orders. Also the Anti-social Behaviour Act 2003, ss18–29, provides for parenting contracts in cases of truancy and exclusion from school and penalty notices in relation to truancy.

Hancock (2000) offered the following comments on parenting orders generally:

'The parenting orders have been greeted with a mixture of interest and scepticism not only in this country but also across Europe and the United States. Whilst studies as far back as the 1970s were being undertaken with parents of young offenders, training them in basic parenting skills, negotiation, rule and boundaries setting, etc and meeting with considerable success, these were nevertheless voluntary and little had been tried with parents on a more mandatory basis. As a result, the introduction of the parenting order is not just a new criminal justice intervention – it is also an experiment in new ways of working with parents, with the Youth Offending Teams acting as something of a guinea pig.

Across the country, pilot Youth Offending Teams have adopted very different models in the delivery of parenting order programmes. In Lewisham, we approached local voluntary sector parenting groups who were already providing support and skills-based programmes to parents on a voluntary basis. We felt that parenting order programmes could be delivered more sensitively and effectively via the voluntary sector in that there would be less social services stigma attached to parents attending, and the groups would be more connected to the local community. We commissioned two different voluntary providers to deliver our group work programmes, with a view to evaluating both models in order to develop an evidence base of "what works". A 10-week programme, covering areas such as active listening, boundary setting, coping strategies, issues around substance misuse, communication and listening, anger management and problem solving, was delivered to all parents on orders. There was also the option of one to one sessions for those parents who were felt to be in need of more individual support. Another key issue was that of ensuring that programmes were sensitive to different cultural and religious dimensions. Parents and carers from different ethnic groups often have different needs and concerns around parenting. These must be acknowledged and addressed at the assessment stage, and Youth Offending Teams must then ensure that a comprehensive and flexible menu of options is available for parents in order that all needs are addressed. In Lewisham, we have appointed a parenting order co-ordinator to develop work with all parents and carers, as well as devising assessment tools for work within pre-sentence reports.' (2000:155)

Child safety orders

The Crime and Disorder Act 1998 made provision for intervention (child safety orders) for those under the age of ten. It is intended to provide supervision, normally for a three-month period but potentially for up to a year, for those at risk of offending or being involved in behaviour that would constitute an offence if of age. The local authority seeks the order through the youth offending team who may have been contacted by other agencies or the police or there may have been a referral from the magistrates' family jurisdiction. Compliance with conditions can also be required. The provision has hardly been used as in reality other systems such as care would be operative or made operative. We perhaps need to have some unease about intervention that is so far from the justice model requirements, but perhaps that is the price of the welfare model. Nevertheless, is a criminal-justice-based intervention the answer for those under the age of ten?

7.8 Analysis of the youth justice system

Improving the process

The Audit Commission (1997) made suggestions as to how the procedures could be improved. They note that the process costs around £2,500 for each young person sentenced. In their view proceedings are too slow, being four months, on average, from arrest to sentence. Also of concern is that half of the proceedings against young people are discontinued, dismissed or end in a discharge. In the short term, the Commission believes that the process could be improved by speeding up the court process with the interval between arrest and sentence being monitored. Persistent offenders on community sentences should be more intensively supervised. Generally, the Commission favours better planning and monitoring. They also argue that prevention is better than cure, and offending by young people at greatest risk could be reduced by targeting, piloting and evaluating schemes such as assistance with parenting skills, structured education for the under fives, support for teachers dealing with badly behaved pupils, and the provision of positive leisure opportunities. All services for children and young people should share information and target areas at greatest risk, and local residents in those areas should be consulted. The resources that would be released if court processes became less important could be used instead to fund local services that reduce offending. All the agencies involved should contribute to monitoring and evaluating preventive programmes.

Preventing children offending

The Crime and Disorder Act 1998 was developed in part out of ideas that were presented in a report called *Preventing Children Offending* (Home Office (1997a)), and some of the material presented there is worth examining in some detail. The report notes that strategies have been multi-faceted – including preventive measures aimed at stopping children and young people from being drawn into crime, measures to encourage those who have committed one or two offences to lead law-abiding lives and measures to deal with the small but significant number of persistent and serious offenders.

Crime prevention

In relation to crime prevention the report states that the government has committed significant resources to help children and young people avoid turning to crime. This includes Phase 1 of the Safer Cities programme, which funded some 800 schemes in England and Wales. This was aimed at young people, with grants totalling around £4.2 million. Phase 2 of the programme, administered by the Department of the Environment since April 1994 (now the Department of the Environment, Transport and the Regions), has provided additional grants of £4 million to 800 crime prevention schemes in 1994/95 and 1995/96. Many of these, are targeted at young people. Under the Grants for Education Support and Training (GEST) programme, the Department for Education and Employment has supported expenditure of over £10 million on the Youth Action Scheme over the period 1993–96. The scheme was designed to help young people at risk of drifting into crime to plan, organise and participate in programmes of challenging activities to develop their self-esteem and sense of responsibility to themselves and the wider community. Proceeds from the National Lottery amounting to £174 million have been paid to 1,149 organisations which are engaged in constructive activities with children, such as the arts, sport and community work. Also the government pays an annual grant of £750,000 to the organisation Crime Concern, and encourages it to take a particular interest in youth crime prevention in England and Wales. Examples of Crime Concern's work are: the carrying out of youth crime audits or surveys on behalf of local authorities; providing education in parenting, to tackle some of the factors affecting families which may contribute to juvenile offending; and the development of youth action groups. Crime Concern and the Prudential Corporation launched a five-year strategy in 1993, costing about £1.5 million, to develop youth action groups in secondary schools across the country. They tackle problems such as bullying, personal safety, vandalism, graffiti and drug abuse; increase young people's interest in crime prevention and encourage a sense of social responsibility. Crime Concern's strategy for youth crime prevention recognises the value of programmes which are designed to address the risk factors associated with offending.

Persistent and serious young offenders

The report notes that there are a small number of young offenders who are responsible for a disproportionate amount of crime in England and Wales. In 1990, for example, 1 per cent of male offenders aged 17 accounted for around 60 per cent of all the convictions of persons of that age. Similarly, a survey undertaken by the Home Office in 1993 suggested that, on average, persistent juvenile offenders committed around 17 offences each. This situation led to a range of interventions to try to control these particularly troublesome youths. These included extending existing legislation so that any child aged ten or over who commits an offence for which an adult could be sentenced to 14 years or more, or life imprisonment, can be sentenced to long periods of detention. Extending from one to two years the maximum period for which a 15–17 year old may be sentenced to detention in a young offender institution was a further innovation. Secure training orders and electronic monitoring were also introduced. The detention and training order has since replaced some of these measures.

Influences on child offending

The influences on people as they grow up may lead them towards, or away from, crime. Through experiences in the family, at school, in the community and at leisure, children can learn the benefits of obeying the law and the costs of not doing so. The ideas of Graham and Bowling (1995), who identified risk factors for offending, were noted in the report. The risk factors are being male, being brought up by a criminal parent or parents, living in a family with multiple problems, experiencing poor parenting and a lack of supervision, poor discipline in the family and at school, playing truant, associating with delinquent friends and having brothers and sisters who offend. Early intervention with children at risk of offending was suggested. The aim is to increase the potential of positive factors and to decrease the impact of negative ones. Pointers are provided as regards the family, schools and leisure activities.

The family. The single most important influence on a child's development is that of the family. Those children who show signs of criminal behaviour at an early age are those who are most likely to end up as serious or persistent offenders. Such children often come from communities and families, which are unstable, chaotic and suffer from a number of problems. Their parents are likely to have criminal record, to neglect their children, or to exercise low levels of supervision and harsh and erratic discipline, and themselves to come from similar families. Children exposed to abuse and neglect within a climate of hostility at home are particularly at risk of becoming violent offenders. Research has also shown, that where children are brought up in a stable environment and have a good relationship with their parents, they are less likely to display delinquent behaviour. The capacity and willingness of the parent or parents to supervise their children and exercise fair and consistent discipline is crucial.

The school. There is evidence to suggest that to an appreciable extent, children's behaviour and attitudes, are shaped and influenced by their experiences at school. The capacity of schools to motivate and integrate their pupils, and offer them a sense of achievement, may help to prevent delinquent behaviour. Research shows that the characteristics of the school such as relationships between pupils and staff, levels of staff and pupil motivation and commitment, the system of rules and how they are enforced, can all play an important part in helping children to stay out of trouble. Schools which have a good relationship between staff and pupils, provide clear and consistently enforced rules, and ensure pupils are offered a wide range of opportunities for achieving success, are most likely to make a positive contribution to preventing criminality.

Leisure use and peer groups. Juvenile offenders often commit offences with others. The use of leisure time, and peer pressure, can influence the likelihood of offending. For example, offending by boys is associated with the amount of time they spend away from home and with their friends. Those who spend their leisure time in unstructured and unsupervised activity on the streets are more at risk of offending. There is also evidence that those whose friends engage in delinquent activity are more likely to do so themselves than those whose friends do not. In contrast, participation in the arts and sports enables young people to use their leisure time in a constructive way. Group activities such as team games can promote a sense of community and pride in achievement, which lead to a heightened awareness of the obligations of citizenship.

The effectiveness of early intervention. The suggestion is made that it is essential to intervene with children at risk of becoming offenders as early as possible. It is also essential to develop strategies for intervention based on sound knowledge about what works. Currently most evidence for the effectiveness of early intervention comes from the USA where a number of initiatives have been independently evaluated. For example, the Syracuse Family Development programme, which provided pre-natal and post-natal advice and support to mothers of children up to the age of five, showed that, by the age of 15, the children in families who received such support had offended less, and less seriously, than children not on the programme. Encouraging results were also achieved in the USA by the LIFT programme (Linking Interests of Families and Teachers), which was set up in Oregon to discourage anti-social behaviour at home and school through parent training, social skills classes for children, measures to improve behaviour and supervision in the playground, and the use of a school-to-home telephone line on which teachers and parents could leave and receive messages. Initial findings suggest that LIFT has reduced aggressive and antisocial behaviour in the short-term.

7.9 Applying 'what works?' principles to young offenders

Utting (1999) identifies strategies for intervention in relation to young offenders and those at risk of becoming young offenders. A key factor is once more identified as being the need for early intervention. This can be at a very early age as in the provision of pre-school programmes in disadvantaged neighbourhoods. These have been shown to reduce criminality in later life. The risk factors include poor parental supervision, family conflict, family attitudes favourable to antisocial behaviour, low family income and a parent or sibling with a criminal record. As to schooling, going to a poorly organised school, a lack of personal commitment, poor school performance and aggressive behaviour are risk factors. Community risk factors are a disadvantaged neighbourhood, community disorganisation and neglect, the availability of drugs and high turnover and lack of neighbourhood attachment. In terms of friends and peers, the risk factors are alienation and lack of social commitment, attitudes that condone criminal behaviour and involvement in criminal behaviour.

A promising approach is home-visiting schemes, which have succeeded in strengthening the bonds of affection between family members. Also successful are family literacy schemes and reading recovery programmes in schools that tackle low educational achievement. The Sheffield anti-bullying initiative is a specific example of a programme that delivered good results. This was evaluated in 23 Sheffield primary and secondary schools. Schools were encouraged to tackle aggressive behaviour and bullying which are known risk factors for violent and criminal behaviour in adolescence and adulthood. This included the creation of a whole school ethos as well as work with individuals. The schools were expected to produce clear and enforceable anti-bullying policies and procedures that were endorsed by governors, staff, parents and pupils. In addition to describing disciplinary measures, schools took steps that included the use of anti-bullying material in the curriculum, classes teaching problem-solving skills, assertiveness training as well as innovative 'no blame' techniques for dealing with bullies. Evaluation a year after the programme was implemented showed a positive impact, with schools that had put the most effort into their strategies generally achieving the best results. Compared with a number of control schools, project schools saw an increase in the number of pupils saying they had not been bullied and a significant decrease in the frequency of bullying, which was most evident in primary schools. An increase in pupils' willingness to take bullying problems to their teachers was clearly evident in secondary schools.

Cognitive-behavioural approaches have been used as a major basis for intervention with youngsters of late. The aim is to get them to understand their situation, to work out what is at the root of their offending, to help them cope with their situations and to move on from them. In short, to fix what is broken but to also about take responsibility for their actions. This approach is much more individualised than would have been the case in the past. Referral orders have such ideas in them, including the guilty plea element. Cognitive-behavioural approaches are characterised as being concerned with: behaviour modification (consistently rewarding socially acceptable behaviour, and ensuring consequences for unacceptable behaviour); social skills training (teaching new skills for dealing with other people in different settings); problem solving (seeking to improve problem awareness, ability to foresee likely consequences of anti-social behaviour and ability to work out and negotiate more acceptable solutions); anger management (improving self-regulation and the ability to relax); and moral reasoning (tackling immature understanding of moral issues, including the effects of crime on victims). These are factors that were identified by Vennard et al (1997).

An example of such an approach is the Inverclyde Intensive Probation Unit programme for 16 to 21 years olds. Young offenders at serious risk of custody were offered the opportunity, on a voluntary basis, to deal with the problems contributing to their offending behaviour and to learn new social and problem-solving skills. Different modules enabled packages to be assembled that were tailored to the individual offender's risk-profile needs which is systematically assessed. A study of reconvictions, 18 months after the participants had completed the programme, found that 33 per cent of those who had completed the course had not been reconvicted. This was significantly lower than the reconviction rate for similar high tariff offenders who were referred for assessment but received a custodial sentence or other disposal. Also identified are strategies that do not work and these include general counselling and therapy sessions, corporal punishment, suspension from school and fear arousal.

7.10 The effectiveness of interventions with young offenders

A major problem that any intervention has to face is that it is not known what the causation of delinquent behaviour is, and in this sense sentencers and policy-makers are of course building on sand. As Rutter and Giller (1981) note most reviews, of what has been a large amount of research dealing with responses, 'have ended with essentially negative conclusions – "no delinquent prevention strategies can be definitely recommended" (Wright and Dixon (1977)); "with few and isolated exceptions the rehabilitative efforts that have been reported so far have had no appreciable effect on recidivism" (Martinson; (1974)); "studies which have produced positive results have been isolated, inconsistent in their evidence, and open to so much methodological criticism that they must remain unconvincing" (Brody (1976))' (1981:267). Rutter and Giller think that such conclusions are slightly too pessimistic. As with Brody much emphasis is placed by Rutter and Giller on the deficiencies of research that has been carried out in terms of factors such as sampling, matching and even doubts as to whether or not the response being assessed actually took place. They favour further experimentation in the future on the grounds that, whilst this is treating people as guinea pigs, given the evidence for present interventions they are all in the nature of an experiment. In terms of types of response their view is that success rates following institutional treatment or care have been generally poor – at least as assessed by re-conviction rates, which have usually run at about 60 to 70 per cent: see for example McMichael (1974), Dunlop (1975), and Millham et al (1975) and (1978). But, of course, that could be no more than a reflection of the seriously recidivist characteristics of youths sent to institutions, just as also it could mean that most institutions are of poor quality or are inappropriately run. A combination of the following features of institutions seem to be linked with beneficial effects: firmness, warmth, harmony, high expectations, good discipline (especially with respect to absconding) and a practical approach to training. But the effects seem to wear off, to a great extent, upon a return to the community. Non-custodial responses seem to produce no worse and indeed marginally better results than custodial responses. Whilst of course there will always be some need for institutions the least interventionist line would seem the ideal to aspire to. For the individual, providing aids to social competence seems a better strategy than attempting to suppress delinquency.

Notions such as 'needs', 'welfare', 'justice', and 'rights' have to be approached with suspicion. They are best seen as mere claims or assertions and this helps in an appreciation of their ideological usage. Rights for example only exist in so far as a person makes an assertion as to their existence. For youngsters they are most likely to be a result of adults deciding both that rights exist and that youngsters should have them. The rights of youngsters are thus the whims of adults. The criminal justice system is not value free and one of its major effects is to provide a control system as regards working-class youth. The various agencies involved act as a filtering mechanism. The result of this is that behaviour which is typical of this group is the most likely behaviour to be defined as criminal. Whilst others may also behave that way, the working-class youths are the most likely to experience reaction when they engage in such behaviour. Factors in the social structure characterised by various forms of disadvantage and powerlessness channel, and in part determine, the participants in the criminal justice system. The criminal justice net is not cast randomly. In *Crime – a Challenge to Us All* (Labour Party (1964)) the view was put that chronic or serious delinquency in a child is, in the main, evidence of lack of the care, the guidance and the opportunities to which every child is entitled. There are very few children who do not behave badly at times; but the children of parents with ample means rarely appear before the juvenile courts. The machinery of law is reserved mainly for working-class children who, more often than not, are also handicapped by being taught in too big classes in unsatisfactory school buildings with few amenities or opportunities for out-of-school activities. Anti-social behaviour in a child may arise from difficulties at home, from unhappiness at school, from physical or mental handicaps or maladjustment, or from a variety of other causes for which the child has no personal responsibility.

If such an analysis were accepted it could be developed in a number of directions. It could lead to suggestions that attention be directed to some extent, and even perhaps to a very great extent, to the social conditions that prevail in the wider society rather than concentrating upon the individual youngster. Whatever the merits of such a suggestion this is unlikely to happen. The point is still worth making. Attention is likely to continue to be focused on the individual. The procedure by which decisions are made within the system for those under the age of 21 clearly has its problems, and questions have been raised as regards the dispositions that are used in relation to youngsters. Examples abound of variation in practice and disparity in the use of procedures and dispositions. Prejudice and discrimination are also to be found in what is a poor system of decision-making which has as its aim the processing of cases and which involves the large-scale exclusion of youngsters and their parents from meaningful involvement in proceedings. The problems of the adult system – such as the means by which guilt is determined, the deficiencies of lay magistrates, the quality of the information available, the deficiencies of lawyers and others in terms of implementing and utilising the safeguards that are available – are also features of the juvenile system. As to the dispositions not only are they sometimes used for purposes for which they were never intended, at times their very role is a matter for conjecture. For both decision-making procedures and dispositions numerous ideas of reform have been presented which envisage small, tinkering-type changes as well as fundamental restructuring. A common theme is to suggest limiting intervention and in particular limiting the use made of custodial measures.

Numerous strategies have been suggested as a means to reduce the use of custodial dispositions. Intensive intermediate treatment and attendance centres could be used in this way. In both cases there would also be the hope that the experience would be helpful for the offender in terms of improving social skills. This probably hopes for far too much as this quite limited intervention cannot really hope to combat the realities of the total social situation which in some cases will be that of long-term, multiple disadvantage which will include family problems and criminally orientated peer-group pressure. Also toughened-up intermediate treatment is just as likely to be used for those for whom a custodial sentence would not have been suitable in the first place. It is this factor that has led commentators to be sceptical about the use of suspended custodial sentences for those under the age of 21. The danger is that it would not be used as an alternative to custody.

It was clear from the Green Paper, *Punishment in the Community* (Home Office (1988b)) that the government at that time also saw merit in the idea of punishment in the community as a means to reduce the use of custodial dispositions. The Green Paper pointed to the difficulties of the 17–20 age group. It noted that 1 per cent of males in this age group receive a custodial sentence. It viewed these youngsters as a group that will largely grow out of crime. The concern was that intervention would have a stigmatising effect and that custodial measures would lead to inappropriate skills and attitudes. The desire was to encourage youngsters out of crime rather than into it. Punishment in the community was seen as being particularly suitable for this age group. Both assistance with problems and in the making of the adjustment to adult life would be provided, as well as a penalty.

The government of the 1980s may have been preaching this sort of message, now they seem to be moving towards faster intervention for good or ill. Punishing parents is also in vogue. Fining parents may worsen the problems of families that are already experiencing difficulties. You have to ask: Are the imposition of convictions and such penalties likely to lead to a change in parental behaviour? It is difficult to see that they would. How much less logical would it be to criminalise and prosecute one or more of the following – schools, the police and other practitioners in the criminal justice system, religious bodies and indeed the government for their failure to control youngsters?

7.11 Conclusion

Dealing with young offenders has proven to be difficult. In particular we just do not know what the causes of the law-breaking behaviour of youngsters are. Given this situation of ignorance it is clear that attempts to reduce such behaviour have been built on sand and it is not surprising that they have largely failed. An absence of proven causes and cures means that in this central facet the welfare model is intellectually bankrupt. There are some glimmers of hope – we are not quite at the stage of saying that nothing works. Some responses seem to be offer some benefits for both society and the individual and it is suggested that these could be utilised. One of the main lessons from research is that non-intervention and the more limited forms of intervention are no worse, and are if anything more successful, than more intrusive measures. As a working principle this would also seem worthwhile. Of course there will always be some offenders whose behaviour is regarded as so outrageous that long-term incapacitation is required. The argument that things would be better with better procedures seems self-evident. The views of the justice model would seem to be the answer. There are however problems with seeing the justice model as the answer. Parsloe (1978) notes that children have needs as well as rights, and protection of rights may have no connection at all with meeting needs. In similar vein Asquith states that

> 'The pursuit of justice and the promotion of the rights of children has usually meant modifying the decision-making process in the attempt to achieve greater procedural equality and is less concerned with the substantial rights of children in terms of taking steps that will truly serve their best interests. If there is genuine concern about the rights of children and their long-term welfare then greater concern has to be directed at the material conditions of social life in which children who offend find themselves.' (1983:221)

A rights-orientated approach is flawed in so far as illusory rights and ineffective safeguards would offer no panacea for the ills of the juvenile justice system. Also, lawyers as one of the protectors of rights, may, as was seen earlier, be one or more of the following – incompetent, primarily motivated by self-interest and attempting to minimise what might well be beneficial intervention. Putting your faith in lawyers is not the most sensible strategy. The courts as protectors of rights leave much to be desired. To summarise it would seem wise to try to minimise intervention, whilst recognising that constructive intervention is possible and indeed should be encouraged. Better procedures as an aspiration is also to be supported. Such an eclectic mishmash may strike you as being a cop-out, and may be regarded as unworkable, but to my mind it is the best suggestion that can be offered at the moment.

The juvenile system has considerable problems and some of the myriad ideas for change that have been suggested have been noted. Indeed, research in the Home Office report *Tackling Youth Crime* (Home Office (1997f)) (which does not speak for the government) stated:

> 'The youth justice system in England and Wales is in disarray. It simply does not work. It can scarcely be called a system at all because it lacks coherent objectives. It satisfies neither those whose principal concern is crime control nor those whose principal priority is the welfare of the young offender.'

Given the extent of the problems and the lack of political will to tackle them that exists, further development of purported solutions is something of an unreal exercise. A mere statement of points in the right direction is all that seems worthwhile. There is, first, a general principle of limiting intervention. Then one would consider improvements to procedure and dispositions in terms of better quality personnel, clear rationales for methods and measurements and a rational rather than prejudiced implementation of them. This would involve a number of things – for example, improving the nature, quality and quantity of information that is used within the system. The final point of principle would seem to be that some regard should be had to the need for intervention in the lives of youngsters in order to provide help rather than punishment.

8 Community Sentences and Orders

8.1   The Criminal Justice Act 2003

8.2   Statistics on community sentences and orders

8.3   Fines

8.4   Absolute and conditional discharge

8.5   Suspended sentence

8.6   Community rehabilitation orders (probation)

8.7   Community punishment orders (community service)

8.8   Community punishment and rehabilitation orders (combination orders)

8.9   Anti-social behaviour orders

8.10 Curfew orders

8.11 Electronic monitoring

8.12 Compensation orders

8.13 Forfeiture

8.14 The effectiveness of community sentences and orders

8.15 The generic community sentence

The Powers of Criminal Courts (Sentencing) Act 2000 provided a consolidation of existing statutory provisions in relation to community sentences and orders – the provisions themselves were not altered. The Criminal Justice Act 1991 was the basis of the system and it made provision for the following community orders: probation orders, community service orders, combination orders, curfew orders, supervision orders and attendance centre orders. These community sentences are only to be imposed where this can be justified by the seriousness of the offence. They stand between a disposal, such as a fine, which would be applicable where the level of seriousness would not justify a community sentence, and much more serious forms of offending which would satisfy the more onerous seriousness criteria required for custodial dispositions. The community order should be one most suitable for the offender and the restrictions on liberty imposed by the order must be commensurate with the seriousness of the offence. The Criminal Justice and Court Services Act 2000 changed the names of certain dispositions. Probation orders became community rehabilitation orders, community service orders became community punishment orders and

276

combination orders would became community punishment and rehabilitation orders. The old names have continued to be used so both will be used where a reminder seems appropriate.

8.1 The Criminal Justice Act 2003

The provisions that relate to the issues in this chapter are detailed below. It is important to note that, since most of the provisions of the Act did not come into force immediately upon Royal Assent, the earlier provisions will still be applicable for some time. In particular, we need to note that the Criminal Justice Act 2003 provides for the notion of a generic community sentence for those aged 16 and over. This will encompass all of the presently available community order options. The court will be able to select the appropriate requirements from a list containing options such as: an unpaid work requirement, an activity requirement or a programme requirement. The new system utilises many of the old ideas. The layout of the chapter is that the details of the original and, indeed, current system are provided first and then a separate treatment of the new developments is included.

This chapter is concerned then with the use of fines, community rehabilitation orders (probation), community punishment orders (community service), community punishment and rehabilitation orders (combination orders), absolute and conditional discharges, suspended sentences, curfew orders, anti-social behaviour orders, curfew orders, compensation orders, forfeiture orders and confiscation orders. This is not quite all of the possibilities but they are certainly the most important ones. Drug treatment orders, sex offender orders and hospital orders are some of the other options that are not considered here. Orders that only apply to those under 21, such as supervision orders and attendance centre orders, were considered in Chapter 7 and imprisonment is explored in Chapter 9. The material can be loosely described as non-custodial or community dispositions. Suspended sentences might be better treated as a custodial disposition, but since about 90 per cent of those who receive a suspension avoid custody, it is treated here as a means of avoiding custody.

Community sentences were portrayed by the government (Home Office (1996)) in the following terms – namely, that offenders have to undergo physically, mentally or emotionally challenging programmes and be required to conform to a structured regime. The courts may specify additional requirements in the interests of securing the rehabilitation of the offender or of protecting the public from harm or further crime. Examples of these are a requirement for drug or alcohol treatment, or to reside in a specified place, or not to approach or contact the victim. The punishment also includes the prospect of a prompt return to court if the offender fails to comply with the requirements of supervision so that the court can decide the appropriate course of action. This may mean a prison sentence if the original offence or offences attracted the possibility of custody.

8.2 Statistics on community sentences and orders

Table 23 provides some basic data on the usage of some of these sentences and orders in 2001: Home Office (2002a). The fine is by far the most used disposition followed by discharges, community rehabilitation orders and community punishment orders.

8.3 Fines

Fines are the most commonly used of the sentences available to the courts. They were used for as many as 69 per cent of offenders in 2001, a total of 934,300 cases. Fines were used for 77 per cent of those sentenced for summary non-motoring offences and 88 per cent of those sentenced for summary motoring offences in 1997. The use of fines is clearly decreasing as the figures for 1986 record a total of 1,598,100 fines being imposed. For indictable offences fines were used for 24 per cent of cases in 2001, whilst the figure was 39 per cent in 1986. Since fines tend to do better than other measures (though perhaps those fined are more likely to be the better risks) in recidivism studies, it does not seem to be progressive to reduce the use that is made of them. The legislative basis for fines is now the consolidating provision: see ss126–129 of the Powers of Criminal Courts (Sentencing) Act (2000).

Table 23

Community Sentences and Orders 2001 (thousands)			
	Magistrates' court	Crown Court	Total
Absolute discharge	15.1	0.1	15.2
Conditional discharge	98.8	2.4	103.2
Fine	927.6	2.6	950.2
Community rehabilitation order	51.0	8.0	59.0
Supervision order	10.5	0.6	11.1
Community punishment order	41.9	7.9	49.8
Attendance centre order	5.8	0.0	5.8
Community punishment and rehabilitation order	13.1	1.6	14.7
Curfew order	3.6	0.2	3.8
Suspended sentence	1.1	1.6	2.7

(Source: Criminal Statistics, England and Wales, 2001)

Magistrates' courts have maximum levels of fines that they can impose for particular offences. In relation to indictable offences there is a £5,000 limit, whilst for summary offences the amount will depend upon their position on a scale introduced by s37 of the Criminal Justice Act 1982. Point 5 is the highest point on the scale and the maximum for that is now £5,000. For Crown Courts there is no system for prescribing maximums, except in the sense that the very limited amount of appellate judgements on non-custodial sentences will provide constraints of a sort. As was seen in Chapter 7 there are separate provisions for young offenders. Since the Criminal Justice Act 1991 fines may be used in combination with community and custodial sentences and orders. In relation to individual defendants a number of decisions will have to be made in relation to the use of a fine. Fines should reflect the gravity of the particular offence, with adjustments being made for aggravating and mitigating circumstances, and then the financial position of the defendant in terms of the ability to pay. The means of the defendant can both increase and decrease the amount to be paid. A term of imprisonment that is appropriate in the case of default will be stated at the time of sentence and in an average case where prison is used for default the person would be there for a week. Time to pay the fine may be a further factor and where this occurs, in normal circumstances, the expectation must be that the fine will be paid within a 12-month period. Measures to collect in the case of default include: distress of goods, attachment of earnings, deduction of benefit, community service, driving disqualification and curfews backed up by electronic tagging. The final three in this list were provided for by the Crime (Sentences) Act 1997.

The advantages of fines

Fines offer many potential advantages as a sentence. They are clearly punitive thus offering a response to criminal behaviour whilst also carrying the hope of both individual and general deterrence. In non-problematic cases they involve no more than an order to pay money – thus they are largely non-interventionist in comparison with measures such as probation. As such the potential sigma of social engineering does not so readily adhere to them. They are flexible, being adaptable to the circumstances of both offences and offenders. Finally, not only are fines cheaper to use than other measures they also produce a very large amount of income.

Unit fines

Fines are not without their problems, the most notable of which is the difficulties involved in ensuring that fines are paid. The Criminal Justice Act 1991 tried to tackle this. The very poor were in the position that some other measure might be used against them, given their ability (or lack of it) to pay a fine. Or, if a fine was used, they might not be able to pay it. The 1991 Act provided for a system of unit fines which to a greater extent took into account the ability of defendants to pay. Offences were graded by seriousness into 50 units, with an amount per unit being prescribed. Then there was a means test, in relation to the person's weekly income, which determined the amount to be paid per unit. The system was based on the idea of the day fine. With a day fine the daily income of the individual would be multiplied by a figure that reflected the seriousness of the offence. The unit fine scheme was abandoned after it had been criticised – the large fines that were being imposed (on the employed) came in for particular criticism. To a lesser extent the small fines that were being imposed (on the unemployed) were also commented upon. One person was given a fine of £1,200 for dropping a crisp packet. Two neighbours who had driven without insurance received fines of £75 in one case and £1,500 in the other. The Criminal Justice Act 1993 provided a system centred more on the seriousness of the offence. Day fine systems have in fact worked well in other countries and there has been evidence from its use in England and Wales that it has merit. The particular scheme introduced (which had rather high amounts in relation to the units), coupled with media hype, probably caused the death of a good idea at that time. In March 2000 there was publicity in the press (Gibb (2000)) in relation to new sentencing guidelines that were to be introduced. These would, once again, more closely link fines to income, but with upper limits in relation to particular offences. So, for example, in a 40-mph speeding case a person could get a fine ranging from £60 to £400. The aims of this system are: to make fines fairer in terms of having the same impact or bite on offenders; to provide a scheme that will reduce the present variations between courts; and to avoid the problems of the first attempts to use unit fines. The 2000 Act provides for reference to financial circumstances in the fixing of fines.

Enforcement difficulties and the problem of disparity

The problem of enforcement leads to both costs for, and strains upon, the criminal justice system in relation to such agencies as the police, the courts, the probation service and most seriously the prison service. Imprisonment as an outcome is somewhat of a tragedy in cases where the original offence was not imprisonable. Figures for 1998 (White (1999)) reveal that 5,400 fine defaulters were received into prison department establishments with an average of 131 at any one time. The use of prison as a means to deal with fine defaulters has seen a welcome large reduction in recent years, the figure for 1985 was 20,500 receptions into prison department establishments. One final problem to be noted is that in a number of respects it is clear that there are different practices and methods operative in fine decision-making and enforcement. The courts have quite a lot of discretion as to the amount of the fine. A statutory scheme which contained more detailed provisions would be a good idea. The disparity is certainly apparent in that some courts are still using systems based on the unit fine ideas. Disparity means injustice for some.

In 2003 Prime Minister, Tony Blair, told an international conference that it is completely unacceptable that less than 60 per cent of fines are enforced. So, as the Lord Chancellor announced this year, there will be no more writing off of fines if they are uncollected after a year, a more robust process for automatically deducting fines from earnings, compulsory work for those who can't pay and contracting-out fine collection to the private sector where the courts can't deliver acceptable performance. It had already been the case that community-based responses were being used in nearly all cases for fine defaulters rather than custody. These included curfew orders and community service. The Courts Act 2003 'makes provisions for changes to the administrative system in relation to fines' enforcement. It is intended that experiments take place with these ideas before final provision is made for nationwide usage. Fines officers are to become the principal administrators of the system, the intention being, in part, the freeing-up of the time of the courts. It is also hoped to introduce a range of new sanctions to improve the effectiveness of fine enforcement. At present, performance in enforcing payment of fines is poor. Much of the work involved in enforcing fines is reserved to magistrates, including tasks that are essentially administrative in nature. The range of incentives and sanctions available to the courts are limited. Courts are constrained by legislation in the approach they can take to enforcing payment of fines and other financial penalties imposed after criminal proceedings. The Act creates the role of a fines officer to take enforcement action in certain circumstances, thus removing the need for all enforcement decisions to be taken by a court. A fines' collection system will be set up which introduces financial incentives to offenders to pay their fines, as well providing a range of new disincentives for fine default. The system is designed to encourage payment but will include new penalties for those who have the means and will not pay. For those who are genuinely unable to pay, the government expects to propose making alternative sentences (such as unpaid work) available to the courts. The overall intention is to ensure that fines are seen as credible and effective punishments.

8.4 Absolute and conditional discharge

Section 7 of the Powers of Criminal Courts Act 1973 provided for absolute and conditional discharges. The Crime and Disorder Act 1998 made some amendments concerning the ability of a court to combine the use of a discharge with other orders. The legislation was consolidated in ss12–15 of the Powers of Criminal Courts (Sentencing) Act 2000. An absolute discharge is where, after a finding of guilt, the court decides that neither punishment nor probation is desirable. Such a decision may be for reasons to do with both the offence and the offender – for example, because the offence is trivial, or the fact of conviction may be sufficient punishment or it may in essence be a comment on the prosecution suggesting that the prosecution was unwise. A conditional discharge has the effect that a person will remain liable to be sentenced for an offence for a specified period of up to three years. If convicted again during that period they may be sentenced for the earlier offence. As Table 23 reveals there were 103,200 conditional discharges and 15,200 absolute discharges in 2001. In 1987 there were 75,600 conditional discharges and 19,000 absolute discharges. There has over the period been an increase in the total numbers being sentenced. For indictable offences, it is a popular sentence for males in the 10–14 age group and for females generally. Breach rates are low for conditional discharges and that prison can very often be avoided in any cases of breach.

8.5 Suspended sentence

The Criminal Justice Act 1967 provided for a system of suspended sentences, which was introduced in 1968. Suspended sentences may be better treated as a custodial disposition, but since about 90 per cent of those who receive a suspension avoid custody, it is treated here as a community disposition. It was intended to operate as an alternative to custody. In 2001 there were 2,700 suspended sentences, a figure that is much lower than that for 1987 when there was 29,200 fully suspended sentences of which 25,800 were for indictable offences. For indictable offences alone in 1977, there were 30,600 suspended sentences. There was a move away from the use of suspended sentences as a result of the Criminal

Justice Act 1991. The figure for 1993 was 2,300 cases, so of late there has been a small increase in its use. For those under 21, suspended sentences have not been possible since 1983. The Criminal Law Act 1977 provided for partly suspended sentences, which were introduced in 1982. The Criminal Justice Act 1982 amended the original legislation. However, this system was to be removed by the Criminal Justice Act 1991 as it did not fit in with the early-release scheme that was being introduced.

It is the Powers of Criminal Courts (Sentencing) Act 2000, ss118–125, that provides for suspended sentences at present. Where a court has decided that a sentence of two years or less is desirable it can suspend the sentence. This will only be possible where the exceptional circumstances of the case justify it and this provision curtailed the use of the suspended sentence. In the period before the 1991 Act, the suspended sentence, had not always been used as an alternative to custody as it should have been. The period of supervision (the operational period) must be between one and two years. The court should consider imposing a fine or a compensation order in addition. The sentence offers the choice of 'behave or else', it can hope to have more teeth than probation as an individual deterrent. The prison sentence cannot be activated unless there is a conviction for an imprisonable offence during the operational period. If there is such a conviction, a court will have to decide if the suspended sentence should be activated in full or in part. It may instead decided to extend the order, to provide for an operational period of up to two years or it may make no order so that the original order continues. When a suspended sentence is used it may not be accompanied by a community rehabilitation order. If the sentence is one of more than six months the Crown Court can use a suspended sentence supervision order for some or all of the operational period. This provides for supervision to the extent that there are requirements of keeping in touch with the supervisor and informing him of any change of address. The offender does not have to consent to this. A breach of the supervision element cannot lead to activation of the suspended sentence – at most a fine can be imposed. In 2001, 11 per cent of suspended sentences were breached, which is a good outcome in comparison to other dispositions.

The Criminal Justice Act 2003 provides for reform of suspended sentences, in relation to short custodial sentences. For these the operation of the suspended sentence will include the addition of requirements of various sorts taken from the community sentence possibilities. At the moment it is a case of being told that you are free and will remain so unless you are convicted again during the life of the order. Under the new suspended sentence the court will have the power to review the progress of the offender if it chooses and alter the requirements accordingly.

The sentence was originally intended to reduce the pressure on the prisons by offering a non-custodial alternative. As with much in the penal system the new initiative had not been thought through – the impact on both sentencers and offenders was not worked out in advance and a detailed prior examination of the issues would have provided warnings of possible pitfalls. Ancel (1971) for example provided details of historical and comparative material which showed that one possibility is that the courts may impose longer initial sentences if they are being asked to suspend sentences. That sentencers may use these options as alternatives to alternatives to custody could also have been foreseen. It is certainly a lesson that seems to have been learnt. Writers are now reluctant to recommend new initiatives in case they would be used in unforeseen or undesirable ways. It soon became clear that the suspended sentence was being used in ways other than as an alternative to custody. The Court of Appeal in *R v O'Keefe* [1969] 2 QB 29 had to remind sentencers that imprisonment must be decided upon first and then the issue of suspension can be raised. The Powers of Criminal Courts Act 1973 gave statutory reinforcement to this. When used for those who would not otherwise have been given a custodial sentence, the result was that more people would be put at risk of custody, with the risk also of increased numbers in prison. Stanley and Baginsky (1984) by examining the sentencing practices of magistrate's courts came to the conclusion that introducing suspended sentences had the effect of putting more people at risk of custody. It seemed that this option was used as an alternative to non-custodial sentences such as fines and probation, as well as an alternative to custody. This can lead to more people receiving custody when breach occurs and the rate of breach was higher in the past. It was stated in a report on sentencing (Home Office (1978)) that 'If the main object of the suspended sentence was to reduce the prison population, there are considerable doubts as to whether it has achieved this effect. It may even have increased the prison population' (1978:117).

Bottoms (1981) indicates there are many unanswered questions about suspended sentences:

'What, then, is the suspended sentence? Is it a let-off, or is it the most serious penalty available to the courts, technically held in abeyance? Is it a custodial or non-custodial sentence? Is it only appropriate for "extremely carefully selected" cases (Leighton (1971)), or is it of much more general application? There are no very clear answers to these questions in the everyday practice of the criminal courts in this country, and foreign experience suggests that others have also found the suspended sentence confusing (Ancel (1971) and Sebba (1969)). Truly there is, as David Thomas once remarked, a marked element of penological ambiguity about the suspended sentence.' (1981:16)

The operation of the suspended sentence since the implementation of the Criminal Justice Act 1991 was examined by Stone (1994). This is still relevant as the Powers of Criminal Courts (Sentencing) Act 2000 was only a consolidating measure. He explored the way in which the requirement of exceptional circumstances, before suspended sentences could be used, was handled in practice by the courts. His evidence was not in line with the view of the Lord Chief Justice in *R v Robinson* (1992) 14 Cr App R (S) 559 who stated 'the instances in which a suspended sentence will be appropriate will be few and far between.' On the contrary it seems that the measure retains an enduring pragmatic appeal and has not been completely marginalised by the 1991 Act. Stone tells us that the courts in his sample:

'... clearly wished to mark the offence with a custodial sentence without requiring the offender to incur the pains of imprisonment. This sentencing tactic was sometimes observable even in the absence of any exceptional factors, for example in dealing with breach of a regulatory court order (such as keeping a dog whilst disqualified or being involved in the management of a company while an undischarged bankrupt). Here the court perhaps hoped to leave the offender in no doubt of the unacceptability of such behaviour, while holding back from the ultimate sanction. In other instances the court seemed simply very reluctant to send the offender to prison and seized upon the suspended sentence as a convenient route of retreat with dignity. For example, in sentencing a woman convicted of cruelty to a child, described in the pre-sentence report as reluctant to take responsibility for her behaviour and very preoccupied with her own emotional needs and drug dependency, the judge justified suspension of sentence by referring to her guilty plea, the fact that the case had been pending for over a year, the unlikelihood that she would resume care of the child in the immediate future and the "lamentable lack of support and advice" from her mother during the critical period. ... Few if any of the cases resulting in a suspended sentence in this study would have satisfied the stringent approach of the Court of Appeal demonstrated in *R v Lowery* (1992) 14 Cr App R (S) 485 and *R v Robinson* (1992) 14 Cr App R (S) 559. However, only 2 per cent of offenders sentenced to suspended sentences at Crown Court in 1992 appealed against sentence and that appeal rate is now likely to be even smaller. As a consequence, although "exceptional circumstances" may seem a somewhat questionable or even spurious concept, it is likely that courts will continue to opt for an exceptional course of sentence for a variety of familiar reasons. Furthermore, the more recent Court of Appeal decisions finding exceptionality may signal greater flexibility and bolster the courts' reluctance to "kill off" the suspended sentence.' (1994:407–408)

8.6 Community rehabilitation orders (probation)

The Criminal Justice and Court Services Act 2000 changed the names of certain dispositions and probation orders became community rehabilitation orders. The Act also provides a major restructuring of the probation service with the existing 54 separate probation services being merged into a national service: the National Probation Service for England and Wales. The aim of the reorganisation is efficiency and so to allow the Home Secretary to give directions to the boards that will operate in the 42 local areas. The areas will correspond with police force areas. This is part of the government's aim of improving efficiency by creating common boundaries across all the agencies in the criminal justice system; the Crown Prosecution Service has recently been reformed in this manner. The boards would be composed of representatives of local communities who understand local needs. The aim of the probation service is to be the protection of the public and to reduce re-offending through the effective enforcement of community sentences. The earlier responsibility for family court work did not fit well with this and so a separate body (the Children And Family Court Advisory and Support Service (CAFCASS)) is responsible for the family work. The Powers of Criminal Courts (Sentencing) Act 2000 included probation in its consolidation in ss41–45.

The work of probation officers

Probation officers and the probation service carry out numerous tasks. They will be considered at various places within this chapter as well as elsewhere in this book. The particular aspect of this work that will be concentrated upon here is their involvement with community rehabilitation orders. This aspect of their work seems to be the best point at which to provide a general account of probation officers and the community rehabilitation service and this will also be undertaken. A non-exhaustive list of their tasks demonstrates both the extent and variety of their activities. To the numerous activities involved in community rehabilitation orders there must be added the similar work carried out in relation to juveniles on supervision orders. Suspended sentence supervision orders, community punishment orders and various financial orders provide other tasks. Social work is carried out in custodial institutions. After release, some prisoners are subject to parole supervision and after-care for prisoners is a further responsibility. Reports and other services are provided for the courts. Various forms of liaison work is carried out, involving for example community schemes, crime prevention and contact with magistrates.

The history of the probation service

A brief account of the history of the probation service is useful as background to the material developed later. The first signs of a probation type of activity in the system were appointees of the Church of England Temperance Society. The first of these was appointed in 1876 and in their position as police court missionaries they sought to save the drunks that were coming before the courts from harsh penalties and then to save their souls. Whilst not part of the formal court structure they were increasingly used by the courts for a variety of tasks – such as providing assistance to those before the courts and providing information to the courts. These developments were to mean that their involvement was not just with drunks, they also started to have responsibilities in relation to prisoners. A more formal system of probation resulted from the Probation of Offenders Act 1907 and the Criminal Justice Acts of 1925 and 1948. The 1925 Act introduced a mandatory system of probation officers and the 1948 Act gave us in essence what we have today – some central direction and control in an essentially local system. There are 54 probation areas but this will change with the enactment of the Criminal Justice and Court Services Act 2000. The period after the 1907 Act up to the 1970s was one of growth in the use of probation and it was a measure that was popular with both the courts and those who commentated upon its use. Matters have been rather different of late. In order to explain why this should be a further excursion into history is required. McWilliams (1983), (1985), (1986) and (1987) in a series of articles identifies certain stages in the development of probation. The period up to 1930 was the 'saving souls' stage which was followed by a period from 1930 to 1970 in which there was a belief in the possibilities of a scientific approach. Probation officers saw their role as one of diagnosis and cure through treatment. The perceived failure of treatment as an approach partly explains why since the 1960s there has been both less confidence in, and less use made of, probation. The 1960s and 1970s were periods in which the tasks of the probation service were considerably increased. The problems for the probation service were to grow in the 1990s as we saw an era in which the desires were the protection of the public, that the punishment should fit the crime and that there was to be punishment in the community. This does not fit in that well with a desire to help clients.

The new National Probation Service which was created in April 2001 was a move towards punishment and a move away from helping offenders. Probation was to be part of delivering the aims of the criminal justice system, such as crime reduction and law enforcement. The 1970s had seen the decline of treatment. Movements were made by the probation service towards providing alternatives to custody and help rather than treatment. From 1979 attempts were made by the government to further change the ethos of the service and the government also wanted more control so they started a move towards centralisation that would assist both accountability and consistency. This was to culminate in the two Acts in 2000. 'What Works' ideas (see Mair (1997)) were starting to be adopted in the 1970s but then punishment in the community became the new government mantra. This would involve more intensive programmes and surveillance. After the Criminal Justice Act 1991 probation was to protect the public, reduce offending and to rehabilitate – quite a change from its historical role.

Raynor and Vanstone (2002) note that:

'By the end of the 1970s the treatment model was being strongly criticised on a number of empirical and ethical grounds. Empirically, studies of the effectiveness of penal sanctions of all kinds had produced generally discouraging results, and while this was not true of all studies, the general impression that nothing works was reinforced by journalistic summaries (Martinson (1974)) and by the overall conclusions of wide-ranging research reviews (Lipton et al (1975); Brody (1976)). These findings also gained strength from what were essentially moral or philosophical arguments against treatments, such as that it dehumanised its subjects, or that it rested on unsubstantiated claims of superior professional wisdom (Bottoms and McWilliams (1979)). Legal scholars were increasingly questioning whether unreliable predictions about future behaviour should continue to influence sentencing and argued instead for proportionate justice based on the seriousness of the offence (Hood (1974); Von Hirsch (1976)). Meanwhile researchers on juvenile justice following the treatment-oriented 1969 Children and Young Persons Act were beginning to document unintended adverse consequences such as increased incarceration following the failure of community-based supervision to prevent further offending (Thorpe et al (1980)). It began to appear that young offenders, like their older counterparts, might actually benefit from proportionate tariff sentencing which did not aim to do them good but would at least avoid the excesses of overambitious compulsory treatment. If the emphasis of the 1970s had been on doing good without much success in demonstrating that good was being done, the 1980s were to be about avoiding harm, in particular by reducing unnecessary incarceration. This seemed a more achievable aim, and one which might commend itself on the grounds of economy even to communities or politicians who were not in sympathy with the underlying humanitarian aim. So began the era of alternatives to custody: probation was to be a non-custodial penalty aiming to increase its market share and reduce imprisonment, rather than a treatment aiming to change people. By the end of the 1980s these principles were well enough accepted to be argued in green and white papers and were embodied in the 1991 Criminal Justice Act, which articulated for the first time in legislation a sentencing rationale based on punishment proportionate to the seriousness of the offence.' (2002:55–56)

Priorities and responsibilities

In 1996 the role of probation was explained in the following terms by the government in *Protecting the Public*: Home Office (1996). It is the probation service's responsibility to supervise adult offenders in the community. This is so that their clients can lead law-abiding lives. Minimising risk to the public is also important. The local probation services in England and Wales provide a wide range of community service placements, providing unpaid work for the benefit of the community, and a wide range of demanding and constructive activities and other forms of supervision. Supervision will include work to confront offending behaviour, so that offenders are aware of the impact of their crimes on their victims and the community and work to instil a greater sense of personal responsibility and discipline, aiding re-integration as a law-abiding member of society.

The government sets priorities for the probation service on the basis of a rolling three-year plan. The Home Secretary's priorities for the probation service at that time were:

1. to ensure that community sentences provide a tough and demanding punishment which is effective in reducing crime;
2. to make community supervision safer for the public by enhanced risk assessment, enforcement and management; and
3. to improve both the quality of service delivery and the use of resources.

Other changes that have been taking place include moving probation away from social work (training is no longer a social work course but rather a community justice degree and vocational training). Integration with the prison service is on the agenda and the government has even considered full merger. The changes to the names of the orders to include punishment were telling and we nearly had a Community Punishment and Rehabilitation Service.

Section 41 of the 2000 Act provides the statutory basis for what are now community rehabilitation orders. It allows probation to be used for a person of or over the age of 16 years who is convicted of an offence. The court has to be of the opinion that the supervision of the offender by a probation officer is desirable in the interests of securing the rehabilitation of the offender, or protecting the public from harm from him or preventing the commission by him of further offences. It is an order requiring him to be under the supervision of a probation officer for a period specified in the order of not less than six months nor more than three years. Before making a probation order, the court has to explain to the offender, in ordinary language, the effect of the order (including any additional requirements proposed to be included in the order) and the consequences which may follow if he fails to comply. Additional requirements, under s42, can cover such as a place of residence, the requirement to undergo drug or psychiatric treatment, to attend a probation centre and either to perform specified activities or to desist from other activities. The person must express his willingness to comply with the order and its requirements. An offender subject to a probation order has to keep in touch with the probation officer responsible for his supervision. This must be in accordance with any instructions given by that officer. Where the offender changes his address he must inform the probation officer.

The National Standards for Probation 2000

The government published the first National Standards for the work of probation services and social services departments in 1992. Further sets of standards were produced in 1995 and 2000. They set the required standards of practice for probation services and social services departments in England and Wales in relation to the supervision of offenders in the community and in providing services to the courts.

Levels of contact

By way of example of the nature of the 2000 Standard, the required levels of contact and how to achieve compliance are described as follows. It states that achieving the minimum required levels of contact, and enforcing supervision rigorously, serves two main purposes – it satisfies the courts and the community that a credible level of disciplined supervision is taking place and also ensures that offenders have the opportunity to engage in effective supervision. The Standards set the minimum requirements and are likely to be exceeded for offenders who pose risks of serious harm to the public, or have a higher probability of reoffending, or for those who may be subject to additional order or licence requirements. In terms of the required levels of contact, for those aged under 22 or serving 12 months or more in custody, the home probation service shall provide the offender with a supervising officer or case manager within ten working days of sentencing. The levels and nature of contact between prisoners, prison staff and the offender's supervising (or managing) officer are not specified in these Standards. Staff are expected to use their judgement to ensure that there is sufficient contact at the pre-release stage to enable the successful resettlement of the offender and the preparation of a supervision plan. Supervising officers shall ensure that they refer to, and act in accordance with official guidance when dealing with arrangements for offenders sentenced to life imprisonment. If an offender has spent sufficient time on remand to be released on licence direct from the court, and no supervising officer has been appointed, the court duty probation officer shall give the supervising probation area as much detail as possible about the offender and the release address, and arrange for the licence to be served. The police shall be given release, licence and address information as soon as practicable and in any case within ten working days of release. Wherever possible the date of the first appointment for those on community orders should be given to the offender, either by the probation service or by the bench (acting on probation service advice) before the offender leaves court. This should be arranged to take place within five working days of the order being made.

The first meeting

At the first meeting the probation service shall ensure that for all offenders the supervising officer shall provide written information setting out what is expected of the offender during the period of supervision and what the offender can expect from the probation service. The probation officer shall explain the instructions to the offender (and provide a copy of the instructions setting out the required standards of behaviour that apply during the period of supervision), which shall prohibit:

1. further offending;
2. violent or aggressive behaviour or threats of violence;
3. other conduct or language that might reasonably give offence to probation staff, other persons on supervision or members of the public;
4. other wilful or persistent non co-operation or behaviour designed to frustrate the purpose of the offender's or others' supervision.

They must also ensure that offenders sign their order or licence (where possible) and indicate that they understand its requirements. Appointments that count towards meeting the Standard are those made in connection with the supervision plan and include appointments with partnership agencies, such as for drug counselling. All such appointments are enforceable and appropriate enforcement action must be taken if any appointment is missed.

Probation statistics

The probation statistics that follow are drawn from Home Office: Home Office (2002e). The first set of data examines the use of community sentences by the courts. In 2001 community sentences were imposed in 32 per cent of sentences for indictable offences, a similar percentage to the 30 per cent in 2000. However, the two types of court had different trends. In the Crown Court the proportion has fallen from 30 per cent in 1995 to 27 per cent in 1996, and then risen to 28 per cent in 1997–1998 before falling back to 27 per cent in 1999 and to 26 per cent in 2000, before returning to 27 per cent in 2001. But, in magistrates' courts, the proportion was steady at 27–28 per cent during 1994 and 1995, before increasing slightly to 29 per cent in 1996–1999 and then to 31 per cent in 2000 and 33 per cent in 2001. Magistrates' courts imposed 88 per cent of all community sentences in 2001. In 2001 magistrates' courts passed 46 per cent of all new prison sentences for indictable offences. The proportion sentenced to community punishment orders (formerly a community service order) or a community rehabilitation order (formerly probation) for indictable violence against the person offences has nearly doubled between 1990 and 2001. For community rehabilitation orders the proportion rose from 7 per cent to 12 per cent and for community punishment orders from 8 per cent to 15 per cent.

Reports prepared for the courts

The number of pre-sentence reports and specific sentence reports written in 2001 (246,000) was 1 per cent lower than in 2000 (249,200). Pre-sentence reports written for adult magistrates' courts fell by 7 per cent in 2001 and the number written for the youth court continued to fall sharply as the youth offending teams took over responsibility for this work. In the Crown Court the number of pre-sentence reports fell 4 per cent to 51,700.

Criminal court orders

The total number of people starting community sentences in 2001 was almost the same as in 2000 at 122,500. However, the types of orders given are changing, with an increase in the use of community punishment orders and community rehabilitation orders but a decrease in the use of community punishment and rehabilitation orders (formerly combination orders). Table 24 provides further details.

Offences

Of those commencing community sentences in 2001, theft and handling stolen goods, represented the largest specific offence group at 22 per cent. However, since 1993 the proportion has decreased significantly, having been 26 per cent at that time.

Previous criminal history

When community punishment and rehabilitation orders were first introduced, the courts used almost half of them (49 per cent in 1993) for offenders who had previously served a

Table 24

Persons Starting Criminal Supervision by the Probation Service (thousands)

Court orders	1996	2001
Community rehabilitation orders	49.1	54.5
Community punishment orders	46.5	52.2
Community punishment and rehabilitation orders	17.0	15.5
Suspended sentence supervision orders	0.5	0.4
Money payment supervision orders	6.4	1.3
All court orders	115.4	122.5

(Source: Probation Statistics, England and Wales 2001)

prison sentence. However, the 1996–2001 figures suggest that there is now little difference between community rehabilitation orders and community punishment and rehabilitation orders in terms of the offender's previous criminal history. For both orders in 2000, about a third of offenders had a previous prison sentence and about a quarter had no previous convictions. Over the last eight years the proportions of the three main orders that have gone to those with no previous convictions have grown considerably. This is part of a general trend towards more severe sentencing.

Orders – additional requirements

In 1991, 24 per cent of new community rehabilitation orders had an additional requirement. This proportion rose to 33 per cent in 1997 and in 2001 was 31 per cent. The requirement to participate in a specified activity has shown steady growth for a number of years. There were 9 per cent of all community rehabilitation orders with such a requirement in 1989 and 25 per cent in 2001.

Average workload per maingrade officer

(Note that a maingrade officer is one that is fully trained as distinct from other employees of the probation service.) These figures give only a rough measure of workload. The actual workload depends not only on the number and length of orders but also on their complexity and the amount of supervision provided. Over time, national standards, for example, will have changed the work involved in preparing pre-sentence reports and supervising offenders on community sentences. Also probation service officers are increasingly being used for some work which would traditionally have been done by maingrade officers. The average number of people supervised per maingrade officer has risen each year since 1992 from 20.7 to 40.7 in 2001. This shows the rising caseloads and falling or stable numbers of fully trained maingrade officers. Total reports completed per officer continued to rise from 51.8 in 1993 to 72.2 in 2001. The average court order caseload per officer rose each year between 1992 and 1998 from 11.3 to 18.3. This reflected the growth in caseload and the fact that numbers of maingrade officers have fallen or remained stable. The average remained unchanged in 1999 at 18.3 but fell for the first time since 1992 to 17.7 at the end of 2000. This fall reflects the fact that a large number of 16–17-year-olds who were formerly the responsibility of the probation service were under the supervision of youth offending teams. However, this figure rose again to 19.0 in 2001. There were some 1,100 trainee probation officers in post at 31 December 2001.

Strategies for effective offender supervision

The Inspectorate of Probation made suggestions (Home Office (1998e)) as regards strategies for effective offender supervision. The following were suggested as points to adopt:

1. programmes which seek to modify offenders' patterns of thinking and behaving are generally more successful than techniques like group or individual counselling;
2. programmes need to be closely matched to the needs and learning styles of offenders;
3. consistency in programme content to allow evaluation.

Points to improve upon included:

1. widening the use of structured risk-assessment processes;
2. availability of a sufficient range of programmes to allow a match with offender needs;
3. dealing with non-attenders at programmes;
4. more use of community service;
5. better quality control of supervisors.

Changing Offenders' Attitudes and Behaviour: What Works?

A Home Office report entitled *Changing Offenders' Attitudes and Behaviour: What Works?* (Mair (1997)) contains a literature review and the findings of a survey into the workings of specific forms of probation practice. Evidence was found that some forms of intervention work better than others – particularly if they are targeted at certain offender types. It is also clear that the performance of some measures are undermined in practice because of lack of rigour in the delivery of them. There was a need for better evaluation of the measures used. As part of this research, Vennard et al (1997) examined the use of cognitive-behavioural approaches with offenders. They reported from a literature search that programmes which draw upon cognitive skills and behavioural methods are reported as achieving higher levels of effectiveness than those which employ group or individual counselling and favour traditional non-directive therapy. The use of cognitive-behavioural methods in a multi-modal programme, which includes life skills and social skills training, shows the most positive results with both juvenile and adult offenders. This combination of components and techniques has also shown some success when targeted on particular groups of offenders – notably, sex offenders and violent offenders – although in most such studies the assessment of effectiveness is confined to clinical outcomes. Certain important caveats surround these seemingly promising findings. The first is that the research literature does not demonstrate that cognitive behavioural approaches, or indeed, any other type of approach, routinely produce major reductions in re-offending among a mixed population of offenders. Caveats aside it does seem that there is some evidence that some things work.

Hedderman and Sugg (1997) also investigated cognitive approaches and they carried out a survey of probation programmes. They sent out a questionnaire to all probation areas

291

asking for information about the extent to which the programmes they operated, or had access to, made use of cognitive skills training. Cognitive skills was defined for the purposes of this survey as an approach which attempted to reduce re-offending by teaching offenders to analyse and modify their thinking. The survey results reveal that since the late 1980s a majority of probation areas have developed or bought programmes with a cognitive skills or cognitive-behavioural dimension. Two-thirds of the areas which ran such programmes were running between five and ten of them. The limited information provided on costs shows that such programmes do not come cheap, yet areas appear to have spent remarkably little time or effort on examining whether such programmes work. In most areas it seems that they do not even know how many people attend, who drops out and why, and who succeeds and why. While offender and staff feedback can be useful ways of examining how user-friendly such programmes are, they are a poor source of data on overall effectiveness in modifying patterns of thinking and reducing reoffending.

The survey also suggests that while the probation service has picked up on the message that 'something works' and recognise that 'cognitive skills' and 'cognitive-behaviourism' are central to this, they have not committed themselves fully to 'what works' principles. In particular, this survey shows a lack of commitment to programme integrity. This is apparent in the fact that the duration and intensity of programmes is commonly altered; and from the fact that staff training is limited or even non-existent. Programmes also seem to function without reference to risk and needs principles. Mixing offenders on parole with others subject to additional requirements and those attending voluntarily may keep programme numbers high, but is unlikely to achieve programmes which are well matched to the levels of risk, and criminogenic needs, of the offenders who attend. While sex-offender programmes tend to be (comparatively) well organised, run by well trained staff, and able to draw on outside expertise, they too are rarely restricted to serious offenders.

Rex (2003) examined the potential of the application of restorative approaches to community-based sanctions and noted:

> 'Several commentators have noted the reparative potential of community service, or the opportunity in cognitive behavioural programmes to make offenders more aware of victims' perspectives or even to have contact with victims of offences similar to those they have committed. But there is clearly scope to go further in developing the restorative aspect of community penalties, which might be linked with promoting the communicative potential of community-based supervision. Thus, Duff (2000) advocates that victim-offender mediation should be routinely built into probation orders, organised and conducted by the supervising probation officer so that the offender communicates to the wider community, as well as to the victim, his apologetic recognition of the wrong that he has done.' (2003:52)

A STOP (straight thinking on probation) programme developed in Mid-Glamorgan, based on cognitive-behavioural ideas achieved better results than similar offenders who were sent to custody. This success was for both the measures used: re-offending rates and changes to attitudes in a positive direction. These ideas became one of the systems adopted, as part of probation's adoption of a 'what works' approach. It became part of the new way forward. Raynor and Vanstone (2002) make the following attempt to provide a recipe for what works:

> 'The message of these various strands of research was encouraging: far from nothing working,

it appeared that appropriate forms of supervision were capable of delivering reductions in offending of between 10 and 20 per cent, or even more in some cases Conversely, the wrong kind of supervision could do harm. Taken together, the research pointed to a number of characteristics of effective supervision which are listed in slightly different ways by different authorities but cover the same ground, and can be summarised as follows. In the present state of our knowledge, it appears likely that the more effective programmes are those which:

1) target high-risk offenders who are otherwise likely to continue to offend, rather than low-risk offenders who may gain little benefit or be harmed. This is Andrews's risk principle, nowadays usually interpreted as guidance to target a medium to high range, as the very highest-risk offenders are likely to be unresponsive except perhaps to very high levels of intervention, beyond what one programme is likely to provide. "Risk" here refers to likelihood of reconviction rather than to dangerousness.

2) focus on criminogenic need, that is, those characteristics or circumstances of offenders which have contributed to their offending (equivalent to dynamic risk factors). This is Andrews's need principle.

3) are highly structured, making clear and explicit demands and following a logical sequence determined by their learning goals.

4) use a directive working approach, so that participants know what they are meant to be doing.

5) use broadly cognitive-behavioural methods, to provide opportunities to learn new thinking and behaviour. This kind of multi-modal, skills-oriented focus is likely to offer a learning style accessible to many offenders, and therefore to help to satisfy Andrews's "responsivity principle" that programmes must promote the engagement and involvement of offenders by using an appropriate learning style and delivery.

6) are best located in the community (though this does not mean they are ineffective in prison).

7) have programme integrity, that is, are delivered as intended, with procedures to ensure this.

8) have committed and effective management.

9) have appropriately trained staff who believe they can be effective.

10) have adequate resources for continuity.

11) have integral evaluation and feedback ideally involving external researchers.' (2002:88–89)

Thus, there was a move in thinking from nothing works to what works. One problem with the 'what works' approach is that experimental programmes may be carried out by the highly motivated whilst the day-to-day practice may be less well motivated or even hostile. Also, it is difficult to ensure that an idea will be implemented as desired. As Chapman and Hough (1998) point out there are many things that can go wrong: supervisor variables generally and in the way they interpret such as additional requirements in orders – amount and type of referral, poor attendance and monitoring and record-keeping, poor selection processes for such as referral etc – to which could be added such as availability of resources. In overall terms resources will be limited but also there is variation of provision. Farrall (2002) adds to this theme and notes that maybe the research on what works is itself perhaps problematic. To get consistent and generalisable results is not going to be easy given that there are so many variables that are difficult, if not impossible, to control.

Rex (2003) suggests that what works seems to be linked to moving towards different life patterns: a steady job, a long term relationship and less contact with those still involved in delinquent/criminal activities. What may also be important for young offenders is the provision of practical help – eg finances, referral for such as drugs or housing, health issues, employment etc. Rex (2003) suggests the need for some changes in direction:

'These suggestions entail a further point. Namely, a step back from the *exclusive* focus on cognitive behavioural work which has dominated the probation work and "What Works?" agendas in recent years. As Rex (1999: 373) has correctly noted, even the original architects of such programmes saw them as *complementing* the social and economic problems faced by probationers. This is not to suggest that cognitive behavioural work is to be abandoned but, rather, that whilst it correctly focuses on increasing probationers' human capital, it is unable to address the wider social contexts in which these probationers live and as such is unable to address such social and economic needs. What is required is a research project which attempts to "fuse" together developments in individual cognitive abilities and changes in their social contexts.

The current project has suggested that probation supervision "works" indirectly through allowing the probationer's life to develop positively. Ensuring how best to enable those developments to occur and designing working practices which will enable probation officers to intervene more readily should form the next stage of research into probation effectiveness.' (2003:228)

Assessing the probation service

A study by Mair and May (1997), *Offenders on Probation,* provides an account of research carried out in 1994 and it provides a further means of assessing the probation service. Instead of the normal reconviction rates, in this study the point of view of those supervised is presented. The survey was restricted to those who had been sentenced to a probation or combination order, and covered 22 of the then 55 probation areas in England and Wales. The sample of offenders in each area was drawn at random. In total the issued sample consisted of 3,300 offenders. Nearly 40 per cent of the sample could not be contacted, mainly because they had been taken into custody, their order had terminated, or they had been transferred to another area. The effective sample, after subtracting those not contactable, was 1,980. Of these, 1,213 interviews were achieved, giving a response rate of 61 per cent. It is possible that those who failed to keep survey appointments will tend to have a less favourable attitude to the probation service than those included. The possibility of bias should be kept in mind when examining the findings.

Offenders were asked why they thought they had been given a probation/combination order rather than another sentence. The most common response (27 per cent) was that the court had wanted the offender to benefit from the services available while on probation. No one mentioned that they had been given their current sentence to stop them re-offending. Nine out of ten thought that their probation order had been useful. The most common reason given for this view was that it gave them someone independent to talk to about problems. A third mentioned getting practical help or advice with specific problems, and about 20 per cent mentioned being helped to keep out of trouble and avoid offending. Over half did not mention any bad points, for those that did it was factors to do with travelling to appointments that was most mentioned. These criticisms help to suggest that orders are achieving the objective of restricting liberty and punishing offenders. More than half the sample did not mention any bad points at all. Women and older offenders were more likely to see their orders as very useful. Nearly three-quarters of respondents said that being on probation had helped them understand their offending behaviour, and almost two-thirds said that they thought being on probation would help them stay out of trouble in the future.

There is no doubt that probation officers are seen in a very positive light by offenders. Previous studies have found this to be the case – albeit for different reasons – and this survey provides confirmation of earlier findings. Such a finding may not please those who desire probation to be more punitive. However, offenders who see probation in a positive light are more likely to turn up for meetings with their probation officers, more willing to listen, and more likely to try to put into practice what is suggested to them. If probation was seen negatively, offenders would be more likely to fail to appear for supervision. This would lead to more breach action and – ultimately – increases in the custodial population.

Previous research has demonstrated the deprived background of those on probation (Stewart and Stewart (1993)), and the survey provides confirmation of this. Most respondents were not working and dependent on state benefits, they had difficulty paying bills, were poorly qualified educationally and not particularly healthy. A significant minority had spent time in care as a child. There is little doubt amongst criminologists that such factors are associated with offending, although the precise relationship between them remains unclear. Their presence cannot be ignored by probation officers and much probation work is focused on trying to alleviate the problems caused by such characteristics. In terms of their background, probationers are very similar to prisoners.

What happened on probation? Offending behaviour was the most commonly discussed topic during supervision, although other matters related to the characteristics of offenders were also talked about – employment, accommodation, money, personal and family problems. Groupwork was not uncommon and outside agencies were used frequently. Such a picture of probation work will not be surprising to those who are familiar with the service. Most offenders considered that they understood their offending behaviour better as a result of probation supervision, yet one-third had committed further offences since being on probation.

In conclusion it is clear that the message contained in this report is a good one for the probation service; it is viewed favourably by most of those it supervises, and seems to work hard at trying to achieve its formal aims and objectives as stated in the National Standards.

This research was valuable in that it did not judge probation by the crude and simple device of reconviction. To do so you would have to tackle issues such as how many crimes of what type over what time period is a failure? There is always the problem of the dark number: the offenders that never come to the attention of the criminal justice system. Such an approach would also not take into account possible positives in terms of improved life chances and attributes. You also have to consider the environment in which the offender finds himself as a variable. People are likely to do best say if they are in an area where good jobs are available rather than bad or no jobs. Given the variables – eg offender and supervisor, the range of factors and problems, the differences in approach which may or may not have been suitable for the particular problem – what can you learn from this type of research and to what extent is every supervision something of a one off? We still do not understand the process of how, say, a one-to-one supervision may have worked. In order to judge the effectiveness of interventions such as probation, we would need to know exactly what was done. If there was a good outcome, we would be able to say that the important variable was the supervision, rather than a favourable environment or some other factor. We would also need to understand exactly what was done so that it could be replicated, assuming it is suitable for a range of offence and offender types. This being based on the premise that all the supervisions went the same way in the experimental programme. This whole approach largely assumes that one size fits all – or do you need different systems for the complex permutation of differing environments, offences, offenders and supervisors? It may be that the supervisor is an important variable and that a good worker, whatever that is, would get good results regardless of the method. It is going to be very difficult to know exactly what you are measuring if you do research into the complexities of the probation service.

The future for probation

This is difficult to predict at the moment. The community rehabilitation order is still popular with the courts, with a notable growth in the extent to which extra requirements are added to community rehabilitation orders. The order is being used for less serious offenders than in the past. Perhaps this shows a lack of faith in probation, as does the decline in its use for property offenders.

8.7 Community punishment orders (community service)

The Criminal Justice and Court Services Act 2000 changed the names of certain dispositions. Community service orders became community punishment orders. At present the orders are available in relation to those aged 16 and above where the offence is imprisonable. The Powers of Criminal Courts Act 1973 was the main statute, the Criminal Justice Act 1982 made its use for 16 year olds possible (originally the minimum age was 17) and the Crime and Disorder Act 1998 also made minor amendments. Now the law is consolidated in ss46–50 of the Powers of Criminal Courts (Sentencing) Act 2000.

The order requires between 40 and 240 hours of unpaid work that is of value to the community. This has to be completed within a period of 12 months. Before an order is made, a report from a probation officer or social worker has to be considered and there has to be suitable work available in the area. The order has to be explained to the offender and consent obtained. Consent is required because of the restrictions in the European Convention on Human Rights on forced labour. Normally the probation service will be responsible for the handling of the order. In the case of non-compliance with the order, an offender may be fined and the order continued, or the order could be revoked in which case resentencing for the original offence is possible.

An examination of statistics provides a picture of community service being a popular measure, use of which has in general grown over the years. For indictable offences it amounted to 2 per cent of total dispositions in 1977 and this had increased to 8 per cent in 1987. In 1987 it was used in 35,900 cases, whereas by 1997 it was used in 47,100 cases in relation to all offences. This had risen to 49,800 by 2001.

In a guide to sentencers produced by the Home Office, an account of what is involved is provided:

'All work is unpaid and of a sort normally undertaken by voluntary effort; some tasks involve offenders working alongside volunteers. The extent to which tasks involve contact with beneficiaries varies widely: helping in outdoor conservation projects, building adventure playgrounds, repairing toys for children in need, painting and decorating houses and flats for the elderly and handicapped are examples of tasks at one end of the spectrum. At the other are tasks which involve close personal contact such as swimming coaching for handicapped children, visiting and helping the elderly and helping at disabled people's sports clubs.' (1986b: 44)

What are community punishment orders for?

The requirement that it can only be used in relation to an imprisonable offence was a result of the original intention that it should be used as an alternative to a custodial sentence and this is not surprising given its development during a period of concern about prison numbers. Pease and McWilliams (1980a) stated that it had reduced the prison population by no more than 2,000 people, whilst Pease and McWilliams (eds) (1980b) still viewed it as being the best bet for decarceration. In practice it was not used in that way and it is now clearly seen as being a sentence in its own right. The Criminal Justice Act 1991 made it clear both that it was a sentence in its own right and that it was intended as a punishment. The punitive element was also seen in the National Standards published in 1989, which stressed the need for good time-keeping, rigour in enforcement and emphasised hard work as an attractive element for programmes. This message was repeated when a fresh set of National Standards were issued in 1994. The aim now is that the order provides punishment in the community. It is worth investigating how we got to this stage.

The purpose of the order and the manner in which it would relate to the existing system (for example its relationship to probation orders) was not worked out in advance. The Advisory Council on the Penal System, the Wooton Report (Home Office (1970)), considered the issue of community service and stated:

'To some it would be simply a more constructive and cheaper alternative to imprisonment; by others it would be seen as introducing into the penal system a new dimension with an emphasis on reparation to the community; others again would regard it as a means of giving effect to the old adage that the punishment should fit the crime; while still others would stress the value of bringing offenders into close touch with those members of the community who are most in need of help and support ... We have not attempted to categorise precisely the types of offender for whom community service might be appropriate, nor do we think it possible to predict what use might be made by the courts of this new form of sentence.' (1970:3)

Their ambivalence continued as regards, for example, the issue of whether or not it should only be used as an alternative to a custodial sentence. This report left much in the dark and little attempt was made before the introduction of community service to clarify its intended purposes. The fact that it seems to be possible to view it in so many different ways seems to have been part of its attraction, and this appears to have helped in its inception and assisted growth to its present status as a statistically important measure. After its introduction the lack of clarity continued. The guide to sentencers (Home Office (1986b)) on its possible rehabilitative qualities saw this as being only something to be hoped for given that 'the likelihood of this happening cannot be predicted in respect of any particular offence' (1986b:45). Probably offender rather than offence was intended – in any case the message is clear, on this as on some other issues no guidance was provided.

Praise for community service

Community service attracted praise despite, and often in full knowledge of, its shortcomings in both theory and practice. Pease – 'the most promising new penal measure for a long time' (1981a:57); Wright – 'one of the most constructive innovations ever made in penal theory and practice' (1982:98); West – 'The sentence is an effective and credible penalty, which also contains rehabilitative opportunities for the offender' (1976:88). Young stated 'it does impose a real, and sometimes extensive, obligation upon the offender, while usually reaping considerable benefits for the community as well' (1979:138).

The position of community punishment in the tariff

It is clear that a short period of community service seems to be used at present for cases in which the court is not of a mind to impose a custodial sentence. In this sense it has moved down tariff. This needs to be borne in mind in relation to the following information from Burney. She noted that 'Community service was most often mentioned by sentencers as the most common substitute for a suspended sentence' (1985:24). She found that its place in the tariff seemed to be at the top end – just before prison. She also noted that it was being used as an alternative to fines for the unemployed. The effect was to squander scarce places on community service schemes. Of 11 adult courts she examined, six used it as an alternative to custody. In the other five there were divided views or it was seen as being a separate sentence in its own right rather than just being an alternative to custody. A problem that arises is that if a court dealing with a default does not know what the other court intended, and often they would not, they will be left to take their own view as to the appropriate sentence for the original offence. Thus, for example, an order may have been made when custody was not in issue, whilst a later court may use custody. Pease (1978) in the light of such problems suggested that community service should only be used as an alternative to custody. Or, alternatively, that the lower end of the number of hours should be reserved for situations where it was not used as an alternative to custody. Later, Pease (1981a) suggested that the problem could be tackled by means of courts making their intentions clear and providing an account of these to be used at any default hearing . Vass (1986) suggested that there seems to be no reason why it should only be used as an alternative to custody and stated that given present practice the imprisonability criteria should be removed.

The problems with community punishment

The vague philosophy of community service and the lact of guidance associated with it produced inconsistency, disparity and thus injustice in practice. Attempts at individualising sentences will of itself produce differences and, as Pease and McWilliams (eds) (1980b) indicate, there were bound to be differences between schemes. This does not excuse what has in fact occurred. Vass in a review stated that the situation was one in which 'rampant discretion in the administration and enforcement of CSOs has led to undesirable and inconsistent practices and lax regimes' (1986:100). Young looked at five probation areas in England concentrating on magistrates' courts, and found disparity both between areas and in courts – 'in each court the sentence was imposed upon offenders who had committed crimes of widely differing degrees of seriousness' (1979:135). Burney (1985) in her research also found differences in practice both within and between courts. Pease (1978) found variations in enforcement practices and Young (1979) found on this issue that in one case, despite a failure to comply with requirements on 12 occasions, the offender was still allowed to continue with the order. Pease (1978) also found differences of view being held within the probation service. In practice this will be important given their influence on the courts. The courts agree with about three quarters of recommendations for community service.

Vass provides a good and wide ranging review of problems with community service. He notes for example that 'in many instances work done by offenders is menial in character, undesirable and degrading to the point where the notion of doing "work for the community" becomes devoid of substance' (1986:100). He sees the fact of menial tasks as having come about because of an expansion of orders without a matched development of resources and supply of suitable schemes. He also raises the issue of consent. On this matter I think it is clear that offenders opt for community service because in their view there may be worse alternatives – such as a fine or custody. Consent obtained by coercion is of dubious worth. Whilst it is not clear what percentage actually want to do community service the problem of absenteeism suggests a lack of commitment. Unless this is a result of disappointment with the schemes it suggests that the original consent was in some cases coerced. Vass also raises the issue of how do you decide who is suitable for community service? He notes that various methods are used and, given that schemes and people differ, prediction is going to be difficult. Pease (1981a) pointed out that practice is based on assumption as to suitability rather than hard evidence. The final point to note from Vass concerns the problems faced by probation practitioners in the field. They are commonly disenchanted being a race apart, marginalised within the service and concerned about the conflict between the policing aspects of community service and the probation officer/client relationship. It is clear that such problems have continued as was reported in a Home Office study by Thomas et al (1990) which found plenty of differences in the way that schemes were operating.

8.8 Community punishment and rehabilitation orders (combination orders)

The Criminal Justice and Court Services Act 2000 changed the names of certain dispositions. Combination orders became community punishment and rehabilitation orders. Combination orders, introduced by the Criminal Justice Act 1991, allowed the joint use of community rehabilitation and community punishment. It was targeted at the problem of persistent offenders particularly property offenders who were in danger of going to prison. The probation element has to be between one and three years and the community service is to be between 40 and 100 hours. They are available in relation to those aged 16 and above where the offence is imprisonable. The court must use the order as a means to rehabilitate, or to protect the public or to prevent further offending. The order should be completed within a year. As seen in Table 23, the order was used for 14,700 cases in 2001.

8.9 Anti-social behaviour orders

The system for anti-social behaviour orders came into force on 1 April 1999. The orders were created by the Crime and Disorder Act 1998. They involve a system similar to an injunction that is intended to deal with local problems. An application will be made by the police or the local authority to the local magistrates' court. An application can be made in relation to any person aged ten or over. It has to be on the basis that a person has acted in an anti-social manner. This means that their behaviour has caused or was likely to cause harassment, alarm or distress to one or more persons not of the same household as himself. This is to exclude domestics. The type of behaviour to be targeted is intimidation of neighbours, unruly and abusive behaviour – perhaps fuelled by alcohol or drugs – racist taunts, and bullying. The minimum period that an order will last is two years and breach of the order is a criminal offence, which can lead to detention for up to five years. The behaviour that is to be controlled is such that a prosecution for criminal offences would not have proceeded, because of problems of proving the requisite criminal intent.

The orders often bar people from entering a geographical area or shop and can include bans on specific acts, such as swearing in public. They are designed to prevent theft, intimidation, drunkenness, violence and other nuisance behaviour. Verbal abuse (59 per cent), graffiti and criminal damage (36 per cent) are the main categories in practice. A report by Campbell (2002) suggests that the orders are helping combat unruly behaviour. However, the procedures to be followed are too onerous and further difficulties in their use are caused by the costs of, and delays in, the process – some taking six months to get through the courts. Campbell reports that there have been none in police areas like Cheshire, Essex, Wiltshire and Dyfed Powys; compared to the 65 implemented in the West Midlands. In the first three years following their creation, there have been 466 anti-social behaviour orders used, with a £5,350 average bill for the taxpayer. According to the study, some local councils and police see that cost as value for money as it can save future spending on staffing, insurance claims and legal costs. But the orders are not viewed as cost effective in other respects as usually they do not bring about better behaviour. The patchy use has been reported by other observers and some still have doubts about their legitimacy. The system involves intervention and perhaps detention without trial or normal processes and such a system is clearly questionable. This is perhaps more so as they are being mainly used for those under 21. Also, whilst it's a civil order its breach is a crime with a five-year maximum sentence in the Crown Court.

The Criminal Justice Act 2003 provides for individual support orders for young people subject to anti-social behaviour orders and these would require them to undertake education-related activities. This seems misconceived in that the likely recipients of such orders are probably already failing to engage with the education system and will have histories of exclusion and truancy.

8.10 Curfew orders

The Criminal Justice Act 1991, now ss37–40 of the Powers of Criminal Courts (Sentencing) Act 2000, provided for curfew orders in relation to a person of or over the age of 16 years who is convicted of an offence. They have been available nationally, in conjunction with the use of electronic monitoring, since December 1999. They offer a means of control within the community and are a form of detention without the use of imprisonment. In *Crime, Justice and Protecting the Public* (Home Office (1990)) they were said to enable offenders to go to work, to attend training courses or probation centres, to carry out community service or to receive treatment for drug abuse. Curfews could be useful in reducing some forms of crime, thefts of and from cars, pub brawls and other types of disorder. A curfew order was also claimed to be of use to keep people away from certain places, such a shopping centres or pubs, or to keep them at home in the evenings or at weekends. It seems to me that they may well be attractive where they are used genuinely as an alternative to custody. Also if they were effectively policed, perhaps by electronic monitoring, they could have a valuable incapacitating effect. The order can last up to six months and would require him to remain, for periods specified in the order, at a specified place. It can cover between two and 12 hours in any one day. The requirements in a curfew order are to avoid conflict with the offender's religious beliefs or with the requirements of any other community order to which he may be subject and any interference with the time, if any, at which he normally works or attends school or other educational establishment. A person to monitor the order will be appointed. Before making a curfew order, the court has to explain to the offender in ordinary language, the effect of the order and the consequences of breach. The offender has to express his willingness to comply with the order before it can be made. Before making a curfew order, the court shall obtain and consider information about the place proposed to be specified in the order (including information as to the attitude of persons likely to be affected by the enforced presence there of the offender). Electronic monitoring of curfew orders was also provided for in the 1991 Act and continued by the 2000 Act.

8.11 Electronic monitoring

The results from the first trials of electronic monitoring in relation to the bail system were disappointing. Research by Mair and Nee (1990) reported problems such as equipment failures, a high rate of breach and that there was a low take up by the courts. Confining offenders within their home may well cause domestic friction. The suggestion has been made that the wearing of a bracelet is degrading, though anecdotal evidence is that it is commonly seen as being a trophy. Probation staff have been ambivalent about the system and their role in relation to it.

NACRO (1989) considered arguments for and against the electronic monitoring of offenders. In favour of electronic monitoring is that it is less costly than imprisonment and can reduce the use of custody without putting the public at risk, avoid the contamination effect of imprisonment through which first offenders mix with more experienced offenders, avoid the stigma attached to having served a prison sentence and assist rehabilitation by allowing the offender to support his or her family and maintain social ties. Those opposed to electronic monitoring of offenders argue that for an offender to be eligible for electronic monitoring as part of home confinement you need a home and a telephone. There is a danger of 'widening the net' of social control and an unwarranted escalation of penalties. Courts are likely to use electronic monitoring for offenders who would otherwise receive a less restrictive non-custodial penalty. If electronic monitoring were applied to offenders who would not otherwise have been sent to prison, this would defeat the argument that monitoring is less intrusive and less costly than prison. Little is known about the types of offenders best suited for these programmes, the effect on re-offending and the psychological impact of monitoring or about the impact of electronic monitoring on the offender's family. Electronic monitoring only allows the authorities to know where an offender is, not what he or she is doing. If he or she is committing an offence from home, the authorities are none the wiser. As you can see NACRO found more arguments against rather than for this innovation. The views below are more positive.

The role that electronic monitoring is to play was considered in *Protecting the Public*: Home Office (1996). This document notes that the Criminal Justice and Public Order Act 1994 allowed trials of electronic monitoring of curfew orders to take place in selected areas. Pilot trials of electronic monitoring commenced in July 1995 at three locations: Manchester, Reading and the County of Norfolk. The area of the trials was extended, in November 1995, to include the whole of Greater Manchester and Berkshire. The objectives of the trials, were to establish the technical and practical arrangements necessary to support the electronic monitoring of curfew orders; to ascertain the likely cost and effectiveness of curfew orders in relation to court sentences; and to evaluate the scope for introducing electronic monitoring of curfew orders on a selective or national basis. The way that the system operates is that an offender would wear a device, commonly an ankle bracelet, that he could not take more than a certain distance from a monitoring device that would be fixed at the place of curfew. The system was presented as being a highly flexible, restrictive community sentence with a part to play in punishing offenders and reducing crime. The curfew order is seen as a significant restriction of liberty with the courts empowered to sentence for up to 2,000 hours over a period of six months. The document tells us that the technology has so far proved successful in monitoring offenders whom the courts want off the streets, and has ensured that the courts' sentences cannot be evaded without serious consequences. The slightest breach of a curfew order or attempt to tamper with the equipment is detected, and investigated by the contractors immediately. No violations are ignored, with warnings given for the most minor infringement. Offenders who continue not to comply are returned to court.

Mortimer et al (1999) presented further findings from the trials in Greater Manchester, Berkshire and Norfolk. They indicated that after poor early take-up, sentencers had started to use the order more frequently and overall completion rates were high. However, completions varied considerably between trial areas and low usage persisted in some courts. Sentencers tended to use curfew orders towards the top end of the community sentence band, but questions remained as to which offenders were most suitable for tagging. Research was still needed as regards why there are differences in completion rates, what type of offender benefits most from a curfew order and in what circumstances should a curfew order be used by itself or be combined with another community sentence: see Richardson (1999) for further details of the various forms of use of tagging in the criminal justice system. The government is considering the scope for wider application of electronic monitoring in relation to areas such as bail and early release. You should also note that the Criminal Justice and Court Services Act 2000 contains provisions on electronic monitoring.

8.12 Compensation orders

Compensation orders saw a decline in their use by the courts – in 1997 there were 97,200 orders, a figure down from 103,000 in 1987. However, by 2001 it was back up to 102,300. Of all offenders sentenced, except summary motoring offences, in the magistrates' courts 14 per cent saw compensation orders being used. The average amount of compensation was £144. For particular offences the amount was £228 for offences of violence, £165 for sexual offences and £171 for theft and handling. In the Crown Court they were used in 7 per cent of cases and the average amount was £1,444: Home Office (2002a). Sections 130–134 of the Powers of Criminal Courts (Sentencing) Act 2000 provide for compensation orders which can hope to provide some financial recompense to the victim. The system is one in which the offender has to pay a sum of money which the victim will be the beneficiary of (the loss of the victim having being a result of the offence). The Crown Court has no limit on the amount of compensation that it can award; the magistrates' courts have a £5,000 per offence limit. This order can be used as well as other orders and, if both a compensation order and a fine seem applicable, preference should be given to providing compensation. In the making of the order, regard is to be had to the means of the offender. A feature of the legislation that could have brought great change to the practices of courts is the requirement that reasons must be stated as to why compensation has not been awarded when the court was empowered to do so. Courts tend to use compensation with regard to property rather than for injury to the person. In *R v Inwood* (1974) 60 Cr App R 70 Lord Scarman pointed out that a compensation order should not be used where there was real doubt about the ability of the offender to pay. Futhermore, when such an order is made alongside the use of a prison sentence, the long-term effect might be to force the offender back into crime after his release. In *R v Maynard* [1983] Crim LR 821 the Court of Appeal made it clear that the loss to the victim is the important thing and not to provide extra punishment or to deprive the offender of any profit made. Those aims should be addressed by the system of fines or through confiscation. Courts have to give precedence to compensation in a case where it considers both a fine and compensation to be appropriate, but the offender does not have sufficient means to pay both in full. This allows the proposed fine to be reduced so that the offender can afford to pay compensations to the victim.

Newburn (1988) in a national survey of the use and enforcement of compensation orders in magistrates' courts in 1986 found that magistrates expressed difficulties as regards assessing loss for personal injuries. In the research it was found that whilst compensation was awarded in 75 per cent of cases of criminal damage it was only used for 5 per cent of cases of assault. It can be mentioned in passing that the Criminal Injuries Compensation system provides a further possible means of compensation for victims of crime. Very briefly the issue will be raised as to whether or not priorities need to be changed so that looking after the needs of the victim would be a much higher priority of the criminal justice system rather than being somewhat of an afterthought as it has been historically. These are important issues and elements of them were raised in the 1988 Green Paper *Punishment, Custody and the Community*: Home Office (1988b). This had amongst its themes the desire to promote responsibility amongst offenders, to make them face up to their actions and to provide the means by which recompense by the offender could be made to society and the victim. Compensation provides a means of recompense to the victim and community service offers the means to provide recompense to the community. The notion of recompense or reparation, and linked notions of mediation and conciliation, are being introduced more and more into our jurisdiction. Some attempts at tackling terminological difficulties is called for first. Restitution is the returning of property and restitution orders are already possible. Restitution is a form of reparation. Reparation orders have been introduced for youngsters, though the idea itself may only involve such an apology by the offender to the victim. In this sense it may also amount to conciliation or reconciliation between offender and victim. Mediation is where a third party provides a structure for dispute settlement and this might lead, for example, to reconciliation. Such ideas were seen to be at work in the material on diversion, and also as regards the deferring of a sentence, in that matters such as making amends to the victim may well be one of the things that would be hoped for. There may be merit for both victim and offender with regard to conciliation. The victim would, for example, be for the offender a legitimate non-professional critic of his actions, as well as being a direct challenge to the offender's justifications. There is some evidence that both victims and offenders might welcome mediation and that it works primarily as a means of reconciliation, though it is not difficult to imagine the potential problems that would be involved. Offenders may engage in such activities for self-serving tactical considerations such as it would look good when it was mentioned in court and a lesser sentence might be obtained. Mediation and reparation schemes can operate at various stages of the criminal justice system – for example, at the pre-prosecution stage or instead of prosecution. For juveniles they can be the means of achieving diversion. Later, at court hearings, they can offer avenues by which custodial sentences can be avoided. Such ideas are about doing things for the offender and often the needs of the victim are not a priority. A number of these themes have been explored further in the examination of restorative justice.

8.13 Forfeiture

Forfeiture orders

Forfeiture orders have seen a considerable growth in use – 36,988 in 2001, whereas the figure was 9,100 in 1987. General powers of forfeiture are provided by s143 of the Powers of

Criminal Courts (Sentencing) Act 2000. As well as a general power there are specific powers under other statutes. The power is that after a person has been convicted or has had a matter taken into consideration, where property has been lawfully seized, or was in the possession of or under the control of a person at the time of their apprehension or summons, and that property was used for or to help in the commission of any offence, or was intended for that purpose, then the court can order forfeiture of it. In doing this, the court must have regard to the effect that this will have on the offender.

8.14 The effectiveness of community sentences and orders

Lloyd, Mair and Hough (1994) presented an analysis of the use of reconviction rates as a method for considering the effectiveness of interventions. They also carried out the first national comparative study of reconviction rates for 15 years. As to the use of reconviction rates as a method for considering the effectiveness of interventions, they note the following problems. It is not clear what the most suitable follow-up period is, though two years seems acceptable. There have been a wide range of definitions that have been used to measure reconvictions. How should you take into account the fact that all reconvictions are not of equal severity? Reconvictions do not take account of all of the aims of sentencing. There is the problem that reconvictions do not measure reoffending. How should you take into account the fact that all reconvictions are not of equal severity? Is it in fact feasible to compare the reconviction rates for different sentences or should you just compare different schemes within a particular type of sentence or order such as probation? How can the effects of policing and prosecution practice be accounted for? Can the attitudes and abilities of those who deliver the disposition, which may make a big difference to its success, be taken into account? These are similar issues to those noted specifically in relation to community rehabilitation orders.

The key findings of their study were that the reconviction rates, two years after release or sentence, were:

Imprisonment	54 per cent
Community service orders	49 per cent
Straight probation orders	43 per cent
Probation orders with added requirements	63 per cent

It is clear that there were considerable differences amongst the four disposals – with a gap of 20 per cent between the reconviction rate associated with straight probation and that associated with probation with added requirements (this is called 4A/4B probation). This does not mean that straight probation is far more successful in terms of reconviction rates than probation with a 4A/4B requirement. What it does mean is that offenders with very different characteristics (and therefore different risks of reconviction) are being sentenced to these different disposals – as, in fact, should be the case.

The study also noted that the key factors in reconviction were found to be – age, sex, offence and criminal history. Discovering the individual impact of the variables used is not an easy matter, although it does appear that age remains a particularly strong predictor of reconviction. There was little association between offence seriousness and risk of

305

reconviction. Thus, prisoners, a large proportion of whom were originally convicted of serious offences, tended to be reconvicted of less serious offences, while probationers, who were originally convicted of less serious offences tended to be reconvicted of offences of similar gravity at reconviction.

The following data from the official statistics (Table 25) reveal worryingly high breach rates for some dispositions: Home Office (2002a).

Table 25

Percentages of Those Who Breached Orders in 1994 and 2001

	1994	2001
Suspended sentence	43	11
Community punishment order	24	32
Community rehabilitation order	10	23
Community punishment and rehabilitation order	26	47
Conditional discharge	10	11

(Source: Criminal Statistics, England and Wales, 2001)

8.15 The generic community sentence

The Criminal Justice Act 2003 provides for the notion of a community sentence. Section 147 states that a community sentence is a community order (as defined by s177) or one or more of the youth community orders. Youth community orders are (under s147): a curfew order, an exclusion order, an attendance centre order, a supervision order and an action plan order. Section 177 provides that there will be one community sentence for those aged 16 and over which will encompass all of the presently available community order options. The court will be able to select the appropriate requirements from the following list: an unpaid work requirement, an activity requirement, a programme requirement, a prohibited activity requirement, a curfew requirement, an exclusion requirement, a residence requirement, a mental health treatment requirement (with the consent of the offender), a drug rehabilitation requirement (with the consent of the offender), an alcohol treatment requirement (with the consent of the offender), a supervision requirement and, in a case where the offender is aged under 25, an attendance centre requirement. Use of the requirements is subject to various forms of restrictions.

Where the court makes a community order imposing a curfew requirement or an exclusion requirement, the court must normally (unless, for example, in the particular circumstances of the case, it considers it inappropriate) also impose an electronic monitoring requirement. For the other requirements the possibility of tagging is made available. A community order must specify a date, not more than three years after the date of the order, by which all the requirements in it must have been complied with.

Enforcement of community orders is to be strengthened by giving the court stronger options in the case of breach.

Restrictions on imposing community sentences

Section 148 provides for these restrictions as follows:

'(1) A court must not pass a community sentence on an offender unless it is of the opinion that the offence, or the combination of the offence and one or more offences associated with it, was serious enough to warrant such a sentence.

(2) Where a court passes a community sentence which consists of or includes a community order –

(a) the particular requirement or requirements forming part of the community order must be such as, in the opinion of the court, is, or taken together are, the most suitable for the offender, and

(b) the restrictions on liberty imposed by the order must be such as in the opinion of the court are commensurate with the seriousness of the offence, or the combination of the offence and one or more offences associated with it.

(3) Where a court passes a community sentence which consists of or includes one or more youth community orders –

(a) the particular order or orders forming part of the sentence must be such as, in the opinion of the court, is, or taken together are, the most suitable for the offender, and

(b) the restrictions on liberty imposed by the order or orders must be such as in the opinion of the court are commensurate with the seriousness of the offence, or the combination of the offence and one or more offences associated with it.'

Section 149 relates to the passing of community sentence on an offender who has been remanded in custody. Allowance can be made for the remand in custody as it would be in relation to a custodial sentence.

Section 150 provides that community sentences are not available where other provisions impose restrictions on sentencing options, as in the case of life as a sentence for murder.

The Criminal Justice Act 2003 also provides for the notion of a responsible officer in relation to the community disposals and it can be such as a probation worker or a youth offending team member. That person must make any necessary arrangements for the offender to be able to meet the requirements of the order, promote the offender's compliance with the requirements, and take enforcement action in the case of non-compliance.

The requirements as provided for by the Criminal Justice Act 2003

Section 199: unpaid work requirement

This section re-enacts, with some modification, s46 of the Powers of Criminal Courts (Sentencing) Act 2000 (which deals with 'community punishment', previously called 'community service'). Unpaid work is done on projects set up by the probation service in consultation with sentencers and the local community. These can include environmental projects, such as clearing canals, removing graffiti, painting and decorating community facilities, working in homes for the elderly or doing shopping for the elderly. No offender can be required to do more than 300 hours of unpaid work or less than 40. The Act increases the current upper limit from 240 hours. The court must not impose an unpaid work requirement unless it is satisfied that the offender is a suitable person to perform work under such a requirement.

Section 201: activity requirement
These provisions are based on the requirements in Schedule 2 of the Powers of Criminal Courts (Sentencing) Act 2000. An activity requirement is a requirement that the offender must either present himself to a specified person, at a specified place, for a certain number of days, and/or take part in specified activities for a certain number of days. An activity requirement may include such tasks as receiving help with employment or group work on social problems. Reparative activities are a particular aim of this requirement. The Act provides that before imposing an activity requirement on an offender, the court must be satisfied that it is feasible to secure compliance with the requirement. The maximum number of days of activity is 60. The offender is required to present himself at a place or places specified by his responsible officer on the number of days specified in the order, and to comply with instructions given by or under the authority of the person in charge of that place. The responsible officer will tell the offender where he needs to go and for how many hours, and that he must comply with the instructions of the person in charge of the place.

Section 202: programme requirement
A programme requirement is a requirement that the offender must participate in an accredited programme on a certain number of days. Programmes are courses which address offending behaviour, covering such topics as anger management, sex offending, substance misuse, etc. An officer of a local probation board (an officer of a local probation board or youth offending team member if the offender is under 18) must recommend that the specified programme is suitable for the offender before the court imposes a programme requirement. The court must also be satisfied that a place on the programme is available for the offender. The offender is required to participate in the programme as specified in the order in accordance with instructions given by his responsible officer. The offender must also comply with any instructions given by, or under the authority of, the person in charge of the programme.

Section 203: prohibited activity requirement
The court can require an offender to refrain from participating in certain activities. For example, it might forbid him to contact a certain person. The offender may be prohibited from participating in specified activities on a certain day or on a number of days or during a period of time. Before setting such a requirement the court must consult an officer of the local probation board, or, in the case of an offender who is under 18, an officer of the local probation board or a member of a youth offending team.

Section 204: curfew requirement
This clause re-enacts, with some modification, s37 of the Powers of Criminal Courts (Sentencing) Act 2000. A curfew requirement is a requirement that the offender must remain at a place specified by the court for certain periods of time. The periods of time must not be less than two hours or more than 12 hours in any given day. The order might, for

example, require the offender to stay at home during the evening and night hours. The court must obtain and consider information about the place specified in the order and the attitude of persons likely to be affected by the presence of the offender.

Section 205: exclusion requirement

A version of this requirement appeared in earlier legislation but it was not brought into operation. An exclusion requirement is a requirement prohibiting the offender from entering an area or place during a period specified in the order. The order may stipulate that the prohibition operates only for certain periods of time and may specify different places for different periods. For example, an offender might be required to stay away from a specified town centre at night. An exclusion requirement cannot last longer than two years.

Section 206: residence requirement

The residence requirement is based on the existing requirements as to residence that can be included in a community rehabilitation order under the Powers of Criminal Courts (Sentencing) Act 2000. It is a requirement that the offender must reside at a place specified in the order for a specified period.

Section 207: mental health treatment requirement

The mental health treatment requirement is based on the requirements as to treatment as part of a community rehabilitation order under the Powers of Criminal Courts (Sentencing) Act 2000. The court will be able to direct an offender to undergo mental health treatment for certain period(s) as part of a community sentence or suspended sentence order.

Section 209: drug rehabilitation requirement

As part of a community sentence or suspended sentence the court may impose a drug rehabilitation requirement, which includes drug treatment and testing. In order to impose such a requirement, the court must be satisfied that the offender is dependent on, or has a propensity to misuse, any controlled drug and as such requires and would benefit from treatment. In addition, the court must be satisfied that the necessary arrangements are or can be made for the treatment and that the offender has expressed a willingness to comply with the drug rehabilitation requirement. The treatment provided may not be for a period of less than six months. A suitably qualified or experienced individual supervises the treatment. It is for the court to decide whether treatment should be residential or non-residential.

Section 212: alcohol treatment requirement

Alcohol treatment is currently available as part of a community rehabilitation order, under the Powers of Criminal Courts (Sentencing) Act 2000. The 2003 Act allows a court to require the offender to undergo alcohol treatment. The treatment must be by or under the direction of a person who is qualified or experienced to reduce or eliminate the offender's dependency on alcohol. This person is to be identified in the order. The court be satisfied that the offender is dependent on alcohol and that this dependency requires and is susceptible to treatment. The court must obtain the offender's consent before imposing an alcohol treatment requirement. The order must last at least six months.

Section 213: supervision requirement

Supervision is a central part of community rehabilitation orders under the Powers of Criminal Courts (Sentencing) Act 2000. The responsible officer might review with the offender his supervision plan, challenge his offending behaviour, hold him to account on the requirements, monitor his progress, and assist him with various problems, such as accommodation, employment, or finance.

Section 214: attendance centre requirement

Attendance centre orders are currently free standing orders for certain young offenders, under the Powers of Criminal Courts (Sentencing) Act 2000. At an attendance centre, practical activities, including sport, can be run to occupy offenders for a certain number of hours to keep them out of trouble. This is often on Saturdays as attendance centres were originally set up for football-related offenders. The 2003 Act enables the court to require an offender to attend an attendance centre for a specified number of hours. The total number of hours an order may specify is to be between 12 and 36. The offender cannot be required to attend more than once a day or for more than three hours on any one day.

Section 215: electronic monitoring requirement

The court can order the electronic monitoring of an offender, as a means to assist in the compliance of an offender with any of the other requirements set out in the order. Electronic monitoring has been available throughout England and Wales since 1999, following a series of pilot projects which operated in selected areas during the previous ten years. In almost all cases of electronic monitoring, the technical equipment uses radio frequency transmissions. It consists of a transmitter (the 'tag'), which is usually worn round the ankle, and a receiver unit which is either connected to a landline telephone or which incorporates mobile phone technology. The receiver unit communicates with a central computer system at a monitoring centre. The transmitter sends signals to the receiver at regular intervals and these are sent on to the central computer. The signal strength of the transmitter is calibrated to the receiver so that if the subject goes out of range (generally this means outside the building where the receiver is located), there is a break in signal and this is also registered by the central computer which generates follow-up action. The transmitter can be removed only by breaking its strap. This interferes with the fibre-optic circuitry inside the strap and is immediately registered as a tamper, also generating follow-up action.

9 Prisons

9.1 The historical background and proposals for change

9.2 The statutory framework

9.3 Criminal Justice Act 2003

9.4 Prison statistics

9.5 The aims and functions of prisons

9.6 Overcrowding, prison conditions and prison security

9.7 Coping with long-term prisoners

9.8 Incapacitation as a benefit of imprisonment

9.9 Deterioration as a possible problem with the use of long-term imprisonment

9.10 Unwanted side-effects of prison

9.11 Praise where praise is due

9.12 The lessons of reconviction data

9.13 Should prison numbers be decreased?

9.14 Conclusion

In this chapter the use of prisons as a system of custodial detention for those aged over 21 years of age is considered. Suspended sentences of imprisonment were considered in relation to community sentences. Most of the material will relate to male prisoners as they make up such a high proportion of the prison population – 94 per cent of the 2002 prison population. Prisons have generated a substantial literature, which raises many issues, not all of which can be tackled here. The central themes that are developed concern possible justifications for, and the aims of, prisons. The practices that make up the system of imprisonment are also examined with emphasis being placed on particular issues – the difficulties caused by long-term incarceration and the problem of overcrowding in prisons. The latter is a part cause of various problems within prisons, such as poor conditions for the prisoners. Both the analytical and descriptive material is utilised in the presentation of an evaluation of the present and possible future uses of imprisonment. Material on the philosophy of sentencing, which was presented in Chapter 6, should be borne in mind when issues such as deterrence and punishment are being considered in this chapter. Much of the material that is presented is critical of prisons and this reflects both the approach taken by the majority of writers and indeed the reality that there is much about prisons that is in need of criticism. It needs to be made clear that prisons do have some merit and that good work is done within them. Attention is directed to contemporary matters, virtually all the material concerns the period since 1945, though a very brief historical background is provided.

9.1 The historical background and proposals for change

It was in the nineteenth century that the basis for the present prison system was established. Hanging, which had been a commonly used penalty, came to be regarded as an excessive reaction to offences such as stealing a loaf of bread and its use declined. Also the use of transportation had ceased by 1867, one of the reasons being that places to send people were no longer readily available. After the American War of Independence in 1776, for example, there was a refusal to accept shipments of convicts. Prisons were developed to fill the gap and prisons as we know them today emerged in a rush in the 1840s. Fifty-four new prisons in six years followed on from the opening of Pentonville in 1842. One obvious reason why we would recognise the nineteenth-century prisons is that they constitute a part of the prison estate at the present time. The nineteenth century also saw, in 1877, the introduction of direct central control of prisons which took over from what had been a local system. This evolved into the present-day system in which prison administration is carried out under the auspices of the Prison Department within the Home Office. The twentieth century saw a period of optimism for prisons. This grew out of the recommendations of the Gladstone Committee of 1895 (*Report from the Departmental Committee on Prisons* (1895)). It was not until the period of office of Sir Alexander Paterson as a Prison Commissioner in the period 1922–1947 that reformative ideas were really pushed. As will soon become apparent it is now very difficult to be optimistic about prisons.

The Criminal Justice Act 2003 provisions that relate to the issues in this chapter are detailed below. It is important to note that, since most of the provisions of the Act did not come into force immediately upon Royal Assent, the earlier provisions will still be applicable for some time. Both this alternative system and what is still the existing system are presented.

The government White Paper, *Justice for All* (Home Office (2002d)), provides details of their intentions for this stage of the criminal justice system. They intend to provide more effective punishment and rehabilitation and start by noting that the prison population is at record levels. Many prisoners receive short sentences that do not help with effective rehabilitation and resettlement, and often increase the chances of reoffending. The White Paper sets out the challenges faced by the correctional services and how by more collaborative working with other statutory agencies and the voluntary and community sectors they can deliver a sentence that reduces crime and help build safer, more cohesive communities. In the light of this there are proposals:

1. to give greater flexibility to probation officers to drug test offenders on release from custody;

2. to pilot the 'Going Straight' contract, a new rehabilitation programme for 18-20-year-olds, including reparation to victims and incentives to participate;
3. to review reception and release procedures for all prisoners to ensure departing prisoners have the appropriate help to resettle;
4. to embark on a modernisation programme to expand capacity in existing prisons, to build new multi-functional community prisons and to close prisons that are not fit for purpose;
5. to benchmark public sector prisons and close or contract out those that do not meet the necessary standards;
6. to review the categorisation of prisoners to balance the needs of security with effective resettlement (this must be a good idea as we have had a security obsession for far too long);
7. to extend the remit of multi-agency public protection panels, appointing independent lay members to the panels and including a statutory requirement to include a wider range of agencies and local bodies.

9.2 The statutory framework

Criminal Justice Act 1991 as consolidated in the Powers of Criminal Courts (Sentencing) Act 2000, s79

The statutory provisions envisaged other sentences or orders being tried wherever possible. The length of the sentence is to relate to the seriousness of the offence, though for the violent or sexual offences a longer term to protect the public from serious harm is possible. Section 79 of the 2000 Act (restrictions on imposing custodial sentences) states:

'(1) This section applies where a person is convicted of an offence punishable with a custodial sentence other than one –
(a) fixed by law ...
(2) Subject to subsection (3) below, the court shall not pass a custodial sentence on the offender unless it is of the opinion:
(a) that the offence, or the combination of the offence and one or more offences associated with it, was so serious that only such a sentence can be justified for the offence, or,
(b) where the offence is a violent or sexual offence, that only such a sentence would be adequate to protect the public from serious harm from him.'

Mandatory sentences under ss109–111 of the Powers of Criminal Courts (Sentencing) Act 2000

The Act provides for mandatory and minimum custodial sentences in the case of repeat offending in the case of certain offences. Section 109 (mandatory life sentence for second serious offence) states:

'(1) This section applies where –
(a) a person is convicted of a serious offence committed after 30th September 1997; and

313

(b) at the time when that offence was committed, he was 18 or over and had been convicted in any part of the United Kingdom of another serious offence.

(2) The court shall impose a life sentence, that is to say –

(a) where the person is 21 or over when convicted of the offence mentioned in subsection (1)(a) above, a sentence of imprisonment for life,

(b) where he is under 21, a sentence of custody for life under section 94 above,

unless the court is of the opinion that there are exceptional circumstances relating to either of the offences or to the offender which justify its not doing so.

(3) Where the court does not impose a life sentence, it shall state in open court that it is of that opinion and what the exceptional circumstances are.

(4) An offence the sentence for which is imposed under subsection (2) above shall not be regarded as an offence the sentence for which is fixed by law.

(5) An offence committed in England and Wales is a serious offence for the purposes of this section if it is any of the following, namely –

(a) an attempt to commit murder, a conspiracy to commit murder or an incitement to murder;

(b) an offence under section 4 of the Offences Against the Person Act 1861 (soliciting murder);

(c) manslaughter;

(d) an offence under section 18 of the Offences Against the Person Act 1861 (wounding, or causing grievous bodily harm, with intent);

(e) rape or an attempt to commit rape;

(f) an offence under section 5 of the Sexual Offences Act 1956 (intercourse with a girl under 13);

(g) an offence under section 16 (possession of a firearm with intent to injure), section 17 (use of a firearm to resist arrest) or section 18 (carrying a firearm with criminal intent) of the Firearms Act 1968; and

(h) robbery where, at some time during the commission of the offence, the offender had in his possession a firearm or imitation firearm within the meaning of that Act.'

Section 110 makes similar provisions in the case of a third class A drug-trafficking offence. Here there is to be a seven-year minimum sentence unless this would, in all the circumstances, be unjust. Section 111 makes similar provisions for a third domestic burglary, with a three-year minimum being provided for.

Early release, parole and home detention curfew

The Crime and Disorder Act 1998 provided for a system of home detention curfew. It relates to prisoners over 18 serving between three months and four years. It can allow release up to two months earlier than normal under the other release schemes. Prisoners spend the rest of the custodial part of their sentence in the community wearing an electronic tag and under curfew arrangements. Over 59,000 prisoners were placed on home detention curfew in a period just short of four years from the start of the scheme in January 1999. In 2002 about 3 per cent of prisoners were on home detention curfew. Ninety per cent of curfewees have completed their curfew period successfully: 3 per cent of prisoners have offended on curfew, of which only a very small proportion of these offences were serious in nature. The idea was extended in 2002 for those serving between three and 12 months in that it became presumptive home detention curfew. Also in 2002 the maximum curfew period was extended to 90 days for prisoners serving sentences of between eight months and four years.

The Criminal Justice Act 1991 provided for a new system of early release and parole. For those serving less than four years, who are known as short-term prisoners, there is automatic release at the halfway point of the sentence. There are two categories of short-term prisoner. The first is those with a sentence of a year or more who are subject to supervision, up to the three-quarter point of the sentence. The second category, on sentences of less than a year, are not subject to supervision. The release is conditional for short-term prisoners in that they can be recalled to prison for offences committed during the term of the original sentence or for breach of supervision requirements. The breach of supervision requirements would normally have been dealt with as a summary offence by magistrates. Since 2000 the Home Secretary is to deal with these matters. The Home Secretary is to act on the advice of the Parole Board. This brings the short-term prisoners back into the same system as that applicable to the long-term prisoners. However, the Criminal Justice Act 2003 makes recall to custody an executive decision, rather than having to be approved by the Parole Board as currently. The Parole Board would scrutinise all recall decisions, to ensure they are fairly taken.

The Parole Board decides on the suitability of prisoners for parole where they had a sentence of between four and seven years. They are eligible for parole at the halfway stage of their sentence but automatic release would come at the two-thirds point. Supervision operates up to the three-quarter point of the sentence for both those released on parole and those who have to wait till the two-thirds point. Recall for offences that are committed during the period up to the end of the sentence, and for breach of licence conditions, is by the Home Secretary acting on the advice of the Parole Board. Since 1998 the Parole Board can deal with those sentenced to less than 15 years rather than the previous shorter period of seven years. In relation to other prisoners on a determinate sentence the Parole Board makes recommendations to the Home Secretary. There are separate provisions for life sentence prisoners and those who are detained at Her Majesty's pleasure under ss90–95 of the Powers of Criminal Courts (Sentencing) Act 2000. A feature change to note is the use of electronic tagging as part of the system of early release.

9.3 Criminal Justice Act 2003

The Criminal Justice Act 2003 makes provision for the following changes to the use of custody.

General restrictions on discretionary custodial sentences

These provisions may not be applicable in all circumstances, in so far as other provisions impose restrictions on sentencing options, as in the case of life as a sentence for murder.
Section 152 provides that:

'(2) The court must not pass a custodial sentence unless it is of the opinion that the offence, or the combination of the offence and one or more offences associated with it, was so serious that neither a fine alone nor a community sentence can be justified for the offence.
(3) Nothing in subsection (2) prevents the court from passing a custodial sentence on the offender if –

(a) he fails to express his willingness to comply with a requirement which is proposed by the court to be included in a community order and which requires an expression of such willingness, or

(b) he fails to comply with an order requiring pre-sentence drug testing.'

Length of discretionary custodial sentences

Section 153 is a general provision and particular offences may have specific provisions in relation to the use of custody. The custodial sentence must be for the shortest term (not exceeding the permitted maximum) that in the opinion of the court is commensurate with the seriousness of the offence, or the combination of the offence and one or more offences associated with it.

Custodial sentences of less than 12 months

These will be replaced by a new sentence, which Halliday called Custody Plus. This would be a system of a short period of custody followed by release on a licence which would include community order options. These sentences would be part custodial and part community dispositions and would consist of a custodial period of between two and 13 weeks, followed by a period of at least six months served in the community on licence within an overall sentence envelope of less than 12 months. A variation on this is Custody Minus. With this a prison sentence of two to 13 weeks could be suspended for up to two years. There would be community requirements as set by the court, breach of which would activate the custodial element. It would then be like Custody Plus. This is a variant on suspended sentences but with more intervention. Committing a further offence during the entire length of suspension would also count as breach.

Sentences of imprisonment of over 12 months

These will be served in full, half in custody, half in the community, with supervision extended to the end of the sentence rather than the three-quarter point as now. The supervision period will include being subject to requirements of various sorts.

Home detention curfew

This will continue to be available in most circumstances. It allowed for a release subject to electronic monitoring up to 60 days earlier than would otherwise have been the case. The new provision extends the period to up to 135 days.

Intermittent custody

New types of intermittent custodial sentence, such as weekend custody, are to be introduced. The Act creates a new sentence of intermittent custody which will permit periods of custody and release, with the release periods being on licence with provision for requirements as part of the licence period.

Mandatory life sentences

The minimum period of detention is to be determined by the court, by reference to statutory criteria, rather than the Home Secretary. The Parole Board would make decisions as to when release was appropriate subject to the minimum period.

Dangerous offenders

Serious violent and sexual offenders will be given new sentences which will ensure that they are kept in prison, or under supervision, for longer periods than currently. These offenders will get one of two new sentences for dangerous offenders (one each for where the maximum sentence is either under or over ten years) or a discretionary life sentence. Release from all of these sentences would be at the discretion of the Parole Board. Those who continue to pose a risk to the public may be kept in prison for an indeterminate period. The provisions as described below are those applicable to adults, but similar arrangements will apply to those under 18 years of age.

Life sentence or imprisonment for public protection for serious offences

Section 225 of the Act provides for a new sentence of imprisonment for public protection, which is an indeterminate sentence. This sentence may only be passed by a court if the offender is convicted of a specified sexual or violent offence carrying a maximum sentence of ten years or more and the court considers that the offender poses a significant risk of serious harm. Where the offence carries a maximum sentence of life imprisonment, the court must pass a life sentence if the seriousness of the offence justifies it. In other cases the court is to impose a sentence of imprisonment for public protection if it considers that no other sentencing options are adequate for the purposes of public protection.

Extended sentence for certain violent and sexual offences: persons 18 or over

Section 227 of the Act replaces the current provisions for extended sentences for sexual and violent offenders in the Powers of Criminal Courts (Sentencing) Act 2000. The conditions which must be met in order for this sentence to be passed are that the offender is over 18, has committed a specified sexual or violent offence carrying a maximum sentence of less than ten years and is judged by the court to pose a significant risk of serious harm to the public. The extended sentence is made up of the appropriate custodial term (ie in terms of seriousness of the offence) and an extension period. During the second half of the appropriate custodial term the offender may be released on the recommendation of the Parole Board. The court must also specify an extended period of supervision on licence to be added to the sentence for the purpose of public protection. The court may add an extension period of up to five years for violent offenders and nine years for sexual offenders. The total term of the extended sentence must not be more than the maximum sentence for the offence in question.

9.4 Prison statistics

The Prison Population in 2002

Hollis and Goodman (2003) reported that the prison population in custody in December 2002 was 69,612, a 5 per cent increase from the previous year. In 1993, it had been much lower at 44,570, although that had been considered a high figure at the time. By the start of August 2003 it had climbed even further to 73,911. The increase in prison numbers is a result of both greater use of custody and longer sentences. The various types of prisoner are detailed in Table 26. There were 65,535 male prisoners in December 2002 and 4,007 female prisoners. Juvenile prisoners aged 15–17 increased by 10 per cent over the year to 2,442. Remand prisoners increased by 8 per cent from 11,265 to 12,208. Sentenced prisoners increased by 5 per cent over the year from 53,982 to 56,439. Five per cent were serving sentences of less than six months, 6 per cent were serving from six months to less than 12 months, 38 per cent were serving from 12 months to less than four years, and 42 per cent were serving sentences of four years and over (excluding life sentence prisoners). There were 5,314 life sentence prisoners in 2002 (9 per cent of all sentenced prisoners) and of these 161 were young persons. There were 5,419 males and 165 females serving life sentences. The prison population was 4,625 (7 per cent) higher than the Certified Normal Accommodation of 64,987. The ethnic origins of prisoners were as follows: 83 per cent of the male British nationals in prison were white, 12 per cent were black, 3 per cent were South Asian and 2.0 per cent were Chinese or from other ethnic groups. Compare this with the male population aged 15–64 as a whole, where 95 per cent were white, 1 per cent were black, 3 per cent were South Asian and 1 per cent were Chinese or from other ethnic groups. The offences for which prisoners were sentenced are detailed in Table 27.

Table 26

Prison Population as at 31 December 2002		
	Male	Female	Total
Aged 15–17	2,327	115	2,442
On remand	413	18	431
Sentenced	1,914	97	2,011
Civil prisoners	0	0	0
Aged 18–20	8,044	477	8,521
On remand	1,793	120	1,913
Sentenced	6,180	353	6,533
Civil prisoners	71	4	75
Adult	55,164	3,485	58,649
On remand	9,129	735	9,864
Sentenced	45,196	2,699	47,895
Civil prisoners	839	51	890

318

	Male	Female	Total
Total	65,535	4,077	69,612
All remand	11,335	873	12,208
All sentenced	53,290	3,149	56,439
All civil	910	55	965

(Source: Prison Population Brief: December 2002)

Table 27

Prison Population December 2001 and December 2002 for Males and Females by Same Offence Types

Offence	Number of males		Number of females	
	2001	2002	2001	2002
Violence against the person	11,384	11,917	494	532
Burglary	8,306	8,719	170	207
Robbery	6,575	7,573	283	403
Theft and handling	4,138	3,783	426	368
Drug offences	8,231	8,507	1,215	1,271

(Source: Prison Population Brief: December 2002)

Counsell and Simes (2002) present the latest prison population projections for England and Wales up to the year 2009. The 2002 figure is projected to increase to 91.400 in 2009 if custody rates and sentence rates remained at 2002 levels. Things rarely stay exactly as they were before and two further plausible scenarios are explored. First, where it is assumed that custody rates increase at 2.5 per cent per year for males and 5 per cent for females to 2005, with the increase halving after that, and that sentence lengths increase annually by 3 per cent for males and 9 per cent for females to 2005, with the increase halving after that. This leads to a prison population of 109,600 in 2009. Second, where it is assumed that custody rates increase at 1.25 per cent per year for males and 2.55 per cent for females to 2005, with the increase halving after that, and that sentence lengths increase annually by 1.5 per cent for males and 4.5 per cent for females to 2005, with the increase halving after that. This leads to a prison population of 98,900 in 2009.

The variety of prisons, prison experiences and prisoner characteristics

Two broad types of prison can be noted – local prisons and training prisons. Local prisons are closed holding prisons which will deal with remand prisoners and may also hold people for the whole of their sentence. Of the training prisons, some are open. Training prisons are for sentenced prisoners but as will be seen later the notion of a training prison is a rather misleading label. Some institutions carry out more than one type of function. Stern

319

provides a useful insight into the types of people and tasks that prisons have to cope with and the variations in what the experience of prison can be for inmates.

'It holds the untried, the unsentenced, the civil prisoners. It acts as a social service, a hospital, a place where reports are written ... a nursery for mothers and their babies, a maternity hospital and a drug-rehabilitation facility. It contains prisoners whom many other prisoners would like to injure because of the nature of their offences, and prisoners who want to injure or kill themselves ... spending time in prison can mean many different experiences – being locked up with two other young men in a smelly cell for most of the day, waiting seven weeks to go to court for trial and then being released and given a community service order, bringing up a newborn baby in the mother and baby unit at Holloway, coping with mental illness in a prison hospital, working in the green houses of an open prison and sharing a dormitory with the most middle-class elements of the population ... or settling down for a long spell in an electronically controlled not over-crowded, top-security prison on the Isle of Wight.' (1987:31 and 35)

Walmsley, Howard and White (1991) in *The National Prison Survey* discovered that the prison population had a disproportionate amount of people from the working class and ethnic minorities. As many as 23 per cent reported themselves as having been in care as a child. Other disadvantages that afflicted the custodial population were higher than normal rates of family, abode and employment difficulties. Gunn et al (1991) noted the problems of mental illness. Psychoses affected 2 per cent of the prisoners in their survey, 5 per cent had neurotic disorders and 8 per cent had personality disorders. When drug problems were added in their estimate was that over 1,100 prisoners were in urgent need of medical treatment for such matters. Statistics on the ethnic background of prisoners (Home Office (1999d)) report that, in 1998, 12 per cent of male prisoners were black and that ethnic prisoners made up 18 per cent of the male population and 24 per cent of the female population. They also tended to be in prison at a younger age and to have received longer sentences than the average. These surveys of social factors are by no means untypical. It is also clear that there is a considerable percentage who are in some senses social inadequates, having a catalogue of social problems.

Women in prison

Statistics on Women and the Criminal Justice System (Home Office (2002b)) reported that women made up only 5 per cent of the prison population in 2001, but that this small amount was growing as the figure had been 3.5 per cent in 1993. The 2001 figure of 3,740 was double the 1993 figure of 1,560. Forty-one per cent of sentenced female prisoners were there for theft and handling, whilst 14 per cent were in prison for drug offences. It is the latter category of drugs that is playing a major part in the growing population in female prisons.

Further data was provided in Home Office (1997b), a thematic review by HM Chief Inspector of Prisons called *Women in Prison*. Whilst the review deals with a wide range of issues, the material here concentrates on the backgrounds of female prisoners. Before this is presented it can be noted that at the end of 1996 there were 15 prison establishments for women consisting of ten women-only prisons and five wings of male prisons. They contained 1,799 sentenced and 645 unsentenced prisoners. The sentence for 61 per cent of them was three years or less. The data was gained in part from a survey by means of interviews with 234 women prisoners who were selected at random. Nearly two-thirds of the women interviewed were mothers, with the majority having at least one child aged under 16. The average number of children which each of these women had was just under three. Approximately 4 per cent had their child with them in prison, all these children were under 18 months old. Only a quarter of the children were being cared for by either their biological father or their mother's current partner. The main carers were the women's own mothers (27 per cent) and or family and friends (29 per cent). More than one in ten of the women had children either in local authority care, fostered or adopted. Over 70 per cent of the women were living in, or had been living in, rented premises of which half was either council-owned or housing-association accommodation. Nearly one in ten of the women claimed to have been homeless before coming to prison. As many as 70 per cent of the women said they had had no previous employment before coming to prison. The majority (71 per cent) said they had not received a prison sentence before and nearly half reported having no previous convictions. Twenty per cent of the women said they had experienced time in care, this is in comparison to 2 per cent for the general population. As to the prison experience, a third said that they had been bullied. The majority of sentenced women reported that they had not experienced sentence planning at all.

Suggestions made for the future were that the female side of prisons should be a separate system, as far as possible, with complete physical separation Also suggested was a separate administrative system, with its own director, and its own worked-out needs and priorities. It was noted that most women who are in prison could be held in open conditions or could have been given a community penalty. Accommodation also needed to be provided closer to urban centres to allow visiting to be facilitated. Examples of the ideas in the report, in relation to the regime, include that, normally, sentenced women should be required to work as full a day as possible and there should be suitable work activities available. Finally, more vocational training courses, in manual skills, should be provided.

9.5 The aims and functions of prisons

In order to tackle the issue of what prisons are for, an outline of possible aims and functions of prisons from both official and non-official sources will be provided. These possibilities will provide a backcloth for the presentation of material on the actual workings of the prison system. The issue of aims and functions will then be returned to as part of an attempt at an evaluation of prisons. Two major hopes that could be held as regards prison would be that they would provide punishment and deterrence. Punishment provides a response to crime, enhancing respect for the law by demonstrating that it will be enforced. It also provides a fulfilment of public desires for revenge. Fines and prisons are the major sources of powers of retribution available to the courts. The former generally operating in the sphere of less serious offences with prison being for the serious offences. Deterrence of both the individual imprisoned and of people generally are other benefits that the existence of and use of prison can hope to offer. In the case of the individual this can involve both incapacitation (severely limiting but not completely removing the opportunity to commit crime) during the period when the person is in prison as well as the hope that the experience of prison will prevent offending after release.

Walker and Padfield (1996:125–126) provide a good list that suggest other possible purposes of prison:

1. To hold people – for example, until trial, or until they can be sentenced or be sent to the place where they will serve their sentence.
2. To coerce people to conform with court orders such as fines.
3. To protect members of the public from offenders by taking them out of circulation.
4. To hold a person long enough to make possible a prolonged course of treatment.
5. To show disapproval of the offence.
6. To protect a very unpopular offender against retaliation by victims or sympathisers of victims.

As regards official views of what prisons are for, it was stated in r1 of the Prison Rules in 1964 that the purpose of the training and treatment of convicted offenders shall be to encourage and assist them to lead a good and useful life. In 1969 the government White Paper *People in Prison* (Home Office (1969)) saw prisons as being there to hold people in conditions that were acceptable to society and in so far as is possible to encourage them to lead a good and useful life. The 1969 document wanted prisoners to have dignity and self-respect and there were still signs of hope as regards the idea of changing people for the better – reformation, rehabilitation and treatment still had mileage in them. By the time of the next official review in 1977 the view had changed and here it was stated that 'Research findings have given little support for the view that imprisonment can directly alter the long-term behaviour of prisoners': Home Office (1977b:136). The May Report in 1979 (Home Office (1979)), in its review of the United Kingdom Prison Services, stated that 'We think that the rhetoric of "treatment and training" has had its day and should be replaced' (1979:67). It was suggested in the May Report that prison should involve positive custody and that prisons should be 'hopeful and purposive communities' (1979:72). Also suggested was a new r1.

'The purpose of the detention of convicted prisoners shall be to keep them in prison which is both secure and yet positive, and to that end the behaviour of all the responsible authorities and staff toward them shall be such as to:

a) create an environment which can assist them to respond and contribute to society as positively as possible;
b) preserve and promote their self respect;
c) minimise, to the degree of security necessary in each particular case, the harmful effects of their removal from normal life;
d) prepare them for and assist them on their discharge.' (1979:67)

Despite the move away from ideas of treatment and training in official statements, r1 has not been changed.

Criminal Justice: A Working Paper (Home Office (1986a)) came up with the following view as to the functions of prisons.

'The Prisons Board has issued a statement of the task of the prison service which identifies four main functions. Briefly stated, they are to hold unsentenced prisoners in custody and produce them to court; to hold sentenced prisoners with a suitable degree of security and release them on the due date; to provide not only the physical necessities but as full a life as is consistent with the facts of custody; and to enable prisoners to retain links with the community and, where possible, help them to prepare for their return to it.' (1986a:30)

Apart from the lack of empirical support for reformative ideas, overcrowding and the poor conditions in prisons meant that such ideas did not really stand a chance. A further development also overshadowed ideas of reform – the development of an obsession with security. These matters will be returned to later in the context of the problems of long-term prisoners. One of the consequences of the obsession with security was prison disturbances and this led to a call for another enquiry into prisons.

The Woolf Report

This Report (Home Office (1991)) was specifically into the disturbances in prisons in April 1991. It was more wide-ranging than was probably intended and it came up with 12 central recommendations.

These are that there should be:

1. Closer co-operation between the different parts of the criminal justice system. For this purpose a national forum and local committees should be established.
2. More visible leadership of the Prison Service by a Director-General who is and is seen to be the operational head and in day-to-day charge of the Service. To achieve this there should be a published 'compact' or 'contract' given by ministers to the Director-General of the Prison Service who should be responsible for the performance of that 'contract' and publicly answerable for the day to day operations of the Prison Service.
3. Increased delegation of responsibility to governors of establishments.
4. An enhanced role for prison officers.
5. A 'compact' or 'contract' for each prisoner setting out the prisoner's expectations and responsibilities in the prison in which he or she is held.
6. A national system of accredited standards, with which, in time, each prison establishment would be required to comply.
7. A new rule that no establishment should hold more prisoners than is provided for in its certified normal level of accommodation, with provisions for Parliament to be informed if exceptionally there is to be a material departure from that rule.
8. A public commitment from ministers to set a timetable to provide access to sanitation for all inmates at the earliest practicable date, not later than February 1996.
9. Better prospects for prisoners to maintain their links with families and the community through more visits and home leaves and through being located in community prisons as near to their homes as possible.
10. A division of prison establishments into small and more manageable and secure units.
11. A separate statement of purpose, separate conditions and generally a lower security categorisation for remand prisoners.
12. Improved standards of justice within prisons involving: the giving of reasons to a

prisoner for any decision which materially and adversely affects him; a grievance procedure and disciplinary proceedings which ensure that the governor deals with most matters under his present powers; relieving Boards of Visitors of their adjudicatory role; and providing for final access to an independent Complaints Adjudicator.

The Report was well received and some change resulted from it. On point 1 we have signs of joined up criminal justice with area committees and a national council introduced. Point 8 happened as slopping out was ended. As regards point 6 there are no signs of legally enforceable standards. Point 7 has certainly not happened as overcrowding is still a big problem.

To be contrasted with the Woolf Report is the Learmont Report (1995), In the Learmont Report it was made clear that custody must be the primary purpose of prisons. This report proposed increasing the number of prisoners who should be subjected to high levels of security and an overall increase in levels of security. This included proposals to limit inmate possessions, the use of magnetic or electronic locks, more surveillance and searches and daily audits of workshop materials and tools.

9.6 Overcrowding, prison conditions and prison security

The issue of overcrowding is one of the major problems that the prison system has had to face since the end of the Second World War. In 1987, 41,994 spaces were available but the population was 6,969 greater at 48,963. More recently, the available accommodation in December 2002 was 64,987, whilst the population was 69,612. The overcrowding is concentrated in the local prisons and remand centres, whereas some types of establishments such as open prisons have spare capacity. These figures can be compared with the data in Table 28 from earlier in the century. From these figures it is clear that there has been a considerable increase in the number of people who are held in prisons.

Table 28

Average Populations for Custodial Establishments	
1920–1945	10–15,000
1950	20,000
1960	27,000
1970	39,028
1980	43,760

(Source: Prison Statistics, England and Wales for (1969, 1970 and 1980))

The most recent increases in the number of people who are held in prisons are a consequence of increases in the remand population and in the number of offenders receiving longer sentences. Trying to deal with the problem of overcrowding in prisons has been one of the central themes of penal policy in recent times. Sentencers were urged to use custody less often and for shorter periods. For example, Douglas Hurd, the then Home Secretary, told a meeting of magistrates in January 1988 that custody is the last resort. The Court of Appeal also made it clear that courts should not sentence on a purely punitive or deterrent basis without regard to the costs or the individual characteristics of the offender. In order to assist this strategy non-custodial sentences have been made available to the courts. When change to the bail and parole systems was introduced, concern over prison numbers has been much in issue. On the other hand there have also been developments that meant that more people would be in danger of going to prison and also that sentences would be longer. There have been various signs of a desire to get tough on crime, and an aspiration of protecting the public has also been expressed: Home Office (1996). The claim was also made by Michael Howard, whilst he was Home Secretary, that prison works. The Criminal Justice Act 1991, which had presented prison as a sentence of last resort, was undermined in a number of ways by the Criminal Justice Act 1993. Maximum sentences were increased and previous convictions and offences having been committed whilst on bail were to be factors in sentencing. The Criminal Justice and Public Order Act 1994, and even more so the Crime (Sentences) Act 1997, were to be further examples of such thinking. Finally, mention can be made of the prison-building programme. This shows a commitment to prisons. Whilst all of this was happening, tactics to reduce prison numbers were still being introduced. In 1997 it was announced that thousands of prisoners were to be electronically tagged and released early. Tagging systems were also to be used to increase the viability of non-custodial sentences and to enhance the prospects of bail rather than a remand in custody by the courts.

The impact of overcrowding

The main problem of overcrowding is that it can have such a generally limiting effect on the regime within prisons. It will limit the availability of work, education, visits and association within the prison. In the worst cases this can mean spending 23 hours of the day locked up in a cell. The conditions in some prisons have at times reached crisis proportions as is evidenced by the statements of those who have responsibilities in relation to them. The Director-General of the Prison Department said in 1981 (Home Office (1982)):

> 'In last year's report, I described the conditions arising from a population well in excess of the available accommodation as an "… affront to a civilised society." Those conditions did not improve in 1981. In some establishments, and particularly when the population rose to its peak of 45,500, they worsened. The subsequent decline in the population provided a measure of relief; it reduced the state of prisons from imminent catastrophe to chronic crisis.'

It is not just those in prison who suffer because of the limited provision of facilities. Shirley Adams explains how it also affects those outside prison as well. Shirley Adams married Peter Adams, who was the first life-sentence prisoner to result from the abolition (initially in 1957 and finally in 1969) of capital punishment for murder. She had met him in prison in the capacity of prison visitor. Adams and Adams (1982) relates their experiences of the penal system. She described the difficulties involved in visiting a prisoner as follows. That no directions were given as to how to get to the prison, so she ended up having to face the embarrassment of asking on a bus as to its whereabouts. Upon arrival she found that you had to wait outside the prison, a situation also being faced by a mother with an infant who had a cold. In the winter the transport situation was such that if a taxi was not taken and paid for then there was a risk that half the visit would be missed.

Conditions in prisons

Insight into prison conditions is to be found in the reports of the Chief Inspector of Prisons, and material here is provided from three reports. In the report on Liverpool Prison (Home Office (1999f)) we are told that with a population of 1,500 prisoners it is the largest prison in England and Wales. It is described as a local prison, but in fact Liverpool is no longer a local prison but a vast training prison containing 1,200 sentenced prisoners. It is still resourced as a local prison, a situation affecting many other large, Victorian, inner-city local prisons around the country. What this suggests is that HMP Liverpool is in need of a clearly defined role and purpose, towards which management and staff can work and for which it should be staffed and resourced. Those resources must be related to the needs of prisoners, within the overall criminal justice system aim of protecting the public by preventing crime. For example, 80 per cent of the prisoner population admit to being heroin users before coming into prison. This suggests not just the need for treatment facilities within the prison, but also the need to tackle the public health issue of the association of blood-transmitted diseases such as Hepatitis C with those who use the drug. If you include social exclusion and parental neglect, 85 per cent of the population have suffered from some form of abuse in their lives. An example of resources not matching needs within Liverpool Prison is a lack of classrooms, which means that education only succeeds in touching 15 per cent of the prison population. There are PE facilities, and an enthusiastic and capable staff, but both are too small to cope with the numbers who wish to use them.

The Chief Inspector in the Preface to the report on Bristol Prison (Home Office (1999g)) stated:

'I have lost count of the number of reports that I have written on local prisons in which I have said and recommended exactly the same things. Collectively and individually they are the most overcrowded prisons in the system, and all are under resourced to look after the range and mix of prisoners who are committed to them. These include remanded prisoners, convicted but unsentenced prisoners, life, long, medium and short sentenced prisoners, mentally disordered prisoners, drug and other substance addicts and, in the case of Bristol, prisoners whose risk to the public and other prisoners is such as to qualify them for Category A status ... I have tried many times, most recently in my 1997–98 Annual Report, to encourage the Prison Service to do something about this situation, and to consider reorganising the prison estate to provide better treatment and conditions for prisoners in local prisons, thus better protecting the public. I continue to do so because they remain without direction or a clear aim, which makes life enormously difficult for Governors. All they have to fall back on is keeping within budget and satisfying Key Performance Indicators, which have little relevance to the realities of life in an overcrowded and under resourced prison. They are not there solely to serve the courts witness the fact that, on average, only 25–30 per cent of their population are awaiting trial or sentence. In theory, therefore, they are training prisons required, in addition, to hold unsentenced prisoners.'

Finally, in the report on Exeter Prison (Home Office (1999h)), he states:

'I fear that those who have read other, recent, local prison inspection reports will not be surprised at much of the content of this one on Exeter. There is the usual mixture of good and bad – many good staff trying to do their best for prisoners, but an already impoverished regime being affected by what are euphemistically called efficiency savings; a good senior management team frustrated by industrial relations problems, high levels of staff sickness and the additional workload put on them by Prison Service Headquarters; good education and PE but not enough work for prisoners – in Exeter's case no work for prisoners.'

A further source of information on prison conditions are the reports of the Prison Ombudsman. The Ombudsman system for prisons, as with the system of prison inspections, is a robust one. He investigates complaints and has a strong persuasive influence in relation to issues where a complaint is upheld. The following information comes from the third report of Sir Peter Woodhead in his position of Prisons Ombudsman which covered 1997: Home Office (1998c). He found it disappointing that he continues to deal with many of the same type of grievances as in previous years. He is still upholding almost half of the complaints investigated and it seems that the Prison Service is not learning from its past mistakes. Problems were identified in the Prison Service's internal complaints system, these being failures to investigate complaints adequately and in taking far too long to deal with relatively simple grievances. Also, the Prison Service is not even able to say how many complaints it deals with and what the outcomes are. The Prison Service ignores at its peril the finding of Lord Woolf, in his inquiry into the prison disturbances of April 1990, that one of the root causes of the riots was that prisoners believed they had no other effective method of ventilating their grievances. In all nearly 2,000 complaints had been received in the year. Some cases raised serious concerns. In one of the cases a woman prisoner had been held inappropriately for 48 hours in an unfurnished cell without basic sanitation and had been denied food and water for 24 hours. Sir Peter said:

'This is one of the worst cases of maltreatment of a prisoner I have seen and I find it disturbing that, although the facts were accepted by the Prison Service, no disciplinary action was taken against any of the staff involved'. The Ombudsman was also unhappy, in some other cases he had dealt with, that the Prison Service was not always handling issues surrounding strip searching appropriately. In one case a prisoner had been strip searched twice within a matter of minutes of his arrival at the prison, contrary to the laid down procedures.'

The following cases come from the *Prisons and Probation Ombudsman Annual Report 2002–2003*, (2003). Mr Z (11708/02) complained about his transfer to another prison following his suspected involvement in consuming alcohol. He was one of several prisoners believed to be intoxicated in a workshop. Mr Z said he had not been drinking but white spirits and spray paints he was using had caused his eyes to become inflamed. An adjudication had been adjourned for production of a witness, but had not been continued with. Instead, Mr Z had been transferred. The charge against Mr Z had been dismissed and there was little, if any, evidence that he had been drinking. The Ombudsman could not know for certain the truth of the matter, but concluded that to transfer a prisoner for suspicion of being drunk was excessive, especially as this appeared to have been a one-off incident. The Ombudsman discovered that part of the prison's zero tolerance policy with regard to alcohol was routinely to transfer transgressors, other than in exceptional circumstances. He objected to this blanket policy and noted that the prison was category B and should be capable of dealing with such problems. Thus he upheld Mr Z's complaint.

A case that was decided differently was that of Mr A (13046/02), who complained that a compact prohibiting him from approaching females was unreasonably restrictive. Mr A said the compact was a farce and asked that it be dropped. He said he had done nothing to justify being on the compact. Mr A's Inmate Intelligence Card and wing history sheets recorded numerous incidents when his behaviour in relation to women caused concern. A further four entries related to inappropriate behaviour towards women since the compact had been imposed. The Ombudsman also saw letters Mr A had written to an outside acquaintance. The recipient (not surprisingly) considered the contents to be both offensive and an intrusion into her private life. The Ombudsman also discovered that the prison used compacts when the only alternative would be to segregate the prisoner. All available information was carefully considered before invoking a contract, the position was regularly reviewed, and the decision of the review was explained to the prisoner. The contract clearly placed stringent restrictions on Mr A and meant he did not have access to the full range of church services or education. Evidence of Mr A's inappropriate behaviour towards and around women was, however, abundant. The Ombudsman considered that the compact and procedures for review were a reasonable way of containing risk and addressing inappropriate behaviour.

The security obsession

The issue of security in prisons is the next matter to be considered and it leads into an account of the long-term detention of prisoners. Security became a major concern after a series of escapes by top security prisoners in the mid-1960s. These included: the Great Train Robbers, Ronnie Biggs and Charlie Wilson (Wilson's escape involved a prison break in); Frank Mitchell, described by the press as being the mad axe-man; and George Blake, the Russian spy. Blake, had been sentenced to 42 years' imprisonment in order to ensure that he would not be at liberty for a long time. A report under Lord Mountbatten (Home Office (1966)) suggested that top-security prisoners should be concentrated in an Alcatraz-like fortress prison. The very secure perimeter would allow for a liberal and constructive regime inside. As we will see in a moment a dispersal system was preferred. However, the concentration idea was to be utilised many years later. Woodhill Prison, near Milton Keynes, was opened in 1998. It is a new high-security establishment designed to house together the most disruptive and dangerous prisoners. The aim is to provide therapy with a view to being able to eventually accommodate the prisoners in other prisons.

The Mountbatten Report also produced a classification system for prisoners.

1. Category A is for those whose escape would be highly dangerous to the public, to the police or to the security of the state.
2. Category B are those for whom escape has to be made difficult.
3. Category C are those who are not suitable for category D but who do not have the ability or resources to make a determined escape bid.
4. Category D is for those who can be trusted in open conditions.

This classification system, built around notions of security, is in use in the prison system. Classification in terms of treatment and training needs would make more sense. The idea of a single fortress prison was not liked by the Home Office in 1996 and a new report was commissioned. The Radzinowicz Report (Home Office (1968b)) suggested that long-term prisoners were best kept in very secure conditions at long-term prisons. This system was introduced and it was called the dispersal system because of its use of a number of prisons rather than just one or two. It was felt that by spreading the high-risk prisoners around the prison system, the calamity of a mass escape would be avoided. Also, it was thought that a fortress system would not be able to foster a liberal and constructive regime. Of course as it happened the dispersal system has not managed this either. Concern with security became the order of the day and this has had invidious and counter-productive effects upon the system for the long-term detention of offenders and, indeed, throughout the prison system as a whole. Matters relating to long-term detention are considered next.

9.7 Coping with long-term prisoners

Abolition of capital punishment for murder, initially in 1957 and finally in 1969, linked with an increasing problem of terrorism and a more restrictive use of parole for very serious offenders, have all meant that there are more prisoners facing long periods in custody. Sentences have also tended to become longer for the more serious offences in recent times. All of this added to concerns about security and control. A very limiting regime was provided for prisoners.

The tactic of control turned out to be counter-productive as evidenced by a series of prison riots – Gartree (1972 and 1978), Hull (1976), both Wormwood Scrubs and Parkhurst (in 1979) and Albany (in 1983) – and of course the 1990 riots which were the worst manifestations of a general problem of prison disturbances. The issues of security and control have become confused. This point was made clear by a report on the long-term prison system drawn up by Prison Department staff, the Control Review Committee: Home Office (1984b). They suggested that, whilst of course there has to be appropriate security, the available resources should be used so as to provide amongst other things a life in prison that should be as close as possible to normal life. They wanted a flexible and responsive system in which human relationships and development could be enhanced rather than an authoritarian and conflict-inducing regime. They felt that a prisoner's time in prison should be planned centrally so as to make best use of resources and so as to make clear to the prisoner both what was expected of him and available to him. Experience from the United States led them to suggest that a number of small units of different character could be provided on one secure site. The hope was that developments of this type could lead to reduced need for the dispersal system. As regards those prisoners who persistently present several control problems, they suggested that special control facilities would have to be made available. These were not intended to be like the infamous control units but rather were to offer safe and humane containment. The control units, which were used in the 1970s, involved amongst other things a minimum period of 90 days' (of 23 hours a day) isolation from other prisoners.

Inertia within a system that as Stern (1987) pointed out fears political embarrassment and revelations in newspapers about prisoners enjoying themselves watching colour television more than it fears revelations about prisoners locked up for twenty-three hours a day has meant that little has happened in the light of the Control Review Committee's report. Whilst the prospects of change being introduced are not good I will nevertheless present some further material which demonstrates the possibilities of smaller humanised and individualised units. The example offered by Grendon Underwood Prison can be noted first. This provides a purposive open atmosphere in which both activities and community contact are encouraged. The possibilities of other regimes are also noted by Downes (1988). In a comparison of the system in England and Wales with that of The Netherlands he quoted an English prisoner in a Dutch closed prison:

'They treat you like a human being. They say "Enjoy your meal", "Good morning". They treat you like a man, they let you do things the way you like, they're not always looking up your arse for drugs, they don't guard you to see the Governor, with two warders either side. Even when you go to solitary, you take yourself there. You think "It can't be true, there must be a catch" but there isn't. I just can't believe they don't despise you because you're a criminal. In England they punish you for being a criminal. Then they punish you while they're punishing you. Then you're punished for the rest of your life.' (1988:163)

He also provided the view of a Dutch prisoner in an English training prison:

'Dutch prisons are much better, especially at thinking how to bring prisoners back to the normal life. There is home leave every weekend or so – here there is no way you can get that experience. If they realise that you are not a thoroughgoing criminal, they will do their best to re-establish you in society. Here there is no real attempt to do that, and for the English prisoners this is very bad. He goes out to nothing, so he goes back to crime ...' (1988:163)

In similar vein Mott (1985) pointed out that changes to regimes in terms of encouraging integration of prison staff and prisoners and in providing activities can have beneficial effects as regards limiting control problems. Hawkins (1974) is one of a number of writers who suggested that prisoners should be integrated into rather than isolated from society and that individualised treatment programmes that offer realistic prospects of benefits should be made available even if they are expensive. It may well be cheaper in the long run to adopt such an approach.

The final example of the possibilities of alternative approaches is that of the special unit at Barlinnie Prison in Scotland. Jimmy Boyle was one of the prisoners in this Special Unit and he describes his experiences of it in Boyle (1984) and to a lesser extent Boyle (1977). The material in relation to the unit is most effectively portrayed when contrasted with other provisions made for long-term prisoners in Scotland (the Special Unit has now been closed down). Jimmy Boyle, after a violent criminal past, was sentenced to life imprisonment for murder in 1967. Within the Scotttish prison system there were a number of prisoners who in effect had nothing to lose and who protested against their conditions and the brutality that was used against them. For this they were punished which led to further incidents in which people were being seriously injured. Boyle (1984) tells well his experience of Inverness Prison:

'I found myself connecting with other prisoners who were in the same boat. We had a lot in common and built up personal relationships when in solitary through an archaic ventilator system that was linked to each cell. In this way we began to plan and co-ordinate our actions. We soon learned that the system which copes well with individual troublemakers doesn't when these same individuals begin to organise and co-operate with each other. In response to this the authorities became more reactionary and oppressive in their measures to contain us. After a succession of fights, riots and demonstrations five of us found ourselves held in the Cages in Inverness prison. These were iron-barred cage fronts that sub-divided a prison cell; reminiscent of those used to hold animals in a travelling circus. We were, at times, kept naked and given one book per week to read. The decor and structure of the whole block was built for sensory deprivation. The rules, blatantly plastered on the wall, stated that no prisoner would be kept in the cages for less than two months or more than six. This was flagrantly abused. ...

The climax of this downward spiral took the form of a bloody riot in the Cages. Many prison officers and prisoners were injured. The doctors announced that I wasn't expected to last the night. Four of us were eventually charged with the attempted murder of six prison officers. It made no difference to any of us. I simply worked my body back to physical fitness in preparation for the next bloody occasion. I thought there was no alternative.

Behind the scenes, outwith our sphere of knowledge, the authorities were stretched to the limit. A number of prison officers in Inverness resigned from the Service in the aftermath of the riot. Prison staff in other prisons were saying they wouldn't have the hard core of us back. The pressure was on to get the Special Unit opened.' (1984:7–8)

As regards the unit, MacDonald and Sim (1977) noted that the Special Unit had evolved into a self-styled therapeutic community. In terms of physical conditions and personal relationships between prisoners and the staff the unit had progressed away from the traditional authoritarian non-relationships and spartan conditions that the majority of long-term prisoners in Scotland face. There is a great deal of freedom, responsibility and personal choice given to prisoners within the confines of the unit. The men wear their own clothes rather than prison uniform. They can decorate their own cells and keep books and record players. They can cook their own food, supplementing prison rations with food bought with their own money. Their mail, unlike that of prisoners in the traditional system, is unrestricted and uncensored. Access to visitors is also unrestricted except when the men are locked up at night. Each prisoner plans his own routine for the day and democratic community meetings take place weekly to discuss any issues that may have arisen. Any member of the community – either staff or prisoner – who 'lets the side down' by breaking the rules, can end up in the 'hot-seat' where his actions are discussed, criticised and chastised by the other members of the community, again whether staff or prisoner. These weekly meetings function as a place where people learn to talk out any problems they might have in an open and objective way – something which is impossible in the traditional system. When a decision affecting domestic issues has to be made, each man, staff or prisoner, has one vote. One of the earliest and most symbolic taken was to remove the door of the punishment cell, which meant that reliance on the old method of punishing an individual by locking him up in solitary confinement was abandoned in favour of the new community based 'hot-seat'. This, according to both the staff and the inmates, is a much more effective means of control than the measures used in the traditional system, measures which, in the majority of cases, serve only to make the prisoner more resentful and bitter.

Ultimately, it is this ability to make democratic decisions and the positive staff-prisoner relationships, together with the physical environment far removed from the obsolete conditions of the majority of prison buildings, which makes the Special Unit unique. Barlinnie is quite simply a different type of system to that of Inverness. There have been problems there, including violence and the death of a prisoner from a drug over-dose. Again context is required and the report of a prison governor on Boyle prior to his transfer to the Special Unit is instructive. 'I am firmly of the opinion that this man is so dangerous that he should never, under any circumstances, be liberated from prison and further, despite the assaults and incidents in which he has been involved in the past, he is still, even at this moment, planning further assaults and further incidents. He is liable at any time if given the slightest opportunity, to attack and kill anybody with whom he is liable to come in contact': Boyle (1984:Preface). Such clientele did not offer the Special Unit an easy ride. Eventually Boyle was released from prison and has had success as an author and sculptor and made a useful contribution in terms of an involvement with both grassroots social problems and as a commentator upon social issues. The key seems to be humanity. Boyle relates one of the experiences of his first day in the unit:

> 'I was then "asked" by the screw if I would come round and sort out my personal property with him. I went, and while we opened the parcels containing old clothing he did something that to him was so natural but to me was something that had never been done before. He turned to me and handed me a pair of scissors and asked me to cut open some of them. He then went about his business. I was absolutely stunned. This was the first thing that made me feel human again. It was the completely natural way that it was done. This simple gesture made me think. In my other world, the penal system in general, such a thing would never happen.' (1977:24)

Given that Boyle was facing trial for six charges of attempted murder on prison staff it was certainly an optimistic approach. Suffice to say that the lessons of such experiences have not been adopted by the prison system.

Close supervision centres

The Prison Service's system of close supervision centres, for the management of disruptive prisoners, was introduced in February 1998. Research on the centres was carried out by Clare and Bottomley et al (2001). The centres were to replace the former network of special units established in the late 1980s, following the recommendations of the Control Review Committee (1984), and generally known as CRC units. The close supervision centres were also intended to take prisoners previously placed on the continuous assessment scheme. The original role of the centres was to operate as part of a national management strategy which aims to secure the return of problematic or disruptive prisoners to a settled and acceptable pattern of institutional behaviour. To this end the system has the following functions:

1. to remove the most seriously disruptive prisoners from mainstream dispersal or training prisons;
2. to contain highly dangerous or disruptive individuals in small highly supervised units with safety for staff and prisoners;
3. to provide the opportunity for individuals to address their anti-social disruptive behaviour in a controlled environment;

4. to stabilise behaviour and prepare for a return to the mainstream with minimum disruption;
5. to assist in the long term containment of those who continue to pose a serious threat to the safety of staff and prisoners.

The researchers in this report argue that the close supervision centres' central underlying principle of prisoner progression, through a variety of incentives and earned privileges, is seriously flawed with respect to the management of these particular prisoners, and that their management should be based on a set of rather different operational principles and processes. The key elements should include:

1. a comprehensive assessment process which includes substantial and integrated clinical input from forensic psychiatric services and others, in order to identify personality disorder and mental illness, and to assess risk;
2. the establishment of differential regimes with safe and humane conditions in which the minimum threshold should be standards and conditions that at least equate to those found in dispersal segregation units;
3. the long-term containment of a small number of high risk prisoners whom it would be unsafe to return to normal location, even when they have spent many years in the system and have progressed to the top level.

9.8 Incapacitation as a benefit of imprisonment

Prison has a considerable, though not totally incapacitating, effect as regards the ability to commit crime. Given present levels of the use of imprisonment the vast majority of criminals will not be in prison and will not be so incapacitated. To suggest an increased use of prisons, such as a doubling of the prison population, would not significantly alter the situation and the costs involved would be very large. Murray (1997), an American writer on the underclass, is a proponent of a rigorous use of such an approach. He suggests that prison works so long as you use it correctly. By this he means with sufficient ruthlessness. Prison would for example deter shop-lifters, if all shop-lifters who were convicted were sentenced to a year in prison. Shop-lifting would become exceedingly rare. Deterrence fails only because the odds of being caught and imprisoned are not high enough, or because the sentence is not harsh enough. Can imprisonment prevent people from committing crimes? Of course it can. The technical term is incapacitation. Burglars who are locked up do not commit burglaries. Murray suggests that lessons are to be learnt from the United States. Like Britain it first tried a sustained, large-scale reduction in the use of prison. It then embarked on a large-scale increase in the use of prison, that has lasted much longer and been much more massive than Britain's recent shift in prison policy. During the period of reduction the crime rate was rising. In 1974 things changed in the United States. The courts began sending criminals to prison in wholesale lots. The number of prisoners in state and federal prisons in 1974 stood at 218,205. It reached 300,000 five years later. It took four more years to reach 400,000, and three more to reach 500,000 in 1986. Since then, the United States has been adding about 100,000 prisoners every two years. As of 1995 there were more than one million people in American prisons. Does this mean that prison does not work? It would appear so given that there is still a high crime rate there. Murray argues that such an approach shows a failure to understand what happened in the United States. He suggests that it is the risk of going to prison that matters. In the United States, starting in 1961, the risk fell by 64 per cent in just 10 years, because the American crime rate shot up. At the same time the policy was to reduce the use of imprisonment. By the time the United States started increasing the number of people in prison in the mid-1970s, huge increases were required just to make the risk of imprisonment keep up with the continuing increases in crime. Only in the past few years, with more than 1 million in prison, has the ratio of prisoners to crimes reached the level that prevailed in 1961. Britain would have to quintuple the prison population to get back to 1954 risk levels.

Murray suggests that prison can stop a rising crime rate and then begin to push it down. The American crime rate hit its peak in 1980, a few years after the risk of imprisonment had bottomed out. Since then, with only a few exceptions, rates for the various serious crimes, have generally been returning to the levels of 20 years ago. The academics are still arguing about how much of this is because of prison. Murray cites academics who suggest that it is a lot to do with prison. For example, Levitt, a Harvard economist, concluded that a 1,000 inmate increase prevents about four murders, 53 rapes, 1,200 assaults, 1,100 robberies, 2,600 burglaries and 9,200 thefts. Academics can reach such conclusions by comparing offenders who are left on the streets with offenders who are imprisoned. More than 60 per cent of American defendants accused of violent crimes are released while awaiting trial. Some will not receive a custodial sentence and some prisoners will be released early. For example, a federal study of state prisoners found that 45 per cent of them were in prison for a crime they had committed while on probation or parole. Most of those on probation had never been in prison (one cannot invoke 'the prison only makes them worse' argument to explain their behaviour). It is possible to work out how many offences they commit during periods that they could otherwise have been in custody. Such an analysis would not of course have taken into account the extra undetected crimes.

It is true that crime in America has receded during the 1980s and 1990s, but it is still extremely high compared with the 1950s. Prison has stopped the rot. Murray does not suggest that it will defeat crime in itself. If you are looking for a return to 1950s crime levels through increased use of prison he suggests that you are going to be disappointed. He knows that raising the imprisonment rate does not affect many of the 'root causes' of crime. He realises that there are social causes, his big idea on this is welfare dependency. Incarcerating people will not, by itself, solve the crime problem. But an intelligent approach to prison does not require that it does so. Murray suggests that you must ask what do we want prison to accomplish? He cites John Dilulio, a leading American criminologist, who weary of hearing the critics of prison repeat that "incarceration is not the answer" got to the heart of the matter:

'If incarceration is not the answer what, precisely, is the question? If the question is "how can we restore the fabric of family life and socialise a new generation of young males to civilised behaviour?" then prison is not the answer. If the question is: "how can we make unemployable youths employable?" prison is not the answer. If the question is "how can we rehabilitate habitual criminals so that they become law-abiding citizens?", prison is only rarely the answer.

But if the question is "how can we deter people from committing crimes?"then prison is an indispensable part of the answer. If the question is "how can we restrain known, convicted criminals from murdering, raping; assaulting and thieving?", prison is just about the perfect answer.'

By way of comment it has to be said that it makes for a plausible argument. It is certainly another point of view. But treat these ideas with some suspicion, there is too much evidence, as we will see later, to doubt that severe penalties will deter. This has been seen in relation to capital punishment for murder and indeed, for a whole range of offences, in the past. For deterrence to operate the potential offender needs to have the penalty in mind at the time that the offence is about to be committed. The reality is that most offenders do not have penalties in mind at that stage, at most they have a fear of being caught. Also to take note of is a report by Amnesty International (Bannister et al (1998)) which details widespread problems of sex abuse and torture within the overstretched United States prison system. The pressure on the system has come from overcrowding – itself the product of the explosion in the number of inmates in recent years. The findings were based on a two-year investigation of United States prisons. A particular feature of the problem is the disproportionate impact it has on poor and ethnic sectors of the population. There is indiscriminate use of control devices such as stun guns. Amongst the catalogue of concerns are accounts of sexual abuse of women.

Where the idea of incapacitation might have particular merit is in relation to dangerous offenders from whom the public need particular protection. Thus, an especially long sentence could be given for this purpose. Sentences which are directed to the purpose of protecting the public would not be a new innovation. The Criminal Justice Act 1948 provided for preventive detention and the Powers of the Criminal Courts Act 1973, by means of a system of extended sentences, also sought to protect the public from persistent recidivists. The Crime (Sentences) Act 1997 is a further example of such thinking. Another example is George Blake's 42-year sentence for spying, intended to ensure that he would never be able to pass on damaging information. It is an unfortunate example given that he escaped. The Criminal Justice Act 2003 makes provision for a category of dangerous offenders. A merit of capital punishment is that as a sentence it ensures that the individual will not offend again. In the United Kingdom debate as to the merits of protective sentences followed the Floud report (Floud and Young (1981)), and the July (1982) issue of the *British Journal of Criminology* (Volume 22, No 3) was wholly concerned with the matter. Academics have found the issue a happy hunting-ground with fears of totalitarianism being raised and scotched and claims as to rival methods of defining dangerousness being advanced, whilst others wish to deride such endeavours, problems of prediction have been raised and been declared both solvable and insurmountable and, finally, different groups of people have been selected as being both suitable and unsuitable for the various types of decision-making that would be involved in both the Floud and alternative schemes.

Protective sentences were suggested as being suitable in relation to grave harm which comprises: death; serious bodily injury; serious sexual assaults; severe or prolonged pain or mental stress; loss of or damage to property which causes severe personal hardship; damage to the environment which has a severely adverse effect on public health or safety; and serious damage to the security of the state. Before the sentence could be used a number of pre-conditions had to be satisfied of which the following are some. The offender would have had to have done, attempted, risked, threatened or conspired to do grave harm. He would also have had to have committed an act of a similar kind on another occasion. The court would also have to be satisfied both that the person was more likely, than other grave offenders of similar age and sex, to do further grave harm and that there was no other permissible means available to offer the necessary degree of protection to the public. What would be aimed for was that there was a better than even chance of being correct. The mistakes made would have to be regarded as one of the costs of the system though it would be desirable that steps be taken in terms of the refinement of predictive techniques. It was thought that such a sentence would only be applicable to a small number of offenders. In 1978 for example it would have been in the order of 140. Such a sentence would be put on a statutory footing and operate in a system of generally shorter sentences for other offenders.

It was fully accepted that the notion of dangerous was a difficult concept and that there were difficulties involved in predicting which people required preventative sentences. The approach taken was to say that risks have to be balanced and redistributed within society and that quite simply choices have to be made. Such choices would have to take into account factors such as public opinion, which has its own peculiar notions of risk and danger as seen in public attitudes to motor cars. Motor cars are potentially dangerous objects and yet are much misused in terms of dangerous behaviour such as speeding. Factors which can limit the risks – such as wearing seat-belts and not drinking and driving – have had to face public resistance. It would be a brave and politically foolish government that legislated for devices to be fitted to cars that would prevent them exceeding the 70 mph speed limit. In the Floud report it was thought that the risk of danger would be largely equated with violence but they had other matters in mind as well in that they included damage to property. The operation of such a system involves sacrificing the interests of the offender. Such an approach was used in 1973 in the case of Paul Storey, a 16 year old who was given a 20-year sentence for mugging. The offence had been particularly severe and appeared to be explainable only in terms of deriving enjoyment from inflicting pain. The sentence was to protect the public, to ensure that the offender would not be released until it was safe to do so. It was not intended to operate as an exemplary or general deterrent sentence, though it was widely portrayed as such.

9.9 Deterioration as a possible problem with the use of long-term imprisonment

A possible problem with long-term imprisonment is that it will cause prisoners to become institutionalised and to deteriorate mentally. Cohen and Taylor's (1981) account of a maximum-security prison (E wing of Durham jail from 1968–1971) would point in that direction. Noting particular features, such as the control aspects and the surveillance by means of television cameras, does not really convey the message of the book. The prisoners were attempting to survive in extreme conditions so as to avoid deterioration and to cope with isolation from the wider society to which in most cases they will have to return – with diminished abilities to cope with everyday life. Jimmy Boyle effectively portrayed the brutalising effects of Peterhead and Inverness prisons: see Boyle (1977 and 1984). Despite such material the weight of evidence points to other conclusions. Zamble and Popporino (1990) found that in general that long-term prisoners, whilst more introverted during their time in prison, did not lose their previous social skills. Rather they are stored up for the future and are available upon release. Bukstel and Kilmann (1980) examined 90 pieces of research from the United States and concluded that the findings do not unequivocally support the popular notion that correctional confinement is harmful to most individuals. Mott (1985:Chapter 3) examined a number of studies from England and Wales and suggested that prisons do not seem to make people deteriorate. Sapsford (1978) in a study of life-sentence prisoners found that interest in the outside world and apathy were not a function of length of sentence. Some changes did occur – that there was a tendency to talk about the past rather than the future, that introversion increases, that institutionalisation develops and that contact with the outside world decreases. This could be said to amount to deterioration, but there is evidence that it is reversible. Sapsford and Banks (1979) examined some Home Office research and noted that changes of attitudes and personality occurred as the time spent in prison increased, but that this did not amount to institutionalisation. They also reported that a wide variety of styles of coping with prison were adopted by prisoners. Coker and Martin (1985) carried out a study of lifers and found that the men, who had served an average of nine years before they were released, had not been seriously damaged or incapacitated by their experiences. This conclusion is supported by other studies that, although men fear it, they do not deteriorate, though their contacts with the outside world may atrophy through enforced neglect. Indeed, the view expressed by one of the men in their research, that prison encourages adequacy and a desire for independence rather than social incompetence and dependency, merits further investigation. Considerable personal resources are needed to cope with institutional regimes whose destructiveness may lie more in their power to isolate than injure, for men are cut off from their families and communities. In light of such studies it seems that for the long-term prisoner prison would appear to be a generally unpleasant and mainly unconstructive experience, particularly in its effect of isolating the person from the outside world. In many cases it will not cause long term psychological damage and where damage does occur it can be reversible.

9.10 Unwanted side-effects of prison

Deterioration if it occurred would be an example of an unwanted side-effect of prison. The possibility of other side-effects needs to be considered. These might include problems for the prisoner with inter-personal relationships, stigma, loss of income and reduced prospects of employment as well as future difficulties in securing accommodation. These effects may also be experienced by the family of the prisoner. Walker (1983), in an examination of such matters, warns of the dangers of assuming both damaging effects and the extent to which this might be long-lasting. Prison may offer families a respite from their relative, the prisoner may receive treatment for health problems that he would not otherwise have had and skills may be developed in prison. Of course, one type of skill is that which can be put to use in crime. An unwanted side-effect of prison would be in so far as it operates as a university of crime. The argument for this has not however been proven. Whilst clearly many prisoners are reconvicted it is not known whether this is a result of one or more of the following factors, or indeed other factors. The police may pay special attention to the behaviour of ex-prisoners such that the police behaviour may be an important variable. For the prisoner he may have had a higher education in the techniques and attitudes of criminality, equally he may have learned bad techniques which would help to explain the reconviction rates! A further possible effect of prison is to harden anti-authority attitudes and to leave the prisoner with a sense of grievance.

9.11 Praise where praise is due

Morgan (1997) provides a short reminder that there is much to praise in British prisons and that talk of crisis has been overdone:

'Over two decades the British prison services have perennially been said by commentators to be in crisis (see, for example, Evans, 1980; Shaw, 1992) – a crisis of order, of legitimacy, of staff morale. Use of the word crisis represents dramatic licence. The British prison services fulfill their intrinsically difficult mandate relatively efficiently most of the time, and they do so in a manner which is publicly a good deal more accountable than most systems in Europe (Morgan, 1993). They are remarkably free from corruption. In spite of the high security lapses of 1994–5 the number of escapes by prisoners who pose a genuine threat to the public is small and declining (Prison Service, 1996:11–12). Following the disturbances in 1990 there had, by the end of 1996, been only one major subsequent disturbance – that at Wymott in 1993. And though there is of course violence, and fear of violence, in British prisons, no prisoner has been killed in a British prison, by either staff or fellow prisoners, for over ten years (King and McDermott, 1995:chapter 3) and no officer has died while on duty at the hands of prisoners in recent memory. Moreover, the material conditions in which most prisoners now live are undoubtedly better in 1997 than for many years. There is only modest overcrowding, the indignities of slopping out are largely a thing of the past and most prisoners are able today to receive visits more frequently in accommodation more pleasant than ever previously known. These improvements in prisoners' living conditions have been matched by improved industrial relations and staff working conditions. The long overtime hours worked until the 1980s have gone and staff turnover is low and declining (Prison Service, 1996:27).

Yet though our prisons can by no stretch of the imagination be said to be in crisis – on the verge of breakdown – their problems are many and the gains of recent years are at grave risk of being lost. The recent massive surge in the prison population, a surge which no reputable commentator has been able to justify in terms of public protection, threatens the stability of the system. The background to the surge, and the mechanics of its production, are discussed in Ashworth (1997) and Downes and Morgan (1997). It has politically been talked into being – the rhetoric of "prison works" – and engineered by judicial decisions taken without crime preventive justification. Space does not permit analysis of how the prison population could without prejudice to public safety be reduced, but at various points in this chapter indications have been given. The recent growth in the number of juvenile prisoners who, it is generally agreed, should not be held in prison. The large number of mentally disordered prisoners who similarly do not belong. The explosion in the number of women prisoners the characteristics of whom suggest that many need not have been confined.' (1997:1183–1184)

Research by Friendship et al (2002) sought to establish if it could replicate the findings of earlier research in North America in terms of improving reconviction rates of prisoners by the use of cognitive behavioural treatment. The programme used involved reasoning and rehabilitation, enhanced thinking skills and had treatment targets of self-control, inter-personal problem solving skills, social perspective taking, critical reasoning skills, cognitive style and understanding the values which govern behaviour. They found that reconviction rates fell considerably in relation to expected rates from a matched control group. The two-year reconviction rates were, for example, up to 14 per cent lower.

9.12 The lessons of reconviction data

Prison has often been assessed in terms of the reconviction rates of ex-prisoners. It allows observations such as the following from Briggs:

> 'If over fifty per cent of the planes sold by aircraft factory X were to crash within two years of delivery, factory X would have to change the model drastically or else go out of business. Planes falling from the sky are both unpopular and frightening. So are people who commit criminal acts. Yet more than half the men and women who are imprisoned for eighteen months or more in the United Kingdom, for example, commit another crime and are back inside within two years. For young people it can run as high as eighty per cent.' (1975:9)

This approach views prison as being a means to change people into law-abiding citizen either through fear of further sanctions or because of a changed attitude towards criminal behaviour. In the former case it relies on the idea that a potential offender will have the sanction in mind in a future potential crime-committing situations. Some of the numerous problems with research in this field need to be indicated. The relevant length of time (if any) which is to act as the cut-off point for success or failure has to be selected. Equally, questions such as the following are raised: Is a reconviction for forgery three years after a sentence for arson a success or a failure? What allowance is to be made for maturational reform as it is clear that offending decreases as age increases? Finally, the data available is likely to be an incomplete and inaccurate record of actual criminality, a problem which even the use of methods such as self-report studies will not be able to fully remedy. This has led some writers to suggest that a different type of criteria should be used, for example the leading of a 'good life' as utilised by Bottoms and McClintock (1973). Such alternative approaches have difficulties of their own. Despite such problems reconviction data does provide some guidance and we also know that crime rates have increased during a time that the use of imprisonment has also increased. On the reconviction data, Bottomley and Pease (1986) warn of the danger of assuming that the reconviction is for a serious offence and they also point out that when a court sends a person back to prison it may be doing no more than punishing persistent offending.

Kershaw, Goodman and White (1999) examined the data on the reconvictions of offenders sentenced or discharged from prison in 1995. The message to be derived from the evidence in this report is that imprisonment and indeed other sentences fail in terms of preventing recidivism. Table 29 provides the data for a two-year follow up.

Table 29

Percentage Reconviction Rate by Sentence

Imprisonment	58
Community penalties	56
Conditional discharge	44
Fines	43
Probation	59
Community service	52
Combination orders	60

(Source: Reconvictions of Offenders Sentenced or Discharged from Prison in 1995)

Some of the differences can be accounted for by such as offender variables and some categories of offender are just bad risks regardless of the disposal used. For some offences the chances of reconviction are much higher than for others – burglary has a 77 per cent rate, whilst sex offences have an 18 per cent rate. Of the sex offenders reconvicted, only 9 per cent were reconvicted for a sex offence. It would make more sense to have a burglar's register rather than a sex offender's register. For young males, generally 77 per cent will reoffend, whereas for adult males the figure is 53 per cent. Reconviction rates were lower where the sentence length was longer, but of course the longer sentence would have increased their age upon release. Another important variable in recidivism was having previous convictions, and even more so the larger the amount of previous convictions. Amongst the adult males who were released, 30 per cent received a custodial sentence within two years of release. Table 30 provides some details for reconviction rate by gender and disposal.

Table 30

Percentage Reconvicted by Gender and Disposal

	Male	Female
Probation	62	44
Community service	52	38
Combination order	62	41
All community penalties	58	42
Immediate custody	58	47

(Source: Reconvictions of Offenders Sentenced or Discharged from Prison in 1995)

As a means of putting people off crime, prison failed. The finding that longer periods in custody produces better reconviction levels does not help. The fact is that a longer sentence will in general lead to people so sentenced being older on release than those on short sentences and are thus more likely to be affected by maturational reform. Those on longer sentences are also more likely to be on early release. Such factors, as well as offence variables, all undermine the argument that a longer period in prison has had a beneficial effect. As regards comparing imprisonment with other sentences Bottomley and Pease (1986) indicate that the difficulties involved in such research are considerable. Having said that, prison comes out of such comparisons the worst, though none of the sentences have any sort of claim to being a success in reconviction terms. Brody (1979) provides insight as to why prison is bound to be of limited use as both an individual and a general deterrent. Quite simply the available evidence tells us that offenders do not have the penalty in mind (far less its nature or severity) at the time of the offence. What they are concerned with (in so far as they consider negative outcomes) are the chances of being caught rather than the consequences of a conviction. Defending prisons on the basis of general deterrence has other difficulties. It involves the moral problem of treating incarcerated offenders as a means to an end that may well not materialise.

Prison then does not appear to offer a general deterrent. This is hardly surprising given that it does not offer much of an individual deterrent. About half of all prisoners will be sent back to prison within two years of release. To go beyond the effect of incapacitating individual offenders, to consider the effectiveness of imprisonment in reducing crime, is even more complex. It is impossible to say how many unsolved crimes are committed by offenders who are never caught. They will not be affected by the imprisonment of less elusive offenders.

How can the rise in prison numbers be explained?

First, it has to be made clear that the numbers in question are those in relation to the total number of people in prison. Whilst these have risen, the rate per 100,000 of the population is much lower than in the past. Davies et al (1996) note that the use of imprisonment was at the rate of 526 per 100,000 in 1894 but by 1997 it was 118. As regards the total numbers some points have already been raised. The matter is clearly complex but factors can be identified. Prison numbers are a product of firstly the number of offenders who commit the number of imprisonable offences (the second variable), the length of the sentence (third) and, fourthly, the impact of early-release systems. In recent decades the government has been confused in its attitudes to the use of imprisonment. The limitations of prisons have been appreciated at times and the courts have received instructions to use prison as a sentence of last resort. Systems of early release were also encouraged and bail as an alternative to custody was promoted. But in various ways the government has also adhered to the 'prison works' philosophy. Certainly longer sentences for the more serious offenders has been a policy as in the case of systems of minimum sentences for certain repeat offenders. The early-release system has also been restricted. New parole criteria were introduced in 1992 as a result of the Criminal Justice Act 1991. For sentences of four years or more there is now discretionary release at the halfway stage of a sentence. With the previous system there was discretionary release after one-third of the sentence. The new system also introduced criteria for release that had to be met, whereas in the old system reasons for refusal had to be found. Clearly both of these changes could have led to fewer or later releases from prison.

9.13 Should prison numbers be decreased?

The problems of prisons such as overcrowding and poor conditions, coupled with a lack of positive findings in their favour and the worry that there may well be negative effects, has led to suggestions that less use, or indeed much less use, should be made of prisons. Brody and Tarling (1980) have calculated that recorded crime rates would not be substantially affected if fewer offenders were sent to prison. The fact that a new building programme is under way shows that recent governments have not accepted this view. Nevertheless, the case for a reduced use of prisons should still be explored. This is not so much because of the obvious merit of the proposition – indeed, as we shall see, there are problems with it – but rather because prison itself appears to be such a disaster that trying the tactic of limiting its use seems an attractive alternative. Two items which highlight some of the difficulties can be noted at the outset.

Young (1986) looked at the literature relating to influences upon the use of imprisonment and ended up stating:

> 'In summary, the present state of our knowledge about those factors which dictate or impinge upon the use of custodial sanctions is fragmentary and inconsistent. The number or length of prison sentences do not necessarily seem to be a direct function of external societal factors such as levels of recorded crime or economic conditions. Nor do particular penal philosophies or the adoption of deliberate policy choices in favour of a greater or lesser use of custody, necessarily seem to have the expected or intended effect in one jurisdiction or explain why its use of imprisonment differs from that of another jurisdiction.' (1986:133–134)

Newman (1974) writing in the context of the United States made points that are pertinent to England and Wales at the present time:

> 'In summary, any significant moves in the direction of diversion and decarceration, as attractive as they sound, have a long way to go and numerous obstacles to overcome. No one, myself included, is in favour of present-day prisons, but until feasible and effective alternatives which meet all the needs of crime control and which respect all its safeguards are developed, then to simply postulate decarceration is not only foolish but dangerous.
>
> Prisons need not and should not be human warehouses, nor ugly and brutalising. Nor should they be used to chill political dissent or sincere efforts to change our social order in the direction of a more equitable, just and crime-free culture. Neither should they be used cosmetically, to remove "nuisances" from our streets, to hold the inept, unpleasant or unemployed who present no real physical danger to others. But until the millennium when the crime-producing factors in our world have been eliminated, incarceration of the dangerous and the deliberate-the violent, the professional, the organised and the wilful, persistent offender-is not only necessary but is itself an alternative to worse choices.' (1974: 339–340)

Decriminalisation

This offers the potential not just of being a means to reduce the custodial population but also a means to completely remove certain behaviour from the criminal justice sphere. The problem with the idea is trying to think of crimes to decriminalise and in particular to be able to identify such crimes where imprisonment is a regular outcome. Non-problematic examples do not spring to mind. In 1967 homosexual behaviour was decriminalised in certain circumstances without social catastrophe (the issue of Aids provides a new dimension to the debate). It is one of the few examples of decriminalisation to date and given the very limited use of imprisonment for such behaviour it had no effect as regards the issue of prison numbers. Future prospects of decriminalisation as a means to reduce prison numbers are no brighter. So-called victimless crimes, as in the case of prostitution and drug-users, are a popular territory for those who seek out targets for decriminalisation. It is not however implausible to view both the prostitute and the drug-user as being victims. Tackling the issue of what should be criminalised may well turn out to be counter-productive in that you may discover behaviour that you want something done about. Desires to protect the environment have been fashionable of late and increased use of the criminal law might be attractive in this sphere.

Non-custodial alternatives

Numerous suggestions have been made as to how the use of prison could be replaced by the use of non-custodial alternatives. For example, Smith et al (1984) in an experimental project in Hampshire in 1981–82 found that the provision of more information to the courts (particularly the Crown Court) could lead, if introduced on a national basis, to approximately 5,000 less people a year being sent to prison.

Another approach is to come up with a list of types of people who should not be sent to prison. A good example of this type of approach is the report of the Parliamentary All Party Penal Affairs Group (1980). In their view society is not protected by keeping prisoners in squalid and overcrowded physical conditions. They wanted prison to be wholly exceptional and to be used only for those who posed a real threat to society. They objected to prison being used for mentally ill and disordered offenders and for habitual drunks and those with a drug dependency. They also questioned the suitability of prison for petty persistent and average offenders. Where prison was to be used the suggestion was a move to shorter sentences. For those on remand who are untried or unsentenced prison was considered to be unsuitable and this line was also taken for those detained in relation to immigration and fine and maintenance defaulters. As regards the mentally ill and disordered offenders, Stern (1987) notes that there is an average of 300 prisoners who could be detained in hospital under the Mental Health legislation. It is not difficult to arrive at a conclusion that many of these should not be in prison. The reality is that often they are in prison because of a lack of alternative facilities. The obvious answer is to ensure that tailor-made alternative facilities are made available which might at least offer the prospect of some positive outcome. Suffice to say that prison as a relatively cheap safety-net for the worst excesses in a society which is trying to reduce expenditure on the mentally ill has unfortunately got mileage in it yet. For the other groups (those with drink and drug problems, the remand population, immigration cases and defaulters) similar conclusions are arrived at. A different form of specialist provision would seem to be required as an alternative to the use of prison as 'a jack of all trades and master of none locking people up place'. Shorter sentences could be produced in a number of ways – for example, by legislation to reduce the maximum penalties available which would be expected to have an effect throughout the tariff. A liberalisation of the early-release system could also be entertained as a thought.

As to the suggestion that prisons should not be used, or used so much, for the petty persistent or average offender, quite simply the problems involved have to be recognised. A point noted by Pease (1981b) in a general critique of the Parliamentary All Party Penal Affairs Group (1980) report was that, as with most of the other suggestions, in practice the proposal would have only a limited impact upon prison populations. This is because as Bottomley and Pease (1986) made clear, when you exclude fine and other defaulters from prison receptions in 1983 and look at those in the up to, and including, six-month sentence bracket you find that 51 per cent of those sentenced came into that bracket. But they make up only 17 per cent of the population. A massive change in sentencing policy would be required to produce only a limited effect. In order to argue for considerably reduced prison populations it seems that you have to argue for a revolutionary change in the way the system operates. This works much better. Quite simply you say that large prison populations are a matter of choice and it is possible to choose to make considerable reductions. The data in Rutherford (1984) shows that in a period in which both England and The Netherlands experienced rising crime rates considerable reductions were possible in The Netherlands whilst we chose to make considerable increases. The word 'choice' is used, given as Rutherford notes, that in England between 1908 and 1938 recorded crime rates increased by 160 per cent while prison population declined by 50 per cent. Such a revolution might well cause disquiet in terms of fears as regards the consequences of such change. However, the experiences of England between 1908 and 1938 and The Netherlands between 1950 and 1978 demonstrates that calamity is not inevitable. Equally, the fears are not groundless. Data on the offence characteristics of prisoners and their record of previous convictions is far from reassuring.

Walmsley (2003) provides data on the use of imprisonment throughout the world and it reveals there are wide differences in the use of imprisonment: see Table 31. Our use of prison is neither high nor low if these figures are the context.

A further matter that seems to be worth exploring is the use of intermittent custody so that a sentence could be served for example at weekends, at nights or during holiday periods. We have elements of such an idea in the present use of probation day centres and attendance centres. This has prospects of being a means of showing disapproval and providing punishment, whilst possible harmful side-effects in spheres such as the family, employment and abode are reduced or removed. Whilst I can see attractions with such an idea it has the capacity to produce net-widening – its effect may be to increase the number of people who experience custody.

344

Table 31

Country	Comparative World Prison Populations Prison Population		Rate per 100,000 of the population
Australia	22,458	(2001)	116
China	1,428,126	(2001)	111
England and Wales	72,269	(2002)	139
France	50,714	(2002)	85
Gambia	450	(2002)	34
Germany	78,707	(2000)	96
India	281,380	(1999)	28
Italy	55,136	(2001)	95
Russia	919,330	(2002)	638
United States	1,962,220	(2001)	686

(Source: World Prison Population List)

9.14 Conclusion

Prisons have been seen to be varied in terms of types, tasks and inmates. To my mind the strongest images that come across from an examination of the literature are the catalogue of social problems that characterise many offenders, the problems of overcrowding and conditions within prisons and the generally negative findings that are commonplace in relation to prisons. To provide assessment of prisons presupposes that some view is held as regards what prisons are for. Various official views as to the purpose of prisons have been presented, and the reality of prisons exposes some of them as being largely platitudes.

The following statements summarise quite well the earlier findings as to the possible tasks of prisons. In relation to prisons Brody and Tarling state that:

> '... their rehabilitative value is negligible (Brody, 1976; Greenberg, 1977) ... capacity to deter individuals is probably over-estimated or at least misunderstood (Beyleveld, 1978; Brody, 1979), and their use as a punishment is too often unjust and unconstructive (Von Hirsch, 1976; Advisory Council on the Penal System, 1977).' (1980:1)

The Director-General of the Prison Service stated in 1981 (Home Office (1982)):

> 'It is, however, one of the consequences of the pressures placed upon the Prison Service by excessive demands and inadequate resources that we have become decreasingly able to meet virtually any of the objectives expected of us other than the simple "incapacitation" of the offender for the period of his sentence. Certainly there is no evidence that prison has either any systematic deterrent or rehabilitate effect: as the May Committee noted, the words of Prison Rule 1 that the purpose of the treatment and training of convicted prisoners shall be "to encourage them to lead a good and useful life" are in present conditions simply a pious aspiration.'

We can expect little positive from the present system as regards rehabilitation and deterrence. Also of concern are the negative side-effects of prison and the great financial cost that is involved in providing prison facilities. Prisons seem to be largely an expensive mistake and the expenditure would seem better put to alternative use. Prisons should not of course be completely abolished – there seems an obvious need to provide a means of containment for some. Equally, it has to be recognised that prison does provide a means of punishment. In this role it seems that the loss of liberty is the punishment and that the conditions should not in themselves be punitive. To provide such extra punishment, either by design or default, is counter-productive in terms of producing control problems in prisons and in so far as it further undermines the capacity of the prisoners to reduce their criminal activities upon release. It has quite simply a brutalising effect upon prisoners. Punishment might be deliverable in other ways by, for example, strategies for punishment in the community or less punishment could be proscribed as part of a general movement to reducing the use of prisons. Prison does seem to have a sanitising function, being used as a temporary dumping ground for social misfits and casualties who have achieved the status of nuisance. You may or may not regard this as an indictment of both prisons and of society as a whole. In any case it seems to be inefficient as the problems are not removed on a permanent basis and are indeed likely to be exacerbated. Different tactics would seem to be required. Hawkins develops some suitable ideas as follows:

> '… all the evidence points to the conclusion that the penitentiary system was, quite literally as it happens, a monumental mistake. The most obvious practical corollaries of that conclusion are firstly a substantial diminution in the use of imprisonment and the further expansion of alternatives to institutionalisation; and secondly the development of much smaller, specialised custodial establishments designed to meet the diversity of our penal needs and purposes.' (1974:115)

I am happy to adopt the notion of substantial diminution, it is far from being an exact statement, but it does make it clear where you stand in the debate. As well as suggesting considerably reduced use of prison by means of some mixture of the tactics examined earlier, it also seems desirable to call for changes in the type of regime operative in prisons. Systems which would hope to be positive rather than negative in effect should be introduced. A move away from the obsession with security and control is called for – for many prisoners the conditions should be as free of limitations as possible. As Hawkins suggests, attempts should be made to individualise the prison experience. Improving conditions so as to enhance positive factors and to limit harmful effects would be of benefit. As regards many of these suggestions there are of course problems of various types. As a basic approach the above ideas would still seem to be worthwhile. We have tried large-scale warehousing of problems and it has not worked. However, the outlook is grim. The building programme for prisons reflects a desire to compound errors. The regime provided within prisons will continue to be poor given the absence of political will to do anything about this matter.

Bibliography

Adams, P and Adams, S (1982) *Knockback*, London: Duckworth.

Advisory Council on the Penal System (1977) *The Length of Prison Sentences*, London: HMSO.

Alderson, J (1979) *Policing Freedom*, London: MacDonald and Evans.

Allatt, P (1984) 'Residential Security: Containment and Displacement of Burglary', *Howard Journal of Criminal Justice*, 23:99.

Ancel, M (1971) *Suspended Sentences*, London: Heinemann.

Andrews, G (1986) 'Dodgers Fare Badly in Railway Sting', *The Guardian*, 4 April 1987, p1.

Anthony, C (1984) 'Diversion from the Court Process', *Justice of the Peace*, p156.

Arnold, T (1962) *The Symbols of Government*, Fort Worth: Harcourt.

Ashworth, A (1982) *Reducing the Prison Population in the 1980s: The Need for Sentencing Reform*, London: NACRO.

Ashworth, A (1983) *Sentencing and Penal Policy*, London: Weidenfeld and Nicolson.

Ashworth, A (1984) 'Prosecution, Police and Public – A Guide to Good Gatekeeping?', *The Howard Journal of Criminal Justice*, p65.

Ashworth, A (1987) 'Devising Sentencing Guidance for England', in Pease and Wasik (eds) (1987) *Sentencing Reform*, Manchester: Manchester University Press.

Ashworth, A (1997) 'Sentencing', in M Maguire et al (eds) (1997) *The Oxford Handbook of Criminology*, 2nd ed, Oxford: Oxford University Press.

Ashworth, A (1998) *The Criminal Process*, Oxford: Oxford University Press.

Ashworth, A and Hough, M (1996) 'Sentencing and the Climate of Opinion', *Criminal Law Review*, p780.

Ashworth, A et al (1984) *Sentencing in the Crown Court*, Oxford: Oxford Centre for Criminological Research.

Asquith, S (1983) *Children and Justice*, Edinburgh: Edinburgh University Press.

Attorney-General (1983) *Criteria for Prosecution*, London: Home Office.

Audit Commission (1997) *Misspent Youth: Young People and Crime*, London: Audit Commission Publications.

Auld, LJ (2001) *A Review of the Criminal Courts in England and Wales,* London: HMSO.

Ayres, M, Hayward, P and Perry, D (2003) *Motoring Offences, England and Wales, 2001*, London: Home Office.

Ayres, M, Perry, D and Hawyard P (2002) *Arrests for Notifiable Offences and the Operation of Certain Police Powers under PACE in England and Wales*, London: Home Office.

Baber, M (2000) *The Criminal Justice (Mode of Trial) (No 2) Bill*, London: House of Commons Library.

Baldwin, J (1992) *The Role of Legal Representatives at the Police Station*, London: HMSO.

Baldwin, J (1997) 'Understanding Judge Ordered and Directed Acquittals in the Crown Court', *Criminal Law Review*, p536.

Baldwin, J and Bedward, J (1991) 'Summarising Tape Recordings of Police Interviewing', *Criminal Law Review*, 671–9.

Baldwin, J and McConville, M (1977) *Negotiated Justice*, London: Martin Robertson.

Baldwin, J and McConville, M (1979) *Jury Trials*, Oxford: Clarendon Press.

Bannister, P et al (1998) *Rights for All*, London: Amnesty International.

Barber, D and Gordon, G (1976) *Members of the Jury*, London: Wildwood House.

Barclay, G and Tavares, C (2002) *International Comparisons of Criminal Justice Statistics*, London: Home Office.

Becker, H (1963) *Outsiders*, Glencoe: Free Press.

Belloni, F and Hodgson, J (2000) *Criminal Injustice*, Basingstoke: Macmillan.

Belson, W (1975) *Juvenile Theft: The Causal Factors*, London: Harper and Row.

Bennett, T (1979) 'The Social Distribution of Criminal Labels', *British Journal of Criminology*, p134.

Bennett, T (ed) (1983) *The Future of Policing*, Cropwood Conference Series No 15, Cambridge: Institute of Criminology.

Bennett, T (1986) 'Situational Crime Prevention from the Offenders' Perspective', pp41–53 of Heal, K and Laycock, G (eds) (1986) *Situational Crime Prevention: From Theory into Practice*, Home Office Research and Planning Unit, London: HMSO.

Berk, R, Brackman, H and Lesser S (1977) *A Measure of Justice*, New York: Academic Press.

Beylveld, D (1978) *The Effectiveness of General Deterrents against Crime: An Annotated Bibliography of Evaluative Research*, Cambridge: Institute of Criminology.

Beylveld, D (1979) *A Bibliography on General Deterrence Research*, Farnborough: Saxon House.

Bittner, E (1967) 'The Police on Skid-Row: A Study of Peace Keeping', *American Sociological Review*, p699.

Black, D (1971) 'The Social Organisation of Arrest', *Stanford Law Review*, p1087.

Black Committee (1979) *Report of the Children and Young Persons Review Group*, Belfast: HMSO.

Block, B, Corbett, C and Peay, J (1993) 'Ordered and Directed Acquittals in the Crown Court: A Time of Change?' *Criminal Law Review*, p95.

Blom-Cooper, L (1974) *Progress in Penal Reform*, Oxford: Clarendon Press.

Bockell, D (1976) *Probation and After-Care*, Edinburgh, Scottish Academic Press.

Bottomley, A K (1970), *Prison Before Trial*, London: Bell.

Bottomley, K and Coleman, C (1981) *Understanding Crime Rates*, Farnborough: Gower.

Bottomley, K and Coleman, C (1984) 'Law and Order: Crime Problem, Moral Panic or Penal Crisis' in Norton, P (ed) (1984) *Law, Order and British Politics*, Aldershot: Gower.

Bottomley, K and Pease, K (1986) *Crime and Punishment*, Milton Keynes: Open University Press.

Bottoms, A (1981) 'The Suspended Sentence in England' *British Journal of Criminology*, 21:1.

Bottoms, A and McClean, J (1976) *Defendants in the Criminal Process*, London: Routledge and Kegan Paul.

Bottoms, A and Mc Clintock, F (1973) *Criminals Coming of Age*, London: Heinemann.

Bottoms, A, Gelsthorpe, L and Rex, S (eds) (2001) *Community Penalties: Change and Challenges,* Cullompton: Willan.

Bowden, T (1978) *Beyond the Limits of the Law*, Harmondsworth: Penguin.

Bowling, B and Foster, J (2002) 'Policing and the Police' in M Maguire et al (eds) (2002) *The Oxford Handbook of Criminology*, 3rd ed, Oxford: Oxford University Press.

Boyle, J (1977) *A Sense of Freedom*, London: Pan.

Boyle, J (1984) *The Pain of Confinement*, Canongate: Edinburgh.

Braithwaite J (1989) *Crime, Shame and Reintegration*, Melbourne: Cambridge University Press.

Braithwaite J (2001) *Restorative Justice and Responsive Regulation*, New York: Oxford University Press.

Brand, S and Price, R (2000) *The Economic and Social Costs of Crime*, London: Home Office.

Brantingham, P (1986) 'Trends in Canadian crime prevention', pp103–112 of Heal, K and Laycock, G (eds) (1986) *Situational Crime Prevention: From Theory into Practice*, Home Office Research and Planning Unit, London: HMSO.

Brantingham, P and Blomberg, T (eds) (1979) *Courts and Diversion*, Beverly Hills: Sage.

Briggs, D (1975) *In Place of Prisons*, London: Maurice Temple Smith.

Brittan, L (1984) 'A Strategy for Criminal Justice', *Howard Journal*, p3.

Brody, S (1976) *The Effectiveness of Sentencing*, London: HMSO.

Brody, S (1979) *Research into the Efficacy of Deterrents*, London: HMSO.

Brody, S and Tarling, R (1980) *Taking Offenders out of Circulation*, London: HMSO.

Brogden, M, Jefferson, T and Walklate, S (1988) *Introducing Policework*, London: Unwin.

Brown, D et al (1992) *Changing the Code*, London: HMSO.

Brown, D (1997) *Offending on Bail and Police Use of Conditional Bail,* Research findings No 72, London: Home Office.

Brown, D (1997) *PACE 10 Years On: A Review of the Research*, London: Home Office.

Brown, D and Isles, S (1985) *Community Constables: A Study of a Policing Initative*, London: HMSO.

Brown, D et al (1994) *Policing Low Level Disorder*, London: HMSO.

Bucke, T and Brown, D (1997) *In Police Custody*, London: Home Office.

Bukstel, L and Kilmann, P (1980) 'Psychological Effects of Imprisonment on Confined Individuals', *Psychological Bulletin*, p469.

Bunyan, T (1976) *The Political Police in Britain*, London: Friedmann.

Burney, E (1985) *Sentencing Young People: What Went Wrong with the Criminal Justice Act 1982?,* Aldershot: Gower.

Burrows, J and Heal, K (1979) 'Police Car Security Campaigns', pp1–16 of Burrows, J, Ekblom, P and Heal, K (eds) (1979) *Crime Prevention and the Police*, London: HMSO.

Cain, M (1973) *Society and the Policeman's Role*, London: Routledge and Kegan Paul.

Campbell, S (2002) *A Guide to Anti-Social Behaviour Orders and Acceptable Behaviour Contracts*, London: Home Office.

Cape, E (2002) 'Assisting and Advising Defendants before Trial', in McConville, M and Wilson, G (eds) (2002) *The Handbook of the Criminal Justice Process*, Oxford: Oxford University Press.

Chaiken, J, Lawless, M, Stevenson, K (1974) *Impact of Police Activity on Crime: Robberies on the New York City Subway System*, Report No R–1424–NYC, Santa Monica, California: Rand Corporation.

Chambliss, W (1964) 'A Sociological Analysis of the Law of Vagrancy', *Social Problems*, p46.

Chambliss, W and Nagasawa, R (1969) 'On the Validity of Official Statistics', *Journal of Research on Crime and Delinquency*, January 1969.

Chambliss, W and Seidman, R (1971) *Law, Order, and Power*, Reading, Massachusetts: Addison-Wesley.

Chapman, T and Hough, M (1998) *Evidence Based Practice: A Guide to Effective Practice*, London: Home Office.

Chatterton, M (1987) 'Assessing Police Effectiveness – Future Prospects', *British Journal of Criminology*, p80.

Choongh, S (1997) *Review of Delay in the Criminal Justice System*, London: Lord Chancellor's Department.

Christie, N (1977) 'Conflicts as Property', *British Journal of Criminology*, 17:1.

Clare, E and Bottomley, A et al (2001) *Evaluation of Close Supervision Centres*, London: Home Office.

Clarke, R and Hough, M (1984) *Crime and Police Effectiveness*, London: HMSO.

Clarke, R and Mayhew, P (eds) (1980) *Designing out Crime*, London: HMSO.

Clarkson, C et al (1994) 'Criminalising Assault', *British Journal of Criminology*, 34:15.

Cohen, S and Taylor, L (1981) *Psychological Survival*, 2nd ed, Harmondsworth: Penguin.

Coker, J and Martin, J (1985) *Licensed to Live*, Oxford: Basil Blackwell.

Comrie, M and Kings, E (1975) *Study of Urban Workloads: final report*, London: Home Office Police Research Services Unit.

Cornish, D and Clarke, R (1986) 'Situational Prevention, Displacement of Crime and Rational Choice Theory', Chapter 1 of Heal, K and Laycock, G (eds) (1986) *Situational Crime Prevention: From Theory into Practice*, Home Office Research and Planing Unit, London: HMSO.

Cotton, J and Povey, D (1999) *Police Complaints and Discipline, April 1998 – March 1999*, London: Home Office.

Cotton, J and Smith, C (2003) *Police Service Strength England and Wales, 31 March 2003*, London: Home Office.

Counsell, R and Simes, J (2002) *Projections of Long Term Trends in the Prison Population to 2009*, London: Home Office.

Crawford A., Jones, T and Woodhouse, T (1990) *The Second Islington Crime Survey*, London: Middlesex Polytechnic Centre for Criminology.

Crawford, A (1998), *Crime Prevention and Community Safety*, London: Longman.

Cray, E (1972) *The Enemy in the Street*, New York: Anchor.

Criminal Cases Review Commission (2003) *Provisional Figures to 30th June 2003*, Website press release.

Crisp, D and Moxon D (1994) *Case Screening by the Crown Prosecution Service*, London: HMSO.

Crown Prosecution Service (2003) *Crown Prosecution Service Annual Report 2002-03*, London: HMSO.

Cumming, E et al (1965) 'The Policeman as Philosopher Guide and Friend', *Social Problems*, p276.

Cutts, A (1982) 'Has the Bail Act Made Any Difference?' *New Law Journal*, 23:1089.

Dahrendorf, R (1985) *Law and Order*, London: Sweet and Maxwell.

Daly, K (2001) 'Conferencing in Australia and New Zealand: Variations, Research Findings and Prospects', in Morris, A and Maxwell, G (eds) (2001) *Restorative Justice for Juveniles*, Oxford: Hart.

Daly, K (2002) 'Restorative Justice', in Wing Hong Chui and Nellis, M (eds) (2003) *Moving Probation Forward*, London: HMSO.

Davies, C (1971) 'Pre-Trial Imprisonment', *British Journal of Criminology*, 11:32.

Davies, M et al (1996) *Penological Esperanto and Sentencing Parocialism*, Aldershot: Dartmouth.

Derbyshire, P (2002) 'Magistrates', in McConville, M and Wilson, G (eds) (2002) *The Handbook of the Criminal Justice Process*, Oxford: Oxford University Press.

Devons, E (1965) 'Serving as a Juryman in England' *Modern Law Review*, p561.

Dickens, B (1970) 'Discretion in Local Authority Prosecutions', *Criminal Law Review*, p618.

Dickson, D (1968) 'Bureacracy and Morality: An Organisational Perspective on a Moral Crusade', *Social Problems*, p143.

Dingwall, G and Harding, C (1998) *Diversion in the Criminal Process*, London: Sweet and Maxwell.

Ditchfield, J (1976) *Police Cautioning in England and Wales*, London: HMSO.

Dixon, D et al (1989) 'Reality and Rules in the Construction and Regulation of Police Suspicion', *International Journal of the Sociology of Law*, p185.

Dodge, C (1979) *A World Without Prisons*, New York, Random House.

Doherty, M and East, R (1985) 'Bail Decisions in Magistrates' Courts', *British Journal of Criminology*, p251.

Doherty, M (2004) *Criminology Sourcebook,* 3rd ed, London: Old Bailey Press.

Doherty, M (2002) *Criminology Textbook,* 4th ed, London: Old Bailey Press.

Downes, D (1988) *Contrasts in Tolerance*, Oxford: Clarendon Press.

Downes, D and Morgan, R (1997) 'Dumping the 'Hostages to Fortune'? The Politics of Law and Order in Post-War Britain', in M Maguire et al (eds) (1997) *The Oxford Handbook of Criminology*, 2nd ed, Oxford: Oxford University Press.

Downes, D and Rock, P (1997) *Understanding Deviance*, Oxford: Oxford University Press.

Drapkin, I (ed) (1969) 'Studies in Criminology', *Scripta Heirosolymitana vol 21*, Jerusalem: Magnus Press.

Duff, P (1997) 'Diversion from Prosecution into Psychiatric Care', *British Journal of Criminology*, 37:15.

Duff, A and Garland, G (1994a) 'Introduction', in Duff and Garland (eds) (1994b).

Duff, A and Garland, G (1994b) *A Reader on Punishment*, Oxford: Oxford University Press.

Dunlop, A (1975) *The Approved School Experience*, London: HMSO.

Dunlop, A (1980) *Junior Attendance Centres*, London: HMSO.

Durkheim, E (1984) *The Division of Labour in Society*, London: Macmillan.

East, R and Doherty, M (1984) 'The Practical Operation of Bail', *Legal Action*, 12:16.

Ehrlich, E (1936) *Fundamental Principles of the Sociology of Law*, New York: reprinted in 1975 by Arno Press.

Ekblom, P and Heal, K (1982) *The Police Response to Calls from the Public*, London: HMSO.

Engels, F (1890a) 'Engels to Bloch in Konigsberg', pp682–683 of *Karl Marx and F Engels Selected Works* (1973), London: Lawrence and Wisehart.

Engels, F (1890b) 'Engels to Schmidt', pp684–689 of *Karl Marx and F Engels Selected Works* (1973), London: Lawrence and Wisehart.

Erickson, R (1982) *Reproducing Order: A Study of Police Patrol Work*, Toronto: University of Toronto Press.

Evan, W M (ed) (1962) *Law and Sociology*, Glencoe: Free Press.

Evans, P (1980) *Prison Crisis,* London: Allen and Unwin.

Evans, R and Ellis, R (1997) *Police Cautioning in the 1990s*, London: Home Office.

Evans, R and Wilkinson, C (1990) 'Variations in Police Cautioning, Policy and Practice in England and Wales', *Howard Journal of Criminal Justice,* p155.

Farrall, S (2002) *Rethinking What Works with Offenders*, Cullompton: Willan.

Farrington, D et al (2002) *Two Intensive Regimes for Young Offenders: A Follow-up Evaluation*, London: Home Office.

Farrington, D and Bennett, T (1981) 'Police Cautioning of Juveniles in London', *British Journal of Criminology*, p123.

Fielding, N (1994) 'The Organisational and Occupational Troubles of Community Police', *Policing and Society*, 4:305.

Fine, B and Millar, R (eds) (1985) *Policing the Miner's Strike*, London: Lawrence and Wishart.

Fisher, C and Mawby, R (1982) 'Juvenile Delinquency and Police Discretion in an Inner-City Area', *British Journal of Criminology*, p63.

Fitzgerald, M and Hough, M (2002) *Policing for London*, Uffculme: Willan.

Floud, J and Young, W (1981) *Dangerousness and Criminal Justice*, London: Heinemann.

Foucault, M (1977) *Discipline and Punish: the Birth of the Prison,* London: Allen Lane.

Friendship, C et al (2002) *An Evaluation of Cognitive Behavioural Treatment for Prisoners*, London: Home Office.

Gelsthorpe, L and Giller, H (1990) 'More Justice for Juveniles: Does More mean Better?', *Criminal Law Review*, pp153–164.

Gelsthorpe, L and Morris, A (1983) 'Attendance Centres: Policy and Practice', *Howard Journal*, p101.

Gelsthorpe, L and Tutt, N (1986) 'The Attendance Centre Order', *Criminal Law Review*, p146.

Gibb, F (2000) 'Courts Will Link Fines to Income', *The Times*, 27 March, p1.

Gibson, B (1987) 'Why Bournemouth?', *Justice of the Peace*, p520.

Goldblatt, P and Lewis, C (eds) (1998) *Reducing Offending,* London: HMSO.

Grace, C and Wilkinson, P (1978) *Sociological Enquiry and Legal Phenomena*, New York: Collier Macmillan.

Graef, R (1990) *Talking Blues*, London: Fontana.

Graham, J and Bowling, B (1995) *Young People and Crime*, London: HMSO.

Greenberg, D (ed) (1977) *Corrections and Punishment*, Beverley Hills: California Sage.

Greenberg, D (1977) 'The Correctional Effects of Correction: A Survey of Evaluations', pp111–148 of Greenberg, D (ed) (1977).

Gunn, J et al (1991) *Mentally Disordered Prisoners*, London: Home Office.

Gunningham, N (1974) *Pollution, Social Interest and the Law*, London: Martin Robertson.

Gusfield, J (1963) *Symbolic Crusade*, Urbaba: University of Illinois Press.

Hall Williams J E (1970) *The English Penal System in Transition*, London: Butterworths.

Hall Williams, J E (1982) *Criminology and Criminal Justice*, London: Butterworths.

Halliday, J (2001) *Making Punishment Work: Report of a Review of the Sentencing Framework of England and Wales*, London: HMSO.

Hancock, S (2000) 'Practical Implications of the Crime and Disorder Act for Youth Offending Teams – A Youth Offending Team's Perspective', in Pickford, J (ed) (2000) *Youth Justice, Theory and Practice*, London: Cavendish.

Haskins, G (1960) *Law and Authority in Massachusetts*, New York: Macmillan.

Hawkins, G (1974) 'The Ideology of Imprisonment', Chapter 7 of Blom-Cooper, L (ed) (1974) *Progress in Penal Reform*, Oxford: Clarendon Press.

Hay, D et al (1975) *Albion's Fatal Tree*, London: Allen Lane.

Heal, K and Laycock G (eds) (1986) *Situational Crime Prevention: From Theory into Practice*, Home Office Research and Planning Unit, London: HMSO.

Healey, M (1985) 'What Are Local Government Services For?' *Local Government Studies*, November/December.

Hedderman, C and Gelsthorpe, L (1997) *Understanding the Sentencing of Women*, London: HMSO.

Hedderman, C and Moxon, D (1992) *Magistrates' Court or Crown Court? Mode of Trial Decisions and Sentencing*, London: HMSO

Hedderman, C and Sugg, D (1997) 'The Influence of Cognitive Approaches: A Survey of Probation Programmes', in Mair, G et al (1997).

Henham, R (1990) *Sentencing Principles and Magistrates' Sentencing Behaviour*, Aldershot: Avebury.

HM Inspectorate of Constabulary, (1998) *Beating Crime*, London: HMSO.

Holdaway, S (1983), *Inside the British Police*, Oxford: Basil Blackwell.

Hollis, V and Goodman, M (2003) *Prison Population Brief: December 2002*, London: Home Office.

Home Office (1957) *Alternatives to Short Terms of Imprisonment*, A Report by the Advisory Council on the Treatment of Offenders, London: HMSO.

Home Office (1959) *Penal Practice in a Changing Society*, Cmnd 645, London: HMSO.

Home Office (1964) *The War against Crime in England and Wales 1959–'64*, Cmnd 2276, London: HMSO.

Home Office (1965a) *The Child, the Family and the Young Offender*, London: HMSO.

Home Office (1965b) *The Adult Offender*, London: HMSO.

Home Office (1966) *Report of the Inquiry into Prison Escapes and Security* (the Mountbatten Report), Cmnd 3175, London: HMSO.

Home Office (1968a) *Children in Trouble*, London: HMSO.

Home Office (1968b) *The Regime for Long Term Prisoners in Conditions of Maximum Security*, London: HMSO.

Home Office (1969) *People in Prison*, London: Home Office.

Home Office (1970) *Report on Non-Custodial and Semi-Custodial Penalties* (the Wooton Report), Advisory Council on the Penal System, London: HMSO.

Home Office (1974) *Bail Procedures in Magistrates' Courts*, London: HMSO.

Home Office (1976) *Children and Young Persons Act 1969: Observations on the Eleventh Report of the Expenditure Committee*, London: HMSO.

Home Office (1977a) *A Review of Criminal Justice Policy*, London: HMSO.

Home Office (1977b) *Prisons and the Prisoner*, London: HMSO.

Home Office (1978) *Sentences of Imprisonment: A Review of Maximum Penalties*, London: HMSO.

Home Office (1979) *Report of the Committee of Inquiry into the United Kingdom Prison Services* (the May Report), London: HMSO.

Home Office (1980a) *The Reduction of Pressure on the Prison System: Observations on the fifteenth report of the Expenditure Committee,* London: HMSO.

Home Office (1980b) *Young Offenders*, London: HMSO.

Home Office (1982) *Report of the Work of the Prison Department*, London: HMSO.

Home Office (1983) *An Independent Prosecution Service for England and Wales*, London: HMSO.

Home Office (1984a) *Criminal Justice: A Working Paper*, London: HMSO.

Home Office (1984b) *Managing the Long Term Prison System*, London: HMSO.

Home Office (1986a) *Criminal Justice: A Working Paper (Revised edition),* London, HMSO.

Home Office (1986b) *The Sentence of the Court*, 4th ed, London: HMSO.

Home Office (1988a) *Criminal Statistics*, London: HMSO.

Home Office (1988b) *Punishment in the Community*, London: HMSO.

Home Office (1990) *Crime, Justice and Protecting the Public*, London: HMSO.

Home Office (1991) *Prison Disturbances* (Woolf Report), London: HMSO.

Home Office (1996) *Protecting the Public: The Government's Strategy on Crime in England and Wales*, London: HMSO.

Home Office (1997a) *Preventing Children Offending,* London, HMSO.

Home Office (1997b) *Women in Prison: A Thematic Review*, London: Home Office.

Home Office (1997c) *Report of the Chief Inspector of Prisons on Feltham YOI*, London, HMSO.

Home Office (1997d) *No More Excuses*, London, HMSO.

Home Office (1997e) *Review of Delay in the Criminal Justice System*, London: HMSO.

Home Office (1997f) *Tackling Youth Crime*, London: HMSO.

Home Office (1998a) *Criminal Statistics 1997*, London: HMSO.

Home Office (1998b) *The Glidewell Report into the Crown Prosecution Service*, London: HMSO.

Home Office (1998c) *Prisons Ombudsman's Annual Report*, London: Home Office.

Home Office (1998d) *Report of the Chief Inspector of Prisons on Werrington YOI: An Unannounced Short Inspection*, London, HMSO.

Home Office (1998e) *Strategies for Effective Offender Supervision*, London: HMSO.

Home Office (1999b) *The 1998 British Crime Survey*, London: HMSO.

Home Office (1999c) *Car Theft Index,* London: HMSO.

Home Office (1999d) *Statistics on Race and the Criminal Justice System,* London: HMSO.

Home Office (1999e) *Statistics on Women and the Criminal Justice System,* London: HMSO.

Home Office (1999f) *Report on H M Prison Liverpool.*

Home Office (1999g) *Report on H M Prison Bristol.*

Home Office (1999h) *Report on H M Prison Exeter.*

Home Office (1999i) *Report of the Parole Board 1998–1999*, London: HMSO.

Home Office (1999j) *Crime Reduction Strategy,* London: HMSO.

Home Office (2000) *The Strategic Plan for the Criminal Justice System 1999–2002*, London: HMSO.

Home Office (2002a) *Criminal Statistics England and Wales 2001*, London: HMSO.

Home Office (2002b) *Statistics on Women and the Criminal Justice System*, London: Home Office.

Home Office (2002c) *Statistics on Race and the Criminal Justice System*, London: Home Office.

Home Office (2002d) *Justice for All*, London: HMSO.

Home Office (2002e) *Probation Statistics, England and Wales 2001*, London: Home Office.

Home Office/Youth Justice Board (2002) *Final Warning Schemes: Guidance for the Police and Youth Offending Teams*, London: Home Office/Youth Justice Board.

Honess T, and Maguire, M (1993) *Vehicle Watch and Car Theft: an Evaluation*, London, HMSO.

Hood, R (1992) *Race and Sentencing*, Oxford: Clarendon Press.

Hope, T (1985) *Implementing Crime Prevention Measures*, Home Office Research Study No 86, London: HMSO.

Hope, T (1986) 'School Design and Burglary', pp73–79 of Heal, K and Laycock, G (eds) (1986) *Situational Crime Prevention: From Theory into Practice*, Home Office Research and Planning Unit, London: HMSO.

Hopkins, A (1975) 'On the Sociology of Criminal Law', *Social Problems*, p608.

Horton, C and Smith, D, (1988) *Evaluating Police Work*, London: Policy Studies Institute.

Hosking, R and Smith, C (2003) *Police Service Strength England and Wales, as at 30th September 2002*, London: Home Office.

Hough, J (1980) *Uniformed Police Work and Management Technology*, London: HMSO.

Hough, M (1987) 'Thinking about Effectiveness', *British Journal of Criminology*, p70.

Hough, M and Mayhew, P (1983) *The British Crime Survey*, London: HMSO.

Hough, M and Mayhew, P (1985) *Taking Account of Crime*, London: HMSO.

Hoyle, C (1997) *Policing Domestic Violence: The Role of the Victim*, Oxford: Oxford University Press.

Hucklesby, A (1997) 'Remand Decision-Makers', *Criminal Law Review*, p269.

Hucklesby, A (2002) 'Bail in Criminal Cases', in McConville, M and Wilson, G (eds) (2002) *The Handbook of the Criminal Justice Process*, Oxford: Oxford University Press..

Hume, D (1969) *A Treatise of Human Nature*, Penguin: Harmondsworth.

Ingelby Committee (1960) *Children and Young Persons*, London, HMSO.

Jacobs, J (1962) *The Death and Life of Great American Cities*, New York: Jonathan Cape.

James, A (1987) 'Performance and the Planning Process' *Social Services Insight*, 6 March.

Jefferson, T and Walker, M (1992) 'Ethnic Minorities in the Criminal Justice System', *Criminal Law Review*, pp83–85.

Johnston, N and Savitz, L (1982) *Legal Process and Corrections*, New York: John Wiley.

Joint Consultative Committee of the Police Staff Associations of England and Wales (1990) *Operational Policing Review*, Surbiton: Joint Consultative Committee.

Jordan, J (1998) 'Effective Policing Strategies for Reducing Crime', in Goldblatt, P and Lewis, C (eds) (1998) *Reducing Offending*, London: HMSO.

Jones, R (1983) 'Justice, Social Work and Statutory Supervision', in Morris, A and Giller, H (eds) (1983) *Providing Criminal Justice for Children*, London: Arnold.

Jones, S (1983) 'Community Policing in Devon and Cornwall: Some Research Findings on the Relationship between the Police and the Public' in Bennett T (ed) (1983) *The Future of Policing*, Cropwood Conference Series No 15, Cambridge: Institute of Criminology.

Jones, S and Levi, M (1983) 'The Police and the Majority: The Neglect of the Obvious', *Police Journal*, 56, 4:351–364.

Jones, P (1985) 'Remand Decisions at Magistrates Courts' in Moxon, D (ed) (1985) *Managing Criminal Justice*, London: HMSO.

Jones, S et al (1986) 'Caught in the Act', *Policing*, 2, 2:129–140.

Justice (1970) *The Prosecution Process in England and Wales*, London: Justice.

Kavanagh, S (1986) 'Crown Prosecution Service', *Legal Action*, November, p8.

Kershaw, C., Goodman, J and White, S (1999) *Reconvictions of Offenders Sentenced or Discharged from Prison in 1995*, London: Home Office.

Kettle, M (1979) 'Anderton's Way', *New Society*, 8 March 1979, p550.

King, G and Morgan, R (eds) (1976) *A Taste of Prison*, London: Routledge.

King, G and Mc Dermott, K (1995) *The State of Our Prisons*, Oxford: Clarendon Press.

King, M (1971) *Bail or Custody*, London: Cobden Trust.

Kinsey, R (1984) *The Merseyside Crime Survey*, Liverpool: Merseyside County Council.

Knutsson, J and Kuhlhorn, E (1981) *Macro Measures against Crime*, Information Bulletin No 1, Stockholm: National Swedish Council for Crime Prevention.

Kuhlhorn, E and Svensson, B (eds) (1982) *Crime Prevention*, Report No 9, Stockholm: Research and Development Division, The National Swedish Council for Crime Prevention.

Labour Party (1964) *Crime – A Challenge to Us All*, London: Labour Party.

Landau, S (1981) 'Juveniles and the Police', *British Journal of Criminology*, p27.

Landau, S and Nathan, G (1983) 'Selecting Juveniles for Cautioning in the London Area', *British Journal of Criminology*, p128.

Laycock, G (1986) 'Property Marking as a Deterrent to Domestic Burglary', pp55–71 of Heal, K and Laycock, G (eds) (1986) *Situational Crime Prevention: From Theory into Practice*, Home Office Research and Planning Unit, London: HMSO.

Learmont Report (1995) *Review of Prison Service Security in England and Wales*, London: HMSO.

Lee, J (1981) 'Some Structural Aspects of Police Deviance in relations with Minority Groups', in C. Shearing (ed) (1981) *Organisational Police Deviance*, Toronto: Butterworths.

Leighton, B (1971) 'Suspended Sentences', *The Magistrate*, p24.

Leng, R (1992) *The Right to Silence in Police Interrogation*, London: HMSO.

Liberty (2000) *Liberty Briefing, Mode of Trial Bill*, London: Liberty.

Lidstone, K, Hogg, R and Sutcliffe, S (1980) *Prosecutions by Private Individuals and Non-Police Agencies*, Royal Commission on Criminal Procedure Research Study No 10, London: HMSO.

Light, R (1984) 'Cautioning the Drunken Offender', *Justice of the Peace*, p793.

Lindesmith, A (1965) *The Addict and the Law*, New York: Vintage.

Lloyd, C, Mair, G and Hough, M (1994) *Explaining Reconviction Rates: A Critical Analysis*, Home Office Research Study 136, London: HMSO.

MacDonald, D and Sim, J (1977) *Scottish Prisons and the Special Unit*, Edinburgh: Scottish Council for Civil Liberties.

Maguire, M and Norris, C (1992) *The Conduct and Supervision of Criminal Investigations*, London: HMSO

Maguire, M et al (eds) (1997) *The Oxford Handbook of Criminology*, 2nd ed, Oxford: Oxford University Press.

Maguire, M et al (eds) (2002) *The Oxford Handbook of Criminology*, 3rd ed, Oxford: Oxford University Press.

Maguire, M et al (2003) *Reducing Alcohol-Related Violence and Disorder: An Evaluation of the 'TASC' Project*, London: Home Office.

Mair, G et al (1997) *Changing Offenders' Attitudes and Behaviour: What Works?*, London: Home Office.

Mair, G and May, C (1997) *Offenders on Probation*, Home Office Research Study 167, London: HMSO.

Mair, G and Nee, C (1990) *Electronic Monitoring; The Trials and Their Results*, London: HMSO.

Mann, M (1970) 'The Social Cohesion of Liberal Democracy', *American Sociological Review*, p423.

Marshall, T (1985) *Alternatives to Criminal Courts*, Aldershot: Gower.

Marshall, T (1996) 'Criminal Mediation in Great Britain 1980–1996', *European Journal on Criminal Policy and Research,* 4:4:21.

Martinson, R (1974) 'What Works – Questions and Answers about Prison Reform', *Public Interest*, p22.

Marx, K (1961) *Capital Volume One*, Moscow: Foreign Publishing House.

Marx, K (1971) *Critique of Political Economy*, London: Lawrence and Wisehart.

Matza D (1969) *Becoming Deviant*, New York: Prentice Hall.

Mawby, R (1977) 'Defensible Space: A Theoretical and Empirical Appraisal', *Urban Studies*, 14:169.

Mawby, R (1979) *Policing the City*, Farnborough: Saxon House.

Mayhew, P (1979) 'Defensible Space: The Current Status of a Crime Prevention Theory', *Howard Journal*, 18:150.

Mayhew P, Clarke R, Hough J and Winchester S (1980) 'Natural Surveillance and Damage to Telephone Kiosks', pp67–74 of Clarke and Mayhew (eds) (1980) *Designing out Crime*, London: HMSO.

Mayhew, P, Clarke, R, Sturman, A and Hough J (1976) *Crime as Opportunity*, Home Office Research Study No 34, London: HMSO.

McCabe, S and Purves, R (1972) *The Jury at Work*, Oxford: Blackwell.

McClintock, F and Avison, N (1968) *Crime in England and Wales*, London: Heinemann.

McCold, P (2001) 'Primary Restorative Justice Practices', in Morris, A and Maxwell, G (eds) (2001) *Restorative Justice for Juveniles*, Oxford: Hart.

McConville, M et al (1991) *The Case for the Prosecution*, London: Routledge.

McConville, M et al (1994) *Standing Accused: The Organisation and Practice of Criminal Defence Lawyers*, London: Clarendon Press.

McConville, M and Baldwin, J (1982a) 'The Role of Interrogation in Crime Discovery and Conviction, *British Journal of Criminology*, p165.

McConville, M and Baldwin, J (1982b) 'The Influence of Race on Sentencing in England', *Criminal Law Review*, p652.

McConville, M and Wilson, G (eds) (2002) *The Handbook of the Criminal Justice Process*, Oxford: Oxford University Press.

McKittrick, N and Eysenck, S (1984) 'Diversion: A Big Fix?', *Justice of the Peace*, pp377 and 393.

McMichael, P (1974) 'After-Care, Family Relationships and Reconviction in a Scottish Approved School', *British Journal of Criminology*, p236.

McWilliams, W (1983) 'The Probation Officer at Court: From Friend to Acquaintance', *Howard Journal*, 20:97.

McWilliams, W (1985) 'The Mission to the English Police Courts', *Howard Journal*, 22:129.

McWilliams, W (1986) 'The Mission Transformed: Professionalisation of Probation Between the Wars', *Howard Journal*, 24:257.

McWilliams, W (1987) 'The English Probation System and the Diagnostic Ideal', *Howard Journal*, 25:241.

Mead, M (1961) 'Some Anthropological Considerations Concerning Natural Law', *Natural Law Forum*, p51.

Millham, S et al (1975) *After Grace-Teeth: A Comparative Study of the Residential Experiences of Boys in Approved Schools*, London: Human Context Books.

Millham, S et al (1978) *Locking up Children; Secure Provision within the Child-Care System*, Farnborough: Saxon House.

Mirfield, P (1985) *Confessions*, London: Sweet and Maxwell.

Mitchell, B (1984) 'The Role of the Public in Criminal Detection', *Criminal Law Review*, p459.

Molony Committee (1927) *Report of the Departmental Committee on the Treatment of Young Offenders*, London: HMSO.

Moodie, S and Tombs, J (1982) *Prosecution in the Public Interest*, Edinburgh: Edinburgh University Press.

Morgan, M (1997) 'Imprisonment: Current Concerns', in M Maguire et al (eds) (1997) *The Oxford Handbook of Criminology*, 2nd ed, Oxford: Oxford University Press.

Morgan, P and Henderson, P (1998) *Remand Decisions and Offending on Bail*, London: Home Office.

Morgan, R (1993) 'Prisons Accountability Revisited', *Public Law*, pp314–332.

Morgan, R and Jones, S (1992) 'Bail or Jail', in Stockdale E and Casale S (eds) (1992) *Criminal Justice under Stress*, London: Blackstone.

Morgan, R and Russell, N (2000) *The Judiciary in the Magistrates' Courts*, London: Home Office.

Morgan, R, Reiner, R and McKenzie, I (1990) *Police Powers and Policy: A Study of Custody Officers*, unpublished Final Report to the Economic and Social Research Council: London.

Morris, A (1978) 'Diversion of Juvenile Offenders from the Criminal Justice System', Chapter 3 of Tutt, N (ed) (1978) *Alternative Strategies for Coping with Crime*, Oxford: Basil Blackwell and Martin Robertson.

Morris, A (1996) *Policing Problem Housing Estates*, London: Home Office.

Morris, A and Giller, H eds (1983) *Providing Criminal Justice for Children*, London: Arnold.

Morris, A and Giller, H (1987) *Understanding Juvenile Justice*, Beckenham: Croom Helm.

Morris, A and Maxwell, G (2001) 'Implementing Restorative Justice: What Works?', in Morris, A. and Maxwell, G (eds) (2001) *Restorative Justice for Juveniles*, Oxford: Hart.

Morris, A and Maxwell, G (eds) (2001) *Restorative Justice for Juveniles*, Oxford: Hart.

Morris, H (1993) 'A Paternalistic Theory of Punishment', in Duff and Garland (eds) (1994) *A Reader on Punishment*, Oxford: Oxford University Press.

Mortimer et al (1999) *Making the Tag Fit*, London: HMSO.

Morton, J (1989) 'The case for the CPS', *Solicitors Journal*, p6.

Mott, J (1983) 'Police Decisions for dealing with Juvenile Offenders', *British Journal of Criminology*, p249.

Mott, J (1985) *Adult Prisons and Prisoners in England and Wales 1970–1982: a Review of the Findings of Social Research*, London: HMSO.

Moxon, D (ed) (1985) *Managing Criminal Justice*, London: HMSO.

Moxon, D (1988), *Sentencing Practice in the Crown Court*, London: HMSO.

Munro, C and Wasik, M eds (1992) *Sentencing, Judicial Discretion and Training*, London: Sweet and Maxwell.

Murray, C (1997) 'The Ruthless Truth: Prison Works', *Sunday Times*, 12 January 1997.

Musto, D (1973) *The American Disease*, New Haven: Yale University Press.

NACRO (1989) *The Electronic Monitoring of Offenders*, London.

NACRO, (1997) *The Tottenham Experiment*, London: NACRO.

National Audit Office Report on the Crown Prosecution Service, (1998) London: National Audit Office.

Nee, C and Taylor, M (1988) 'Residential Burglary in the Republic of Ireland', *Howard Journal*, 105.

Newburn, T (1988) *The Use and Enforcement of Compensation Orders in Magistrates' Courts*, London: HMSO.

Newburn, T (2002) 'Young People, Crime and Youth Justice' in Maguire, M et al (eds) (2002) *The Oxford Handbook of Criminology*, 3rd ed, Oxford: Oxford University Press.

Newburn, T et al (2002) *The Introduction of Referral Orders into the Youth Justice System*, London: Home Office.

Newburn, T (2003) *Crime and Criminal Justice Policy*, Harlow: Pearson.

Newman, D (1974) 'In Defence of Prison', pp333–340 of Johnston and Savitz (eds) (1982) *Legal Process and Corrections*, New York: John Wiley.

Newman, O (1972) *Defensible Space*, London: Architecture Press.

Newman, O (1976) *Defensible Space: People and Design in the Violent City*, London: Architecture Press.

Newman, O (1980) *Community of Interest*, New York: Anchor Press.

Newman, O (1997) *Creating Defensible Space*, London: Diana Publishing.

Norris, C et al (1992) 'Black and Blue: An Analysis of the Influence of Race on Being Stopped by the Police', *British Journal of Sociology*, 43: 207.

O'Reilly, J and Calvert, J (2002) 'The Secret Witness', *Sunday Times*, 28 April.

O'Reilly, J and Stevens, J (2002) 'Bandit Country UK: Why Criminals Win', *Sunday Times*, 10 March.

Parker, H et al (1989) *Unmasking the Magistrates*, Milton Keynes: Open University Press.

Parliamentary All Party Penal Affairs Group, (1980) *Too Many Prisoners*, London: Barry Rose.

Parliamentary All Party Penal Affairs Group (1983) *The Prevention of Crime among Young People*, London: Barry Rose.

Parsloe, P (1978) *Juvenile Justice in Britain and the United States: The Balance of Needs and Rights*, London: Routledge and Kegan Paul.

Parsons, T (1960) *Structure and Process in Modern Societies*, Glencoe: Free Press.

Parsons, T (1962) 'The Law and Social Control' in Evan, W M (ed) (1962) *Law and Sociology*, Glencoe: Free Press.

Pasternoster, R et al (1979) 'The Stigma of Diversion: Labeling in the Juvenile Justice System', Chapter 8 of Brantingham and Blomberg (eds) (1979) *Courts and Diversion*, Beverley Hills: Sage.

Patchett, K and McClean, L (1965) 'Decision-Making in Juvenile Cases', *Criminal Law Review*, p699.

Pease, K (1978) 'Community Service and the Tarrif', *Criminal Law Review*, 269.

Pease, K (1981a) *Community Service Orders- A First Decade of Promise*, London: Howard League.

Pease, K (1981b) 'The Size of the Prison Population', *British Journal of Criminology*, p71.

Pease, K (1997) 'Crime Prevention' in Maguire, M et al (eds) *The Oxford Handbook of Criminology*, 2nd ed, Oxford: Oxford University Press.

Pease, K and McWilliams, W (1980a) 'The Future of Community Service' in Pease, K and McWilliams, W (1980b).

Pease, K and McWilliams, W (eds) (1980b) *Community Service by Order*, Edinburgh: Scottish Academic Press.

Pease, K and Wasik, M eds (1987) *Sentencing Reform*, Manchester: Manchester University Press.

Pettit, P and Braithwaite, J (1993) 'Not Just Desserts Even in Sentencing', *Current Issues in Criminal Justice*, 4:222.

Phillips, C and Brown, D (1998) *Entry into the Criminal Justice System: A Survey of Police Arrests and Their Outcomes,* Home Office Research Study Number 185, London: Home Office.

Pickford, J (2000) 'Introduction: A New Youth Justice for a New Century?', in Pickford, J (ed) (2000) *Youth Justice: Theory and Practice*, London: Cavendish..

Pickford, J (ed) (2000) *Youth Justice: Theory and Practice*, London: Cavendish.

Piliavin, I and Briar, S (1964)'Police Encounters with Juveniles', *American Journal of Sociology*, p206.

Pinchbeck, I and Hewitt, M (1973) *Children in English Society*, London: Routledge and Kegan Paul.

Platt, A. (1969) *The Child Savers*, Chicago: University of Chicago Press.

Plowden, P (2003) *Criminal Litigation in Practice,* Newcastle: Northumbria Law Press.

Pound, R (1940) *Contemporary Juristic Theory*, Claremont: Claremont Colleges.

Pound, R (1942) *Social Control Through Law*, New Haven: Yale University Press.

Pound, R (1954) *An Introduction to the Philosophy of Law*, New Haven: Yale University Press.

Pound, R (1959) *Jurisprudence* (5 volumes), St Paul, Minnesota: West Publishing.

Povey, D and Cotton, J (2003) *Police Complaints and Discipline, 12 months to March 2002,* London: Home Office

Povey, D and Prime, J (1999) *Recorded Crime Statistics, England and Wales, April 1998 to March 1999*, London: HMSO.

Powis, D (1977) *The Signs of Crime: A Field Manual for Police*, London: McGraw Hill.

Poyner, B (1983) *Design against Crime: Beyond Defensible Space*, London: Butterworths.

Poyner, B (1986) 'A Model for Action', pp25–39 of Heal, K and Laycock, G (eds) (1986) *Situational Crime Prevention: From Theory into Practice*, Home Office Research and Planning Unit, London: HMSO.

Pratt, J (1986) 'Diversion from the Juvenile Court: A History of Inflation and a Critique of Progress', *British Journal of Criminology*, p212.

Pratt, J and Bray, K (1985) 'Bail Hostels – Alternatives to Custody', *British Journal of Criminology*, 25:160.

Prescott, M (2000) 'One Pupil in Five Admits to Committing Crime', *Sunday Times*, 26 March, Section 1, p7.

Prime, J, White, S, Liriano, S and Patel, K (2001) *Criminal Careers of Those Born between 1953 and 1978*, London: Home Office.

Prison Reform Trust, (1986) *The Bail Lottery*, London: Prison Reform Trust.

Prison Service, (1996) *Corporate Plan 1996–9*, London: Prison Service.

Prisons and Probation Ombudsman Annual Report 2002–2003 (2003) London: HMSO.

Punch, M and Naylor, T (1973) 'The Police: A Social Service', *New Society*, p358.

Quinney, R (1970) *The Social Reality of Crime*, Boston: Little Brown.

Quinney R (1974) *Criminal Justice in America*, Boston: Little Brown.

Raine, J and Willson, M (1996) 'The Imposition of Conditions in Bail Decisions: From Summary Punishment to Better Behaviour on Remand', *Howard Journal of Criminal Justice*, p256.

Rainton, D (1974) 'Police Discretion', *Police Review*, pp878, 912 and 945.

Ramsay, M (1986) 'Preventing Disorder', pp81–89 of Heal, K and Laycock, G (eds) (1986) *Situational Crime Prevention: From Theory into Practice*, Home Office Research and Planning Unit, London: HMSO.

Rawls, J (1972) *A Theory of Justice*, Oxford: Oxford University Press.

Raynor, P and Vanstone, M (2002) *Understanding Community Penalties*, Buckingham; Open University Press.

Reiner, R (1997) 'Policing and the Police', in Maguire, M et al (eds) (1997) *The Oxford Handbook of Criminology*, 2nd ed, Oxford: Oxford University Press.

Reiss, A (1971) *The Police and the Public*, New Haven: Yale University Press.

Report from the Departmental Report on Prisons (1895) (the Gladstone Report), London: HMSO.

Report of the Criminal Cases Review Committee (1999) *Annual Report 1999*, Birmingham: Criminal Cases Review Committee.

Report of the Stewart Committee in Scotland (1983) *Keeping Offenders Out of Court: Further Alternatives to Prosecution*, Cmnd 8959, Edinburgh: HMSO.

Report of the Youth Justice Board (1998) *Preventing Offending by Young Persons*, London: HMSO.

Rex, S (1998) 'A New form of Rehabilitation', in Von Hirsch and Ashworth (eds) (1998) *Principled Sentencing*, Oxford: Hart.

Rex, S (2003) 'What Works in Theories of Punishment?', in Wing Hong Chui and Nellis, M (eds) (2003) *Moving Probation Forward*, London: HMSO.

Richardson, F (1999) 'Electronic Tagging of Offenders: Trials in England', *Howard Journal*, 38:2:158.

Riley, D (1980) 'An Evaluation of a Campaign to Reduce Vandalism', pp127–137 of Clarke, R and Mayhew, P (eds) (1980) *Designing out Crime*, London: HMSO.

Riley, D and Vennard, J (1988) *Triable Either Way Cases: Crown Court or Magistrates' Court?*, London: HMSO.

Roche, D (2003) *Accountability in Restorative Justice*, Oxford: Oxford University Press.

Rock, P (1973) *Deviant Behaviour*, London: Hutchinson.

Rose, D (1996) *In The Name of the Law*, London: Vintage.

Rose R (ed) (1969), Policy Making in Britain, London, Macmillan.

Royal Commission on Criminal Justice (1993) The Runciman Commission, *Report of the Royal Commission on Criminal Justice*, London: HMSO.

Royal Commission on Criminal Procedure Report, (1981) London: HMSO.

Rutherford, A (1984) *Prisons and the Process of Justice*, London: Heinemann.

Rutter, M and Giller, H (1981) *Juvenile Delinquency*, Harmondsworth: Penguin.

Ryan, M (1983) *The Politics of Penal Reform*, London: Longmans.

Samuels, A (1986) 'Non Crown Prosecutions: Prosecutions by Non-Police Agencies and by Private Individuals', *Criminal Law Review*, p33.

Sanders, A (1985) 'Class Bias in Prosecutions', *The Howard Journal of Criminal Justice*, p176.

Sanders, A (1986) 'An Independent Crown Prosecution Service', *Criminal Law Review*, p16.

Sanders, A (2002) 'From Suspect to Trial', in Maguire M et al (2002) *The Oxford Handbook of Criminology*, 3rd ed, Oxford: Oxford University Press.

Sanders, A et al (1997) *Victims with Learning Disabilities: Negotiating the Criminal Justice System*, Oxford: Centre for Criminological Research.

Sanders, A and Bridges, L (1990) 'Access to Police Advice and Police Malpractice', *Criminal Law Review*, p494.

Sanders, A and Young, R (1994) *Criminal Justice*, London: Butterworths.

Sapsford, R. (1978) 'Life Sentence Prisoners: Psychological Changes During Sentence', *British Journal of Criminology*, p128.

Sapsford, R and Banks, C (1979) 'A Synopsis of Some Home Office Research', Part 3 of Smith, D (ed) (1979) *Life Sentence Prisoners*, London: HMSO.

Sarri, R (1979) 'Juvenile Aid Panels: The Australian Approach to Juvenile Diversion', Chapter 7 of Brantingham and Blomberg (eds) (1979) *Courts and Diversion*, Beverley Hills: Sage.

Schafer, H (1982) 'Women by Night', pp207–226 of Kuhlhorn, E and Svensson, B (eds) (1982) *Crime Prevention*, Report No 9, Stockholm: Research and Development Division, The National Swedish Council for Crime Prevention.

Scheleff, L (1975) 'From Restitutive Law to Repressive Law' *European Journal of Sociology* p29.

Schwartz, R and Miller, J (1964) 'Legal Evolution and Societal Complexity', *American Journal of Sociology*, p159.

Sebba, L (1967) 'Decision-Making in Juvenile Cases', *Criminal Law Review*, p347.

Sebba, L (1969) 'Penal Reform and Court Practice: The Case of the Suspended Sentence' pp133–170 of Drapkin, I (ed) (1969) 'Studies in Criminology', *Scripta Heirosolymitana vol 21*, Jerusalem: Magnus Press.

Sellin, T and Wolfgang, M (1964) *The Measurement of Delinquency*, New York: Wiley.

Shapland, J and Vagg, J (1988) *Policing by the Public*, London: Routledge.

Shaw, S (1992) 'Prisons', in E Stockdale and S Casale, (eds) (1992) *Criminal Justice under Stress*, London: Blackstone.

Sherman, L et al (1997) *Preventing Crime: What Works, What Doesn't, What's Promising*, Office of Justice Programmes Research Report: US Department of Justice.

Sherrif, P (1998) *Summary Probation Statistics, England and Wales 1997*, London: Home Office.

Simmons, J and Dodd, T (2003) *Crime in England and Wales 2002/2003*, London: Home Office.

Sisson, S et al (1999) *Cautions, Court Proceedings and Sentencing, England and Wales*, London: Home Office.

Skogan, W (1990) *The Police and Public in England and Wales: A British Crime Survey Report*, London: HMSO

Skogan, W (1996) 'Public Opinion and the Police', in W Saulsbury, J Mott and T Newburn, (eds) (1996) , *Themes in Contemporary Policing*, London: Police Foundation/Policy Studies Institute.

Skolnick, J (1966) *Justice without Trial*, New York: Wiley.

Smith, D (ed) (1979) *Life Sentence Prisoners*, London, HMSO.

Smith, D et al (1983) *Police and People in London*, London: Policy Studies Institute.

Smith, D et al (1984) *Reducing the Prison Population*, London: HMSO.

Smith, M (2001) 'What Future for Public Safety and Restorative Justice in a System of Community Penalties?' in Bottoms, A, Gelsthorpe, L and Rex, S (eds) (2001) *Community Penalties: Change and Challenges*, Cullompton: Willan.

Softley, P et al (1980) 'Police Interrogation', London: HMSO.

Somerville, J (1969) 'A Study of the Preventative Aspect of Police Work with Juveniles', *Criminal Law Review*, pp407 and 472.

Southgate, P and Ekblom, P (1984) *Contacts between Police and Public: Findings from the British Crime Survey*, Home Office Research Study No 77, London: HMSO.

Spenser, S (1992) *Car Crime and Young People on a Sunderland Housing Estate*, London: HMSO.

Stanley, S and Baginsky, M (1984) *Alternatives to Prison*, London: Peter Owen.

Steer, D (1970) *Police Cautions*, Oxford: Blackwell.

Steer, D (1980) *Uncovering Crime: the Police Role*, London: HMSO.

Stern, V (1987) *Bricks of Shame*, Harmondsworth: Penguin.

Stewart, G and Stewart, J (1993) *Social Circumstances of Younger Offenders under Supervision*, London: Association of Chief Officers of Probation.

Stewart G. and Tutt N (1987) *Children in Custody*, Aldershot, Gower.

Stinchcombe, A (1963) 'Institutions of Privacy in the determination of Police Administrative Practice', *American Journal of Sociology*, 69, 2: 150–60.

Stockdale, E and Casale, S (eds) (1992) *Criminal Justice under Stress*, London: Blackstone.

Stone, N (1994) 'The Suspended Sentence since the Criminal Justice Act 1991', *Criminal Law Review*, p399.

Strang, H (2002) *Repair or Revenge: Victims and Restorative Justice*, Oxford: Clarendon Press.

Sturman, A (1980) 'Damage on Buses: The Effects of Supervision', pp31–38 of Clarke, R and Mayhew P (eds) (1980) *Designing out Crime*, London: HMSO.

Tarling, R (1979) *Sentencing Practices in Magistrates' Courts*, London: HMSO.

Tarling, R (1988) *Police Work and Manpower Allocation*, Research and Planning Unit Paper 47, London: HMSO.

Tendler, S (1989) 'Pursue Justice Not Economics, Police Tell Crown Service', *The Times*, 19 May, p5.

The Magistrate (1989) 'Crown Prosecution Service', Report of a speech by the Attorney General, p4.

The Sunday Times (1988) 'Crown Prosecution Faces a Crisis', 6 November, pA12.

The Times (2000) *When More Means Less*, Editorial in *The Times*, 22 February.

Thomas, N et al (1990) *Study of Community Service Orders*, Birmingham: University of Birmingham.

Thompson, E P (1975) *Whigs and Hunters: The Origins of the Black Act*, London: Allen Lane.

Thornton, A et al (2003) *Distraction Burglary amongst Older Adults and Ethnic Minority Communities*, London: Home Office.

Timmons, J (1986) 'The Crown Prosecution Service in Practice', *Criminal Law Review*, p28.

Trojanowicz, J and Bucqueroux, B (1998) *Community Policing: How to Get Started*, Dayton: Anderson Publishing.

Turk, A (1969) *Criminality and the Legal Order*, Chicago: Rand McNally.

Turner, A (1992) 'Sentencing in Magistrates' Courts' in Munro and Wasik (eds) (1992) *Sentencing, Judicial Discretion and Training*, London: Sweet and Maxwell.

Tutt, N (ed) (1978) *Alternative Strategies for Coping with Crime*, Oxford: Basil Blackwell and Martin Robertson.

Tweedie, I (1982) 'Police Cautioning of Juveniles', *Criminal Law Review*, p168.

Uglow, S (2002) *Criminal Justice*, London: Sweet and Maxwell.

Umbreit, M, Coates, R and Vos, B (2001) 'Victim Impact of Meeting with Young Offenders; Two Decades of Victim Offender Mediation Practice and Research', in Morris, A and Maxwell, G (eds) (2001) *Restorative Justice for Juveniles*, Oxford: Hart.

Utting, D (1999) *What Works in the United Kingdom?*, London: HMSO.

Van Maanen, J (1973) 'Observations on the Making of a Policeman', *Human Organisation*, 32, 4:407–418.

Van Ness, D, Morris, A and Maxwell, G (2001) 'Introducing Restorative Justice', in Morris, A and Maxwell, G (eds) (2001) *Restorative Justice for Juveniles*, Oxford: Hart.

Vass, A (1986) 'Community Service: Areas of Concern and Suggestions for Change', *Howard League*, 25: 100.

Vennard, J (1981) *Acquittal Rates in Magistrates' Courts*, London: HMSO

Vennard, J et al (1997) 'The Use of Cognitive-Behavioural Approaches with Offenders: Messages from the Research', in Mair, G et al (1997) *Changing Offenders' Attitudes and Behaviour: What Works?*, London: Home Office.

Vogler, R (1983) 'The Changing Nature of Bail', *Legal Action Group Bulletin*, 11 February, London: Legal Action Group.

Vold, G et al (2002) *Theoretical Criminology*, 5th ed, Oxford: Oxford University Press.

Von Hirsch, A (1976) *Doing Justice: the choice of punishments*, New York: Hill and Wang.

Von Hirsch, A (1993) *Censure and Sanctions*, Oxford: Oxford University Press.

Von Hirsch, A and Ashworth, A eds (1998) *Principled Sentencing*, Oxford: Hart.

Von Hirsch, A et al (1999) *Criminal Deterrence and Sentence Severity*, Oxford: Hart.

Walgrave, L (2001) 'On Restoration and Punishment: Favourable Similarities and Fortunate Differences', in Morris, A and Maxwell, G (eds) (2001) *Restorative Justice for Juveniles*, Oxford: Hart.

Walker, C (2002) 'Miscarriages of Justice', in McConville, M and Wilson, G (eds) (2002) *The Handbook of the Criminal Justice Process*, Oxford: Oxford University Press.

Walker, N (1983) 'Side-Effects of Incarceration', *British Journal of Criminology*, p61.

Walker, N and Padfield, N (1996) *Sentencing: Theory, Law and Practice*, London: Butterworths.

Walmsley, R (2003) *World Prison Population List*, London: Home Office.

Walmsley, R and White, S (1979) *Sexual Offences, Consent and Sentencing*, London: HMSO.

Wasik, M (1992) 'Sentencing: A Fresh Look at Aims and Objectives', in Stockdale and Casale eds (1992) *Criminal Justice Under Stress*, London: Blackstone.

Wasik, M (1993) *Emmings on Sentencing*, London: Blackstone.

Wasik, M (1999) 'Reparation: Sentencing and the Victim', *Criminal Law Review*, p470.

Wasik, M et al (1999) *Criminal Justice: Text and Materials*, London: Longman.

Weatheritt, M (1986) *Innovations in Policing*, London: Croom Helm.

Weitekamp, E (2001) 'Mediation in Europe: Paradoxes, Problems and Promises', in Morris, A and Maxwell, G (eds) (2001) *Restorative Justice for Juveniles*, Oxford: Hart.

Weitekamp, E and Kerner, H (eds) (2003) *Restorative Justice in Context*, Cullompton: Willan.

Weitekamp, E, Kerner, H and Meier U (2003) 'Community and Problem-Orientated Policing in the Context of Restorative Justice', in Weitekamp, E and Kerner, H (eds) (2003) *Restorative Justice in Context*, Cullompton: Willan.

Welsh Campaign for Civil and Political Liberties and the NUM South Wales (1985) *Striking Back,* Cardiff: Welsh Campaign for Civil and Political Liberties and the NUM South Wales.

West, D J (1976) 'Community Service', in King and Morgan (eds) (1976) *A Taste of Prison*, London: Routledge.

West, D J and Farrington, D P (1977) *The Delinquent Way of Life*, London: Heinemann.

Westley, W (1970) *Violence and the Police*, Cambridge, Massachusetts: MIT Press.

White, K and Brody, S (1980) 'The Use of Bail Hostels', *Criminal Law Review*, p420.

White, P (1999) *The Prison Population in 1998: A Statistical Overview*, London: HMSO.

Wilkins, G and Addicott, C (1999) *Motoring Offences, England and Wales, 1997*, London: HMSO.

Wilkinson, P (1977) *Terrorism and the Liberal State*, London: Macmillan.

Williams, K (2001) *Criminology*, 4th ed, London: Blackstone.

Willis, C (1984) *The Tape Recording of Police Interviews with Suspects*, London: HMSO.

Wilson, J Q (1968) *Varieties of Police Behaviour*, Cambridge, Mass: Harvard University Press.

Wilson, S (1980) 'Vandalism and "Defensible Space" on London Housing Estates', pp39–66 of Clarke, R and Mayhew, P (eds) (1980) *Designing out Crime*, London: HMSO.

Wing Hong Chui and Nellis, M (eds) (2003) *Moving Probation Forward*, London: Pearson.

Wolchover, D and Heaton-Armstrong, A (1998) 'New Labour's Attack on Trial by Jury', *New Law Journal*, 30 October.

Wooton, B (1977) 'Official Advisory Bodies' pp13–31 of Walker N (ed) (1977) *Penal Policy Making in England*, Cambridge: Institute of Criminology.

Wright, M (1982) *Making Good*, London: Burnett.

Wright, W and Dixon, M (1977) 'Community Prevention and Treatment of Juvenile Delinquency: A Review of Evaluation Studies', *Journal of Research in Crime and Delinquency*, p235.

Wright, R and Logie, R (1988) 'How Young House Burglars Choose Targets', *Howard Journal of Criminal Justice*, 27:92.

Young, M (1991) *An Inside Job*, Oxford: Oxford University Press.

Young, R (2001) 'Just Cops Doing "Shameful" Business: Police-Led Restorative Justice Schemes', in Morris, A and Maxwell, G (eds) (2001) *Restorative Justice for Juveniles*, Oxford: Hart.

Young, W (1979) *Community Service Orders*, London: Heinemann.

Young, W (1986) 'Influences upon the use of Imprisonment: A Review of the Literature', *Howard Journal*, p125.

Zamble, and Popporino, (1990) 'Coping, Imprisonment and Rehabilitation', *Criminal Justice and Behaviour*, 17:1.

Zander, M (1979a) 'The Investigation of Crime: A Study of Cases Tried at the Old Bailey', *Criminal Law Review*, p203.

Zander, M (1979b) 'Operation of the Bail Act in London Magistrates' Courts', *New Law Journal*, 129:108.

Zander, M (1991) 'What the Annual Statistics Tell Us about Pleas and Acquittals', *Criminal Law Review*, p252.

Zander, M and Henderson, P (1993) *The Crown Court Study*, London: HMSO.

Index

Absolute discharge, *281*
Action plan orders, *264*
Admissibility of evidence, *185–187*
Alcohol-related violence and disorder, *63–65*
Anti-social behaviour orders, *300–301*
Appeals, *187–188*
Approved schools, *234–235*
Arnold, *44–45*
Attendance centres, *261–263*
Auld report, *28, 188*

Bail, *156–167*
    Bail Act 1976, *158*
    conditional, *162–164*
    Crown Prosecution Service, and, *165*
    custodial remands, *160*
    disparity in bail decision-making, *164*
    empirical studies, *164*
    hostels, *161–162*
    low-quality information in, *166–167*
    offending on, *160–161*
    police, and, *165*
    pressure on prisons, *161*
    problems in bail decision-making, *157–167*
    quality of bail decsion-making, *165–166*
    retreat from presumption of, *159*
Baldwin, *114*
Beating Crime, *122–123*
Borstals, *234–235*
British Crime Survey 1998, *12*
British Crime Survey 2002–2003, *12–13*
Burglary, *51, 55–59, 222–223*

Car theft,
    data, *66*
    Vehicle Watch, *65*
    youth, *65–66*
Carl Bridgewater case, *94–96*
Cautions, *126–136*
    aims, *132–133*
    Crime and Disorder Act 1998, *127–128*
    controlling discretion, *132*
    disadvantages, *133–136*
    disparity in decision-making, *131*
    Home Office Circular 181/1994, *129–131*
    justifications, *132–133*
    official guidance, *128–132*
    problems, *133–136*

Cautions (*contd.*)
    statistics, *128*
    understanding cautioning rates, *131–132*
Chief constable, *99*
Child safety orders, *267*
City centre disorder, *62–63*
Combination orders *see* Community punishment
    and rehabilitation orders
Community punishment orders, *296–299*
Community punishment and rehabilitation
    orders, *299–300*
Community rehabilitation orders *see* Probation
Community sentences and orders, *276–310*
    absolute discharge, *281*
    anti-social behaviour orders, *300–301*
    community punishment orders, *296–299*
        orders, purpose of, *297–298*
        position in the tariff, *298*
        praise for, *298*
        problems with, *299*
        Wooton Report, *297*
    community punishment and rehabilitation
        orders, *299–300*
    community rehabilitation orders,
        284–296. See also Probation
    compensation orders, *303–304*
    conditional discharge, *281*
    Criminal Justice Act 2003, *278*
    curfew orders, *301*
    effectiveness, *305–306*
    electronic monitoring, *301–303*
    fines, *278–281*
        advantages of, *279*
        disparity, *280–281*
        enforcement, *280–281*
        unit, *279–280*
    forfeiture orders, *304–305*
    generic community sentence, *306–310*
        requirements provided by Criminal
           Justice Act 2003, *307–310*
        restrictions on imposing, *307*
    suspended sentence, *281–284*
    statisitics, *82*
Community service *see* Community punishment
    orders
Compensation orders, *303–304*
Conditional discharge, *281*
Crime prevention, *46–71*
    community strategies, *67–70*

Crime prevention (*contd.*)
   conclusions, *70–71*
   displacement, *52–53*
   evaluating schemes, *49–50*
   examples, *47–49*
   government thinking on, *50–51*
      burglary, *51*
   nature of, *47*
   rational choice model, *49*
   social strategies, *67–70*
      importance of early intervention, *68–69*
         Dorset Healthy Alliance Project, *69*
         Home Start, *69*
      On Track, *69–70*
      risks factors regarding potential criminality, *67–68*
   specific studies, *53–67*
      burglary, *55–59*
      campaigns, *53–54*
      car theft data, *66*
      city centre disorder, *62–63*
      defensible space, *59–62*
      pick-pocketing, *62*
      problem housing estates, *66–67*
      reducing alcohol-related violence, *63–65*
      small shops, *67*
      vandalism, *59–62*
      Vehicle Watch, *65*
      youth car crime, *65–66*
   success stories, *51–52*
Criminal Cases Review Commission, *192–193*
Criminal courts, review of, *174–175*
Criminal justice system, *1–45*
   aims, *19–22*
   characterisitics of a particular society, *18*
   costs, *9–10*
   crime causation, *18*
   development of penal policy since 1945, *22–32*
   factors influencing creation of criminal law, *41–45*
   insitutions, *2*
   models, *35–41*
      Durkheim, *35–36*
      Ehrlich, *36*
      Engels, *39–40*
      Marx, *39–40*
      Parsons, *37–39*
      Pound, *37*
      Quinney, *40–41*
   nature of man, *18*

Criminal justice system (*contd.*)
   new managerialism, *34–35*
   pandering to the public, *32–34*
   research into, *19*
   stages, *2*
   statistical account, *3–15*
      British Crime Survey 1998, *12*
      British Crime Survey 2002–2003, *12–13*
      costs, *9–10*
      international comparisons, *8*
      motoring offences, *4*
      Official Crime Statistics 2001, *4–5*
      race, *7–8*
      response of courts, *15*
      self-report studies, *10–13*
      victim studies, *10–13*
      women, *6*
   values, *16–17*
      Mead, *16–17*
      Rawls, *17*
Criminal trial, *168–193*
   admissibility of evidence, *185–187*
   appeals, *187–188*
      Auld report, *188*
      Criminal Justice Act 2003, *188*
      following trial on indictment, *187–188*
   Criminal Cases Review Commission, *192–193*
   human rights, *188–192*
      art 5, *189–190*
      art 6, *191–192*
   jury, *179–185*
      advantages, *184*
      competence, *181–184*
         research on, *182–184*
      disadvantages, *184–185*
      disqualifications, *180–181*
      functions, *179*
      qualifications, *180–181*
      verdict, *181*
   mode of, *169–173*
      conclusion, *173*
   pleas, *173–174*
      guilty, *173–174*
      Royal Commission on Criminal Justice 1993, *174*
   quality of defence in Crown Court, *178–179*
   review of criminal courts, *174–175*
   role of magistrates, *175–178*
      criticisms of, *176–178*
Crown Prosecution Service, *139–140, 141, 142, 144, 145, 145–156, 165*

Curfew orders, *301*

Defensible space, *59–62*
Detention and training order, *261*
Deterrence, *198–200*
Displacement, *52–53*
Diversion, *136–139*
Dorset Healthy Alliance Project, *69*
Drug use, sentencing guidelines, *222*
Durkheim, *35–36*

Ehrlich, *36*
Electronic monitoring, *301–303*
Engels, *39–40*

Fines, *278–281*
   advantage of, *279*
   disparity, *280–281*
   enforcement, *280–281*
   unit, *279–280*
Forfeiture orders, *304–305*

Gender, *219–220*
Glidewell Report, *139–140*
Guildford Four, *94*
Gusfield, *45*

Haskins, *44*
Hay et al, *44–45*
Home Start, *69*
Human rights, *188–192*

Jury, *179–185*
   advantages, *184*
   competence, *181–184*
     research on, *182–184*
   disadvantages, *184–185*
   disqualifications, *180–181*
   functions, *179*
   qualifications, *180–181*
   verdict, *181*

Lindesmith, *43–44*
Long-term detention, *261*
Long-term prisoners, *329–333*
   close supervision centres, *332–333*
   deterioration problem, *336–337*

McConville et al, *115–117*
Magistrates, *175–178*
   criticisms of, *176–178*
Marijuana Tax Act 1937, *42–43*
Marx, *39–40*

Mead, *16–17*
Miscarriages of justice, factors in, *96*
Motoring offences, *4*
Mountbatten Report, *23, 328–329*

On Track, *69–70*

Narey Report, *169*

Parenting orders, *239–240, 266–267*
Parsons, *37–39*
Paternalism, *201–202*
Penal policy, developments since 1945, *22–32*
Pervasiveness of crime, *13–15*
Pick-pocketing, *62*
Platt, *44*
Pleas, *173–174*
Police, *72–125*
   assessing performance of, *123–124*
   bail, and, *165*
   cautions *see* Cautions
   community policing, *117–118*
   complaints, *96–98*
   discretion, *104–109*
     studies, *106, 108–109, 109*
   discrimination, *104–109*
   expectations, *90–98*
     abuse of power, *93–96*
     law enforcement, *91–92*
     order maintenance, *91*
     police vs public view, *93*
     role of public, *91–92*
     service functions, *92–93*
   factors in arrest decisions, *105–106*
   factors influencing policing, *98–104*
     chief constable, *99*
     complexity and variety, *102*
     cop culture, *100–102*
     Kilburn study, *103*
     London in new millennium, *103–104*
     pressures on police organisation, *99–100*
     real police work, *101–102*
   gatekeepers to criminal justice system, as, *106–108*
   interview, *111–112*
   numbers, *74*
   powers, *74–90*
     access to legal advice, *89*
     arrest, *75–82, 109*
     detention, *87–89*
     entry, search and seizure, *84–87*
     right to silence, *89–90*

Police, powers (*contd.*)
 stop and search, *82–83, 109*
 provision of legal services to defendant,
  113–117
  Baldwin, *114*
  McConville et al, *115–117*
  Sanders, *114–115*
  types of assistance available, *113–114*
 Reform Act 2002, *73–74*
 remedies, *96–98*
 stereotypes, *104–109*
 suspect in police station, *109–112*
  inequality of arms, *111*
  interview environment, *111–112*
 suspicion, use of, *108–109*
 what works?, *119–123*
  Beating Crime, *122–123*
  strategies, *121–122*
Police complaints, *96–98*
Pound, *37*
Pre-sentence reports, *215–217*
Preventing Children Offending, *268–270*
Prisons, *311–346*
 aims, *321–324*
 conclusions, *345–346*
 conditions, *326–328*
 Criminal Justice Act 2003, *315–317*
  custodial sentences less than 12 months,
  316
  dangerous offenders, *317*
  general restrictions on discretionary
   custodial sentences, *315–316*
  dangerous offenders, *317*
  general restrictions on discretionary
   custodial sentences, *315–316*
  home detention curfew, *316*
  intermittent custody, *316*
  mandatory life sentences, *317*
 functions, *321–324*
 history, *312*
 home detention curfew, *314–315, 316*
 incapacitation as a benefit of
  imprisonment, *333–336*
 long-term prisoners, *329–333*
  close supervision centres, *332–333*
  deterioration problem, *336–337*
 overcrowding, *324–326*
 praise, *338–339*
 proposals for change, *312–313*
 reconviction data, lessons of, *339–342*
 reduction of prison numbers, *342–345*
  decriminalisation, *343*
  non-custodial alternatives, *343–344*

Prisons (*contd.*)
 security, *328–329*
 side-effects, unwanted, *337–338*
 statistics, *318–321*
  population 2002, *318–319*
  prison experiences, *319–320*
  prisoner characteristics, *319–320*
  variety of prisons, *319–320*
  women prisoners, *320–321*
 statutory framework, *313–315*
  early release and parole, *314–315*
 Woolf Report, *323–324*
Probation, *284–296*
 assessing the service, *294–296*
 Changing Offenders' Attitudes and
  Behaviour: What Works?, *291–294*
 effective offender supervision, *291*
 future, *296*
 history of service, *285–286*
 National Standards for 2000, *215,*
  287–289
 priorities, *286–287*
 responsibilities, *286–287*
 statistics, *289–291*
 work of officers, *284–285*
Prosecution system, *139–156*
 Crown Prosecution Service, *139–140,*
  141, 142, 144, 145, 145–146, 165
  acquittals, *150–153*
  bureaucratic/other pressures on, *154*
  Code for Crown Prosecutors (2000),
  145–148
  National Audit Office Report (1998),
  156
  police power in relation to, *154–155*
  police view of, *150*
  problems of, *148–156*
  retreat from prosecution, *153–154*
 Glidewell Report, *139–140*
 prosecutions by private individuals and
  institutions, *144–145*
 reform, *142–145*
  Prosecution of Offences Act 1985, *144*
  prosecutions by private individuals and
   institutions, *144–145*
  Royal Commission on Criminal
   Procedure (1981), *143*
  1982 White Paper, *143–144*
 statistics, *140–142*

Quinney, *40–41*

Race, *220–221*

Radzinowicz Report,   *329*
Rational choice model,   *49*
Rawls,   *17*
Referral orders,   *244–258*
  legislative provisions,   *250–258*
Rehabilitation,   *200–201*
Reparation orders,   *264–266*
Reprimands,   *239, 243–244*
Restorative justice,   *202–213*
  accountability,   *212*
  effectiveness,   *212–213*
  examples,   *205–210*
  good practice,   *211*
  parameters,   *210*
  philosophical considerations,   *210–211*
Retribution,   *197–198*
Royal Commission on Criminal Justice
      1993,   *169, 174*
Royal Commission on Criminal Procedure
      (1981),   *143*

Sanders,   *114–115*
Sentences,   *214 see* Sentencing
  community,   *214*
  custodial,   *214*
Sentencing,   *194–226*
  aims,   *197*
  deferral of sentence,   *195–196*
  disparity,   *221*
  factors taken into account in,   *214–221*
    age,   *217*
    aggravating,   *218*
      examples,   *218–219*
    gender,   *219–220*
    information,   *215–217*
    legal limits,   *214*
    mitigating factors,   *217*
      examples,   *218–219*
    Powers of Criminal Courts (Sentencing)
        Act 2000,   *214–215*
    pre-sentence reports,   *215–217*
    principles of sentencing,   *214*
    race,   *220–221*
    reasons for,   *219*
    response to previous sentences and
        orders,   *217*
  guidelines,   *222–224, 225–226*
    burglary,   *222–223*
    drugs,   *222*
    theft and false accounting,   *223–224*
  principles,   *196–213*
    aims,   *197*
    deterrence,   *198–200*

Sentencing, principles, deterrence (*contd.*)
    research,   *199–200*
  incapacitation,   *200*
  paternalism,   *201–202*
  rehabilitation,   *200–201*
  restorative justice,   *202–213*
  retribution,   *197–198*
  sanitising society,   *200*
Sentencing Advisory Panel,   *225, 226*
Sentencing Council,   *224, 225*
  statistics,   *195*
  who should sentence?,   *224–225*
Sentencing Advisory Panel,   *225, 226*
Sentencing Council,   *224, 225*
Supervision orders,   *263–264*
Suspended sentence,   *281–284*

Thompson,   *44–45*

Vandalism,   *59–62*
Vehicle Watch,   *65*

Warnings,   *239, 243–244*
Woolf Report,   *161, 166, 323–324*
Wooton Report,   *297*

Young offenders,   *227–275*
  analysis of youth justice system,   *267–270*
    improving the process,   *267–268*
    Preventing Children Offending,
        268–270
  conclusion,   *274–276*
  courts,   *230–232*
    Practice Direction (2000),   *231–232*
  effectiveness of interventions with,
      272–274
  framework 1982–2004 *see* Youth justice
      framework 1982–2004
  history of systems for,   *234–237*
    approved schools,   *234–235*
    borstals,   *234–235*
    Children and Young Persons Act
        1969,   *236–237*
    Criminal Justice Act 1982,   *237*
    The 1960s,   *235–236*
  justice model,   *233–234*
  sentences/orders,   *241–267*
    action plan orders,   *264*
    attendance centres,   *261–263*
    checklist,   *241–242*
    child safety orders,   *267*
    detention and training order,   *261*
    long-term detention,   *261*

Young offenders, sentences/orders (*contd.*)
    parenting orders, *266–267*
    referral orders, *244–258*
    reparation orders, *264–266*
    reprimands, *239, 243–244*
    supervision orders, *263–264*
    warnings, *239, 243–244*
    young offender institutions, *259–261*
  statisitics, *228–230*
  welfare model, *232–233*
  'what works?', *270–272*
Youth Justice Board, *240–241*
  objectives, *241*

Youth justice framework 1982–2004, *237–240*
  Crime and Disorder Act 1998, *239–240*
    new systems of control, *239*
    parenting orders, *239–240*
    reprimands, *239*
    warnings, *239*
  Crime (Sentences) Act 1997, *239*
  Criminal Justice Act 1988, *238*
  Criminal Justice and Public Order Act
    1994, *238*
  Youth Justice and Criminal Evidence Act
    1999, *240*
Young offender institutions, *259–261*

Unannotated Cracknell's Statutes for Use in Examinations

New Editions of Cracknell's Statutes

Only £11.95 Due 2004

Cracknell's Statutes provide a comprehensive series of essential statutory provisions for each subject. Amendments are consolidated, avoiding the need to cross-refer to amending legislation. Unannotated, they are suitable for use in examinations, and provide the precise wording of vital Acts of Parliament for the diligent student.

Commercial Law
ISBN: 1 85836 562 7

Family Law
1 85836 566 X

Company Law
ISBN: 1 85836 563 5

Medical Law
ISBN: 1 85836 567 8

Conflict of Laws
ISBN: 1 85836 564 3

Public International Law
ISBN: 1 85836 568 6

Evidence
ISBN: 1 85836 565 1

Revenue Law
ISBN: 1 85836 569 4

Succession
ISBN: 1 85836 570 8

For further information or to place an order, please contact:

Mail Order
Old Bailey Press at Holborn College
Woolwich Road
Charlton
London
SE7 8LN

Telephone: 020 8317 6039/6200
Fax: 020 8317 6004
Website: www.oldbaileypress.co.uk
E-Mail: mailorder@oldbaileypress.co.uk

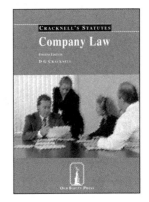

101 Questions & Answers Series

Designed for the undergraduate, the 101 Questions & Answers series is for all those who have a positive commitment to passing their law examinations. Each chapter covers a different examinable topic and comprises an introduction and a selection of questions and answers. The majority of questions represent examination 'bankers' and are supported by full-length essay solutions. There are also a generous number of interrograms designed to pinpoint examination fundamentals, which are supported by skeleton answers summarising the basics that need to be known for examination purposes.

Only £7.95 Published December 2003

Constitutional Law
ISBN: 1 85836 522 8

Law of Contract
ISBN: 1 85836 517 1

Criminal Law
ISBN: 1 85836 432 9

Law of Tort
ISBN: 1 85836 516 3

Land Law
ISBN: 1 85836 515 5

For further information or to place an order, please contact:

Mail Order
Old Bailey Press at Holborn College
Woolwich Road
Charlton
London
SE7 8LN

Telephone: 020 8317 6039/6200
Fax: 020 8317 6004
Website: www.oldbaileypress.co.uk
E-Mail: mailorder@oldbaileypress.co.uk

Learning Resources
Centre

Suggested Solutions to Past Examination Questions 2001–2002

The Suggested Solutions series provides examples of full answers to the questions regularly set by examiners. Each suggested solution has been broken down into three stages: general comment, skeleton solution and suggested solution. The examination questions included within the text are taken from past examination papers set by the University of London. The full opinion answers will undoubtedly assist you with your research and further your understanding and appreciation of the subject in question.

Only £6.95 Published December 2003

Company Law
ISBN: 1 85836 519 8

Evidence
ISBN: 1 85836 521 X

Employment Law
ISBN: 1 85836 520 1

Family Law
ISBN: 1 85836 525 2

European Union Law
ISBN: 1 85836 524 4

Suggested Solutions are also published on the core LLB subjects for different years – please contact us for details.

For further information or to place an order, please contact:

Mail Order
Old Bailey Press at Holborn College
Woolwich Road
Charlton
London
SE7 8LN

Telephone: 020 8317 6039/6200
Fax: 020 8317 6004
Website: www.oldbaileypress.co.uk
E-Mail: mailorder@oldbaileypress.co.uk

Company Law
2001–2002 LLB Examination Questions and Suggested Solutions
University of London External Examinations
Solutions by Susan Barber

Old Bailey Press

The Old Bailey Press Integrated Student Law Library is tailor-made to help you at every stage of your studies, from the preliminaries of each subject through to the final examination. The series of Textbooks, Revision WorkBooks, 150 Leading Cases and Cracknell's Statutes are interrelated to provide you with a comprehensive set of study materials.

You can buy Old Bailey Press books from your University Bookshop, your local Bookshop, directly using this form, or you can order a free catalogue of our titles from the address shown overleaf.

The following subjects each have a Textbook, 150 Leading Cases, Revision WorkBook and Cracknell's Statutes unless otherwise stated.

Administrative Law
Commercial Law
Company Law
Conflict of Laws
Constitutional Law
Conveyancing (Textbook and 150 Leading Cases)
Criminal Law
Criminology (Textbook and Sourcebook)
Employment Law (Textbook and Cracknell's Statutes)
English and European Legal Systems
Equity and Trusts
Evidence
Family Law
Jurisprudence: The Philosophy of Law (Textbook, Sourcebook and Revision WorkBook)
Land: The Law of Real Property
Law of International Trade
Law of the European Union
Legal Skills and System (Textbook)
Obligations: Contract Law
Obligations: The Law of Tort
Public International Law
Revenue Law (Textbook, Revision WorkBook and Cracknell's Statutes)
Succession

Mail order prices:	
Textbook	£15.95
150 Leading Cases	£11.95
Revision WorkBook	£9.95
Cracknell's Statutes	£11.95
Suggested Solutions 1999–2000	£6.95
Suggested Solutions 2000–2001	£6.95
Suggested Solutions 2001–2002	£6.95
101 Questions and Answers	£7.95
Law Update 2004	£10.95

Please note details and prices are subject to alteration.

To complete your order, please fill in the form below:

Module	Books required	Quantity	Price	Cost
		Postage		
		TOTAL		

For the UK and the rest of Europe, add 15% postage and packing.
For the rest of the world, add 50% for airmail.

ORDERING

By telephone to Mail Order at 020 8317 6039/6200, with your credit card to hand.

By fax to 020 8317 6004 (giving your credit card details).

Website: www.oldbaileypress.co.uk
E-Mail: mailorder@oldbaileypress.co.uk

By post to: Mail Order, Old Bailey Press at Holborn College, Woolwich Road, Charlton, London, SE7 8LN.

When ordering by post, please enclose full payment by cheque or banker's draft, or complete the credit card details below. You may also order a free catalogue of our complete range of titles from this address.

We aim to despatch your books within 3 working days of receiving your order. All parts of the form must be completed.

Name

Address

Postcode

E-Mail
Telephone

Total value of order, including postage: £

I enclose a cheque/banker's draft for the above sum, or

charge my   ☐ Access/Mastercard   ☐ Visa   ☐ American Express

Cardholder: ....

Card number

☐☐☐☐ ☐☐☐☐ ☐☐☐☐ ☐☐☐☐

Expiry date ☐☐☐☐

Signature: ....Date: ....